Essential Concepts and Applications

Fundamentals of MANAGEMENT

THIRD EDITION

Stephen P. Robbins
San Diego State University

David A. DeCenzo
Towson University

Upper Saddle River, New Jersey 07458

Robbins, Stephen P.,
Fundamentals of management / Stephen P. Robbins, David A. DeCenzo.—3rd ed.
p. cm.
Includes bibliographical references and index.
ISBN 0-13-017601-X
1. Management. I. DeCenzo, David A. II. Title.
HD31.R5643 2001
658—dc21 99-057549

Managing Editor (Editorial): *Melissa Steffens*
Editor-in-Chief: *Natalie Anderson*
Editorial Assistant: *Samantha Steel*
Assistant Editor: *Jessica Sabloff*
Media Project Manager: *Michele Faranda*
Executive Marketing Manager: *Michael Campbell*
Production Editor: *Cindy Spreder*
Associate Managing Editor (Production): *Judy Leale*
Production Coordinator: *Keri Jean*
Manufacturing Supervisor: *Arnold Vila*
Manufacturing Buyer: *Diane Peirano*
Senior Prepress/Manufacturing Manager: *Vincent Scelta*
Senior Designer: *Cheryl Asherman*
Design Manager: *Patricia Smythe*
Photo Researcher: *Teri Stratford*
Cover Design: *John Romer*
Cover and Icon Art: *Robert Pizzo*
Senior Print/Media Production Manager: *Karen Goldsmith*
Print Production Manager: *Christina Mahon*
Composition: *Rainbow Graphics*

Copyright © 2001 by Prentice-Hall, Inc., Upper Saddle River, New Jersey 07458. All rights reserved. Printed in the United States of America. This publication is protected by Copyright and permission should be obtained from the publisher prior to any prohibited reproduction, storage in a retrieval system, or transmission in any form or by any means, electronic, mechanical, photocopying, recording, or likewise. For information regarding permission(s), write to: Rights and Permissions Department.

10 9 8 7 6 5 4 3 2 1
ISBN 0-13-017601-X

Brief Contents

Contents

Preface

Welcome to the third edition of *Fundamentals of Management*. In the first two editions of this book, we said we thought there was a market for a "different" kind of management textbook. Not different just for the sake of being different but a book that was truly reflective of the contemporary trends in management and organizations. To us, that meant a book that focused on the foundations of management—covering the essential concepts in management, providing a sound foundation for understanding the key issues, offering a strong practical focus, and yet also covering the latest research studies in the field. It should also be able to be completed in a one-term course. In essence, we wanted to create a book that provided significant value both in relevance and cost to its readers. We believe our first two editions fulfilled these goals. We think this revision continues this tradition.

We use this preface to address three critical questions:

1. What assumptions guided the development of this book?
2. What's new in this revision?
3. How does the book encourage learning?

What Were Our Assumptions in Writing This Book?

Every author who sits down to write a book has a set of assumptions—either explicit or implicit—that guide what is included and what is excluded. We want to state ours up front.

Management is an exciting field. The subject matter encompassed in an introductory management text is inherently exciting. We're talking about the real world. We're talking about why Amazon.com is revolutionizing the book-selling industry; how SiloCaf, a coffee bean–processing plant, uses sophisticated technologically based controls to enhance productivity and ensure consistent quality in their work; why companies like London Fog are struggling to survive; how teams at Hewlett-Packard redesigned a production process, cut waste, controlled costs, and increased productivity; and what techniques can make a university more efficient and responsive to its students. A good management text should capture this excitement. How? Through a crisp and conversational writing style, elimination of nonessential details, a focus on issues that are relevant to the reader, and inclusion of examples and visual stimuli to make concepts come alive.

It's our belief that management shouldn't be studied solely from the perspective of "top management," "billion-dollar companies," or "U.S. corporations." The subject matter in management encompasses everyone from the lowest supervisor to the chief executive officer. The content should give as much attention to the challenges and opportunities in supervising a staff of 15, some of whom may be telecommuting, as those in directing a staff of MBA-educated vice presidents. Similarly, not everyone wants to work for a Fortune 500 company. Readers who are interested in working in small businesses, entrepreneurial ventures, or not-for-profit organizations should find the descriptions of management concepts applicable to their needs. Finally, organizations operate today in a global village. Readers must understand how to adjust their practices to reflect differing cultures. Our book addresses each of these concerns.

Before we committed anything to paper and included it in this book, we made sure it met our "so what?" test. Why would someone need to know this fact? If the relevance isn't overtly clear, either the item should be omitted or its relevance should be directly explained. In addition, content must be timely. We live in dynamic times. Changes are taking place at an unprecedented pace. A textbook in a dynamic field such as management must reflect this fact by including the latest concepts and practices. Our does!

This book is organized around the four traditional functions of management—planning, organizing, leading, and controlling. It is supplemented with material that addresses current issues affecting managers. For example, we take the reader through Managing in Today's World (Chapter 2), Understanding Work Teams (Chapter 9), and Leadership and Trust (Chapter 11). We also integrate throughout the text such contemporary topics as work process engineering, empowerment, diversity, and continuous improvements. There are a total of 14 chapters, plus 3 modules that describe the evolution of management thought, focus on popular quantitative techniques used in business today, and provide some special information to students regarding how to build their management careers.

Fundamentals of Management, third edition, is lean and focused. To get down to 14 chapters, we had to make some difficult decisions regarding the cutting and reshaping of material. We were assisted in this process by feedback from previous users. The result, we believe, is a text that identifies the essential elements students need in an introductory management course.

What's New in This Third Edition?

Several features and content topics have been added or expanded in this revision.

New and relevant topics We continue to present material that is current and relevant. These include:

Management competencies (Chapter 1)
Knowledge workers (Chapter 2)
Electronic commerce and e-business (Chapter 2)
Six sigma (Chapter 3)
Labor–management cooperation (Chapter 6)
Workplace violence (Chapter 6)
Internet job searches (Career Module)
Internships (Career Module)
Emotional intelligence (Chapter 8)
Motivating professionals (Chapter 10)
Visionary leadership (Chapter 11)
Building Trust (Chapter 11)
Team leadership (Chapter 11)
Technology transfer (Chapter 14)
Supply chain management (Chapter 14)
Project management (Chapter 14)

A skill-focused approach It's not enough to know about management. Today's students want the skills to succeed in management. So we expanded on our skill component in this edition. You'll see this in the Management Workshop at the end of each chapter.

The Management Workshop is designed to help students build analytical, diagnostic, team-building, investigative, Internet, and writing skills. We address these skill areas in several ways. For example, we include experiential exercises to develop team building skills; cases to build diagnostic, analytical, and decision-making skills; suggested topical writing assignments to enhance writing skills; and Internet search exercises to develop Internet research skills.

Management Workshop

Team Skill-Building Exercise

Individual versus Group Decisions

Objective: To contrast individual and group decision making.

Time: 15 minutes.

Step 1: You have 5 minutes to read the following story and individually respond to each of the 11 statements as either true, false, or unknown. Begin.

The Story: A salesclerk had just turned off the lights in the store when a man appeared and demanded money. The owner opened a cash register. The contents of the cash register were scooped up, and the man sped away. A member of the police force was notified promptly.

STATEMENTS ABOUT THE STORY

1 A man appeared after the owner had turned off his store lights. True, false, or unknown?
2 The robber was a man. True, false, or unknown?
3 The man did not demand money. True, false, or unknown?
4 The man who opened the cash register was the owner. True, false, or unknown?
5 The store owner scooped up the contents of the cash register and ran away. True, false, or unknown?
6 Someone opened a cash register. True, false, or unknown?
7 After the man who demanded the money scooped up the contents of the cash register, he ran away. True, false, or unknown?
8 The cash register contained money, but the story does not state how much. True, false, or unknown?
9 The robber demanded money of the owner. True, false, or unknown?
10 The story concerns a series of events in which only three persons are referred to: the owner of the store, a man who demanded money, and a member of the police force. True, false, or unknown?
11 The following events in the story are true: Someone demanded money; a cash register was opened; its contents were scooped up; a man dashed out of the store. True, false, or unknown?

Step 2: After you have answered the 11 questions individually, form groups of four or five members each. The groups have 10 minutes to discuss their answers and agree on the correct answers to each of the 11 statements.

Step 3: Your instructor will give you the actual correct answers. How many correct answers did you get at the conclusion of step 1? How many did your group achieve at the conclusion of step 2? Did the group outperform the average individual? The best individual? Discuss the implications of these results.

Developing Your Skill at Conducting a Meeting

Running an Effective Meeting

ABOUT THE SKILL

As a manager, you will spend a large portion of your workday in meetings. And, undoubtedly, there will be instances when you will be responsible for running meetings. Below are some suggestions for making sure your meetings run properly.

STEPS IN PRACTICING THE SKILL

- **Prepare and distribute an agenda well in advance of the meeting.** An agenda defines the meeting's purpose for participants and the boundaries between relevant and irrelevant discussion topics. Also, the agenda can serve as an important vehicle for premeeting discussions with participants.
- **Consult with participants before the meeting to ensure proper participation.** Let all participants know that their input is valuable and that you welcome their speaking up at the meeting when they have something to offer.
- **Establish specific time parameters for the meeting; specify when it will start and end.** This step helps keep the meeting on time and focused on the important matters.
- **Maintain focused discussion during the meeting.** Items not on the agenda should not be given substantial time during the meeting. If an issue is important, maybe another meeting, with its own agenda, should be held to address that issue.
- **Encourage and support participation by all members.** If you have done a good job in the second step, participants should come prepared to talk but still may need some encouragement at the meeting. Sometimes, direct questions about what they think will get them to talk.
- **Encourage the clash of ideas.** Remember, you want as much information about a topic to surface as possible. Disagreements are fine. They indicate that different voices are being heard. Better to work the differences out now than to have them surface later.
- **Discourage the clash of personalities.** Disagreements can enhance the process, but they should be substantive disputes. Differences caused by personal issues are a disaster in a meeting.
- **Bring closure by summarizing accomplishments and allocating follow-up assignments.** This step lets participants understand what occurred in the meeting and what they may have to do before the next meeting. This is, in essence, planning.

Practicing the Skill

CONDUCTING A MEETING

You manage a group of six skilled technicians in the radiology department of a large hospital. You need to meet with them all to discuss the hospital's unpopular new vacation policy and to devise your department's vacation schedule for the coming year. In keeping with the new policy, only one person will be allowed to take vacation at any given time.

Anna, the newest member of the department, is out sick but has agreed to participate in the meeting by telephone. Ravi and Helen, senior members of the department, both want to take the same week off.

Draft your agenda for the meeting and allocate specific time intervals for each topic or discussion.

A Case Application

Developing Your Diagnostic and Analytical Skills

BEATRICE INTERNATIONAL HOLDINGS

Research over the past few decades has shown us the need for understanding the sociocultural factors among people from different countries. Individuals from countries where power distance is high, for example, are frequently accustomed societies composed of "Haves" and "Have-nots." The Haves possess significant power to make decisions. Yet, when these Haves leave the comforts of their homeland, they, too, often must make some adjustments in their decision-making styles. That's precisely what Loida Nicolas Lewis did.[38]

Lewis grew up in the Philippines. She was born into a politically well-connected family that still operates the country's largest and most successful furniture company. Her early years were filled with all the privileges and amenities associated with high society: the best schools,

136 PLANNING Part Two

FOUNDATIONS OF DECISION MAKING Chapter Four 137

A practicing perspective Our experience has led us to conclude that students like to see and read about people who have made a contribution to their organization and use the management techniques we discuss. So we've included "One Manager's Perspective" boxes. Managers from all types of organizations contribute their perspective on how they use one or more tools discussed in the relevant chapter.

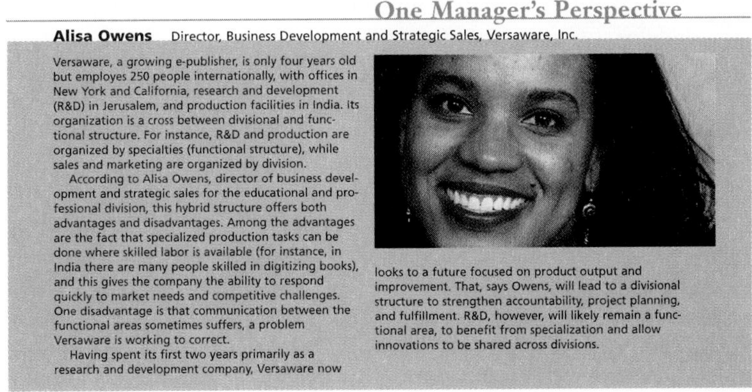

One Manager's Perspective

Alisa Owens Director, Business Development and Strategic Sales, Versaware, Inc.

Versaware, a growing e-publisher, is only four years old but employs 250 people internationally, with offices in New York and California, research and development (R&D) in Jerusalem, and production facilities in India. Its organization is a cross between divisional and functional structure. For instance, R&D and production are organized by specialties (functional structure), while sales and marketing are organized by division.

According to Alisa Owens, director of business development and strategic sales for the educational and professional division, this hybrid structure offers both advantages and disadvantages. Among the advantages are the fact that specialized production tasks can be done where skilled labor is available (for instance, in India there are many people skilled in digitizing books), and this gives the company the ability to respond quickly to market needs and competitive challenges. One disadvantage is that communication between the functional areas sometimes suffers, a problem Versaware is working to correct.

Having spent its first two years primarily as a research and development company, Versaware now looks to a future focused on product output and improvement. That, says Owens, will lead to a divisional structure to strengthen accountability, project planning, and fulfillment. R&D, however, will likely remain a functional area, to benefit from specialization and allow innovations to be shared across divisions.

How have we encouraged understanding with in-text learning aids? Just what do students need to facilitate their learning? We began to answer that question by pondering some fundamental issues: Could we make this book both "fun" to read and pedagogically sound? Could it motivate students to read on and facilitate learning? Our conclusion was that an effective textbook could and should teach, as well as present ideas. Toward that end, we designed this book to be an effective learning tool. Let's specifically describe some of the pedagogical features—in addition to what we've mentioned previously—that we included to help students better assimilate the material.

Learning outcomes Before you start a trip, it's valuable to know where you're headed. That way, you can minimize detours. The same holds true in reading a text. To make learning more efficient, we open each chapter of this book with a list of outcomes that describe what the student should be able to do after reading the chapter. These outcomes are designed to focus students' attention on the major issues within each chapter. Each outcome is a key learning element for readers.

Chapter summaries Just as outcomes clarify where one is going, chapter summaries remind you where you have been. Each chapter of this book concludes with a concise summary organized around the opening learning outcomes.

Review and discussion questions Every chapter in this book ends with a set of review and discussion questions. If students have read and understood the contents of a chapter, they should be able to answer the review questions. These "Reading for Comprehension" review questions are drawn directly from the material in the chapter.

The discussion questions go beyond comprehending chapter content. They're designed to foster higher-order thinking skills. That is, they require the reader to apply, integrate, synthesize, or evaluate management concepts. The "Linking Concepts to Practice" discussion questions will allow students to demonstrate that they not only know the facts in the chapter but also can use those facts to deal with more complex issues.

Supplements Package

Visit:
www.prenhall.com/robbins

Fundamentals comes with a complete, high-tech support package for faculty and students. This includes a comprehensive instructor's manual and test bank; a dedicated Web site <www.prenhall.com/robbins>; inclusion on PHLIP (Prentice Hall Learning on the Internet Partnership), a faculty-support Web site featuring Instructor's Manual, PowerPoint slides, current news articles, and links to related Internet sites; an on-line student study guide; electronic transparencies; and the Robbins Self-Assessment Library, which provides students with insights into their skills, abilities, and interests.

Instructor's Manual with Video Guide Designed to guide the educator through the text, each chapter in the instructor's manual includes learning objectives, chapter contents, a detailed lecture outline, questions for discussion, and boxed materials.

Instructor's Resource CD-ROM This all inclusive multimedia product is an invaluable asset for professors who prefer to work with electronic files rather than traditional print supplements. On this single CD-ROM, instructors will find the Instructor's Manual, the complete set of PowerPoint slides, the Test Item File, and the Prentice Hall Test Manager program.

Test Item File Each chapter contains true/false, multiple choice, short answer/essay questions, and situation-based questions. Together the questions cover the content of each chapter in a variety of ways providing flexibility in testing the students' knowledge of the text.

Windows/Prentice Hall Test Manager Contains all of the questions in the printed TIF. Test Manager is a comprehensive suite of tools for testing and assessment. Test Manager allows educators to easily create and distribute tests for their courses, either by printing and distributing through traditional methods, or by on-line delivery via a Local Area Network (LAN) server.

PowerPoint Electronic Transparencies with Teaching Notes A comprehensive package, these PowerPoint transparencies are designed to aid the educator and supplement in-class lectures. To further enhance the lecture, teaching notes for each slide are included both electronically, and as a printed, punched, and perforated booklet for insertion into a three-ring binder, allowing the educator to customize the lecture.

Color Transparencies Designed to aid the educator and enhance classroom lectures, 100 of the most critical PowerPoint electronic transparencies have been chosen for inclusion in this package as full-color acetates.

The Video Package offers two different options for enhanced learning:

Skills Videos Five videos (one for each part of the text) offer dramatizations that highlight various management skills. The videos provide excellent starting points for classroom discussion and debate. These videos are available on VHS for classroom presentation.

Company Videos Additional videos focus on the management practices at small and medium-size companies. These videos are from the *Small Business 2000* series (as seen on PBS). Video notes are found in the Instructor's Manual, and offer a summary of each video with discussion points and suggested responses.

WebCT On-Line Course This third edition offers a fully developed on-line course for management.

Study Guide Designed to aid student comprehension of the text, the study guide contains chapter objectives, detailed chapter outlines, review, discussion, and study questions.

Self-Assessment Library CD-ROM Free as a value pack, this valuable tool includes 45 individual self-assessment exercises, organized around individuals, groups, and organizations. Each exercise can be taken electronically and scored immediately, giving students individual feedback.

PHLIP/CW Web Site *Fundamentals* is supported by PHLIP (Prentice Hall Learning on the Internet Partnership) the book's companion Web site. An invaluable resource for both instructors and students, PHLIP features a wealth of up-to-date, on-line resources at the touch of a button! A research center, current events articles, an interactive study guide, exercises, and additional resources all combine to give you the most advanced text-specific Web site available.

Acknowledgments

Writing a textbook is often the work of a number of people whose names generally never appear on the cover. Yet, without their help and assistance, a project like this would never come to fruition. We'd like to recognize some special people who gave so unselfishly to making this book a reality.

First are our friends at Prentice Hall. Specifically, we want to thank Melissa Steffens, David Shafer, Judy Leale, Cindy Spreder, Michael Campbell, Jim Boyd, Natalie Anderson, Sandy Steiner, Diane Peirano, Cheryl Asherman, Teri Stratford, Irene Hess, and Samantha Steel. We appreciate their support and efforts to make this book successful.

We also want to thank our previous users and students who provided us with a number of suggestions for this revision.

Reviewers

Artegal R. Camburn	Buena Vista University
David W. Hart	Mary Washington College
Edward A. Johnson	University of North Florida
Barbara McIntosh	University of Vermont
Marta Mooney	Fordham University
C. Dewitt Peterson	Burlington County College
Jerry L. Thomas	Arapahoe Community College
Mark Youndt	University of Connecticut

Their constructive comments and suggestions have made this a much better book.

Finally, we'd like to add a personal note. Each of us has some special people we'd like to recognize.

From Steve's corner: I want to thank Laura Ospanik, Dana Murray, and Jennifer Robbins. My wife, Laura, continues to be a source of ideas and support. And my daughters, Dana and Jennifer, provide a rich source of suggestions on how to make my texts more relevant and student accessible.

From Dave's: I have given a lot of thought to what I'd like to say to my family that I haven't said before. And the more that I think about it, I keep coming back to the realization that the key word in all of my thoughts is "family." Through life's struggles, we often don't understand that there's always one constant—the love that a family has. To my wife Terri, you have an inner strength that is unequaled. We are all lucky to have you in our lives. To Mark, getting ready for that senior year in high school is amazing. It's been a pleasure to watch you grow into such a terrific young man. Keep your focus and you'll go far in life. To Meredith, you continue to teach us how to deal with difficult situations, to stand up for what you know is right, and have the conviction to make this world a better place. You are more beautiful today and an honor to have as a daughter. To Gabriella, the Mouse, you bring sunshine to everyone around you. If only I had one tenth of your energy. There's never a rainy day when I'm around you. And Natalie, you keep me in line. Keep up with that bubbling personality and the world is your's. I know my life is better because you are in it! Thanks again to all of you for making me who I am.

A Short Note To Students

Now that our writing chores are over, we can put our feet up on the table and offer a few brief comments to those of you who will be reading and studying this book. First, this text provides you exposure to the fundamentals of management. As you'll see in our first chapter, *fundamentals* implies coverage of the basic functions of management. We've made every effort to give you the essential information a student will need to solidly build a knowledge foundation. A knowledge base, however, is not easily attained unless you have a text that is straightforward, timely, and interesting to read. We have made every effort to achieve those goals with a writing style that tries to capture the conversational tone that you would get if you were personally attending one of our lectures. That means logical reasoning, clear explanations, and lots of examples to illustrate concepts.

A book, in addition to being enjoyable to read and understand, should help you learn. Reading for reading's sake, without comprehension, is a waste of your time and effort. So, we've done a couple of things in this book to assist your learning. We've introduced major topic headings in each chapter. These green underlined heads provide exposure to a broad management concept. Most of these leading heads are followed by questions. Each "question" heading was carefully chosen to reinforce understanding of very specific information. Accordingly, as you read each of these sections, material presented will address the question posed. Thus, after reading a chapter (or a section for that matter), you should be able to return to these headings and respond to the question. If you can't answer a question or are unsure of your response, you'll know exactly what sections you need to reread or where more of your effort needs to be placed. All in all, this format provides a self-check on your reading comprehension.

We've added other check points that you should find useful. Our review and discussion questions (called Reading for Comprehension and Linking Concepts to Practice, respectively) are designed to reinforce the chapter outcomes from two perspectives. First, review questions focus on material covered in the chapter. These are another way to reinforce your comprehension of the important concepts in the chapter. The discussion questions require you to go one step further. Rather than asking you to recite facts, discussion questions require you to integrate, synthesize, or apply a management concept. True understanding of the material is revealed when you can apply these more complex issues to a variety of situations.

There is another element of this text that we hope you'll enjoy. These are the Management Workshop sections at the end of each chapter. Managing today requires sound competencies—competencies that can be translated into specific skills. These sections are designed to help you enhance your analytical, diagnostic, investigative, team-building, Internet, and writing skills. We hope that you find them useful and use them as a source of self-development. You'll also find step-by-step skill guidance to help you learn such skills as how to build a power base, interview candidates, build trust, and provide performance feedback. We encourage you to carefully review each of these, practice the behaviors, and keep them handy for later reference.

We conclude by extending an open invitation to you. If you'd like to give us some feedback, we encourage you to write. Send your correspondence to Professor Dave DeCenzo at the College of Business and Economics, Towson University, Towson, Maryland 21252-0001. Dave is also available on e-mail <ddecenzo@towson.edu>.

Good luck this semester and we hope you enjoy reading this book as much as we did preparing it for you.

One

Managers and Management

LEARNING OUTCOMES After reading this chapter, I will be able to:

1. Describe the difference between managers and operative employees.
2. Explain what is meant by the term *management.*
3. Differentiate between efficiency and effectiveness.
4. Describe the four primary processes of management.
5. Classify the three levels of managers and identify the primary responsibility of each group.
6. Summarize the essential roles performed by managers.
7. Discuss whether the manager's job is generic.
8. Describe the four general skills necessary for becoming a successful manager.
9. Describe the value of studying management.
10. Identify the relevance of popular humanities and social science courses to management practices.

In today's fiercely competitive marketplace, an organization can fail at a moment's notice. What distinguishes those organizations that succeed from those that don't? Good managers. Managers come from all walks of life. They differ in terms of shape, color, age, and gender. They work to produce a profit or to achieve some social good. Yet managers don't accomplish these goals by themselves. Goals are achieved through and with the efforts of others. Managers make sure plans are laid out, activities are kept on track, and the environment is conducive for productive work. One such manager is Wiin Wu.[1]

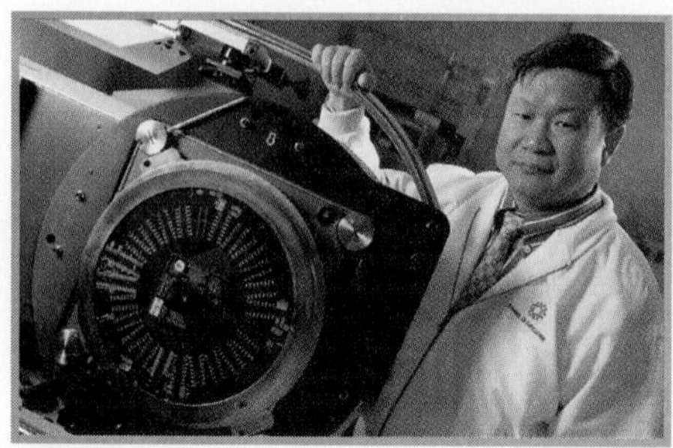

Educated in the United States at MIT and Stanford University, Wu began his career in California at Intel. After several years of working at this high-tech giant, he felt he was ready to move on. He had a vision of how to make better computer chips, and he felt he could make that vision happen if he had his own company. Wu made his vision a reality in 1989 when he founded Macronix International, Ltd., in Taiwan's Hsinchu Science Park.

From the very beginning, Wu understood the value of good management. As the founder, he knew he needed to surround himself with high-quality people to fulfill his vision. He did this by offering several workers an opportunity to join him in Taiwan—giving them a chance to return home and to have a "piece" of the company. Many gave up comfortable and stable jobs in the United States for this chance.

Wu also realized that no organization could remain complacent in the volatile microchip market and survive. He knew that long-term success came from identifying opportunities and staking out a growth plan. So Wu created alliances with other companies and invested heavily in research and development, spending nearly 16 percent of company revenues on product development.

While making decisions about the company, its directions and how its money is spent, Wu never overlooks the role of the human factor. He constantly seeks ways to re-create the organization, making it possible for employees to do the best job they can while facing the fewest hassles. He fosters a work environment that promotes enthusiasm—one in which employees excitedly look forward to coming to work. And he knows that he must "grow" his people, providing them opportunities to develop so they'll stay knowledgeable and able to respond to change.

Have Wiin Wu's efforts proven successful for Macronix International? The answer appears to be yes. Company sales exceeded $320 million in 1998, and its share of the Asian microchip market has nearly doubled from 2.8 to 5.4 percent. These results—and Wu's positioning of the company to reach $1 billion in sales in the next several years—have earned Macronix the recent honor of being chosen one of Taiwan's thriving high-tech companies.

Wiin Wu provides a good example of what a successful manager does. The key word, however, is example. There is no universally accepted model of what a successful manager looks like. Managers today can be under age eighteen or over eighty. Nowadays, they are as likely to be women as they are to be men.[2] They manage large corporations, small businesses, government agencies, hospitals, museums, schools, and such nontraditional organizations as cooperatives. Some hold positions at the top of their organizations; some are middle managers, and others are first-line supervisors who oversee employees. And today's managers can be found in every country on the globe.

This book is about the work activities of Wiin Wu and the tens of millions of other managers like him. In this chapter, we introduce you to managers and management by answering, or at least beginning to answer, these questions: Who are managers, and where do they work? What is management, and what do managers do? And why should you spend your time studying management?

Managers work in organizations. Therefore, before we identify who managers are and what they do, we must clarify what we mean by the term *organization*.

An **organization** is a systematic arrangement of people brought together to accomplish some specific purpose. Your college or university is an organization. So are sororities, the United Way, churches, your neighborhood convenience store, the New York Yankees baseball team, the MCI–Worldcom Corporation, the Mexico-based retailer Commercial Mexicana,[3] and Royal Dutch Shell. These are all organizations because each has three common characteristics.

organization
A systematic arrangement of people brought together to accomplish some specific purpose

operatives
People who work directly on a job or task and have no responsibility for overseeing the work of others

managers
Individuals in an organization who direct the activities of others

WHAT THREE COMMON CHARACTERISTICS DO ALL ORGANIZATIONS SHARE?

Every organization has a *purpose* and is made up of *people* who are *grouped* in some fashion (see Exhibit 1-1). The distinct purpose of an organization is typically expressed in terms of a goal or set of goals. For example, Richard McGinn, president of Lucent Technologies, has set his sights on achieving a greater market share in the $600 billion telecommunications market;[4] whereas Xerox CEO Rick Thoman expects the company to achieve "double-digit revenue growth."[5] Second, no purpose or goal can be achieved by itself. People must make decisions to establish the purpose and to perform a variety of activities to make the goal a reality. Third, all organizations develop a systematic structure that defines and limits the behavior of its members. Developing structure may include, for example, creating rules and regulations, giving some members supervisory control over other members, forming work teams, or writing job descriptions so that organizational members know what they are supposed to do. The term organization, therefore, refers to an entity that has a distinct purpose, has people or members, and has a systematic structure.

HOW ARE MANAGERS DIFFERENT FROM OPERATIVE EMPLOYEES?

Managers work in organizations, but not everyone who works in an organization is a manager. For simplicity's sake, we can divide organizational members into two categories: operatives and managers. **Operatives** are people who work directly on a job or task and have no responsibility for overseeing the work of others. The people who make the automotive parts at the Dana assembly plant, ring up your sale at Foot Locker, or process your course registration in your college's registrar office are all operatives. In contrast, **managers** direct the activities of other people in the organization. Customarily classified as top, middle, or first-line managers, these individuals supervise both operative employees and

How does an organization like the New York Yankees become successful? By having in place a systematic arrangement of quality people—both on and off the field—focusing their efforts on achieving some goal. For them, that's winning the World Series.

Exhibit 1-1
Common Characteristics of Organizations

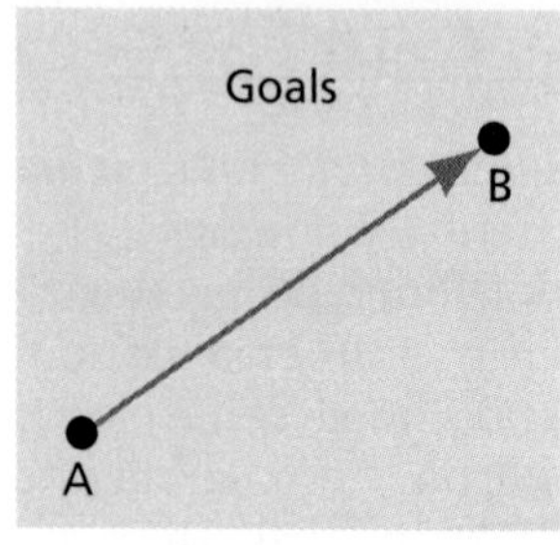

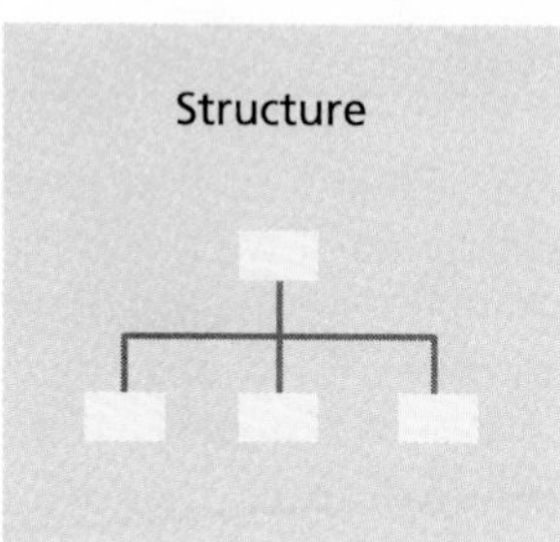

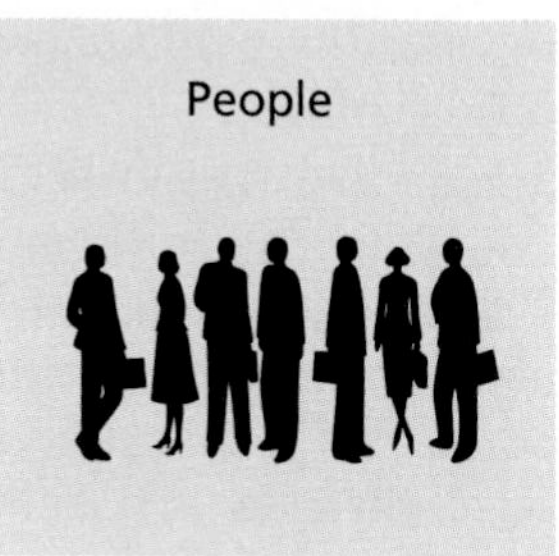

lower-level managers (see Exhibit 1-2). That does not mean, however, that managers don't work directly on tasks. Some managers also have operative responsibilities themselves. For example, district sales managers for Moen Faucets also have basic responsibilities of servicing some accounts in addition to overseeing the activities of the other sales associates in their territory. The distinction, then, between the two groups—operatives and managers—is that managers have employees who report directly to them.

first-line managers
Supervisors responsible for directing the day-to-day activities of operative employees

middle managers
Individuals at levels of management between the first-line manager and top management

top managers
Individuals who are responsible for making decisions about the direction of the organization and establishing policies that affect all organizational members

WHAT TITLES DO MANAGERS HAVE IN ORGANIZATIONS?

Identifying exactly who managers are in an organization is often not a difficult task, although you should be aware that management positions come with a variety of titles. **First-line managers** are usually called supervisors. They are responsible for directing the day-to-day activities of operative employees. In your college, for example, the department chair would be a first-line supervisor overseeing the activities of the departmental faculty (the operatives). **Middle managers** represent levels of management between the first-line manager (the supervisor) and top management. These individuals manage other managers—and possibly some operative employees—and are typically responsible for translating the goals set by top management into specific details that lower-level managers can perform. In organizations, middle managers may have such titles as department or agency head, project leader, unit chief, district manager, dean, bishop, or division manager.

At or near the top of an organization are **top managers.** These individuals, like Wiin Wu, Robert McGinn, or Rick Thoman, are responsible for making decisions about the direction of the organization and establishing policies that affect all

Exhibit 1-2
Organizational Levels

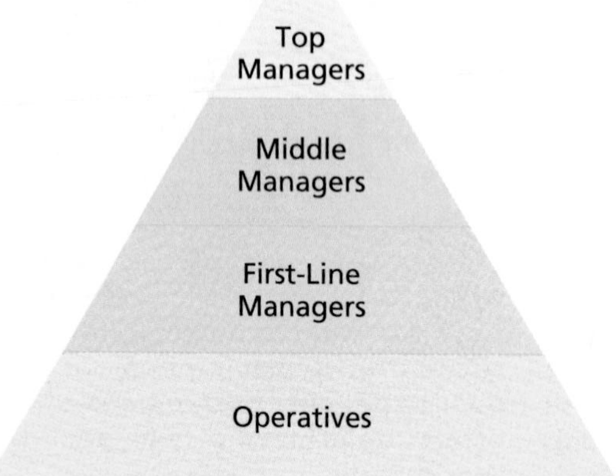

organizational members. Top managers typically have titles such as vice president, president, chancellor, managing director, chief operating officer, chief executive officer, or chairperson of the board.

What Is Management, and What Do Managers Do?

Just as organizations have common characteristics, so, too, do managers. Despite the fact that their titles vary widely, there are several common elements to their jobs—regardless of whether the manager is a head nurse in the intensive care unit of Cedars-Sinai Hospital who oversees a staff of 11 critical care specialists or the president of the 608,000-member General Motors Corporation.[6] In this section we will look at these commonalities as we define management, present the classical management functions, review recent research on managerial roles, and consider the universal applicability of managerial concepts.

management
The process of getting things done, effectively and efficiently, through and with other people

efficiency
Means doing the thing correctly; refers to the relationship between inputs and outputs. Seeks to minimize resource costs

effectiveness
Means doing the right thing; goal attainment

HOW DO WE DEFINE MANAGEMENT?

The term **management** refers to the process of getting things done, effectively and efficiently, through and with other people. Several components in this definition warrant discussion. These are the terms *process, effectively,* and *efficiently.*

The term *process* in the definition of management represents the primary activities managers perform. We explore these in the next section.

Effectiveness and efficiency deal with what we are doing and how we are doing it. **Efficiency** means doing the task correctly and refers to the relationship between inputs and outputs. For instance, if you get more output for a given input, you have increased efficiency. So, too, do you increase efficiency when you get the same output with fewer resources. Since managers deal with input resources that are scarce—money, people, equipment—they are concerned with the efficient use of those resources. Management, therefore, is concerned with minimizing resource costs.

Although minimizing resource costs is important, it is not enough simply to be efficient. Management is also concerned with completing activities. In management terms, we call this ability **effectiveness.** Effectiveness means doing the right task. In an organization, that translates into goal attainment (see Exhibit 1-3).

Although efficiency and effectiveness are different terms, they are interrelated. For instance, it's easier to be effective if one ignores efficiency. Hewlett-Packard could produce more sophisticated and longer-lasting toner cartridges for its

Not all organizational members have management responsibilities. Some are operative employees—individuals responsible for working directly on a job. For example, this Dana employee works in the company's Lancaster, Pennsylvania automotive parts assembly plant where he assembles car parts used by a number of automobile manufacturers. While he has specific job responsibilities, this Dana operative does not oversee the work of others.

Exhibit 1-3
Efficiency and Effectiveness

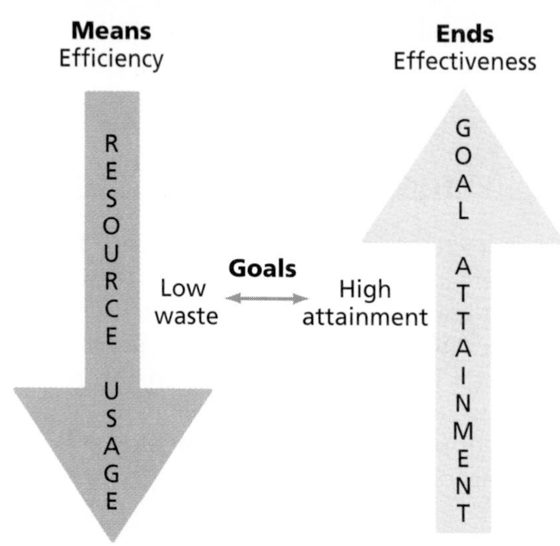

laser printers if it disregarded labor and material input costs. Similarly, some government agencies have been regularly attacked on the grounds that they are reasonably effective but extremely inefficient. That is, they accomplish their goals but do so at a very high cost. Our conclusion: Good management is concerned with both attaining goals (effectiveness) and doing so as efficiently as possible.[7]

Can organizations be efficient and yet not be effective? Yes, by doing the wrong things well! A number of colleges have become highly efficient in processing students. Through the use of computer-assisted learning, distance-learning programs, or a heavy reliance on part-time faculty, administrators may have significantly cut the cost of educating each student. Yet some of these colleges have been criticized by students, alumni, and accrediting agencies for failing to educate students properly. Of course, high efficiency is associated more typically with high effectiveness. And poor management is most often due to both inefficiency and ineffectiveness or to effectiveness achieved through inefficiency.

WHAT ARE THE MANAGEMENT PROCESSES?

In the early part of this century, the French industrialist Henri Fayol wrote that all managers perform five management activities referred to as the management process. They plan, organize, command, coordinate, and control.[8] In the mid-1950s, two professors at UCLA used the terms planning, organizing, staffing, directing, and controlling as the framework for a textbook on management that for twenty years was unquestionably the most widely sold text on the subject.[9] The most popular textbooks still continue to be organized around the **management processes,** though these have generally been condensed to the basic four: planning, organizing, leading, and controlling (see Exhibit 1-4). Let us briefly define what each of these encompasses. Keep in mind before we begin, however, that, although we will look at each as an independent task, managers must be able to perform all four activities simultaneously and realize that each has an effect on the others. That is, these processes are interrelated and interdependent.

management process
Planning, organizing, leading, and controlling

If you don't much care where you want to get to, then it doesn't matter which way you go, the Cheshire cat said in *Alice in Wonderland.* Since organizations exist to achieve some purpose, someone has to define that purpose and the means for its achievement. A manager is that someone. The **planning** component encompasses defining an organization's goals, establishing an overall strategy for achiev-

planning
Includes defining goals, establishing strategy, and developing plans to coordinate activities

Exhibit 1-4
Management Process Activities

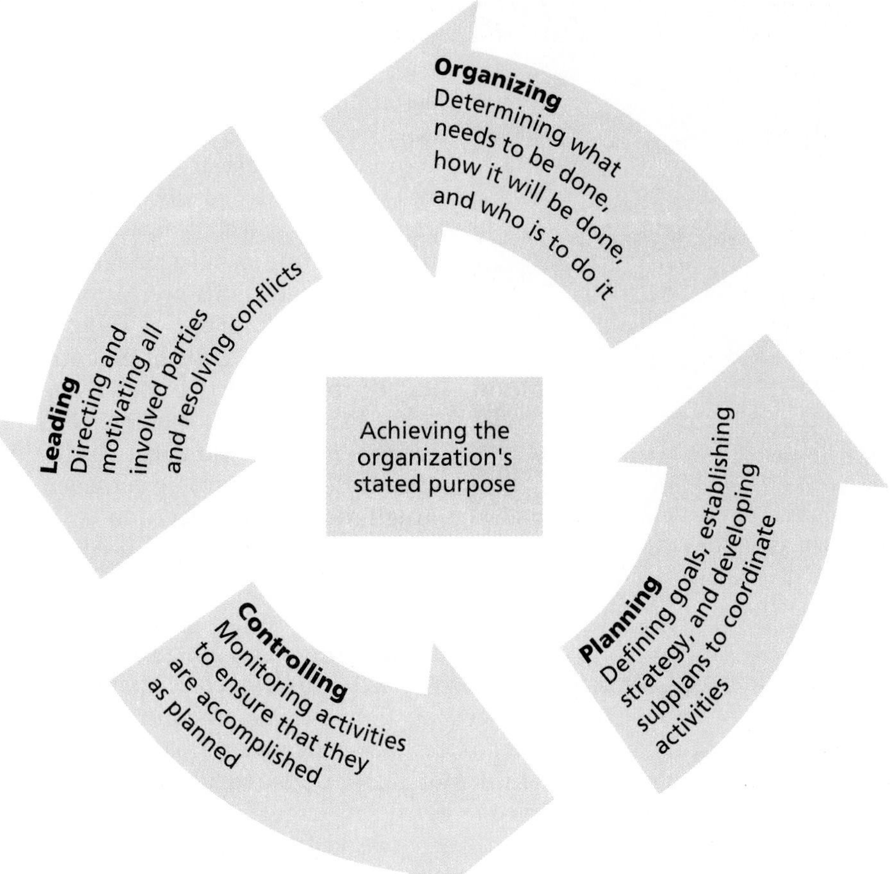
Organizing
Determining what needs to be done, how it will be done, and who is to do it
Leading
Directing and motivating all involved parties and resolving conflicts
Achieving the organization's stated purpose
Planning
Defining goals, establishing strategy, and developing subplans to coordinate activities
Controlling
Monitoring activities to ensure that they are accomplished as planned

ing those goals, and developing a comprehensive hierarchy of plans to integrate and coordinate activities. Setting goals keeps the work to be done in its proper focus and helps organizational members keep their attention on what is most important.

Managers like Wiin Wu are also responsible for designing an organization's structure. We call this management activity **organizing.** Organizing includes determining what tasks are to be done, who is to do them, how the tasks are to be grouped, who reports to whom, and where decisions are to be made.

We know that every organization contains people. And it is part of a manager's job to direct and coordinate those people. Performing this activity is the **leading** component of management. When managers motivate employees, direct the activities of others, select the most effective communication channel, or resolve conflicts among members, they are leading.

The final activity managers perform is **controlling.** After the goals are set, the plans formulated, the structural arrangements determined, and the people hired, trained, and motivated, something may still go amiss. To ensure that things are going as they should, a manager must monitor the organization's performance. Actual performance must be compared with the previously set goals. If there are any significant deviations, it is the manager's responsibility to get the organization back on track. This method of monitoring, comparing, and correcting is what we mean when we refer to the controlling process.

organizing
Includes determining what tasks are to be done, who is to do them, how the tasks are to be grouped, who reports to whom, and where decisions are to be made

leading
Includes motivating employees, directing the activities of others, selecting the most effective communication channel, and resolving conflicts

controlling
The process of monitoring performance, comparing it with goals, and correcting any significant deviations

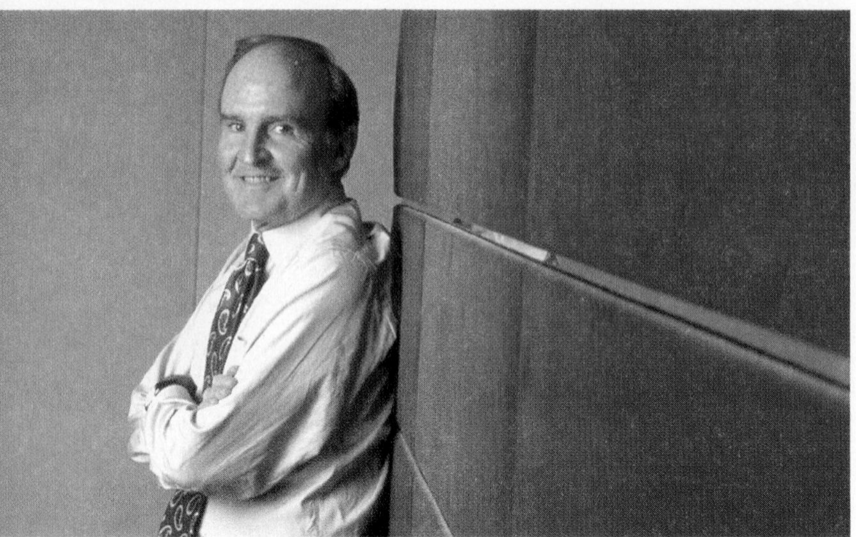

Whenever a manager, like CEO Jack Welch of General Electric, represents his organization to the community at large, he is performing the management role of spokesperson.

The continued popularity of the process approach is a tribute to its clarity and simplicity. But is it an accurate description of what managers actually do?[10] Following this management approach, it's easy to answer the question, "What do managers do?" They plan, organize, lead, and control. But is this really true of all managers? Fayol's original applications were not derived from a careful survey of thousands of managers in hundreds of organizations. Rather, they merely represented observations based on his experience in the French mining industry. In the late 1960s, Henry Mintzberg provided fresh insight on the manager's job.[11]

WHAT ARE MANAGEMENT ROLES?

Henry Mintzberg undertook a careful study of five chief executives at work. What he discovered challenged several long-held notions about the manager's job. For instance, in contrast to the predominant views at the time that managers were reflective thinkers who carefully and systematically processed information before making decisions, Mintzberg found that the managers he studied engaged in a large number of varied, unpatterned, and short-duration activities. There was little time for reflective thinking because the managers encountered constant interruptions. Half of these managers' activities lasted less than nine minutes. But in addition to these insights, Mintzberg provided a categorization scheme for defining what managers do on the basis of actual managers on the job. These are commonly referred to as Mintzberg's **managerial roles.**

managerial roles
Specific categories of managerial behavior; often grouped under three primary headings: interpersonal relationships, transfer of information, and decision making

Mintzberg concluded that managers perform 10 different but highly interrelated roles. The term managerial roles refers to specific categories of managerial behavior. These 10 roles, as shown in Exhibit 1-5, can be grouped under three primary headings—interpersonal relationships, the transfer of information, and decision making.

IS THE MANAGER'S JOB UNIVERSAL?

Previously, we mentioned the universal applicability of management activities. So far, we have discussed management as if it were a generic activity. That is, a manager is a manager regardless of where he or she manages. If management is truly a generic discipline, then what a manager does should be essentially the same regardless of whether he or she is a top-level executive or a first-line supervisor; in a business firm or a government agency; in a large corporation or a small business; or located in Berlin, Germany or Berlin, Maryland. Let's take a closer look at the generic issue.

Level in the organization We have already acknowledged that the importance of managerial roles varies depending on the manager's level in the organization. But the fact that a supervisor in a research laboratory at Pfizer

Exhibit 1-5 Mintzberg's Managerial Roles

Role	Descrption	Identifiable Activities
Interpersonal		
Figurehead	Symbolic head; obliged to perform a number of routine duties of a legal or social nature	Greeting visitors; signing legal documents
Leader	Responsible for the motivation and activation of employees; responsible for staffing, training, and associated duties	Performing virtually all activities that involve employees
Liaison	Maintains self-developed network of outside contacts and informers who provide favors and information	Acknowledging mail; doing external board work; performing other activities that involve outsiders
Informational		
Monitor	Seeks and receives wide variety of special information (much of it current) to develop thorough understanding of organization and environment; emerges as nerve center of internal and external information about the organization	Reading periodicals and reports; maintaining personal contacts
Disseminator	Transmits information received from other employees to members of the organization—some information is factual, some involves interpretation and integration of diverse value positions of organizational influencers	Holding informational meetings; making phone calls to relay information
Spokesperson	Transmits information to outsiders on organization's plans, policies, actions, results, etc.; serves as expert on organization's industry	Holding board meetings; giving information to the media
Decisional		
Entrepreneur	Searches organization and its environment for opportunities and initiates "improvement projects" to bring about change; supervises design of certain projects as well	Organizing strategy and review sessions to develop new programs
Disturbance handler	Responsible for corrective action when organization faces important disturbances	Organizing strategy and review sessions that involve disturbances and crises
Resource allocator	Responsible for the allocation of organizational resources of all kinds—in effect, the making or approval of all significant organizational decisions	Scheduling; requesting authorization; performing any activity that involves budgeting and the programming of employees' work
Negotiator	Responsible for representing the organization at major negotiations	Participating in union contract negotiations or in those with suppliers

SOURCE: *The Nature of Managerial Work* (paperback) by H. Mintzberg, Table 2, pp. 92–93. Copyright © 1973 Addison Wesley Longman. Reprinted by permission of Addison Wesley Longman.

Pharmaceuticals doesn't do exactly the same things that the president of Pfizer does should not be interpreted to mean that their jobs are inherently different. The differences are of degree and emphasis but not of activity.

As managers move up the organization, they do more planning and less direct overseeing of others. This distinction is visually depicted in Exhibit 1-6. All managers, regardless of level, make decisions. They perform planning, organizing, leading, and controlling activities, but the amount of time they give to each activity is not necessarily constant. In addition, the content of the managerial activities changes with the manager's level. For example, as we will demonstrate in Chapter 5, top managers are concerned with designing the overall organization's structure, whereas lower-level managers focus on designing the jobs of individuals and work groups.

Profit versus not-for-profit Does a manager who works for the U.S. Bureau of Engraving, the Royal Canadian Mounted Police, or the AMVETS Foundation do the same things that a manager in a business firm does? Put another way, is the manager's job the same in both profit and not-for-profit organizations? The answer is, for the most part, yes.[12] Regardless of the type of organization a manager works in, the job has commonalities with all other managerial positions. All managers make decisions, set objectives, create workable organization structures, hire and motivate employees, secure legitimacy for their organization's existence, and develop internal political support in order to implement programs. Of course, there are some noteworthy differences. The most important is measuring performance. Profit, or the "bottom line," acts as an unambiguous measure of the effectiveness of a business organization. There is no such universal measure in not-for-profit organizations. Measuring the performance of schools, museums, government agencies, or charitable organizations, therefore, is more difficult. But don't interpret this difference to mean that managers in those organizations can ignore the financial side of their operation. Even not-for-profit organizations need to make money to survive. It's just that making a profit for the "owners" of not-for-profit organizations is not the primary focus. Consequently, managers in these organizations generally do not face a profit-maximizing market test for performance.

Our conclusion is that, while there are distinctions between the management of profit and not-for-profit organizations, the two are far more alike than they are different. Managers in both are similarly concerned with planning, organizing, leading, and controlling.

Exhibit 1-6
Distribution of Time per Activity by Organizational Level

Source: Adapted from T. A. Mahoney, T. H. Jerdee, and S. J. Carroll, "The Job(s) of Management," *Industrial Relations* 4, No. 2 (1965), p. 103.

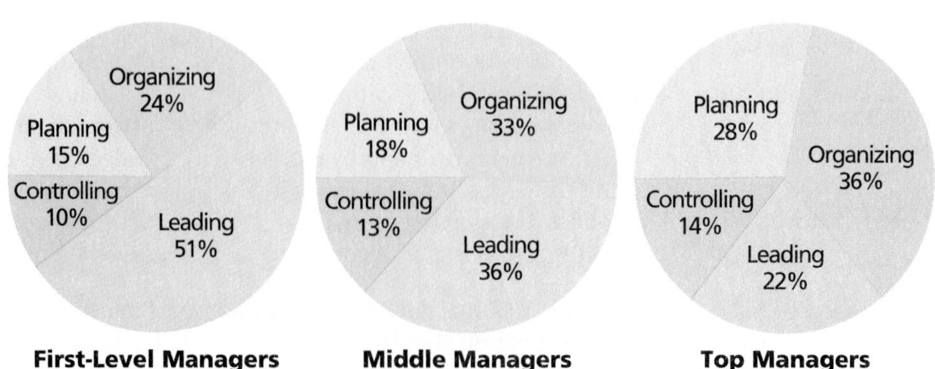

Size of organization Would you expect the job of a manager in a print shop that employs 12 people to be different from that of a manager who runs a 1,200-person printing plant for the *New York Times*? This question is best answered by looking at the job of managers in small business firms and comparing them with our previous discussion of managerial roles. First, however, let's define small business and the part it plays in our society.

There is no commonly agreed-upon definition of a small business because of different criteria used to define *small*. For example, an organization can be classified as a small business using such criteria as number of employees, annual sales, or total assets. For our purposes, we will call a **small business** any independently owned and operated profit-seeking enterprise that has fewer than 500 employees. Small businesses may be little in size, but they have a major effect in the world economy. Statistics tell us that small businesses account for about 97 percent of all nonfarm businesses in the United States; they employ over 60 percent of the private workforce; they dominate such industries as retailing and construction; and they will generate half of all new jobs during the next decade. Moreover, small businesses are where the job growth has been in recent years. Between 1980 and 2000, *Fortune* 100 companies cut several million jobs, but companies with fewer than 500 employees have created more than 2 million jobs annually.[13] This phenomenon is not confined solely to the United States. Similar small business start-ups have been witnessed in such countries as China, Japan, and Great Britain.[14]

small business
Any independently owned and operated profit-seeking enterprise that has fewer than 500 employees

Now to the question at hand: Is the job of managing a small business different from that of managing a large one? A study comparing the two found that the importance of roles differed significantly.[15] As illustrated in Exhibit 1-7, the small business manager's most important role is that of spokesperson. The small business manager spends a large amount of time performing outwardly directed actions such as meeting with customers, arranging financing with bankers, searching for new opportunities, and stimulating change. In contrast, the most important concerns of a manager in a large organization are directed internally—

Importance of Roles

Roles Played by Managers in Small Firms	Importance	Roles Played by Managers in Large Firms
Spokesperson	High	Resource allocator
Entrepreneur Figurehead Leader	Moderate	Liaison Monitor Disturbance handler Negotiator
Disseminator	Low	Entrepreneur

Exhibit 1-7
Importance of Managerial Roles in Small and Large Businesses

SOURCE: Adapted from J. G. P. Paolillo, "The Manager's Self Assessments of Managerial Roles: Small vs. Large Firms," *American Journal of Small Business*, January–March 1984, pp. 61–62.

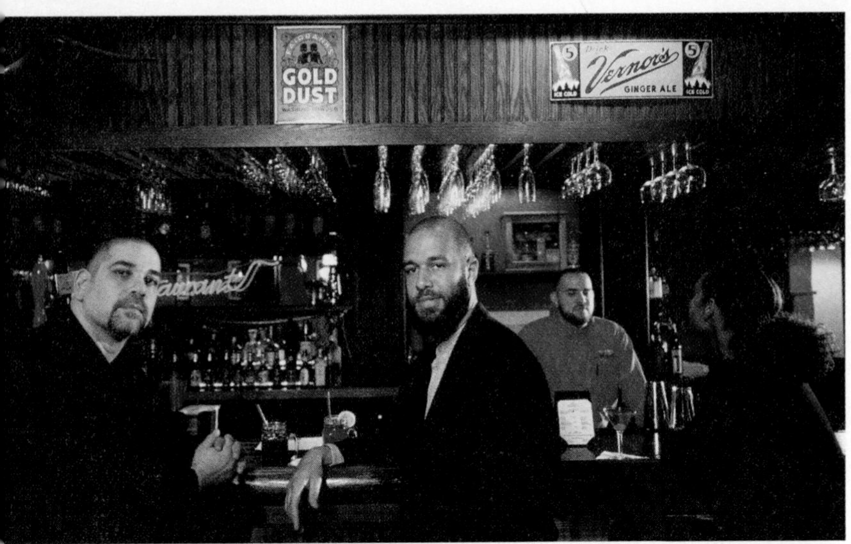

Robert and Benjamin Bynum, founders of fine-dining and first-rate entertainment establishments, are the epitome of today's small business manager. They spend a considerable amount of their time as spokespersons and entrepreneurs, which they find beneficial in helping them grow their business.

deciding which organizational units get what available resources and how much of them. According to this study, the entrepreneurial role—looking for business opportunities and planning activities for performance improvement—is least important to managers in large firms.

Compared with a manager in a large organization, a small business manager is more likely to be a generalist. His or her job will combine the activities of a large corporation's chief executive with many of the day-to-day activities undertaken by a first-line supervisor. Moreover, the structure and formality that characterize a manager's job in a large organization tend to give way to informality in small firms. Planning is less likely to be a carefully orchestrated ritual. The organization's design will be less complex and structured. And control in the small business will rely more on direct observation than on sophisticated computerized monitoring systems.[16]

Again, as with organizational level, we see differences in degree and emphasis but not in activities. Managers in both small and large organizations perform essentially the same activities; only how they go about them and the proportion of time they spend on each are different.

Management concepts and national borders The last generic issue concerns whether management concepts are transferable across national borders. If managerial concepts were completely generic, they would also apply universally in any country in the world, regardless of economic, social, political, or cultural differences. Studies that have compared managerial practices between countries have not generally supported the universality of management concepts.[17] In Chapter 2, we will examine some specific differences between countries and describe their effect on managing. At this point, it is sufficient to say that most of the concepts we will be discussing in future chapters primarily apply to the United States, Canada, Great Britain, Australia, and other English-speaking democracies. We should be prepared to modify these concepts if we want to apply them in India, China, Chile, or other countries whose economic, political, social, or cultural environment differs greatly from that of the so-called free-market democracies.

Making decisions and dealing with change Two final points of view need to be considered regarding what managers do. Managers make decisions, and managers are agents of change. Almost everything managers do requires them to make decisions. Whether it involves setting goals in the organization, deciding how to structure jobs, determining how to motivate and reward employees, or determining where significant performance variances exist, a manager must make a decision. The best managers, then, are the ones who can identify critical problems, assimilate the appropriate data, make sense of the information, and choose the best course of action to take for resolving the problem. We'll address the proper way to make decision in Chapter 4.

Organizations today also operate in a world of dynamic change. Managing chaos has become the rule—not the exception. Successful managers acknowledge the rapid changes around them and are flexible in adapting their practices to deal with those changes. For instance, successful managers recognize the potential effect of technological improvements on a work unit's performance, but they also realize that people often resist change. Accordingly, managers need to be in a position to "sell" the benefits of the change while, simultaneously, helping their employees deal with the uncertainty and anxiety that the changes may bring. This example illustrates how managers act as agents of change. We'll look at this change phenomenon in greater detail in Chapter 7.

WHAT SKILLS AND COMPETENCIES DO SUCCESSFUL MANAGERS POSSESS?

Even though we recognize that all managers—regardless of level, organization size, profit or nonprofit enterprise—perform the four basic activities of management to some degree, a more crucial question becomes, "What are the critical skills that are related to managerial competence?" In the 1970s, management researcher Robert L. Katz attempted to answer that question.[18] What Katz and others have found is that managers must possess four critical management skills.[19] Management skills identify those abilities or behaviors that are crucial to success in a managerial position. These skills can be viewed on two levels—general skills a manager must possess and the specific skills that are related to managerial success. Let's look at these two categories.

General skills There seems to be overall agreement that effective managers must be proficient in four general skill areas.[20] These are conceptual, interpersonal, technical, and political skills.

Conceptual skills refer to the mental ability to analyze and diagnose complex situations. They help managers see how things fit together and facilitate making good decisions. **Interpersonal skills** encompass the ability to work with, understand, mentor, and motivate other people, both individually and in groups (see Developing Your Mentoring Skills on p. 23). Since managers get things done through other people, they must have good interpersonal skills to communicate, motivate, and delegate. Additionally, all managers need **technical skills.** These are abilities to apply specialized knowledge or expertise. For top-level managers, these abilities tend to be related to knowledge of the industry and a general understanding of the organization's processes and products. For middle and lower-level managers, they are related to the specialized knowledge required in the areas with which they work—finance, human resources, manufacturing, computer systems, law, marketing, and the like. Finally, managers need **political skills.** This area is related to the ability to enhance one's position, build a power base, and establish the right connections. Organizations are political arenas in which people compete for resources. Managers with good political skills tend to be better at getting resources for their group than are managers with poor political skills. They also receive higher evaluations and get more promotions.[21]

conceptual skills
A manager's mental ability to coordinate all of the organization's interests and activities

interpersonal skills
A manager's ability to work with, understand, mentor, and motivate others, both individually and in groups

technical skills
A manager's ability to use the tools, procedures, and techniques of a specialized field

political skills
A manager's ability to build a power base and establish the "right" connections

Specific skills Research has also identified six sets of behaviors that explain a little bit more than 50 percent of a manager's effectiveness.[22]

- **Controlling the organization's environment and its resources** This includes demonstrating, in planning and allocation meetings as well as in on-the-spot decision making, the ability to be proactive and stay ahead of environmental changes. It also involves basing resource decisions on clear, up-to-date, accurate knowledge of the organization's objectives.
- **Organizing and coordinating** In this skill, managers organize around tasks and then coordinate interdependent relationships among tasks wherever they exist.
- **Handling information** This set of behaviors comprises using information and communication channels for identifying problems, understanding a changing environment, and making effective decisions.
- **Providing for growth and development** Managers provide for their own personal growth and development, as well as for the personal growth and development of their employees, through continual learning on the job.
- **Motivating employees and handling conflicts** Managers enhance the positive aspects of motivation so that employees feel impelled to perform their work and eliminate those conflicts that may inhibit employees' motivation.
- **Strategic problem solving** Managers take responsibility for their own decisions and ensure that subordinates effectively use their decision-making skills.

management competencies
A cluster of related knowledge, skills, and attitudes related to effective managerial performance

Management competencies The most recent approach to defining the manager's job focuses on **management competencies.**[23] These are defined as a cluster of related knowledge, skills, and attitudes related to effective managerial performance. One of the most comprehensive competency studies has come out of the United Kingdom.[24] It's called the management charter initiative (MCI). Based on an analysis of management activities and focusing on what effective managers should be able to do rather than on what they know, the MCI sets generic standards of management competence. Currently, there are two sets of standards. Management I is for first-level managers. Management II is for middle managers. Standards for top management are under development.

Exhibit 1-8 lists standards for middle management. For each area of competence there is a related set of specific elements that define effectiveness in that area. For instance, one area of competence is recruiting and selecting personnel. Successful development of this competence area requires that managers be able to define future personnel requirements, to determine specifications to secure quality people, and to assess and select candidates against team and organizational requirements.

One of the important skills a manager must develop is that of mentoring employees. At Ingersoll-Rand, being a mentor is an important competency for all managers to have. Mentoring has become an important part of Ingersoll-Rand's development programs.

Exhibit 1-8 Management Charter Initiative Competencies for Middle Managers

Basic Competence	Specific Associated Elements (Sample)
1. Initiate and implement change and improvement in services, products, and systems	Identify opportunities for improvement in services, products, and systems Negotiate and agree on the introduction of change
2. Monitor, maintain, and improve service and product delivery	Establish and maintain the supply of resources into the organization/department Establish and agree on customer requirements
3. Monitor and control the use of resources	Control costs and enhance value Monitor and control activities against budgets
4. Secure effective resource allocation for activities and projects	Justify proposals for expenditures on projects Negotiate and agree on budgets
5. Recruit and select personnel	Define future personnel requirements Determine specifications to secure quality people
6. Develop teams, individuals, and self to enhance performance	Develop and improve teams through planning and activities Identify, review, and improve developmental activities for individuals
7. Plan, allocate, and evaluate work carried out by teams, individuals, and self	Set and update work objectives for teams and individuals Allocate work and evaluate teams, individuals, and self against objectives
8. Create, maintain, and enhance effective working relationships	Establish and maintain trust and support of one's employees Identify and minimize interpersonal conflict
9. Seek, evaluate, and organize information for action	Obtain and evaluate information to aid decision making Record and store information
10. Exchange information to solve problems and make decisions	Lead meetings and group discussions Advise and inform others

The MCI standards are attracting global interest. The Australian Institute of Management, for example, has already started using the standards, and the Management Development Center of Hong Kong is considering introducing them to help managers become more mobile after China's recent takeover of Hong Kong.

How Much Importance Does the Marketplace Put on Managers?

Good managers can turn straw to gold. Poor managers can do the reverse. This realization has not been lost on those who design compensation systems for organizations. Managers tend to be more highly paid than operatives. As a manager's authority and responsibility expand, so typically does his or her pay. Moreover, many organizations willingly offer extremely lucrative compensation packages to get and keep good managers.

If you were privy to the compensation paid employees at large toy-manufacturing firms such as Mattel and Fisher Price, you would discover an interesting fact. Their best sales associates rarely earn more than $95,000 a year. In contrast, the annual income of their senior managers is rarely less than $225,000, and, in some cases, it may exceed $750,000. The fact that these firms pay managers considerably more than nonmanagers is a measure of the importance placed on effective management skills. What is true at these toy-manufacturing firms is true in most organizations. Good managerial skills are a scarce commodity, and compensation packages are one measure of the value that organizations place on them.

However, realize that not all managers make six-figure incomes. Such salaries are usually reserved for senior executives. What, then, could you expect to earn as a manager? The answer depends on your level in the organization, your education and experience, the type of business the organization is in, comparable pay standards in the community, and how effective a manager you are. Most first-line supervisors earn between $30,000 and $55,000 a year. Middle managers often start near $45,000 and top out at around $120,000. Senior managers in large corporations can earn $1 million a year or more.[25] In 1998, for instance, the average cash compensation (salary plus annual bonus) for 483 of the top two executives at the 392 largest publicly held U.S. corporations was well over $1 million.[26] The top 20 of these individuals (CEOs from Walt Disney, CBS, and America Online) averaged more than $100 million in total compensation (including their stock options).[27] In many cases, this compensation was also enhanced by other means—such as stock options. Management compensation reflects the market forces of supply and demand. Management superstars, like superstar athletes in professional sports, are wooed with signing bonuses, interest-free loans, performance incentive packages, and guaranteed contracts. Of course, as in the case of athletes, some controversy surrounds the large dollar amounts paid to these executives[28] (see Ethical Dilemma in Management).

Ethical Dilemma in Management

Are U.S. Executives Overpaid?

Are we paying U.S. executives too much?[29] Is an average salary in excess of $60 million justifiable? There are two sides to the issue. One side of the issue believes that these executives have tremendous organizational responsibilities. They not only have to manage the organization in today's environment, they must keep it moving into the future. Their jobs are not 9-to-5 jobs, but rather 6 to 7 days a week, often 10 to 14 hours a day. If jobs are evaluated on the basis of skills, knowledge, abilities, and responsibilities, executives should be highly paid.[30] Furthermore, there is the issue of motivation and retention. If you want these individuals to succeed and stay with the company, you must provide a compensation package that motivates them to stay. Incentives based on various measures also provide the impetus for them to excel.

On the other hand, most of the research done on executive salaries questions the linkage to performance. Even when profits are down, many executives are paid handsomely. In fact, American company executives are regarded as some of the highest paid people in the world. On average, their salaries have increased in the last decade by more than 40 percent per year, but the average worker's salary has increased only about 3 percent during the same time. Furthermore, U.S. executives make two to five times the salaries of their foreign counterparts. That's an interesting comparison, especially when you consider that a number of executives in Japanese and European organizations perform better.

Do you believe that U.S. executives are overpaid? What's your opinion?

Why Study Management?

Management, as an academic field of study, offers a number of insights into many aspects of our daily organizational lives. Consequently, there are several reasons why we may want to study this topic.

The first reason for studying management is that we all have a vested interest in improving the way organizations are managed. Why? Because we interact with them every day of our lives. Does it frustrate you when you have to spend a couple of hours in a Department of Motor Vehicles office to get your driver's license renewed? Are you perplexed when none of the salespeople in a department store seem interested in helping you? Are you angered when you call an airline three times and their representatives quote you three different prices for the same trip? As a taxpayer, doesn't it seem as if something is wrong when you read about companies that have overbilled the federal government for defense-related equipment? These are all examples of problems that can largely be attributed to poor management. Organizations that are well managed—such as Wal-Mart, Siemens, Southwest Airlines, Motorola, Merck Pharmaceuticals, Toys "Я" Us, and Ssangyong Investment and Securities Company—develop a loyal constituency, grow, and prosper. Those that are poorly managed often find themselves with a declining customer base and reduced revenues. Eventually, the survival of poorly managed organizations becomes threatened. Thirty years ago, Gimbels, W.T. Grant, and Eastern Airlines were thriving corporations. They employed tens of thousands of people and provided goods and services on a daily basis to hundreds of thousands of customers. But weak management did them in. Today those companies no longer exist.

The second reason for studying management is that once you graduate from college and begin your career, you will either manage or be managed. For those

One Manager's Perspective

Susan Harrison Associate Director, Human Resources, Fitch IBCA, Inc.

People skills are by far the most important of the many skills required of today's managers, says Susan Harrison of Fitch IBCA, Inc., an international credit rating agency. The ability to keep employees happy, challenged, and informed is vital in a competitive labor market, and today's managers must also add mentoring and training skills to help them develop and retain talented employees.

Harrison knows the value of having a wide range of liberal arts and humanities courses in preparing for a management career. Sociology, psychology, and even anthropology enhance the future manager's understanding of people, both as individuals and in groups. Particular courses Harrison finds especially useful include Managing Human Resources, Managing Diversity in Organizations, and Managing Communication in Organizations.

Since practical work experience hones skills over time, Harrison also feels that summer internships in industries of interest are invaluable. Not only does an internship provide a first-hand glimpse of the dynamics of the professional environment, but it also offers a dynamic lesson in the value of using people skills to create a productive, satisfying, and challenging work life in today's organizations. As Harrison says, "A staff is only as good as its manager."

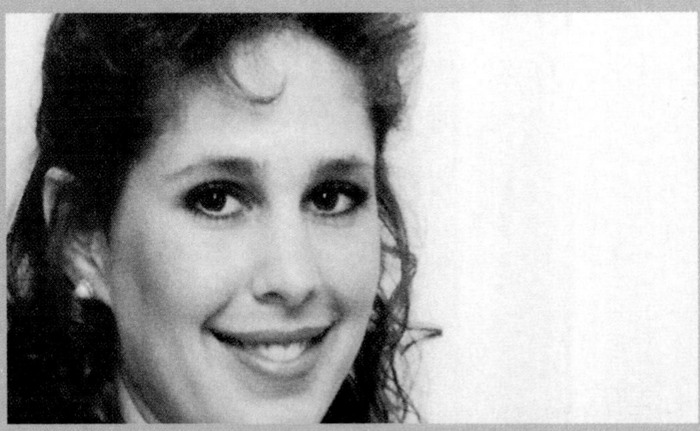

who plan on careers in management, an understanding of the management process forms the foundation upon which to build their management skills, but it would be naive to assume that everyone who studies management is planning a career in management. A course in management may only be a requirement for a desired degree, but that needn't make the study of management irrelevant. Assuming that you will have to work for a living and that you will almost certainly work in an organization, you will be a manager or work for a manager. You can gain a great deal of insight into the way your boss behaves and the internal workings of organizations by studying management. The point is that you needn't aspire to be a manager to gain something valuable from a course in management.

Before we leave this chapter, it's important to put this whole topic of studying management into a proper perspective. That's because management as a field doesn't exist in isolation. Rather, it embodies the work and practices from individuals from a wide variety of disciplines. In the next section, we'll look at some of these linkages.

How Does Management Relate to Other Disciplines?

College courses frequently appear to be independent bodies of knowledge. Too often, little of what is taught in one course is linked to past or future courses. As a result, many students don't believe that they should retain what they've previously learned. This has been especially true in most business curriculums. There is typically a lack of connectedness between core business courses and between courses in business and the liberal arts. Accounting classes, for instance, make little reference to marketing; and marketing classes typically make little reference to courses in economics or political science. College curriculums resemble a group of silos, with each silo representing a separate and distinct discipline.

A number of management educators have begun to recognize the need to build bridges between these silos by integrating courses across the college curriculum. Toward this end, we offer the following interdisciplinary overview.

We've integrated topics around the *humanities and social science* courses you may have taken as part of your general education requirements. This is designed to help you see how courses in disciplines such as economics, psychology, sociology, political science, philosophy, and speech communications relate to topics in management.

The big picture is often lost when management concepts are studied in isolation. By adding this cross-disciplinary perspective, you'll gain a greater appreciation of how general education classes and other business courses are useful to students of organizations. This, in turn, can help you to be a more effective manager.

WHAT CAN STUDENTS OF MANAGEMENT GAIN FROM HUMANITIES AND SOCIAL SCIENCE COURSES?

Let's briefly look by discipline at popular humanities and social science courses that directly affect management practices.

Anthropology Anthropology is the study of societies, which helps us learn about human beings and their activities. Anthropologists' work on cultures and environments, for instance, has helped managers to better understand differences in fundamental values, attitudes, and behavior between people in different countries and within different organizations.

Economics Economics is concerned with the allocation and distribution of scarce resources. It provides us with an understanding of the changing economy as well as the role of competition and free markets in a global context. For example, why are most athletic shoes made in Asia? Or why does Mexico now have more automobile plants that Detroit? Economists provide the answer to these questions when they discuss comparative advantage. Similarly, an understanding of free trade and protectionist policies is absolutely essential to any manager operating in the global marketplace, and these topics are addressed by economists.

Learning from the humanities and business core concepts. That's precisely what helped an individual like Doug Ivester, former CEO of Coca-Cola, as he spent time in Shanghai. By having a broader perspective, Ivester was able to better understand another country's culture, the political environment, and the wants and needs of people who live in those countries. His successor, Douglas Daft, will benefit from these too.

Philosophy Philosophy courses inquire into the nature of things, particularly values and ethics. Ethics are standards governing human conduct. Ethical concerns go directly to the existence of organizations and what constitutes proper behavior within them. For instance, the liberty ethic (John Locke) proposed that freedom, equality, justice, and private property were legal rights; the Protestant ethic (John Calvin) encouraged individuals to be frugal, work hard, and attain success, and the market ethic (Adam Smith) argued that the market and competition, not government, should be the sole regulators of economic activity. These ethics have shaped today's organizations by providing a basis for legitimate authority, linking rewards to performance and justifying the existence of business and the corporate form.

Political science Political science studies the behavior of individuals and groups within a political environment. Specific topics of concern to political scientists include structuring of conflict, allocating power, and manipulating power for individual self-interest.

Capitalism is just one economic system. The economies of the former Soviet Union and much of Eastern Europe, for example, were based on socialistic concepts. Planned economies were not free markets. Rather, government owned most of the goods-producing businesses. And organizational decision makers essentially carried out the dictates of government policies. Efficiency had little meaning in such economies. There was no competition in most of the basic industries because they were government controlled. In many cases, effectiveness was defined by how many people a plant employed rather than by basic financial criteria.

Management is affected by a nation's form of government—whether it allows its citizens to hold property, by citizens' ability to engage in and enforce contracts, and by the appeal mechanisms available to redress grievances. In a democracy, for instance, people typically have the right of private property, the freedom to enter or not enter into contracts, and an appeal system for justice. A nation's stand on property, contracts, and justice, in turn, shapes the type, form, and policies of its organizations.

Psychology Psychology is the science that seeks to measure, explain, and sometimes change the behavior of humans and other animals. Psychologists concern themselves with studying and attempting to understand individual behavior.

The field of psychology is leading the way in providing managers with insights into human diversity. Today's managers confront both a diverse customer base and a diverse set of employees. Psychologists' efforts to understand gender and cultural diversity provide managers with a better understanding of the needs of their changing customer and employee populations. Psychology courses are also relevant to managers in terms of gaining a better understanding of motivation, leadership, trust, employee selection, performance appraisals, and training techniques.

Sociology Sociology studies people in relation to their fellow human beings. What are some of the sociological issues that have relevance to managers? Here's a few. How are societal changes such as globalization, increasing cultural diversity, changing gender roles, and varying forms of family life affecting organizational practices? What are the implications of schooling practices and education trends on future employees' skills and abilities? How are changing demographics altering customer and employment markets? What will the information-age society look like? Answers to questions such as these have a major effect on how managers operate their business.

A Concluding Remark

We've attempted to provide some insight into the need to integrate the college courses you have taken. That's because what you learn in humanities and social science courses can assist you in becoming better prepared to manage in today's dynamic marketplace.

PHLIP Companion Web Site

We invite you to visit the Robbins/DeCenzo companion Web site at *www.prenhall.com/robbins* for this chapter's Internet resources.

Chapter Summary

How will you know if you fulfilled the Learning Outcomes on page 1? You will have fulfilled the Learning Outcomes if you are able to:

1 *Describe the difference between managers and operative employees.*
Managers direct the activities of others in an organization. They have such titles as supervisor, department head, dean, division manager, vice president, president, and chief executive officer. Operatives are nonmanagerial personnel. They work directly on a job or task and have no responsibility for overseeing the work of others.

2 *Explain what is meant by the term management.*
Management refers to the process of getting activities completed efficiently with and through other people. The process represents the primary activities of planning, organizing, leading, and controlling.

3 *Differentiate between efficiency and effectiveness.*
Efficiency is concerned with minimizing resource costs in the completion of activities. Effectiveness is concerned with getting activities successfully completed—that is, goal attainment.

4 *Describe the four primary processes of management.*
The four primary processes of management are planning (setting goals), organizing (determining how to achieve the goals), leading (motivating employees), and controlling (monitoring activities).

5 *Classify the three levels of managers and identify the primary responsibility of each group.*
The three levels of management are first-line supervisors, middle managers, and top managers. First-line supervisors are the lowest level of management and are typically responsible for directing the day-to-day activities of operative employees. Middle managers represent the levels of management between the first-line supervisor and top management. These individuals—who manage other managers and possibly some operative employees—are primarily responsible for translating the goals set by top management into specific details that lower-level managers can perform. Top managers, at or near the pinnacle of the organization, are responsible for making decisions about the direction of the organization and establishing policies that affect all organizational members.

6 *Summarize the essential roles performed by managers.*
Henry Mintzberg concluded that managers perform ten different roles or behaviors. He classified them into three sets. One set is concerned with interpersonal relationships (figurehead, leader, liaison). The second set is related to the transfer of information (monitor, disseminator, spokesperson). The third set deals with decision making (entrepreneur, disturbance handler, resource allocator, negotiator).

7 *Discuss whether the manager's job is generic.*
Management has several generic properties. Regardless of level in an organization, all managers perform the same four activities; however, the emphasis given to each function varies with the manager's position in the hierarchy. Similarly, for the most part, the manager's job is the same regardless of the type of organization he or she is in. The generic properties of management are found mainly in the world's democracies. One should be careful in assuming that management practices are universally transferable outside so-called free-market democracies.

8 *Describe the four general skills necessary for becoming a successful manager.*
The four critical types of skills necessary for becoming a successful manager are conceptual (the ability to analyze and diagnose complex situations); interpersonal (the ability to work with and understand others); technical (applying specialized knowledge); and political (enhancing one's position and building a power base).

9 *Describe the value of studying management.*
People in all walks of life have come to recognize the important role that good management plays in our society. For those who aspire to managerial positions, the study of management provides the body of knowledge that will help them to

be effective managers. For those who do not plan on careers as managers, the study of management can give them considerable insight into the way their bosses behave and into the internal activities of organizations.

10 *Identify the relevance of popular humanities and social science courses to management practices.*
Management does not exist in isolation. Rather, management practices are directly influenced by research and practices in such fields as anthropology (learning about individuals and their activities); economics (understanding allocation and distribution of resources); philosophy (developing values and ethics); political science (understanding behavior of individuals and groups in a political setting); psychology (learning about individual behavior); and sociology (understanding relationships among people).

Review and Application Questions

READING FOR COMPREHENSION

1. What is an organization? Why are managers important to an organization's success?
2. What four common activities comprise the process approach to management? Briefly describe each of them.
3. What are the four general skills and the six specific skills that affect managerial effectiveness?
4. How does a manager's job change with his or her level in the organization?
5. What value do courses in anthropology, economics, philosophy, political science, psychology, and sociology have for managers? Give an example of one application to management practice from each of these disciplines.

LINKING CONCEPTS TO PRACTICE

1. Are all effective organizations also efficient? Discuss. If you had to choose between being effective or being efficient, which one would you say is more important? Why?
2. Contrast planning, organizing, leading, and controlling with Henry Mintzberg's 10 roles.
3. Is your college instructor a manager? Discuss in terms of both planning, organizing, leading, and controlling and of Mintzberg's managerial roles.
4. In what ways would the activities of an owner of a bicycle repair shop that employs two people and the president of the Schwinn bicycle company's job be similar? In what ways would they be different?
5. Some individuals today have the title of project leader. They manage projects of various size and duration and must coordinate the talents of many people to accomplish their goals, but none of the workers on their projects reports directly to them. Can these project leaders really be considered managers if they have no employees over whom they have direct authority? Discuss.

Management Workshop

Team Skill-Building Exercise

A New Beginning

One of the more unnerving aspects of beginning a new semester is gaining an understanding of what is expected in each class.[31] By now, your instructor has probably provided you with a course syllabus, which gives you some necessary information about how the class will function. Understandably, this information is important to you. Yet, there is another component: giving your instructor some indication of what you want or expect from the class. Specifically, some data can be useful for providing insight into this class. To collect these data, you will need to answer some questions. First, take out a piece of paper and place your name at the top; then respond to the following:

1. What do I want from this course?
2. Why is this class important to me?
3. How does this course fit into my career plans?
4. How do I like an instructor to "run" the class?
5. What do I think is my greatest challenge in taking this class?

When you have finished answering these questions, pair up with another class member (preferably someone you do not already know) and exchange papers. Get to know one another (using the information on these sheets as a starting point). Prepare an introduction of your partner, and share your partner's responses to the five questions with the class and your instructor.

Developing Your Mentoring Skill

Guidelines for Mentoring Others

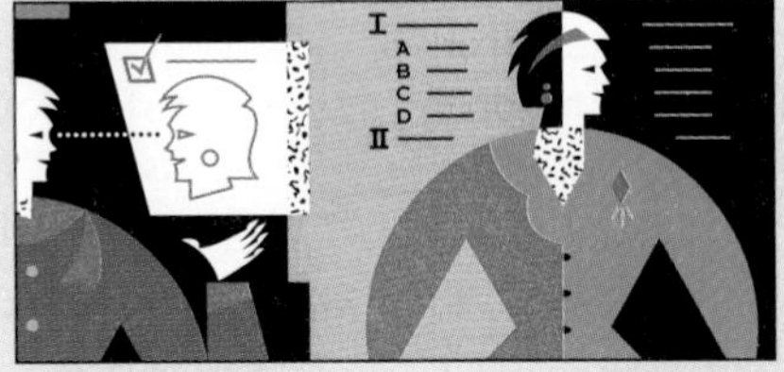

ABOUT THE SKILL

A mentor is usually someone in the organization who is more experienced and in a higher level position and sponsors or supports another employee (frequently called a protégé). A mentor can teach, guide, and encourage. Some organizations have formal mentoring programs, but even if your organization does not, mentoring should be an important skill for you to develop.

STEPS IN PRACTICING THE SKILL

- **Communicate honestly and openly with your protégé.** If your protégé is going to learn from you and benefit from your experience, you're going to have to be open and honest as you talk about what you've done. Bring up the failures as well as the successes. Remember that mentoring is a learning process and in order for learning to take place, you're going to have to "tell it like it is."
- **Encourage honest and open communication from your protégé.** You need to know what your protégé hopes to gain from this relationship. You should encourage the protégé to ask for information and to be specific about what he or she wants to gain.
- **Treat the relationship with the protégé as a learning opportunity.** Don't pretend to have all the answers and all the knowledge, but do share what you've learned through your experiences. And in your conversations and interactions with your protégé, you may be able to learn as much from that person as he or she does from you. So listen to what your protégé is saying.
- **Take the time to get to know your protégé.** As a mentor, you should be willing to take the time to get to know your protégé and his or her interests. If you're not willing to spend extra time, you should probably not embark on a mentoring relationship.

Practicing the Skill

MENTORING

Select a relative, neighbor, or friend and ask your protégé to spend an hour teaching you a new skill such as playing a musical instrument, rollerblading, or cooking a meal. Then teach your protégé a skill you've mastered, such as playing a video game, singing a song in a foreign language, or balancing a checkbook.

Write a brief set of notes about each mentoring experience. Be sure to record what you learned from your protégé and how you might have improved your own learning opportunity. Could you have prepared ahead of time? How would that have helped you learn better? In assessing your performance as a mentor, evaluate your skill in organizing and presenting the necessary information. Did your protégé ask questions you could not immediately answer? How did you handle these? How do you think you could have done better?

A Case Application

Developing Your Diagnostic and Analytical Skills

BODY SHOP INTERNATIONAL

Anita Roddick and her husband, Gordon, opened their first Body Shop in 1976 in Brighton, England.[32] Their product was unique at the time—soaps and lotions that were made primarily from natural ingredients. They merged cosmetics sales with environmental activism. From the very beginning, their strategy was to build a successful company that was environmentally friendly and driven by principles, not by profits. For example, the company supported and promoted a wide range of environmental and human rights projects—from Greenpeace's save-the-whales campaign, to Survival International's rain forest project, to a boycott of Shell Oil for its human rights abuses in Nigeria.

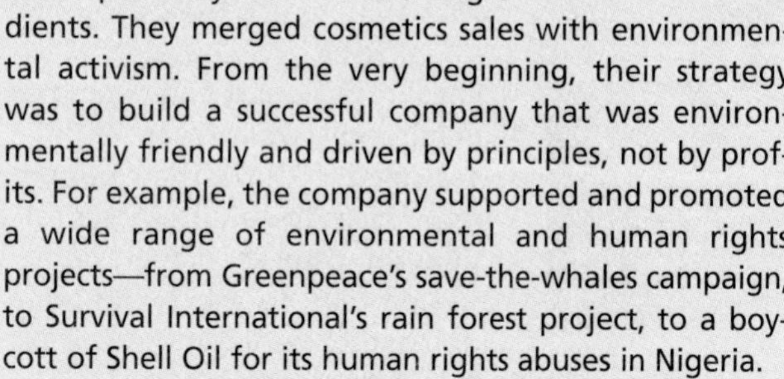

For years the concept worked. The company grew from its single store in Brighton to 1,366 stores in 46 countries. In fact, by 1995, Body Shop International was Britain's most successful company, with annual sales of approximately $360 million. But recent problems have forced Ms. Roddick to bring in Stuart Rose, a professional manager, as the company's managing director. Here are Stuart Rose's major challenges:

- The company's image was tarnished by a television documentary that charged the Body Shop made false claims about its stand against animal testing. However, the Roddicks sued for libel and won.
- The Limited has aggressively expanded its Body Shop competitor—Bath and Body Works. Between 1992 and 1997, the Limited opened more than 400 stores in the United States, mostly in high-rent malls. With its aggressive marketing and The Limited's deep pockets, they have cut into Body Shop's growth.
- U.S. operations have suffered badly. Many of the U.S. stores are losing money. Part of the problem is that these stores are owned by the Body Shop, unlike other countries where stores are franchised. Another part of the problem is that costs have risen as new stores have been located in malls to gain a foothold against Bath and Body Works.

Although Body Shop appears to have problems, all is not gloomy. The Body Shop's Asian market has grown rapidly and is profitable. Additionally, although the British market is nearly saturated, it generates 44 percent of the company's revenues and produces a solid profit.

QUESTIONS

1. Describe how Stuart Rose performs planning, organizing, leading, and controlling activities in his dealings with the major challenges the company faces.
2. What management roles does Stuart Rose play in dealing with a) the Roddicks, b) customers, and c) environmental activists? Give an example of each role.
3. Describe how "lessons" learned from disciplines such as economics, philosophy, and sociology could be of benefit to Stuart Rose.

Developing Your Investigative Skills

Using the Internet

Visit *www.prenhall.com/robbins* for updated Internet Exercises.

Enhancing Your Writing Skills

Communicating Effectively

1 Develop a 3- to 4-page response to the following question: "Are U.S. executives overpaid?" Present both sides of the argument and include supporting data. Conclude your discussion by defending and supporting one of the two arguments you've presented.

2 Describe how the president of your college fulfills the 10 managerial roles identified by Henry Mintzberg (refer to Exhibit 1-5). In your discussion, provide specific references to actual activities by your college's president—not just the "identifiable activities" we've listed in the exhibit.

3 Schedule a meeting with three faculty members—one who teaches economics, one who teaches psychology, and one who teaches political science. Ask each of them how their respective courses relate to today's business environment, and what are the most critical elements from their courses that a business student should understand. Write up your findings in a 3- to 4-page report.

History Module

The Historical Roots of Contemporary Management Practices

This module will demonstrate that a knowledge of management history can help you understand contemporary management theory and practice. We'll introduce you to the origins of many contemporary management concepts and show how they evolved to reflect the changing needs of organizations and society as a whole.

The Premodern Era

Organized activities and management have existed for thousands of years. The Egyptian pyramids and the Great Wall of China are evidence that projects of tremendous scope, employing tens of thousands of people, were undertaken well before modern times. The pyramids are a particularly interesting example. The construction of a single pyramid occupied over 100,000 people for 20 years.[1] Who told each worker what he or she was supposed to do? Who ensured that there would be enough stones at the site to keep workers busy? The answer to such questions is management. Regardless of what managers were called at the time, someone had to plan what was to be done, organize people and materials to do it, and provide direction for the workers.

When you hear the name Michelangelo, what comes to your mind? Renaissance artist? Genius? How about manager? Recent evidence tells us that the traditional image of Michelangelo—the lonely genius trapped between agony and ecstasy, isolated on his back on a scaffold, single-handedly painting the ceiling of the Sistine Chapel—is a myth.[2] Some 480 years ago, Michelangelo was actually running a medium-sized business. Thirteen people helped him paint the Sistine Chapel ceiling, about 20 helped carve the marble tombs in the Medici Chapel in Florentine, and at least 200 men, under his supervision, built the Laurentian Library in Florence. Michelangelo personally selected his workers, trained them, assigned them to one or more teams, and kept detailed employment records. For example, he recorded the names, days worked, and wages of every employee, every week. Meanwhile,

Michelangelo played the role of the trouble-shooting manager. He would daily dart in and out of the various work areas under his supervision, check on workers' progress, and handle any problems that arose.

These historical examples demonstrate that organized activities and managers have been with us since before the Industrial Revolution. However, it has been only in the past several hundred years, particularly in the last century, that management has undergone systematic investigation, acquired a common body of knowledge, and become a formal discipline.

WHAT WAS ADAM SMITH'S CONTRIBUTION TO THE FIELD OF MANAGEMENT?

division of labor
The breakdown of jobs into narrow, repetitive tasks

Adam Smith's name is typically cited in economics courses for his contributions to classical economic doctrine, but his discussion in *Wealth of Nations* (1776) included a brilliant argument on the economic advantages that organizations and society would reap from the **division of labor.**[3] He used the pin-manufacturing industry for his examples. Smith noted that 10 individuals, each doing a specialized task, could produce about 48,000 pins a day among them. However, if each worked separately and independently, those 10 workers would be lucky to make 200—or even 10—pins in one day.

Smith concluded that division of labor increased productivity by increasing each worker's skill and dexterity, by saving time that is commonly lost in changing tasks, and by the creation of labor-saving inventions and machinery. The general popularity today of job specialization—in service jobs such as teaching and medicine as well as on assembly lines in automobile plants—is undoubtedly due to the economic advantages cited over 200 years ago by Adam Smith.

HOW DID THE INDUSTRIAL REVOLUTION INFLUENCE MANAGEMENT PRACTICES?

Industrial Revolution
The advent of machine power, mass production, and efficient transportation begun in the late eighteenth century in Great Britain

Possibly the most important pre-twentieth-century influence on management was the **Industrial Revolution.** Originating in late-eighteenth-century Great Britain, the Revolution had crossed the Atlantic to America by the end of the Civil War. Machine power was rapidly substituted for human power. Using machines, in turn, made it economical to manufacture goods in factories.

The advent of machine power, mass production, the reduced transportation costs that followed the rapid expansion of the railroads, and lack of governmental regulation also fostered the development of big organizations. John D. Rockefeller was putting together the Standard Oil monopoly, Andrew Carnegie was gaining control of two thirds of the steel industry, and similar entrepreneurs were creating other large businesses that would require formalized management practices. A formal theory to guide managers in running their organizations was needed. However, it was not until the early 1900s that the first major step toward developing such a theory was taken.

Classical Contributions

The roots of modern management lie with a group of practitioners and writers who sought to formulate rational principles that would make organizations more efficient. Because they set the theoretical foundations for a discipline called management, we call their contributions the **classical approach** to management. We can break the classical approach into two subcategories: scientific management and general administrative theory. Scientific management theorists looked at the field from the perspective of how to improve the productivity of operative personnel. The general administrative theorists, on the other hand, were concerned with the overall organization and how to make it more effective.

classical approach
The term used to describe the hypotheses of the scientific management theorists and the general administrative theorists

WHAT CONTRIBUTIONS DID FREDERICK TAYLOR MAKE?

If one had to pinpoint the year that modern management theory was born, one could make a strong case for 1911, the year that Frederick Winslow Taylor's *The Principles of Scientific Management* was published.[4] Its contents would become widely accepted by managers throughout the world. The book described the theory of **scientific management**—the use of the scientific method to define the "one best way" for a job to be done. The studies conducted before and after the book's publication would establish Taylor as the father of scientific management. Frederick Taylor did most of his work at the Midvale and Bethlehem Steel companies in Pennsylvania (see Details on a Management Classic). As a mechanical engineer with a Quaker/Puritan background, he was consistently appalled at the inefficiency of workers. Employees used vastly different techniques to do the same job. They were prone to "taking it easy" on the job. Taylor believed that worker output was only about one third of what was possible. Therefore, he set out to correct the situation by applying the scientific method to jobs on the shop floor. He spent more than two decades pursuing with a passion the "one best way" for each job to be done.

scientific management
The use of the scientific method to define the "one best way" for a job to be done

Details on a Management Classic

Frederick Taylor

Probably the most widely cited example of scientific management is Taylor's pig iron experiment. Workers loaded "pigs" of iron weighing 92 pounds onto rail cars. Their average daily output was 12.5 tons. Taylor believed that if the job was scientifically analyzed to determine the one best way to load pig iron, the output could be increased to 47 or 48 tons per day.

Taylor began his experiment by looking for a physically strong subject who placed a high value on the dollar. The individual Taylor chose was a big, strong Dutch immigrant, whom he called "Schmidt." Schmidt, like the other loaders, earned $1.15 a day, which even at the turn of the century was barely a subsistence wage. Taylor offered Schmidt $1.85 a day if he would do what Taylor asked.

Using money to motivate Schmidt, Taylor asked him to load the pig irons, alternating various job factors to see what impact the changes had on Schmidt's daily output. For instance, on some days, Schmidt would lift the pig irons by bending his knees; on other days, he would keep his legs straight and use his back. Taylor experimented with rest periods, walking speed, carrying positions, and other variables. After a long period of methodically trying various combinations of procedures, techniques, and tools, Taylor obtained the level of productivity he thought possible. By putting the right person on the job with the correct tools and equipment, by having the worker follow his instructions exactly, and by motivating the worker with a significantly higher daily wage, Taylor was able to reach his 48-ton objective.

It's important to understand what Taylor saw at Midvale Steel that aroused his determination to improve the way things were done in the plant. At the time, there were no clear concepts of worker and management responsibilities. Virtually no effective work standards existed. Workers purposely worked at a slow pace. Management decisions were of the "seat-of-the-pants" variety, based on hunch and intuition. Workers were placed on jobs with little or no concern for matching their abilities and aptitudes with the tasks required. Most important, management and workers considered themselves to be in continual conflict. Rather than cooperating to their mutual benefit, they perceived their relationship as a zero-sum game—any gain by one would be at the expense of the other.

Taylor sought to create a mental revolution among both the workers and management by creating clear guidelines for improving production efficiency. He defined four principles of management (see Exhibit HM-1). He argued that following these principles would result in the prosperity of both management and workers. Workers would earn more pay and management more profits.

Using scientific management techniques, Taylor was able to define the one best way of doing each job. He could then select the right people for the job and train them to do it precisely in this one best way. To motivate workers, he favored incentive wage plans. Overall, Taylor achieved consistent improvements in productivity in the range of 200 percent or more, and he reaffirmed the function of managers to plan and control and that of workers to perform as instructed.

The impact of Taylor's work cannot be overstated.[5] During the first decade of the century, Taylor delivered numerous public lectures to convey scientific management to interested industrialists. Between 1901 and 1911, at least 18 firms adopted some variation of scientific management. In 1908, the Harvard Business School declared Taylor's approach the standard for modern management and adopted it as the core around which all courses were to be organized. Taylor, himself, began lecturing at Harvard in 1909. Between 1910 and 1912, two events catapulted scientific management into the limelight. In 1910, the Eastern Railroad requested a rate increase from the Interstate Commerce Commission. Appearing before the commission, an efficiency expert claimed that railroads could save $1 million a day (equivalent to about $17 million today) through the application of scientific management. This assertion became the centerpiece of the hearings and created a national audience for Taylor's ideas. Then in 1911, *The Principles of Scientific Management* became an instant best-seller. By 1914, Taylor's principles had become so popular that an "efficiency exposition" held in New York City, with Taylor as the keynote speaker, drew a crowd estimated at 69,000. Although Taylor spread his ideas not only in the United States but also in France, Germany, Russia, and Japan, his greatest influence was on U.S. manufacturing. His method gave U.S. companies a comparative advantage over foreign firms that made U.S. manufacturing efficiency the envy of the world—at least for 50 years or so.

Exhibit HM-1
Taylor's Four Principles of Management

1. Develop a science for each element of an individual's work, which replaces the old rule-of-thumb method.
2. Scientifically select and then train, teach, and develop the worker. (Previously, workers chose their own work and trained themselves as best they could.)
3. Heartily cooperate with the workers so as to ensure that all work is done in accordance with the principles of the science that has been developed.
4. Divide work and responsibility almost equally between management and workers. Management takes over all work for which it is better fitted than the workers. (Previously, almost all the work and the greater part of the responsibility were thrown upon the workers.)

WHO WERE THE OTHER MAJOR CONTRIBUTORS TO SCIENTIFIC MANAGEMENT?

Taylor's ideas inspired others to study and develop methods of scientific management. His most prominent disciples were Frank and Lillian Gilbreth,[6] and Henry Gantt.

A construction contractor by background, Frank Gilbreth gave up his contracting career in 1912 to study scientific management after hearing Taylor speak at a professional meeting. Along with his wife Lillian, a psychologist, he studied work arrangements to eliminate wasteful hand-and-body motions. The Gilbreths also experimented with the design and use of the proper tools and equipment for optimizing work performance.[7] Frank Gilbreth is probably best known for his experiments in reducing the number of motions in bricklaying.

The Gilbreths were among the first to use motion picture films to study hand-and-body motions. They devised a microchronometer that recorded time to 1/2,000 of a second, placed it in the field of study being photographed, and thus determined how long a worker spent enacting each motion. Wasted motions missed by the naked eye could be identified and eliminated. The Gilbreths also devised a classification scheme to label 17 basic hand motions—such as "search," "select," "grasp," and "hold"—which they called **therbligs** (Gilbreth spelled backward with the *th* transposed). This scheme allowed the Gilbreths to more precisely analyze the exact elements of worker's hand movements.

therbligs
The Gilbreths' classification scheme for labeling 17 basic hand motions

Another associate of Taylor's at Midvale and Bethlehem Steel was a young engineer named Henry L. Gantt. Like Taylor and the Gilbreths, Gantt sought to increase worker efficiency through scientific investigation. He extended some of Taylor's original ideas and added a few of his own. For instance, Gantt devised an incentive system that gave workers a bonus for completing their jobs in less time than the allowed standard. He also introduced a bonus for a foreman to be paid for each worker who made the standard plus an extra bonus if all of that foreman's workers made it. In so doing, Gantt expanded the scope of scientific management to encompass the work of managers as well as that of operatives. Gantt is probably most noted for creating a graphic bar chart that could be used by managers as a scheduling device for planning and controlling work. We'll look at the Gantt Chart in more detail in Chapter 14.

WHY DID SCIENTIFIC MANAGEMENT RECEIVE SO MUCH ATTENTION?

Many of the guidelines Taylor and others devised for improving production efficiency appear today to be common sense. For instance, one can say that it should have been obvious to managers in those days that workers should be carefully screened, selected, and trained before being put into a job.

To understand the importance of scientific management, you have to understand the times in which Taylor, the Gilbreths, and Gantt lived. The standard of living was low. Production was highly labor-intensive. Midvale Steel, at the turn of the century, may have employed 20 or 30 workers who did nothing but load pig iron onto rail cars. Today, their entire daily production could probably be done in several hours by one person with a hydraulic-lift truck, but they didn't have such mechanical devices. Similarly, the breakthroughs Frank Gilbreth achieved in bricklaying are meaningful only when you recognize that most quality buildings at that time were constructed of brick, that land was cheap, and that the major cost of a plant or home was the cost of the materials (bricks) and the labor cost to lay them.

WHAT DID HENRI FAYOL AND MAX WEBER CONTRIBUTE TO MANAGEMENT THEORY?

Henri Fayol and Max Weber were two important individuals who helped to develop the general administrative theory. We mentioned Henri Fayol in Chapter 1 as having designated management as a universal set of activities—specifically, planning, organizing, commanding, coordinating, and controlling. Because his writings were important, let's take a more careful look at what he had to say.[8]

Fayol wrote during the same period that Taylor did. However, whereas Taylor was concerned with management at the shop level (or what we today would describe as the job of a supervisor) and used the scientific method, Fayol's attention was directed at the activities of all managers, and he wrote from personal experience. Taylor was a scientist. Fayol, the managing director of a large French coal-mining firm, was a practitioner.

Fayol described the practice of management as distinct from accounting, finance, production, distribution, and other typical business functions. He argued that management was an activity common to all human undertakings in business, in government, and even in the home. He then proceeded to state 14 **principles of management**—fundamental or universal truths—that could be taught in schools and universities. These principles are listed in Exhibit HM-2.

principles of management
Fayol's fundamental or universal principles of management practice

Max Weber was a German sociologist. Writing in the early part of this century, Weber developed a theory of authority structures and described organizational activity on the basis of authority relations.[9] He described an ideal type of organization that he called a **bureaucracy,** characterized by division of labor, a clearly defined hierarchy, detailed rules and regulations, and impersonal relationships. Weber recognized that this ideal bureaucracy didn't exist in reality but, rather, represented a selective reconstruction of the real world. He used it as a basis for theorizing about work and the way that work could be done in large groups. His theory became the design prototype for many of today's large organizations. The features of Weber's ideal bureaucratic structure are outlined in Exhibit HM-3.

bureaucracy
Weber's ideal type of organization characterized by division of labor, a clearly defined hierarchy, detailed rules and regulations, and impersonal relationships

WHAT WERE THE GENERAL ADMINISTRATIVE THEORISTS' CONTRIBUTIONS TO MANAGEMENT PRACTICE?

A number of our current ideas and practices in management can be directly traced to the contributions of the **general administrative theorists.** For instance, the functional view of the manager's job owes its origin to Henri Fayol. Although many of his principles may not be applicable to the wide variety of organizations that exist today, they were a frame of reference for many current concepts.

general administrative theorists
Writers who developed general theories of what managers do and what constitutes good management practice

Weber's bureaucracy was an attempt to formulate an ideal model for organization design and a response to the abuses that Weber observed within organizations. Weber believed that his model could remove the ambiguity, inefficiencies, and patronage that characterized most organizations at that time. Weber's bureaucracy is not as popular as it was a decade ago, but many of its components are still inherent in large organizations.

Human Resources Approach

Managers get things done by working with people, which explains why some writers and researchers have chosen to look at management by focusing on the

Exhibit HM-2 Fayol's Fourteen Principles of Management

1. **Division of Work** This principle is the same as Adam Smith's "division of labor." Specialization increases output by making employees more efficient.
2. **Authority** Managers must be able to give orders. Authority gives them this right. Along with authority, however, goes responsibility. Wherever authority is exercised, responsibility arises.
3. **Discipline** Employees must obey and respect the rules that govern the organization. Good discipline is the result of effective leadership, a clear understanding between management and workers regarding the organization's rules, and the judicious use of penalties for infractions of the rules.
4. **Unity of Command** Every employee should receive orders from only one superior.
5. **Unity of Direction** Each group of organizational activities that have the same objective should be directed by one manager using one plan.
6. **Subordination of Individual Interests to the General Interest** The interests of any one employee or group of employees should not take precedence over the interests of the organization as a whole.
7. **Remuneration** Workers must be paid a fair wage for their services.
8. **Centralization** Centralization refers to the degree to which subordinates are involved in decision making. Whether decision making is centralized (to management) or decentralized (to subordinates) is a question of proper proportion. The task is to find the optimum degree of centralization for each situation.
9. **Scalar Chain** The line of authority from top management to the lowest ranks represents the scalar chain. Communications should follow this chain. However, if following the chain creates delays, cross-communications can be allowed if agreed to by all parties and superiors are kept informed.
10. **Order** People and materials should be in the right place at the right time.
11. **Equity** Managers should be kind and fair to their subordinates.
12. **Stability of Tenure of Personnel** High employee turnover is inefficient. Management should provide orderly personnel planning and ensure that replacements are available to fill vacancies.
13. **Initiative** Employees who are allowed to originate and carry out plans will exert high levels of effort.
14. **Esprit de Corps** Promoting team spirit will build harmony and unity within the organization.

organization's human resources. Much of what currently makes up the field of personnel or human resources management, as well as contemporary views on motivation and leadership, has come out of the work of theorists we have categorized as part of the human resources approach to management.

WHO WERE SOME EARLY ADVOCATES OF THE HUMAN RESOURCES APPROACH?

Undoubtedly, many people in the nineteenth and the early part of the twentieth century recognized the importance of the human factor to an organization's success, but five individuals stand out as early advocates of the human resources approach. They are Robert Owen, Hugo Munsterberg, Mary Parker Follett, Chester Barnard, and Elton Mayo.

Exhibit HM-3 Weber's Ideal Bureaucracy

1 **Division of Labor** Jobs are broken down into simple, routine, and well-defined tasks.
2 **Authority Hierarchy** Offices or positions are organized in a hierarchy, each lower one being controlled and supervised by a higher one.
3 **Formal Selection** All organizational members are to be selected on the basis of technical qualifications demonstrated by training, education, or formal examination.
4 **Formal Rules and Regulations** To ensure uniformity and to regulate the actions of employees, managers must depend heavily on formal organizational rules.
5 **Impersonality** Rules and controls are applied uniformly, avoiding involvement with personalities and personal preferences of employees.
6 **Career Orientation** Managers are professional officials rather than owners of the units they manage. They work for fixed salaries and pursue their careers within the organization.

What claim to fame does Robert Owen hold? Robert Owen was a successful Scottish businessman who bought his first factory in 1789 when he was just eighteen. Repulsed by the harsh practices he saw in factories across Scotland—such as the employment of young children (many under the age of 10), 13-hour workdays, and miserable working conditions—Owen became a reformer. He chided factory owners for treating their equipment better than their employees. He said that they would buy the best machines but then buy the cheapest labor to run them. Owen argued that money spent on improving laboring conditions was one of the best investments that business executives could make. He claimed that a concern for employees was both highly profitable for management and would relieve human misery.

Owen proposed a utopian workplace. Owen is not remembered in management history for his successes but rather for his courage and commitment to reducing the suffering of the working class.[10] He was more than a hundred years ahead of his time when he argued, in 1825, for regulated hours of work for all, child labor laws, public education, company-furnished tools and equipment, and business involvement in community projects.[11]

For what is Hugo Munsterberg best known? Hugo Munsterberg created the field of industrial psychology—the scientific study of individuals at work to maximize their productivity and adjustment. In his text, *Psychology and Industrial Efficiency* (1913)[12] he argued for the scientific study of human behavior to identify general patterns and to explain individual differences. Munsterberg suggested the use of psychological tests to improve employee selection, the value of learning theory in the development of training methods, and the study of human behavior to determine what techniques are most effective for motivating workers. Interestingly, he saw a link between scientific management and industrial psychology: Both sought increased efficiency through scientific work analyses and through better alignment of individual skills and abilities with the demands of various jobs. Much of our current knowledge of selection techniques, employee training, job design, and motivation is built on the work of Munsterberg.

What contributions did Mary Parker Follett make to management? One of the earliest writers to recognize that organizations could be viewed from the perspective of individual and group behavior was Mary Parker Follett.[13] A transitional figure who wrote in the time of scientific management but proposed more people-oriented ideas, Follett was a social philosopher whose ideas had clear implications for management practice. Follett thought that organizations should be based on a group ethic rather than on individualism. Individual potential, she argued, remained as potential until released through group association. The manager's job was to harmonize and coordinate group efforts. Managers and workers should view themselves as partners—as part of a common group. As such, managers should rely more on their expertise and knowledge to lead subordinates than on the formal authority of their position. Her humanistic ideas influenced the way we look at motivation, leadership, power, and authority.

Who was Chester Barnard? A transitional figure like Follett, Chester Barnard proposed ideas that bridged classical and human resources viewpoints. Like Fayol, Barnard was a practitioner—he was the president of New Jersey Bell Telephone Company. He had read Weber and was influenced by his work. But unlike Weber, who had an impersonal view of organizations, Barnard saw organizations as social systems that require human cooperation. He expressed his views in his book *The Functions of the Executive* (1938).[14]

Barnard believed that organizations were made up of people with interacting social relationships. The manager's major functions were to communicate and stimulate subordinates to high levels of effort. A major part of an organization's success, as Barnard saw it, depended on the cooperation of its employees. Barnard also argued that success depended on maintaining good relations with the people and institutions with whom the organization regularly interacted. By recognizing the organization's dependence on investors, suppliers, customers, and other external stakeholders, Barnard introduced the idea that managers had to examine the external environment and then adjust the organization to maintain a state of equilibrium. Regardless of how efficient an organization's production might be, if management failed to ensure a continuous input of materials and supplies or to find markets for its output, then the organization's survival would be threatened.

The current interest in building cooperative work groups, making business firms more socially responsible, and matching organizational strategies to opportunities in the environment can be traced to ideas originally proposed by Barnard.

What were the Hawthorne studies? Without question, the most important contribution to the human resources approach to management came out of the **Hawthorne studies** undertaken at the Western Electric Company's Hawthorne Works in Cicero, Illinois.[15]

Hawthorne studies
A series of studies during the 1920s and 1930s that provided new insights into group norms and behaviors

The Hawthorne studies, begun in 1924 but expanded and continued through the early 1930s, were initially devised by Western Electric industrial engineers to examine the effect of different illumination levels on worker productivity. Control and experimental groups were established. The experimental group was presented with different levels of illumination intensity, and the control group worked under a constant intensity. The engineers expected individual output to be directly related to the intensity of light. However, they found that as the light level was increased in the experimental group, output for both groups rose. To the surprise of the engineers, as the light level was dropped in the experimental group, productivity continued to increase in both groups. In fact, productivity decreased in the experimental group only after the light intensity had been reduced to that of moonlight. The engineers concluded that illumination intensity was not directly related to group productivity, but they could not explain the behavior they had witnessed.

In 1927, the Western Electric engineers asked Harvard professor Elton Mayo and his associates to join the study as consultants, a relationship that would last through 1932 and encompass numerous experiments covering the redesign of jobs, changes in the lengths of the workday and workweek, the introduction of rest periods, and individual versus group wage plans.[16] For example, one experiment evaluated the effect of a piecework incentive pay system on group productivity. The results indicated that the incentive plan had less effect on workers' output than did group pressure and acceptance and the concomitant security. Social norms or standards of the group, therefore, were concluded to be the key determinants of individual work behavior.

Scholars generally agree that the Hawthorne studies, under the leadership of Elton Mayo, had a dramatic impact on the direction of management thought. Mayo concluded that behavior and sentiments are closely related, that group influences significantly affect individual behavior, that group standards establish individual worker output, and that money is less a factor in determining output than are group standards, group sentiments, and security. These conclusions led to a new emphasis on the human factor in the functioning of organizations and the attainment of their goals. They also led to increased paternalism by management.

The Hawthorne studies, however, have not been without critics. Attacks have been made on procedures, analyses of the findings, and the conclusions drawn.[17] From a historical standpoint, it is of little importance whether the studies were academically sound or their conclusions justified. What is important is that they stimulated an interest in human factors. The Hawthorne studies went a long way in changing the dominant view of the time that people were no different than machines; that is, you put them on the shop floor, cranked in the inputs, and caused them to produce a known quantity of outputs. Furthermore, the legacy of Hawthorne is still with us today. Current organizational practices that owe their roots to the Hawthorne studies include attitude surveys, employee counseling, management training, participative decision making, and team-based compensation systems.

Why was the Human Relations Movement important to management history? Another group within the human resources approach is important to management history for its unflinching commitment to making management practices more humane. Members of the human relations movement uniformly believed in the importance of employee satisfaction—a satisfied worker was believed to be a productive worker. For the most part, the people associated with this movement—Dale Carnegie, Abraham Maslow, and Douglas McGregor—were individuals whose views were shaped more by their personal philosophies than by substantive research evidence.

Dale Carnegie is often overlooked by management scholars, but his ideas and teachings have had an enormous effect on management practice. His book *How to Win Friends and Influence People*[18] was read by millions in the 1930s, 1940s, and 1950s. In addition, during this same period, thousands of managers and aspiring managers attended his management speeches and seminars. What was the theme of Carnegie's book and lectures? Essentially, he said that the way to succeed was to (1) make others feel important through a sincere appreciation of their efforts, (2) make a good first impression, (3) win people over to your way of thinking by letting others do the talking, being sympathetic, and "never telling a man he is wrong," and (4) change people by praising good traits and giving the offender the opportunity to save face.[19]

Abraham Maslow, a humanistic psychologist, proposed a hierarchy of five needs: physiological, safety, social, esteem, and self-actualization.[20] In terms of motivation, Maslow argued that each step in the hierarchy must be satisfied before the next level can be activated and that once a need was substantially satisfied, it no longer motivated behavior.

A survey of management professors in the early 1970s found that Maslow's 1943 publication on the needs hierarchy was cited as the second most influential article in all of management research.[21] The needs hierarchy is arguably still the best-known theory of general motivation, despite the fact that "the available research does not support the Maslow theory to any significant degree."[22] Even today, no author of an introductory textbook in management, organizational behavior, human relations, supervision, psychology, or marketing is likely to omit a discussion of the needs hierarchy.

Douglas McGregor is best known for his formulation of two sets of assumptions—Theory X and Theory Y—about human nature.[23] Theory X presents an essentially negative view of people. It assumes that they have little ambition, dislike work, want to avoid responsibility, and need to be closely supervised to work effectively. On the other hand, Theory Y offers a positive view, assuming that people can exercise self-direction, accept responsibility, and consider work to be as natural as rest or play. McGregor believed that Theory Y assumptions best captured the true nature of workers and should guide management practice.

A story about McGregor does a good job of capturing the essence of the human relations perspective. McGregor had taught for a dozen years at the Massachusetts Institute of Technology (M.I.T.) before he became president of Antioch College. After six years at Antioch, McGregor seemed to recognize that his philosophy had failed to cope with the realities of organizational life.

> I believed, for example, that a leader could operate successfully as a kind of advisor to his organization. I thought I could avoid being a "boss." Unconsciously, I suspect, I hoped to duck the unpleasant necessity of making difficult decisions, of taking the responsibility for one course of action, among many uncertain alternatives, of making mistakes and taking the consequences. I thought that maybe I could operate so that everyone would like me—that "good human relations" would eliminate all discord and disagreement. I couldn't have been more wrong. It took a couple of years but I finally began to realize that a leader cannot avoid the exercise of authority any more than he can avoid responsibility for what happens to his organization.[24]

The irony in McGregor's case was that he went back to M.I.T. and began preaching his humanistic doctrine again. And he continued to do so until his death. Like Maslow's, McGregor's beliefs about human nature have had a strong following among management academics and practitioners. For instance, the previously cited survey on important contributions to management identified McGregor's book as the most influential book.[25]

What common thread linked advocates of the human relations movement? The common thread that united human relations supporters, including Carnegie, Maslow, and McGregor, was an unshakable optimism about people's capabilities. They believed strongly in their cause and were inflexible in their beliefs, even when faced with contradictory evidence. No amount of contrary experience or research evidence would alter their views. Despite this lack of objectivity, advocates of the human relations movement had a definite influence on management theory and practice.

Who were the behavioral science theorists? One final category within the human resources approach encompasses a group of psychologists and sociologists who relied on the scientific method for the study of organizational behavior. Unlike the theorists of the human relations movement, behavioral science theorists engaged in objective research on human behavior in organizations. They carefully attempted to keep their personal beliefs out of their work. They sought to develop rigorous research designs that could be replicated by other behavioral scientists. In so doing, they hoped to build a science of organizational behavior.[26]

A list of important behavioral science theorists and their contributions would number into the hundreds. But beginning after World War II and continuing today, they have created a wealth of studies that allow us to make fairly accurate predictions about behavior in organizations. Our current understanding of such issues as leadership, employee motivation, personality differences, the design of jobs and organizations, organizational cultures, high-performance teams, performance appraisals, conflict management, and negotiation techniques are largely due to the contributions of behavioral scientists.

The Quantitative Approach

The quantitative approach to management, sometimes referred to as operations research (OR) or management science, evolved out of the development of mathematical and statistical solutions to military problems during World War II. For instance, when the British had to get the maximum effectiveness from their limited aircraft capability against the massive forces of the Germans, they asked their mathematicians to devise an optimum allocation model. Similarly, U.S. antisubmarine warfare teams used operations research (OR) techniques to improve the odds of survival for Allied convoys crossing the North Atlantic and for selecting the optimal depth-charge patterns for aircraft and surface vessel attacks on German U-boats.

After the war, many of the quantitative techniques that had been applied to military problems were moved into the business sector. One group of military officers, labeled the "Whiz Kids," joined Ford Motor Company in the mid-1940s and immediately began using statistical methods to improve decision making at Ford. Two of the most famous Whiz Kids were Robert McNamara and Charles "Tex" Thornton. McNamara rose to the presidency of Ford and then became U.S. Secretary of Defense. At the Department of Defense, he sought to quantify resource allocation decisions in the Pentagon through cost-benefit analyses. He concluded his career as head of the World Bank. Tex Thornton founded the billion-dollar conglomerate Litton Industries, again relying on quantitative techniques to make acquisition and allocation decisions. Dozens of other operations researchers from the military went into consulting. The consulting firm of Arthur D. Little, for instance, began applying OR techniques to management problems in the early 1950s. By 1954, at least 25 firms had established formal OR groups, and as many as 300 OR analysts worked in industry.[27]

What are quantitative techniques, and how have they contributed to current management practice? The quantitative approach to management includes applications of statistics, optimization models, information models, and computer simulations. Linear programming, for instance, is a technique that managers can use to improve resource allocation. Work scheduling can become more efficient as a result of critical-path scheduling analysis. Decisions on determining optimum inventory levels have been significantly influenced by the economic order quantity model. In general, the quantitative approaches have contributed directly to management decision making, particularly to planning and control decisions.

Analysis: How Social Events Shape Management Approaches

We conclude this historical review by showing you how social events shape what theorists write about and what practicing managers focus on. Although some management historians may quarrel with the following cause–effect analysis, few would disagree that societal conditions are the primary driving forces behind the emergence of the different management approaches.

WHAT STIMULATED THE CLASSICAL APPROACH?

The common thread in the ideas offered by people like Taylor, the Gilbreths, Fayol, and Weber was increased efficiency. The world of the late nineteenth and early twentieth century was highly inefficient. Most organizational activities were unplanned and unorganized. Job responsibilities were vague and ambiguous. Managers, when they existed, had no clear notion of what they were supposed to do. There was a crying need for ideas that could bring order out of this chaos and improve productivity. And the standardized practices offered by the classicists was a means to increase productivity. Take the specific case of scientific management. At the turn of the century, the standard of living was low; wages were modest, and few workers owned their own homes. Production was highly labor-intensive. It wasn't unusual, for instance, for hundreds of people to be doing the same repetitive, back-breaking job, hour after hour, day after day. So Taylor could justify spending six months or more studying one job and perfecting a standardized "one best way" to do it because the labor-intensive procedures of the time had so many people performing the same task. And the efficiencies on the production floor could be passed on in lower prices for steel, thus expanding markets, creating more jobs, and making products such as stoves and refrigerators more accessible to working families. Similarly, Frank Gilbreth's breakthroughs in improving the efficiency of bricklayers and standardizing those techniques meant lower costs for putting up buildings and, thus, more buildings being constructed. The cost of putting up factories and homes dropped significantly. So more factories could be built, and more people could own their own homes. The end result: The application of scientific management principles contributed to raising the standard of living of entire countries.

WHAT STIMULATED THE HUMAN RESOURCE APPROACH?

The human resources approach really began to roll in the 1930s when two related forces were instrumental in fostering this interest. First was a backlash to the overly mechanistic view of employees held by the classicists. Second was the Great Depression.

The classical view treated organizations and people as machines. Managers were the engineers who ensured that the inputs were available and that the machines were properly maintained. Any failure by the employee to generate the desired output was viewed as an engineering problem: It was time to redesign the job or grease the machine by offering the employee an incentive wage plan. Unfortunately, this kind of thinking created an alienated workforce. Human beings were not machines and did not necessarily respond positively to the cold and regimented work environment of the classicists' perfectly designed organization. The human resources approach offered managers solutions for decreasing this alienation and for improving worker productivity.

The Great Depression swept the globe in the 1930s and dramatically increased the role of government in individual and business affairs. For instance, in the United States, Franklin Roosevelt's New Deal sought to restore confidence to a stricken nation. Between 1935 and 1938 alone, the Social Security Act was created to provide old-age assistance; the National Labor Relations Act was passed to legitimize the rights of labor unions; the Fair Labor Standards Act introduced the guaranteed hourly wage; and the Railroad Unemployment Insurance Act established the first national unemployment protection. This New Deal climate increased the importance of the worker. Humanizing the workplace had become congruent with society's concerns.

WHAT STIMULATED THE QUANTITATIVE APPROACHES?

The major impetus to the quantitative approaches was World War II. Government-funded research programs were created to develop mathematical and statistical aids for solving military problems. The success of these operations research techniques in the military was impressive. After the war, business executives became more open to applying these techniques to their organizational decision making. And, of course, as these techniques improved the quality of decisions and increased profits in those firms that used them, managers in competing firms were forced to adopt these same techniques.

New organizations were created to disseminate information to managers on these quantitative techniques. The Operations Research Society of America was founded in 1952 and began publishing its journal, *Operations Research.* In 1953, The Institute of Management Science stated its objectives were "to identify, extend, and unify scientific knowledge that contributes to the understanding of the practice of management" and began publishing the journal *Management Science.*[28]

By the late 1960s, courses in mathematics, statistics, and operations management had become required components of most business school curricula. The new generation of managers was knowledgeable in such techniques as probability theory, linear programming, queuing theory, and games theory.

Building on History: Studying Management Today

The material in this module has focused on very specific schools of management thought. Although each school of management was formed in response to the social climate of the period, each stood in isolation of each other. However, three integrative frameworks have evolved that can help you organize and better understand the subject matter of management. These are the process, systems, and contingency approaches.

WHAT IS THE PROCESS APPROACH?

In December 1961, Harold Koontz published an article in which he carefully detailed the diversity of approaches to the study of management—functions, quantitative emphasis, human relations approaches—and concluded that there existed a "management theory jungle."[29] Koontz conceded that each of the diverse approaches had something to offer management theory, but he then proceeded to demonstrate that many were only managerial tools. He felt that a process approach could encompass and synthesize the diversity of the day. The **process approach,** originally introduced by Henri Fayol, is based on the management activities discussed in Chapter 1. The performance of these activities—planning, organizing, leading, and controlling—is seen as circular and continuous (refer to Exhibit 1-4, p. 7).

process approach
The performance of planning, leading, and controlling activities is seen as circular and continuous

Although Koontz's article stimulated considerable debate, most management teachers and practitioners held fast to their own individual perspectives.[30] But Koontz had made a mark. The fact that most current management textbooks employ the process approach is evidence that it continues to be a viable integrative framework.

HOW CAN A SYSTEMS APPROACH INTEGRATE MANAGEMENT CONCEPTS?

The mid-1960s began a decade in which the idea that organizations could be analyzed in a systems framework gained a strong following. The **systems approach** defines a system as a set of interrelated and interdependent parts arranged in a manner that produces a unified whole. Societies are systems and so, too, are computers, automobiles, organizations, and animal and human bodies.

systems approach
Defines a system as a set of interrelated and interdependent parts arranged in a manner that produces a unified whole

There are two basic types of systems: closed and open. **Closed systems** are not influenced by and do not interact with their environment. In contrast, an **open systems** approach recognizes the dynamic interaction of the system with its environment (see Exhibit HM-4). Today, when we talk of organizations as systems, we mean open systems. That is, we acknowledge the organization's constant interaction with its environment.

closed system
A system that is not influenced by and does not interact with its environment

open system
A system that dynamically interacts with its environment

An organization (and its management) is a system that interacts with and depends upon its environment. In management terms, we call this relationship dealing with the organization's stakeholders. **Stakeholders** are any group that is affected by organizational decisions and policies, including government agencies, labor unions, competing organizations, employees, suppliers, customers and clients, local community leaders, or public interest groups. The manager's job is to coordinate all these parts to achieve the organization's goals. For example, most organizational members realize that customers are the lifelines of organizations, and bringing a new product to market without first ensuring that it is needed, and desired, by customers could lead to disaster. If failing to anticipate what customers want leads to a reduction in revenues, there may be less financial resources to pay wages and taxes, buy new equipment, or repay loans. The systems approach recognizes that such relationships exist and that management must understand them and the potential constraints that they may impose.

stakeholders
Any group that is affected by organizational decisions and policies

The systems approach also recognizes that organizations do not operate in isolation. Organizational survival often depends on successful interactions with the external environment,[31] which encompasses economic conditions, the global marketplace, political activities, technological advancements, and social customs. Ignoring any of these over a long period of time can have a detrimental effect on the organization.

Exhibit HM-4
The Organization and Its Environment

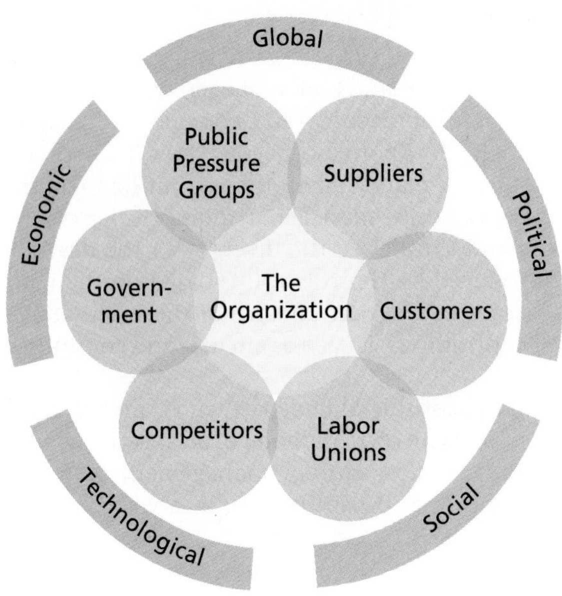

Just how relevant is the systems approach for a manager? It appears to be quite relevant, particularly because a manager's job entails coordinating and integrating various work activities so that the system of interrelated and interdependent parts (the organization) meets its goals. Although the systems perspective does not provide specific descriptions of what managers do, it does provide a broader picture than the process approach does. Moreover, viewing the manager's job as linking the organization to its environment makes the organization more sensitive and responsive to key stakeholders such as customers, suppliers, government agencies, and the community in which it operates.

WHAT IS A CONTINGENCY APPROACH TO THE STUDY OF MANAGEMENT?

Management, like life itself, is not based on simplistic principles. Insurance companies know that not all people have the same probability of becoming seriously ill. Factors such as age, fitness, and the use of alcohol or tobacco are contingencies that influence one's health. Similarly, you cannot say that students always learn less in a distance-learning course than in one in which a professor is physically present. An extensive body of research tells us that contingency factors such as course content and the way in which individuals learn influence learning effectiveness.

contingency approach
The situational approach to management that replaces more simplistic systems and integrates much of management theory

The **contingency approach** (sometimes called the situational approach) has been used in recent years to replace simplistic principles of management and to integrate much of management theory.[32] A contingency approach to the study of management is logical. Because organizations are diverse—in size, objectives, tasks being done, and the like—it would be surprising to find universally applicable principles that would work in all situations. In other words, managing Oracle's software design engineers would be different from managing sales clerks at Nordstrom and would even be different from managing Oracle's own marketing staff. But, of course, it is one thing to say, "It all depends," and another to say what it depends upon. Advocates of the contingency approach—a group that includes most management researchers and practitioners—have been trying to identify the "what" variables. Exhibit HM-5 describes four popular contingency

Exhibit HM-5 Four Popular Contingency Variables

Organization size The number of people in an organization is a major influence on what managers do. As size increases, so do the problems of coordination. For instance, the type of organization structure appropriate for an organization of 50,000 employees is likely to be inefficient for an organization of 50 employees.

Routineness of task technology In order for an organization to achieve its purpose, it uses technology; that is, it engages in the process of transforming inputs into outputs. Routine technologies require organizational structures, leadership styles, and control systems that differ from those required by customized or nonroutine technologies.

Environmental uncertainty The degree of uncertainty caused by political, technological, sociocultural, and economic changes influences the management process. What works best in a stable and predictable environment may be totally inappropriate in a rapidly changing and unpredictable environment.

Individual differences Individuals differ in terms of their desire for growth, autonomy, tolerance for ambiguity, and expectations. These and other individual differences are particularly important when managers select motivational techniques, leadership styles, and job designs.

variables. This list is not comprehensive—at least 100 different variables have been identified—but it represents those most widely used and gives you an idea of what we mean by the term *contingency variable.* As you can see from the list, the contingency variables can have a significant effect on what managers do—that is, on the way work activities are coordinated and integrated.

Two

Managing in Today's World

LEARNING OUTCOMES After reading this chapter, I will be able to:

1. Describe the three waves in modern social history and their implications for organizations.
2. Explain the importance of viewing management from a global perspective.
3. Identify how technology is changing the manager's job.
4. Define *social responsibility* and *ethics.*
5. Explain what is meant by the term *entrepreneurial spirit.*
6. Describe the management implications of a diversified workforce.
7. Explain why companies focus on quality and continuous improvement.
8. Describe why many corporations have downsized.

Doing business today is radically different than it was just 20 years ago. For that matter, it's different today than it was just a few short years ago. Increased global competition, the advent of electronic business over the Internet, economic crises, and the like are all requiring organizations to rethink how they do business. That's because to be effective in this rapidly moving and ever-changing environment, organizations need to do things better, faster, have higher quality, and meet the increasing demands of their customers. One such organization, Amazon.com, founded by Jeff Bezos, is a good example of how an organization can successfully compete in a global marketplace.[1]

In 1994, Bezos was a successful computer programmer on Wall Street. His entrepreneurial spirit, however, kept him focused on the expansive growth occurring on the Internet. At the time, the Internet was growing 2,300 percent each month. He decided to quit his job and began looking for business opportunities on the Internet. Bezos drew up a list of 20 products that he figured could be sold on-line. Included in this list were music, magazines, software, and books. After some research on his part, he settled on the notion that books would offer the best opportunity. His rationale for this decision was based on two simple facts. First, books offered a number of products to sell—nearly two million titles were in print. Second, giant bookstores were not as competitive as companies in other industries such as music.

Bezos piled his belongings into a moving van and headed west. He chose Seattle because the area offered a talented pool of computer professionals (Microsoft and many other computer software start-up companies are located in Seattle). Furthermore, it was near two major book wholesalers. In 1995, Jeff sold his first book through his Web site <*www.amazon.com*>.

How does Amazon.com work? When customers log onto the company's Web page, they can search for a book by title, author, or subject. Customers who are not looking for a particular book can browse through the database of over 2.5 million books to find something of interest. When customers find the book they want to buy, they use on-line forms to specify hardcover or paperback, gift wrapping, and mode of shipment. Payment is made by credit card submitted over their secured Internet site (or by phone, if desired). After the transaction is made, Amazon.com requests the books from a distributor or publisher, and the books are delivered to the company's Seattle warehouse. The order is then packed and shipped to the customer—usually within three days. The most fascinating thing about Amazon.com is that it is truly a virtual organization. It employs approximately 2,100 people, has no physical storefront, and a relatively small inventory. Everyone does what's needed to get the job done and satisfy the customer.

Jeff Bezos began with a vision—to create the earth's biggest bookstore. What he developed was an organization that today not only sells books, but CDs and computer products. It even offers customers the opportunity to sell their property through auctions. As a result, Amazon.com has become one of the leaders in Web-based commerce. Its 1998 sales were in excess of $600 million, and the stock market recently valued the company at over $22 billion!

A generation ago, successful managers valued stability, predictability, and efficiency achieved through economies of large size. But many of yesterday's stars—for instance, Sears and Bell & Howell—have faded because they did not adapt to what was happening around them. In Exhibit 2-1, we have identified the 1960s star and the current star in a number of industries.

What common factors characterize the stars of the 2000s? They are lean, fast, and flexible. They are dedicated to quality, organize work around teams, create ethical work environments, minimize hierarchical overhead, and exhibit entrepreneurial skills when facing change.

In this chapter, we will establish a foundation for understanding this changing world of work. No successful organization, or its management, can operate without understanding and dealing with the dynamic environment that surrounds it.

We will look at the forces that are causing organizations to change, what contemporary organizations are like, and how managers in these contemporary organizations are responding.

The Changing Economy

The histories of our 1960s stars in Exhibit 2-1 demonstrate that organizations that are stagnant and bound by tradition are increasingly fading from the limelight. Why? Because one of the biggest problems in managing an organization today is failing to adapt to the changing world. Economies throughout the world are going through turbulent change. To better understand the current change, let's look back on the road we've taken.

It's easy to forget that just 25 years ago, no one had a fax machine, a cellular phone, or a laptop. Terms we now use in our everyday vocabulary, like *e-mail* and *modem,* were known to maybe, at best, a few hundred people. Computers often took up considerable space, quite unlike today's 4-pound laptop. Moreover, if you were to talk about networks 25 years ago, people would have assumed you were talking about ABC, CBS, or NBC—the major television networks.

The silicon chip and other advances in technology have permanently altered the economies of the world, and as we'll show momentarily, the way people work. Digital electronics, optical data storage, more powerful and portable computers, and the ability for computers to communicate with each other are changing the way information is created, stored, used, and shared. One individual who has studied these changes and predicted some of their implications is futurist Alvin Toffler.

Toffler has written extensively about social change.[2] Classifying each period of social history, Toffler has argued that modern civilization has evolved over three "waves." With each wave came a new way of doing things. Some groups of people gained from the new way; others lost.

The first wave was driven by *agriculture.* Until the late nineteenth century, all economies were agrarian. For instance, in the 1890s, approximately 90 percent of people were employed in agriculture-related jobs. These individuals were typically

Exhibit 2-1 Corporate Stars: 1960 Versus 2000

Industry	1960s Star	21st Century Star
Airlines	Pan Am	Southwest
Automobiles	General Motors	DaimlerChrysler
Broadcasting	CBS	CNN
Cameras	Bell & Howell	Minolta
Computers	IBM	Dell Computer
Film	Eastman Kodak	Fuji
General retailing	Sears	Wal-Mart
Information access	Local public library	America Online
Mail delivery	U.S. Post Office	Federal Express
Newspapers	*New York Times*	*USA Today*
Security brokerage	Merrill Lynch	Charles Schwab
Steel	USX (U.S. Steel)	Nucor Steel

their own bosses and were responsible for performing a variety of tasks. Their success, or failure, was contingent on how well they produced. Since the 1890s, the proportion of the population engaged in farming has consistently dropped. Now less than five percent of the global workforce is needed to provide our food; in the United States, it's under three percent.

The second wave was *industrialization.* From the late 1800s until the 1960s, most developed countries moved from agrarian societies to industrial societies. In doing so, work left the fields and moved into formal organizations. The industrial wave forever changed the lives of skilled craftsmen. No longer did they grow something or produce a product in its entirety. Instead, workers were hired into tightly structured and formal workplaces. Mass production, specialized jobs, and authority relationships became the mode of operation. It gave rise to a new group of workers—the blue-collar industrial workers—individuals who were paid for performing routine work that relied almost exclusively on physical stamina. By the 1950s, industrial workers had become the largest single group in every developed country. They made products such as steel, automobiles, rubber, and industrial equipment. Ironically, "no class in history has ever risen faster than the blue-collar worker. And no class in history has ever fallen faster."[3] Today, blue-collar industrial workers account for less than 30 percent of the U. S. workforce and will be less than half that in just a few years.[4] The shift since World War II has been away from manufacturing work and toward service jobs. Manufacturing jobs, as a proportion of the total civilian workforce, today are highest in Japan at 24.3 percent. In the United States, manufacturing jobs make up about 18 percent of the civilian workforce. In contrast, services make up 59 percent of jobs in Italy (the lowest percentage of any industrialized country) and more than 80 percent in the United States and Canada.[5]

By the start of the 1970s a new age was gaining momentum. This is based on *information.* Technological advancements were eliminating many low-skilled, blue-collar jobs. Moreover, the information wave was transforming society from a manufacturing focus to one of service. People were increasingly moving from jobs on the production floor to clerical, technical, and professional jobs. Job growth in the past 20 years has been in low-skilled service work (such as fast-food employees, clerks, and home health aides) and knowledge work. This latter group includes professionals such as registered nurses, accountants, teachers, lawyers, and engineers. It also includes technologists—people who work with their hands and with theoretical knowledge—commonly referred to an information technologists.[6] Computer programmers, software designers, and systems analysts are examples of jobs in this category. Knowledge workers as a group currently make up about a third of the U.S. workforce.[7]

knowledge workers
Workers whose jobs are designed around the acquisition and application of information

Knowledge workers are at the cutting edge of the third wave. Their jobs are designed around the acquisition and application of information. The economy needs people who can fill these jobs—the demand for them is great. And because the supply of information technologists is low, those in the field are paid a premium for their services.[8] Meanwhile, the number of blue-collar workers has shrunk dramatically. Unfortunately, some of the blue-collar workers don't have the education and flexibility necessary to exploit the new job opportunities in the information revolution. They don't have the specific skills to move easily into high-paying technologist jobs. This situation contrasts with the shift from the first wave to the second. The transition from the farm to factory floor required little additional skill—oftentimes just a strong back and a willingness to learn, follow directions, and work hard.

Exhibit 2-2 The Changing Economy

Old Economy	New Economy
National borders limit competition	National borders are nearly meaningless in defining an organization's operating boundaries
Technology reinforces rigid hierarchies and limits access to information	Technology changes in the way information is created, stored, used, and shared have made it more accessible
Job opportunities are for blue-collar industrial workers	Job opportunities are for knowledge workers
Population is relatively homogeneous	Population is characterized by cultural diversity
Business is estranged from its environment	Business accepts its social responsibilities
Economy is driven by large corporations	Economy is driven by small entrepreneurial firms
Customers get what business chooses to give them	Customer needs drive business

As these waves influenced society, so too have they affected how we do business (see Exhibit 2-2). International markets, technological improvements, changes in workforce composition, and the like are giving rise to new organizational issues. In the following section, as well as throughout this chapter, we will explore some of the more important forces that are creating challenges for contemporary managers.

A Global Marketplace

Part of the rapidly changing environment that managers face is the globalization of business. Management is no longer constrained by national borders. BMW, a German-owned firm, builds cars in South Carolina. Similarly, McDonald's sells hamburgers in China. Exxon, a so-called American company, receives more than three fourths of its revenues from sales outside the United States. Toyota makes cars in Kentucky. General Motors makes cars in Brazil. And Mercedes sport-utility vehicles are made in Alabama.[9] Parts for Ford Motor Company's Crown Victoria come from all over the world: Mexico (seats, windshields, and fuel tanks), Japan (shock absorbers), Spain (electronic engine controls), Germany (antilock brake systems), and England (key axle parts). These examples illustrate that the world has become a **global village.** To be effective in this boundaryless world, managers need to adapt to cultures, systems, and techniques that are different from their own.[10]

global village
Refers to the concept of a boundaryless world; the production and marketing of goods and services worldwide

In the 1960s, Canada's prime minister described his country's proximity to the United States as analogous to sleeping with an elephant, "You feel every twitch the animal makes." In the 2000s, we can generalize this analogy to the entire world. A rise in interest rates in Japan, for example, instantly affects managers and organizations throughout the world. The fall of communism in Eastern Europe and the collapse of the Soviet Union created exciting opportunities for business firms throughout the free world.

International businesses have been with us for a long time. For instance, Siemens, Remington, and Singer were selling their products in many countries in the nineteenth century. By the 1920s, some companies, including Fiat, Ford, Unilever, and Royal Dutch/Shell, had gone multinational. But it was not until the mid-1960s that **multinational corporations (MNCs)** became commonplace.

multinational corporations (MNCs)
Companies that maintain significant operations in two or more countries simultaneously but are based in one home country

National boundaries no longer confine today's organizations. The global village enables companies like McDonald's to sell hamburgers anywhere in the world. This fast-food restaurant in Japan is just one of nearly 5,000 restaurants McDonald's opened outside of the United States. As a result of moving into the global village, McDonald's revenues have increased by almost $20 billion from overseas sales.

These corporations, which maintain significant operations in two or more countries simultaneously but are based in one home country, initiated the rapid growth in international trade. Today, companies such as Gillette, Mobil Oil, Coca-Cola, and Aflac are among a growing number of U.S.-based firms that earn more than 60 percent of their revenues from foreign operations.[11]

The expanding global environment has extended the reach and goals of MNCs to create an even-more-generic global organization called the **transnational corporation (TNC).** This type of organization does not seek to replicate its domestic successes by managing foreign operations from home. Instead, decisions in TNCs are made at the local level. Nationals (individuals born and raised in a specific country) are typically hired to run operations in each country. The products and marketing strategies for each country are tailored to that country's culture. Nestlé, for example, is a transnational corporation. With operations in almost every country on the globe, it is the world's largest food company, yet its managers match their products to their consumers. In part of Europe, Nestlé sells products that are not available in the United States or Latin America. Another example is Frito-Lay, which markets a Dorito chip in the British market that differs in both taste and texture from the U.S. and Canadian version.

transnational corporation (TNC)
A company that maintains significant operations in more than one country simultaneously and decentralizes decision making in each operation to the local country

borderless organization
A management structure in which internal arrangements that impose artificial geographic barriers are broken down

Many large, well-known companies are moving to more effectively globalize their management structure by breaking down internal arrangements that impose artificial geographic barriers. This type of organization is called a **borderless organization.** For instance, IBM dropped its organizational structure based on country and reorganized into 14 industry groups. Ford merged its culturally distinct European and North American auto operations and plans to add a Latin America and an Asia-Pacific division in the future. Bristol-Myers Squibb changed its consumer business to become more aggressive in international sales and installed a new executive in charge of worldwide consumer medicines such as Bufferin and Excedrin. The move to borderless management is an attempt by organizations to increase efficiency and effectiveness in a competitive global marketplace.[12]

HOW DOES GLOBALIZATION EFFECT ORGANIZATIONS?

Organizations are mostly effected by globalization when their management decides to enter into the global marketplace. An organization going global typically proceeds through three stages as shown in Exhibit 2-3. In Stage I, managers make the first push toward going international merely by exporting the organization's products to foreign countries. This is a passive step toward international

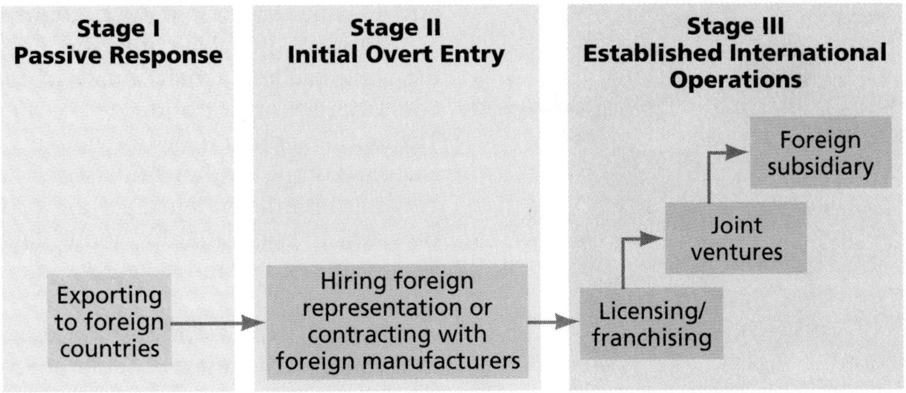

Exhibit 2-3
Stages of Going Global

Stage I Passive Response	Stage II Initial Overt Entry	Stage III Established International Operations
Exporting to foreign countries →	Hiring foreign representation or contracting with foreign manufacturers →	Licensing/franchising → Joint ventures → Foreign subsidiary

involvement involving minimal risk because managers make no serious effort to tap foreign markets. Rather, the organization fills foreign orders only when it gets them. This may be the first and only international involvement many firms in the mail-order business have.

In Stage II, managers make an overt commitment to sell products in foreign countries or to have them make in foreign factories. Yet, there is still no physical presence of company employees outside the company's home country. On the sales side, Stage II typically is done either by sending domestic employees on regular business trips to meet foreign customers or by hiring foreign agents or brokers to represent the organization's product line. On the manufacturing side, managers contract with a foreign firm to produce the organization's products.

Stage III represents a strong commitment by managers to pursue international markets aggressively.[13] As shown in Exhibit 2-3, managers can do this in different ways. They can license or franchise to another firm the right to use the organization's brand name, technology, or product specifications. This approach is used widely by pharmaceutical companies and fast-food chains such as Pizza Hut. Joint ventures involve larger commitments; a domestic and a foreign firm share the cost of developing new products or building production facilities in a foreign country. These are called **strategic alliances.**[14] These partnerships provide a fast and less expensive way for companies to compete globally than would doing it on their own. Recent cross-border alliances include British Airways and American Airlines, Polaroid and Minolta, and Nestlé and General Mills. Managers make the greatest commitment, and assume the greatest risk, when the organization sets up a foreign subsidiary. Such subsidiaries can be managed as an MNC (with domestic control), a TNC (with foreign control), or a borderless organization (with global control). Acura, a free-standing company fully owned by Honda, is an example of a foreign subsidiary.

strategic alliances
A domestic and a foreign firm share the cost of developing new products or building production facilities in a foreign country

WHAT EFFECT DOES GLOBALIZATION HAVE ON MANAGERS?

When you hear the name Whirlpool, what comes to mind? A large U.S. manufacturer of appliances such as washers, dryers, and refrigerators? That description is somewhat correct, but Whirlpool's activities are not confined to the United States. It is also the top manufacturer and distributor of appliances in Europe and Asia.[15]

In terms of the changing global environment, the spread of capitalism makes the world a smaller place. Business has new markets to conquer. And well-trained

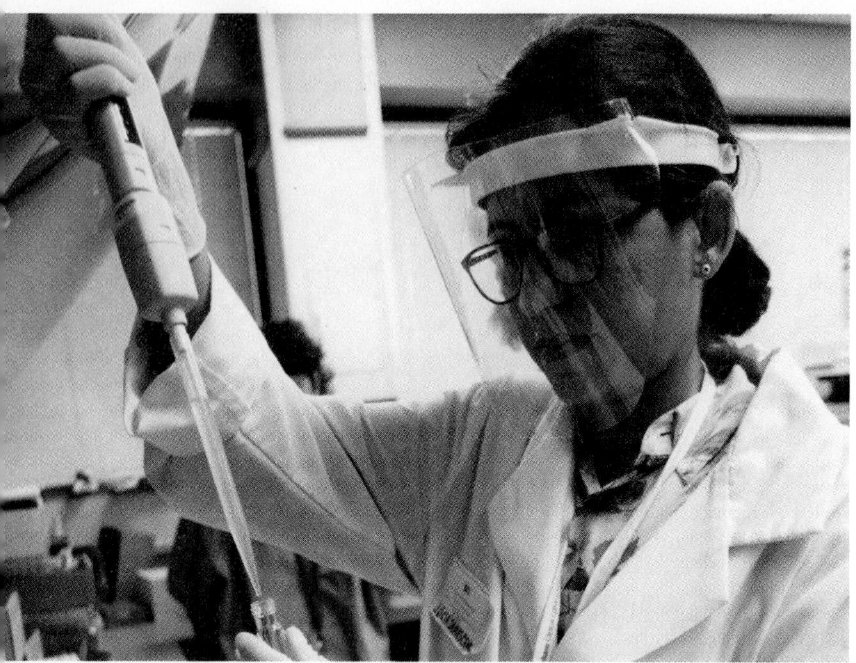

Operating in the global village requires organizations to fully understand the laws of the land. An action at SmithKline Beecham to deny an employee a promotion because of age may have been appropriate under laws in England, however, the same action in the United States would surely have led to discrimination claims.

and reliable workers in such countries as Hungary, Slovakia, and the Czech Republic become a rich source of low-cost labor for organizations everywhere. The implementation of free markets in Eastern Europe further underscores the growing interdependence among countries and the potential for goods, labor, and capital to move easily across national borders.

A boundaryless world introduces new challenges for managers. One specific challenge is managing in a country where there's a different national culture.[16] The specific challenge is recognizing the differences that might exist and finding ways to make interactions effective. One of the first issues to deal with, then, is the perception of "foreigners."

U.S. managers once held a rather parochial view of the world of business. **Parochialism** is a narrow focus; these managers saw things solely through their own eyes and within their own perspectives.[17] They believed that their business practices were the best in the world. They did not recognize that people from other countries had different ways of doing things or that they lived differently from Americans. In essence, parochialism is an **ethnocentric view.** Of course, this view cannot succeed in a global village—nor is it the dominant view held today. But changing U.S. managers' perception first required understanding of the different cultures and their environments.

parochialism
Refers to a narrow focus in which one sees things solely through one's own eyes and within one's own perspective

ethnocentric view
A parochial view in which one sees one's own culture as better than any other

All countries have different values, morals, customs, political and economic systems, and laws. Traditional approaches to studying international business have sought to advance each of these topic areas. However, a strong case can be made that traditional business approaches need to be understood within their social context. That is, organizational success can come from a variety of managerial practices—each of which is derived from a different business environment.[18] For example, status is perceived differently in different countries. In France, for instance, status is often the result of factors important to the organization, such as seniority, education, and the like. This emphasis is called ascribed status.[19] In the United States, status is more a function of what individuals have personally accomplished (achieved status). Managers need to understand societal issues (such as status) that might affect operations in another country.

Countries also have different laws. For instance, in the United States, laws guard against employers' taking action against employees solely on the basis of an employee's age. Similar laws do not exist in all other countries. As a case in point, an employee of SmithKline Beecham, PLC, a British firm that operates in the United States, was denied a promotion for jobs outside the United States because company officials determined him to be "too old." Such action would be discriminatory and illegal in the United States, but the law was not applicable to the United Kingdom.[20] Of course, if SmithKline officials had made that same decision about an employee for a job in the United States, they would have been breaking the law. The issue this example raises for organizations is that viewing the global environment from any single perspective may be too narrow and potentially problematic. A more appropriate approach is to recognize the cultural dimensions of a country's environment.

An illuminating study of the differences of cultural environments was conducted by Geert Hofstede.[21] He surveyed over 116,000 employees in 40 countries—all of whom worked for IBM. By analyzing various dimensions of a country's culture, Hofstede was able to provide a framework for managing in the global village. His data indicated that, in general, national culture has a major impact on employees' work-related values and attitudes. He was able to classify those values and attitudes into four specific dimensions of national culture. These are (1) individualism versus collectivism, (2) power distance, (3) uncertainty avoidance, and (4) quantity versus quality of life (see Exhibit 2-4).[22]

What implications does Hofstede's research have for American managers? Into which countries will U.S. managers fit best? Where are they likely to have the biggest adjustment problems? All we have to do is identify those countries that are most and least like the United States on the four dimensions. The United States is strongly individualistic but low on power distance. This same pattern was exhibited in Hofstede's study by England, Australia, Canada, the Netherlands, and New Zealand. The countries least similar to the United States on these two dimensions were Venezuela, Colombia, Pakistan, Singapore, and the Philippines.

The United States scored low on uncertainty avoidance and high on quantity of life. This same pattern was shown by Ireland, England, Canada, New Zealand, Australia, India, and South Africa. The countries least similar to the United States on these dimensions were Chile and Portugal.

Exhibit 2-4 Hofstede's Cultural Dimensions

Individualism Refers to a loosely knit social framework in which people are supposed to look after their own interests and those of their immediate family. **Collectivism** is characterized by a tight social framework in which people expect others in their group (such as the family or organization) to look after them and to protect them.

Power distance A measure of the extent to which a society accepts the fact that power in institutions and organizations is distributed unequally. A high power distance society accepts wide differences in power in organizations. Employees show a great deal of respect for those in authority. Titles and rank carry a lot of weight.

Uncertainty avoidance A society that is high in uncertainty avoidance is characterized by a high level of anxiety among its people, which manifests itself in great nervousness, stress, and aggressiveness. Because people in these societies feel threatened by uncertainty and ambiguity, mechanisms are created to provide security and reduce risk. Their organizations are likely to have formal rules; there will be little tolerance for deviant ideas and behaviors; and members will strive to believe in absolute truths.

Quantity versus quality of life Some cultures emphasize the quantity of life and value such concepts as assertiveness and the acquisition of money and material goods. Other cultures emphasize the quality of life, placing importance on relationships and the expression of sensitivity and concern for the welfare of others.

These results empirically support part of what many of us suspected—that the U.S. manager transferred to London, Toronto, Melbourne, or a similar city would have to make the fewest adjustments. Hofstede's results allow us to identify countries in which "culture shock" is likely to be the greatest and where managers would most likely have to significantly change their style.

But not all dealings with individuals from other cultures occur when managers cross national borders. Most such encounters are likely to involve interactions between managers in the United States and individuals who come to work here. What then can these managers do? When working with individuals from different cultures, a manager must understand that individuals informally learn about their cultures and that most such learning is unconscious. The Mars Company (the candy maker), for example, recognizes and builds on this informal development. It provides formalized training to its U.S. employees that focuses on the "major differences which may lead to problems," such as communication barriers and ways in which differences can be resolved.[23] Managers need to be flexible in their dealings with their foreign-born employees. Because of cultural differences, these employees just may not understand you. Managers must, therefore, recognize and acknowledge that differences do exist in their backgrounds, customs, and work schedules and make adjustments accordingly.[24]

Emphasis on Technology

Suppose you need information on how well your unit is meeting its production standards. Thirty years ago you probably would have had to submit a requisition to the operations-control department. Their response may have taken as long as a month, and the information would have been in whatever format that the operations department dictated. Today, however, a few keystrokes on your computer will get that information almost instantaneously. Moreover, it will be precisely the information you want—which may be entirely different than the information one of your colleagues needs on a similar account.

Since the 1970s, U.S. companies such as General Electric, CitiGroup Technologies, Wal-Mart, and 3M have been using automated offices, robotics in manufacturing, computer-assisted design software, integrated circuits, microprocessors, and electronic meetings. These technological advances make the organizations more productive and help them create and maintain a competitive advantage.[25]

technology
Any equipment, tools, or operating methods that are designed to make work more efficient

Technology includes any equipment, tools, or operating methods that are designed to make work more efficient. Technological advances involve the integration of technology into a process for changing inputs into outputs. For example, to sell its goods or services, an organization must first take certain inputs—labor, raw materials, and the like—and transform them into outputs. In years past, many of these transforming operations were performed by human labor. Technology, however, has made it possible to enhance this production process by replacing human labor with electronic and computer equipment. For instance, assembly operations at General Motors rely heavily on robotics. Robots perform repetitive tasks—such as spot welding and painting—much more quickly than humans can. And the robots are not subject to health problems caused by exposure to chemicals or other hazardous materials. Technology is also making it possible to better serve customers. For example, state-of-the-art steelmaking technology enables Lukens, Inc., to customize customer orders, so that "making a one-of-a-kind product" can be done as efficiently as producing a whole shipload of a standardized product.[26] Technology, however, is not used just in manufacturing enterprises. The banking industry, for instance, has been able to replace thousands of tellers with ATM machines and electronic bill-paying systems.

Technological advancements are also used to provide better, more useful information. Most cars built today, for example, have an on-board computer circuit that a technician can plug into to determine operating problems—saving countless diagnostic hours for a mechanic. And at Frito-Lay, technology has meant getting better and more timely information. Sales representatives enter inventory and sales data into a hand-held computer; the data are then transmitted daily to company headquarters. As a result, company officials have complete information on their product lines in several hundred thousand stores within 24 hours.[27]

How does an organization benefit from information technology? Technological changes, especially those related to information technology (IT), have had and continue to have a significant effect on the way that organizations are managed. For instance, Dell Computer Corporation designed its newest factory without any space for inventory storage. General Electric, too, plans to save millions of dollars by buying spare parts for its facilities over the Internet. Both of those decisions and actions were made possible by IT.[28] In addition, IT has created the ability to circumvent the physical confines of working only in a specified organizational location. With notebook and desktop computers, fax machines, high-speed modems, organizational Intranets, and other forms of IT, organizational members can do their work anyplace, anytime.[29]

What are the implications of this vast spread of IT? One important implication is that employees' job skill requirements will increase.[30] Workers will need the ability to read and comprehend software and hardware manuals, technical journals, and detailed reports. Another implication is that IT tends to level the competitive playing field.[31] It provides organizations (no matter their size or market power) with the ability to innovate, bring products to market rapidly, and respond to customer requests.[32] For example, Tommy Boy Records, a small hip hop record producer, uses IT to control its own marketing, sales, pricing, and distribution. In doing so, it is able to compete successfully against the most powerful global entertainment conglomerates.[33] And we can't talk about IT without mentioning the impact of the Internet and e-commerce.

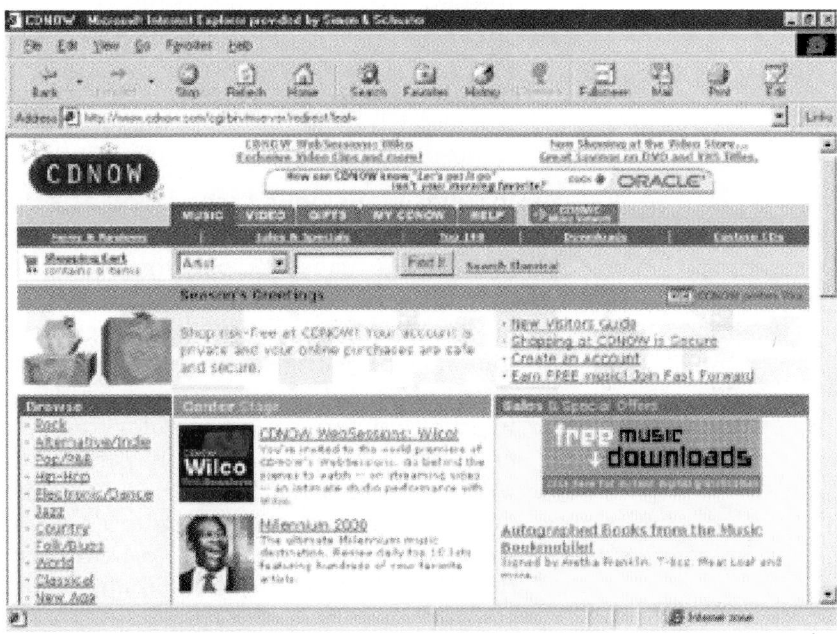

Having trouble finding the latest release of your favorite group? Don't fret and don't get in your car and drive to a music store at your local mall. Rather, simply log-on to *www.cdnow.com* and place your order. You'll have your CD in a few days. What you're experiencing here is e-commerce. Through the advent of technology, you're able to access information and make purchases from your personal computer. And you can do this 24/7!

One of the greatest phenomena we've witnessed in business today

e-commerce
Any computer transaction that occurs when data are processed and transmitted over the Internet

is the proliferation of activities over the Internet.[34] These activities, commonly referred to as **e-commerce**, involve any computer transaction that occurs where data are processed and transmitted over the Internet.[35] For instance, individuals today can make airline reservations, download recent court cases or Security and Exchange Commission filings, purchase a car, invest in the stock market, check their bank account balances, or even pay their taxes over the Internet. Organizations, too, are using the Internet to enhance business-to-business transactions. Purchasing and procurement activities, tracking shipments, and the like are more efficient through e-commerce opportunities.[36] At Dell Computer, for example, more than 80 percent of its corporate sales come through e-commerce.[37] The enormity of e-commerce cannot be overlooked. E-commerce is "changing our society and how we conduct our business."[38] Over just a few short years, e-commerce has grown from nonexistence to a major "player" in business today. Consider that in 1998 more than 10 million people made purchases over the Internet. Additionally, more than 16 percent of all car buyers in 1998 made their purchase through e-commerce.[39] And let's not forget the fastest growing stocks on Wall Street have been the Internet stocks—companies like Yahoo!, eBay, and Amazon.com.

E-commerce is changing customers' expectations about convenience, speed, comparability, price, and service.

One of the greatest effects e-commerce will have on organizations is the realization that customers will be empowered.[40] Customers will have access to more information than they've had at any time in history. They will be able to interact with an organization without the assistance of a "human." And they will generally be able to do this 24 hours a day, 7 days a week. As a result, "customers' expectations about convenience, speed, comparability, price, and service" will be greatly changed.[41] Organizations that continually adapt to meet customers' needs will succeed. Those that don't will likely fail—especially considering the increased competition from other Internet companies.

In what ways does technology alter a manager's job? Technology has had a positive effect on the internal operations of organizations, but it has also changed the manager's job. Organizations today have become integrative communication centers. By linking computers, telephones, fax machines, copiers, printers, and the like, managers can get complete information quickly. With that information, managers can better formulate plans, make faster decisions, more clearly define the jobs that workers need to perform, and monitor work activities. In essence, information technology today has enhanced a manager's ability to more effectively and efficiently perform the four primary activities associated with a manager's job.

Technology is also changing how a manager's work is performed. Historically, the work site was located close to a source of skilled labor, so employees were near their bosses. Management could observe what work was being done and could easily communicate with employees face to face. Through the advent of technological advancements, managers are able to supervise employees in remote locations, and the need for face-to-face interaction has decreased dramatically.[42] Work, for many, occurs where their computers are. **Telecommuting** capabilities—linking a worker's computer and modem with those of coworkers and management at an office—have made it possible for employees to live anywhere.[43] With this potential, many employers no longer have to consider locating a business

telecommuting
The linking of a worker's computer and modem with those of coworkers and management at an office

near its workforce. For example, if Aetna Insurance in Idaho finds that it is having problems attracting qualified local applicants for its claims-processing jobs, and a pool of qualified workers is available in Denver, Aetna doesn't need to establish a facility in Colorado. Instead, by providing these employees with computer equipment and appropriate ancillaries, the work can be done hundreds of miles away and then be transmitted to the "home" office. However, effectively communicating with individuals in remote locations and ensuring that performance objectives are being met have become two of managers' biggest challenges.[44] In addressing these challenges, organizations will focus on training managers to establish performance standards and ensure appropriate work quality and on-time completion. Traditional "face-time" is removed in decentralized work sites, and managers' need to "control" the work will have to change. Instead, there will have to be more employee involvement, allowing workers to make those decisions that affect them. For instance, although the work assigned to employees has a due date, managers must recognize that home workers will work at their own pace. Instead of an individual focusing work efforts over an eight-hour period, the individual may work two hours here, three hours at another time, and another three late at night. The emphasis, then, will be on output, not means.

What Does Society Expect from Organizations and Managers?

The importance of corporate social responsibility surfaced in the 1960s when the activist movement began questioning the singular economic objective of business. For instance, were large corporations irresponsible because they discriminated against women and minorities as shown by the obvious absence of female and minority managers at that time? Was a company like Dow Corning ignoring its social responsibility by marketing breast implants when data indicated that leaking silicone could be a health hazard? Were tobacco companies ignoring health risks associated with nicotine and its addictive properties? Before the 1960s, few people asked such questions. Even today, good arguments can be made for both sides of the social responsibility issue (see Exhibit 2-5). Arguments aside, times have changed. Managers are now regularly confronted with decisions that have a dimension of social responsibility; philanthropy, pricing, employee relations, resource conservation, product quality, and operations in countries with oppressive governments are some of the more obvious factors. They are addressing these areas by reassessing forms of packaging, recyclability of products, environmental safety practices, and the like. The idea of being environmentally friendly or "green" will have an effect on all aspects of business—from the conception of products and services to use and subsequent disposal by customers.[45] In a globally competitive world, few organizations can afford the bad press or potential economic ramifications of being seen as socially irresponsible.[46]

Few terms have been defined in as many different ways as social responsibility. Some of the more popular meanings include "profit maximization," "going beyond profit making," "voluntary activities," "concern for the broader social system," and "social responsiveness."[47] Most of the debate has focused on the extremes. On one side, there is the classical—or purely economic—view that management's only social responsibility is to maximize profits.[48] On the other side stands the socioeconomic position, which holds that management's responsibility goes well beyond making profits to include protecting and improving society's welfare.[49]

Exhibit 2-5 Arguments For and Against Social Responsibility

The major arguments for the assumption of social responsibilities by business are:

1. **Public expectations** Social expectations of business have increased dramatically since the 1960s. Public opinion in support of business pursuing social as well as economic goals is now well solidified.
2. **Long-run profits** Socially responsible businesses tend to have more secure long-run profits. This is the normal result of the better community relations and improved business image that responsible behavior brings.
3. **Ethical obligation** A business firm can and should have a conscience. Business should be socially responsible because responsible actions are right for their own sake.
4. **Public image** Firms seek to enhance their public image to gain more customers, better employees, access to money markets, and other benefits. Since the public considers social goals to be important, business can create a favorable public image by pursuing social goals.
5. **Better environment** Involvement by business can solve difficult social problems, thus creating a better quality of life and a more desirable community in which to attract and hold skilled employees.
6. **Discouragement of further government regulation** Government regulation adds economic costs and restricts management's decision flexibility. By becoming socially responsible, business can expect less government regulation.
7. **Balance of responsibility and power** Business has a large amount of power in society. An equally large amount of responsibility is required to balance it. When power is significantly greater than responsibility, the imbalance encourages irresponsible behavior that works against the public good.
8. **Stockholder interests** Social responsibility will improve the price of a business's stock in the long run. The stock market will view the socially responsible company as less risky and open to public attack. Therefore, it will award its stock a higher price-earnings ratio.
9. **Possession of resources** Business has the financial resources, technical experts, and managerial talent to provide support to public and charitable projects that need assistance.
10. **Superiority of prevention over cures** Social problems must be dealt with at some time. Business should act on them before they become serious and costly to correct and take management's energy away from accomplishing its goal of producing goods and services.

The major arguments against the assumption of social responsibilities by business are:

1. **Violation of profit maximization** This is the essence of the classical viewpoint. Business is most socially responsible when it attends strictly to its economic interests and leaves other activities to other institutions.
2. **Dilution of purpose** The pursuit of social goals dilutes business's primary purpose: economic productivity. Society may suffer as both economic and social goals are poorly accomplished.
3. **Costs** Many socially responsible activities do not pay their own way. Someone has to pay these costs. Business must absorb these costs or pass them on to consumers in higher prices.
4. **Too much power** Business is already one of the most powerful institutions in our society. If it pursued social goals, it would have even more power. Society has given business enough power.
5. **Lack of skills** The outlook and abilities of business leaders are oriented primarily toward economics. Business people are poorly qualified to cope with social issues.

Exhibit 2-5 Arguments For and Against Social Responsibility

6 **Lack of accountability** Political representatives pursue social goals and are held accountable for their actions. Such is not the case with business leaders. There are no direct lines of social accountability from the business sector to the public.

7 **Lack of broad public support** There is no broad mandate from society for business to become involved in social issues. The public is divided on the issue. In fact, it is a topic that usually generates a heated debate. Actions taken under such divided support are likely to fail.

SOURCE: Adapted from R. J. Monsen Jr., "The Social Attitudes of Management," in J. M. McGuire, ed. *Contemporary Management: Issues and Views* (Upper Saddle River, NJ: Prentice Hall, 1974), p. 616; and K. Davis and W. Frederick, *Business and Society: Management, Public Policy, Ethics,* 5th ed. (New York: McGraw-Hill, 1984), pp. 28–41.

HOW CAN ORGANIZATIONS DEMONSTRATE SOCIALLY RESPONSIBLE ACTIONS?

What do we mean when we talk about **social responsibility?** It's a business firm's obligation, beyond that required by the law and economics, to pursue long-term goals that are good for society.[50] Note that this definition assumes that business obeys the law and pursues economic interests. We take as a given that all business firms—those that are socially responsible and those that are not—will obey all laws that society imposes. Also note that this definition views business as a moral agent. In its effort to do good for society, it must differentiate between right and wrong.

social responsibility
A firm's obligation, beyond that required by the law and economics, to pursue long-term goals that are good for society

We can understand social responsibility better if we compare it with two similar concepts: social obligation and social responsiveness.[51] **Social obligation** is the foundation of a business's social involvement. A business has fulfilled its social obligation when it meets its economic and legal responsibilities and no more. It does the minimum that the law requires. A firm pursues social goals only to the extent that they contribute to its economic goals. In contrast to social obligation, both social responsibility and social responsiveness go beyond merely meeting basic economic and legal standards. For example, both might mean respecting the community in which the company operates, treating all employees fairly, respecting the environment, supporting career goals and special work needs of women and minorities, or not doing business in countries in which there are human rights violations.

social obligation
The obligation of a business to meet its economic and legal responsibilities and no more

Social responsibility also adds an ethical imperative to do those things that make society better and not to do those that could make it worse. **Social responsiveness** refers to the capacity of a firm to adapt to changing societal conditions.[52] Social responsibility requires business to determine what is right or wrong and thus seek fundamental ethical truths. Social responsiveness is guided by social norms that can provide managers with a meaningful guide for decision making.

social responsiveness
The ability of a firm to adapt to changing societal conditions

HOW DO MANAGERS BECOME MORE SOCIALLY RESPONSIBLE?

Ethics commonly refers to a set of rules or principles that define right and wrong conduct.[53] Understanding ethics may be difficult, depending on the view that one holds of the topic (see Developing Your Ethics Skill, p. 74). Exhibit 2-6 presents three views of ethical standards.[54] Regardless of one's own view, whether a manager acts ethically or unethically will depend on several factors. These factors

ethics
A set of rules or principles that define right and wrong conduct

Exhibit 2-6 Three Views of Ethics

Utilitarian view of ethics	Refers to a situation in which decisions are made solely on the basis of their outcomes or consequences. The goal of utilitarianism is to provide the greatest good for the greatest number. On one side, utilitarianism encourages efficiency and productivity and is consistent with the goal of profit maximization. On the other side, however, it can result in biased allocations of resources, especially when some of those affected lack representation or voice.
Rights view of ethics	Refers to a situation in which the individual is concerned with respecting and protecting individual liberties and privileges, including the rights to privacy, freedom of conscience, free speech, and due process. The positive side of the rights perspective is that it protects individuals' freedom and privacy. But it has a negative side in organizations: It can present obstacles to high productivity and efficiency by creating an overly legalistic work climate.
Theory of justice view of ethics	Refers to a situation in which an individual imposes and enforces rules fairly and impartially. A manager would be using a theory of justice perspective in deciding to pay a new entry-level employee $1.50 an hour over the minimum wage because that manager believes that the minimum wage is inadequate to allow employees to meet their basic financial commitments. Imposing standards of justice also comes with pluses and minuses. It protects the interests of those stakeholders who may be underrepresented or lack power, but it can encourage a sense of entitlement that reduces risk taking, innovation, and productivity.

SOURCE: G. F. Cavanaugh, D. J. Moberg, and M. Valasquez, "The Ethics of Organizational Politics," *Academy of Management Journal,* June 1981, pp. 363–74.

include the individual's morality, values, personality, and experiences; the organization's culture; and the issue in question.[55] People who lack a strong moral sense are much less likely to do the wrong things if they are constrained by rules, policies, job descriptions, or strong cultural norms that discourage such behaviors. For example, someone in your class has stolen the final exam and is selling a copy for $50. You need to do well on this exam or risk failing the course. You expect some classmates have bought copies—and that could affect any possibility of the exam being "curved" by the professor. Do you buy a copy because you fear that without it you'll be disadvantaged, or do you refuse to buy a copy and try your best?

code of ethics
A formal document that states an organization's primary values and the ethical rules it expects managers and operatives to follow

The example of the final exam illustrates how ambiguity about what is ethical can be a problem for managers. Codes of ethics are an increasingly popular tool for reducing that ambiguity.[56] A **code of ethics** is a formal document that states an organization's primary values and the ethical rules it expects managers and operative employees to follow.[57] Ideally, these codes should be specific enough to guide organizational personnel in what they are supposed to do yet loose enough to allow for freedom of judgment.[58] Nearly 90 percent of *Fortune* 1000 companies have a stated code of ethics.[59]

In isolation, ethics codes are not likely to be much more than window dressing.[60] Their effectiveness depends heavily on whether management supports them and how employees who break the codes are treated. If management considers them to be important, regularly reaffirms their content, and publicly reprimands rule breakers, ethics codes can supply a strong foundation for an effective corporate ethics program.[61]

Why the emphasis on the entrepreneurial spirit? In Chapter 1, we introduced the small business. Although some differences between managing in a small business and a large one were noted, the focus was primarily on size. But, as the environment surrounding business continues to change, one trend becomes evident: more and more people are starting their own businesses—about 2 million of them annually in the United States alone.[62] It's also happening in all of North America, in Latin America, and in countries such as Russia, Hungary, and China.[63]

Entrepreneurship is the process of initiating a business venture, organizing the necessary resources, and assuming the risks and rewards. Because entrepreneurial businesses usually start small, most can be defined as a "small business"—one that has fewer than 500 employees.

entrepreneurship
The process of initiating a business venture, organizing the necessary resources, and assuming the risks and rewards

What explains the increased popularity of individuals starting their own business? There has always been a segment of the population that wanted to control its own destiny. Such people have long chosen entrepreneurship, but recent changes in the economy have stimulated interest in being one's own boss. The downsizing of large corporations has displaced million of workers and managers. Many of these employees have taken the trauma of being laid off and turned it into a self-employment opportunity, frequently financed in large part by their severance pay or early retirement bonus. Other members of the corporate world have seen colleagues and friends lose their jobs and have concluded that future opportunities in downsized corporations will be limited.[64] Therefore, they have voluntarily cut their corporate ties and chosen self-employment. Another force boosting entrepreneurship is the increasing options in franchising. Purchasing a franchise such as Blockbuster Video, Dunkin' Donuts, Merry Maids, or Super 8 Motels allows an entrepreneur to run his or her own business but with less risk.[65] That's because franchises have a lower failure rate than the typical new business because the marketing, operations, and management support are provided by the franchiser.

The entrepreneurial spirit, however, is not limited solely to the small business. Some companies are attempting to model the activities of the entrepreneur. Why? In general, entrepreneurs are better able to respond to a changing environment than are managers in a traditional hierarchical organization. The owner-manager is involved in the day-to-day operations and is usually close to the customer. Furthermore, the owner-manager is the main decision maker, and all employees report to him or her. The result is a "flatter" organization—with few layers of hierarchy.

In large organizations, people who demonstrate entrepreneurial characteristics are called **intrapreneurs.**[66] Should this imply then that entrepreneurs can exist in every large, established organization? The answer depends on one's definition of the term. The noted management guru Peter Drucker, for instance, argues that they can exist there.[67] He describes an entrepreneurial manager as someone who is confident in his or her abilities, who seizes opportunities for change, and who not only expects surprises but capitalizes on them. He contrasts this person with the traditional manager, who feels threatened by change, is bothered by uncertainty, prefers predictability, and is inclined to maintain the status quo. Drucker's use of the term entrepreneurial, however, is misleading. By almost any definition of good management, his entrepreneurial type would be preferred over the traditional type. Yet intrapreneurship can never capture the autonomy and riskiness inherent in true entrepreneurship, because intrapreneurship takes place within a larger organization. All financial risks are carried by the parent company. Rules,

intrapreneurs
Persons within an organization who demonstrate entrepreneurial characteristics

policies, and other constraints are imposed by the parent company; intrapreneurs report to bosses, and the payoff for success is not financial independence but career advancement.[68] We will come back to entrepreneurs in the next chapter.

What Will the Workforce of 2010 Look Like?

diversity
The varied background of organizational members in terms of gender, race, age, sexual orientation, and ethnicity

family-friendly benefits
A wide range of work and family programs to help employees; includes on-site day care, child and elder care, flexible work hours, job sharing, part-time employment, relocation programs, adoption benefits, parental leave, and other programs

Until very recently, managers took a "melting-pot" approach to personnel differences in organizations. They assumed that people who were different would somehow automatically want to assimilate. But today's managers have found that employees do not set aside their cultural values and lifestyle preferences when they come to work. The challenge for managers, therefore, is to make their organizations more accommodating to diverse groups of people by addressing different lifestyles, family needs, and work styles. The melting-pot assumption is being replaced by the recognition and celebration of differences.[69]

HOW DOES DIVERSITY AFFECT ORGANIZATIONS?

As organizational **diversity** in terms of gender, race, age, sexual orientation, and ethnicity increases, management adapts its human resource practices to reflect those changes. Many organizations today, like BankAmerica, have workforce diversity programs. They tend to "hire, promote and retain minorities,"[70] as well as focus on training employees. Some, like Motorola, actually conduct cultural audits to ensure that diversity is pervasive in the organization.[71] Furthermore, other organizations—both large and small—are modifying their benefit programs to make them more "family-friendly."[72]

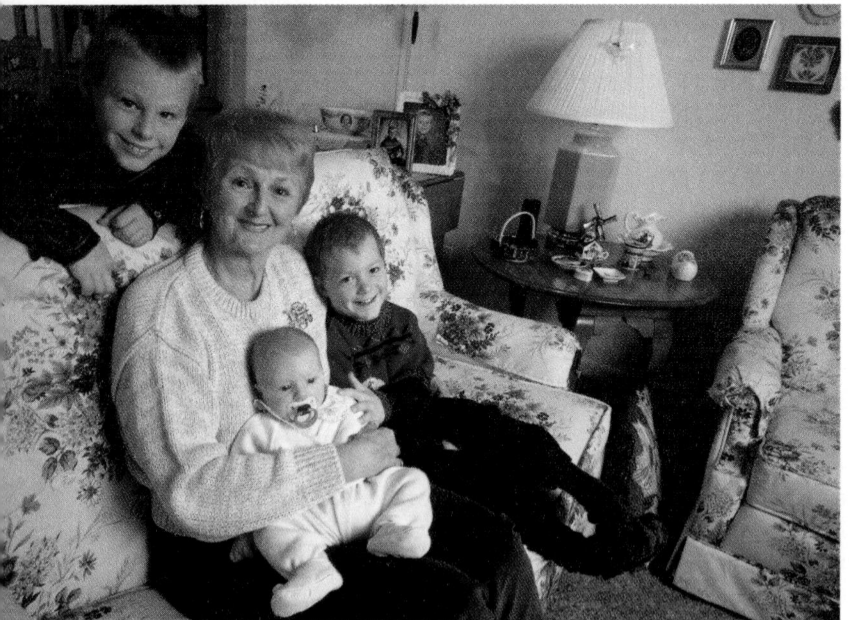

Family-friendly benefits can include many diverse benefit offerings. At Merck, recognized as one of the nation's 100 best companies for employees, one family-friendly benefit is a stock option program. By providing employees an opportunity to have a "piece of the business" stock options enable employees like Madeline Etzold to retire early and spend more time with her family.

To better meet the needs of the diverse workforce, some organizations, such as AT&T, the Merck, Qualcomm, and Marriott are also offering family-friendly benefits.[73] **Family-friendly benefits** include a wide range of work and family programs such as on-site day care, child and elder care, flexible work hours, job sharing, telecommuting, temporary part-time employment, unpaid leaves of absences, personal concierge services, relocation programs, adoption benefits, and parental leave.[74] With more women working and more two-career couples, family-friendly benefits are a means of helping employees better balance their work and family lives.[75] And studies indicate that helping employees resolve work and family conflicts boosts morale, increases productivity, reduces absenteeism, and makes it easier for employers to recruit and retain skilled workers.[76] For example, a study at Johnson & Johnson found that absenteeism among employees who used flexible work hours and family-leave policies was on average 50 percent less than those who did not take advantage of these family-friendly benefits.[77]

HOW DO WE MAKE MANAGERS MORE SENSITIVE TO DIFFERENCES?

The diversity that exists in the workforce requires managers to be more sensitive to the differences each group brings to the work setting. For example, managers will have to shift their philosophy from treating everyone alike to recognizing individual differences and responding to those differences in ways that will ensure employee retention and greater productivity. They must be in a position to recognize and deal with the different values, needs, interests, and expectations of employees. They must avoid any practice or action that can be interpreted as being sexist, racist, or offensive to minorities. Of course, at the same time, they must not illegally discriminate against any employees.

Such organizations as Levi Strauss, Hewlett-Packard, Lotus Development, and U.S. West are providing sophisticated diversity training programs for their managers to help them better communicate, motivate, and lead. These training programs are designed to raise diversity consciousness among current employees. For example, Hewlett-Packard conducts training on cultural differences between American Anglos, Mexicans, Indochinese, and Filipinos at a San Diego plant. Monsanto's two-day diversity program directly addresses racial, ethnic, and gender stereotypes.[78]

How Do Organizations Make the Customer King?

Henry Ford said his customers could have any color car they wanted—as long as it was black. Stew Leonard, owner of the world's largest dairy store in southern Connecticut, says there are only two rules in his business. "Rule 1—the customer is always right. Rule 2—If the customer is ever wrong, reread Rule 1."[79]

Managers in today's organizations are being influenced by the Stew Leonards of the world. They realize that long-term success can be achieved only by satisfying the customer.[80] For it's the customer who ultimately pays the bills. And as we have mentioned several times so far in this chapter, customers have more choices than ever before and are, therefore, more difficult to please. That is, customers are demanding quicker service, high quality, and value for their money. Mass customization, toll-free service hotlines, the growth of e-commerce and mail order, discount superstores, and managers who have become obsessed with quality are all responses to the concept that quality is what the customer says it is.[81] To make this theory a reality, organizations and their managers have embarked on several critical activities—continuous improvements in quality, work process engineering, downsizing, and flexibility and rapid response.

> *Stew Leonard's Dairy 2 rules: Rule 1—the customer is always right. Rule 2—If the customer is ever wrong, reread Rule 1.*

HOW HAVE ORGANIZATIONS SHOWN AN INCREASED CONCERN WITH QUALITY?

There is a quality revolution taking place in both the private and the public sectors.[82] The generic term that has evolved to describe this revolution is **total qual-**

total quality management (TQM)
A philosophy of management that is driven by customer needs and expectations and that is committed to continuous improvement

ity management (TQM) or continuous improvement. The revolution was inspired by a small group of quality experts—individuals like Joseph Juran and the late W. Edwards Deming.[83] For our discussion, we'll focus our attention on Deming's work.

An American who found few managers in the United States interested in his ideas, Deming went to Japan in 1950 and began advising many top Japanese managers on ways to improve their production effectiveness. Central to his management methods was the use of statistics to analyze variability in production processes. A well-managed organization, according to Deming, was one in which statistical control reduced variability and resulted in uniform quality and predictable quantity of output. Deming developed a 14-point program for transforming organizations. Today, Deming's original program has been expanded into a philosophy of management that is driven by customer needs and expectations[84] (see Exhibit 2-7). Total quality management expands the term *customer* beyond the traditional definition to include everyone involved with the organization, either internally or externally—encompassing employees and suppliers as well as the people who buy the organization's products or services.[85] The objective is to create an organization committed to continuous improvement or, as the Japanese call it, **kaizen.**[86]

kaizen
The Japanese term for an organization committed to continuous improvement

Although TQM has been criticized by some for overpromising and underperforming, its overall record is impressive.[87] Varian Associates, Inc., a maker of scientific equipment, used TQM in its semiconductor unit to cut the time it took to put out new designs by 14 days. Another Varian unit, which makes vacuum systems for computer dust-free clean rooms, boosted on-time delivery from 42 percent to 92 percent through continuous improvement methods. Globe Metallurgical, Inc., a small Ohio metal producer, credits TQM for having helped it become 50 percent more productive. And the significant improvements made over the past decade in the quality of cars produced by GM, Ford, and DaimlerChrysler can be directly traced to the implementation of total quality methods.

Exhibit 2-7 Components of Total Quality Management

1. Intense focus on the *customer.* The customer includes not only outsiders who buy the organization's products or services but also internal customers (such as shipping or accounts payable personnel) who interact with and serve others in the organization.
2. Concern for *continuous improvement.* TQM is a commitment to never being satisfied. "Very good" is not good enough. Quality can always be improved.
3. Improvement in the *quality of everything* the organization does. TQM uses a very broad definition of quality. It is related not only to the final product but also to how the organization handles deliveries, how rapidly it responds to complaints, how politely the phones are answered, and the like.
4. Accurate *measurement.* TQM uses statistical techniques to measure every critical variable in the organization's operations. These are compared against standards, or benchmarks, to identify problems, trace them to their roots, and eliminate their causes.
5. *Empowerment of employees.* TQM involves the people on the line in the improvement process. Teams are widely used in TQM programs as empowerment vehicles for finding and solving problems.

One Manager's Perspective

Martin Morrison Manager of Technical Writing, Shared Medical Systems

Shared Medical Systems (SMS) provides information solutions for the worldwide health industry. Its more than 5,000 customers include hospitals, physicians' offices, clinics, and major health provider networks and organizations in 20 countries. Continuous improvement, a quality management process with a strong emphasis on the customer, forms a basic part of the organization's mission, as this quote from SMS's mission statement reveals, "Through long-term partnerships in the health industry, we help our customers improve their quality of care, financial performance, and strategic position by providing superior, cost-effective solutions based on information systems and services."

When it comes to putting those words into practice with user groups, Martin Morrison, manager of technical writing, puts it this way, "SMS partners with the user groups to provide presentations, demonstrations, and workshops, but especially to *listen.* That is how we identify those areas of our products and services that can be improved to match more closely our customers' growing and changing needs."

Morrison goes on to describe how SMS's managers in particular play a significant role in continuous improvement. Each manager must be personally involved in the process, and all employees are encouraged to participate, whether at a user-group meeting or on a process improvement team. In addition, SMS's employees maintain a constant customer-first attitude in their daily work. In this way, the organization is able to make partnerships with its customers paramount.

WHEN MUST MANAGERS THINK IN TERMS OF QUANTUM CHANGES RATHER THAN CONTINUOUS IMPROVEMENT?

Although continuous improvement methods are useful innovations in many of our organizations, they generally focus on incremental change. Such action—a constant and permanent search to make things better—is intuitively appealing. Many organizations, however, operate in an environment of rapid and dynamic change. As the elements around them change so quickly, a continuous improvement process may keep them behind the times.

The problem with a focus on continuous improvements is that it may provide a false sense of security. It may make managers feel as if they are actively doing something positive, which is somewhat true. Unfortunately, ongoing incremental change may allow managers to avoid facing up to the possibility that what the organization may really need is radical or quantum change, referred to as **work process engineering.**[88] Continuous change may also make managers feel as if they are taking progressive action while, at the same time, avoiding having to implement quantum changes that will threaten organizational members. The incremental approach of continuous improvement, then, may be today's version of rearranging the deck chairs on the *Titanic.*[89]

work process engineering
radical or quantum change in an organization

If you have been reading this chapter carefully, you may be asking yourself, "Aren't these authors contradicting what they said a few paragraphs ago about TQM?" It may appear so, but consider this. Although continuous improvement can often lead to organizational improvements, it may not always be the right approach initially. That's

Kaizen, the Japanese term and organizational concept is not just for Japanese firms. U.S. companies like AlliedSignal use kaizen too. Here, these AlliedSignal workers provide progress reports on their team's project accomplishments in an effort to ensure that they will produce a high-quality outcome.

the case if you are producing an improved version of an outdated product. Instead, a complete overhaul might be required. Once this has been done, then continuous improvement can have its rightful place. Let's see how this operates.

Assume that you are the manager responsible for implementing design changes in your roller skate business. If you take the continuous improvement approach, your frame of reference will be a high-toe leather shoe on top of a steel carriage with four wooden wheels. Your continuous improvement program may lead you to focus on innovations such as a different grade of cowhide for the shoe, speed laces for the uppers, or a different type of ball bearing in the wheels. Of course, your skate may be better than the one you previously made, but is that enough? Compare your product with that of a competitor who reengineers the design process.

To begin, your competitor poses the following question: How can we design a skate that is safe, fun, fast, and provides greater mobility? Starting from scratch and not being constrained by her current manufacturing process, your competitor completes her redesign with something she calls "in-line skates." Instead of leather and metal skates, you are now competing against a molded boot, similar to that used in skiing. Your competitor's skate is better than one made from leather and has no laces to tie. In addition, it uses four to six high-durability plastic wheels, which are placed in line for greater speed and mobility.

In this theoretical example, both companies made progress. But which do you believe made the most progress given the dynamic environment they face? Our example demonstrates why companies such as Thermos, Ryder Trucks, and Casio Computer are opting for work process engineering rather than incremental change.[90] It is imperative in today's business environment that all managers consider the challenge of reengineering their organizational processes. Why? Because work process engineering can lead to "major gains in cost, service, or time"[91] as well as assist an organization in preparing to meet the challenges technology changes foster.[92]

WHY DO ORGANIZATIONS LAY OFF WORKERS?

There was a time in corporate America when organizations followed a relatively simple rule: In good times you hire employees; in bad times, you fire them. Since the late 1980s that "rule" no longer holds true, at least for most of the largest companies in the world. Throughout the 1990s, for instance, most *Fortune* 500 companies made significant cuts in their overall staff. IBM cut staff by 122,000 workers, and at AT&T, 83,000 employees were let go. Boeing reduced its staff by 61,000; Sears cut 50,000 jobs, and Eastman Kodak reduced its workforce by more than 34,000 positions.[93] This **downsizing** phenomenon is not going on just in the United States. Jobs are being eliminated in almost all industrialized nations. For example, Peugeot (France) cut nearly 10 percent of its workforce over a five-year period; Renault (France) eliminated 17 percent of its jobs, and Volkswagen (Germany) eliminated about 30,000

downsizing
An activity in an organization designed to create a more efficient operation through extensive layoffs

jobs and cut the remaining employees' pay by 16 percent.[94] In Japan, Sony eliminated 17,000 workers, NEC cut 15,000 jobs, and Toyo Engineering eliminated 29 percent of its workforce.[95]

Cutting jobs for any organization's president is never an easy task. But conditions in the marketplace sometimes demand it. That's what Sony's President Nobuyuki Idei has found. The once-flourishing company has been experiencing falling profits. As a result, Idei has decided to cut 17,000 jobs over a three-year period.

Why this trend for downsizing? Organizations are attempting to increase their flexibility to better respond to change. Continuous improvement and work process engineering are creating flatter structures and redesigning work to increase efficiency. The result is a need for fewer employees. Are we implying that big companies are disappearing? Absolutely not! It is how they are operating that is changing. Big isn't necessarily inefficient. Companies such as PepsiCo, Home Depot, and Motorola manage to blend large size with agility by dividing their organization into smaller, more flexible units.

Downsizing as a strategy is here to stay. It's part of a larger goal of balancing staff to meet changing needs.[96] When organizations become overstaffed, they will likely cut jobs. At the same time, they are likely to increase staff if doing so adds value to the organization. A better term for this organizational action, then, might be **rightsizing.** Rightsizing involves linking staffing levels to organizational goals. For example, in one recent year, AT&T cut 8,000 jobs—mostly operators who were replaced by voice-recognition technology—while at the same time, adding staff in marketing and network systems. Accordingly, rightsizing promotes greater use of outside firms for providing necessary products and services, called **outsourcing,** in an effort to remain flexible and responsive to the ever-changing environment.[97]

rightsizing
Linking staffing levels to organizational goals

outsourcing
An organization's use of outside firms for providing necessary products and services

HOW DO ORGANIZATIONS CREATE FLEXIBLE AND RAPID RESPONSE SYSTEMS?

Lou Capolzzola worked full time, for 10 years, at *Sports Illustrated*. He was a photographic lighting specialist. One day his job was eliminated. Well, the job was not exactly eliminated—just Lou's permanent position in the organization. Lou was given the choice to continue as an independent contractor, but his base pay would be about half what it was as a full-time employee. He wouldn't be paid most of the overtime pay he had previously been entitled to, and he would lose all of his $20,000-a-year benefit package and whatever security goes with a full-time, permanent job. Why did this happen? Time Warner, the publisher of *Sports Illustrated,* decided it could save money and increase flexibility by converting a lot of jobs like Lou's into temporary positions.[98]

Time Warner and thousands of other organizations in the global village have decided they could save money and increase their flexibility by converting many jobs like Lou's into temporary or part-time positions—giving rise to what is com-

contingent workforce
Part-time, temporary, and contract workers who are available for hire on an as-needed basis

monly referred to as the **contingent workforce** (see Exhibit 2-8).[99] Today, temporary workers can be found in secretarial, nursing, accounting, assembly-line, legal, dentistry, computer programming, engineering, marketing, and even senior management positions.[100]

Why the organizational emphasis on contingent employees? Many large companies are converting some permanent jobs into temporary ones (see Ethical Dilemma in Management). For example, 27 percent of Microsoft's Seattle-area employees are temporaries.[101] Organizations facing a rapidly changing environment must be in a position to adjust rapidly to those changes. Having a large number of permanent full-time employees limits management's ability to react. For example, an organization that faces significantly decreased revenues during an economic downturn may have to cut staff. Deciding who is to be laid off and what effect the layoffs will have on productivity and on the rest of the organization will be extremely complex in organizations that have a large permanent workforce. On the other hand, organizations that rely heavily on contingent workers will have greater flexibility because workers can be easily added or taken off as needed. In addition, staffing shortages, opportunities to capitalize on new markets, obtaining someone who possesses a special skill for a particular project, and the like, all point to a need for the organization to be able to rapidly adjust its staffing level.

Nearly two decades ago there were 619,000 temporary jobs in the United States. Today that number is over 2.6 million.[102] In Europe, companies have shifted overwhelmingly to hiring temporary workers. About 11 percent of all jobs in France and more than 33 percent of those in Spain are now filled by temporary workers.[103] How do employees feel about this growth in temporary work? Many

Exhibit 2-8 Contingent Workers

Part-time employees	Part-time employees work fewer than 40 hours a week. In general, part-timers are afforded few, if any, employee benefits. Part-time employees are generally a good source of employees for organizations to staff their peak hours. For example, the bank that expects its heaviest clientele between 10 A.M. and 2 P.M. may bring in part-time tellers for those four hours. Part-time employees may also be involved in job sharing, in which two employees split one full-time job.
Temporary employees	Temporary employees, like part-timers, are generally employed during peak production periods. Temporary workers also fill in for employees who are off work for an extended period of time. For example, a secretarial position may be filled by a "temp" while the secretary is off work during his 12-week unpaid leave of absence for the birth of his daughter. Temporary workers create a fixed cost to an employer for labor "used" during a specified period.
Contract workers	Contract workers, subcontractors, and consultants (may be referred to as freelance individuals) are hired by organizations to work on specific projects. These workers, typically very skilled, perform certain duties for an organization. Often their fee is set in the contract and is paid when the organization receives particular deliverables. Organizations use contract workers because their labor cost is fixed, and they do not incur any of the costs associated with a full-time employee population. In addition, some contract arrangements may exist because the contractor can provide virtually the same good or service in a more efficient manner than could a permanent employee.

employees prefer their contingent status. Yet the prime reason United Parcel Service's 185,000 workers went on strike in August 1997 was to protest UPS's filling the majority of its new positions with temporaries, who were paid significantly lower wages than full-timers.[104] It's probably accurate to say that the majority of the workforce prefers permanent, full-time employment, but in a world of rapid change, permanent employees limit management's flexibility. A large permanent workforce, for example, restricts management's options and raises costs for firms that suffer the ups and downs of market cycles. So we can expect employers to increasingly rely on temporaries to fill new and vacated positions.

What issues do contingent workers create for managers? Temporaries and the flexibility they foster present special challenges for managers. Each contingent worker may need to be treated differently in terms of practices and policies. For instance, one worker may have to be on site, but another may be able, given the nature of the work, to work at home. Managers must also make sure that contingent workers do not perceive themselves as second-class workers. Because they often do not receive many of the amenities—such as health and paid-leave benefits—that full-time **core employees** do, contingent workers may tend to view their work as not being critically important. Accordingly, they may not be as loyal, as committed to the organization, or as motivated on the job as permanent workers are. That tendency may be especially relevant to those individuals, like Lou Capolzzola, who have been forced to join the temporary workforce. Today's managers must recognize that it will be their responsibility to motivate their entire workforce—full-time and temporary employees—and to build their commitment to doing good work!

core employees
The small group of full-time employees of an organization who provide some essential job tasks for the organization

Ethical Dilemma in Management

The Contingent Workforce

Contingent work can be a blessing for both organizations and the individuals involved. Contingent workers provide employers with a rich set of diverse skills on an as-needed basis. In addition, hiring precisely when the specific work is to begin is very cost effective. Moreover, individuals who desire to work less than full time are also given the opportunity to keep their skills sharp. Simultaneously, being contingent workers permits them to balance their commitment to personal matters and their careers.

Many of the blessings for individuals, however, revolve around a central theme: An individual chooses to be a contingent worker. Unfortunately, that is not always the case. Jobs in the United States have shifted in terms of requisite skills and locations, and that trend is expected to continue. Consequently, the involuntary contingent workforce will be expected to grow in the years ahead.

Being part of the contingent workforce—even if not by choice—might not be so bad if employees received benefits typically offered to full-time core employees. Although hourly rates sometimes are higher for the contingent workers, these individuals have to pay for the benefits that organizations typically provide to their full-time permanent employees. For instance, as a contract worker, you are required to pay all of your Social Security premiums. For core and some part-time employees, the employee and the employer share in this "tax." So some of that "extra" hourly rate of the contingent worker is taken away as an expense. Added to Social Security are such things as health insurance payments. Buying health insurance through an organization that receives group rates is generally cheaper than having to buy the insurance yourself. This is yet another expense for the contingent worker. So, too, is having to pay for office supplies and equipment. As for time off with pay, forget about it. Vacation, holidays, sick leave? It's simple. Take all you want. But remember, when you don't work, you don't get paid!

Do you believe organizations that hire contingent workers who would rather have permanent employment are guilty of exploitation? Should organizations be legally required to provide some basic level of benefits—such as health insurance, vacation, sick leave, and retirement—to contingent workers? What's your opinion?

Some Concluding Remarks

If you stop for a moment and digest what you have been reading in this chapter, you might wonder if organizations and managers as we described them in Chapter 1 still exist. They do but with some significant modifications. Both organizations and managers need to be more flexible and respond to change.

Frederick Taylor, the "father of scientific management" (see History Module), argued nearly a century ago for the division of work and responsibility between management and workers. He wanted managers to do the planning and thinking. Workers were just to do what they were told. That prescription might have been good advice at the turn of the century, but workers today are far better educated and trained than they were in Taylor's day. In fact, because of the complexity and changing nature of many jobs, today's workers may be considerably more knowledgeable than those who manage them about how best to do their jobs. This fact is not being ignored by management. Managers are transforming themselves from bosses into team leaders. Instead of telling employees what to do, an increasing number of managers are finding that they become more effective when they focus on motivating, coaching, and cheerleading. Managers also recognize that they can often improve quality, productivity, and employee commitment by redesigning jobs to increase the decision-making discretion of workers. We call this process **empowering** employees.[105]

empowering
The redesigning of jobs in order to increase the decision-making discretion of workers

For much of the twentieth century, most organizations stifled the capabilities of their workforce. They overspecialized jobs and demotivated employees by treating them like unthinking machines. Recent successes at empowering employees in companies such as Colgate-Palmolive, Fiat, Wal-Mart, and Quad/Graphics, Inc. suggest that the future lies in expanding the worker's role in his or her job rather than in practicing Taylor's segmentation of responsibilities.[106]

If organizations are to successfully compete in a global village, they have to be able to make decisions and implement changes quickly.

The empowerment movement is being driven by two forces. First is the need for quick decisions by those people who are most knowledgeable about the issues. That requires moving decision making to individuals closest to the problems. If organizations are to successfully compete in a global village, they have to be able to make decisions and implement changes quickly. Second is the reality that the large layoffs in the middle-management ranks that began in the late 1980s have left many managers with considerably more people to supervise than they had in the past. And they may not have formal control over the work activities of some of these individuals.

The same manager who today oversees a staff of 35 cannot micromanage in the ways that were possible when he or she supervised 10 people. For example, one manager at AT&T, which has undergone extensive downsizing, had to assume responsibilities for three areas that previously had been handled by three managers. This manager had to empower her people, "because you can't know every data system and every policy. It's been a letting-go process and stretching."[107] That letting go and stretching process can be likened to the role of a sports team **coach.**

coach
A manager who motivates, empowers, and encourages his or her employees

Consider the job of head coach of a college basketball team. This individual is the one who establishes the game plan for an upcoming game and readies the players for the task. Even though the coach prepares the plans and the players, he or she cannot go out on Saturday afternoon and play the game. Instead, it is the players who execute the game plan. So what does the coach do during the game? It depends on how well the plan is working. When the competition is doing something that is counter to the game plan, the coach must quickly formulate new plans to give the players another competitive advantage. Thus, the coach deals with the exceptions. And, regardless of the game's outcome, as the players play the game, the coach becomes one of the major cheerleaders—recognizing outstanding performance toward fulfilling the plan and boosting player morale. This coaching role is increasingly becoming an accurate description of the jobs of today's managers!

PHLIP Companion Web Site

We invite you to visit the Robbins/DeCenzo companion Web site at *www.prenhall.com/robbins* for this chapter's Internet resources.

Chapter Summary

How will you know if you fulfilled the Learning Outcomes on page 45? You will have fulfilled the Learning Outcomes if you are able to:

1 *Describe the three waves in modern history and their implications for organizations.*
The first wave was agriculture (up to the 1890s). During the agricultural wave, individuals were their own bosses and were responsible for performing a variety of tasks. The second was industrialization (about 1900 to the 1960s). Work left the fields and moved into formal organizations with workers hired into tightly structured and formal workplaces dominated by mass production, specialized jobs, and authority relationships. The third wave is information technology (beginning in the 1970s). The information age has significantly reduced low-skilled, blue-collar jobs in manufacturing, but it has created abundant opportunities for educated and skilled technical specialists, professionals, and other knowledge workers.

2 *Explain the importance of viewing management from a global perspective.*
Competitors are no longer defined within national borders. New competition can suddenly appear at any time, from anywhere in the world. Accordingly, managers must think globally if their organizations are to succeed over the long term.

3 *Identify how technology is changing the manager's job.*
Technology is changing a manager's job in several ways. Managers will have immediate access to information that will help them in making decisions. In addition, through the advent of technological advancements, managers may be supervising employees in remote locations, reducing the face-to-face interaction with these individuals. Consequently, effectively communicating with individuals in remote locations as well as ensuring that performance objectives are being met will become major challenges.

4 *Define social responsibility and ethics.*
Social responsibility refers to an obligation, beyond that required by law and economics, for a firm to pursue long-term goals that are good for society. Ethics refers to rules or principles that define right or wrong conduct.

5 *Explain what is meant by the term entrepreneurial spirit.*
Entrepreneurial spirit refers to individuals who are independent workers who initiate a business venture, have a tendency to take calculated risk, and accept the fact that mistakes occur in business.

6 *Describe the management implications of a diversified workforce.*
The workforce of 2010 will witness heterogeneity of gender, race, and ethnicity. It will also include the physically disabled, gays and lesbians, the elderly, and those who are significantly overweight. The most important requirement for managers is sensitivity to the differences among individuals. That means they must shift their philosophy from treating everyone alike to recognizing differences and responding to those differences in ways that will ensure employee retention and greater productivity.

7 *Explain why organizations focus on quality and continuous improvement.*
Organizations focus on quality and continuous improvement for several reasons. First, today's educated consumer demands it. Accordingly, a company that lacks quality products and services may be unsuccessful in achieving its goals. Second, quality and continuous improvements are strategic initiatives in an organization designed to make the operation more efficient and effective.

8 *Describe why many corporations have downsized.*
Many corporations have downsized in an attempt to increase their flexibility. Continuous improvements and work process engineering activities have created flatter structures and redesigned work to increase efficiency. As a result, organizations need fewer employees.

Review and Application Questions

READING FOR COMPREHENSION

1 Describe the shifts in the types of jobs in the workforce during the past 100 years.

2 Explain the managerial implications of a global village.

3 What are the managerial implications of Hofstede's research on cultural environments? In what countries do you believe managers from the United States are likely to have to make the fewest adjustments? In what countries do you believe they'd have to make the most adjustments?

4 Describe the managerial implications of growing organizational diversity.

5 Identify the characteristics and behaviors of an ethical manager.

6 Explain the increased popularity of entrepreneurial spirit in the past 20 years.

LINKING CONCEPTS TO PRACTICE

1 "Entrepreneurs are born, not made." Do you agree or disagree with the statement? Explain.

2 "Continuous improvement programs include contributions from all historical management contributors." Do you agree or disagree with this statement? Discuss.

3 "Work process engineering is just a fad for organizations to reduce their payrolls and increase their profits." Do you agree or disagree with this statement? Explain.

4 "Coaching and empowering employees will replace the traditional management functions of planning, organizing, leading, and controlling." Do you agree or disagree with this statement? Explain.

5 Discuss the implications of hiring contingent workers from both the organizational and contingent worker perspective.

Management Workshop

Team Skill-Building Exercise

Understanding Cultural Differences

Workforce diversity has become a major issue for managers. Although there are often similarities among individuals, obvious differences do exist. A means of identifying some of those differences is to get to know individuals from the diverse groups. For this exercise, you will need to contact people from a different country. If you don't know any, the office of your college that is responsible for coordinating international students can give you a list of names. Interview at least three people to get responses to such questions as:

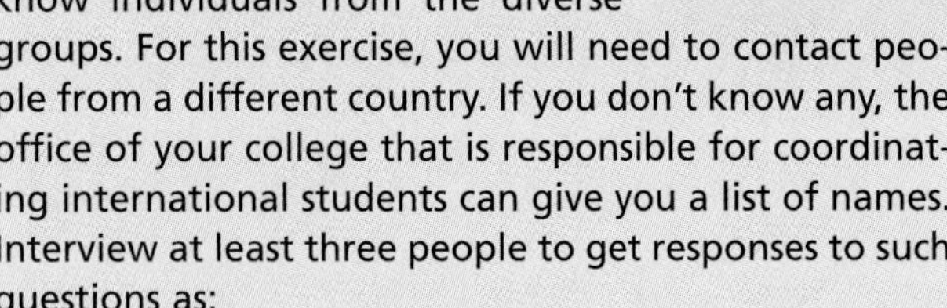

1 What country do you come from?

2 What is your first language?

3 Describe your country's culture in terms of, for example, form of government, emphasis on individual versus group, role of women in the workforce, benefits provided to employees, and how managers treat their employees.

4 What were the greatest difficulties in adapting to your new culture?

5 What advice would you give me if I had a management position in your country?

In groups of three to five class members, discuss your findings. Are there similarities in what each of you found? If so, what are they? Are there differences? Describe them. What implications for managing in the global village has this exercise generated for you and your group?

Developing Your Ethics Skills

Guidelines for Acting Ethically

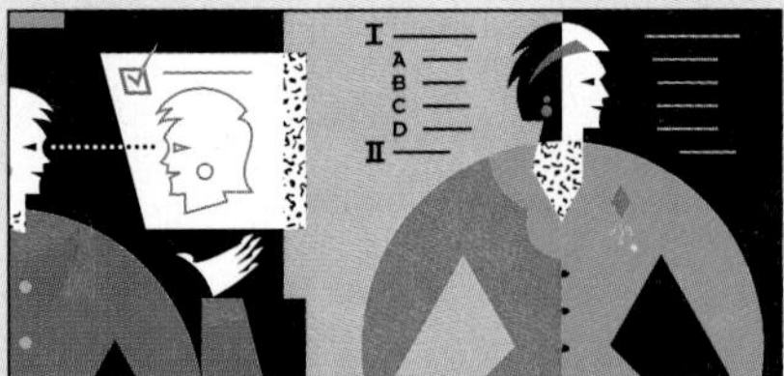

ABOUT THE SKILL

Making ethical choices can often be difficult for managers. Obeying the law is mandatory, but acting ethically goes beyond mere compliance with the law. It means acting responsibly in those "gray" areas, where right and wrong are not defined. What can you do to enhance your managerial abilities in acting ethically? We offer some guidelines.

STEPS IN PRACTICING THE SKILL

1 **Know your organization's policy on ethics.** Company policies on ethics, if they exist, describe what the organization perceives as ethical behavior and what it expects you to do. This policy will help you to clarify what is permissible and the managerial discretion you will have. This becomes your code of ethics!

2 **Understand the ethics policy.** Just having the policy in your hand does not guarantee that it will achieve what it is intended to do. You need to fully understand it. Behaving ethically is rarely a cut-and-dried process. But the policy can act as a guiding light, providing a basis from which you act within the organization. Even if a policy does not exist, there are still several steps you can take before you deal with the difficult situation.

3 **Think before you act.** Ask yourself, "Why am I going to do what I'm about to do? What led up to the problem? What is my true intention in taking this action? Is my reason valid? Or are there ulterior motives behind it—such as demonstrating organizational loyalty? Will my action injure someone? Would I disclose to my boss or my family what I'm going to do?" Remember, it's your behavior and your actions. You need to make sure that you are not doing something that will jeopardize your role as a manager, your organization, or your reputation.

4 **Ask yourself what-if questions.** If you are thinking about why you are going to do something, you should also be asking yourself what-if questions. For example, the following questions may help you shape your actions: "What if I make the wrong decision? What will happen to me? To my job?

"What if my actions were described, in detail, on the local TV news show or in the newspaper? Would it bother or embarrass me or those around me?

"What if I get caught doing something unethical? Am I prepared to deal with the consequences?"

5 **Seek opinions from others.** If it is something major that you must do, and about which you are uncertain, ask for advice from other managers. Maybe they have been in a similar situation and can give you the benefit of their experience. Or maybe they can just listen and act as a sounding board for you.

6 **Do what you truly believe is right.** You have a conscience, and you are responsible for your behavior. Whatever you do, if you truly believe it was the right action to take, then what others say or what the "Monday morning quarterbacks" say is immaterial. You need to be true to your own internal ethical standards. Ask yourself: Can I live with what I've done?

Practicing the Skill

ETHICS

Find a copy of your school's code of conduct or the code of ethics of any organization to which you belong. Or, obtain a copy of the code of ethics for a professional organization you hope to join after graduating. Evaluate the code's provisions and policies. Are there any that you are uncomfortable with? Why? Are there any that are routinely violated? Why do you think this is happening? What are the usual consequences of such violations? Do you think they are appropriate?

If you had trouble obtaining the code of conduct, find out why. Under what circumstances is it normally distributed, posted, or otherwise made available to members?

A Case Application

Developing Your Diagnostic and Analytical Skills

ZANE'S CYCLES

Who would you believe sells the most bikes in the New Haven, Connecticut, area? If you guessed Sears, Wal-Mart, or the local toy store you'd be wrong. The honor goes to Zane's Cycles, an independent bicycle shop run by its 30-something founder, Chris Zane.[108] To many people, Chris Zane is the epitome of today's manager. Chris wanted to control his destiny by being his own boss. So he started his own business, and, from the beginning, had a vision of what he wanted the business to become. After mustering up the necessary resources to get the operation up and running, he entered into a highly competitive and risky retail venture. He understood, too, that being satisfied with any success today could lead to doom tomorrow. The interesting thing was that Chris began this process at the ripe old age of twelve!

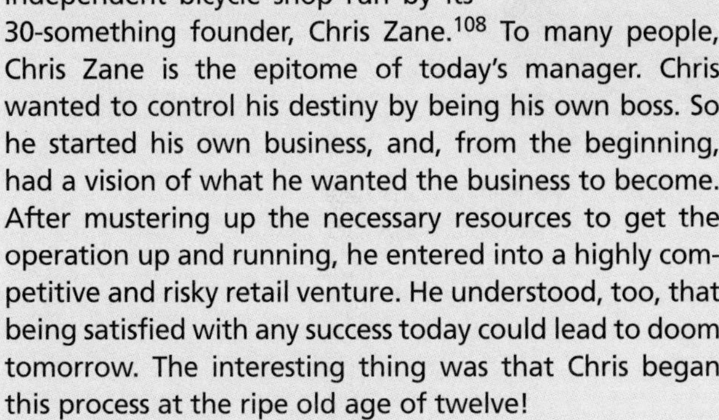

Zane had a lot of faith in his ability to be successful. He knew, though, that to be successful he would have to take some risks. After all, a small bike shop competing against large retailers seemed unlikely to survive, but Chris would not accept failure. He learned all he could in college about running a business—particularly focusing on satisfying customers and implementing new and creative techniques to achieve his goals. For instance, when two main competitors in town offered 90-day warranties on bike sales and repairs, Zane offered a one-year warranty. When they matched him, he raised the ante—giving a lifetime guarantee on all transactions at the store. He will even come and pick up the bike at a customer's house. When those two competitors went out of business, he negotiated a deal with the phone company. He agreed to pay the remainder of the two companies' Yellow Pages advertising. Callers to either of those numbers heard not only, "The number you are calling is no longer in service," but also, "If you are in need of a bicycle dealer, Zane's Cycles will be happy to serve you." By pressing zero, the caller is automatically transferred to Chris!

Even with fewer competitors, Zane realized he couldn't stop moving forward. He had to contend with the large discount retailers and a growing bicycle mail-order business. Chris recognized that he had to give the appearance of being a larger business—especially if he wanted to expand nationwide and possibly abroad. But he wanted to do so without hurting his "small" business appeal. To that end, he contracted with a marketing co-op firm to develop a 32-page mail-order catalog. By using the co-op, Zane customized several pages specifically to his shop while advertising and offering for sale many of the same items that other mail-order bike dealers do. And his newly installed computer tracking system can tell him precisely what zip code areas are producing the highest sales volumes.

Although his creativity had boosted sales, Zane recognized that most of his business came from customers who visited the shop, and he wanted them to feel special. Now, while customers browse, they can enjoy free refreshments at his in-store coffee and juice bar. Even the kids have a toy corner, so parents can shop at their own pace without being distracted. He has hired sales representatives and given them the freedom to make whatever decisions they need to please the customer and make a sale. But ringing up an "immediate" sale is not the primary focus. For example, Chris recognizes that, in his business, some customers feel nickled-and-dimed to death for having to purchase the most mundane things. So Chris does not charge for any item in his store that sells for less than $1. If customers need a bike part—a tire valve cap or a chain link—salespeople simply give it to them. The store also gives away cellular phones so bike riders can keep in touch with others or be prepared to make a call for assistance if needed.

Zane also believes that any successful business owes its success to the community that supports it. It's a relationship that must be nurtured. So, for example, when a Connecticut law was passed requiring helmets to be worn by all bicyclers, Zane supported the cause by selling his bike helmets to customers at cost. And to give even more back to the community, he established five $1,000 annual scholarships for local high school students who wanted to go to college. Do these expenditures have a bearing on his success? You bet they do. For instance, he calculates that his giveaways, community support, lifetime warranties, and coffee and juice bar have resulted in a 700 percent return on his investment—and a committed and loyal clientele.

QUESTIONS

1 Identify and describe the entrepreneurial spirit exhibited by Chris Zane. How has this affected his business?

2 Do you believe that Chris Zane endorses the concept that the "customer is king"? Support your position with examples.

3 Is Chris Zane a socially responsible employer? Does your opinion change when you consider that some of his socially responsible actions have helped him achieve a 700 percent return on investment? Discuss.

Developing Your Investigative Skills

Using the Internet

Visit *www.prenhall.com/robbins* for updated Internet Exercises.

Enhancing Your Writing Skills

Communicating Effectively

1 Select an industrialized country. Research information about a particular business practices in that country. For instance, you might compare U.S. employment discrimination laws with laws in your selected country and the differences that may exist. Or you may want to explore the ethics of "gift-giving" to political leaders.

2 Provide a two- to three-page write-up on an e-commerce business (e.g., Amazon.com; Dell, IBM) and the effect e-commerce is having on the operation of business. Emphasize the way the business has had to change to become an e-commerce business and the benefits that have accrued or are anticipated.

3 Family-friendly benefits have a tendency to be perceived as benefits that are primarily offered to female employees, but fathers have rights too. Research what organizations are doing to provide male employees with family-friendly benefits. In presenting your results, include a discussion on the benefits and the costs accruing to organizations from offering these benefits.

Three

Foundations of Planning

LEARNING OUTCOMES After reading this chapter, I will be able to:

1 Define *planning.*

2 Explain the potential benefits of planning.

3 Identify potential drawbacks to planning.

4 Distinguish between strategic and tactical plans.

5 State when directional plans are preferred over specific plans.

6 Define *management by objectives* and identify its common elements.

7 Outline the steps in the strategic management process.

8 Describe the four grand strategies.

9 Explain SWOT analysis.

10 Compare how entrepreneurs and bureaucratic managers approach strategy.

Kristen Schaffner-Irvin sees opportunities in the changing world.[1] A native of Huntington Beach, California, Schaffner-Irvin was a stay-at-home mom, but money was tight in the family, and she felt that she had to go to work. She wanted to find a job that would allow her to care for her children while simultaneously producing some extra income for the household. Having grown up in a family-owned fuel business, Kristen knew the ins and outs of the fuel-delivery industry. She didn't want, however, to go to work for her father. Instead, she wanted to "make it" on her own—fulfilling a life-long dream of being her own boss, in her own company. So with just a laptop computer and a telephone, she started Team Petroleum in 1992.

Having worked in the industry, Schaffner-Irvin recognized that a more efficient fuel delivery system was possible. Although she doesn't own any oil wells, fuel depots, or even fuel trucks, she felt that her company could be successful if she could demonstrate that Team Petroleum added value to its customers. Shaffner-Irvin envisioned this happening by buying fuel for her customers from suppliers and having it delivered to them, but delivery alone was not sufficient enough to "add value." What she did was to offer her customers a special service that her competitors didn't. She has linked their fuel tanks to her computer system, which monitors the customer's fuel consumption and automatically notifies Schaffner-Irvin's office when another delivery is needed. With some 80 fuel suppliers nationwide in her network, she is able to schedule fuel deliveries more effectively and efficiently than her customers could with their own staff. And she offers this service and makes scheduled deliveries on a 24/7 basis.

Since 1992, Kristen Schaffner-Irvin has nurtured a thriving business. She now employs eight people and has revenues in excess of $34 million. Her desire, focus, and ability to plan effectively and to use technology has turned her opportunity into a reality. She also now has more time to be with her children, and her family enjoys the lifestyle that her income provides.

This chapter presents the basics of planning. You will learn the difference between formal and informal planning, why managers plan, and the various types of plans managers use. We will explore the strategic planning process and look at the various strategies available to organizations and ways they can develop and maintain a competitive advantage. Finally, we will discuss entrepreneurship and why it is a special type of strategic planning.

Planning Defined

What is meant by the term *planning?* As we stated in Chapter 1, planning encompasses defining the organization's objectives or goals, establishing an overall strategy for achieving those goals, and developing a comprehensive hierarchy of plans to integrate and coordinate activities. It is concerned, then, with ends (what is to be done) as well as with means (how it is to be done).

Planning can be further defined in terms of whether it is *informal* or *formal.* All managers engage in planning, even if it is only the informal variety. In informal planning, very little, if anything, is written down. What is to be accomplished is in the head of one or a few people. Furthermore, the organization's objectives are rarely verbalized. This generally describes planning in many small businesses: The owner-manager has a private vision of where he or she wants to go and how he or she expects to get there. The planning is general and lacks continuity. Of course, informal planning exists in some large organizations, while some small businesses have very sophisticated formal plans.

When we use the term *planning* in this book, however, we are implying formal planning. Specific objectives are written down and made available to organization members. This means that management clearly defines the path it wants to take to get from where it is to where it wants to be.

Planning in Uncertain Environments

If managers performed their jobs in organizations that never faced changes in the environment, there would be little need for planning. What a manager did today, and well into the future, would be precisely the same as it was decades ago. There would be no need to think about what to do. It would be spelled out in some manual. In such a world, planning efforts would be unnecessary, but that world doesn't exist. Technological, social, political, economic, and legal changes are ever-present. The environment managers face is too dynamic and has too great an effect on an organization's survival to be left to chance. Accordingly, contemporary managers must plan—and plan effectively.

WHY SHOULD MANAGERS FORMALLY PLAN?

Managers should engage in planning for several reasons. Four of the more popular reasons are that planning provides direction, reduces the impact of change, minimizes waste and redundancy, and sets the standards to facilitate control (see Exhibit 3-1).

Planning establishes coordinated effort. It gives direction to managers and nonmanagers alike. When all organizational members understand where the organization is going and what they must contribute to reach the objectives, they can begin to coordinate their activities and cooperation and teamwork are fostered. On the other hand, a lack of planning can cause various organizational

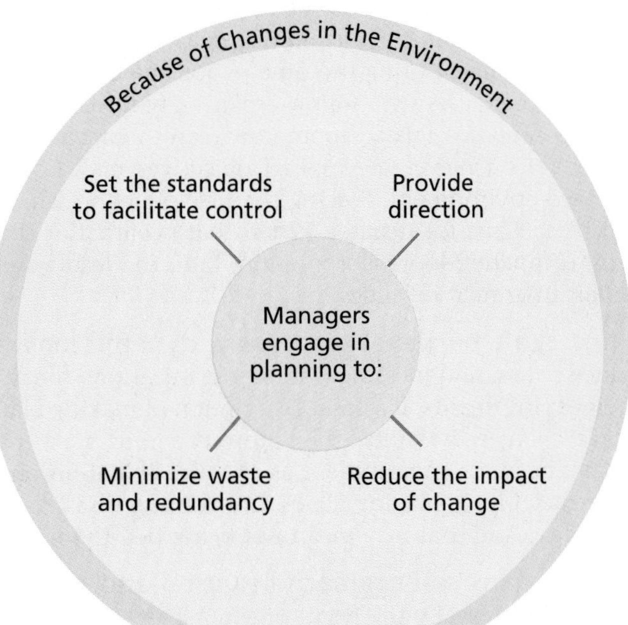

Because of Changes in the Environment
Set the standards to facilitate control
Provide direction
Managers engage in planning to:
Minimize waste and redundancy
Reduce the impact of change

Exhibit 3-1
Reasons for Planning

If . . . organizations . . . never faced changes in the environment, there would be little need for planning.

members or their units to work against one another. Consequently, the organization may be prevented from moving efficiently toward its objectives.

By forcing managers to look ahead, anticipate change, consider the impact of change, and develop appropriate responses, planning reduces uncertainty. It also clarifies the consequences of the actions managers might take in response to change. Planning, then, is precisely what managers need in a chaotic environment.

Planning also reduces overlapping and wasteful activities. Coordination before the fact is likely to uncover waste and redundancy. Furthermore, when means and ends are clear, inefficiencies become obvious.

Finally, planning establishes objectives or standards that facilitate control. If organizational members are unsure of what they are attempting to achieve, how can they determine whether they have achieved it? In planning, objectives are developed. In the controlling function of management, performance is compared against the established objectives. If and when significant deviations are identified, corrective action can be taken. Without planning, then, there truly cannot be effective control.

WHAT ARE SOME CRITICISMS OF FORMAL PLANNING?

Formal planning became very popular in the 1960s. And, for the most part, it still is today. It makes sense to establish some direction. After all, as the Cheshire cat said to Alice, the way you ought to go "depends a good deal on where you want to get to." But critics have begun to challenge some of the basic assumptions underlying planning. Let's look at the major arguments that have been offered against formal planning.

Planning may create rigidity[2] Formal planning efforts can lock an organization into specific goals to be achieved within specific timetables. When these objectives were set, the assumption may have been made that the environment wouldn't change during the time period the objectives cover. If that assumption is faulty, managers who follow a plan may have trouble. Rather than remaining flexible—and possibly scrapping the plan—managers who continue to do what is required to achieve the original objectives may not be able to cope with the changed environment. Forcing a course of action when the environment is fluid can be a recipe for disaster. When that occurred at the Toronto-based business-form company Moore Corporation, Ltd., the result was a loss of several million dollars in annual revenues.[3]

Plans can't be developed for a dynamic environment[4] As we mentioned a few sentences ago, most organizations today face dynamic change in their environments. If a basic assumption of making plans—that the environment won't change—is faulty, then how can one make plans? We have described today's business environment as chaotic. By definition, that means random and unpredictable. Managing chaos and turning disasters into opportunities require flexibility. And that may mean not being tied to formal plans.

Formal plans can't replace intuition and creativity[5] Successful organizations are typically the result of someone's vision, but these visions have a tendency to become formalized as they evolve. Formal planning efforts typically follow a methodology that includes a thorough investigation of the organization's capabilities and opportunities and a mechanistic analysis that reduces the vision to a programmed routine. That can spell disaster for an organization. For instance, the rapid rise of Apple Computer in the late 1970s and throughout the 1980s was attributed, in part, to the creativity and anticorporate attitudes of one of its cofounders, Steven Jobs. But as the company grew, Jobs felt a need for more formalized management—something he was uncomfortable performing. He hired a CEO, who ultimately ousted Jobs from his own company. With Jobs's departure came increased organizational formality—the very thing Jobs despised because it hampered creativity.

Planning focuses managers' attention on today's competition, not on tomorrow's survival[6] Formal planning has a tendency to focus on how to best capitalize on existing business opportunities within the industry. It often does not allow for managers to consider creating or reinventing the industry. Consequently, formal plans may result in costly blunders and incur catch-up costs when others take the lead. On the other hand, companies such as Intel and ABB (Asea Brown Boveri) have found much of their success to be the result of forging into uncharted waters, designing and developing new industries as they go![7]

Formal planning reinforces success, which may lead to failure[8] We have been taught that success breeds success. That has been an American tradition. After all, if it's not broken, don't fix it. Right? Well, maybe not! Success may, in fact, breed failure in an uncertain environment. It is hard to change or discard successful plans—to leave the comfort of what works for the anxiety of the unknown. Successful plans, however, may provide a false sense of security—generating more confidence than they deserve. Managers often won't deliberately face that unknown until they are forced to do so by changes in the environment. But by then, it may be too late.

Kenneth L. Lay, CEO of Enron Corporation, a Houston, Texas-based energy company, has witnessed firsthand the volatility of global business. The uncertainty surrounding Enron's nearly $3 billion contract in Dabhol, India, nearly resulted in the contract being canceled and investor lawsuits against the company.

THE BOTTOM LINE: DOES PLANNING IMPROVE ORGANIZATIONAL PERFORMANCE?

Do managers and organizations that plan outperform those that don't? Or have the critics of planning won the debate? Let's look at the evidence.

Contrary to the reasons the critics of planning cite, the evidence generally supports the position that organizations should have formal plans. But that's not to be interpreted as a blanket endorsement of planning. It would be inaccurate to say that organizations that formally plan always outperform those that don't.

Many studies have explored the relationship between planning and performance.[9] On the basis of those studies, we can draw the following conclusions. First, formal planning in an organization generally means higher profits, higher return on assets, and other positive financial results. Second, the quality of the planning process and the appropriate implementation of the plans probably contribute more to high performance than does the extent of planning. Finally, in those organizations in which formal planning did not lead to higher performance, the environment was typically the culprit. For instance, government regulations and similar environmental constraints reduce the impact of planning on an organization's performance. Why? Because managers will have fewer viable alternatives. For example, planning efforts by top managers at Enron Corporation (a Houston-based energy company) suggested that it was a good decision to enter into an agreement to build a power plant in Dabhol, India. However, when the Indian government abruptly canceled the $2.8 billion contract as a result of "a rising backlash against foreign investments," the value of Enron's planning effort was significantly reduced.[10] When uncertainty is high, there's no reason to anticipate that organizations that plan will outperform those that do not.

Types of Plans

The most popular ways to describe plans are in terms of their *breadth* (strategic versus tactical), *time frame* (long term versus short), *specificity* (directional versus specific), and *frequency of use* (single use versus standing). Keep in mind, however, these planning classifications are not independent of one another. For instance, there is a close relationship between the short- and long-term categories and the strategic and tactical categories. Exhibit 3-2 illustrates the relationship among types of plans.

HOW DO STRATEGIC AND TACTICAL PLANNING DIFFER?

strategic plans
Plans that are organizationwide, establish overall objectives, and position an organization in terms of its environment

tactical plans
Plans that specify the details of how an organization's overall objectives are to be achieved

Plans that apply to the entire organization, that establish the organization's overall objectives, and that seek to position the organization in terms of its environment are **strategic plans.** Strategic plans drive the organization's efforts to achieve its goals. As these plans filter down in the organization, they serve as a basis for the tactical plans. **Tactical plans** (sometimes referred to as operational plans) specify the details of how the overall objectives are to be achieved. Strategic and tactical plans differ in three primary ways—their time frame, scope, and whether they include a known set of organizational objectives.[11] Tactical plans tend to cover shorter periods of time. For instance, an organization's monthly, weekly, and day-to-day plans are almost all tactical. On the other hand, strategic plans tend to cover an extended time period—usually five years or more. They also cover a broader area and deal less with specifics. Finally, strategic plans include the formulation of objectives, whereas tactical plans assume the existence of objectives. Tactical plans describe how those objectives will be attained.

IN WHAT TIME FRAME DO PLANS EXIST?

short-term plans
Plans that cover less than one year

long-term plans
Plans that extend beyond five years

Financial analysts traditionally describe investment returns as short and long term. The short term covers less than one year. Any time frame beyond five years is classified as long term. Managers have adopted the same terminology for plans. For clarity, we will emphasize **short-term plans** and **long-term plans** in this discussion.

The difference between short- and long-term plans is important given the length of future commitments and the degree of variability organizations face. For example, the more an organization's current plans affect future commitments, the longer the time frame that management should use. That is, plans should extend far enough to carry through those commitments that are made today. Planning over too long or too short a period is inefficient.

Exhibit 3-2
Types of Plans

Breadth	Time Frame	Specificity	Frequency of Use
Strategic	Long term	Directional	Single use
Tactical	Short term	Specific	Standing

With respect to the degree of variability, the greater the uncertainty, the more plans should be of the short-term variety. That is, if rapid or important technological, social, economic, legal, or other changes are taking place, well-defined and precisely chartered routes are more likely to hinder an organization's performance than to aid it. Shorter-term plans allow for more flexibility.

WHAT IS THE DIFFERENCE BETWEEN SPECIFIC AND DIRECTIONAL PLANS?

It appears intuitively correct that specific plans are always preferable to directional, or loosely guided, plans. **Specific plans** have clearly defined objectives. There is no ambiguity, and there are no problems with misunderstandings. For example, a manager who seeks to increase her firm's sales by 8 percent over a given 12-month period might establish specific procedures, budget allocations, and schedules of activities to reach that objective. These actions represent specific plans.

specific plans
Plans that have clearly defined objectives and leave no room for misinterpretation

However, specific plans are not without drawbacks. They require a clarity and a predictability that often does not exist. When uncertainty is high and management must maintain flexibility in order to respond to unexpected changes, directional plans are preferable.[12] As shown in Exhibit 3-3, both directional and specific plans can lead you from point A to point B. If there were a detour on Sussex Road, however, the specific plans might create confusion. **Directional plans,** on the other hand, identify general guidelines. They provide focus but do not lock managers into specific objectives or specific courses of action. A specific plan might aim to cut costs by 10 percent and increase revenues by 8 percent in the next six months; a directional plan might aim at improving corporate profits by 6 percent to 12 percent during the next six months. The flexibility inherent in directional plans is obvious. This advantage must be weighed against the loss in clarity provided by specific plans.

directional plans
Flexible plans that set out general guidelines

Exhibit 3-3 Directional versus Specific Plans

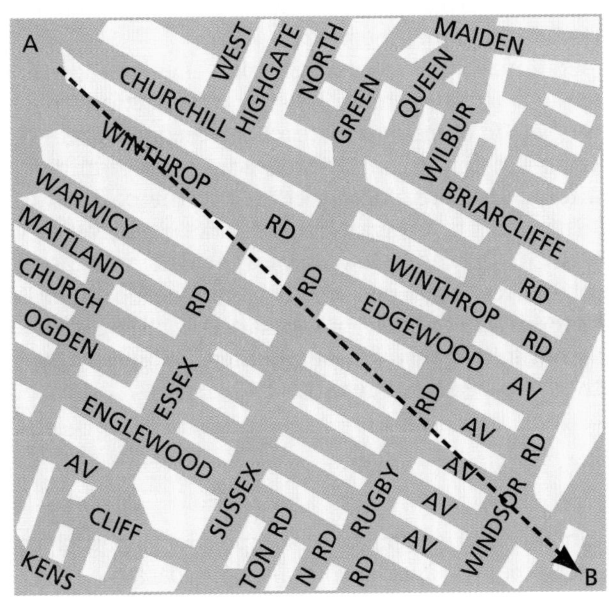

Directional plan

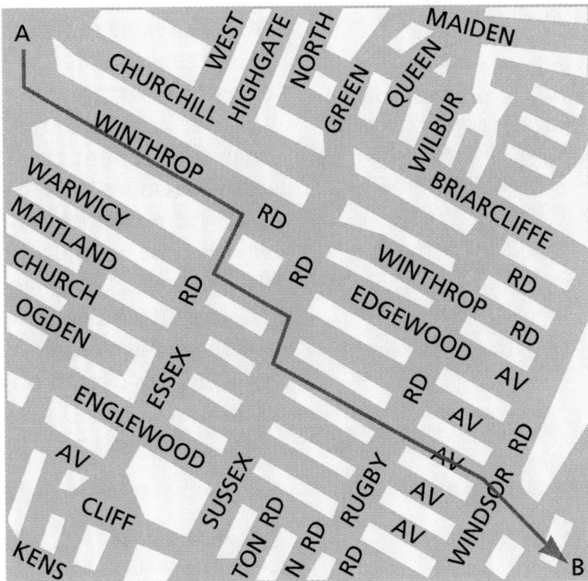

Specific plan

HOW DO SINGLE-USE AND STANDING PLANS DIFFER?

single-use plans
A plan that is used to meet the needs of a particular or unique situation

Some plans are meant to be used only once; others are used repeatedly. A **single-use plan** is used to meet the need of a particular or unique situation. For example, when Charles Schwab (a discount brokerage firm) introduced its Internet-based transaction service, top managers devised a single-use plan to guide the acquisition. In addition, in response to continued interest competitive pressures, Schwab's managers designed a single-use plan to retool the company's customer service area. Part of this plan included a study of fast-food companies like McDonald's to see how they managed their franchises and how their approach might help Schwab's interaction with its branch offices.

standing plan
A plan that is ongoing and provides guidance for repeatedly performed actions in an organization

Standing plans, in contrast, are ongoing. They provide guidance for repeatedly performed actions in the organization. For example, when you register for classes for the coming semester, you are using a standing registration plan at your college or university. The dates change, but the process works in the same way semester after semester.

Management by Objectives

Several organizations today are helping their employees set performance objectives in an effort to achieve organizational goals. One means of doing this is through a process called **management by objectives (MBO),** a system in which specific performance objectives are jointly determined by subordinates and their superiors; progress toward objectives is periodically reviewed, and rewards are allocated on the basis of that progress. Instead of using goals to control, MBO uses them to motivate.

Instead of using goals to control, MBO uses them to motivate.

management by objectives (MBO)
A system in which specific performance objectives are jointly determined by subordinates and their supervisors, progress toward objectives is periodically reviewed, and rewards are allocated on the basis of that progress

WHAT IS MBO?

Management by objectives is not new. The concept goes back almost 50 years.[13] Its appeal lies in its emphasis on converting overall objectives into specific objectives for organizational units and individual members.

MBO makes objectives operational by a process in which they cascade down through the organization. As depicted in Exhibit 3-4, the organization's overall objectives are translated into specific objectives for each succeeding level—divisional, departmental, individual—in the organization. Because lower-unit managers participate in setting their own goals, MBO works from the bottom up as well as from the top down. The result is a hierarchy that links objectives at one level to those at the next level. For the individual employee, MBO provides specific personal performance objectives. Each person, therefore, has an identified specific contribution to make to his or her unit's performance. If all the individuals achieve their goals, then the unit's goals will be attained. Subsequently, the organization's overall objectives will become a reality.

WHAT ARE THE COMMON ELEMENTS IN AN MBO PROGRAM?

Four ingredients are common to MBO programs: goal specificity, participative decision making, an explicit time period, and performance feedback.

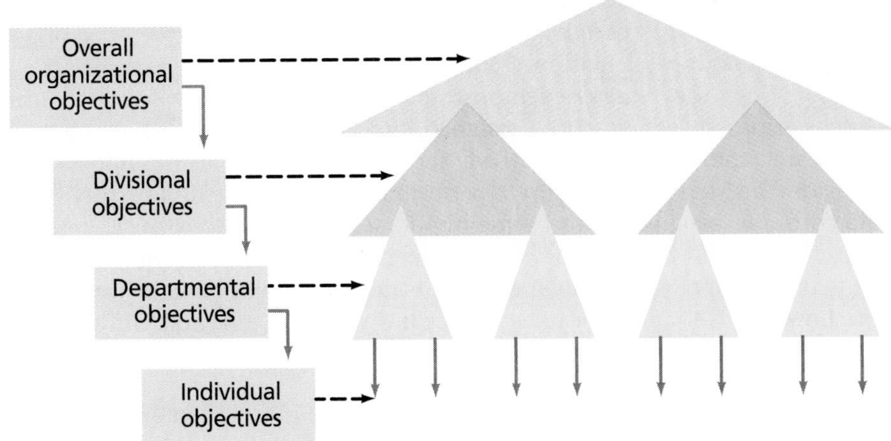

Exhibit 3-4
Cascading of Objectives

The objectives in MBO should be concise statements of expected accomplishments. It is not adequate, for example, merely to state a desire to cut costs, improve service, or increase quality. Such desires need to be converted into tangible objectives that can be measured and evaluated—to cut departmental costs by 8 percent, to improve service by ensuring that all insurance claims are processed within 72 hours of receipt, or to increase quality by keeping returns to less than .05 percent of sales.

In MBO, the objectives are not unilaterally set by the boss and assigned to employees, as is characteristic of traditional objective setting. MBO replaces these imposed goals with participatively determined goals. The manager and employee jointly choose the goals and agree on how they will be achieved.

Each objective has a concise time period in which it is to be completed. Typically, the time period is three months, six months, or a year.

The final ingredient in an MBO program is continuous feedback on performance and goals. Ideally, this is accomplished by giving ongoing feedback to individuals so they can monitor and correct their own actions. This is supplemented by periodic formal appraisal meetings in which superiors and subordinates can review progress toward goals and which lead to further feedback.

DOES MBO WORK?

Assessing the effectiveness of MBO is a complex task. Let's briefly review a growing body of literature on the relationship between goals and performance.[14] If factors such as a person's ability and acceptance of goals are held constant, more difficult goals lead to higher performance. Although individuals with very difficult goals achieve them far less often than those who have very easy goals, they, nevertheless, perform at a consistently higher level.

Moreover, studies consistently support the finding that specific difficult-to-achieve goals produce a higher level of output than do no goals or generalized goals such as "do your best." Feedback also favorably affects performance. Feedback lets a person know whether his or her level of effort is sufficient or needs to be increased. It can induce a person to raise his or her goal level after attaining a previous goal and indicate ways to improve performance.

The results cited here are all consistent with MBO's emphasis on specific goals and feedback. MBO implies, rather than explicitly states, that goals must be perceived as feasible. Research on goal setting indicates that MBO is most effective if the goals are difficult enough to require some stretching.

But what about participation? MBO strongly advocates that goals be set participatively. Does the research demonstrate that participatively set goals lead to higher performance than those assigned by a manager? Somewhat surprisingly, the research comparing participatively set with assigned goals has not shown any strong or consistent relationship to performance.[15] When goal difficulty has been held constant, assigned goals frequently do as well as participatively determined goals, contrary to MBO ideology. Therefore, it is not possible to argue for the superiority of participation as MBO proponents do. One major benefit from participation, however, is that it appears to induce individuals to set more difficult goals.[16] Thus, participation may have a positive effect on performance by increasing one's goal-aspiration level.

Studies of actual MBO programs confirm that MBO effectively increases employee performance and organizational productivity. A review of 70 programs, for example, found organizational productivity gains in 68 of them.[17] This same review also identified top management commitment to MBO as critical if programs are to reach their potential. When top managers had a high commitment to MBO and were personally involved in its implementation, the average gain in productivity was 56 percent. When commitment and involvement were low, the average gain in productivity dropped to only 6 percent.

HOW DO YOU SET EMPLOYEE OBJECTIVES?

Employees should have a clear understanding of what they're attempting to accomplish. Furthermore, as a manager, you have the responsibility for seeing that this task is achieved by helping your employees set work goals. Although these two statements appear to be common sense, that's not always the case. Setting objectives is a skill that every manager needs to perfect. You can better facilitate this process by following these guidelines:

- **Identify an employee's key job tasks** Goal setting begins by defining what you want your employees to accomplish. The best source for this information is each employee's job description.
- **Establish specific and challenging goals for each key task** Identify the level of performance expected of each employee. Specify the target for the employee to hit. Specify the deadlines for each goal. Putting deadlines on each goal reduces ambiguity. Deadlines, however, should not be set arbitrarily. Rather, they need to be realistic given the tasks to be completed.
- **Allow the employee to actively participate** When employees participate in goal setting, they are more likely to accept the goals. However, it must be sincere participation. That is, employees must perceive that you are truly seeking their input, not just going through the motions.
- **Prioritize goals** When you give someone more than one goal, it is important to rank the goals in order of importance. Prioritizing encourages the employee to take action and expend effort on each goal in proportion to its importance. Rate goals for difficulty and importance. Goal setting should not encourage people to choose easy goals. When goals are rated, individuals can be given credit for trying difficult goals, even if they don't fully achieve them.
- **Build in feedback mechanisms to assess goal progress** Feedback lets employees know whether their level of effort is sufficient to attain the goal.

Feedback should be both self- and supervisor generated. In either case, feedback should be frequent and recurrent.

- **Link rewards to goal attainment** It's natural for employees to ask "What's in it for me?" Linking rewards to the achievement of goals will help answer that question.

IS THERE A DOWNSIDE TO SETTING OBJECTIVES?

Despite some strong evidence indicating that specific employee goals are linked to higher performance, not everyone supports the value of setting objectives. One of the most vocal critics of processes like MBO was the late W. Edwards Deming (of TQM fame).[18] Deming argued that specific goals may, in fact, do more harm than good. He felt that employees tend to focus on the goals by which they will be judged, so they may direct their efforts toward quantity of output (what's being measured) and away from quality. Specific goals also, say some critics, encourage individual achievement rather than a team focus.[19] In addition, Deming believed that, when objectives are set, employees tend to view them as ceilings rather than as floors. That is, after setting a goal and achieving it, employees will tend to relax. Consequently, specific goals may have a tendency to limit employees' potential and discourage efforts for continuous improvement.

The critics of objectives are potentially correct. However, they can be overcome.[20] One way for managers to assist in this matter is to ensure that employees have multiple goals—all of which have a quality component. For instance, an insurance claims adjuster could be evaluated not only on the total number of claims processed but also on the number of errors made. Managers should treat MBO as an ongoing activity. This means that they should regularly review goals with employees and make changes when warranted. Furthermore, managers should reward employees for setting difficult goals—even if they aren't fully achieved. In doing so, managers reduce or eliminate the perception that failing to achieve goals results in punishment. If fear of reprisal dominates employees' thinking, they are likely to set easier, more attainable goals. As a result, employees won't stretch themselves with ambitious goals, and, ultimately, productivity will be reduced.

The Importance of an Organizational Strategy

Before the early 1970s, managers who made long-range plans generally assumed that better times lay ahead. Plans for the future were merely extensions of where the organization had been in the past. However, the energy crisis, deregulation, accelerating technological change, and increasing global competition as well as other environmental shocks of the 1970s and 1980s undermined this approach to long-range planning.[21] These changes in the rules of the game forced managers to develop a systematic means of analyzing the environment, assessing their organization's strengths and weaknesses, and identifying opportunities where the organization could have a competitive advantage. The value of thinking strategically began to be recognized.[22]

One survey of business owners found that 61 percent had strategic plans, and, among those who had plans, 88 percent responded that they had found their plans to be effective.[23] Other studies have also supported the premise that companies that plan strategically have better financial measurements than those without plans.[24]

Today, strategic planning has moved beyond the private sector to include government agencies, hospitals, and educational institutions. For example, the skyrocketing costs of a college education, competition from companies offering alternative educational forums, and cutbacks in federal aid for students and research have led many university administrators to assess their colleges' aspirations and identify a market niche in which they can survive, prosper, and implement an effective strategy.[25]

A Strategic Framework: Choosing a Niche

strategic management process
A nine-step process that involves strategic planning, implementation, and evaluation

When an organization attempts to develop its strategy, senior management goes through the **strategic management process** (see Exhibit 3-5), a nine-step process that involves strategic planning, implementation, and evaluation. Strategic planning encompasses the first seven steps, but even the best strategies can go awry if management fails either to implement them properly or to evaluate their results. Let's look at the various steps in the strategic management process.

HOW DOES THE STRATEGIC MANAGEMENT PROCESS OPERATE?

mission statement
The purpose of an organization

In order to develop their strategy, organizational members must first identify the organization's current mission, objectives, and strategies (step 1). Every organization has a **mission statement** that defines its purpose and answers the question, "What business or businesses are we in?" Defining the organization's mission forces management to identify the scope of its products or services carefully. For example, Oticon Holding A/S of Hellerup, Denmark, set its sights on becoming the world's premier hearing-aid manufacturer. Achieving that mission "drives the business, mobilizes the workers, and gets the high-quality product to the market."[26]

Determining the nature of one's business is as important for not-for-profit organizations as it is for business firms. Hospitals, government agencies, and colleges must also identify their missions. For example, is a college training students for the professions, training students for particular jobs, or providing students with a well-rounded, liberal education? Is it seeking students from the top 5 percent of high school graduates, students with low academic grades but high aptitude-test scores, or students in the vast middle ground? Answers to questions such as these clarify the organization's current purpose (see Team Skill-Building Exercise in the Management Workshop section of this chapter). Once its mission has been identified, the organization can begin to look outside the company to ensure

All organizations, including educational institutions like Johns Hopkins University, need to plan strategically. Cutbacks in government funding of research projects, for example, have resulted in Hopkins' officials assessing their strengths and further defining their niche in which they can survive and prosper.

Exhibit 3-5 The Strategic Management Process

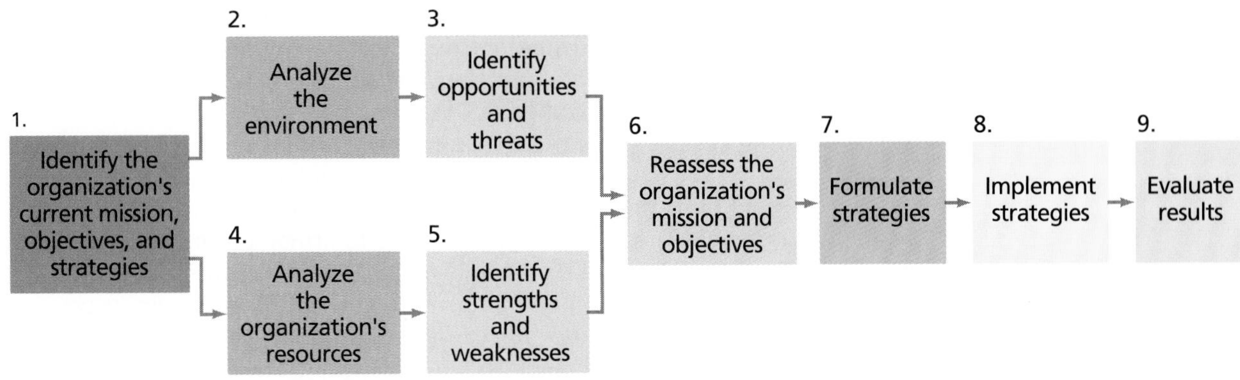

that its strategy aligns well with the environment.[27] As a case in point, Panasonic is a major producer of home entertainment systems. But beginning in the mid-1980s, technological breakthroughs in miniaturization and the trend toward smaller homes dramatically increased the demand for powerful, but very compact, sound systems. The success of Panasonic's home audio strategy depends on understanding the technological and social changes that are taking place.

Management of every organization needs to analyze its environment (step 2). In the Netherlands, by law, proprietary information is public. But organizations in other countries—such as the United States—must obtain that information on their own.[28] That means that these organizations need to find out, for instance, what their competition is up to, what pending legislation might affect them, what their customers desire, and what the supply of labor in locations where they operate is like. By analyzing the external environment, managers are in a better position to define the available strategies that best align with their environment.[29] For example, to address a customer desire for an environmentally friendly grill, Thermos (the Schaumburg, Illinois, bottle and lunch box company) developed an electric barbecue grill that cooked foods that tasted as if they were cooked on gas and charcoal grills but did not cause air pollution.[30] By understanding their environment, Thermos was able to capitalize on a product that increased its total revenues by more than 13 percent. That's what understanding an organization's environment is all about!

Step 2 of the strategy process is complete when management has an accurate grasp of what is taking place in its environment and is aware of important trends that might affect its operations. This is aided by environmental scanning activities and competitive intelligence.

What is environmental scanning? Russell Boss, CEO of A.T. Cross, knows the importance of environmental scanning.[31] The maker of luxury pens, the organization enjoyed much success in the 1970s and 1980s, a success attributed primarily to Cross's slender, thin-profiled pens. By the late 1980s, however, customers' preferences had changed. They wanted fatter, sturdier writing instruments. A.T. Cross failed to recognize that trend. Competing pens, such as Gillette Company's Waterman S.A. fountain pens and Germany's Montblanc pen took over the luxury pen market; Cross was moved to the middle of the pack. Boss recognizes the company's error in failing to scan the environment and must now play catch-up.

environmental scanning
Screening large amounts of information to detect emerging trends and create a set of scenarios

Managers like Russell Boss, in both small and large organizations, are increasingly turning to **environmental scanning** to anticipate and interpret changes in their environment.[32] The term refers to screening large amounts of information to detect emerging trends and create a set of scenarios. There is some evidence to indicate that companies that scan the environment achieve higher profits and revenue growth than companies that don't.[33]

The importance of environmental scanning was first recognized (outside of national security agencies such as the Central Intelligence Agency or National Security Agency) by firms in the life insurance industry in the late 1970s.[34] Life insurance companies found that the demand for their product was declining even though all the key environmental signals strongly favored the sale of life insurance. The economy and population were growing. Baby boomers were finishing school, entering the labor force, and getting married. The market for life insurance should have been expanding, but it wasn't. The insurance companies had failed to recognize a fundamental change in family structure in the United States.

Young families, who represented the primary group of buyers of new insurance policies, tended to be dual-career couples who were increasingly choosing to remain childless for a longer time. The life insurance needs of a family with one income, a dependent spouse, and a houseful of kids are much greater than those of a two-income family with few, if any, children. That a multibillion-dollar industry could overlook such a fundamental social trend underscored the need to develop techniques for monitoring important environmental developments.

competitive intelligence
Accurate information about competitors that allows managers to anticipate competitors' actions rather than merely react to them

How is competitive intelligence useful? One of the fastest growing areas of environmental scanning is competitive intelligence.[35] It seeks basic information about competitors: Who are they? What are they doing? How will what they are doing affect us? As managers at A.T. Cross should have recognized, accurate information about the competition can allow managers to anticipate competitors' actions rather than merely react to them.

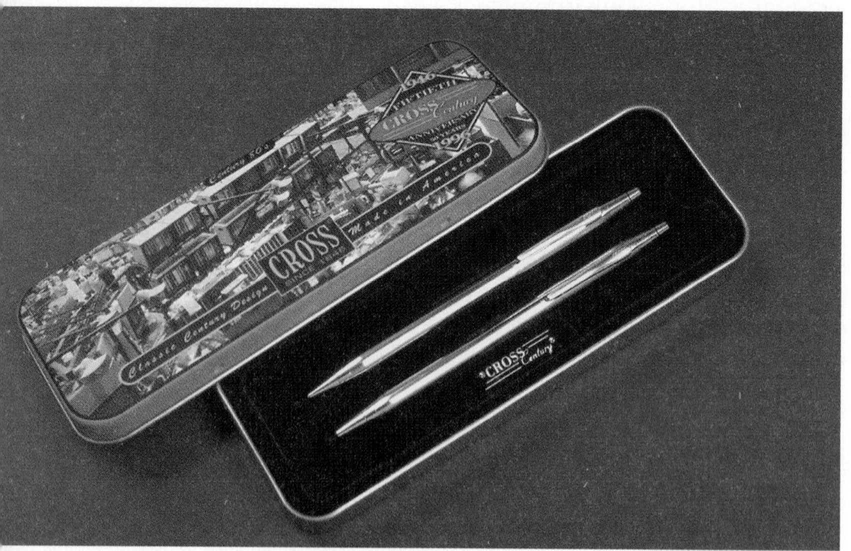

Cross pens and pencils were once the industry standard, but management's failure to properly scan the environment and gather competitive intelligence led to significant losses in the market. Had they gathered such data, they would have identified the market demand for fatter, sturdier pens that consumers were craving.

One researcher who has closely studied **competitive intelligence** suggests that 95 percent of the competitor-related information an organization needs to make crucial strategic decisions is available and accessible to the public.[36] In other words, competitive intelligence isn't organizational espionage. Advertisements, promotional materials, press releases, reports filed with government agencies, annual reports, want ads, newspaper reports, information on the Internet, and industry studies are readily accessible sources of information. Specific information on an industry and associated organizations is increasingly available through electronic databases. Managers can literally tap into a wealth of competitive information by purchasing access to databases sold by companies such as Nexus and Knight-Ridder—or obtained free through information on corporate or the Securities and Exchange Commission Web sites. Trade shows and the debriefing of your own sales staff can be good sources of information on competitors. Many organizations even regularly buy competitors' products and ask their own employees to evaluate them to learn about new technical innovations.

The techniques and sources listed above can reveal a number of issues and concerns that can affect an organization, but in a global business environment, environmental scanning and obtaining competitive intelligence are more complex.[37] Because global scanning must gather information from around the world, many of the previously mentioned information sources may be too limited. One means of overcoming this difficulty is for management to subscribe to news services that review newspapers and magazines from around the globe and provide summaries to client companies.

WHAT ARE THE PRIMARY STEPS IN THE STRATEGIC MANAGEMENT PROCESS?

opportunities, strategic
Positive external environmental factors

threats
Negative external environmental factors

After analyzing and learning about the environment, management needs to evaluate what it has learned in terms of **opportunities** that the organization can exploit and **threats** that the organization faces (step 3).[40] In a very simplistic way, opportunities are positive external environmental factors, and threats are negative ones.

Ethical Dilemma in Management

When Is Competitive Intelligence Unethical?

Knowing as much as you can about your competition is simply good business sense, but how far can you go to obtain that information? It's clear that over the past few years, competitive intelligence activities have increased—but sometimes these same well-intended actions have crossed the line to corporate spying.[38] For example, when a company pays for information that was obtained by someone who hacked a company's computer system, receiving that data is illegal. By the late 1990s, nearly 1,500 U.S. companies were victims of some type of corporate espionage, resulting in more than $300 billion in losses for these organizations.[39]

Most individuals understand the difference between what is legal and what's not. That's not the issue. Although some competitive intelligence activities may be legal, they may not be ethical. Consider the following scenarios:

1 You obtain copies of lawsuits and civil cases that have been filed against a competitor. Although the information is public, you use some of the surprising findings against your competitor in bidding for a job.

2 You pretend to be a journalist who's writing a story about the company. You call company officials and seek responses to some specific questions regarding the company's plans for the future. You use this information in designing a strategy to compete better with this company.

3 You apply for a job at one of your competitors. During the interview, you ask specific questions about the company and its direction. You report what you've learned back to your employer.

4 You dig through a competitor's trash and find some sensitive correspondence about a new product release. You use this information to launch your competing product before your competitor's.

5 You purchase some stock in your competitor's company in order to get the annual report and other company information that is sent out. You use this information to your advantage in developing your marketing plan.

Which if any of these events are unethical? Defend your position. What ethical guidelines would you suggest for competitive intelligence activities? Explain.

Keep in mind, however, that the same environment can present opportunities to one organization and pose threats to another in the same or a similar industry because of their different resources or different focus. Take communications, for example. Telecommuting technologies have enabled organizations that sell computer modems, fax machines, and the like to prosper. But organizations such as the U.S. Postal Service and even Federal Express, whose business it is to get messages from one person to another, have been adversely affected by this environmental change.

Next, in step 4, we move from looking outside the organization to looking inside.[41] That is, we are evaluating the organization's internal resources. What skills and abilities do the organization's employees have? What is the organization's cash flow? Has it been successful at developing new and innovative products? How do customers perceive the image of the organization and the quality of its products or services?

This fourth step forces management to recognize that every organization, no matter how large and powerful, is constrained in some way by its resources and the skills it has available. An automobile manufacturer, such as Ferrari, cannot start making minivans simply because its management sees opportunities in that market. Ferrari does not have the resources to successfully compete against the likes of DaimlerChrysler, Ford, Toyota, and Nissan. On the other hand, Renault and a Peugeot-Fiat partnership can, and they may begin expanding their European markets by selling minivans in North America.[42]

The analysis in step 4 should lead to a clear assessment of the organization's internal resources—such as capital, worker skills, patents, and the like. It should also indicate organizational departmental abilities such as training and development, marketing, accounting, human resources, research and development, and management information systems. Internal resources or things that the organization does well are its **strengths.** And any of those strengths that represent unique skills or resources that can determine the organization's competitive edge are its **core competency.** Calgary's Big Rock Brewery has built a core competency simply by creating a special taste for its beers and giving them "ugly names like Warthog and Grasshopper."[43] On the other hand, those resources that an organization lacks or activities that the firm does not do well are its **weaknesses.**

strengths, strategic
Internal resources that are available or things that an organization does well

core competency
Any of the strengths that represent unique skills or resources that can determine the organization's competitive edge

weaknesses
Resources that an organization lacks or activities that it does not do well

An understanding of the organization's culture and the strengths and weaknesses of its culture is a crucial part of step 5 that has only recently been getting the attention it deserves.[44] Specifically, managers should be aware that strong and weak cultures have different effects on strategy and that the content of a culture has a major effect on the content of the strategy.

In a strong culture, for instance, almost all employees will have a clear understanding of what the organization is about. In a strong culture, it should be easy for management to convey to new employees the organization's core competency. A department store chain such as Nordstrom, which has a very strong culture that embraces service and customer satisfaction, should be able to instill its cultural values in new employees in a much shorter time than can a competitor with a weak culture. The negative side of a strong culture, of course, is that it is difficult to change. A strong culture may act as a significant barrier to acceptance of a change in the organization's strategies. In fact, the strong culture at Wang Labs undoubtedly kept top management from perceiving the need to adopt a new corporate strategy in the 1980s in response to changes in the computer industry—and led, in part, to the demise of the organization. Successful organizations with strong cultures can become prisoners of their own past successes.

WHAT IS SWOT ANALYSIS?

A merging of the externalities (steps 2 and 3) with the internalities (steps 4 and 5) results in an assessment of the organization's opportunities (see Exhibit 3-6). This merging is frequently called **SWOT analysis** because it brings together the organization's **S**trengths, **W**eaknesses, **O**pportunities, and **T**hreats in order to identify a strategic niche that the organization can exploit. Having completed the SWOT analysis, the organization reassesses its mission and objectives (Exhibit 3-5, step 6). For example, as the demand for film continues to rise worldwide, managers at Kodak have developed plans to begin selling "yellow boxes of film" in such countries as Russia, India, and Brazil, where many of the "people . . . have yet to take their first picture."[45] Although risk is associated with this venture, company executives feel that they have to exploit this strategic niche and take advantage of an opportunity in the external environment.

SWOT analysis
Analysis of an organization's strengths, weaknesses, opportunities, and threats in order to identify a strategic niche that the organization can exploit

In light of the SWOT analysis and identification of the organization's opportunities, management reevaluates its mission and objectives. Are they realistic? Do they need modification? If changes are needed in the organization's overall direction, this is where they are likely to originate. On the other hand, if no changes are necessary, management is ready to begin the actual formulation of strategies.[46]

HOW DO YOU FORMULATE STRATEGIES?

Strategies need to be set for all levels in the organization (step 7). Management needs to develop and evaluate alternative strategies and then select a set that is compatible at each level and will allow the organization to best capitalize on its resources and the opportunities available in the environment. For most organizations, four primary strategies are available. Frequently called the **grand strategies,** they are growth, stability, retrenchment, and combination strategies.

grand strategies
The four primary types of strategies: growth, stability, retrenchment, and combination

The growth strategy If management believes that bigger is better, then it may choose a growth strategy. A **growth strategy** is one in which an organization attempts to increase the level of the organization's operations.[47] Growth can take the form of more sales revenues, more employees, or more market share. Many "growth" organizations achieve this objective through direct expansion, new product development, quality improvement,[48] or by diversifying—merging with or acquiring other firms.

growth strategy
A strategy in which an organization attempts to increase the level of its operations; can take the form of increasing sales revenue, number of employees, or market share

Exhibit 3-6
SWOT: Identifying Organizational Opportunities

One means of implementing a growth strategy is to focus on new product lines. At IKEA, the Swedish furniture retailer, they've embarked on a growth strategy by starting a child furniture line.

Growth through direct expansion involves increasing company size, revenues, operations, or workforce. This effort is internally focused and does not involve other firms. For example, Dunkin' Donuts is pursuing a growth strategy when it expands. As opposed to purchasing other "donut" chains, Dunkin' Donuts expands by opening restaurants in new locations or by franchising to entrepreneurs who are willing to accept and do business the "Dunkin'" way. Growth, too, can also come from creating businesses within the organization. When Northwest Airlines decided to create and supply its own in-flight meals—as opposed to contracting with an external vendor—the airline was exhibiting a growth strategy by expanding its operations to include food distribution. And when IKEA, the Swedish furniture outlet expanded its offerings to include furniture for children, it, too, was focusing on a growth strategy.[49]

Companies may also grow by merging with other companies or acquiring similar firms. A **merger** occurs when two companies—usually of similar size—combine their resources to form a new company. For example, when the Lockheed and Martin-Marietta Corporations merged to form Lockheed-Martin, they did so to compete more effectively in the aerospace industry. Organizations can also acquire another firm. An **acquisition,** which is similar to a merger, usually happens when a larger company buys a smaller one—for a set amount of money or stocks, or both—and incorporates the acquired company's operations into its own. Examples include Samsung Electronic's acquisition of Array, Harris Microwave Semiconductors, Lux, Integrative Telecom Technologies, and AST Research,[50] and Seagram Company's acquisition of MCA (a film, television, and recording company).[51] These acquisitions demonstrate a growth strategy whereby companies expand through diversification.

merger
Occurs when two companies, usually of similar size, combine their resources to form a new company

acquisition
Occurs when a larger company buys a smaller one and incorporates the acquired company's operations into its own

stability strategy
A strategy that is characterized by an absence of significant change

The stability strategy A stability strategy is best known for what it is not. That is, the **stability strategy** is characterized by an absence of significant changes. This means that an organization continues to serve its same market and customers while maintaining its market share. When is a stability strategy most appropriate? It is most appropriate when several conditions exist: a stable and unchanging environment, satisfactory organizational performance, a presence of valuable strengths and absence of critical weaknesses, and nonsignificant opportunities and threats.

Are there examples of organizations that are successfully employing a stability strategy? Yes. But most do not get the "press" that companies using other strategies get. One reason might be that no change means no news. Another might be that the company itself wants to keep a low profile; stakeholders may consider the status quo to be inappropriate, or the strategy may be an indication of rigidity of the planning process. Nonetheless, a company such as Kellogg's does use the stability strategy very well. Kellogg's, intent on exploiting its unique niche, has not moved far from its breakfast food market emphasis. The company also has not demonstrated a desire to diversify into other food markets as some of its competitors have.

The retrenchment strategy Before the 1980s, very few North American companies ever had to consider anything but how to grow or maintain what they currently had. But, because of technological advancements, global competition, and other environmental changes, mergers and acquisitions growth and stability strategies may no longer be viable for some companies. Instead, organizations such as Sears, General Motors, the U.S. Army, and Apple Computer have had to pursue a **retrenchment strategy.** This strategy is characteristic of an organization that is reducing its size or selling off less profitable product lines. For instance, Black & Decker sold off its small household appliances and sporting equipment product lines in an effort to bolster its core business of power tools.[52]

retrenchment strategy
A strategy characteristic of a company that is reducing its size, usually in an environment of decline

The combination strategy A **combination strategy** is the simultaneous pursuit of two or more strategies described above. That is, one part of the organization may be pursuing a growth strategy while another is retrenching. For example, Pennzoil has sold off (retrenchment) declining business operations such as its Purolator oil-filter business. Simultaneously, it has expanded (growth) its oil marketing efforts into foreign markets and is developing new exploration efforts in such areas as Azerbaijan and Qatar.[53]

combination strategy
The simultaneous pursuit by an organization of two or more of growth, stability, and retrenchment strategies

Determining a competitive strategy The selection of a grand strategy sets the stage for the entire organization. Subsequently, each unit within the organization has to translate this strategy into a set of strategies that will give the organization a competitive advantage. That is, to fulfill the grand strategy, managers will seek to position their units so that they can gain a relative advantage over the company's rivals. This positioning requires a careful evaluation of the competitive forces that dictate the rules of competition within the industry in which the organization operates.

One of the leading researchers into strategy formulation is Michael Porter of Harvard's Graduate School of Business.[54] His competitive strategies framework demonstrates that managers can choose among three generic competitive strategies. According to Porter, no firm can successfully perform at an above-average profitability level by trying to be all things to all people. Rather, Porter proposed that management must select a **competitive strategy** that will give its unit a distinct advantage by capitalizing on the strengths of the organization and the industry it is in. These three strategies are: **cost leadership** (low-cost producer), **differentiation** (uniqueness in a broad market), and **focus** (uniqueness in a narrow market).

According to Porter, when an organization sets out to be the low-cost producer in its industry, it is following a cost-leadership strategy. Success with this strategy requires that the organization be the cost leader, not merely one of the contenders for that position. In addition, the product or service being offered must be perceived as comparable to that offered by rivals or at least acceptable to buyers. How does a firm gain such a cost advantage? Typical means include efficiency of operations, economies of scale, technological innovation, low-cost labor, or preferential access to raw materials. Firms that have used this strategy include Wal-Mart, Canadian Tire, E & J Gallo Winery, and Southwest Airlines.[55]

competitive strategy
A strategy to position an organization in such a way that it will have a distinct advantage over its competition; three types are cost leadership, differentiation, and focus strategies

cost-leadership strategy
The strategy an organization follows when it wants to be the lowest-cost producer in its industry

differentiation strategy
The strategy an organization follows when it wants to be unique in its industry within a broad market

focus strategy
The strategy an organization follows when it wants to establish an advantage in a narrow market segment

The firm that seeks to be unique in its industry in ways that are widely valued by buyers is following a differentiation strategy. It might emphasize high quality, extraordinary service, innovative design, technological capability, or an unusually positive brand image. The attribute chosen must be different from those offered by rivals and significant enough to justify a price premium that exceeds the cost of differentiating. There is no shortage of firms that have found at least one attribute that allows them to differentiate themselves from competitors. Intel (technology), Maytag (reliability), Mary Kay Cosmetics (distribution), and L.L. Bean (service) are a few.

The first two strategies sought a competitive advantage in a broad range of industry segments. The focus strategy aims at a cost advantage (cost focus) or differentiation advantage (differentiation focus) in a narrow segment. That is, management will select a segment or group of segments in an industry (such as product variety, type of end buyer, distribution channel, or geographical location of buyers) and tailor the strategy to serve them to the exclusion of others. The goal is to exploit a narrow segment of a market. Of course, whether a focus strategy is feasible depends on the size of a segment and whether it can support the additional cost of focusing. Stouffer's used a cost-focus strategy in its Lean Cuisine line to reach calorie-conscious consumers seeking both high-quality products and convenience.

Which strategy management chooses depends on the organization's strengths and its competitors' weaknesses. Management should avoid a position in which it has to slug it out with everybody in the industry. Rather, the organization should put its strength where the competition isn't. Success, then, depends on selecting the right strategy, the one that fits the complete picture of the organization and the industry of which it is a part. In so doing, organizations can gain the most favorable competitive advantage.

What if an organization cannot use one of these three strategies to develop a competitive advantage? Porter uses the term *stuck in the middle* to describe that situation. Organizations that are stuck in the middle often find it difficult to achieve long-term success. When they do, it's usually the result of competing in a highly favorable market or having all their competitors similarly stuck in the middle. Porter notes, too, that successful organizations may get into trouble by reaching beyond their competitive advantage and end up stuck in the middle.

Sustaining a competitive advantage Long-term success with any one of Porter's competitive strategies requires that the advantage be sustainable. That is, it must withstand both the actions of competitors and the evolutionary changes in the industry. That isn't easy, especially in environments as dynamic as the ones organizations face today. Technology changes. So too, do customers' product preferences. And competitors frequently try to imitate an organization's success. Managers need to create barriers that make imitation by competitors difficult or reduce the competitive opportunities. The use of patents, copyrights, or trademarks may assist in this effort. For example, to protect its "environmentally friendly computer chip process" the Radiance Service Company has secured patents in 37 countries.[56] Similarly, Kendall-Jackson has trademarked its packaging of its Turning Leaf chardonnay wine and has used that trademark in an effort to keep E & J Gallo Winery from selling its chardonnay in similar packaging.[57]

In addition, when there are strong efficiencies from economies of scale, reducing price to gain volume is a useful tactic. Organizations can also "tie up" suppliers with exclusive contracts that limit their ability to supply materials to rivals. Or organizations can encourage and lobby for government policies that impose import tariffs that are designed to limit foreign competition.

The one thing management cannot do is to become complacent. Resting on past successes may be the beginning of serious trouble for the organization. Sustaining a competitive advantage requires constant action by management in order to stay one step ahead of the competition. For example, to keep ahead of the competition and to ensure a closeness with its customers, Harley-Davidson started the Harley Owners Group (HOG), which now boasts more than 360,000 feedback-providing members.[58]

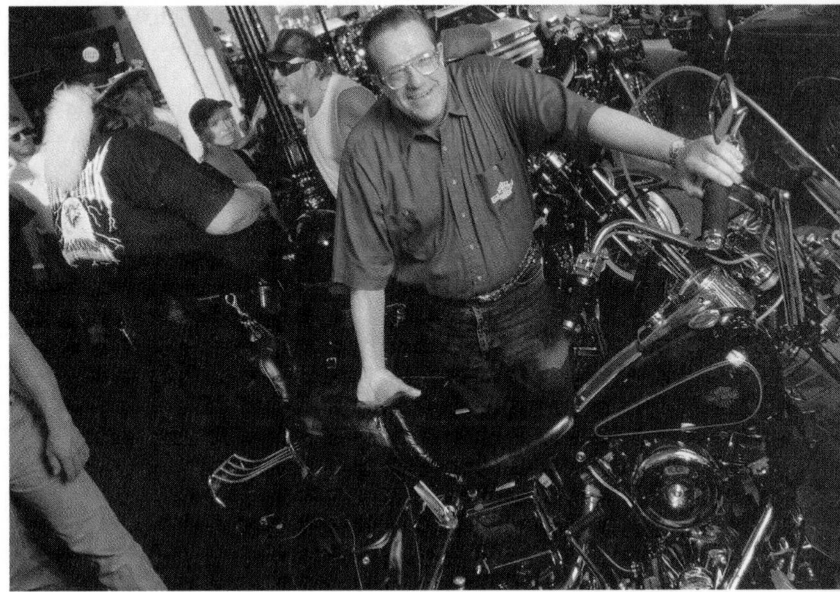

How can an organization sustain a competitive advantage? At Harley-Davidson, this is done in part by having senior managers get involved with their customers. As a member of the Harley Owners Group (HOG), managers like CEO Richard Teerlink interact with other owners to get their feedback and suggestions.

WHAT HAPPENS AFTER STRATEGIES ARE FORMULATED?

The next-to-last step in the strategic management process is implementation (step 8). No matter how good a strategic plan is, it cannot succeed if it is not implemented properly. Top management leadership is a necessary ingredient in a successful strategy. So, too, is a motivated group of middle- and lower-level managers to carry out senior management's specific plans.

Finally, results must be evaluated (step 9). How effective have the strategies been? What adjustments, if any, are necessary? In Chapter 13, we will review the control process. The concepts and techniques that we introduce in that chapter can be used to assess the results of strategies and to correct significant deviations.

Quality as a Strategic Weapon

An increasing number of organizations are applying quality practices to build a competitive advantage.[59] To the degree that an organization can satisfy a customer's need for quality, it can differentiate itself from the competition and attract and hold a loyal customer base. Moreover, constant improvement in the quality and reliability of an organization's products or services can result in a competitive advantage others cannot steal.[60] Product innovations, for example, offer little opportunity for sustained competitive advantage. Why? Because usually they can be quickly copied by rivals.[61] But incremental improvement is something that becomes an integrated part of an organization's operations and can develop into a considerable cumulative advantage. To illustrate how continuous improvement can be used as a strategic tool, let's look at the Watsonville, California, Granite Rock Company, winner of a prestigious U.S. award for quality.

Granite Rock "produces and sells crushed stone, mixes concrete and asphalt products, and does some highway paving."[62] There did not appear to be a serious need for Granite to change its operations, but its management team, headed by Bruce and Steve Woolpert, would not sit still. They knew they had to continuously get to know their customers in terms of what quality meant to them. What they found was startling. They learned that each product line had special customers' needs tied to it. For example, in its concrete operations, customers demanded "on-time delivery," which meant that Granite had to be prepared to deliver its product whenever the customer wanted. This required an around-the-clock operation—the beginning of Granite Xpress. Granite Xpress is now open 24 hours a day, 7 days a week. How does it work? Customers simply drive their trucks under a loader, insert a card, and tell the machine how much of a product they want. It is then automatically dispensed, and a bill is sent to the customer later. The Woolperts recognized that this change was needed to satisfy their customers. This strategic innovation, as well as some others, not only helped them weather the construction recession in the early 1990s but also led them to double their market share.

Quality can result in a competitive advantage others cannot steal!

Using quality for developing a competitive advantage does not apply only to firms in industries like Granite Rock. Organizations worldwide—from Whirlpool in the United States to Daewoo in South Korea to educational institutions such as Oregon State University—are recognizing the value of quality as a competitive advantage.[63]

HOW CAN BENCHMARKING HELP PROMOTE QUALITY?

benchmarking
The search for the best practices among competitors or noncompetitors that lead to their superior performance

Benchmarking involves the search for the best practices among competitors or noncompetitors that lead to their superior performance.[64] The basic idea underlying benchmarking is that management can improve quality by analyzing and then copying the methods of the leaders in various fields. As such, benchmarking is a very specific form of environmental scanning.

In 1979, Xerox undertook what is widely regarded as the first benchmarking effort in the United States. Until then, the Japanese had been aggressively copying the successes of others by traveling around, watching what others were doing, and then using their new knowledge to improve their products and processes. Xerox's management couldn't figure out how Japanese manufacturers could sell mid-size copiers in the United States for considerably less than Xerox's production costs. So the company's head of manufacturing took a team to Japan to make a detailed study of their competition's costs and processes. They got most of their information from Xerox's own joint venture, Fuji-Xerox, which knew its competition well. What the team found was shocking. Their Japanese rivals were light-years ahead of Xerox in efficiency. Benchmarking these efficiencies marked the beginning of Xerox's recovery in the copier field. Today, in addition to Xerox, companies such as Southwest Airlines, Du Pont, Alcoa, Ford, Eastman Kodak, and Motorola use benchmarking as a standard tool in their quest for quality improvement.

To illustrate benchmarking in practice, let's look at its application at Ford Motor Company. Ford used benchmarking in the early 1980s in developing its highly successful Taurus. The company compiled a list of some 400 features that its customers said were the most important and then set about finding the car with the best of each. Then it tried to match or top the best of the competition. For instance, the door handles on the Taurus were benchmarked against those of the Chevrolet Lumina; the easy-to-change taillight bulbs, against those of the Nissan Maxima; and the tilt steering wheel, against the wheel of Honda Accord. The Taurus has been the best-selling passenger vehicle since 1992 in the United

States.[65] When the Taurus was redesigned for 1996, Ford benchmarked all over again. This time, however, the Taurus was repositioned to compete more directly with the Toyota Camry in a more expensive market niche.

Employees at Borg-Warner Automotive have met the rigorous standards for ISO 9000 certification. As a result of this registration, Borg-Warner is one of a select few companies that can use this "quality" identifier as competitive advantage.

WHAT IS THE ISO 9000 SERIES?

During the 1980s, there was an increasing push among global corporations to improve their quality. They knew that, to compete in the global village, they had to offer some assurances to purchasers of their products and services that what they were buying was of the quality they expected. In years past, purchasers had to accept individual "guarantees" that what was being sold met their needs and standards. Those individual guarantees changed in 1987, with the formation of the **ISO 9000 series,** designed by the International Organization for Standardization, based in Geneva, Switzerland.[66] The ISO standards reflect a process whereby "independent auditors attest that a company's factory, laboratory, or office has met quality management requirements."[67] These standards, once met, assure customers that a company uses specific steps to test the products it sells; continuously trains its employees to ensure they have up-to-date skills, knowledge, and abilities; maintains satisfactory records of its operations; and corrects problems when they occur.[68] Some of the multinational and transnational companies that have met these standards are Texas Petrochemical; British Airways; Shanghai-Foxboro Company, Ltd.; Braas Company; Betz Laboratories; Hong Kong Mass Transit Railway Corporation; BP Chemicals International Ltd.; Cincinnati Milacron's Electronic Systems Division; Borg-Warner Automotive; and Taiwan Synthetic Rubber Corporation.

ISO 9000 series
Designed by the International Organization for Standardization, these standards reflect a process whereby "independent auditors attest that a company's factory, laboratory, or office has met quality management standards"

A company that obtains an ISO certification can boast that it has met stringent international quality standards and is one of a select group of companies worldwide to achieve that designation. Certification can be more than just a competitive advantage; it also permits entry into some markets not otherwise accessible. For example, 89 nations have adopted the ISO standards. Uncertified organizations attempting to do business in those countries may be unable to successfully compete against certified companies. Many customers in the global village want to see the certification, and it becomes a dominant customer need. And in 1997, ISO 14000 went into effect. Companies achieving this certification will have demonstrated that they are environmentally responsible.[69]

Achieving ISO certification is far from cost-free. Most organizations that want certification spend nearly one year and incur several hundreds of thousands of dollars to achieve that goal.[70] For example, Betz Laboratories in Trevor, Pennsylvania, spent over eight months and more than $500,000 to obtain an ISO certification. Betz company officials, as well as hundreds of individuals like them, recognize that obtaining such certification is quickly becoming a necessity to export goods to any organization in the nations that support the ISO 9000 series standards.

HOW CAN ATTAINING SIX SIGMA SIGNIFY QUALITY?

Wander around organizations like General Electric, AlliedSignal, Intel, or Eastman Kodak, and you're likely to find green and black belts. Karate classes? Hardly. These green and black belts[71] signify individuals trained in six sigma processes.[72]

six sigma
A philosophy and measurement process that attempts to "design in" quality as a product is being made

Six sigma is a philosophy and measurement process developed in the 1980s at Motorola. The premise behind **six sigma** is to "design, measure, analyze, and control the input side of a production process."[73] That is, rather than measuring the quality of a product after it is produced, six sigma attempts to "design in" quality as the product is being made (see Exhibit 3-7). It is a process that uses statistical models, coupled with specific quality tools, high levels of rigor, and know-how when improving processes.[74] How effective is six sigma at ensuring quality? Let's answer that by posing a question. In your opinion, is 99.9 percent effective enough? Consider this: At 99.9 percent effectiveness, 12 babies will be given to the wrong parents each day; 22,000 checks would be deducted from the incorrect checking accounts each hour, and 2 planes a day would fail to land safely at Chicago's O'Hare International Airport.[75] That's definitely not what anyone intends. Accordingly, six sigma is designed to decrease defects to fewer than 4 per million items produced. That's a significant improvement considering that just 10 years ago, three sigma was a fairly standard objective by most Americans. Three sigma results in more than 66,000 defects per million.[76]

How have organizations that have implemented six sigma methodologies fared? Considering that AlliedSignal saved more than $1.5 billion through a six sigma effort, and GE has increased profits by more than $1 billion, six sigma is successful. Moreover, companies like GE are now looking into asking their suppliers to be six sigma compliant to maximize the benefits of this quality program.[77]

Exhibit 3-7
Six Sigma
12-Process Steps

- Select the critical-to-quality characteristics.
- Define the required performance standards.
- Validate measurement system, methods, and procedures.
- Establish the current processes capability.
- Define upper and lower performance limits.
- Identify sources of variation.
- Screen potential causes of variation to identify the vital few variables needing control.
- Discover variation relationship for the vital variables.
- Establish operating tolerances on each of the vital variables.
- Validate the measurement system's ability to produce repeatable data.
- Determine the capability of the process to control the vital variables.
- Implement statistical process control on the vital variables.

SOURCE: Cited in D. Harold and F. J. Bartos, "Optimize Existing Processes to Achieve Six Sigma Capability," reprinted with permission from *Control Engineering,* March 1998, p. 87, © Cahners Business Information.

One Manager's Perspective

Geoff Gilpin Director of Affinity Marketing, GTE Communications Corp.

Planning, as Geoff Gilpin sees it, is an ongoing process. "It's our road map," he says, "but the destination is constantly changing due to dynamic market conditions." In his role as director of affinity marketing for GTE Communications, Gilpin works with outside organizations to jointly market GTE's communication products to end customers. The market moves quickly, making flexibility an important characteristic of a good manager and of good plans. "If you can't make a quick decision," says Gilpin, "you get left behind."

Planning is critical in keeping up with a market like telecommunications, in which things can change daily, and Gilpin also relies on planning to support his team's internal communication and the coordination of their efforts. In addition, measuring performance against the plan—and learning from any gaps that appear—is a big part of GTE's continuous improvement process.

Objectives provide direction for the planning Gilpin's group must do. His objectives must both fit with the overall business plan and be clear enough to be communicated well throughout the company. "I try to create easily understandable statements that will drive specific, measurable behaviors" to support GTE's goals, he says.

Entrepreneurship: A Special Case of Strategic Planning

You have heard the story dozens of times. With only an idea, a few hundred dollars, and use of the family garage, someone starts what eventually becomes a multibillion-dollar global corporation. Take the case of Linda Lang.[78]

Linda Lang founded Arizona Rotocraft, Inc., a helicopter engine repair shop, in 1993 with $25,000. She started her company after divorcing her husband and liquidating the concrete business they had run. Some people think that a woman would be unlikely to be successful in the field of helicopter repair, but Lang has built her company to 21 employees and over $6 million in annual revenues. Although she realistically accepts the possibility that this business could fail, Lang takes steps to see it does not. In a large company, a manager with the responsibility of managing a division or product line might not take the risks that Lang and other such entrepreneurs take and might not be as firmly committed to seeing the venture succeed.

Strategic planning often carries a big-business bias. It implies a formalization and structure appropriate for large, established organizations that have abundant resources, but many people are not interested in managing such organizations. That desire, coupled with changes in technology, the economy, and social conditions (i.e., two-income families), has fostered an increase in start-up companies.[79] Like Linda Lang or Dave Thomas of Wendy's, Douglas Becker of Sylvan Learning Systems, or Stan Smith of Acer Computer International, they are excited about the idea of starting their own business from scratch—an action that is called entrepreneurship.

WHAT IS ENTREPRENEURSHIP?

There is no shortage of definitions of *entrepreneurship*.[80] Some, for example, apply the term to the creation of any new business. Others focus on intentions, claiming that entrepreneurs seek to create wealth, which is different from starting businesses merely as a means of income substitution (that is, working for yourself rather than working for someone else). When most people describe entrepreneurs, they use adjectives such as bold, innovative, initiative taking, venturesome, and risk taking.[81] They also tend to associate entrepreneurs with small businesses. We will define entrepreneurship as a process by which individuals pursue opportunities, fulfilling needs and wants through innovation, without regard to the resources they currently control.[82]

It is important not to confuse managing a small business with entrepreneurship. Not all small business managers are entrepreneurs.[83] Many do not innovate. A great many managers of small businesses are merely scaled-down versions of the conservative, conforming bureaucrats who staff many large corporations and public agencies.

DO ENTREPRENEURS POSSESS SIMILAR CHARACTERISTICS?

business plan
A document that explains the business founder's vision and describes the strategy and operations of that business

One of the most researched topics in entrepreneurship has been the determination of what, if any, psychological characteristics entrepreneurs have in common. A number of common characteristics have been found. These include hard work, self-confidence, optimism, determination, a high energy level,[84] and even good luck.[85] But three factors regularly sit on the top of most lists that profile the entrepreneurial personality. Entrepreneurs have a high need for achievement, believe strongly that they can control their own destinies, and take only moderate risks.[86] The research allows us to draw a general description of entrepreneurs. They tend to be independent types who prefer to be personally responsible for solving problems, for setting goals, and for reaching those goals by their own efforts. They plan extensively, oftentimes laying out their goals and activities in a **business plan.**[87] A business plan is a document that "explains the entrepreneur's vision, describes the strategy and operations of the venture"[88] (see Developing Your Business Plan Skill, p. 108). Entrepreneurs also value independence and particularly do not like being controlled by others. They are not afraid of taking chances, but they are not wild risk takers. Entrepreneurs prefer to take calculated risks where they feel that they can control the outcome.

What is an entrepreneur and how does one differ from a "traditional" manager? For people like Douglas Becker (left) of Sylvan Learning that question is relatively easy to answer. Becker is bold and innovative. He takes initiative and calculated risks to move into new ventures. All this in his effort to pursue opportunities and control his own destiny.

The evidence on entrepreneurial personalities leads us to several conclusions. First, people with this personality makeup are not likely to be contented, productive employees in the typical large corporation or government agency. The rules, regulations, and controls that these bureaucracies impose on their members frustrate entrepreneurs. Sec-

	Traditional Managers	Entrepreneurs
Primary motivation	Promotion and other traditional corporate rewards such as office, staff, and power	Independence, opportunity to create, financial gain
Time orientation	Achievement of short-term goals	Achievement of 5- to 10-year growth of business
Activity	Delegation and supervision	Direct involvement
Risk propensity	Low	Moderate
View toward failures and mistakes	Avoidance	Acceptance

Exhibit 3-8
Comparison of Entrepreneurs and Traditional Managers

SOURCE: Adapted from D. Hisrich, "Entrepreneurship/Intrapreneurship," *American Psychologist,* February 1990, p. 218.

ond, the challenges and conditions inherent in starting one's own business mesh well with the entrepreneurial personality. Starting a new venture, which they control, appeals to their willingness to take risks and determine their own destinies. But, because entrepreneurs believe that their future is fully in their own hands, the risk they perceive as moderate is often seen as high by nonentrepreneurs. Finally, the cultural context in which individuals were raised will have an effect.[89] For instance, in the former East Germany, where the cultural environment exhibits high power distance and high uncertainty avoidance (see Geert Hofstede, Chapter 2), many of the entrepreneurial characteristics—such as initiative and risk taking—are lacking.

HOW DO ENTREPRENEURS COMPARE WITH TRADITIONAL MANAGERS?

Exhibit 3-8 summarizes some key differences between entrepreneurs and traditional bureaucratic managers. The latter tend to be custodial, but entrepreneurs actively seek change by exploiting opportunities. When searching for these opportunities, entrepreneurs often put their personal financial security at risk. The hierarchy in large organizations typically insulates traditional managers from these financial wagers and rewards them for minimizing risks and avoiding failures.

PHLIP Companion Web Site

We invite you to visit the Robbins/DeCenzo companion Web site at *www.prenhall.com/robbins* for this chapter's Internet resources.

Chapter Summary

How will you know if you fulfilled the Learning Outcomes on page 79? You will have fulfilled the Learning Outcomes if you are able to:

1 *Define planning.*
Planning is the process of determining objectives and assessing the way those objectives can best be achieved.

2 *Explain the potential benefits of planning.*
Planning gives direction, reduces the impact of change, minimizes waste and redundancy, and sets the standards to facilitate controlling.

3 *Identify potential drawbacks to planning.*
Planning is not without its critics. Some of the more noted criticisms of planning are: it may create rigidity; plans cannot be developed for a dynamic environment; formal plans cannot replace intuition and creativity; planning focuses managers' attention on today's competition, not on tomorrow's survival; and because formal planning reinforces success, it may lead to failure.

4 *Distinguish between strategic and tactical plans.*
Strategic plans cover an extensive time period (usually five or more years), encompass broad issues, and include the formulation of objectives. Tactical plans cover shorter periods of time, focus on specifics, and assume that objectives are already known.

5 *State when directional plans are preferred over specific plans.*
Directional plans are preferred over specific plans when managers face uncertainty in their environments and desire to maintain flexibility in order to respond to any unexpected changes.

6 *Define management by objectives and identify its common elements.*
Management by objectives (MBO) is a system in which specific performance objectives are jointly determined by employees and their bosses; progress toward objectives is periodically reviewed, and rewards are allocated on the basis of the progress. The four ingredients common to MBO programs are goal specificity, participative decision making, explicit time periods, and performance feedback.

7 *Outline the steps in the strategic management process.*
The strategic management process is made up of nine steps: (1) identify the organization's current mission, objectives, and strategies, (2) analyze the environment, (3) identify opportunities and threats in the environment, (4) analyze the organization's resources, (5) identify the organization's strengths and weaknesses, (6) reassess the organization's mission and objectives on the basis of its strengths, weaknesses, opportunities, and threats, (7) formulate strategies, (8) implement strategies, and (9) evaluate results.

8 *Describe the four grand strategies.*
The four grand strategies are (1) growth (increasing the level of the organization's operations), (2) stability (making no significant change in the organization), (3) retrenchment (reducing the size or variety of operations), and (4) combination (using two or more grand strategies simultaneously).

9 *Explain SWOT analysis.*
SWOT analysis refers to analyzing the organization's internal strengths and weaknesses as well as external opportunities and threats in order to identify a niche that the organization can exploit.

10 *Compare how entrepreneurs and bureaucratic managers approach strategy.*
Entrepreneurs approach strategy by first seeking out opportunities that they can exploit. Bureaucratic managers approach strategy by first determining the availability of their resources.

Review and Application Questions

READING FOR COMPREHENSION

1 Contrast formal with informal planning.

2 Under what circumstances are short-term plans preferred? Under what circumstances are specific plans preferred?

3 Compare an organization's mission with its objectives.

4 Describe the nine-step strategic management process.

5 What is a SWOT analysis?

6 How can quality provide a competitive advantage? Give an example.

7 What differentiates small business managers from entrepreneurs? Explain your answer.

LINKING CONCEPTS TO PRACTICE

1 "Organizations that fail to plan are planning to fail." Do you agree or disagree with the statement? Explain your position.

2 Under what circumstances do you believe MBO would be most useful? Discuss.

3 Using Michael Porter's generic strategies, describe the strategy used by each of the following companies to develop a competitive advantage in its industry: Home Depot, Nordstrom, and Disney. Provide specific examples.

4 "The primary means of sustaining a competitive advantage is to adjust faster to the environment than your competitors do." Do you agree or disagree with the statement? Explain your position.

5 Arie P. DeGues, head of planning for the Royal Dutch/Shell Group Companies, once suggested that the ability to "learn faster than competitors" may be the only sustainable competitive advantage. Do you agree? Why or why not.

Management Workshop

Team Skill-Building Exercise

Your College's Mission

You might not pay much attention to your college's goals and objectives because you are focusing on your studies. But your college had to carve out its niche in an effort to provide something of value to its students and must continue to monitor its performance.

For this exercise, break up into small groups. The charge of each small group is to prepare responses to the following questions and present its findings to the class.

1 What is your college's mission? What resources does your college have that support its mission?

2 How would you describe your college's environment in terms of technology and of government regulations?

3 What do you believe are the strengths and weaknesses of your college?

4 Which grand strategy is your college following? Which of Porter's generic strategies is evident at your college?

5 What do you believe to be your college's competitive advantage? What do you think your college should do to sustain its competitive advantage?

Developing Your Business Plan Skill

Writing a Business Plan

ABOUT THE SKILL

One of the first steps in starting a business is to prepare a business plan. Not only does the business plan aid you in thinking about what you're going to do and how you're going to do it, it provides a sound basis from which you can obtain funding and resources for your organization. In fact, a well-prepared business plan can be submitted to a financial institution in its entirety as the basis of why you should get a loan to start your business.

STEPS IN WRITING THE BUSINESS PLAN[90]

1 **Describe your company's background and purpose.** Provide the history of the company. Briefly describe the company's history and what this company does that's unique. Describe what your product or service will be, how you intend to market it, and what you need to bring your product or service to the market.

2 **Identify your short- and long-term objectives.** What is your intended goal for this organization? Clearly, for a new company three broad objectives are relevant—creation, survival, and profitability.[91] Specific objectives can include such things as sales, market share, product quality, employee morale, or social responsibility. Identify how you plan to achieve each objective, how you intend to determine whether you met the objective, and when you intend the objective to be met (e.g., short or long term).

3 **Provide a thorough market analysis.** You need to convince readers that you understand what you are doing, what your market is, and what competitive pressures you'll face. In this analysis, you'll need to describe the overall market trends, the specific market you intend to compete in, and who the competitors are. In essence, in this section you'll perform your SWOT analysis.

4 **Describe your development and production emphasis.** Explain how you are going to produce your product or service. Include time frames from start to finish. Describe the difficulties you may encounter in this stage as well as how much you believe activities in this stage will cost. Provide an

explanation of what decisions (e.g., make or buy?) you will face and what you intend to do.

5 **Describe how you'll market your product or service.** What is your selling strategy? How do you intend to reach your customers? In this section, you'll want to describe your product or service in terms of your competitive advantage and demonstrate how you'll exploit your competitor's weaknesses. In addition to the market analysis, you'll also want to provide sales forecasts in terms of the size of the market, how much of the market you can realistically capture, and how you'll price your product or service.

6 **Establish your financial statements.** What is your bottom line? Investors want to know this. In the financial section, you'll need to provide projected profit-and-loss statements (income statements) for approximately three to five years. You will also need to include a cash-flow analysis as well as the company's projected balance sheets. In the financial section, you should also give thought to how much the start-up costs will be as well as to developing a financial strategy—how you intend to use funds received from a financial institution and how you'll control and monitor the financial well-being of the company.

7 **Provide an overview of the organization and its management.** Identify the key executives, summarizing their education, experience, and any relevant qualifications. Identify their positions in the organization and their job roles. Explain how much salary they intend to earn initially. Identify any others who may assist the organization's management (e.g., company lawyer, accountant, board of directors, and the like). This section should also include, if relevant, a section on how you intend to deal with employees. For example, how will employees be paid, what benefits will be offered, and how will employee performance be assessed?

8 **Describe the legal form of the business.** Identify the legal form of the business. For example, is it a sole proprietor, a partnership, a corporation? Depending on the legal form, information may need to be provided regarding equity positions, shares of stock issued, and the like.

9 **Identify the critical risks and contingencies facing the organization.** In this section you'll want to identify what you'll do if problems arise. For instance, if you don't meet sales forecasts, what will you do? Similar responses to such questions as problems with suppliers, inability to hire qualified employees, poor-quality products, etc., should be addressed. Readers want to see if you've anticipated potential problems and if you have contingency plans. This is the "what if" section.

10 **Put the business plan together.** Using the information you've gathered from the previous nine steps, it's now time to put the business plan together into a well-organized document. A business plan should contain a *cover page* that contains the company name, address, contact person, and numbers at which the individual can be reached. The cover page should also contain the date the business was established and, if one exists, the company logo. The next page of the business plan should be a *table of contents.* Here you'll want to list and identify the location of each major section and subsection in the business plan. Remember to use proper outlining techniques. Next comes the *executive summary,* the first section the readers will actually read. Accordingly, it is one of the more critical elements of the business plan because if the executive summary is poorly done, readers may not read any further. Highlight in a two- to three-page summary information about the company, its management, its market and competition, the funds requested, how the funds will be used, financial history (if available), financial projections, and when investors can expect to get their money back (called the *exit*). Now it's time to provide the main sections of your business plan, the material you've researched and written about in steps 1 through 9 above. Close out the business plan with a section that summarizes the highlights of what you've just presented. Finally, if you have charts, exhibits, photographs, tables, and the like, you may also include an appendix in the back of the business plan. If you do, remember to cross reference this material to the relevant section of the report.

Practicing the Skill

BUSINESS PLAN

You have come up with a great idea for a business and need to create a business plan to present to a bank. Choose one of the following products or services and draft the part of your plan that describes how you will price and market it (see step 5).

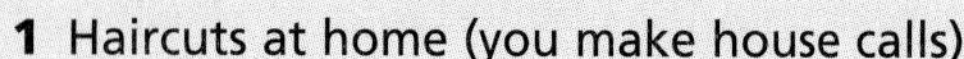

1 Haircuts at home (you make house calls)
2 Olympic snowboarding computer game
3 On-line apartment rental listing
4 Ergonomic dental chair
5 Voice-activated house alarm
6 Customized running shoes

Now choose a different product or service from the list and identify critical risks and contingencies (see step 9).

A Case Application

Developing Your Diagnostic and Analytical Skills

WATSON PHARMACEUTICALS

Allen Chao grew up in Taiwan.[92] His parents owned and operated a large pharmaceutical manufacturing business. Their dream was for their son to study pharmacy sciences at a U.S. institution and then return home to succeed his father. But along the way, their plans changed. After earning a doctorate from Purdue University in 1973 in industrial and physical pharmacy, Chao chose to work as a researcher for G. D. Searle & Company. Five years later, after being recognized for his creative abilities, he was promoted to director of new product and new pharmaceutical technology development. Meanwhile, his parents had sold their business and decided to relocate to California. In 1983, Chao followed in his parents' footsteps and started his own company, giving it his mother's family name, Hwa, and adding the word "son." Americanizing the name, he called it Watson Pharmaceuticals. His company would specialize in the manufacturing of generic drugs.

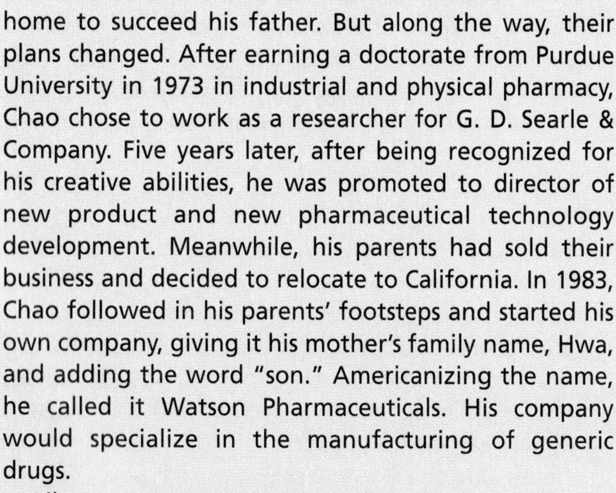

Like many entrepreneurs, Allen Chao found that starting a company was difficult. He needed more than $4 million just to set up labs—yet no lenders would invest in him. The risk was too great in the fiercely competitive pharmaceutical business—especially for a company specializing in manufacturing generic drugs. But, like a true entrepreneur, Chao was not deterred by setbacks. He knew he could be successful, so he turned to his family and friends in Taiwan—giving up almost 90 percent of the equity in the business in exchange for start-up capital.

Chao's strategy was unlike that of most other companies in the generic drug business. Large competitors targeted multimillion-dollar markets and high-volume drugs such as Tagamet and Valium. Watson Pharmaceuticals specialized in producing generic equivalents of hard-to-copy medicines such as Lederle's Asendin (an antidepressant) and Loxitane's Loxapine (a tranquilizer). Furthermore, most of Chao's competition sought to compete in the generic markets in which annual sales were at least $150 million, and they went after named drugs. Chao, on the other hand, chose to go after market segments in which sales rarely exceeded $10 million and where little drug name recognition existed.

Has his strategy paid off? You bet! Since introducing its first generic drug in 1985, Watson Pharmaceuticals now has 47 different products available in nearly 100 different dosage strengths on the market, and many of them have no direct competition. In fact, Chao's plan to go after the smaller markets has led Watson Pharmaceuticals to control almost 50 percent of those markets. His strategy has resulted in annual revenues approaching $600 million and net income exceeding $120 million.

QUESTIONS

1 What type of grand strategy(ies) has Chao pursued? Cite specific examples.

2 Michael Porter identified three generic strategies that companies can follow to develop a competitive advantage. Which one of the three do you believe Chao is primarily using? Discuss and support your choice.

3 What characteristics does Allen Chao possess that indicate he is an entrepreneur? Give specific examples.

Developing Your Investigative Skills

Using the Internet

Visit *www.prenhall.com/robbins* for updated Internet Exercises.

Enhancing Your Writing Skills

Communicating Effectively

1 Develop a two- to three-page response to the following statement: "Formal planning reduces flexibility and hinders success." Present both sides of the argument and include supporting data. Conclude your paper by defending and supporting one of the two arguments you've presented.

2 Describe how your class syllabus is used as an objective tool. Refer to the "setting employee objectives" section in the text (see pp. 88–89). In your discussion, provide specific references regarding how the guidelines we've offered apply to your class.

3 We've witnessed a few corporate mega-mergers in the past few years. Organizations like Daimler-Benz and Chrysler or Travelers Insurance and Citicorp, for example, have used the merger as a strategic tool. Pick one of these two mergers and describe the strategic implications. Highlight why the merger made strategic sense, what benefits the combined company expects to accrue because of the merger, and the potential drawbacks, if any, the merger may have.

Four

Foundations of Decision Making

LEARNING OUTCOMES After reading this chapter, I will be able to:

1. Describe the steps in the decision-making process.
2. Identify the assumptions of the rational decision-making model.
3. Explain the limits to rationality.
4. Define *certainty, risk,* and *uncertainty* as they relate to decision making.
5. Describe the actions of the bounded-rational decision maker.
6. Identify the two types of decision problems and the two types of decisions that are used to solve them.
7. Define *heuristics* and explain how they affect the decision-making process.
8. Identify four decision-making styles.
9. Describe the advantages and disadvantages of group decisions.
10. Explain three techniques for improving group decision making.

During the physical fitness boom of the 1970s, millions of previously unathletic people became interested in exercise. During this time, the fastest-growing segment of the physical fitness market was jogging. In fact, it's estimated that almost 30 million people now jog, and another 10 million wear running shoes for leisure wear. Most of these 40 million people have one preferred choice in athletic shoes—Nike.[1] And that appears to be the shoe of choice at the 2000 European soccer championship and the 2000 Summer Olympics in Sydney, Australia.

Nike was founded by Philip Knight, a track star from the University of Oregon. Nike's big breakthrough came in 1975 with the development of the "waffle" sole—soles with tiny rubber studs that made the shoe spongier than any other shoe on the market. From that point on, Nike's sales skyrocketed. Today, Nike has annual sales in excess of $9.5 billion and enjoys over a 40 percent market share in the U.S. market and a 37 percent market share globally.

Nike's success can be traced to several core values of Knight's. First, Knight values innovation, so Nike emphasizes research and development to continually improve its products. Nike's managers never sit back and assume that what they have is "good enough." Rather, borrowing from Moore's Law (the realization that computer chip capacity doubles every 18 months), Nike looks to bring new products and designs to the market every two years. Second, Knight values diversity. Nike provides a variety of styles and models to satisfy everyone's taste—from the professional athlete to the elderly person looking for a comfortable pair of walking shoes. Nike also makes products that cater to a diverse buying group—targeting, for example, women and various international markets. But most notably, behind Knight's actions was his desire for the company to be on the "hearts, minds, and feet" of every individual. To achieve that goal, Nike relied heavily on a phenomenal marketing campaign.

Being a former athlete, Knight recognized that professional sports heroes could influence a lot of people. He believed that if he could get high-profile athletes—such as the former Chicago Bull Michael Jordan, baseball's home-run king Mark McGwire, and the soccer player extraordinaire Mia Hamm—to become part of the Nike team, the company could "build new product lines and marketing campaigns around them." The athletes' dominating presence and the consumers' passion for imitating their idols enabled Knight to achieve his goal of operating the number one athletic shoe and apparel company in the world.

In spite of occasional setbacks, like the economic turmoil in Asia and criticism of its Asian labor practices, the decisions that Phil Knight has made appear to have worked, but Knight remains alert and vigilant. He hasn't lost sight of one fact—that when you are number one, everyone else is after you.

Phil Knight, like all managers, makes a lot of decisions—some small and some large. The overall quality of those decisions goes a long way in determining an organization's success or failure.[2] In this chapter, we examine the foundations of decision making.

In the last chapter, we discussed how companies plan—for both the long-term survival of the organization and the short-term day-to-day operations. Implied in these planning activities were the decisions managers make. Plans should not come out of thin air; they should be the result of careful analyses. After weighing the advantages and disadvantages of various alternatives, managers select the ones that will best serve the interests of the organization. This selection process is called decision making. What kinds of planning decisions do managers like Phil Knight make? We have listed a few examples in Exhibit 4-1.

- What are the organization's long-term objectives?
- What strategies will best achieve those objectives?
- What should the organization's short-term objectives be?
- What is the most efficient means of completing tasks?
- What might the competition be considering?
- What budgets are needed to complete department tasks?
- How difficult should individual goals be?

Exhibit 4-1 Examples of Planning-Function Decisions

The Decision-Making Process

Decision making is typically described as "choosing among alternatives," but this view is overly simplistic. Why? Because decision making is a process rather than the simple act of choosing among alternatives. Exhibit 4-2 illustrates the **decision-making process** as a set of eight steps that begins with identifying a problem, moves through selecting an alternative that can alleviate the problem, and concludes with evaluating the decision's effectiveness. This process is as applicable to your decision about what you're going to do on spring break as it was to Citicorp and Travelers Insurance executives who were considering combining their companies. The process can also be used to describe both individual and group decisions. Let's take a closer look at the process in order to understand what each step encompasses.

decision-making process
A set of eight steps that includes identifying a problem, selecting a solution, and evaluating the effectiveness of the solution

WHAT DEFINES A DECISION PROBLEM?

The decision-making process begins with the identification of a **problem** (step 1) or, more specifically, a discrepancy between an existing and a desired state of affairs.[3] Let's develop an example that illustrates this point to use throughout this section. For the sake of simplicity, let's make the example something to which most of us can relate: the decision to buy a vehicle. Take the case of a new-product manager for the Finland-based wireless communications company, Nokia. The manager has spent nearly $3,000 on auto repairs over the past few years, and now the car has a blown engine. Repair estimates indicate that it is not economical to repair the car. Furthermore, convenient public transportation is unavailable.

problem
A discrepancy between an existing and a desired state of affairs

So now we have a problem. There is a disparity between the manager's need to have a functional vehicle and the fact that her current one isn't working. Unfortunately, this example doesn't tell us much about how managers identify

Exhibit 4-2 The Decision-Making Process

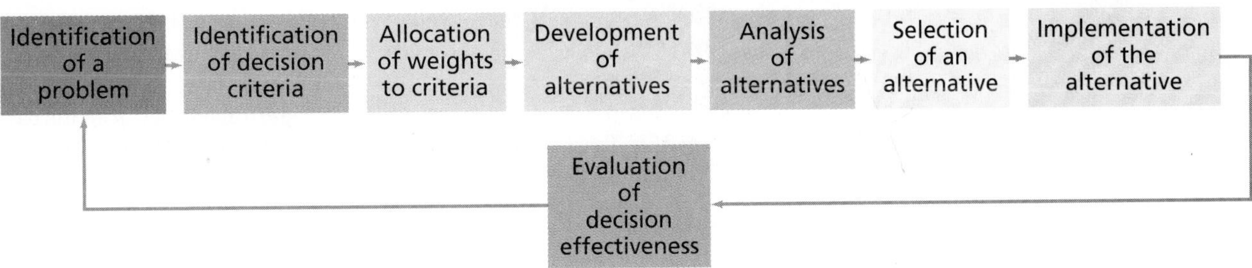

problems. In the real world, most problems don't come with neon signs identifying them as such. A blown engine is a clear signal to the manager that she needs a new car, but few problems are so obvious. Instead, problem identification is subjective. Furthermore, the manager who mistakenly solves the wrong problem perfectly is as likely to perform just as poorly as the manager who fails to identify the right problem and does nothing. Problem identification is neither a simple nor an unimportant part of the decision-making process.[4] How do managers become aware that they have a discrepancy? Managers have to make a comparison between their current state of affairs and some standard. What is that standard? It can be past performance, previously set goals, or the performance of some other unit within the organization or in other organizations. In our car-buying example, the standard is a previously set goal—a vehicle that runs.

WHAT IS RELEVANT IN THE DECISION-MAKING PROCESS?

decision criteria
Factors that are relevant in a decision

Once a manager has identified a problem that needs attention, the **decision criteria** that will be important in solving the problem must be identified (step 2).

In our car-buying example, the product manager has to assess what factors are relevant in her decision. These might include criteria such as price, model (two-door or four-door), size (compact or intermediate), manufacturer (French, German, American), optional equipment (automatic transmission, side-protection impact system, leather interior), and repair records. These criteria reflect what she thinks is relevant in her decision. Every decision maker has criteria—whether explicitly stated or not—that guide his or her decision. Note that, in this step in the decision-making process, what is not identified is as important as what is. If the product manager doesn't consider fuel economy to be a criterion, then it will not influence her choice of car. Thus, if a decision maker does not identify a particular factor in this second step, then it is treated as if it were irrelevant to the decision maker.

HOW DOES THE DECISION MAKER WEIGHT THE CRITERIA?

The criteria are not all equally important. It is necessary, therefore, to allocate weights to the items listed in step 2 in order to give them their relative priority in the decision (step 3).

A simple approach is merely to give the most important criterion a weight of 10 and then assign weights to the rest against that standard. Thus, in contrast to a criterion that you gave a 5, the highest-rated factor would be twice as important. The idea is to use your personal preferences to assign priorities to the relevant criteria in your decision as well as to indicate their degree of importance by assigning a weight to each. Exhibit 4-3 lists the criteria and weights that our manager developed for her car-replacement decision. Price is the most important criterion in her decision, with performance and handling having low weights.

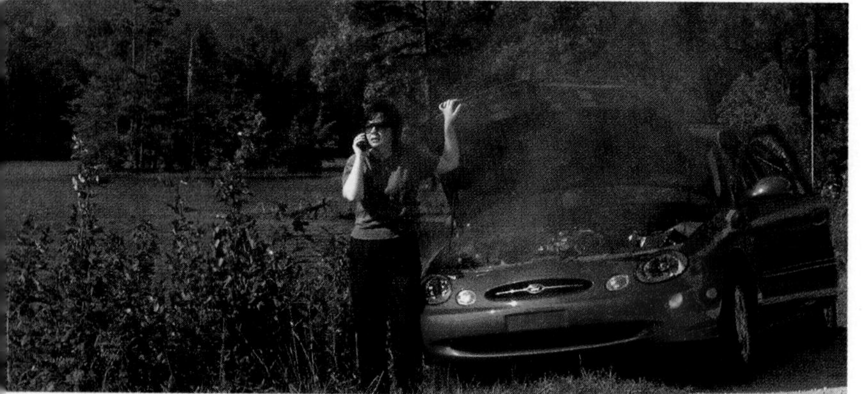

Problems in business rarely jump out at us like this one. But even here, is it a blown engine or simply a burst radiator hose? Problems may or may not be what they appear to be. Consequently, the first thing one needs to do in making a decision is to identify the problem.

Criterion	Weight
Price	10
Interior comfort	8
Durability	5
Repair record	5
Performance	3
Handling	1

Exhibit 4-3 Criteria and Weight in Car-Buying Decision (Scale of 1 to 10)

Then the decision maker lists the alternatives that could succeed in resolving the problem (step 4). No attempt is made in this step to appraise these alternatives, only to list them. Let's assume that our manager has identified 12 vehicles as viable choices: Jeep Cherokee, Ford Mustang, Mercedes C230, Chevrolet Camaro, Mazda 626, Dodge Intrepid, Volvo V70, Isuzu Rodeo, BMW 318, Audi 90, Toyota Camry, and the Volkswagen Passat.

Once the alternatives have been identified, the decision maker must critically analyze each one (step 5). The strengths and weaknesses of each alternative become evident as they are compared with the criteria and weights established in steps 2 and 3. Each alternative is evaluated by appraising it against the criteria. Exhibit 4-4 shows the assessed values that the manager put on each of her 12 alternatives after she had test driven each car. Keep in mind that the ratings given the 12 cars shown in Exhibit 4-4 are based on the assessment made by the new-product manager. Again, we are using a 1–10 scale. Some assessments can be achieved in a relatively objective fashion. For instance, the purchase price represents the best price the manager can get from local dealers, and consumer magazines report data from owners on frequency of repairs. However, the assessment of handling is clearly a personal judgment. The point is that most decisions contain judgments. They are reflected in the criteria chosen in step 2, the weights given to the criteria, and the evaluation of alternatives. This explains why two

Exhibit 4-4 Assessment of Car Alternatives

Alternatives	Initial Price	Interior Comfort	Durability	Repair Record	Performance	Handling	Total
Jeep Cherokee	2	10	8	7	5	5	37
Ford Mustang	9	6	5	6	8	6	40
Mercedes C230	8	5	6	6	4	6	35
Chevrolet Camaro	9	5	6	7	6	5	38
Mazda 626	5	6	9	10	7	7	44
Dodge Intrepid	10	5	6	4	3	3	31
Volvo V70	4	8	7	6	8	9	42
Isuzu Rodeo	7	6	8	6	5	6	38
BMW 318	9	7	4	4	4	5	33
Audi 90	5	8	5	4	10	10	42
Toyota Camry	6	5	10	10	6	6	43
Volkswagen Passat	8	6	6	5	7	8	40

vehicle buyers with the same amount of money may look at two totally distinct sets of alternatives or even look at the same alternatives and rate them differently.

Exhibit 4-4 is only an assessment of the 12 alternatives against the decision criteria; it does not reflect the weighting done in step 3. If one choice had scored 10 on every criterion, you wouldn't need to consider the weights. Similarly, if the weights were all equal, you could evaluate each alternative merely by summing up the appropriate lines in Exhibit 4-4. For instance, the Camaro would have a score of 38, and the Toyota Camry a score of 43. If you multiply each alternative assessment against its weight, you get the figures in Exhibit 4-5. For instance, the Isuzu Rodeo scored a 40 on durability, which was determined by multiplying the weight given to durability (5) by the manager's appraisal of Isuzu on this criterion (8). The summation of these scores represents an evaluation of each alternative against the previously established criteria and weights. Notice that the weighting of the criteria has changed the ranking of alternatives in our example. The Mazda 626, for example, has gone from first to third. From our analysis, both initial price and interior comfort worked against the Mazda.

WHAT DETERMINES THE "BEST" CHOICE?

Step 6 is the critical act of choosing the best alternative from among those enumerated and assessed. Since we determined all the pertinent factors in the decision, weighted them appropriately, and identified the viable alternatives, we merely have to choose the alternative that generated the highest score in step 5. In our car example (Exhibit 4-5), the decision maker would choose the Toyota Camry. On the basis of the criteria identified, the weights given to the criteria, and the decision maker's assessment of each vehicle's achievement on the criteria, the Toyota scored highest (224 points) and thus became the best alternative.

Exhibit 4-5 Weighting of Vehicles (Assessment × Criteria Weight)

Alternatives	Initial Price (10)		Interior Comfort (8)		Durability (5)		Repair Record (5)		Performance (3)		Handling (1)		Total
Jeep Cherokee	2	**20**	10	**80**	8	**40**	7	**35**	5	**15**	5	**5**	**195**
Ford Mustang	9	**90**	6	**48**	5	**25**	6	**30**	8	**24**	6	**6**	**223**
Mercedes C230	8	**80**	5	**40**	6	**30**	6	**30**	4	**12**	6	**6**	**198**
Chevrolet Camaro	9	**90**	5	**40**	6	**30**	7	**35**	6	**18**	5	**5**	**218**
Mazda 626	5	**50**	6	**48**	9	**45**	10	**50**	7	**21**	7	**7**	**221**
Dodge Intrepid	10	**100**	5	**40**	6	**30**	4	**20**	3	**9**	3	**3**	**202**
Volvo V70	4	**40**	8	**64**	7	**35**	6	**30**	8	**24**	9	**9**	**202**
Isuzu Rodeo	7	**70**	6	**48**	8	**40**	6	**30**	5	**15**	6	**6**	**209**
BMW 318	9	**90**	7	**56**	4	**20**	4	**20**	4	**12**	5	**5**	**203**
Audi 90	5	**50**	8	**64**	5	**25**	4	**20**	10	**30**	10	**10**	**199**
Toyota Camry	6	**60**	5	**40**	10	**50**	10	**50**	6	**18**	6	**6**	**224**
Volkswagen Passat	8	**80**	6	**48**	6	**30**	5	**25**	7	**21**	8	**8**	**212**

WHAT IS DECISION IMPLEMENTATION?

Although the choice process is completed in the previous step, the decision may still fail if it is not implemented properly (step 7). Therefore, this step is concerned with putting the decision into action. **Decision implementation** includes conveying the decision to those affected and getting their commitment to it. As we will demonstrate later in this chapter, groups or committees can help a manager achieve commitment. The people who must carry out a decision are most likely to enthusiastically endorse the outcome if they participate in the decision-making process.

decision implementation
Putting a decision into action; includes conveying the decision to the persons who will be affected by it and getting their commitment to it

WHAT IS THE LAST STEP IN THE DECISION PROCESS?

The last step in the decision-making process (step 8) appraises the result of the decision to see whether it has corrected the problem. Did the alternative chosen in step 6 and implemented in step 7 accomplish the desired result? The evaluation of the results of decisions is detailed in Chapter 13 where we will look at the control function.

rational
Describes choices that are consistent and value-maximizing within specified constraints

Making Decisions: The Rational Model

Managerial decision making is assumed to be **rational** in that managers make consistent, value-maximizing choices within specified constraints.[5] In this section, we take a close look at the underlying assumptions of rationality and then determine how valid those assumptions actually are.

A decision maker who was perfectly rational would be fully objective and logical. He or she would define a problem carefully and would have a clear and specific goal. Moreover, the steps in the decision-making process would consistently lead toward selecting the alternative that maximizes that goal. Exhibit 4-6 summarizes the assumptions of rationality.

Remember that the assumptions of rationality often do not hold true, because the level of certainty that the rational model demands rarely exists. That is, **certainty** implies that a manager can make an accurate decision because the outcome of every alternative is known. In the real world, we know that is not the case. Most managers, then, must try to assign probabilities to outcomes that may result. We call this process dealing with **risk.**[6] When decision makers do not have full knowledge of the problem and cannot determine even a reasonable probability of alternative outcomes, they must make their decisions under a condition of **uncertainty.**

certainty
The implication that, in making a decision, the decision maker knows the outcome of every possible alternative

risk
The probability that a particular outcome will result from a given decision

uncertainty
A condition in which managers do not have full knowledge of the problem they face and cannot determine even a reasonable probability of alternative outcomes

Exhibit 4-6 Assumptions of Rationality

The problem is clear and unambiguous	A single, well-defined goal is to be achieved	All alternatives and consequences are known	Preferences are clear	Preferences are constant and stable	No time or cost constraints exist	Final choice will maximize economic payoff

Lead to

Rational Decision Making

The Real World of Managerial Decision Making: Modification of the Rational Model

When you were deciding where to attend college, did you obtain catalogs from the more than 10,000 colleges and universities that exist throughout the world? Obviously not. Did you carefully identify all the relevant criteria—tuition costs, scholarships offered, location, majors offered, and so forth—in making your decision? Did you evaluate each potential college against these criteria in an effort to make an optimum selection? We doubt it. But don't take this as an indictment of you or your decision-making ability. Most of us make decisions on the basis of incomplete information. Why? When we are faced with complex problems, most of us respond by reducing the problem to something we can readily understand. People often have limited abilities to process and assimilate massive amounts of information to reach an optimal solution. As a result, they *satisfice.* That is, they seek solutions that are satisfactory and sufficient—or just good enough.

People . . . often seek decision solutions . . . that are good enough.

Do managers engage in satisficing behavior? Or do they act rationally by carefully assessing problems, identifying all the relevant criteria, using their creativity to identify all viable alternatives, and, after a meticulous review of each alternative, finding the optimum choice? When managers are faced with a simple problem with few alternatives, when time pressures are minimal, and when the cost of seeking out and evaluating alternatives is low, the rational model provides a good description of the decision-making process.[7] But such situations are the exception rather than the rule.

Numerous studies have added to our understanding of managerial decision making.[8] These studies often challenge one or more of the assumptions of rationality. They suggest that decision making often veers from the logical, consistent, and systematic process that rationality implies. Do these limits to rationality mean that managers ignore the eight-step decision process we described at the beginning of this chapter? Not necessarily. Why? Because despite the limits to perfect rationality, managers are expected to appear to follow the rational process.[9] They know that "good" decision makers are supposed to do certain things: identify problems, consider alternatives, gather information, behave thoughtfully, and act decisively but prudently. By doing so, managers signal to their bosses, peers, and employees that they are competent and that their decisions are the result of intelligent and rational deliberation. The process they follow is frequently referred to as bounded rationality.

WHAT IS BOUNDED RATIONALITY?

Management theory is built on the premise that individuals act rationally and that managerial jobs revolve around the rational decision-making process. However, the assumptions of rationality are rather optimistic. Few people actually behave rationally. Given this fact, how do managers make decisions if it is unlikely that they are perfectly rational? Herbert Simon, an economist and management scholar, found that within certain constraints, managers do act rationally. Because it is impossible for human beings to process and understand all the information necessary to meet the test of rationality, what they do is construct simplified models that extract the essential features from problems without capturing all of their complexities.[10] Simon called this decision-making process **bounded rationality.** Under the definition of bounded rationality, decision makers can behave rationally (the rational decision-making model) within the limits of the simplified or bounded model.[11] The result of their actions is a satisficing decision rather than a maximizing one—a decision in which "good-enough" solutions are selected. As a result, instead of optimizing a choice, decision makers select alternatives that satisfy the problem.[12]

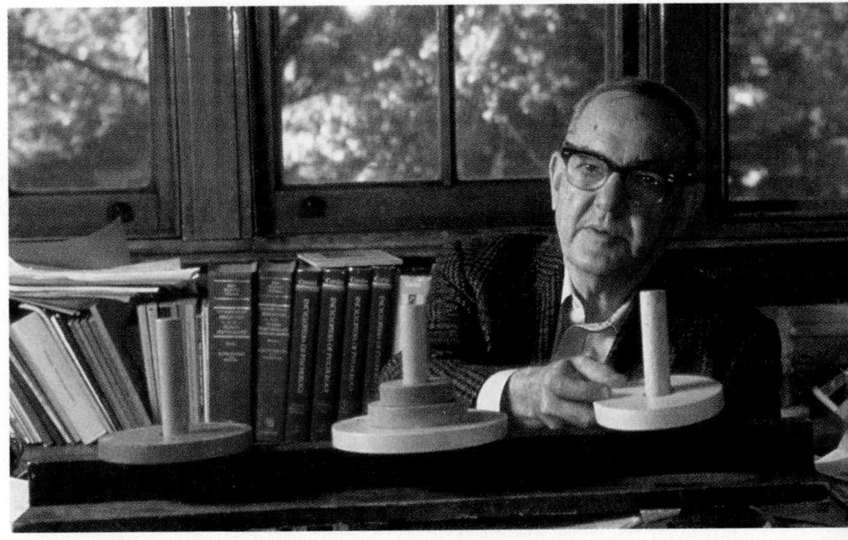

Herbert Simon recognized that decisions typically don't follow the assumptions of rationality. But, that wasn't an indictment of the model itself. Although environmental factors may act as barriers to these assumptions, decision makers can still act rationally but in a constrained way. To do this, Simon says managers make decisions in what is called *bounded rationality.*

How do managers' actions within these boundaries differ from actions within the rational model? Once a problem is identified, the search for criteria and alternatives begins. But this list of criteria is generally limited to the more conspicuous choices. That is, Simon found that decision makers will focus on easy-to-find choices—those that tend to be highly visible. In many instances, this means developing alternatives that vary only slightly from decisions that have been made in the past to deal with similar problems.

bounded rationality
Behavior that is rational within the parameters of a simplified model that captures the essential features of a problem

Once this limited set of alternatives is identified, decision makers will begin reviewing them, but that review will not be exhaustive. Rather, they will proceed to review the alternatives only until an alternative that is sufficient, or good enough, to solve the problems at hand is found. Thus, the first alternative to meet the good-enough criterion ends the search, and decision makers can then proceed to implement this acceptable course of action. For example, suppose as a double major in finance and human resource management, you're looking for a job in benefit administration. You would like to find employment within 75 miles of your hometown at a starting salary of $29,000. You accept a job offer as an industrial relations specialist from a mid-sized firm nearly 60 miles from home at a starting salary of $29,500. A more comprehensive job search would have revealed a job in benefit administration in a *Fortune* 1000 firm just 25 miles from your hometown and starting at $31,000. Because the first job offer was satisfactory (or good enough), you behaved in a bounded rational manner by accepting it, although, according to the assumptions of perfect rationality, you didn't maximize your decision by searching all possible alternatives.

What are the implications of bounded rationality on the manager's job? In situations in which the assumptions of perfect rationality do not apply (including many of the most important and far-reaching decisions that a manager makes), the details of the decision-making process are strongly influenced by the decision maker's self-interest, the organization's culture, internal politics, and power considerations.

One Manager's Perspective

Shirley DeLibero Executive Director, New Jersey Transit

When we think of decision making as a formal management process, we sometimes imagine that we have a single problem to solve and all the time in the world to solve it. For Shirley DeLibero, however, decision making is a nonstop process with multiple and simultaneous challenges.

Like many employees in the public sector, DeLibero faced some unhappy customers when she took over the position of executive director of the New Jersey Transit Department. The department's trains and buses had a long history of poor maintenance and continual breakdowns, which meant they frequently ran late. While government funds for upkeep and repair were being eroded by budget cuts, customers were fuming at rising fares and continued deterioration in both the level and the quality of service.

None of these problems helped morale within the department. The members of the transit workers' union were vocal about their concerns, dissatisfactions, and anxiety. Yet no improvements could be made without their efforts.

DeLibero faced many challenges in her previous transportation management posts. In her newest position, it almost seemed as if too many decisions needed to be made at once. Her first decision, however, was to focus on employee morale as the key to improving service. Once plans to overcome low morale were in place, other decisions could follow.

ARE COMMON ERRORS COMMITTED IN THE DECISION-MAKING PROCESS?

When individuals make decisions, they must make choices. But doing so requires careful thought and a lot of information. Complete information, however, would overload us. Consequently, we often engage in behaviors that speed up the process. That is, in order to avoid information overload, we rely on judgmental shortcuts called **heuristics.**[13] Heuristics commonly exist in two forms—availability and representative. Both types create biases in a decision maker. Another bias is the decision maker's tendency to escalate commitment to a failing course of action.

heuristics
Judgmental shortcuts

availability heuristic
The tendency for people to base their judgments on information that is readily available to them

Availability heuristic **Availability heuristic** is the tendency to base judgments on information that is readily available. Events that invoke strong emotions, are vivid to the imagination, or have recently occurred create a strong impression on us. As a result, we are likely to overestimate the frequency of the occurrence of unlikely events. For instance, many people have a fear of flying. Although traveling in commercial aircraft is statistically safer than driving a car, aircraft accidents get much more attention. The media coverage of an air disaster causes individuals to overstate the risk of flying and understate the risk of driving. For managers, availability heuristic can also explain why, when conducting performance appraisals (see Chapter 6), they tend to give more weight to more recent behaviors of an employee than the behaviors of six or nine months ago.

representative heuristic
The tendency for people to base judgments of probability on things with which they are familiar

Representative heuristic Literally millions of recreational league players dream of becoming a professional basketball player one day. In reality, most of these youngsters have a better chance of becoming medical doctors than they do of ever playing in the NBA. These dreams are examples of what we call **representative heuristic.** Representative heuristic causes individuals to match the likelihood of an occurrence with something that they are familiar with. For example, our young ballplayers may think about someone from their local league who 15 years ago went on to play in the NBA. Or they think, while watching players on television, that they could perform as well.

In organizations, we can find several instances of representative heuristic. Decision makers may predict the future success of a new product by relating it to a previous product's success. Managers may also be affected by representative heuristic when they no longer hire graduates from a particular college program because the last three persons hired from that program were poor performers.

Go to almost any basketball court and you'll likely find one thing in common. Someone is playing basketball wearing the jersey of Michael Jordan. Why? Because many of these players are trying to be like Mike, formerly of the Chicago Bulls. After all, wearing his jersey and playing like him will help them one day go to the NBA—after a successful college career and at least one NCAA championship! That dream is what we call *representative heuristic.*

Escalation of commitment A popular strategy in playing blackjack is to guarantee you can't lose. When you lose a hand, double your next bet. This strategy, or decision rule, may appear innocent enough, but if you start with a $5 bet and lose six hands in a row (not uncommon for many of us), you will be wagering $320 on your seventh hand merely to recoup your losses and win $5.

The blackjack strategy illustrates a phenomenon called **escalation of commitment,** an increased commitment to a previous decision despite negative information. That is, the escalation of commitment represents the tendency to stay the course, despite negative data that suggest one should do otherwise.[14]

escalation of commitment
An increased commitment to a previous decision despite negative information

Some of the most notorious events involving escalation of commitment were decisions made by presidents of the United States.[15] For example: Lyndon Johnson's administration increased the tonnage of bombs dropped on North Vietnam despite constant information that bombing was not bringing the war any closer to conclusion. Richard Nixon refused to destroy his secret White House tapes. George Bush believed that, given his popularity after Operation Desert Storm and the fall of the Soviet Union, he had only to pay attention to foreign affairs to win the 1992 presidential election. History now tells us that staying the course proved detrimental to Johnson, Nixon, and Bush. In an organizational setting, David Peterson, the premier of Ontario, committed an additional $4 billion to complete the Darlington nuclear plant even though there was evidence that consumption estimates and, thus, revenue projections were too optimistic.[16] Rather than cut his losses, Peterson continued to commit funds to the project—eventually spending double the original estimate.

In organizations, managers like David Peterson may recognize that their previous solution is not working, but, rather than search for new alternatives, they simply increase their commitment to the original solution. Why do they do this? In many cases, it's an effort to demonstrate that their initial decision was not wrong.[17]

Decision Making: A Contingency Approach

The types of problems managers face in decision-making situations often determine how a problem is treated. In this section, we present a categorization scheme for problems and for types of decisions. Then we show how the type of decision a manager uses should reflect the characteristics of the problem.

HOW DO PROBLEMS DIFFER?

Some problems are straightforward. The goal of the decision maker is clear, the problem familiar, and information about the problem easily defined and complete. Examples might include a supplier's tardiness with an important delivery, a customer's wanting to return a mail-order purchase, a news program's having to respond to an unexpected and fast-breaking event, or a university's handling of a student who is applying for financial aid. Such situations are called **well-structured problems.** They align closely with the assumptions underlying perfect rationality.

well-structured problems
Straightforward, familiar, easily defined problems

Many situations faced by managers, however, are **ill-structured problems.** They are new or unusual. Information about such problems is ambiguous or incomplete. The decision to enter a new market segment such as e-commerce or to hire an architect to design a new office park is an example of an ill-structured problem. So, too, is the decision to invest in a new, unproven technology.

ill-structured problems
New problems in which information is ambiguous or incomplete

WHAT IS THE DIFFERENCE BETWEEN PROGRAMMED AND NONPROGRAMMED DECISIONS?

Just as problems can be divided into two categories, so, too, can decisions. As we will see, programmed, or routine, decision making is the most efficient way to handle well-structured problems. However, when problems are ill structured, managers must rely on nonprogrammed decision making in order to develop unique solutions.

A Sears automotive mechanic breaks an alloy wheel rim while installing new tires on a vehicle. What does the manager do? There is probably some standardized method for handling this type of problem. For example, the manager may replace the rim at the company's expense. This is a **programmed decision.** Decisions are programmed to the extent that they are repetitive and routine and to the extent that a specific approach has been worked out for handling them. Because the problem is well structured, the manager does not have to go to the trouble and expense of working up an involved decision process. Programmed decision making is relatively simple and tends to rely heavily on previous solutions. The develop-the-alternatives stage in the decision-making process is either nonexistent or given little attention. Why? Because once the structured problem is defined, its solution is usually self-evident or at least reduced to a very few alternatives that are familiar and that have proved successful in the past. In many cases, programmed decision making becomes decision making by precedent. Managers simply do what they and others have done previously in the same situation. The broken wheel rim does not require the manager to identify and weight decision criteria or to develop a long list of possible solutions. Rather, the manager falls back on a systematic procedure, rule, or policy.

programmed decision
A repetitive decision that can be handled by a routine approach

WHAT ARE PROCEDURES, RULES, AND POLICIES, AND WHEN ARE THEY BEST USED?

A **procedure** is a series of interrelated sequential steps that a manager can use when responding to a well-structured problem. The only real difficulty is identi-

procedure
A series of interrelated sequential steps that can be used to respond to a well-structured problem

fying the problem. Once the problem is clear, so is the procedure. For instance, a purchasing manager receives a request from computing services for licensing arrangements to install 16 copies of Microsoft Outlook. The purchasing manager knows that there is a definite procedure for handling this decision. Has the requisition been properly filled out and approved? If not, one can send the requisition back with a note explaining what is deficient. If the request is complete, the approximate costs are estimated. If the total exceeds $7,500, three bids must be obtained. If the total is $7,500 or less, only one vendor need be identified and the order placed. The decision-making process is merely the execution of a simple series of sequential steps.

A **rule** is an explicit statement that tells a manager what he or she ought or ought not to do. Rules are frequently used by managers who confront a well-structured problem because they are simple to follow and ensure consistency. In the illustration above, the $7,500 cutoff rule simplifies the purchasing manager's decision about when to use multiple bids.

rule
An explicit statement that tells managers what they ought or ought not to do

A third guide for making programmed decisions is a **policy.** It provides guidelines to channel a manager's thinking in a specific direction. The statement that "we promote from within, whenever possible" is an example of a policy. In con-

policy
A general guide that establishes parameters for making decisions

Ethical Dilemma in Management

Bausch & Lomb Leaves Town

Bausch & Lomb, the Rochester, New York, eyewear company, made some major changes that had a number of western Maryland citizens seeing red. A Bausch & Lomb sunglass-lens plant in the area was targeted for closure. As a result, approximately 600 jobs were cut.[18] Company representatives decided to close the plant because it was too expensive to maintain the current operation in the Maryland area and shift the operations to plants in San Antonio, Texas, and Hong Kong.

Is Bausch & Lomb justified in its actions? Company officials certainly have a right to manage the operations in the most profitable way they can. Bausch & Lomb watched corporate profits fall from $171.4 million to $31.1 million in a two-year period. The company's chief executive was ousted but that did little to boost profits. Moving to areas where employee pay was lower was viewed as an effective way to reduce costs. Therefore, the bottom line warranted their actions. Furthermore, management argued that the company brought more to the community—specifically, high-paying jobs that allowed the community to grow and prosper—than the community gave back. And, in today's global economy, hometown loyalties rarely override economic considerations.

Why was employee pay so high in the Maryland plant? When a company such as Bausch & Lomb establishes an operation in an area, it wants to attract a skilled, dedicated, and committed workforce. But, because Bausch & Lomb was the primary employer in the region, turnover was almost nonexistent and pay levels kept climbing upward. At the San Antonio plant, in contrast, turnover is significant, and new employees can be hired at lower wage rates than the person who left the job. As a result of employee longevity, the average hourly wage rate in Maryland was nearly 33 percent higher than it was in Texas; the percentage was even higher when the Maryland plant was compared with the Hong Kong plant.

Employees in the Maryland plant did make more money than their counterparts in Texas and Hong Kong, but they had given the company something that other plants did not have—high-recognition quality products. Over the years, the western Maryland plant had been recognized by several independent groups for producing some of the highest-quality sunglass lenses in the world. In fact, employees were awarded a prestigious international designation of quality that few other organizations anywhere in the world achieve as well as the organization having been a recipient of a productivity award from the U.S. government.

What role, if any, should social responsibility have played in Bausch & Lomb's decision to close its western Maryland plant? Should companies like Bausch & Lomb have a legal right to move to another area simply to cut costs, knowing their actions will create an economic hardship for the community? What if they are given tax incentives to locate in their original location? What's your opinion on this topic?

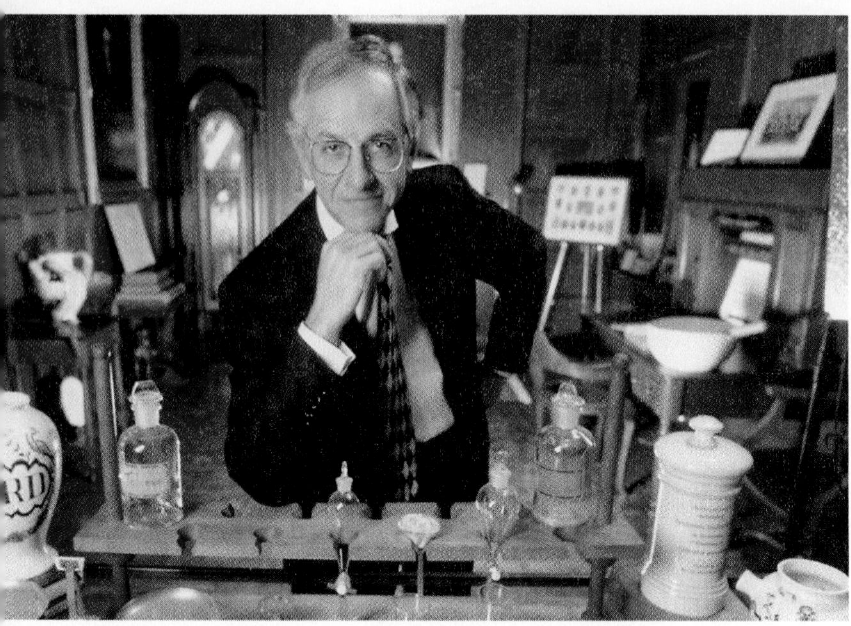

To succeed in the future, companies like Eli Lilly have had to make nonprogrammed decisions about their future. Faced with declining revenues from its popular antidepressant, Prozac, Chairman and CEO Sidney Taurel has looked at creating alliances with other businesses to help position the company for the next decade.

trast to a rule, a policy establishes parameters for the decision maker rather than specifically stating what should or should not be done. It's at this point that one's ethical standards will come into play. As an analogy, think of the Ten Commandments as rules and the U.S. Constitution as policy. The latter requires judgment and interpretation; the former do not.

WHAT DO NONPROGRAMMED DECISIONS LOOK LIKE?

Deciding whether to acquire another organization, deciding which global markets offer the most potential, selecting of an architect to design a new corporate headquarters building, engineering work processes to improve efficiency, or deciding whether to sell off an unprofitable division are examples of **nonprogrammed decisions.** Such decisions are unique and nonrecurring. When a manager confronts an ill-structured problem, there is no cut-and-dried solution. A custom-made, nonprogrammed response is required.

nonprogrammed decisions
Decisions that must be custom-made to solve unique and nonrecurring problems

The creation of a new organizational strategy is a nonprogrammed decision. This decision is different from previous organizational decisions because the issue is new; a different set of environmental factors exists, and other conditions have changed. For example, Eli Lilly & Company's decision to seek strategic alliances with other pharmaceutical companies in the late 1990s was unlike any other strategic decision the company had previously made.[19] Eli Lilly had enjoyed excellent earnings from a number of its drugs, especially the well-known antidepressant Prozac. Yet Prozac's sales over the past few years have been decreasing as competing products have appeared on the market even though Prozac has accounted for more than one third of Eli Lilly's revenues. Furthermore, the patent on Prozac expires in 2003. The hundreds of decisions that went into Eli Lilly's strategic alliances had never been made before; they were clearly of the nonprogrammed variety.

HOW CAN YOU INTEGRATE PROBLEMS, TYPES OF DECISIONS, AND LEVEL IN THE ORGANIZATION?

Exhibit 4-7 describes the relationship among types of problems, types of decisions, and level in the organization. Well-structured problems are responded to with programmed decision making. Ill-structured problems require nonprogrammed decision making. Lower-level managers essentially confront familiar and repetitive problems; therefore, they most typically rely on programmed decisions such as standard operating procedures. However, the problems confronting managers are more likely to become ill structured as the managers move up the organizational hierarchy. Why? Because lower-level managers handle the routine

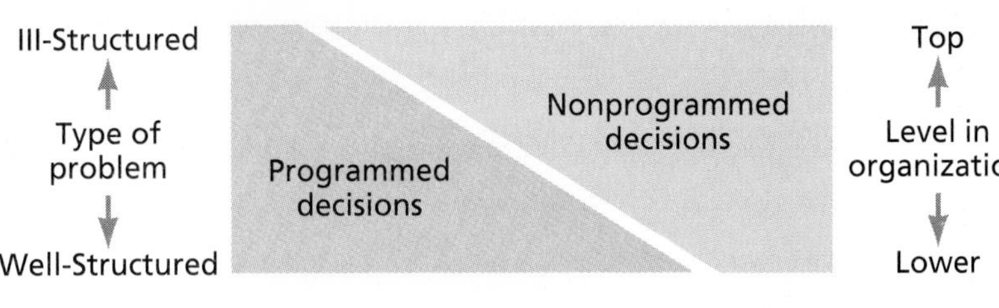

Exhibit 4-7
Types of Problems, Types of Decisions, and Level in the Organization

decisions themselves and pass upward only decisions that they find unique or difficult. Similarly, managers pass down routine decisions to their employees in order to spend their time on more problematic issues.

Few managerial decisions in the real world are either fully programmed or fully nonprogrammed. Most decisions fall somewhere in between. Few programmed decisions are designed to eliminate individual judgment completely. At the other extreme, even the most unusual situation requiring a nonprogrammed decision can be helped by programmed routines.

A final point on this topic is that organizational efficiency is facilitated by programmed decision making—a fact that may explain its wide popularity. Whenever possible, management decisions are likely to be programmed. Obviously, this approach is not too realistic at the top of the organization, because most of the problems that top management confront are of a nonrecurring nature. However, there are strong economic incentives for top management to create policies, standard operating procedures, and rules to guide other managers.

Programmed decisions minimize the need for managers to exercise discretion. This is important because discretion costs money. The more nonprogrammed decision making a manager is required to do, the greater the judgment needed. Because sound judgment is an uncommon quality, it costs more to acquire the services of managers who possess it.

Decision-Making Styles

Every decision maker brings a unique set of personal characteristics to his or her problem-solving efforts. For example, a manager who is creative and comfortable with uncertainty is likely to develop and evaluate decision alternatives differently from someone who is more conservative and less likely to accept risk. As a result of this information, researchers have sought to identify different decision-making styles.[20]

The basic premise for this decision-making model is the realization that individuals differ along two dimensions. The first is the way they *think*.[21] Some decision makers are logical and rational. Being such, they process information in a sequential manner. In contrast, some individuals think creatively and use their intuition.[22] These decision makers have a tendency to see matters from a big-picture perspective. The second dimension focuses on individuals' *tolerance for ambiguity*. Some individuals have a high need for consistency and order in making decisions so that ambiguity is minimized. Others, however, are able to tolerate high levels of uncertainty and can process many thoughts at the same time. When we diagram these two dimensions, four decision-making styles are formed. These styles are *directive, analytic, conceptual,* and *behavioral* (see Exhibit 4-8).

Exhibit 4-8
Decision-Making Styles

SOURCE: S. P. Robbins, *Supervision Today* (Upper Saddle River, NJ: Prentice Hall, 1995), p. 111.

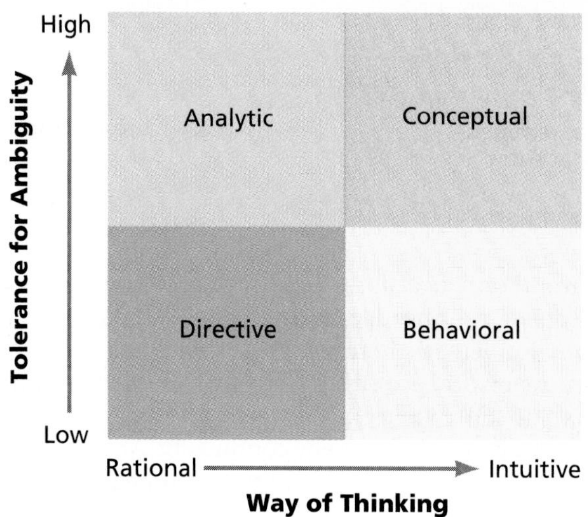

The directive style represents a decision-making style characterized by low tolerance for ambiguity and a rational way of thinking. These individuals are logical and efficient and typically make fast decisions that focus on the short term. The analytic decision-making style is characterized by high tolerance for ambiguity combined with a rational way of thinking. These individuals prefer to have complete information before making a decision. As a result, they carefully consider many alternatives. The conceptual style of decision-making represents someone who tends to be very broad in outlook and to look at many alternatives. These decision makers tend to focus on the long run and often look for creative solutions. The behavioral style reflects an individual who thinks intuitively but has a low tolerance for uncertainty. These decision makers work well with others, are open to suggestions, and are concerned about the individuals who work for them.

Although the four decision-making styles appear independent, most managers possess characteristics of more than one style. That is, although they usually have a dominant style, the other three styles can be alternatives—to be used when a situation may be best resolved by using a particular style.

Making Decisions in Groups

Do managers make a lot of decisions in groups? You bet they do! Many decisions in organizations, especially important decisions that have far-reaching effects on organizational activities and personnel, are typically made in groups. It's a rare organization that doesn't at some time use committees, task forces, review panels, work teams, or similar groups as vehicles for making decisions. Why? In many cases, these groups represent the people who will be most affected by the decisions being made. Because of their expertise, these people are often best qualified to make decisions that affect them.

Studies tell us that managers spend up to 40 percent or more of their time in meetings.[23] Undoubtedly, a large portion of that time is involved with defining problems, arriving at solutions to those problems, and determining the means for implementing the solutions. It's possible, in fact, for groups to be assigned any of the eight steps in the decision-making process.

WHAT ARE THE ADVANTAGES OF GROUP DECISION MAKING?

Individual and group decisions have their own set of strengths. Neither is ideal for all situations. Let's begin by reviewing the advantages that group decisions have over individual decisions.

Group decisions provide more complete information than do individual ones.[24] There is often truth to the axiom that two heads are better than one. A group will bring a diversity of experience and perspectives to the decision process that an individual, acting alone, cannot. Groups also generate more alternatives. Because groups have a greater quantity and diversity of information, they can identify more alternatives than can an individual. Quantity and diversity of information are greatest when group members represent different specialties. Furthermore, group decision making increases acceptance of a solution. Many decisions fail after the final choice has been made because people do not accept the solution. However, if the people who will be affected by a certain solution, and who will help implement it, participate in the decision they will be more likely to accept the decision and to encourage others to accept it. And finally, this process increases legitimacy. The group decision-making process is consistent with democratic ideals; therefore, decisions made by groups may be perceived as more legitimate than decisions made by a single person. The fact that the individual decision maker has complete power and has not consulted others can create a perception that a decision was made autocratically and arbitrarily.

WHAT ARE THE DISADVANTAGES OF GROUP DECISION MAKING?

If groups are so good, how did the phrase "a camel is a racehorse put together by a committee" become so popular? The answer, of course, is that group decisions are not without their drawbacks. There are several major disadvantages. First, they are *time-consuming.* It takes time to assemble a group. In addition, the interaction that takes place once the group is in place is frequently inefficient. Groups almost always take more time to reach a solution than an individual would take to make the decision alone. There may also be *minority domination,* where members of a group are never perfectly equal. They may differ in rank in the organization, experience, knowledge about the problem, influence on other members, verbal skills, assertiveness, and the like. This imbalance creates the opportunity for one or more members to dominate others in the group. A minority that dominates a group frequently has an undue influence on the final decision.

Will this group of individuals make a better decision collectively than they would as any one individual? The answer to that question lies in what you're evaluating. If it's completeness, legitimacy, and more creative solutions, it would be "better." However, if speed and efficiency of the decision are the most important, then the group would not be as quick. Accordingly, having a group or an individual make the decision is determined by what the outcome of the decision needs.

Another problem focuses on the *pressures to conform* in groups. For instance, have you ever been in a situation in which several people were sitting around discussing a particular item and you had something to say that ran contrary to the consensus views of the group, but you remained silent? Were you surprised to learn later that others shared your views and also had remained silent? What you experienced is what Irving Janis termed **groupthink.**[25] This is a form of conformity in which group members withhold deviant, minority, or unpopular views in order to give the appearance of agreement. As a result, groupthink undermines critical thinking in the group and eventually harms the quality of the final decision. And, finally, there is *ambiguous responsibility.* Group members share responsibility, but who is actually responsible for the final outcome? In an individual decision, it is clear who is responsible. In a group decision, the responsibility of any single member is watered down.

groupthink
The withholding by group members of different views in order to appear to be in agreement

Groupthink undermines critical thinking and harms the final decision.

Groupthink applies to a situation in which a group's ability to appraise alternatives objectively and arrive at a quality decision is jeopardized. Because of pressures for conformity, groups often deter individuals from critically appraising unusual, minority, or unpopular views. Consequently, an individual's mental efficiency, reality testing, and moral judgment deteriorate.

How does groupthink occur? The following are examples of situations in which groupthink is evident:

1 Group members rationalize any resistance to the assumptions they have made.
2 Members apply direct pressures on those who momentarily express doubts about any of the group's shared views or who question the validity of arguments favored by the majority.
3 Those members who have doubts or hold differing points of view seek to avoid deviating from what appears to be group consensus.
4 There is an illusion of unanimity. If someone does not speak, it is assumed that he or she is in full accord.

Does groupthink really hinder decision making? Yes. Several research studies have found that groupthink symptoms were associated with poorer-quality decision outcomes.[26] But, groupthink can be minimized if the group is cohesive, fosters open discussion, and has an impartial leader who seeks input from all members.

WHEN ARE GROUPS MOST EFFECTIVE?

Whether groups are more effective than individuals depends on the criteria you use for defining effectiveness. Group decisions tend to be more accurate. The evidence indicates that, on the average, groups make better decisions than individuals.[27] However, if decision effectiveness is defined in terms of speed, individuals are superior. If creativity is important, groups tend to be more effective than individuals. And if effectiveness means the degree of acceptance the final solution achieves, the nod again goes to the group.[28]

The effectiveness of group decision making is also influenced by the size of the group. The larger the group, the greater the opportunity for heterogeneous representation. On the other hand, a larger group requires more coordination and more time to allow all members to contribute. What this means is that groups probably should not be too large: A minimum of five to a maximum of about fifteen members is best. Evidence indicates, in fact, that groups of five and, to a lesser extent, seven are the most effective.[29] Because five and seven are odd numbers, strict deadlocks are avoided. Effectiveness should not be considered without also assessing efficiency. Groups almost always stack up as a poor second in efficiency to the individual decision maker. With few exceptions, group decision making consumes more work hours than does individual decision making. In deciding whether to use groups, then, primary consideration must be given to assessing whether increases in effectiveness are more than enough to offset the losses in efficiency.

HOW CAN YOU IMPROVE GROUP DECISION MAKING?

When members of a group meet face to face and interact with one another, they create the potential for groupthink. They can censor themselves and pressure other group members into agreement. Three ways of making group decision making more creative are brainstorming, the nominal group technique, and electronic meetings.

What is brainstorming? **Brainstorming** is a relatively simple technique for overcoming the pressures for conformity that retard the development of creative alternatives.[30] It utilizes an idea-generating process that specifically encourages any and all alternatives while withholding any criticism of those alternatives. In a typical brainstorming session, a half-dozen to a dozen people sit around a table. Of course, technology is changing where that "table" is. The group leader states the problem in a clear manner that is understood by all participants. Members then "freewheel" as many alternatives as they can in a given time. No criticism is allowed, and all the alternatives are recorded for later discussion and analysis. Brainstorming, however, is merely a process for generating ideas. The next method, the nominal group technique, helps groups arrive at a preferred solution.[31]

brainstorming
An idea-generating process that encourages alternatives while withholding criticism

How does the nominal group technique work? The **nominal group technique** restricts discussion during the decision-making process, hence the term. Group members must be present, as in a traditional committee meeting, but they are required to operate independently. They secretly write a list of general problem areas or potential solutions to a problem. The chief advantage of this technique is that it permits the group to meet formally but does not restrict independent thinking as so often happens in the traditional interacting group.

nominal group technique
A decision-making technique in which group members are physically present but operate independently

How can electronic meetings enhance group decision making? The most recent approach to group decision making blends the nominal group technique with sophisticated computer technology.[32] It is called the **electronic meeting.**

electronic meeting
A type of nominal group technique in which participants are linked by computer

Once the technology for the meeting is in place, the concept is simple. Up to 50 people sit around a horseshoe-shaped table that is empty except for a series of computer terminals. Issues are presented to the participants, who type their responses onto their computer screens. Individual comments, as well as aggregate votes, are displayed on a projection screen in the room.

The major advantages of electronic meetings are anonymity, honesty, and speed. Participants can anonymously type any message they want, and it will flash on the screen for all to see at the push of a board key. It allows people to be brutally honest with no penalty. And it is fast—chitchat is eliminated, discussions do not digress, and many participants can "talk" at once without interrupting the others.

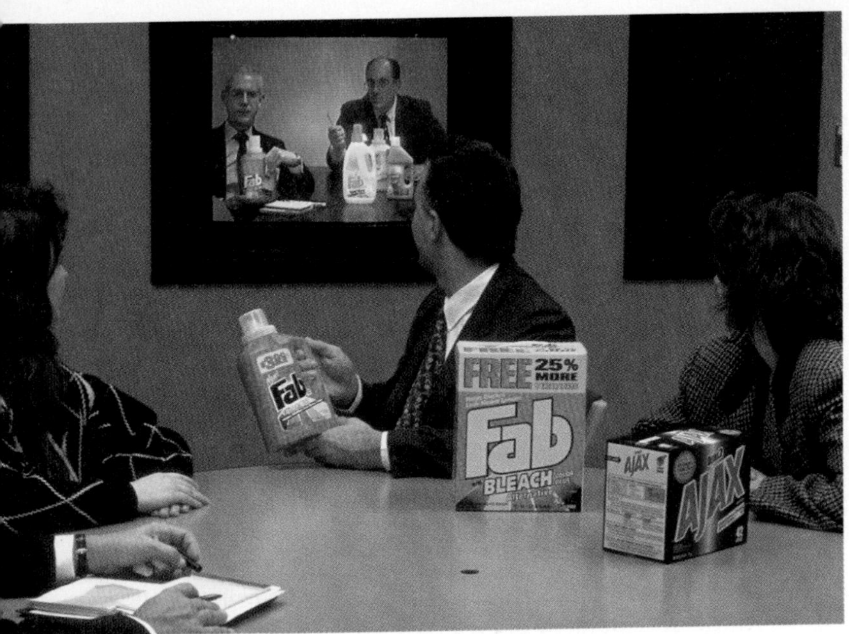

Companies such as Colgate use video conferencing as a means of bringing people from all parts of the world together to have input into a decision that is being made. This process is quicker than bringing everyone physically together—and clearly a cost savings for companies who use the technology.

Experts claim that electronic meetings are as much as 55 percent faster than traditional face-to-face meetings.[33] Phelps Dodge Mining, for instance, used the approach to cut its annual planning meeting from several days down to 12 hours. However, there are drawbacks. Those who type quickly can outshine those who may be verbally eloquent but lousy typists; those with the best ideas don't get credit for them; and the process lacks the informational richness of face-to-face oral communication. However, this technology is just starting to catch on; the future of group decision making is very likely to include extensive usage of electronic meetings.

A variation of the electronic meeting is the video conference. By linking together media from different locations, people can have face-to-face meetings even when they are thousands of mile apart. This has enhanced feedback among the members, saved countless hours of business travel, and ultimately saved companies like Colgate hundreds of thousands of dollars.[34] As a result, they are more effective in their meetings and have increased the efficiency in which decisions are made.

National Culture and Decision-Making Practices

Research shows that, to some extent, decision-making practices differ from country to country.[35] The way decisions are made—whether by group, by team members, participatively, or autocratically by an individual manager—and the degree of risk a decision maker is willing to take are just two examples of decision variables that reflect a country's cultural environment. For example, in India, power distance and uncertainty avoidance (see Chapter 2) are high. There, only very senior-level managers make decisions, and they are likely to make safe decisions. In contrast, in Sweden, power distance and uncertainty avoidance are low. Swedish managers are not afraid to make risky decisions. Senior managers in Sweden also push decisions down in the ranks. They encourage lower-level managers and employees to take part in decisions that affect them. In countries such as Egypt, where time pressures are low, managers make decisions at a slower and more deliberate pace than managers do in the United States. And in Italy, where history and traditions are valued, managers tend to rely on tried and proven alternatives to resolve problems.

ringisei
Japanese consensus-forming group decisions

Decision making in Japan is much more group oriented than in the United States.[36] The Japanese value conformity and cooperation. Before making decisions, Japanese CEOs collect a large amount of information, which is then used in consensus-forming group decisions called **ringisei.** Because employees in

Japanese organizations have high job security, managerial decisions take a long-term perspective rather than focus on short-term profits as is often the practice in the United States.

Senior managers in France and Germany also adapt their decision styles to their country's culture. In France, for instance, autocratic decision making is widely practiced, and managers avoid risks. Managerial styles in Germany reflect the German culture's concern for structure and order. Consequently, there are extensive rules and regulations in German organizations. Managers have well-defined responsibilities and accept that decisions must go through channels.

As managers deal with employees from diverse cultures, they need to recognize what is common and accepted behavior when asking them to make decisions. Some individuals may not be as comfortable with being closely involved in decision making as others, or they may not be willing to experiment with something radically different. Managers who accommodate the diversity in decision-making philosophies and practices can expect a high payoff if they capture the perspectives and strengths that a diverse workforce offers.[37]

PHLIP Companion Web Site

We invite you to visit the Robbins/DeCenzo companion Web site at *www.prenhall.com/robbins* for this chapter's Internet resources.

Chapter Summary

How will you know if you fulfilled the Learning Outcomes on page 113? You will have fulfilled the Learning Outcomes if you are able to:

1. *Describe the steps in the decision-making process.*
   Decision making is an eight-step process: (1) identify a problem, (2) identify decision criteria, (3) allocate weights to the criteria, (4) develop alternatives, (5) analyze alternatives, (6) select an alternative, (7) implement the alternative, and (8) evaluate decision effectiveness.
2. *Identify the assumptions of the rational decision-making model.*
   The rational decision model assumes that the decision maker can identify a clear problem, has no goal conflict, knows all options, has a clear preference ordering, keeps all preferences constant, has no time or cost constraints, and selects a final choice that maximizes his or her economic payoff.
3. *Explain the limits to rationality.*
   Rationality assumptions do not apply in many situations because problems are not simple, goals are not clear, alternatives are many, and there are time and cost constraints. In addition, decision makers sometimes increase commitment to a previous choice to confirm its original correctness; prior decision precedents constrain current choices, and most organizational cultures discourage taking risks and searching for innovative alternatives.

4 *Define certainty, risk, and uncertainty as they relate to decision making.*
Certainty implies that a manager can make an accurate decision because the outcome of every alternative is known. Because this is often not the case, risk involves assigning probabilities to outcomes that may result. When decision makers have neither full knowledge of the problem nor a reasonable probability of what may happen, they must make their decisions under a condition of uncertainty.

5 *Describe the actions of the bounded-rational decision maker.*
In the bounded-rational decision-making process, decision makers construct simplified models that extract essential features from the problems they face without capturing all their complexity. They then attempt to act rationally within this simplified model.

6 *Identify the two types of decision problems and the two types of decisions that are used to solve them.*
Managers face well- and ill-structured problems. Well-structured problems are straightforward, familiar, easily defined, and solved using programmed decisions. Ill-structured problems are new or unusual, involve ambiguous or incomplete information, and are solved using nonprogrammed decisions.

7 *Define heuristics and explain how they affect the decision-making process.*
Heuristics are shortcuts decision makers can take to speed up the decision-making process. Heuristics commonly exist in two forms—availability and representative. Both types create biases in a decision maker's judgment.

8 *Identify four decision-making styles.*
The four decision-making styles are the directive style (characterized by low tolerance for ambiguity and a rational way of thinking), the analytic style (characterized by high tolerance for ambiguity combined with a rational way of thinking), the conceptual style (characterized by a very broad outlook and a tendency to look at many alternatives), and the behavioral style (characterized by intuitive thinking and a low tolerance for uncertainty).

9 *Describe the advantages and disadvantages of group decisions.*
Groups offer certain advantages—more complete information, more alternatives, increased acceptance of a solution, and greater legitimacy. On the other hand, groups are time-consuming, can be dominated by a minority, create pressures to conform, and cloud responsibility.

10 *Explain three techniques for improving group decision making.*
Three ways of improving group decision making are brainstorming (utilizing an idea-generating process that specifically encourages any and all alternatives while withholding any criticism of those alternatives), the nominal group technique (a technique that restricts discussion during the decision-making process), and electronic meetings (the most recent approach to group decision making, which blends the nominal group technique with sophisticated computer technology).

Review and Application Questions

READING FOR COMPREHENSION

1 Explain how decision making is related to the planning process.

2 How is implementation important to the decision-making process?

3 What is a satisficing decision? How does it differ from a maximizing decision?

4 How do certainty, risk, and uncertainty affect individuals when they make a decision?

5 How does escalation of commitment affect decision making?

6 What is groupthink? What are its implications for decision making?

LINKING CONCEPTS TO PRACTICE

1 Describe a decision you have made that closely aligns with the assumptions of perfect rationality. Compare this with the process you used to select your college. Is there a departure from the rational model in your college decision? Explain.

2 Is the order in which alternatives are considered more critical under assumptions of perfect rationality or bounded rationality? Why?

3 Explain how a manager might deal with making decisions under conditions of uncertainty.

4 "With more and more managers using computers, they'll be able to make more rational decisions." Do you agree or disagree with the statement? Why?

5 Why do you think organizations have increased the use of groups for making decisions during the past 20 years? When would you recommend using groups to make decisions?

Management Workshop

Team Skill-Building Exercise

Individual Versus Group Decisions

Objective: To contrast individual and group decision making.

Time: 15 minutes.

Step 1: You have 5 minutes to read the following story and individually respond to each of the 11 statements as either true, false, or unknown. Begin.

The Story: A salesclerk had just turned off the lights in the store when a man appeared and demanded money. The owner opened a cash register. The contents of the cash register were scooped up, and the man sped away. A member of the police force was notified promptly.

STATEMENTS ABOUT THE STORY

1. A man appeared after the owner had turned off his store lights. True, false, or unknown?
2. The robber was a man. True, false, or unknown?
3. The man did not demand money. True, false, or unknown?
4. The man who opened the cash register was the owner. True, false, or unknown?
5. The store owner scooped up the contents of the cash register and ran away. True, false, or unknown?
6. Someone opened a cash register. True, false, or unknown?
7. After the man who demanded the money scooped up the contents of the cash register, he ran away. True, false, or unknown?
8. The cash register contained money, but the story does not state how much. True, false, or unknown?
9. The robber demanded money of the owner. True, false, or unknown?
10. The story concerns a series of events in which only three persons are referred to: the owner of the store, a man who demanded money, and a member of the police force. True, false, or unknown?
11. The following events in the story are true: Someone demanded money; a cash register was opened; its contents were scooped up; a man dashed out of the store. True, false, or unknown?

Step 2: After you have answered the 11 questions individually, form groups of four or five members each. The groups have 10 minutes to discuss their answers and agree on the correct answers to each of the 11 statements.

Step 3: Your instructor will give you the actual correct answers. How many correct answers did you get at the conclusion of step 1? How many did your group achieve at the conclusion of step 2? Did the group outperform the average individual? The best individual? Discuss the implications of these results.

Developing Your Skill at Conducting a Meeting

Running an Effective Meeting

ABOUT THE SKILL

As a manager, you will spend a large portion of your workday in meetings. And, undoubtedly, there will be instances when you will be responsible for running meetings. Below are some suggestions for making sure your meetings run properly.

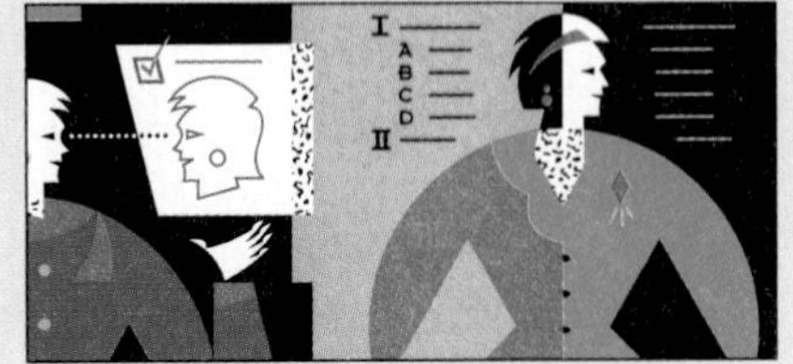

STEPS IN PRACTICING THE SKILL

- **Prepare and distribute an agenda well in advance of the meeting.** An agenda defines the meeting's purpose for participants and the boundaries between relevant and irrelevant discussion topics. Also, the agenda can serve as an important vehicle for premeeting discussions with participants.

- **Consult with participants before the meeting to ensure proper participation.** Let all participants know that their input is valuable and that you welcome their speaking up at the meeting when they have something to offer.
- **Establish specific time parameters for the meeting; specify when it will start and end.** This step helps keep the meeting on time and focused on the important matters.
- **Maintain focused discussion during the meeting.** Items not on the agenda should not be given substantial time during the meeting. If an issue is important, maybe another meeting, with its own agenda, should be held to address that issue.
- **Encourage and support participation by all members.** If you have done a good job in the second step, participants should come prepared to talk but still may need some encouragement at the meeting. Sometimes, direct questions about what they think will get them to talk.
- **Encourage the clash of ideas.** Remember, you want as much information about a topic to surface as possible. Disagreements are fine. They indicate that different voices are being heard. Better to work the differences out now than to have them surface later.
- **Discourage the clash of personalities.** Disagreements can enhance the process, but they should be substantive disputes. Differences caused by personal issues are a disaster in a meeting.
- **Bring closure by summarizing accomplishments and allocating follow-up assignments.** This step lets participants understand what occurred in the meeting and what they may have to do before the next meeting. This is, in essence, planning.

Practicing the Skill

CONDUCTING A MEETING

You manage a group of six skilled technicians in the radiology department of a large hospital. You need to meet with them all to discuss the hospital's unpopular new vacation policy and to devise your department's vacation schedule for the coming year. In keeping with the new policy, only one person will be allowed to take vacation at any given time.

Anna, the newest member of the department, is out sick but has agreed to participate in the meeting by telephone. Ravi and Helen, senior members of the department, both want to take the same week off.

Draft your agenda for the meeting and allocate specific time intervals for each topic or discussion.

A Case Application

Developing Your Diagnostic and Analytical Skills

BEATRICE INTERNATIONAL HOLDINGS

Research over the past few decades has shown us the need for understanding the sociocultural factors among people from different countries. Individuals from countries where power distance is high, for example, are frequently accustomed societies composed of "Haves" and "Have-nots." The Haves possess significant power to make decisions. Yet, when these Haves leave the comforts of their homeland, they, too, often must make some adjustments in their decision-making styles. That's precisely what Loida Nicolas Lewis did.[38]

Lewis grew up in the Philippines. She was born into a politically well-connected family that still operates the country's largest and most successful furniture company. Her early years were filled with all the privileges and amenities associated with high society: the best schools, foreign travel, and a large base of support and assistance. One thing that her upbringing did not include, however, was having decisions made for her.

Lewis has always been an independent woman, making her own choices, not those her family wanted her to make. For example, her father urged her to become a lawyer, a politician, and an instrumental member of the ruling class in the Philippines. She rejected that alternative; she wanted to dedicate her life to two goals—raising a family and helping others less fortunate than herself. She wanted to help Filipinos enter the United States so that they could escape the political repression in the Philippines. She married Reginald F. Lewis, the major owner and chairman of Beatrice International Holdings, Inc., the New York-based global supermarket and specialty foods company.

Lewis was living her dream—raising a family and helping others. Her life was uncomplicated. At least until 1993, when Reginald Lewis—who was known as the world's richest African-American man and had become a national role model—passed away. In his will, he left the job of running Beatrice to his wife. Lewis inherited a $1.7 billion company, but this company was stagnating.

Lewis did not have the business acumen or the experience of her late husband. In fact, this soft-spoken, petite woman has a persona that was directly opposite to Reginald's "macho, bruising style." Understandably anxious, she nevertheless took over the company and began molding it in her image.

She recognized that the company was losing money. Its tremendous growth through diversification in the 1980s was hurting Beatrice. Many of the status symbols her late husband had accumulated—a corporate jet, high-priced New York real estate, and the like—were now financial drains leading in part to a $17 million loss. So she made several major decisions. She pared down the company to enhance its core business operations of making ice cream in the Canary Islands and producing snack foods in Ireland. She also decided to sell off the company limousine and the corporate jet, cut headquarters staff in half, and sell off many of the less profitable ice cream companies that Beatrice held in Denmark, Germany, and Italy. She also focused on reducing Beatrice's debt in an effort to take the company public.

One would think that following a strong leader like Reginald would have posed problems for Lewis. It didn't. Although her style is very different from her husband's, she has achieved remarkable success. She involves her inner group in decisions and uses compassion to develop a "focused, disciplined, sensitive, and collegial atmosphere." And the numbers support that her approach is working. Her actions—while reducing company annual revenues to about $350 million—have led to nearly a 35 percent increase in net earnings.

QUESTIONS

1 What types of problems do you see Loida Lewis having to deal with in this case? Explain your choices.

2 What decisions did Loida Lewis make that helped turn around the ailing company? Would you classify them as programmed or nonprogrammed? Why?

3 How would you describe Lewis' decision-making style? Cite specific examples.

Developing Your Investigative Skills

Using the Internet

Visit *www.prenhall.com/robbins* for updated Internet Exercises.

Enhancing Your Writing Skills

Communicating Effectively

1 "People often make decisions that are good enough, which may not be the best solution." Build a case that presents both sides of this argument. In your discussion, emphasize when "good enough" may be appropriate and when the "best solution" may be critical. Provide specific examples in your paper.

2 Describe a situation in which a decision you made was influenced by availability or representative heuristics. In retrospect, provide an evaluation of how effective that decision was. Given your evaluation, are you more or less inclined to use judgmental shortcuts in your decision-making process? Explain.

3 Do you believe that a company has the "ethical" right to move its plant and operations from one location to another even though the former location was profitable and its employees produced quality products? Defend your position. In your discussion address the social responsibility implications of such an organizational decision.

Quantitative Decision-Making Aids

In this module, we'll look at several decision-making aids and techniques. Specifically we'll introduce you to payoff matrices, decision trees, break-even analysis, ratio analysis, linear programming, queuing theory, and economic order quantity. The purpose of each of these methods is to provide managers with a tool to assist in the decision-making process and to provide more complete information to make better-informed decisions.

Payoff Matrices

In Chapter 4, we introduced you to the topic of uncertainty and how it can affect decision making. Although uncertainty plays a critical role by limiting the amount of information available to managers, another factor is their psychological orientation. For instance, the optimistic manager will typically follow a *maximax* choice (maximizing the maximum possible payoff); the pessimist will often pursue a *maximin* choice (maximizing the minimum possible payoff), and the manager who desires to minimize his "regret" will opt for a *minimax* choice. Let's briefly look at these different approaches using an example.

Consider the case of a marketing manager at Discover International in New York. He has determined four possible strategies (we'll label these S1, S2, S3, and S4) for promoting the Discover card throughout the northeastern United States. However, he is also aware that one of his major competitors, Visa, has three competitive strategies (CA1, CA2, and CA3) of its own for promoting its own card in the same region. In this case, we'll assume that the Discover executive has no previous knowledge that would allow him to place probabilities on the success of any of his four strategies. With these facts, the Discover card manager formulates the matrix in Exhibit QM-1 to show the various Discover strategies and the resulting profit to Discover depending on the competitive action chosen by Visa.

Exhibit QM-1
Payoff Matrix for Discover

Discover Marketing Strategy	Visa's Response (in millions of $)		
	CA1	CA2	CA3
S1	13	14	11
S2	9	15	18
S3	24	21	15
S4	18	14	28

In this example, if our Discover manager is an optimist, he'll choose S4 because that could produce the largest possible gain: ($28 million). Note that this choice maximizes the maximum possible gain (maximax choice). If our manager is a pessimist, he'll assume only the worst can occur. The worst outcome for each strategy is as follows: S1 = $11 million; S2 = $9 million; S3 = $15 million; and S4 = $14 million. These are the most pessimistic outcomes from each strategy. Following the maximin choice, the manager would maximize the minimum payoff—in other words, he'd select S3.

In the third approach, managers recognize that once a decision is made it will not necessarily result in the most profitable payoff. There may be a "regret" of profits foregone (given up)—regret referring to the amount of money that could have been made had a different strategy been used. Managers calculate regret by subtracting all possible payoffs in each category from the maximum possible payoff for each given—in this case, for each competitive action. For our Discover manager, the highest payoff, given that Visa engages in CA1, CA2, or CA3 is $24 million, $21 million, or $28 million respectively (the highest number in each column). Subtracting the payoffs in Exhibit QM-1 from these figures produces the results in Exhibit QM-2.

The maximum regrets are S1 = $17 million; S2 = $15 million; S3 = $13 million; and S4 = $7 million. The minimax choice minimizes the maximum regret, so our Discover manager would choose S4. By making this choice, he'll never have a regret of profits foregone of more than $7 million. This result contrasts, for example, with a regret of $15 million had he chosen S2 and Visa had taken CA1.

Decision Trees

decision trees
Useful quantitative tool to analyze decisions that involve a progression of decisions

Decision trees are a useful way to analyze hiring, marketing, investment, equipment purchases, pricing, and similar decisions that involve a progression of decisions. They're called decision trees because, when diagramed, they look a lot like a tree with branches. Typical decision trees encompass expected value analysis by assigning probabilities to each possible outcome and calculating payoffs for each decision path.

Exhibit QM-2
Regret Matrix for Discover

Discover Marketing Strategy	Visa's Response (in millions of $)		
	CA1	CA2	CA3
S1	11	7	17
S2	15	6	10
S3	0	0	13
S4	6	7	0

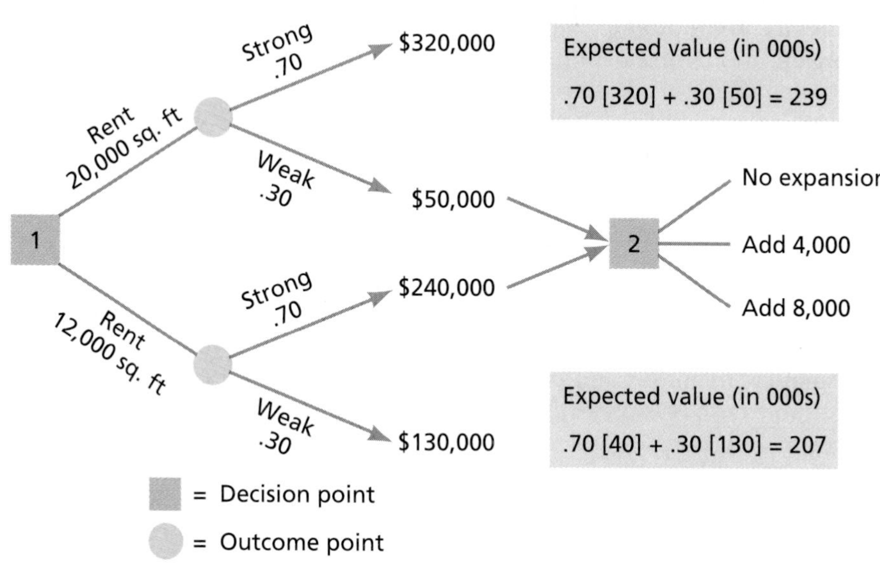

Exhibit QM-3
Decision Tree and Expected Values for Renting a Large or Small Retail Space

Exhibit QM-3 illustrates a decision facing Mike Rosenthal, the Midwestern region site-selection supervisor for Barnes & Noble bookstore. Mike supervises a small group of specialists who analyze potential locations and make store site recommendations to the Midwestern region's director. The lease on the company's store in Cleveland, Ohio, is expiring, and the landlord has decided not to renew it. Mike and his group have to make a relocation recommendation to the regional director.

Mike's group has identified an excellent site in a nearby shopping mall in North Olmsted. The mall owner has offered him two comparable locations: one with 12,000 square feet (the same as he has now) and the other a larger, 20,000 square-foot space. Mike has an initial decision to make about whether to recommend renting the larger or smaller location. If he chooses the larger space and the economy is strong, he estimates the store will make a $325,000 profit. However, if the economy is poor, the high operating costs of the larger store will mean that the profit will be only $50,000. With the smaller store, he estimates the profit at $240,000 with a good economy and $130,000 with a poor one.

As you can see from Exhibit QM-3, the expected value for the larger store is $239,000 [(.70 × 320) × (.30 × 50)]. The expected value for the smaller store is $207,000 [(.70 × 240) × (.30 × 130)]. Given these projections, Mike is planning to recommend the rental of the larger store space. What if Mike wants to consider the implications of initially renting the smaller space and then expanding if the economy picks up? He can extend the decision tree to include this second decision point. He has calculated three options: no expansion, adding 4,000 square feet, and adding 8,000 square feet. Following the approach used for Decision Point 1, he could calculate the profit potential by extending the branches on the tree and calculating expected values for the various options.

Break-Even Analysis

How many units of a product must an organization sell in order to break even—that is, to have neither profit nor loss? A manager might want to know the minimum number of units that must be sold to achieve his or her profit objective or

break-even analysis
A technique for identifying the point at which total revenue is just sufficient to cover total costs

whether a current product should continue to be sold or should be dropped from the organization's product line. **Break-even analysis** is a widely used technique for helping managers make profit projections.[1]

Break-even analysis is a simplistic formulation, yet it is valuable to managers because it points out the relationship among revenues, costs, and profits. To compute the break-even point (*BE*), the manager needs to know the unit price of the product being sold (*P*), the variable cost per unit (*VC*), and the total fixed costs (*TFC*).

An organization breaks even when its total revenue is just enough to equal its total costs. But total cost has two parts: a fixed component and a variable component. Fixed costs are expenses that do not change, regardless of volume, such as insurance premiums and property taxes. Fixed costs, of course, are fixed only in the short term because, in the long run, commitments terminate and are thus subject to variation. Variable costs change in proportion to output and include raw materials, labor costs, and energy costs.

The break-even point can be computed graphically or by using the following formula:

$$BE = \left[\frac{TFC}{P - VC}\right]$$

This formula tells us that (1) total revenue will equal total cost when we sell enough units at a price that covers all variable unit costs, and (2) the difference between price and variable costs, when multiplied by the number of units sold, equals the fixed costs.

When is break-even useful? To demonstrate, assume that, at Todd's Atlanta Espresso, Todd charges $1.75 for an average cup of coffee. If his fixed costs (salary, insurance, etc.) are $47,000 a year and the variable costs for each cup of espresso are $0.40, Todd can compute his break-even point as follows: $47,000/(1.75 – 0.40) = 34,815 (about 670 cups of espresso sold each week), or when annual revenues are approximately $60,926. This same relationship is shown graphically in Exhibit QM-4.

How can break-even serve as a planning and decision-making tool? As a planning tool, break-even analysis could help Todd set his sales objective. For example, he could establish the profit he wants and then work backward to determine what sales level is needed to reach that profit. As a decision-making tool, break-analysis could also tell Todd how much volume has to increase in order to break even if he is currently operating at a loss or how much volume he can afford to lose and still break even if he is currently operating profitably. In some cases, such as the management of professional sports franchises, break-even analysis has shown the projected volume of ticket sales required to cover all costs to be so unrealistically high that management's best choice is to sell or close the business.

Ratio Analysis

We know that investors and stock analysts make regular use of an organization's financial documents to assess its worth. These documents can be analyzed by managers as planning and decision-making aids.

Managers often want to examine their organization's balance and income statements to analyze key ratios: that is, to compare two significant figures from the financial statements and express them as a percentage or ratio. This practice

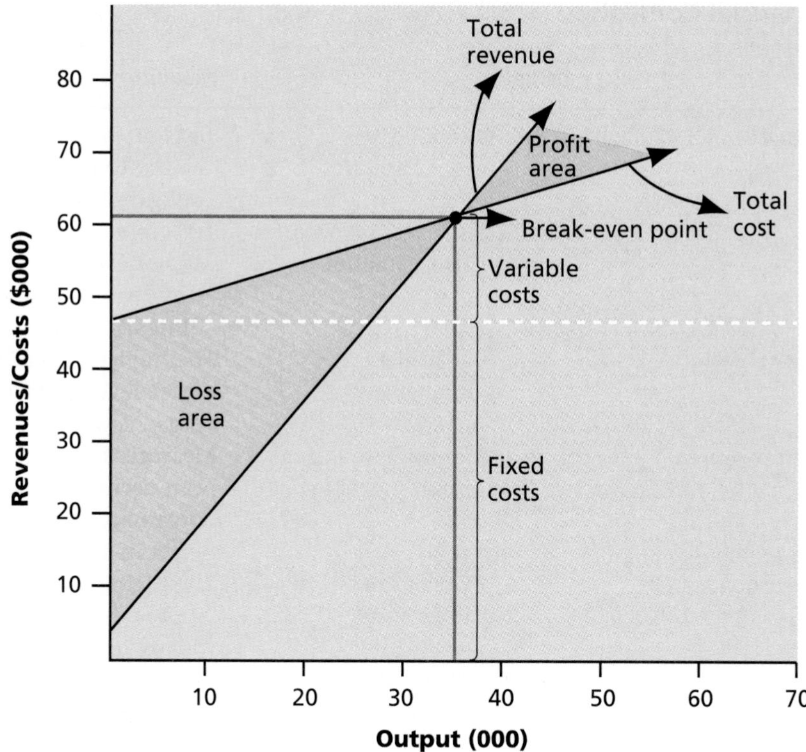

Exhibit QM-4
The Break-Even Analysis

allows managers to compare current financial performance with that of previous periods and other organizations in the same industry. Some of the more useful ratios evaluate liquidity, leverage, operations, and profitability. These are summarized in Exhibit QM-5.

What are liquidity ratios? Liquidity is a measure of the organization's ability to convert assets into cash in order that debts can be met. The most popular liquidity ratios are the current ratio and the acid test ratio.

The current ratio is defined as the organization's current assets divided by its current liabilities. Although there is no magic number that is considered safe, the accountant's rule of thumb for the current ratio is 2:1. A significantly higher ratio usually suggests that management is not getting the best return on its assets. A ratio at or below 1:1 indicates potential difficulty in meeting short-term obligations (accounts payable, interest payments, salaries, taxes, and so forth).

The acid-test ratio is the same as the current ratio except that current assets are reduced by the dollar value of inventory held. When inventories turn slowly or are difficult to sell, the acid test ratio may more accurately represent the organization's true liquidity. That is, a high current ratio that is heavily based on an inventory that is difficult to sell overstates the organization's true liquidity. Accordingly, accountants typically consider an acid test ratio of 1:1 to be reasonable.

Leverage ratios refer to the use of borrowed funds to operate and expand an organization. The advantage of leverage occurs when funds can be used to earn a rate of return well above the cost of those funds. For instance, if management can borrow money at 6 percent and can earn 10 percent on it internally, it makes good sense to borrow, but there are risks to over-leveraging. The interest on the debt can be a drain on the organization's cash resources and can, in extreme cases,

Exhibit QM-5 Popular Financial Controls

Objective	Ratio	Calculation	Meaning
Liquidity test	Current ratio	$\frac{\text{Current assets}}{\text{Current liabilities}}$	Tests the organization's ability to meet short-term obligations
	Acid test	$\frac{\text{Current assets less inventories}}{\text{Current liabilities}}$	Tests liquidity more accurately when inventories turn over slowly or are difficult to sell
Leverage test	Debt-to-assets	$\frac{\text{Total debt}}{\text{Total assets}}$	The higher the ratio, the more leveraged the organization
	Times-interest-earned	$\frac{\text{Profits before interest and taxes}}{\text{Total interest charges}}$	Measures how far profits can decline before the organization is unable to meet its interest expenses
Operations test	Inventory turnover	$\frac{\text{Cost of sales}}{\text{Inventory}}$	The higher the ratio, the more efficiently inventory assets are being used
	Total asset turnover	$\frac{\text{Revenues}}{\text{Total assets}}$	The fewer assets used to achieve a given level of sales, the more efficiently management is using the organization's total assets
Profitability	Profit margin-on-revenues	$\frac{\text{Net profit after taxes}}{\text{Total revenues}}$	Identifies the profits that various products are generating
	Return-on-investment	$\frac{\text{Net profit after taxes}}{\text{Total assets}}$	Measures the efficiency of assets to generate profits

drive an organization into bankruptcy. The objective, therefore, is to use debt wisely. Leverage ratios such as debt-to-assets ratio (computed by dividing total debt by total assets) or the times-interest-earned ratio (computed as profits before interest and taxes divided by total interest charges) can help managers control debt levels.

Operating ratios describe how efficiently management is using the organization's resources. The most popular operating ratios are inventory turnover and total assets turnover.

The inventory turnover ratio is defined as revenue divided by inventory. The higher the ratio, the more efficiently inventory assets are being used. Revenue divided by total assets represents an organization's total assets turnover ratio. It measures the level of assets needed to generate the organization's revenue. The fewer assets used to achieve a given level of revenue, the more efficiently management is using the organization's total assets.

Profit-making organizations want to measure their effectiveness and efficiency. Profitability ratios serve such a purpose. The better known of these are profit-margin-on-revenues and return-on-investment ratios.

Managers of organizations that have a variety of products want to put their efforts into those products that are most profitable. The profit-margin-on-revenues ratio, computed as net profit after taxes divided by total revenues, is a measure of profits per dollar revenues.

One of the most widely used measures of a business firm's profitability is the return-on-investment ratio. It's calculated by multiplying revenues/investments times profits/revenues. This percentage recognizes that absolute profits must be placed in the context of assets required to generate those profits.

Linear Programming

Natalie Lopez owns a software development company. One product line involves designing and producing software that detects and removes viruses. The software comes in two formats: DOS and MAC versions. She can sell all of these products she can produce. That, however, is her dilemma. The two formats go through the same production departments. How many of each type should she make to maximize her profits?

A close look at Lopez's operation tells us she can use a mathematical technique called linear programming to solve her resource allocation dilemma. As we will show, **linear programming** is applicable to her problem, but it cannot be applied to all resource allocation situations. Besides requiring limited resources and the objective of optimization, it requires that there be alternative ways of combining resources to produce a number of output mixes. There must also be a linear relationship between variables.[2] This means that a change in one variable will be accompanied by an exactly proportional change in the other. For Lopez's business, this condition would be met if it took exactly twice the time to produce two diskettes—irrespective of format—as it took to produce one.

linear programming A mathematical technique that solves resource allocation problems

Many different types of problems can be solved with linear programming. Selecting transportation routes that minimize shipping costs, allocating a limited advertising budget among various product brands, making the optimum assignment of personnel among projects, and determining how much of each product to make with a limited number of resources are just a few. To give you some idea of how linear programming is useful, let's return to Lopez's problem. Fortunately, Natalie's problem is relatively simple, so we can solve it rather quickly. For complex linear programming problems, computer software has been designed specifically to help develop solutions.

First, we need to establish some facts about Lopez's business. She has computed the profit margins to be \$18 for the DOS format and \$24 for the MAC. She can therefore express her objective function as: maximum profit = \$18 R + \$24 S, where R is the number of DOS diskettes produced and S is the number of MAC diskettes. In addition, she knows how long it takes to produce each format and the monthly production capacity for virus software [2,400 hours in design and 900 hours in production] (see Exhibit QM-6). The production capacity numbers act as constraints on her overall capacity. Now Lopez can establish her constraint equations:

$$4R + 6S \leq 2{,}400$$

$$2R + 2S \leq 900$$

Of course, because a software format cannot be produced in a volume less than zero, Lopez can also state that $R \geq 0$ and $S \geq 0$. She has graphed her solution as shown in Exhibit QM-7. The yellow shaded area represents the options that do

Exhibit QM-6
Production Data for Virus Software

Department	Number of Hours Required per Unit		Monthly Production Capacity (Hours)
	DOS Version	MAC Version	
Design	4	6	2,400
Manufacture	2.0	2.0	900
Profit per unit	$18	$24	

Exhibit QM-7
Graphical Solution to Lopez's Linear Programming Problem

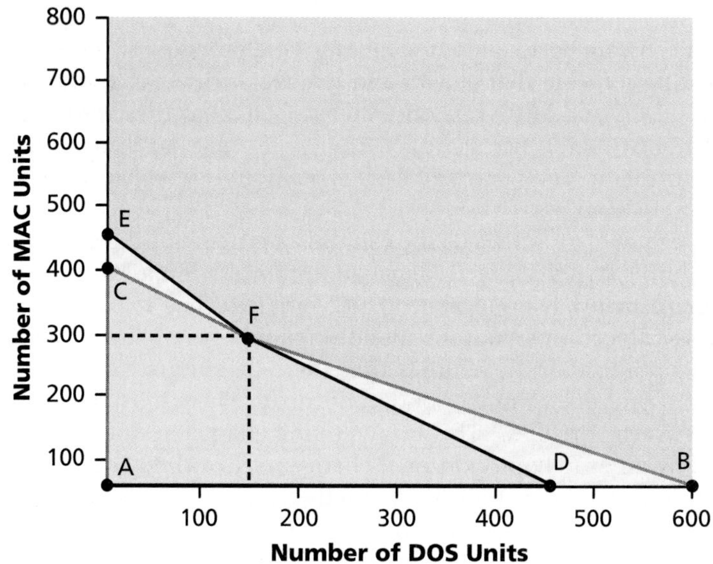

not exceed the capacity of either department. What does this mean? We know that total design capacity is 2,400 hours. So if Natalie decides to design only DOS format, the maximum number she can produce is 600 (2,400 hours ÷ 4 hours of design for each DOS). If she decides to produce all MAC versions, the maximum she can produce is 400 (2,400 hours ÷ 6 hours of design for MAC). This design constraint is shown in Exhibit QM-7 as line *BC*. The other constraint Natalie faces is that of production. The maximum of either format she can produce is 450, because each takes 2 hours to copy, verify, and package. This production constraint is shown in the exhibit as line *DE*. Natalie's optimal resource allocation will be defined at one of the corners of this feasibility region (area ACFD). Point F provides the maximum profits within the constraints stated. At point A, profits would be zero because neither virus software version is being produced. At points C and D, profits would be $9,600 (400 units @ $24) and $8,100 (450 units @ $18), respectively. At point F profits would be $9,900 (150 DOS units @ $18 + 300 MAC units @ $24).[3]

Queuing Theory

You are a supervisor for a branch of NationsBank outside of Boston. One of the decisions you have to make is how many of the nine cashier stations to keep open at any given time. **Queuing theory,** or what is frequently referred to as waiting-line theory, could help you decide.

queuing theory
A technique that balances the cost of having a waiting line against the cost of service to maintain that line

A decision that involves balancing the cost of having a waiting line against the cost of service to maintain that line can be made easier with queuing theory. This includes such common situations as determining how many gas pumps are needed at gas stations, tellers at bank windows, toll takers at toll booths, or check-in lines at airline ticket counters. In each situation, management wants to minimize cost by having as few stations open as possible yet not so few as to test the patience of customers. In our teller example, on certain days (such as the first of every month and Fridays) you could open all nine windows and keep waiting time to a minimum, or you could open only one, minimize staffing costs, and risk a riot.

The mathematics underlying queuing theory is beyond the scope of this book, but you can see how the theory works in our simple example. You have nine tellers working for you, but you want to know whether you can get by with only one window open during an average morning. You consider twelve minutes to be the longest you would expect any customer to wait patiently in line. If it takes four minutes, on average, to serve each customer, the line should not be permitted to get longer than three deep (12 minutes ÷ 4 minutes per customer = 3 customers). If you know from past experience that, during the morning, people arrive at the average rate of two per minute, you can calculate the probability (P) that the line will become longer than any number (n) of customers as follows:

$$P_n = \left[\frac{\text{Arrival Rate}}{1 - \text{Service Rate}}\right] \times \left[\frac{\text{Arrival Rate}}{\text{Service Rate}}\right]^n$$

where n = 3 customers, arrival rate = 2 per minute, and service rate = 4 minutes per customer. Putting these numbers into the above formula generates the following:

$$P_n = \left[1 - 2/4\right] \times \left[2/4\right]^3 = (1/2) \times (8/64) = (8/128) = 0.0625$$

What does a P of 0.0625 mean? It tells you that the likelihood of having more than three customers in line during the average morning is 1 chance in 16. Are you willing to live with four or more customers in line six percent of the time? If so, keeping one teller window open will be enough. If not, you will have to assign more tellers to staff them.

Economic Order Quantity Model

One of the best-known techniques for mathematically deriving the optimum quantity for a purchase order is the **economic order quantity** (EOQ) model (see Exhibit QM-8). The EOQ model seeks to balance four costs involved in ordering and carrying inventory: the purchase costs (purchase price plus delivery charges less discounts); the ordering costs (paperwork, follow-up, inspection when the item arrives, and other processing costs); carrying costs (money tied up in inventory, storage, insurance, taxes, and so forth); and stockout costs (profits foregone from orders lost, the cost of reestablishing goodwill, and additional expenses incurred to expedite late shipments). When these four costs are known, the model identifies the optimal order size for each purchase.

economic order quantity
A technique for balancing purchase, ordering, carrying, and stockout costs to derive the optimum quantity for a purchase order

The objective of the economic order quantity (EOQ) model is to minimize the total costs associated with the carrying and ordering costs. As the amount ordered gets larger, average inventory increases and so do carrying costs. For example, if

Exhibit QM-8
Determining the Most Economic Order Quantity

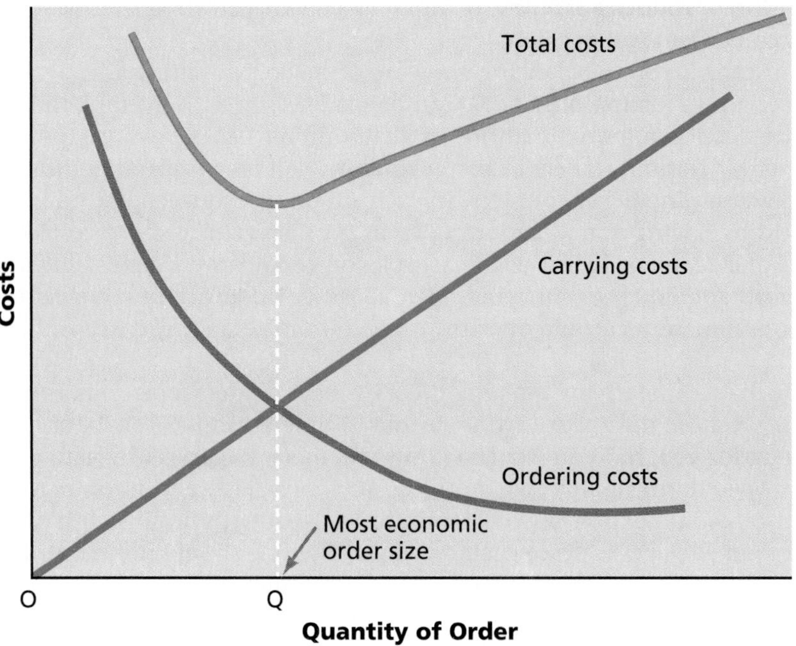

annual demand for an inventory item is 26,000 units, and a firm orders 500 each time, the firm will place 52 (26,000/500) orders per year. This gives the organization an average inventory of 250 (500/2) units. If the order quantity is increased to 2,000 units, there will be fewer orders (13 [26,000/2,000]) placed. However, average inventory on hand will increase to 1,000 (2,000/2) units. Thus, as holding costs go up, ordering costs go down, and vice versa. The most economic order quantity is reached at the lowest point on the total cost curve. That's the point at which ordering costs equal carrying costs—or the economic order quantity (see point Q in Exhibit QM-8).

To compute this optimal order quantity, you need the following data: forecasted demand for the item during the period (*D*); the cost of placing each order (*OC*); the value or purchase price of the item (*V*); and the carrying cost (expressed as a percentage) of maintaining the total inventory (*CC*). Given these data, the formula for *EOQ* is as follows:

$$EOQ = \sqrt{\frac{2 \times D \times OC}{V \times CC}}$$

Let's work an example of determining the *EOQ*. Take, for example, Barnes Electronics, a retailer of high-quality sound and video equipment. The owner, Sam Barnes, wishes to determine the company's economic order quantities of high-quality sound and video equipment. The item in question is a Sony compact radio cassette recorder. Barnes forecasts sales of 4,000 units a year. He believes that the cost for the sound system should be $50. Estimated costs of placing an order for these systems are $35 per order and annual insurance, taxes, and other carrying costs at 20 percent of the recorder's value. Using the *EOQ* formula, and the preceding information, he can calculate the *EOQ* as follows:

$$EOQ = \sqrt{\frac{2 \times 4{,}000 \times 35}{50 \times .02}}$$

$$EOQ = \sqrt{28{,}000}$$

$$EOQ = 167.33 \text{ or } 168 \text{ units}$$

The inventory model suggests that it's most economic to order in quantities or lots of approximately 168 recorders. Stated differently, Barnes should order about 24 (4,000/168) times a year. However, what would happen if the supplier offers Barnes a 5 percent discount on purchases if he buys in minimum quantities of 250 units? Should he now purchase in quantities of 168 or 250? Without the discount, and ordering 168 each time, the annual costs for these recorders would be as follows:

Purchase cost:	\$50 × \$4,000	= \$200,000
Carrying cost (average number of inventory units times value of item times percentage	168/2 × \$50 × 0.02	= 840
Ordering costs (number of orders times cost to place order)	24 × \$35	= 840
Total Cost:		= \$201,680

With the 5 percent discount for ordering 250 units, the item cost (\$50 × [\$50 × 0.05]) would be \$47.5. The annual inventory costs would be as follows:

Purchase cost:	\$47.50 × 4,000	= \$190,000.00
Carrying cost:	250/2 × \$47.5 × 0.02	= 1,187.50
Ordering cost:	16 (4,000/250) × \$35	= 560.00
Total cost:		= \$191,747.50

These calculations suggest to Barnes that he should take advantage of the 5 percent discount. Even though he now has to stock larger quantities, the annual savings amounts to nearly \$10,000. A word of caution, however, needs to be added. The EOQ model assumes that demand and lead times are known and constant. If these conditions can't be met, the model shouldn't be used. For example, it generally shouldn't be used for manufactured component inventory because the components are taken out of stock all at once, in lumps, or odd lots rather than at a constant rate. Does this mean that the EOQ model is useless when demand is variable? No. The model can still be of some use in demonstrating trade-offs in costs and the need to control lot sizes. However, there are more sophisticated lot-sizing models for handling demand and special situations. The mathematics for EOQ, like the mathematics for queuing theory, go far beyond the scope of this text.

Five

Basic Organization Designs

LEARNING OUTCOMES After reading this chapter, I will be able to:

1. Identify and define the six elements of organization structure.
2. Describe the advantages and disadvantages of work specialization.
3. Contrast authority and power.
4. Identify the five different ways by which management can departmentalize.
5. Contrast mechanistic and organic organizations.
6. Summarize the effect on organization structures of strategy, size, technology, and environment.
7. Contrast the divisional and functional structures.
8. Explain the strengths of the matrix structure.
9. Describe the boundaryless organization and what elements have contributed to its development.
10. Describe what is meant by the term *organization culture.*

Not more than a decade or two ago, managers in both small and large organizations typically sought to pattern their organizational structures after such companies as General Motors and IBM. They strove to create hierarchical organizations with mass-production capabilities and efficiencies, standardized rules and regulations, and centralized control. One such industry that promoted this traditional mindset was the accounting profession. Walk into nearly any accounting firm, and you could almost predict what you'd see. As you enter through the pristine chrome-and-glass 12-foot-high doors, you're met by a perfectly coiffed receptionist seated behind a wood-grained circular workstation. As you sit in the leather waiting room chairs, you glance at the rows of bookcases holding the latest Internal Revenue Code books and a whole host of other reference materials. Soon your accountants buzz the receptionist that they are ready to see you, and you're ushered down a long corridor past many offices, around cubicles, and into the conference room where you're met by three individuals, all dressed in dark blue pinstripe suits, standing around their 24-foot solid mahogany conference table in the well-decorated conference room that resembles an art gallery. This is what clients used to see when they visited Lipschultz, Levin and Gray (LLG), a Northbrook, Illinois, CPA firm. The key words here are *used to see.*[1]

For decades, LLG was the prototypical accounting firm. Most of their accountants worked in windowless offices or in 8-by-8 cubicles, dressed meticulously, and did everything by the book—especially following the hierarchy when communicating information. As the firm grew, more and more management layers were added until this 55-member firm had completely outgrown its 17,000-square-foot office, and more importantly, began to lose business. The "bean counters," as LLG prefers to be called, needed to make some drastic changes, but it wasn't until one partner, Steve Siegel, blurted out in a partner meeting to Harold Lipschultz that it was time for Lipschultz to retire that things began to change. Lipschultz, one of the founding partners, recognized that Siegel was right. The world of accounting was changing rapidly. Performing accounting, auditing, and tax services was no longer enough to keep the firm afloat. Moreover, significant turnover and subsequent recruiting difficulties helped Lipschultz make the decision to leave the firm and turn the managing responsibilities over to Siegel. It would be up to Siegel to work his magic, and he immediately embarked on organizational changes that surprised everyone.

One of the first things Siegel did was to cut the staff nearly in half. He then proceeded to eliminate private offices and cubicles—tearing down walls whenever possible. He took away desks and regular seating locations. In their place, he gave every employee a rolling tote cart, a phone, a laptop computer, and some hanging file folders. He thought this change could create a team of workers who could be crossed-trained and offer better client service. Siegel also believed that he could build trust among the firm's employees—trust that had been eroding over the past decade. He changed the dress code from business dress to business casual in an effort to make the work environment more enjoyable. And in the open space provided by tearing down walls and reducing staff, he installed a miniature golf course—radical structural changes in any organization but changes that have proved quite beneficial to LLG.

Has Siegel's experiment been a success? Since he took over as managing partner and made his draconian changes, the bean counters have witnessed considerable growth. Their referrals have more than doubled, and income has more than tripled in the past 10 years. The firm is now located in an office space that is 60 percent smaller than what they had just several years ago, at a significant cost savings to the firm. Equally important, LLG has had remarkable success in recruiting new accountants. Once perceived as taking other firms' "dregs," the firm now employs individuals who are recognized as being the top of their class and come from Scotland, England, South Africa, Russia, and France as well as the United States. Many stay with LLG because of the creativity the work environment offers. As a result, employee longevity has more than doubled, going from 4.75 years to over 10.

Siegel's actions may not work for every accounting firm or for other organizations. Yet in LLG's case, they have worked well. The employees are now accustomed to having an open workspace, working as team members, and carrying their office around with them. The creativity that the work environment inspires has enabled the firm to add such services to their traditional accounting work as business consulting services and e-commerce assistance. But the biggest winners here are the clients, for Siegel has created an organizational structure that provides better client opportunities and services.

The LLG example demonstrates the importance of the right structure and work environment. In this chapter, we present the foundations of organization structure. We define the concept and its key components, introduce organization design options, consider contingency variables that determine when certain design options work better than others, and explore the concept of organization culture.

Once certain organizational members have made decisions regarding corporate strategies, they must develop the structure that will best facilitate the attainment of those goals. Recall from Chapter 1 that we defined organizing as the function of management that creates the organization's structure. When managers develop or change the organization's structure, they are engaging in **organization design.** This process involves making decisions about how specialized jobs should be allocated, the rules to guide employees' behaviors, and at what level decisions are to be made. Organization design decisions are typically made by senior managers. Occasionally, perhaps, they might seek input from mid-level managers, but lower-level managers and operatives rarely have an opportunity to provide input. Nonetheless, it still is important to understand the process. Why? Because each of us works in some type of organization structure, and we need to know why we are grouped as we are. In addition, given the changing environment and the need for organizations to rapidly adapt, we should begin our understanding of what tomorrow's structures may look like.

organization design
A process in which managers develop or change their organization's structure

As you read this chapter, recognize that the organization design material presented applies to any type of organization, whether it's a business enterprise interested in making profits for its owners or a not-for-profit organization that provides service to specialized customers (such as your college) or to the community at large (such as the U.S. Postal Service or your local sanitation department).

The Elements of Structure

The basic concepts of organization design were formulated by management writers in the early 1900s who offered a set of principles for managers to follow in organization design. More than six decades have passed since most of those principles were originally proposed. Given the passing of that much time and all the changes that have taken place in our society, you might think that they would be pretty worthless today. Surprisingly, they're not. For the most part, these principles still provide valuable insights into designing effective and efficient organizations. Of course, we have also gained a great deal of knowledge over the years as to their limitations. In the following sections, we discuss the six elements of structure: work specialization, chain of command, span of control, authority and responsibility, centralization versus decentralization, and departmentalization.

WHAT IS WORK SPECIALIZATION?

Work specialization has been around for centuries in industrialized countries. In fact, back in the 1700s when economist Adam Smith published *Wealth of Nations,* he advocated that jobs should be divided into smaller parts. In **work specialization,** a job is broken down into a number of steps, and each step is completed by a separate individual. In essence, individuals specialize in doing part of an activity rather than the entire activity. Installing only the mother boards and hard-disk drives in a computer assembly line is an example of work specialization.

work specialization
A component of organization structure that involves having each discrete step of a job done by a different individual rather than having one individual do the whole job

Taco Bell employees making tacos and burritos reflect what is commonly referred to by management writers as *work specialization.* This means that each employee has a set of specific steps to do before the "task" is passed on to another person.

So, too, are the specific tasks crew members perform each time they make beef burritos deluxe at Taco Bell.

Work specialization makes efficient use of the diversity of skills that workers hold. In most organizations, some tasks require highly developed skills; others can be performed by the those who have lower skill levels. If all workers were engaged in all the steps of, say, a manufacturing process, all would have to have the skills necessary to perform both the most demanding and the least demanding jobs. Thus, except when performing the most highly skilled or highly sophisticated tasks, employees would be working below their skill level. In addition, skilled workers are paid more than unskilled workers, and, because wages tend to reflect the highest level of skill, all workers would be paid at highly skilled rates to do easy tasks—an inefficient use of resources. That is why you rarely find a cardiac surgeon closing up a patient after surgery. Doctors doing their residency in open-heart surgery and learning the skill usually stitch and staple the patient after the surgeon has performed bypass surgery.

Early proponents of work specialization believed that it could lead to infinitely increasing productivity. At the turn of the twentieth century and earlier, that generalization was reasonable. Because specialization was not widely practiced, its introduction almost always generated higher productivity, but a good thing can be carried too far. There is a point at which the human diseconomies from division of labor that surface as boredom, fatigue, stress, low productivity, poor quality, increased absenteeism, and high turnover exceed the economic advantages (see Exhibit 5-1).

By the 1960s, that point had been reached in a number of jobs. In such cases, productivity could be increased by enlarging, rather than narrowing, the scope of job activities.[2] For instance, successful efforts to increase productivity included giving employees a variety of activities to do, allowing them to do a complete piece of work, and putting them together into teams. Each of those ideas, of course, runs counter to the work-specialization concept. Yet, overall, work specialization is alive and well in most organizations today. We have to recognize the economies it provides in certain types of jobs, but we also have to recognize its limitations.

WHAT IS THE CHAIN OF COMMAND?

chain of command
The management principle that no person should report to more than one boss

The early management writers argued that an employee should have one and only one superior to whom he or she is directly responsible. An employee who has to report to two or more bosses might have to cope with conflicting demands or priorities.[3] In those rare instances when the **chain of command** principle had to be violated, early management writers always explicitly designated a clear separation of activities and a supervisor responsible for each.

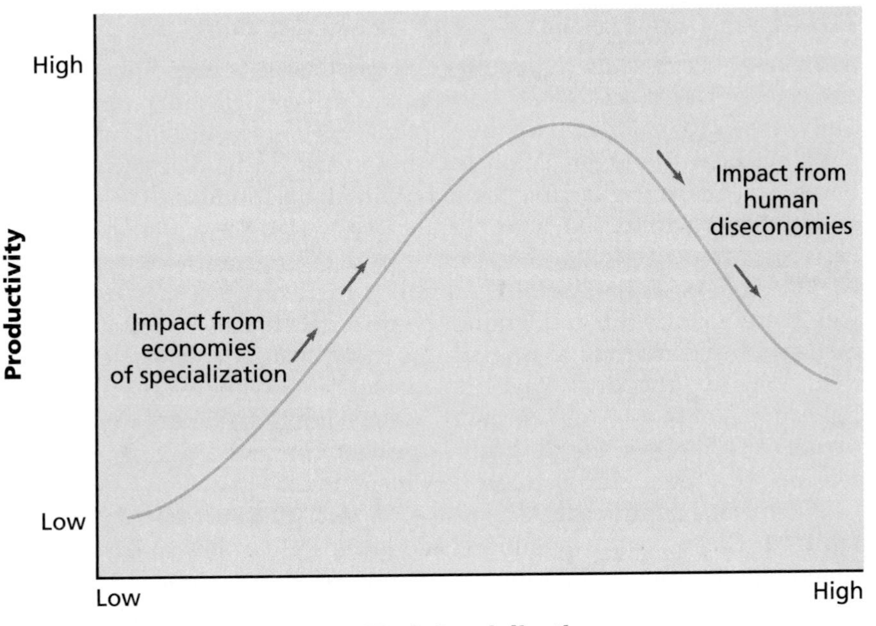

Exhibit 5-1
Economies and Diseconomies of Work Specialization

The chain of command concept was logical when organizations were comparatively simple. Under many circumstances, it is still sound advice; many contemporary organizations continue to adhere to it. Yet there are instances, which we introduce later in this chapter, when strict adherence to the chain of command creates a degree of inflexibility that hinders an organization's performance.[4]

WHAT IS THE SPAN OF CONTROL?

How many employees can a manager efficiently and effectively direct? This question of **span of control** received a great deal of attention from early management writers. Although there was no consensus on a specific number, the early writers favored small spans—typically no more than six workers—in order to maintain close control.[5] However, several writers did acknowledge level in the organization as a contingency variable. They argued that as a manager rises in an organization, he or she has to deal with a greater number of ill-structured problems, so top managers need a smaller span than do middle managers, and middle managers require a smaller span than do supervisors. Over the last decade, however, we are seeing some change in theories about effective spans of control.

span of control
The number of subordinates a manager can direct efficiently and effectively

Many organizations are increasing their spans of control. The span for managers at such companies as General Electric and Reynolds Metals has expanded to 10 or 12 employees—twice the number of 15 years ago.[6] The span of control is increasingly being determined by looking at contingency variables.[7] It is obvious that the more training and experience employees have, the less direct supervision they need. Managers who have well-trained and experienced employees can function with a wider span. Other contingency variables that will determine the appropriate span include similarity of employee tasks, the complexity of those tasks, the physical proximity of employees, the degree to which standardized procedures are in place, the sophistication of the organization's management information system, the strength of the organization's value system, and the preferred managing style of the manager.[8]

WHAT ARE AUTHORITY AND RESPONSIBILITY?

authority
The rights inherent in a managerial position to give orders and expect them to be obeyed

Authority refers to the rights inherent in a managerial position to give orders and expect the orders to be obeyed (see Ethical Dilemma in Management). Authority was a major tenet of the early management writers; it was viewed as the glue that held the organization together. It was to be delegated downward to lower-level managers, giving them certain rights while providing certain prescribed limits within which to operate (see Details on a Management Classic). Each management position has specific inherent rights that incumbents acquire from the position's rank or title. Authority, therefore, is related to one's position within an organization and ignores the personal characteristics of the individual manager. It has nothing to do with the individual. The expression "The king is dead; long live the king" illustrates the concept. Whoever is king acquires the rights inherent in the king's position. When a position of authority is vacated, the person who has left the position no longer has any authority. The authority remains with the position and its new incumbent.

responsibility
An obligation to perform assigned activities

When managers delegate authority, they must allocate commensurate **responsibility.** That is, when employees are given rights, they also assume a corresponding obligation to perform. Allocating authority without responsibility creates opportunities for abuse, and no one should be held responsible for something over which he or she has no authority.

line authority
The authority that entitles a manager to direct the work of an employee

Are there different types of authority relationships? The early management writers distinguished between two forms of authority: line authority and staff authority. **Line authority** entitles a manager to direct the work of an employee. It is the employer-employee authority relationship that extends from the top of the organization to the lowest echelon, according to the chain of command, as shown in Exhibit 5-2. As a link in the chain of command, a manager with line authority has the right to direct the work of employees and to make certain decisions without consulting anyone. Of course, in the chain of command, every manager is also subject to the direction of his or her superior.

Sometimes the term *line* is used to differentiate line managers from staff managers. In this context, *line* refers to managers whose organizational function contributes directly to the achievement of organizational objectives. In a manufacturing firm, line managers are typically in the production and sales functions, whereas managers in human resources and payroll are considered staff managers with staff authority. Whether a manager's function is classified as line or staff depends on the organization's objectives. For example, at Staff-Builders, a supplier

Ethical Dilemma in Management

Following Orders

A survey of U.S. managers has revealed a significant difference in the values, attitudes, and beliefs they personally held and what they encountered in the workplace.[9] And this is not simply a U.S. phenomenon. Managers around the world, in such places as the Pacific Rim, Europe, and India, are all facing the same predicaments.

If you were asked to follow orders that you believed were unconscionable (for instance, if your boss asked you to destroy evidence that he or she had been stealing a great deal of money from the organization), would you comply? What if you merely disagreed with the orders—say, being asked to bring him or her coffee each morning when no such task is included in your job description? What would you do in these instances? Furthermore, what effect do you feel national culture has on your complying with orders?

Details on a Management Classic

Stanley Milgram

Stanley Milgram, a social psychologist at Yale University, wondered how far individuals would go in following orders.[10] If subjects were placed in the role of a teacher in a learning experiment and told by the experimenter to administer a shock each time that a learner made a mistake, would the subjects follow the commands of the experimenter? Would their willingness to comply decrease as the intensity of the shock was increased?

To answer those questions, Milgram hired a set of subjects. Each was told that the experiment was to investigate the effect of punishment on memory. Their job was to act as teachers and administer punishment whenever the learner made a mistake on a learning test. Punishment in this case was an electric shock. The subject sat in front of a shock generator with 30 levels of shock—beginning at zero and progressing in 15-volt increments to a high of 450 volts. The demarcations of these positions ranged from "slight shock" at 15 volts to "danger: severe shock" at 450 volts. The subjects—who had received a sample shock of 45 volts—were able to see the learner strapped in an electric chair in an adjacent room. Of course, the learner was an actor, and the electric shocks were phony, but the subjects didn't know that.

The subjects were instructed to shock the learner each time he made a mistake and that subsequent mistakes would result in an increase in shock intensity. Throughout the experiment, the subject got verbal feedback from the learner. At 75 volts, the learner began to grunt and moan; at 150 volts, he demanded to be released from the experiment; at 180 volts, he cried out that he could no longer stand the pain; and at 300 volts, he insisted he be released because of a heart condition. After 300 volts, the learner did not respond to further questions.

Most subjects protested and, fearful that they might kill the learner if the increased shocks were to bring on a heart attack, insisted that they could not go on. The experimenter responded by saying that they had to, that was their job. Most of the subjects dissented. Dissension, however, wasn't synonymous with disobedience. Sixty-two percent of the subjects increased the shock level to the maximum of 450 volts. The average level of shock administered by the remaining 38 percent was nearly 370 volts—more than enough to kill even the strongest human.

What can we conclude from Milgram's results? One obvious conclusion is that authority is a potent source of getting people to do things. Subjects in Milgram's experiment administered levels of shock far above what they felt comfortable giving because they were told they had to, despite the fact that they could have walked out of the room any time they wanted.

of temporary employees, interviewers have a line function. Similarly, at the payroll firm of ADP, payroll is a line function.

As organizations get larger and more complex, line managers find that they do not have the time, expertise, or resources to get their jobs done effectively. In response, they create **staff authority** functions to support, assist, advise, and generally reduce some of their informational burdens. The hospital administrator cannot effectively handle the purchasing of all the supplies the hospital needs, so she creates a purchasing department, a staff department. Of course, the head of the purchasing department has line authority over the purchasing agents who work for her. The hospital administrator might also find that she is overburdened and needs an assistant. In creating the position of her assistant, she has created a staff position. Exhibit 5-3 illustrates line and staff authority.

staff authority
Positions that have some authority but that are created to support, assist, and advise the holders of line authority

How does the contemporary view of authority and responsibility differ from the historical view? The early management writers were enamored of authority. They assumed that the rights inherent in one's formal position in an organization were the sole source of influence. They believed that managers were all-powerful. This might have been true 30 or 60 years ago. Organizations were simpler. Staff was less important. Managers were only minimally dependent on technical specialists. Under such conditions, influence is the same as authority. And the higher a manager's position in the organization, the more influence he or she had. However, those conditions no longer hold. Researchers and practitioners of man-

Exhibit 5-2
Chain of Command

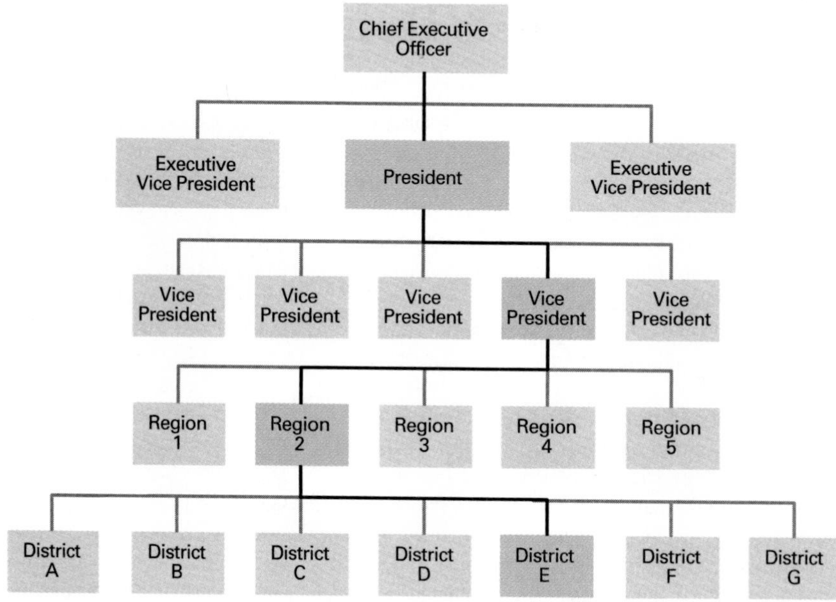

agement now recognize that you do not have to be a manager to have power and that power is not perfectly correlated with one's level in the organization.

Authority is an important concept in organizations, but an exclusive focus on authority produces a narrow, unrealistic view of influence. Today, we recognize that authority is but one element in the larger concept of power.[11]

power
An individual's capacity to influence decisions

How do authority and power differ? The terms authority and power are frequently confused. Authority is a right, the legitimacy of which is based on the authority figure's position in the organization. Authority goes with the job. **Power,** on the other hand, refers to an individual's capacity to influence decisions. Authority is part of the larger concept of power. That is, the formal rights

Exhibit 5-3 Line versus Staff Authority

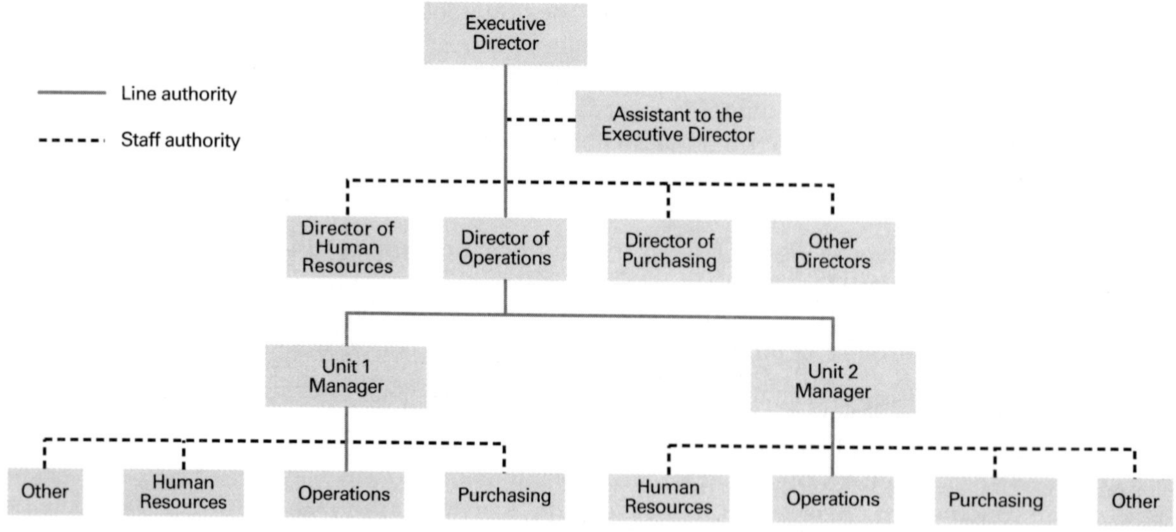

Exhibit 5-4 Authority versus Power

A. Authority

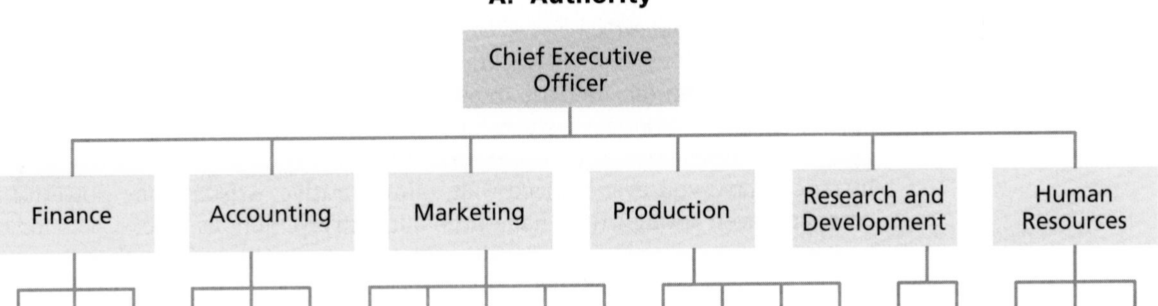

B. Power

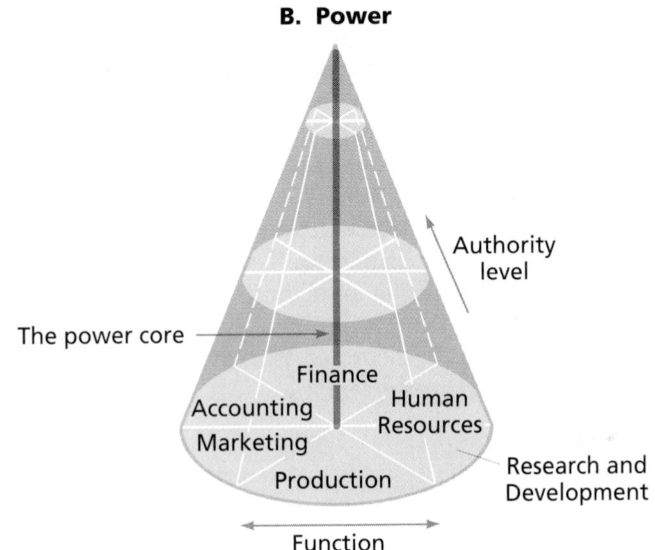

that come with an individual's position in the organization are just one means by which an individual can affect the decision process.

Exhibit 5-4 visually depicts the difference between authority and power. The two-dimensional arrangement of boxes in part A portrays authority. The area in which the authority applies is defined by the horizontal dimension. Each horizontal grouping represents a functional area. The influence one holds in the organization is defined by the vertical dimension in the structure. The higher one is in the organization, the greater one's authority.

Power, on the other hand, is a three-dimensional concept (the cone in part B of Exhibit 5-4). It includes not only the functional and hierarchical dimensions but also a third dimension called centrality. Although authority is defined by one's vertical position in the hierarchy, power is made up of both one's vertical position and one's distance from the organization's power core or center.

Think of the cone in Exhibit 5-4 as an organization. The center of the cone is the power core. The closer you are to the power core, the more influence you have on decisions. The existence of a power core is, in fact, the only difference between A and B in Exhibit 5-4. The vertical hierarchy dimension in A is merely one's level on the outer edge of the cone. The top of the cone corresponds to the top of the hierarchy, the middle of the cone to the middle of the hierarchy, and so on. Similarly, the functional groups in A become wedges in the cone. Each wedge represents a functional area.

The cone analogy explicitly acknowledges two facts: (1) The higher one moves in an organization (an increase in authority), the closer one moves to the power core; and (2) it is not necessary to have authority in order to wield power because one can move horizontally inward toward the power core without moving up. For instance, have you ever noticed that administrative assistants are powerful in a company even though they have little authority? Often, as gatekeepers for their bosses, these assistants have considerable influence over whom their bosses see and when they see them. Furthermore, because they are regularly relied upon to pass information on to their bosses, they have some control over what their bosses hear. It is not unusual for a $95,000-a-year middle manager to tread very carefully in order not to upset the boss's $35,000-a-year administrative assistant. Why? Because the assistant has power. This individual may be low in the authority hierarchy but close to the power core.

Low-ranking employees who have relatives, friends, or associates in high places might also be close to the power core. So, too, are employees with scarce and important skills.[12] The lowly production engineer with 20 years of experience in a company might be the only one in the firm who knows the inner workings of all the old production machinery. When pieces of this old equipment break down, only this engineer understands how to fix them. Suddenly, the engineer's influence is much greater than it would appear from his or her level in the vertical hierarchy. What does this tell us about power? It states that power can come from different areas (see Developing Your Power Base Skill, p. 179). John French and Bertram Raven have identified five sources, or bases, of power: coercive, reward, legitimate, expert, and referent.[13] We have summarized them in Exhibit 5-5.

centralization
A function of how much decision-making authority is pushed down to lower levels in an organization; the more centralized an organization is, the higher is the level at which decisions are made

decentralization
The pushing down of decision-making authority to the lowest levels of an organization

HOW DO CENTRALIZATION AND DECENTRALIZATION DIFFER?

One of the questions that needs to be answered in the organizing function is "At what level are decisions made?" **Centralization** is a function of how much decision-making authority is pushed down to lower levels in the organization. Centralization-decentralization, however, is not an either-or concept. Rather, it's a degree phenomenon. By that we mean that no organization is completely centralized or completely decentralized. Few, if any, organizations could effectively function if all their decisions were made by a select few people (centralization) or if all decisions were pushed down to the level closest to the problems **(decentralization).** Let's look, then, at how the early management writers viewed centralization as well as at how it exists today.

Exhibit 5-5
Types of Power

Coercive power	Power based on fear.
Reward power	Power based on the ability to distribute something that others value.
Legitimate power	Power based on one's position in the formal hierarchy.
Expert power	Power based on one's expertise, special skill, or knowledge.
Referent power	Power based on identification with a person who has desirable resources or personal traits.

Early management writers proposed that centralization in an organization depended on the situation.[14] Their objective was the optimum and efficient use of employees. Traditional organizations were structured in a pyramid, with power and authority concentrated near the top of the organization. Given this structure, historically, centralized decisions were the most prominent, but organizations today have become more complex and are responding to dynamic changes in their environments. As such, many managers believe that decisions need to be made by those individuals closest to the problems faced regardless of their organizational level. In fact, the trend over the past three decades—at least in U.S. and Canadian organizations—has been a movement toward more decentralization in organizations.[15]

Today, managers often choose the amount of centralization or decentralization that will allow them to best implement their decisions and achieve organizational goals. What works in one organization, however, won't necessarily work in another. So managers must determine the amount of decentralization for each organization and work units within it. For instance, at Motorola, although many production decisions are pushed down to lower levels or even outside to some suppliers, financial and product distribution decisions remain in the hands of senior management.[16] You may also recall that, in Chapter 2, one of the central themes of our discussion of empowering employees was to delegate to them the authority to make decisions on those things that affect their work and to change the way that they think about work.[17] That's the issue of decentralization at work. Notice, however, that it doesn't imply that senior management no longer makes decisions.

CAN YOU IDENTIFY THE FIVE WAYS TO DEPARTMENTALIZE?

Early management writers argued that activities in the organization should be specialized and grouped into departments. Work specialization creates specialists who need coordination. This coordination is facilitated by putting specialists together in departments under the direction of a manager. These departments are typically based on the work functions performed, the product or service offered, the target customer or client, the geographic territory covered, or the process used to turn inputs into outputs. No single method of departmentalization was advocated by the early writers. The method or methods used should reflect the grouping that would best contribute to the attainment of the organization's objectives and the goals of individual units.

How are activities grouped? One of the most popular ways to group activities is by functions performed or **functional departmentalization.** A manager might organize his or her plant by separating engineering, accounting, information systems, human resources, and purchasing specialists into departments (see Exhibit 5-6). Functional departmentalization can be used in all types of organizations. Only the functions change to reflect the organization's objectives and

functional departmentalization
The grouping of activities by functions performed

Exhibit 5-6
Functional Departmentalization

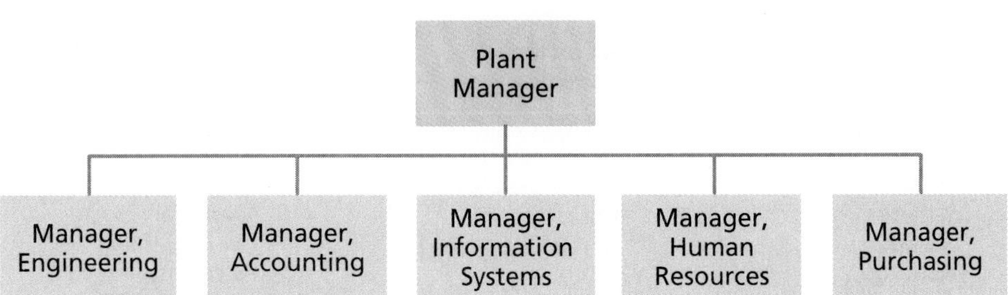

Exhibit 5-7 Product Departmentalization

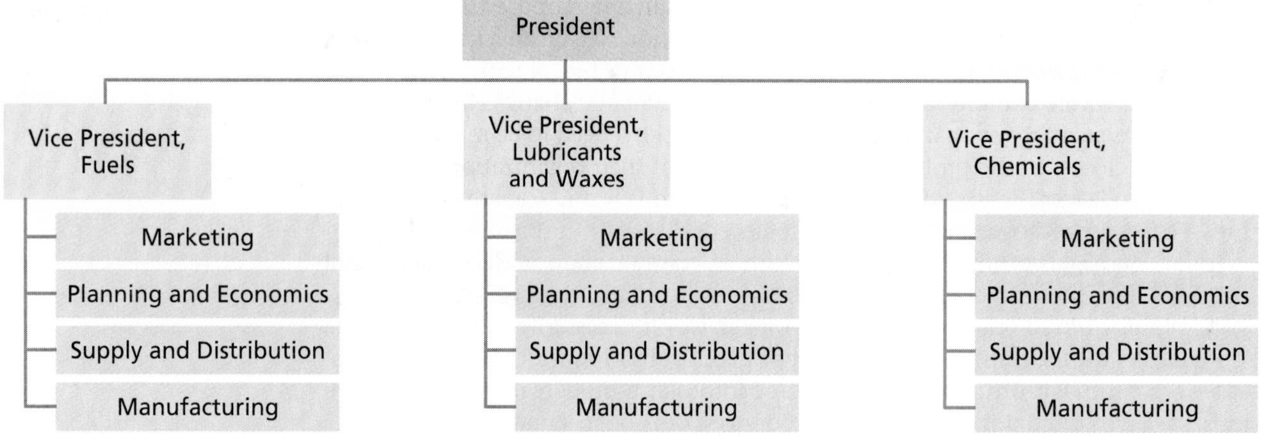

activities. A hospital might have departments devoted to research, patient care, accounting, and so forth. A professional soccer franchise might have departments of player personnel, ticket sales, and travel and accommodations.

product departmentalization
The grouping of activities by product produced

Exhibit 5-7 illustrates the **product departmentalization** method used at Bombardier Ltd., a Canadian company. Each major product area in the corporation is under the authority of a senior manager who is a specialist in, and is responsible for, everything having to do with his or her product line. Another company that uses product departmentalization is L.A. Gear. Its structure is based on its varied product lines, which include women's footwear, men's footwear, and apparel and accessories. If an organization's activities were service related, rather than product related as are those of Bombardier and L.A. Gear, each service would be autonomously grouped. For instance, an accounting firm would have departments for taxes, management consulting, auditing, and the like. In such a case, each department offers a common array of services under the direction of a product or service manager.

customer departmentalization
The grouping of activities by common customers

geographic departmentalization
The grouping of activities by territory

The particular type of customer the organization seeks to reach can also dictate employee grouping. The sales activities in an office supply firm, for instance, can be broken down into three departments that serve retail, wholesale, and government customers (see Exhibit 5-8). A large law office can segment its staff on the basis of whether it serves corporate or individual clients. The assumption underlying **customer departmentalization** is that customers in each department have a common set of problems and needs that can best be met by specialists.

Another way to departmentalize is on the basis of geography or territory—**geographic departmentalization.** The sales function might have western, south-

Exhibit 5-8 Customer Departmentalization

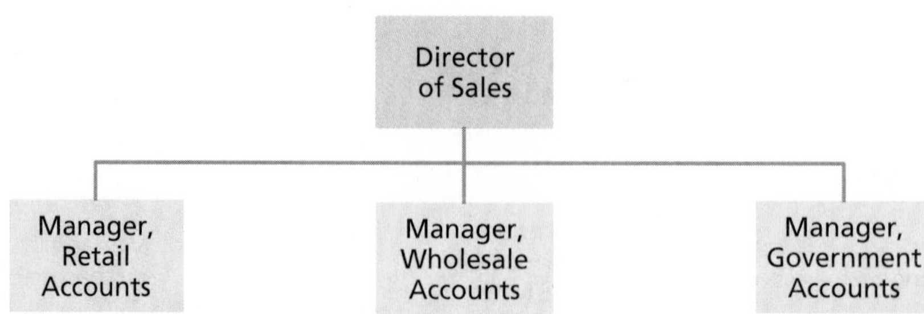

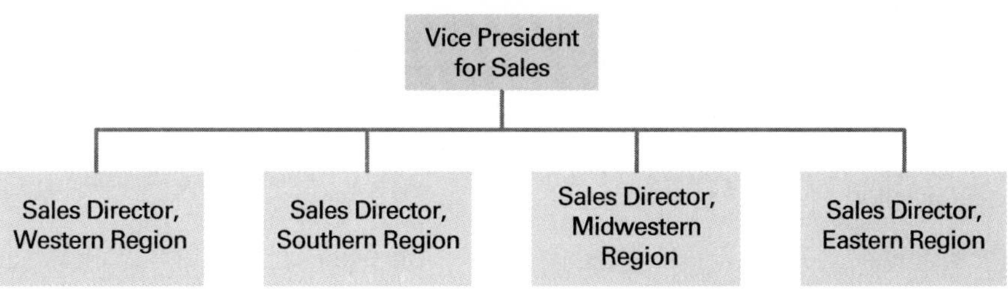

Exhibit 5-9
Geographic Departmentalization

ern, midwestern, and eastern regions (see Exhibit 5-9). A large school district might have six high schools to provide for each of the major geographic territories within the district. If an organization's customers are scattered over a large geographic area, this form of departmentalization can be valuable. For instance, the organization structure of Coca-Cola in the new millennium reflects the company's operations in two broad geographic areas—the North American sector and the international sector (which includes the Pacific Rim, the European Community, Northeast Europe and Africa, and Latin America groups).

process departmentalization
The grouping of activities by work or customer flow

The final form of departmentalization is called **process departmentalization,** which groups activities on the basis of work or customer flow. Exhibit 5-10 represents process departmentalization by depicting the various departments in a motor vehicle department. If you have ever been to a state motor vehicle office to get a driver's license, you probably went through several departments before receiving your license. In some states, applicants go through three steps, each handled by a separate department: (1) validation by the motor vehicles division, (2) processing by the licensing department, and (3) payment collection by the treasury department.

How does the contemporary view of departmentalization differ from the historical view? Most large organizations continue to use most or all of the departmental groups suggested by the early management writers. Black & Decker, for instance, organizes each of its divisions along functional lines, its manufacturing units around processes, its sales around geographic regions, and its sales regions around customer groupings. But a recent trend needs to be mentioned. That is, rigid departmentalization is being complemented by the use of teams that cross traditional departmental lines.

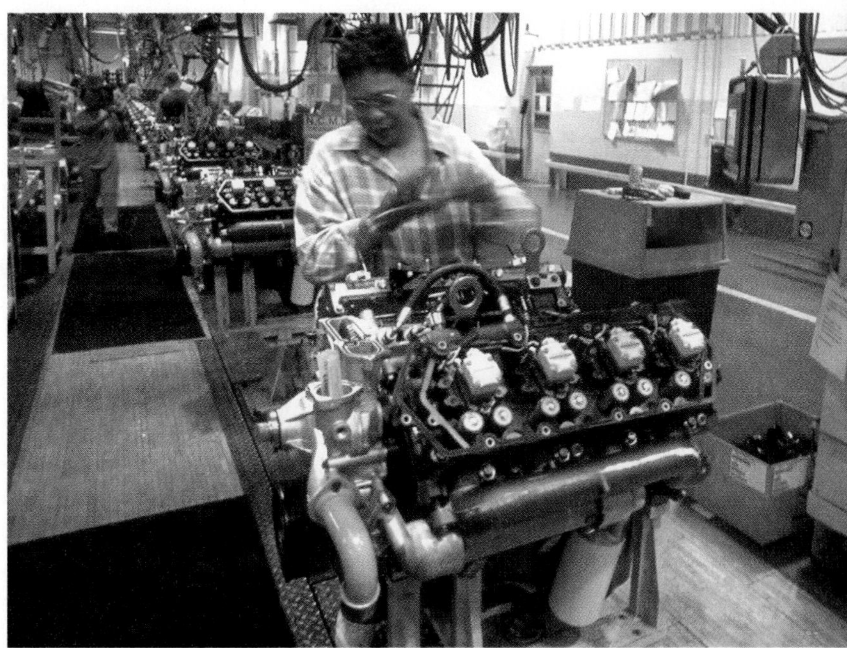

Some organizations today recognize the benefits of grouping their employees into teams. At the Navistar International Transportation Corporation in Indianapolis, the organization's structure is built around work teams. Job classifications have been reduced from 60 titles to 1, production has more than doubled from 126,000 to 290,000 engines annually, and defects have decreased nearly 97 percent.

Today's competitive environment has refocused the attention of management on its customers. To better monitor the needs of customers and to be able to respond to changes in those needs, many organizations have given greater emphasis to customer departmentaliza-

Exhibit 5-10
Process Departmentalization

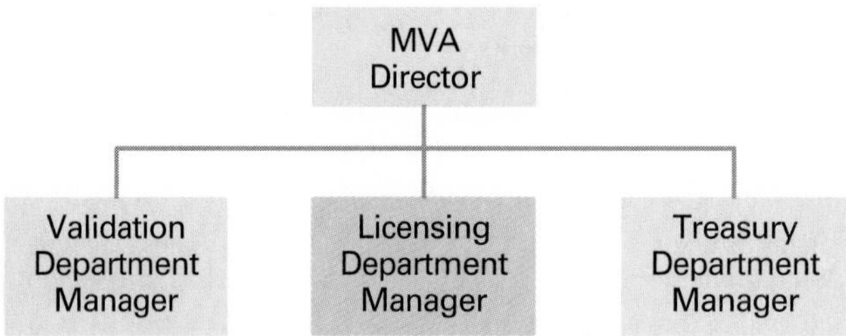

tion. The Dana Corporation, for example, restructured its bureaucracy into six strategic business units that focus on customers,[18] allowing the company to better identify its customers and to respond faster to their requirements.

We are also seeing many more teams today as devices for accomplishing organizational objectives.[19] Nearly 80 percent of the *Fortune* 500 firms are using teams.[20] As tasks have become more complex, and diverse skills are needed to accomplish those tasks, management has increasingly used teams and task forces. We look at the issue of teams in Chapter 9.

If we combine the basic organizational structural elements, we arrive at what most of the early writers believed to be the ideal structural design: the mechanistic or bureaucratic organization. Today we recognize that there is no single ideal organization structure for all situations.

Contingency Variables Affecting Structure

The most appropriate structure to use will depend on contingency factors. In this section, we address two generic organization structure models and then look at the more popular contingency variables—strategy, size, technology, and environment.

mechanistic organization
A bureaucracy; a structure that is high in specialization, formalization, and centralization

HOW IS A MECHANISTIC ORGANIZATION DIFFERENT FROM AN ORGANIC ORGANIZATION?

Exhibit 5-11 describes two organizational forms.[21] The **mechanistic organization** (or bureaucracy) was the natural result of combining the six elements of structure. Adhering to the chain of command principle ensured the existence of

Exhibit 5-11
Mechanistic versus Organic Organizations

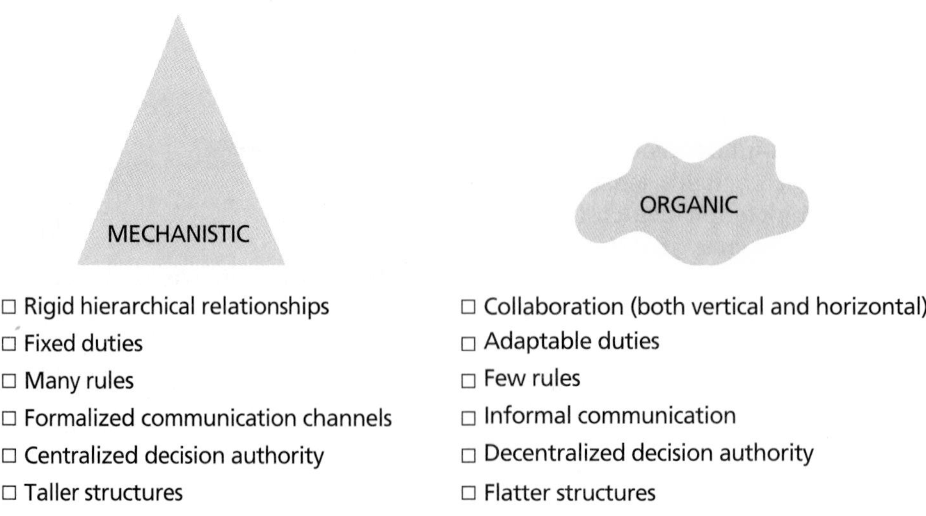

a formal hierarchy of authority, with each person controlled and supervised by one superior. Keeping the span of control small at increasingly higher levels in the organization created tall, impersonal structures. As the distance between the top and the bottom of the organization expanded, top management would increasingly impose rules and regulations. Because top managers couldn't control lower-level activities through direct observation and ensure the use of standard practices, they substituted rules and regulations. The early management writers' belief in a high degree of division of labor created jobs that were simple, routine, and standardized. Further specialization through the use of departmentalization increased impersonality and the need for multiple layers of management to coordinate the specialized departments.

The **organic organization** is a highly adaptive form that is as loose and flexible as the mechanistic organization is rigid and stable. Rather than having standardized jobs and regulations, the organic organization's loose structure allows it to change rapidly as required. They have division of labor, but the jobs people do are not standardized. Employees tend to be professionals who are technically proficient and trained to handle diverse problems. They need very few formal rules and little direct supervision because their training has instilled in them standards of professional conduct. For instance, a petroleum engineer does not need to be given procedures on how to locate oil sources miles offshore. The engineer can solve most problems alone or after conferring with colleagues. Professional standards guide his or her behavior. The organic organization is low in centralization so that the professional can respond quickly to problems and because top management cannot be expected to possess the expertise to make necessary decisions.

organic organization
An adhocracy; a structure that is low in specialization, formalization, and centralization

When is each of these two models appropriate? Let's look at the contingency variables that affect organization structure.

HOW DOES STRATEGY AFFECT STRUCTURE?

An organization's structure is a means to help management achieve its objectives. Because objectives are derived from the organization's overall strategy, it is only logical that strategy and structure should be closely linked. For example, if the organization focuses on providing certain services—say, police protection in a community—its structure will be one that promotes standardized and efficient services. Similarly, if an organization is attempting to employ a growth strategy by entering into global markets, it will need a structure that is flexible, fluid, and readily adaptable to the environment. Accordingly, organizational structure should follow strategy. And, if management makes a significant change in its organization's strategy, it will need to modify structure to accommodate and support that change.

The first important research on the strategy-structure relationship was Alfred Chandler's study of close to 100 large U.S. companies.[22] After tracing the development of these organizations over 50 years and compiling extensive case histories of companies such as Du Pont, General Motors, Standard Oil of New Jersey, and Sears, Chandler concluded that changes in corporate strategy precede and lead to changes in an organization's structure. Specifically, he found that organizations usually begin with a single product or line. The simplicity of the strategy requires only a simple or loose form of structure to execute it. Decisions can be centralized in the hands of a single senior manager, and complexity and formalization will be low. As organizations grow, their strategies become more ambitious and elaborate.

Research has generally confirmed the strategy-structure relationship using the strategy terminology presented in Chapter 3.[23] For instance, organizations pursuing a differentiation strategy (see Chapter 3) must innovate to survive. Unless they can maintain their uniqueness, they may lose their competitive advantage. An organic organization matches best with this strategy because it is flexible and maximizes adaptability. In contrast, a cost-leadership strategy seeks stability and efficiency. Stability and efficiency help to produce low-cost goods and services. This, then, can best be achieved with a mechanistic organization.

HOW DOES SIZE AFFECT STRUCTURE?

There is considerable historical evidence that an organization's size significantly affects its structure.[24] For instance, large organizations—those typically employing 2,000 or more employees—tend to have more division of labor, horizontal and vertical differentiation, and rules and regulations than do small organizations. However, the relationship is not linear; size has less impact as an organization expands. Why? Essentially, once an organization has around 2,000 employees, it is already fairly mechanistic. An additional 500 employees will not have much effect. On the other hand, adding 500 employees to an organization that has only 300 members is likely to result in a shift toward a more mechanistic structure.

HOW DOES TECHNOLOGY AFFECT STRUCTURE?

Every organization uses some form of technology to convert its inputs into outputs. To attain its objectives, the organization uses equipment, materials, knowledge, and experienced individuals and puts them together into certain types and patterns of activities. For instance, college instructors teach students by a variety of methods: formal lectures, group discussions, case analyses, programmed learning, and so forth. Each of these methods is a type of technology. Over the years, several studies regarding the effect of technology have been conducted.[25] For instance, in one study, British scholar Joan Woodward found that distinct relationships exist between size of production runs and the structure of the firm. She also found that the effectiveness of organizations was related to the "fit" between technology and structure.[26] Most of these studies, like Woodward's, have focused on the processes or methods that transform inputs into outputs and how they differ by their degree of routineness. For example, mass production of steel, tires, and automobiles or petroleum refining generally employs routine technology. The more routine the technology, the more standardized the structure can be. Conversely, Rockwell International's development of the Space Shuttle represented a nonroutine technology. Because the technology was less routine, the structure was more organic.[27]

HOW DOES ENVIRONMENT AFFECT STRUCTURE?

In Chapter 2, we discussed the organization's environment as a constraint on managerial discretion. It also has a major effect on the organization's structure. Essentially, mechanistic organizations are most effective in stable environments. Organic organizations are best matched with dynamic and uncertain environments.

The evidence on the environment-structure relationship helps to explain why so many managers have restructured their organizations to be lean, fast, and flexible.[28] Global competition, accelerated product innovation by all competitors, and increased demands from customers for higher quality and faster deliveries are examples of dynamic environmental forces. Mechanistic organizations tend to be ill equipped to respond to rapid environmental change. As a result, managers, like those at the St. Louis–based household appliance company, Emerson Electric, are redesigning their organizations in order to make them more organic.[29] As a result, Emerson Electric has regained market share once lost to low-cost producers in Japan, Brazil, and Korea by giving employees more autonomy to do their jobs and instilling in them a pride of ownership.

Organization Design Applications

What types of organization designs exist in companies such as Toshiba, Liz Claiborne, Hershey Foods, and Sun Life Assurance Company of Canada, Ltd.? Let's look at the various types of organization designs that you might see in contemporary organizations.

WHAT IS A SIMPLE STRUCTURE?

Most organizations start as an entrepreneurial venture with a simple structure. This organization design reflects the owner as president, with all employees reporting directly to her.

A **simple structure** is defined more by what it is not than by what it is. It is not an elaborate structure.[30] If you see an organization that appears to have almost no structure, it is probably of the simple variety. By that we mean that work specialization is low; few rules govern the operations, and authority is centralized in a single person—the owner. The simple structure is a "flat" organization; it usually has only two or three vertical levels and a loose body of empowered employees in whom the decision-making authority is centralized.

simple structure
An organization that is low in specialization and formalization but high in centralization

The simple structure is most widely used in smaller businesses, like San Francisco's One Market restaurant, in which the manager and the owner are often the same. The strengths of the simple structure should be obvious. It is fast, flexible, and inexpensive to maintain, and accountability is clear. However, it is effective only in small organizations. It becomes increasingly inadequate as an organization grows, because its few policies or rules to guide operations and its high centralization result in information overload at the top. As size increases, decision making becomes slower and can eventually come to a standstill as the single executive tries to continue making all the decisions. If the structure is not changed and adapted to its size, the firm is likely to lose momentum and eventually fail. The simple structure's other weakness is that it is risky: Everything depends on one person. If anything happens to the owner-manager, the organization's information and decision-making center is lost.

A simple structure is one in which most, if not all, employees report to the owner. At One Market restaurant in San Francisco, workers report to the owner/chef, who, like employees, performs many of the activities required for quality customer service.

WHAT DO WE MEAN BY A BUREAUCRACY?

Many organizations do not remain simple structures. That decision is often made by choice or because structural contingency factors dictate it. For example, as production or sales increase significantly, companies generally reach a point at which more employees are needed. As the number of employees rises, informal work rules of the simple structure give way to more formal rules. Rules and regulations are implemented; departments are created, and levels of management are added to coordinate the activities of departmental people. At this point, a bureaucracy is formed. Two of the most popular bureaucratic design options grew out of the function and product departmentalizations. These are appropriately called the functional and divisional structures, respectively.

functional structure
An organization in which similar and related occupational specialties are grouped together

Why do companies implement functional structures? We introduced functional departmentalization a few pages ago. The **functional structure** merely expands the functional orientation to make it the dominant form for the entire organization. As displayed in Exhibit 5-6 (page 163) management can choose to organize its structure by grouping similar and related occupational specialties. The strength of the functional structure lies in the advantages that accrue from work specialization. Putting like specialties together results in economies of scale, minimizes duplication of personnel and equipment, and makes employees comfortable and satisfied because it gives them the opportunity to talk the same language as their peers. The most obvious weakness of the functional structure, however, is that the organization frequently loses sight of its best interests in the pursuit of functional goals. No one function is totally responsible for results, so members within individual functions become insulated and have little understanding of what people in other functions are doing.

divisional structure
An organization made up of self-contained units

What is the divisional structure? The **divisional structure** is an organization design made up of self-contained units or divisions. Hershey Foods and PepsiCo have implemented such a structure. Building on product departmentalization (see Exhibit 5-7, page 164), each division is generally autonomous, with a division manager responsible for performance and holding complete strategic and operational decision-making authority. In most divisional structures, central headquarters provides support services—such as financial and legal services—to the divisions. Of course, the headquarters also acts as an external overseer to coordinate and control the various divisions. Divisions are, therefore, autonomous within given parameters.

The chief advantage of the divisional structure is that it focuses on results. Division managers have full responsibility for a product or service. The divisional structure also frees the headquarters staff from being concerned with day-to-day operating details so that they can pay attention to long-term and strategic planning. The major disadvantage of the divisional structure is duplication of activities and resources. Each division, for instance, may have a marketing research department. In the absence of autonomous divisions, all of the organization's marketing research might be centralized and done for a fraction of the cost that divisionalization requires. Thus, the divisional form's duplication of functions increases the organization's costs and reduces efficiency.

CAN AN ORGANIZATION DESIGN CAPTURE THE ADVANTAGES OF BUREAUCRACIES WHILE ELIMINATING THEIR DISADVANTAGES?

The functional structure offers the advantages that accrue from specialization. The divisional structure has a greater focus on results but suffers from duplication

Exhibit 5-12 Sample Matrix Structure

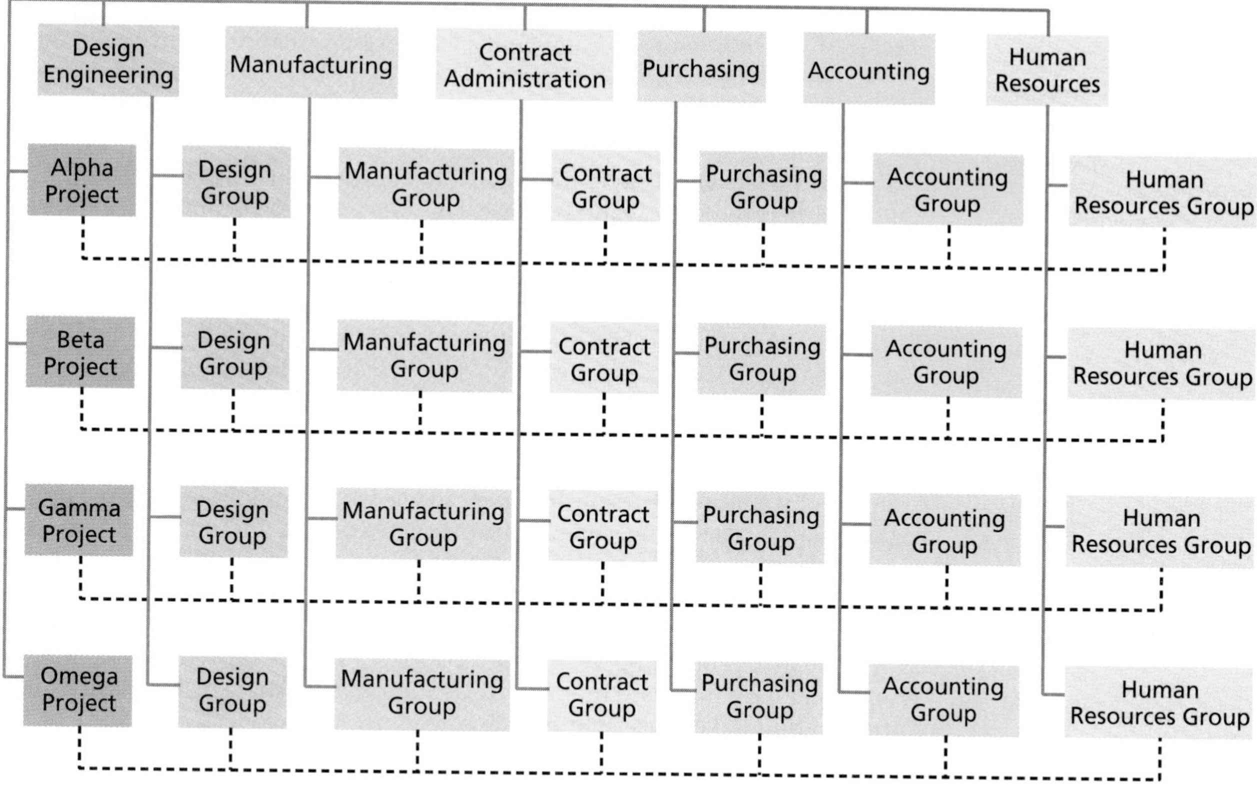

of activities and resources. Does any structure combine the advantages of functional specialization with the focus and accountability that product departmentalization provides? Yes, and it's called the **matrix structure.**[31]

matrix structure
An organization in which specialists from functional departments are assigned to work on one or more projects led by a project manager

Exhibit 5-12 illustrates the matrix structure of an aerospace firm. Notice that along the top of the figure are the familiar functions of engineering, accounting, human resources, manufacturing, and so forth. Along the vertical dimension, however, are the various projects on which the aerospace firm is currently working. Each program is directed by a manager who staffs his or her project with people from the functional departments. The addition of this vertical dimension to the traditional horizontal functional departments, in effect, weaves together elements of function and product departmentalization—hence the term *matrix*.

The unique characteristic of the matrix is that employees in this structure have at least two bosses: their functional departmental manager and their product or project managers. Project managers have authority over the functional members who are part of that manager's project team, but authority is shared between the two managers. Typically, the project manager is given authority over project employees relative to the project's goals, but decisions such as promotions, salary recommendations, and annual reviews remain the functional manager's responsibility. To work effectively, project and functional managers must communicate regularly and coordinate the demands upon their common employees.[32]

The primary strength of the matrix is that it can facilitate coordination of a multiple set of complex and interdependent projects while still retaining the economies that result from keeping functional specialists grouped together.[33] The major disadvantages of the matrix are the confusion it creates and its propensity to foster power struggles. When you dispense with the chain of command principle, you significantly increase ambiguity. Confusion can arise over who reports to whom. This confusion and ambiguity, in turn, plant the seeds of power struggles.

WHAT ARE TEAM-BASED STRUCTURES?

team-based structure
An organization that consists entirely of work groups or teams

In a **team-based structure,** the entire organization consists of work groups or teams that perform the organization's work.[34] In such a structure, it goes without saying that team members have the authority to make decisions that affect them, because there is no rigid chain of command in these work arrangements. How can team structures benefit the organization? Let's look at what happened at Thermos, the Schaumburg, Illinois, bottle and lunch box company.

Company officials became aware of how Thermos's bureaucracy was slowing decision making and constraining innovation, especially in creating new products.[35] Thermos's CEO, Monte Peterson, attacked the problem by revamping the corporate structure. He flattened the organization by developing interdisciplinary team-based structures. These teams were made up of employees from such areas as engineering, marketing, manufacturing, and finance. In addition, each team also had members who were external to the company, such as suppliers or customers. The prime directive was to "listen to customers, and develop products they want." In doing so, the company would be able to satisfy its customers and its performance could improve. In fact, since the company moved to a team-based design, sales have increased dramatically, and its market share in, for instance, the barbecue grill market, has risen from 2 percent to 20 percent.

One Manager's Perspective

Alisa Owens Director, Business Development and Strategic Sales, Versaware, Inc.

Versaware, a growing e-publisher, is only four years old but employs 250 people internationally, with offices in New York and California, research and development (R&D) in Jerusalem, and production facilities in India. Its organization is a cross between divisional and functional structure. For instance, R&D and production are organized by specialties (functional structure), while sales and marketing are organized by division.

According to Alisa Owens, director of business development and strategic sales for the educational and professional division, this hybrid structure offers both advantages and disadvantages. Among the advantages are the fact that specialized production tasks can be done where skilled labor is available (for instance, in India there are many people skilled in digitizing books), and this gives the company the ability to respond quickly to market needs and competitive challenges. One disadvantage is that communication between the functional areas sometimes suffers, a problem Versaware is working to correct.

Having spent its first two years primarily as a research and development company, Versaware now looks to a future focused on product output and improvement. That, says Owens, will lead to a divisional structure to strengthen accountability, project planning, and fulfillment. R&D, however, will likely remain a functional area, to benefit from specialization and allow innovations to be shared across divisions.

WHY IS THERE MOVEMENT TOWARD A BOUNDARYLESS ORGANIZATION?

The last organization design application that we cover is the boundaryless organization. A **boundaryless organization** is not defined or limited by boundaries or categories imposed by traditional structures.[36] It blurs the historical boundaries surrounding an organization by increasing its interdependence with its environment.[37] Sometimes called network organizations, learning organizations, barrier-free, modular, or virtual corporations,[38] boundaryless structures cut across all aspects of the organization.[39] Rather than having functional specialties located in departments working on distinctive tasks, these internally boundaryless organizations group employees to accomplish some core competency (see Chapter 3).[40] For instance, at Sweden's Karolinska Hospital, surgical teams handle all of a patient's needs from diagnosis, to surgery, to recovery. Surgeries once involved 47 departments. Now these surgical teams are performing 3,000 surgeries each year with 15 fewer operating rooms available. And patient waiting times for surgery have been cut from six to eight months to just under three weeks.[41]

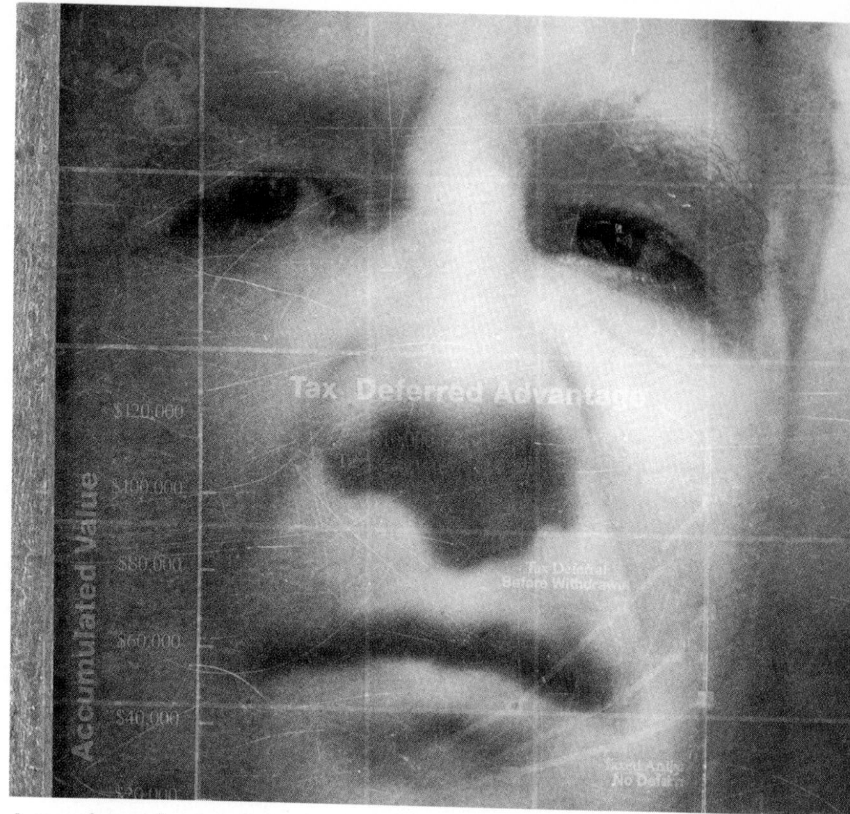

A number of companies are recognizing the value of the virtual corporation. At GeneralLife Insurance Company in Edwardsville, Illinois, CEO Michael Conley and a staff of 13 manage and coordinate some 3,000 insurance agents. Through the use of technology, this organization has been able to significantly cut costs and offer better services to its customers.

But boundaryless organizations are not merely flatter organizations. They attempt to eliminate vertical, horizontal, and interorganizational barriers. To do this, however, frequently requires an internal revolution.[42] That is, managers must break down the traditional hierarchies that have often existed for many decades. Horizontal organizations require multidisciplinary work teams who have the authority to make the necessary decisions and be held accountable for measurable outcomes.[43] What factors have contributed to the rise of boundaryless designs in today's organizations? Undoubtedly, many of the issues we covered in Chapter 2 have had an effect. Specifically, globalization of markets and competitors has played a major role. An organization's need to respond and adapt to the complex and dynamic environment is best served by boundaryless organizations. Changes in technology have also contributed to this movement.[44] Advances in computer power, "intelligent" software, and telecommunications enable boundaryless e-commerce organizations to exist. Each of these supports the information network that makes the virtual workplace possible. For example, at GeneraLife Insurance Company, CEO Michael Conley and his 13 staff members manage and coordinate the activities of 3,000 insurance agents, mostly with the assistance of the Internet.[45] Finally, a rapidly changing environment compels an organization

boundaryless organization
An organization that is not defined or limited by boundaries or categories imposed by traditional structures

to rapidly innovate to survive. A boundaryless organization provides the flexibility and fluid structure that facilitate quick movements to capitalize on opportunities.

Organization Culture

We know that every individual has what psychologists have termed *personality,* a set of relatively permanent and stable traits. When we describe someone as warm, innovative, relaxed, or conservative, we are describing personality traits. An organization, too, has a personality, which we call the organization's culture.

WHAT IS AN ORGANIZATION CULTURE?

organization culture
A system of shared meaning within an organization that determines, to a large degree, how employees act

What do we specifically mean by the term **organization culture?** We refer to a system of shared meaning. Just as tribal cultures have totems and taboos that dictate how each member should act toward fellow members and outsiders, organizations have cultures that govern how their members should behave. In every organization, systems or patterns of values, symbols, rituals, myths, and practices have evolved over time.[46] These shared values determine, in large degree, what employees see and how they respond to their world.[47]

HOW CAN CULTURES BE ASSESSED?

Though we currently have no definitive method for measuring an organization's culture, preliminary research suggests that cultures can be analyzed by rating an organization on 10 characteristics.[48] We have listed these characteristics in Exhibit 5-13. These 10 characteristics are relatively stable and permanent over time. Just as an individual's personality is stable and permanent—if you were outgoing last month, you're likely to be outgoing next month—so, too, is an organization's culture.

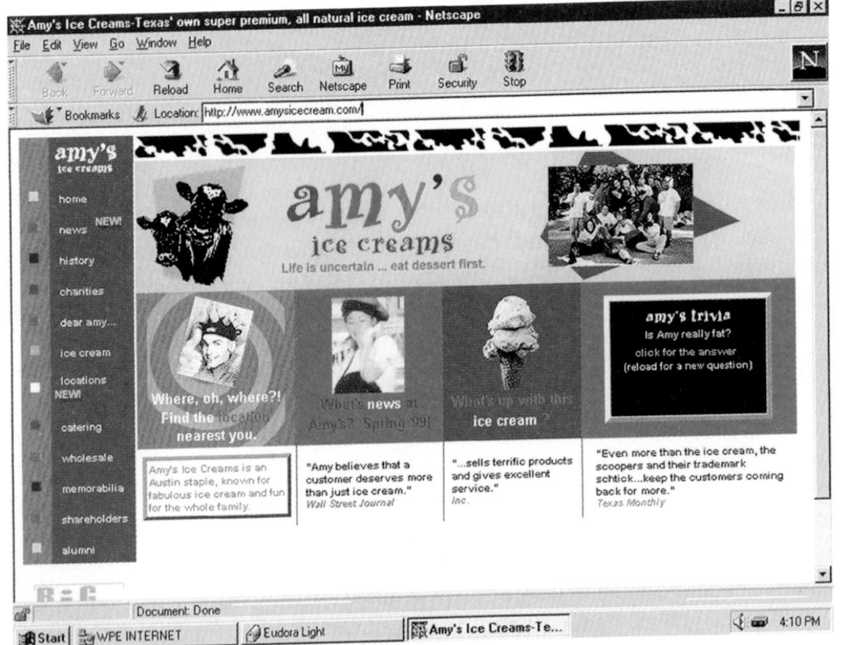

How can culture affect business? At Amy's Ice Creams, Amy Miller has created a culture that promotes family fun and entertainment. Being such, employees "act" at work in ways that promote the enjoyable environment.

WHERE DOES AN ORGANIZATION'S CULTURE COME FROM?

An organization's culture usually reflects the vision or mission of the organization's founders. Because the founders had the original idea, they also have biases on how to carry out the idea. They are unconstrained by previous customs or ideologies. The founders establish the early culture by projecting an image of what the organization should be. The small size of most new organizations also helps the founders impose their vision on all organization members. An organization's culture, then, results from

Exhibit 5-13 Ten Characteristics of Organization Culture

1. **Member identity** The degree to which employees identify with the organization as a whole rather than with their type of job or field of professional expertise
2. **Group emphasis** The degree to which work activities are organized around groups rather than individuals
3. **People focus** The degree to which management decisions take into consideration the effect of outcomes on people within the organization
4. **Unit integration** The degree to which units within the organization are encouraged to operate in a coordinated or interdependent manner
5. **Control** The degree to which rules, regulations, and direct supervision are used to oversee and control employee behavior
6. **Risk tolerance** The degree to which employees are encouraged to be aggressive, innovative, and risk-seeking
7. **Reward criteria** The degree to which rewards such as salary increases and promotions are allocated on employee performance criteria in contrast to seniority, favoritism, or other nonperformance factors
8. **Conflict tolerance** The degree to which employees are encouraged to air conflicts and criticisms openly
9. **Means-end orientation** The degree to which management focuses on results or outcomes rather than on the techniques and processes used to achieve those outcomes
10. **Open-systems focus** The degree to which the organization monitors and responds to changes in the external environment

the interaction between (1) the founders' biases and assumptions and (2) what the first employees learn subsequently from their own experiences.[49] For example, the founder of IBM, Thomas Watson, established a culture based on "pursuing excellence, providing the best customer service, and respect for employees."[50] Ironically, some 75 years later, in an effort to revitalize the ailing IBM, CEO Louis Gerstner dismantled that culture and replaced it with such guiding principles as "the marketplace drives everything we do" and "think and act with a sense of urgency."[51] At Southwest Airlines, Herb Kelleher reinforces the company's "people culture" by doing things and having in place practices—such as compensation and benefits that are above industry averages—to make employees happy.[52] And at Amy's Ice Creams in Austin and Houston, Texas, founder Amy Miller reinforces customer fun by promoting "off-the-wall" employee behavior like tossing ice cream to one another, wearing pajamas at work, juggling, or even break dancing on the countertops.[53]

HOW DOES CULTURE INFLUENCE STRUCTURE?

An organization's culture may have an effect on its structure, depending on how strong, or weak, the culture is. For instance, in organizations that have a strong culture—like that of Barclay PLC, a large British bank characterized as a formal, cold, risk-averse organization—these dominant values create behavioral consistency. In such a case, the organization's culture can substitute for the rules and regulations that formally guide employees.[54] In essence, strong cultures can create predictability, orderliness, and consistency without the need for written documentation. Therefore, the stronger an organization's culture, the less managers need to be concerned with developing formal rules and regulations. Instead, those guides will be internalized in employees when they accept the organization's culture. If, on the other hand, an organization's culture is weak—if there are no dominant shared values—its effect on structure is less clear.

PHLIP Companion Web Site

We invite you to visit the Robbins/DeCenzo companion Web site at *www.prenhall.com/robbins* for this chapter's Internet resources.

Chapter Summary

How will you know if you fulfilled the Learning Outcomes on page 153? You will have fulfilled the Learning Outcomes if you are able to:

1 *Identify and define the six elements of organization structure.*
The six elements of organization structure are: work specialization (having each discrete step of a job done by a different individual rather than one individual do the whole job), chain of command (management principle that no employee should report to more than one boss), span of control (the number of employees a manager can effectively and efficiently manage) authority (rights inherent in a managerial position to give orders and expect them to be followed) and responsibility (an obligation to perform assigned activities), centralization (the higher the level in which decisions are made) versus decentralization (pushing down of decision-making authority to lowest levels in an organization), and departmentalization (the grouping of activities in an organization by function, product, customer, geography, or process).

2 *Describe the advantages and disadvantages of work specialization.*
The advantages of work specialization are related to economic efficiencies. It makes efficient use of the diversity of skills that workers hold. Skills are developed through repetition. Less time is wasted than when workers are generalists. Training is also easier and less costly, but work specialization can result in human diseconomies. Excessive work specialization can cause boredom, fatigue, stress, low productivity, poor quality, increased absence, and high turnover.

3 *Contrast authority and power.*
Authority is related to rights inherent in a position. Power describes all means by which an individual can influence decisions, including formal authority. Authority is synonymous with legitimate power. However, a person can have coercive, reward, expert, or referent power without holding a position of authority. Thus, authority is actually a subset of power.

4 *Identify the five different ways by which management can departmentalize.*
Managers can departmentalize on the basis of function (work being done), product (product or service being generated), customer (group served), geography (location of operations), or process (work flow). In practice, most large organizations use all five ways.

5 *Contrast mechanistic and organic organizations.*
The mechanistic organization, or bureaucracy, rates high on worker specialization, formal work rules and regulations, and centralized decisions. Workers perform specific job duties, their actions guided by formal work regulations, and decisions are typically made by higher levels in the organization. In the organic organization, employees are generalists and perform all parts of a job, face fewer work regulations, and oftentimes have the authority to make decisions on issues directly related to their work.

6 *Summarize the effect on organization structures of strategy, size, technology, and environment.*
The "strategy determines structure" thesis argues that structure should follow strategy. As strategies move from single product, to vertical integration, to product diversification, structure must move from organic to mechanistic. As size increases, so, too, do specialization, formalization, and horizontal and vertical differentiation. But size has less of an impact on large organizations than on small ones because once an organization has around 2,000 employees, it tends to be fairly mechanistic. All other things equal, the more routine the technology, the more mechanistic the organization should be. The more nonroutine the technology, the more organic the structure should be. Finally, stable environments are better matched with mechanistic organizations, but dynamic environments fit better with organic organizations.

7 *Contrast the divisional and functional structures.*
The functional structure groups similar or related occupational specialties together. It takes advantage of specialization and provides economies of scale by allowing people with common skills to work together. The divisional structure is composed of autonomous units or divisions, with managers having full responsibility for a product or service. However, these units are frequently organized as functional structures inside their divisional framework. So divisional structures typically contain functional structures within them—and they are less efficient.

8 *Explain the strengths of the matrix structure.*
By assigning specialists from functional departments to work on one or more projects led by project managers, the matrix structure combines functional and product departmentalization. It thus has the advantages of both work specialization and high accountability.

9 *Describe the boundaryless organization and what elements have contributed to its development.*
The boundaryless organization is a design application in which the structure is not defined by or limited to the boundaries imposed by traditional structures. It breaks down horizontal, vertical, and interorganizational barriers. It's also flexible and adaptable to environmental conditions. The factors contributing to boundaryless organizations include global markets and competition, technology advancements, and the need for rapid innovation.

10 *Describe what is meant by the term* organization culture.
Organization culture is a system of shared meaning within an organization that determines, in large degree, how employees act.

Review and Application Questions

READING FOR COMPREHENSION

1. Describe what is meant by the term *organization design.*
2. How are authority and organization structure related? Authority and power?
3. In what ways can management departmentalize? When should one method be considered over the others?
4. Why is the simple structure inadequate in large organizations?
5. Describe the characteristics of a boundaryless organization structure.
6. What is the source of an organization's culture?

LINKING CONCEPTS TO PRACTICE

1. Which do you think is more efficient—a wide or a narrow span of control? Support your decision.
2. "An organization can have no structure." Do you agree or disagree with this statement? Explain.
3. Show how both the functional and matrix structures might create conflict within an organization.
4. Do you think the concept of organizational structures, as described in this chapter, is appropriate for charitable organizations? If so, which organization design application would you believe to be most appropriate? If not, why not? Explain your position.
5. What effects do you think the characteristics of the boundaryless organization will have on employees in the twenty-first century organizations?
6. Classrooms have cultures. Describe your class culture. How does it affect your instructor? You?

Team Skill-Building Exercise

How Is Your School Organized?

Every university or college displays a specific type of organizational structure. That is, if you are a business major, your classes are often housed in a department, school, or college of business. But have you ever asked why? Or is it something you just take for granted?

In Chapter 3 you had an opportunity to assess your college's strengths, weaknesses, and comparative advantage and see how this fits into its strategy. Now, in this chapter we have built a case that structure follows strategy. Given your analysis in Chapter 3 (if you have not done so, you may want to refer to page 108 for the strategy part of this exercise), analyze your college's overall structure in terms of formalization, centralization, and complexity. Furthermore, look at the departmentalization that exists. Is your college more organic or mechanistic? Now analyze how well your college's structure fits with its strategy. Do the same thing for your college's size, technology, and environment. That is, assess its size, degree of technological routineness, and environmental uncertainty. Based on these assessments, what kind of structure would you predict your college to have? Does it have this structure now? Compare your findings with other classmates. Are there similarities in how each viewed the college? Differences? What do you believe has attributed to these findings?

Developing Your Power Base Skill

Building a Power Base

ABOUT THE SKILL

One of the more difficult aspects of power is acquiring it. For some individuals, power comes naturally, and, for some, it is a function of the job they hold. But what can others do to develop power? The answer is respect others, build power relationships, develop associations, control important information, gain seniority, and build power in stages.[55]

STEPS IN PRACTICING THE SKILL

1 **Respect others.** One of the most crucial aspects of developing power is to treat others the way you would like to be treated. That sentence may be a cliché, but it holds a tremendous key. If others don't respect you, your power will generally be limited. Sure, they may do the things you ask, but only because of the authority of your position. People need to know that you're genuine, and that means respecting others. In today's world, with the great diversity that exists, you must be sensitive to others' needs. Failure to do so may only lead to problems, most of which can be avoided if you see the good in people and realize that most people try their best and want to do a good job.

2 **Build power relationships.** People who possess power often associate with others who have power. It appears to be a natural phenomenon—birds of a feather do flock together! You need to identify these people and model their behavior.[56] The idea is that you want to make yourself visible to powerful people and let them observe you in a number of situations.

3 **Develop associations.** We learn at an early age that there is strength in numbers. In the "power" world, this tenet also applies. By associating with others, you become part of a group in which all the members' energies are brought together to form one large base of power. Often called coalitions, these groups form to influence some event.

4. **Control important information.** Get yourself into a position that gives you access to information other people perceive as important. Access to information is especially critical in a world where people's lives depend so much on information processing. One of the greatest means of developing this power is to continue to learn. Finding new approaches to solve old problems or creating a special process are ways of gaining a level of expertise that can make you indispensable to the organization.
5. **Gain seniority.** Seniority is somewhat related to controlling information. Power can be gained by simply having been around for a long time. People will often respect individuals who have lived through the ups and downs of an organization. Their experience gives them a perspective or information that newcomers don't have.
6. **Build power in stages.** No one goes from being powerless one moment to being powerful the next. That simply doesn't occur. Power comes in phases. As you build your power, remember, it will start off slowly. You will be given opportunities to demonstrate that you can handle the power. After each test you pass, you'll more than likely be given more power.

Practicing the Skill

BUILDING A POWER BASE

Mariel is a supervisor in the Internet sales division of a large clothing retailer. She has let it be known that she is devoted to the firm and plans to build her career there.

Mariel is hard-working and reliable, has volunteered for extra projects, has taken in-house development courses, and joined a committee dedicated to improving employee safety on the job. She undertook an assignment to research ergonomic office furniture for the head of the department and gave up several lunch hours to consult with the head of human resources about her report. Mariel filed the report late, but she excused herself by explaining that her assistant lost several pages that she had to redraft over the weekend. The report was well received and several of Mariel's colleagues think she should be promoted when the next opening arises.

Evaluate Mariel's skill in building a power base. What actions has she taken that are helpful to her in reaching her goal? Is there anything she should have done differently?

A Case Application

Developing Your Diagnostic and Analytical Skills

ASEA BROWN BOVERI

Can an organization be both a global giant and yet act as if it were a small, local business? Most organizations must answer this question in the negative, but don't mention that to the executives at Asea Brown Boveri (ABB), the Switzerland-based multibillion-dollar world leader in electric power generation, high-speed trains, and robotics.[57]

ABB was formed in 1988 through a merger of Asea, a Swedish engineering group, with Brown Boveri, a Swiss competitor. At the time of the merger, company executives were facing a challenge of becoming a world-class global leader. Although they recognized that large size created more possibilities, ABB executives realized that it could also be an impediment. Trying to maintain centralized control over global operations simply created too many efficiencies. Moreover, flatter structures that encouraged lateral communications were needed to create smaller-company dynamics.

To achieve their vision, ABB executives embarked on a number of organizational design activities. Headquarters staff was cut from more than 2,000 employees to just under 180. The company was divided into 1,300 separate companies and 5,000 profit centers, each focusing on a particular customer and market.

And authority, responsibility, and accountability for the success of each of these units are pushed down to the lowest level possible. One of the most striking elements of the ABB restructuring, however, was the introduction of an innovative dual chain of command. ABB has approximately 250 managers, who lead the organizations 250,000 employees. Each of these managers runs his or her operations with a local board of directors. In addition, ABB has approximately 60 global business managers who are organized into eight segments such as financial services, transportation, process automation and engineering, electrical equipment, and electrical power businesses of power generation, transportation, and distribution. This structure makes it easier for local managers to capitalize on information and other technologies from different countries and transport these best practices to various parts of the organization.

Over more than 10 years, ABB has demonstrated that large organizations can flourish in today's dynamic environment. Yet that is mostly accomplished by having an organization structure that is fluid enough to rapidly adjust to the competitive pressures the changing world.

QUESTIONS

1 Would you describe ABB as more of a mechanistic or an organic organization? Explain and use specific examples to support your position.

2 How have technology and communications affected ABB's organizational structure?

3 How would you describe the characteristics of ABB's culture? Use Exhibit 5-13 as a guide in answering this question.

Developing Your Investigative Skills

Using the Internet

Visit *www.prenhall.com/robbins* for updated Internet Exercises.

Enhancing Your Writing Skills

Communicating Effectively

1 Visit a McDonald's on a weekday around lunch time. On your first order, ask for a Big Mac or a chicken sandwich. Record how long it takes to have your order filled. On your second order, request the Big Mac or chicken sandwich and ask for a) no lettuce, b) extra ketchup, and c) extra pickles. Record how long this special order takes. Compare the two times. Discuss the time differences in terms of efficiencies of work specialization. Also note whether the second order was completed correctly. What are the implications of this simple investigation for product standardization?

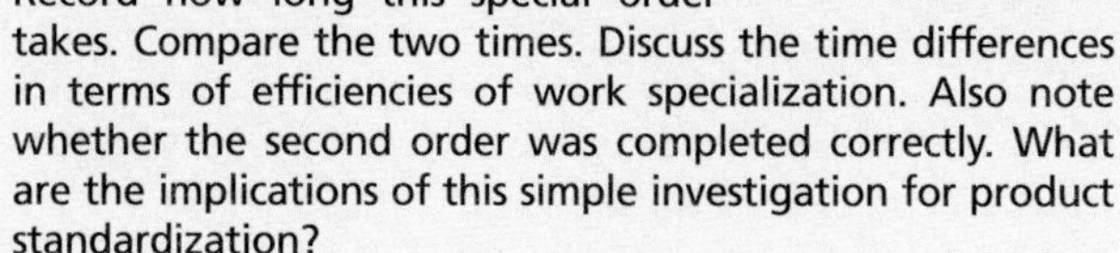

2 Discuss the pros and cons of employees working on projects and reporting to several project managers. Discuss the implications you envision for violating the chain of command principle. Cite specific examples. If you were a project manager who managed project members who reported to other managers, what would you do to make sure that your project would be completed on time?

3 "Employees should follow orders and directives given to them by their managers. Those who don't are subject to being disciplined for insubordination." Develop an argument for both sides of this statement. Complete your paper by stating and supporting your position on whether employees should unquestionably follow orders given to them by their managers.

Six

Staffing and Human Resource Management

LEARNING OUTCOMES After reading this chapter, I will be able to:

1. Describe the human resource management process.
2. Identify the influence of government regulations on human resource decisions.
3. Differentiate between job descriptions and job specifications.
4. Contrast recruitment and downsizing options.
5. Explain the importance of validity and reliability in selection.
6. Describe the selection devices that work best with various kinds of jobs.
7. Identify various training methods.
8. Explain the various techniques managers can use in evaluating employee performance.
9. Describe the goals of compensation administration and factors that affect wage structures.
10. Explain what is meant by the terms *sexual harassment, family-friendly benefits, labor-management cooperation, workplace violence*, and *layoff-survivor sickness.*

What do Starflight Enterprises and AIDA Electronics have in common? Is it that they're successful small businesses that are growing every year? Is it the fact that each has found a particular niche on which to capitalize and meet customer needs? The answer is yes to both questions, but the main thing each of these organizations has in common is that neither of them has their own employees. They lease their employees from HR Tech, a Columbia, Maryland-based professional employee organization.[1]

A professional employee organization (PEO) is a firm that "provides integrated human resource administration and risk management services" to other organizations. That is, a PEO recruits, trains, pays employees, and handles all the necessary insurance and government reporting requirements. PEOs like HR Tech provide an avenue for companies to outsource all their human resource activities. The employees, although they are technically PEO employees, permanently work for client organizations.

HR Tech was founded in 1995 by Scott Thompson, Darren Seward, and Tony Bonacuse. All three recognized that human resource services—especially employee benefits and government compliance programs—were major headaches for small business owners who wanted to do the things they enjoyed most—selling the services of their business. However, they needed employees, and with each employee came a variety of responsibilities. For example, if an organization has 15 employees, it is required to follow a wide variety of government regulations related to hiring, firing, and promoting them. Completing the requisite payroll documentation as well as employee safety forms is generally more involved than most entrepreneurs envision. Furthermore, attracting skilled employees in smaller businesses is more often more difficult because these businesses typically cannot afford to offer the full array of employee benefits that many of today's workers seek. For Thompson, Seward, and Bonacuse, this challenge created an opportunity for them to provide a valuable service to smaller businesses.

HR Tech targets organizations with fewer than 100 employees that need a fully functioning human resource department but can't justify the costs. For a fee ranging from 10 percent to 20 percent of their total payroll costs, HR Tech handles all the human resource activities for a client organization. For example, they issue paychecks, deposit payroll taxes, handle unemployment and workers' compensation claims, provide employee benefits, screen applicants, and develop employee handbooks. HR Tech will also handle terminations if necessary. Freeing small business owners from endless paperwork and government regulations is only one piece of the puzzle. By hiring the employees and leasing them to client organizations, HR Tech is able to provide employee benefits at a much lower cost than if small business owners had to buy them separately, allowing the client organizations to offer the benefits "their" employees desire at a fraction of the cost. This includes comprehensive health insurance plans, retirement programs, credit union membership, and life insurance. These programs alone have helped reduce turnover in many of HR Tech's client organizations.

Have Thompson, Seward, and Bonacuse built a better mousetrap? It looks like it. HR Tech has witnessed revenues increase from $5 million in 1996 to over $110 million in 1998. The company now has more than 200 clients and leases out more than 5,000 employees. In just over three years, the company has gone from an idea in the minds of these three entrepreneurs to the 19th largest private-sector employer in the Mid-Atlantic United States.

Managers and the Human Resource Management Process

The quality of an organization is, to a large degree, determined by the quality of people it employs. Success for most organizations depends on finding the employees with the skills to successfully perform the tasks required to attain the company's strategic goals. Staffing and human resource management decisions and methods are critical to ensuring that the organization hires and keeps the right personnel.

Some of you may be thinking, "Sure, personnel decisions are important. But aren't most of them made by people who specifically handle human resource issues?" It's true that, in many organizations, a number of the activities grouped under the label **human resource management (HRM)** are done by specialists. In other cases, HRM activities may even be outsourced to companies like HR Tech. Not all managers have HRM staff support. Many small business managers, for instance, are obvious examples of individuals who frequently must do their own hiring without the assistance of HRM specialists. Even managers in larger organizations are frequently involved in recruiting candidates, reviewing application forms, interviewing applicants, inducting new employees, making decisions about employee training, providing career advice to employees, and evaluating employees' performance. So, whether or not an organization provides HRM support activities, every manager is involved with human resource decisions in his or her unit.

human resources management (HRM)
The management function that is concerned with getting, training, motivating, and keeping competent employees.

Exhibit 6-1 introduces the key components of an organization's human resource management process. It represents eight activities, or steps (the blue-shaded boxes),

Exhibit 6-1 The Strategic Human Resource Management Process

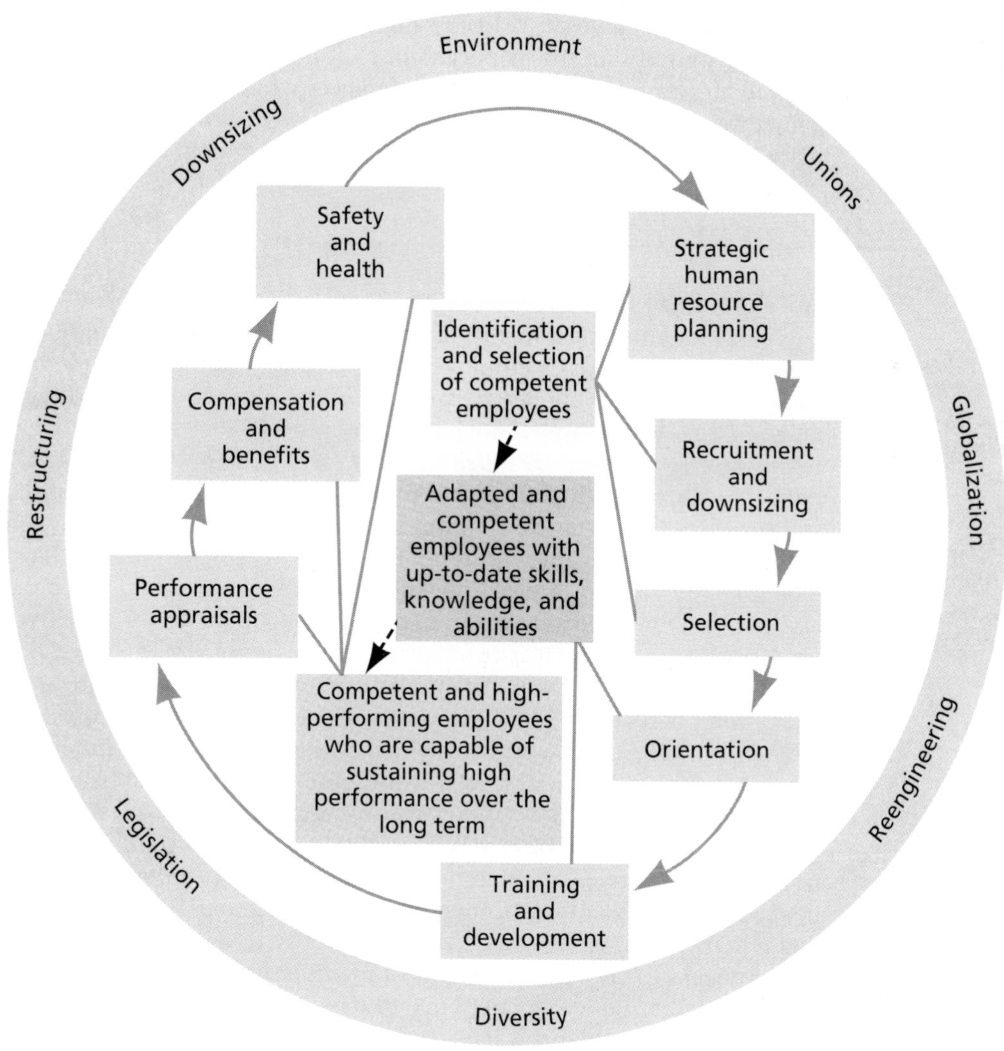

that, if properly executed, will staff an organization with competent, high-performing employees who are capable of sustaining their performance level over the long term.

The first three steps represent employment planning, the addition of staff through recruitment and the reduction in staff through downsizing, and selection. When executed properly, these steps lead to the identification and selection of competent employees and assist organizations in achieving their strategic direction.[2] Accordingly, once an organization's strategy has been established and the organization structure has been designed, it's now time to add the people. That's one of the most critical roles for HRM and one that has increased the importance of human resource managers to the organization.

Once you have selected competent people, you need to help them adapt to the organization and to ensure that their job skills and knowledge are kept current. You do this through orientation and training and development. The last steps in the HRM process are designed to identify performance goals, correct performance problems if necessary, and help employees sustain a high level of performance over their entire work life. The activities involved include performance appraisal, compensation and benefits, and safety and health.

Notice in Exhibit 6-1 that the entire employment process is influenced by the external environment. Many of the factors introduced in Chapter 2 (e.g., globalization, downsizing, diversity) directly affect all management practices, but their effect is probably greatest in the management of human resources, because whatever happens to an organization ultimately influences what happens to its employees. So, before we review the human resource management process, let's examine one primary environmental force that affects HRM—employment and discrimination laws.

The Legal Environment of HRM

Since the mid-1960s, the federal government has greatly expanded its influence over HRM by enacting a wealth of laws and regulations (see Exhibit 6-2 for examples). As a result, today's employers must ensure that equal employment opportunities exist for job applicants and current employees. Decisions regarding who will be hired, for example, or which employees will be chosen for a management training program must be made without regard to race, sex, religion, age, color, national origin, or disability. Exceptions can occur only when special circumstances exist. For instance, a community fire department can deny employment to a firefighter applicant who is confined to a wheelchair, but if that same individual is applying for a desk job, such as a fire department dispatcher, the disability cannot be used as a reason to deny employment. The issues involved, however, are rarely that clear-cut. For example, employment laws protect most employees whose religious beliefs require a specific style of dress—robes, long shirts, long hair, and the like. However, if the specific style of dress may be hazardous or unsafe in the work setting (e.g., when operating machinery), a company could refuse to hire a person who would not adopt a safer dress code.[3]

affirmative action programs
Programs that ensure that decisions and practices enhance the employment, upgrading, and retention of members of protected groups

Trying to balance the "shoulds and should-nots" of these laws often falls within the realm of **affirmative action.** Many organizations have affirmative action programs to ensure that decisions and practices enhance the employment, upgrading, and retention of members from protected groups such as minorities and females. That is, the organization not only refrains from discrimination but actively seeks to enhance the status of members from protected groups.

Managers are not completely free to choose whom they hire, promote, or fire. Although these regulations have significantly helped to reduce employment dis-

Exhibit 6-2 Major U.S. Federal Laws and Regulations Related to HRM

Year	Law or Regulation	Description
1963	Equal Pay Act	Prohibits pay differences based on sex for equal work
1964 (amended in 1972)	Civil Rights Act, Title VII	Prohibits discrimination based on race, color, religion, national origin, or sex
1967 (amended in 1978)	Age Discrimination in Employment Act	Prohibits age discrimination against employees between 40 and 65 years of age
1973	Vocational Rehabilitation Act	Prohibits discrimination on the basis of physical or mental disabilities
1974	Privacy Act	Gives employees the legal right to examine letters of reference concerning them
1978	Pregnancy Discrimination Act, Title VII	Prohibits dismissal because of pregnancy alone and protects job security during maternity leaves
1978	Mandatory Retirement Act	Prohibits the forced retirement of most employees before the age of 70; later amended to eliminate upper limit
1986	Immigration Reform and Control Act	Prohibits unlawful employment of aliens and unfair immigration-related employment practices
1988	Polygraph Protection Act	Limits an employer's ability to use lie detectors
1988	Worker Adjustment and Retraining Notification Act	Requires employers to provide 60 days' notice before a facility closing or mass layoff
1990	Americans with Disabilities Act	Prohibits employers from discriminating against and requires reasonable accommodation of essentially qualified individuals with physical or mental disabilities or the chronically ill
1991	Civil Rights Act	Reaffirms and tightens prohibition of discrimination; permits individuals to sue for punitive damages in cases of intentional discrimination
1993	Family and Medical Leave Act	Permits employees in organizations with 50 or more workers to take up to 12 weeks of unpaid leave each year for family or medical reasons

crimination and unfair employment practices, they have, at the same time, reduced management's discretion over human resource decisions.

Employment Planning

Employment planning is the process by which management ensures that it has the right number and kinds of people in the right places at the right times, people who are capable of effectively and efficiently completing those tasks that will help the organization achieve its overall objectives. Employment planning, then, translates the organization's mission and objectives into a personnel plan that will allow the organization to achieve its goals. Employment planning can be condensed into two steps: (1) assessing current human resources and (2) assessing

employment planning
The process by which management ensures it has the right number and kinds of people in the right places at the right time, capable of helping the organization achieve its goals

future human resource needs and developing a program to meet future human resource needs.

human resource inventory report
A report listing the name, education, training, prior employer, languages spoken, and the like of each employee in the organization

job analysis
An assessment of the kinds of skills, knowledge, and abilities needed to successfully perform each job in an organization

job description
A written statement of what a job holder does, how it is done, and why it is done

job specification
A statement of the minimum acceptable qualifications that an incumbent must possess to perform a given job successfully

HOW DOES AN ORGANIZATION CONDUCT AN EMPLOYEE ASSESSMENT?

Management begins by reviewing its current human resource status. This review is typically done by generating a **human resource inventory.** In an era of sophisticated computer systems, it is not too difficult a task to generate a human resource inventory report in most organizations. The input for this report is derived from forms completed by employees. Such reports might list the name, education, training, prior employment, languages spoken, capabilities, and specialized skills of each employee in the organization. This inventory allows management to assess what talents and skills are currently available in the organization.

Another part of the current assessment is the **job analysis.** Whereas the human resource inventory is concerned with telling management what individual employees can do, job analysis is more fundamental. It is typically a lengthy process, one in which workflows are analyzed and behaviors that are necessary to perform jobs are identified. For instance, what does an international photographer who works for *National Geographic* do? What minimal knowledge, skills, and abilities are necessary for the adequate performance of this job? How do the job requirements for an international photographer compare with those for a domestic photographer or for a photo librarian? These are questions that job analysis can answer. Ultimately, the purpose of job analysis is to determine the kinds of skills, knowledge, and attitudes needed to successfully perform each job. This information is then used to develop, or revise if they already exist, job descriptions and job specifications.

What skills, knowledge, and abilities does this employee need to be successful in her job as a computer programmer? The answer to that question lies in the job analysis. Information from the job analysis is used to develop job descriptions and job specifications, which detail the duties of the job and performance expectations, as well as what the employee must possess to be a successful performer.

A **job description** is a written statement of what a job holder does, how it is done, and why it is done. It typically portrays job content, environment, and conditions of employment. The **job specification** states the minimum qualifications that an incumbent must possess to perform a given job successfully. It identifies the knowledge, skills, and attitudes needed to do the job effectively. The job description and specification are important documents when managers begin recruiting and selecting. For instance, the job description can be used to describe the job to potential candidates. The job specification keeps the manager's attention on the list of qualifications necessary for an incumbent to perform a job and assists in determining whether candidates are qualified. Furthermore, hiring individuals on the basis of the information contained in these two documents helps to ensure that the hiring process is not discriminatory.

HOW ARE FUTURE EMPLOYEE NEEDS DETERMINED?

Future human resource needs are determined by the organization's strategic direction. Demand for human resources (its employees) is a result of demand for the organization's products or services. On the basis of its estimate of total revenue, management can attempt to establish the number and mix of human resources needed to reach that revenue. In some cases, however, the situation may be reversed. When particular skills are necessary and in scarce supply, the availability of satisfactory human resources determines revenues. This might be the case for managers in information technology companies like Intel or Sybase that find themselves with more business opportunities than they can handle. The managers' primary limiting factor in building revenues is their ability to locate and hire staff with the qualifications necessary to satisfy the firm's clients.[4] In most cases, however, the overall organizational goals and the resulting revenue forecast provide the major input in determining the organization's human resource requirements.

After it has assessed both current capabilities and future needs, management is able to estimate shortages—both in number and in kind—and to highlight areas in which the organization is overstaffed. A program can then be developed that matches these estimates with forecasts of future labor supply. Employment planning not only guides current staffing needs but also projects future employee needs and availability.

Recruitment and Selection

Once managers know their current staffing levels—whether they are understaffed or overstaffed—they can begin to do something about it. If one or more vacancies exist, they can use the information gathered through job analysis to guide them in **recruitment**—that is, the process of locating, identifying, and attracting capable applicants.[5] On the other hand, if employment planning indicates a surplus, management will want to reduce the labor supply within the organization and will initiate downsizing or layoff activities.

recruitment
The process of locating, identifying, and attracting capable applicants

WHERE DOES A MANAGER RECRUIT CANDIDATES?

Candidates can be found by using several sources—including the World Wide Web. Exhibit 6-3 offers some guidance. The source that is used should reflect the local labor market, the type or level of position, and the size of the organization.

Are certain recruiting sources better than others? Do certain recruiting sources produce superior candidates? The answer is generally Yes. The majority of studies have found that employee referrals generally produce the best candidates.[6] The explanation for this finding is intuitively logical. First, applicants referred by current employees are prescreened by those employees. Because the recommenders know both the job and the person being recommended, they tend to refer well-qualified applicants. Second, because current employees often feel that their reputation in the organization is at stake with a referral, they tend to make referrals only when they are reasonably confident that the referral won't make them look bad. However, management should not always opt for the employee-referred candidate: Employee referrals may not increase the diversity and mix of employees.

Employees will make a referral when they are reasonably confident that the referral won't make them look bad.

Exhibit 6-3
Traditional Recruiting Sources

Source	Advantages	Disadvantages
Internal searches	Low cost; build employee morale; candidates are familiar with organization	Limited supply; may not increase proportion of protected group employees
Advertisements	Wide distribution can be targeted to specific groups	Generate many unqualified candidates
Employee referrals	Knowledge about the organization provided by current employees; can generate strong candidates because a good referral reflects on the recommender	May not increase the diversity and mix of employees
Public employment agencies	Free or nominal cost	Candidates tend to be lower skilled, although some skilled employees available
Private employment agencies	Wide contacts; careful screening; short-term guarantees often given	High cost
School placement	Large, centralized body of candidates	Limited to entry-level positions
Temporary help services	Fill temporary needs	Expensive
Employee leasing and independent contractors	Fill temporary needs, but usually for more specific, longer-term projects	Little commitment to organization other than current project

How does a manager handle layoffs? In the past decade, most large U.S. corporations, as well as many government agencies and small businesses, have been forced to shrink the size of their workforce or restructure their skill composition. Downsizing has become a relevant means of meeting the demands of a dynamic environment.

What are a manager's downsizing options? Obviously, people can be fired, but other choices may be more beneficial to the organization. Exhibit 6-4 summarizes a manager's major downsizing options. But keep in mind, regardless of the method chosen, employees may suffer. We discuss this phenomenon for employees—both victims and survivors—later in this chapter.

IS THERE A BASIC METHOD OF SELECTING JOB CANDIDATES?

selection process
The process of screening job applicants to ensure that the most appropriate candidates are hired

Once the recruiting effort has developed a pool of candidates, the next step in the employment process is to determine who is best qualified for the job. In essence, then, the **selection process** is a prediction exercise: It seeks to predict which applicants will be "successful" if hired, which candidates will perform well on the criteria the organization uses to evaluate its employees. In filling a network administrator position, for example, the selection process should be able to predict which applicants will be able to properly install, debug, and manage the orga-

Option	Description
Firing	Permanent involuntary termination
Layoffs	Temporary involuntary termination; may last only a few days or extend to years
Attrition	Not filling openings created by voluntary resignations or normal retirements
Transfers	Moving employees either laterally or downward; usually does not reduce costs but can reduce intraorganizational supply-demand imbalances
Reduced workweeks	Having employees work fewer hours per week, share jobs, or perform their jobs on a part-time basis
Early retirements	Providing incentives to older and more-senior employees for retiring before their normal retirement date
Job sharing	Having employees, typically two part-timers, share one full-time position

Exhibit 6-4
Downsizing Options

nization's computer network. For a position as a sales representative, it should predict which applicants will be effective in generating high sales volumes. Consider, for a moment, that any selection decision can result in four possible outcomes. As shown in Exhibit 6-5, two of those outcomes would indicate correct decisions, and two would indicate errors.

A decision is correct (1) when the applicant was predicted to be successful (was accepted) and later proved to be successful on the job or (2) when the applicant was predicted to be unsuccessful (was rejected) and, if hired, would not have been able to do the job. In the former case, we have successfully accepted; in the latter case, we have successfully rejected. Problems occur, however, when we reject candidates who, if hired, would have performed successfully on the job (called reject errors) or accept those who subsequently perform poorly (accept errors). These problems are, unfortunately, far from insignificant. A generation ago, reject errors meant only that the costs of selection were increased because more candidates would have to be screened. Today, selection techniques that result in reject errors can open the organization to charges of employment discrimination, especially if applicants from protected groups are disproportionately rejected. Accept errors, on the other hand, have very obvious costs to the organization, including the cost of training the employee, the costs generated or profits foregone because of the

Later Job Performance	Reject	Accept
Successful	Reject error	Correct decision
Unsuccessful	Correct decision	Accept error
	Selection Decision	

Exhibit 6-5
Selection Decision Outcomes

employee's incompetence, and the cost of severance and the subsequent costs of additional recruiting and selection screening. The major thrust of any selection activity is, therefore, to reduce the probability of making reject errors or accept errors while increasing the probability of making correct decisions. We do this by using selection procedures that are both reliable and valid.

reliability
The degree to which a selection device measures the same thing consistently

What is reliability? **Reliability** addresses whether a selection device measures the same characteristic consistently. For example, if a test is reliable, any individual's score should remain fairly stable over time, assuming that the characteristics it is measuring are also stable. The importance of reliability should be self-evident. No selection device can be effective if it is low in reliability. Using such a device would be the equivalent of weighing yourself every day on an erratic scale. If the scale is unreliable—randomly fluctuating, say, 10 to 15 pounds every time you step on it—the results will not mean much. To be effective predictors, selection devices must possess an acceptable level of consistency.

validity
The proven relationship between a selection device and some relevant criterion

What is validity? Any selection device that a manager uses—such as application forms, tests, interviews, or physical examinations—must also demonstrate **validity.** That is, there must be a proven relationship between the selection device used and some relevant measure. For example, a few pages ago, we mentioned a firefighter applicant who was wheelchair bound. Because of the physical requirements of a firefighter's job, someone confined to a wheelchair would be unable to pass the physical endurance tests. In that case, denying employment could be considered valid, but requiring the same physical endurance tests for the dispatching job would not be job related. Thus, the law prohibits management from using any selection device that cannot be shown to be directly related to successful job performance. That constraint goes for entrance tests, too; management must be able to demonstrate that, once on the job, individuals with high scores on this test outperform individuals with low scores. Consequently, the burden is on management to verify that any selection device it uses to differentiate applicants is related to job performance.

The burden is on management to verify that any selection device it uses is related to successful job performance.

HOW EFFECTIVE ARE TESTS AND INTERVIEWS AS SELECTION DEVICES?

Managers can use a number of selection devices to reduce accept and reject errors. The best-known devices include written and performance-simulation tests, and interviews. Let's briefly review these devices, giving particular attention to the validity of each in predicting job performance. After we review them, we'll discuss when each should be used.

How do written tests serve a useful purpose? Typical written tests include tests of intelligence, aptitude, ability, and interest. Such tests have long been used as selection devices, although their popularity has run in cycles. Written tests were widely used for twenty years after World War II, but beginning in the late 1960s, they fell into disfavor. They were frequently characterized as discriminatory, and many organizations could not validate that their written tests were job related. But, since the late 1980s, written tests have made a comeback. Managers have become increasingly aware that poor hiring decisions are costly and that properly designed tests could reduce the likelihood of making such decisions. In addition, the cost of developing and validating a set of written tests for a specific job has come down markedly.

A review of the evidence finds that tests of intellectual ability, spatial and mechanical ability, perceptual accuracy, and motor ability are moderately valid predictors for many semiskilled and unskilled operative jobs in industrial organizations.[7] And intelligence tests are reasonably good predictors for supervisory positions.[8] However, an enduring criticism of written tests is that intelligence and other tested characteristics can be somewhat removed from the actual performance of the job itself. For example, a high score on an intelligence test is not necessarily a good indicator that the applicant will perform well as a computer programmer. This criticism has led to an increased use of performance-simulation tests.

Here's one to consider when selecting employees. Everything about this candidate's résumé looks great. But when she shows up for the interview, she appears with multiple facial piercings which you know go against the grain of the conservative culture of your organization. Do you believe this individual "fits?" How would you react to her in an interview setting?

What are performance-simulation tests? What better way is there to find out whether an applicant for a technical writing position at Siemens can write technical manuals than to ask him or her to do it? The logic of this question has led to the increasing interest in performance-simulation tests. Undoubtedly, the enthusiasm for these tests lies in the fact that they are based on job-analysis data and, therefore, should more easily meet the requirement of job relatedness than do written tests. **Performance-simulation tests** are made up of actual job behaviors rather than substitutes. The best-known performance-simulation tests are work sampling (a miniature replica of the job) and assessment centers (simulating real problems one may face on the job). The former is suited to persons applying for routine jobs, the latter to managerial personnel.

performance-simulation tests
Selection devices that are based on actual job behaviors; work sampling and assessment centers

The advantage of performance simulation over traditional testing methods should be obvious. Because content is essentially identical to job content, performance simulation should be a better predictor of short-term job performance and should minimize potential employment discrimination allegations.[9] Additionally, because of the nature of their content and the methods used to determine content, well-constructed performance-simulation tests are valid predictors.

Is the interview effective? The interview, along with the application form, is an almost universal selection device.[10] Few of us have ever gotten a job without undergoing one or more interviews (see Ethical Dilemma in Management). The irony of this fact is that the value of the interview as a selection device has been the subject of considerable debate.[11]

Interviews can be reliable and valid selection tools, but too often they are not. When interviews are structured and well organized, and when interviewers are held to relevant questioning, interviews are effective predictors.[12] But those conditions do not characterize many interviews. The typical interview in which appli-

Ethical Dilemma in Management

Stress Interviews

Your interview day has finally arrived. You are all dressed up to make that lasting first impression. You finally meet Mr. Bedford: He shakes your hand firmly and invites you to get comfortable. Your interview has started. This is the moment you've waited for.

The first few moments appear mundane enough. The questions, in fact, seem easy. Your confidence is growing. That little voice in your head keeps telling you that you are doing fine—just keep on going. Suddenly, the questions get tougher. Mr. Bedford leans back and asks why you want to leave your current job—the one you've been in for only 18 months. As you begin to explain that you wish to leave for personal reasons, he starts to probe. His smile is gone. His body language is different. All right, you think, be honest. So you tell Mr. Bedford that you want to leave because your boss is unethical and you don't want your reputation tarnished by being associated with this individual. This situation has led to a number of public disagreements with your boss, and you're tired of dealing with the problem. Mr. Bedford looks at you and replies, "If you ask me, that's not a valid reason for wanting to leave. Appears to me that you should be more assertive about the situation. Are you sure you're confident enough and have what it takes to make it in this company?"

How dare he talk to you that way! Who does he think he is? You respond in an angry tone. And guess what, you've just fallen victim to one of the tricks of the interviewing business—the stress interview.[13]

Stress interviews are becoming more commonplace. Every job produces stress, and at some point, every worker has a horrendous day. So these types of interviews predict how you may react under less-than-favorable conditions. Interviewers want to observe how you'll react when you are put under pressure. Applicants who demonstrate the resolve and strength to handle the stress indicate a level of professionalism and confidence. It's those characteristics that are being assessed. Individuals who react to the pressure interview in a positive manner indicate that they should be able to handle the day-to-day irritations at work. Those who don't, well. . . .

On the other hand, these interviews are staged events. Interviewers deliberately lead applicants into a false sense of security—the comfortable interaction. Then suddenly and drastically, they change. They go on the attack. And it's usually a personal assault on a weakness they've uncovered about the applicant. It's possibly humiliating; at the very least, it's demeaning.

Should stress interviews be used? Should interviewers be permitted to assess professionalism and confidence and how one reacts to the everyday nuisances of work by putting applicants into a confrontational scenario? Should human resources advocate the use of an activity that could possibly get out of control? What's your opinion?

cants are asked a varying set of essentially random questions in an informal setting often provides little in the way of valuable information.

All kinds of potential biases can creep into interviews if they are not well structured and standardized. To illustrate, a review of the research leads us to the following conclusions:

- Prior knowledge about the applicant will bias the interviewer's evaluation.
- The interviewer tends to hold a stereotype of what represents a good applicant.
- The interviewer tends to favor applicants who share his or her own attitudes.
- The order in which applicants are interviewed will influence evaluations.
- The order in which information is elicited during the interview will influence evaluations.
- Negative information is given unduly high weight.
- The interviewer may make a decision concerning the applicant's suitability within the first four or five minutes of the interview.
- The interviewer may forget much of the interview's content within minutes after its conclusion.

- The interview is most valid in determining an applicant's intelligence, level of motivation, and interpersonal skills.
- Structured and well-organized interviews are more reliable than unstructured and unorganized ones.[14]

What can managers do to make interviews more valid and reliable? A number of suggestions have been made over the years. We list some in Developing Your Interviewing Skill, p. 214.

How can you close the deal? Interviewers who treat the recruiting and hiring of employees as if the applicants must be sold on the job and exposed only to an organization's positive characteristics are likely to have a workforce that is dissatisfied and prone to high turnover.[15]

Every job applicant acquires, during the hiring process, a set of expectations about the company and about the job for which he or she is interviewing. When the information an applicant receives is excessively inflated, a number of things happen that have potentially negative effects on the company. First, mismatched applicants are less likely to withdraw from the search process. Second, because inflated information builds unrealistic expectations, new employees are likely to become quickly dissatisfied and to prematurely resign. Third, new hires are prone to become disillusioned and less committed to the organization when they face the unexpected harsh realities of the job. In many cases, these individuals feel that they were duped or misled during the hiring process and may become problem employees.

To increase job satisfaction among employees and reduce turnover, you should consider providing a **realistic job preview (RJP).** An RJP includes both positive and negative information about the job and the company. For example, in addition to the positive comments typically expressed in the interview, the candidate would be told of the less attractive aspects of the job. For instance, he or she might be told that there are limited opportunities to talk to coworkers during work hours, that promotional advancement is slim, or that work hours fluctuate so erratically that employees may be required to work during what are usually off hours (nights and weekends). Research indicates that applicants who have been given a realistic job preview hold lower and more realistic job expectations for the jobs they will be performing and are better able to cope with the frustrating elements of the job than are applicants who have been given only inflated information. The result is fewer unexpected resignations by new employees.

realistic job preview (RJP)
Providing both positive and negative information about the job and the company during the job interview

For managers, realistic job previews offer a major insight into the HRM process. That is, retaining good people is as important as hiring them in the first place. Presenting only the positive aspects of a job to a job applicant may initially entice him or her to join the organization, but it may be an affiliation that both parties will quickly regret.

Orientation, Training, and Development

If we have done our recruiting and selecting properly, we should have hired competent individuals who can perform successfully, but successful performance requires more than the possession of certain skills. New hires must be acclimated to the organization's culture and be trained to do the job in a manner consistent with the organization's objectives. To achieve these ends, HRM embarks on orientation and training.

HOW DO WE INTRODUCE NEW HIRES TO THE ORGANIZATION?

orientation
The introduction of a new employee to the job and the organization

Once a job candidate has been selected, he or she needs to be introduced to the job and organization. This introduction is called **orientation.** The major objectives of orientation are to reduce the initial anxiety all new employees feel as they begin a new job; to familiarize new employees with the job, the work unit, and the organization as a whole; and to facilitate the outsider-insider transition. Job orientation expands on the information the employee obtained during the recruitment and selection stages. The new employee's specific duties and responsibilities are clarified as well as how his or her performance will be evaluated. This is also the time to rectify any unrealistic expectations new employees might hold about the job. Work-unit orientation familiarizes the employee with the goals of the work unit, makes clear how his or her job contributes to the unit's goals, and provides an introduction to his or her coworkers. Organization orientation informs the new employee about the organization's objectives, history, philosophy, procedures, and rules. This information should include relevant personnel policies such as work hours, pay procedures, overtime requirements, and benefits. A tour of the organization's physical facilities is often part of the orientation.

Management has an obligation to make the integration of the new employee into the organization as smooth and as free of anxiety as possible. Successful orientation, whether formal or informal, results in an outsider-insider transition that makes the new member feel comfortable and fairly well adjusted, lowers the likelihood of poor work performance, and reduces the probability of a surprise resignation by the new employee only a week or two into the job.

Several years ago front-line employees, like hotel desk clerks, would have received a one-day orientation only. Today at Marriott, a 90-day orientation program truly adapts employees to their jobs—and to superb customer service.

WHAT IS EMPLOYEE TRAINING?

On the whole, planes don't cause airline accidents, people do. Most collisions, crashes, and other mishaps—nearly three quarters of them—result from errors by the pilot or air traffic controller or inadequate maintenance. Weather and structural failures typically account for the remaining accidents.[16] We cite these statistics to illustrate the importance of training in the airline industry. These maintenance and human errors could be prevented or significantly reduced by better employee training.

Employee training is a learning experience in that it seeks a relatively permanent change in employees such that their ability to perform on the job improves. Thus, training involves changing skills, knowledge, attitudes, or behavior.[17] This may mean changing what employees know, how they work, or their attitudes toward their jobs, coworkers, managers, and the organization. It has been estimated, for instance, that U.S. business firms alone spend over $30 billion a year on formal courses and training programs to develop workers' skills.[18] Management, of course, is responsible for deciding when employees are in need of training and what form that training should take.

Determining training needs typically involves generating answers to several questions (see Exhibit 6-6). If some of these questions sound familiar, you have been paying close attention. It is precisely the type of analysis that took place when managers developed an organization structure to achieve their strategic goals—only now the focus is on the people.

The leading questions in Exhibit 6-6 suggest the kinds of signals that can warn a manager when training may be necessary. The more obvious ones are related directly to productivity. There may be indications that job performance is declining such as decreases in production numbers, lower quality, more accidents, and higher scrap or rejection rates. Any of these outcomes might suggest that worker skills need to be fine tuned. Of course, we are assuming that the employee's performance decline is in no way related to lack of effort. Managers, too, must also recognize that training may be required because the workplace is constantly evolving. Changes imposed on employees as a result of job redesign or a technological breakthrough also require training.

How are employees trained? Most training takes place on the job. The prevalence of on-the-job training can be attributed to its simplicity of such methods and its usually lower cost. However, on-the-job training can disrupt the workplace and result in an increase in errors while learning takes place. Also, some skill training is too complex to learn on the job and should take place outside the work setting.

What are some of the typical methods used? Many different types of training methods are available. For the most part, however, we can classify them as on-the-job or off-the-job training. We have summarized the more popular training methods in Exhibit 6-7.

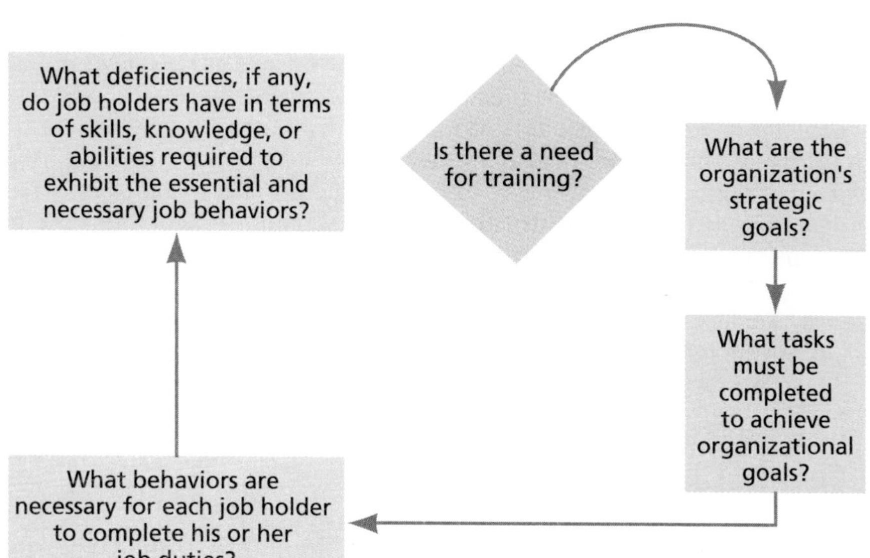

Exhibit 6-6
Determining if Training Is Needed

Exhibit 6-7
Typical Training Methods

Sample On-the-Job Training Methods	
Job rotation	Lateral transfers allowing employees to work at different jobs. Provides good exposure to a variety of tasks.
Understudy assignments	Working with a seasoned veteran, coach, or mentor. Provides support and encouragement from an experienced worker. In the trades industry, this may also be an apprenticeship.

Sample Off-the-Job Training Methods	
Classroom lectures	Lectures designed to convey specific technical, interpersonal, or problem-solving skills.
Films and videos	Using the media to explicitly demonstrate technical skills that are not easily presented by other training methods.
Simulation exercises	Learning a job by actually performing the work (or its simulation). May include case analyses, experiential exercises, role playing, and group interaction.
Vestibule training	Learning tasks on the same equipment that one actually will use on the job but in a simulated work environment.

How can managers ensure that training is working? It is easy to generate a new training program, but if the training effort is not evaluated, any employee-training efforts can be rationalized. It would be nice if all companies could boast the returns on investments in training that Motorola executives do; they claim they receive $30 in increased productivity for every dollar spent on training[19] as well as a 139 percent increase in sales productivity.[20] But such a claim cannot be made unless training is properly evaluated.

Can we determine how training programs are typically evaluated? The following approach is probably generalizable across organizations: Several managers, representatives from HRM, and a group of workers who have recently completed a training program are asked for their opinions. If the comments are generally positive, the program may get a favorable evaluation and the organization will continue it until someone decides, for whatever reason, it should be eliminated or replaced.

The reactions of participants or managers, while easy to acquire, are the least valid; their opinions are heavily influenced by factors that may have little to do with the training's effectiveness—difficulty, entertainment value, or the personality characteristics of the instructor. However, trainees' reactions to the training may, in fact, provide feedback on how worthwhile the participants viewed the training. Beyond general reactions, however, training must also be evaluated in terms of how much the participants learned, how well they are using their new skills on the job (did their behavior change?) and whether the training program achieved its desired results (reduced turnover, increased customer service, etc.).[21]

Performance Management

It is important for managers to get their employees to reach performance levels that the organization considers desirable. How do managers ensure that employees are performing as well as they are supposed to? In organizations, the formal means of assessing the work of employees is through a systematic performance appraisal process.

WHAT IS A PERFORMANCE MANAGEMENT SYSTEM?

A **performance management system** is a process of establishing performance standards and evaluating performance in order to arrive at objective human resource decisions—such as pay increases and training needs—as well as to provide documentation to support any personnel actions. Undoubtedly, performance appraisals are important. But how do you evaluate an employee's performance? That is, what are the specific techniques for appraisal? We have listed them in Exhibit 6-8.[22]

performance management system
A process of establishing performance standards and evaluating performance in order to arrive at objective human resource decisions and to provide documentation to support personnel actions

The *written essay* requires no complex forms or extensive training to complete. However, a "good" or "bad" appraisal may be determined as much by the evaluator's writing skill as by the employee's actual level of performance. The use of *critical incidents* focuses the evaluator's attention on those critical or key behaviors that separate effective from ineffective job performance. The appraiser writes down anecdotes describing whatever the employee did that was especially effective or ineffective. The key here is that only specific behaviors are cited, not vaguely defined personality traits. One of the oldest and most popular methods of appraisal is by *graphic rating scales*. This method lists a set of performance factors such as quantity and quality of work, job knowledge, cooperation, loyalty, attendance, honesty, and initiative. The evaluator then goes down the list and rates each factor on an incremental scale. An approach that has received renewed attention involves behaviorally anchored rating scales (BARS).[23] These scales combine major elements from the critical incident and graphic rating scale approaches. The appraiser rates an employee according to items along a numerical scale, but the items are examples of actual behavior on a given job rather than general descriptions or traits.[24]

Finally, an appraisal device that seeks performance feedback from such sources as the person being rated, bosses, peers, team members, customers, and suppliers has

Exhibit 6-8
Performance Appraisal Methods

Method	Advantage	Disadvantage
Written essay	Simple to use	More a measure of evaluator's writing ability than of employee's actual performance
Critical incidents	Rich examples behaviorally based	Time-consuming; lack quantification
Graphic rating scales	Provide quantitative data; less time-consuming than others	Do not provide depth of job behavior assessed
BARS	Focus on specific and measurable job behaviors	Time-consuming; difficult to develop measures
Multiperson	Compares employees with one another	Unwieldy with large number of employees
MBO	Focuses on end goals; results oriented	Time-consuming
360° Appraisal	More thorough	Time-consuming

360-degree appraisal An appraisal device that seeks feedback from a variety of sources for the person being rated

become very popular in organizations. It's called the **360-degree appraisal.**[25] It's being used in approximately 90 percent of the Fortune 1000 firms, which include such companies as Otis Elevator, DuPont, Nabisco, Warner-Lambert, Mobil Oil, Cook Children Health Care System, General Electric, and UPS.[26]

In today's dynamic organizations, traditional performance evaluations systems may be archaic. Downsizing has given supervisors greater responsibility and more employees who report directly to them. Accordingly, in some instances, it is almost impossible for supervisors to have extensive job knowledge of each of their employees. Furthermore, the growth of project teams and employee involvement in today's companies places the responsibility of evaluation at points at which people are better able to make an accurate assessment.[27]

The 360-degree feedback process also has some positive benefits for development concerns.[28] Many managers simply do not know how their employees view them and the work they have done. For example, Jerry Wallace, GM's Saturn plant's head of personnel, viewed himself as up to date on all the latest management techniques.[29] Although Jerry considered himself open to change and flexible to new ideas, feedback from his employees indicated that Jerry was a control freak. After some soul-searching, plus an assessment from an external leadership group, Jerry realized his employees were right. He finally understood why nobody wanted to be on a team with him and why he had to do everything himself.[30] In this case, the 360-degree feedback instrument eliminated a large barrier to Jerry's career advancement.

Research studies into the effectiveness of 360-degree performance appraisals are reporting positive results from more accurate feedback, empowering employees, reducing the subjective factors in the evaluation process, and developing leadership in an organization.[31]

One Manager's Perspective

Robbin Kalt Vice President, Morgan Stanley Dean Witter

At Morgan Stanley Dean Witter, the global financial services firm, the goal of using the 360° review is to develop people continuously. According to Robbin Kalt, vice president and development manager in information technology, the process has been well received among employees and managers alike. "Feedback is prone to be more fair and well rounded," she says, "if it is not coming just from the person's direct manager."

The system relies on formal, written feedback. This information is collected from a broad group of evaluators at all levels and divisions—senior managers, colleagues and peers, and people they manage. The employee also completes a self-evaluation listing his or her own development needs and career goals.

Specific skills and expected performance levels are defined for each functional area of the firm. When all the evaluations of the employee are received, the employee and an evaluation director, usually his or her boss, discuss the feedback, measure performance against the criteria that have been set, and review career goals. All of the input to the 360° review is kept strictly confidential.

One result of the system, says Kalt, is that "people seem to care more about their careers and are more proactive about improving their areas for development."

Should we compare people with one another or against a set of standards? The methods identified above have one thing in common. They require us to evaluate employees on the basis of how well their performance matches established or absolute criteria. Multiperson comparisons, on the other hand, compare one person's performance with that of one or more individuals. Thus, they are relative, not absolute, measuring devices. The three most popular forms of this method are group-order ranking, individual ranking, and paired comparison.

The *group-order ranking* requires the evaluator to place employees into a particular classification such as "top fifth" or "second fifth." If a rater has 20 employees, only 4 can be in the top fifth, and, of course, 4 must be relegated to the bottom fifth. The *individual ranking approach* requires the evaluator merely to list the employees in order from highest to lowest. Only one can be "best." In an appraisal of 30 employees, the difference between the first and second employee is assumed to be the same as that between the twenty-first and twenty-second. Even though some employees may be closely grouped, there can be no ties. In the *paired comparison approach,* each employee is compared with every other employee in the comparison group and rated as either the superior or weaker member of the pair. After all paired comparisons are made, each employee is assigned a summary ranking based on the number of superior scores he or she achieved. Although this approach ensures that each employee is compared against every other one, it can become unwieldy when large numbers of employees are being assessed.

Isn't MBO an appraisal approach too? We introduced management by objectives during our discussion of planning in Chapter 3. MBO, however, is also a mechanism for appraising performance. In fact, it is the preferred method for assessing managers and professional employees.[32]

Employees are evaluated by how well they accomplish a specific set of objectives that have been determined to be critical in the successful completion of their jobs. As you'll recall from our discussion in Chapter 3, these objectives need to be tangible, verifiable, and measurable. MBO's popularity among managerial personnel is probably due to its focus on end goals. Managers tend to emphasize such results-oriented outcomes as profit, sales, and costs. This emphasis meshes with MBO's concern with quantitative measures of performance. Because MBO emphasizes ends rather than means, this appraisal method allows managers to choose the best path for achieving their goals.

WHAT HAPPENS WHEN PERFORMANCE FALLS SHORT?

So far this discussion has focused on the performance management system. And, although that is designed to help managers ensure a productive workforce, one important question needs to be raised. What if an employee is not performing in a satisfactory manner? What can you do?

If, for some reason, an employee is not meeting his or her performance goals, a manager needs to find out why. If it is because the employee is mismatched for the job (a hiring error) or because he or she does not have adequate training, something relatively simple can be done; the manager can either reassign the individual into a job that better matches his or her skills or train the employee to do the job more effectively. If the problem is associated not with the employee's abilities but with his or her desire to do the job, it becomes a **discipline** problem. In that case, a manager can try counseling and, if necessary, can take disciplinary action such as verbal and written warnings, suspensions, and even terminations.

Employee counseling is a process designed to help employees overcome performance-related problems. Rather than viewing the performance problem from

discipline
Actions taken by a manager to enforce an organization's standards and regulations

employee counseling
A process designed to help employees overcome performance-related problems

a punitive point of view (discipline), employee counseling attempts to uncover why employees have lost their desire or ability to work productively. More important, it is designed to find ways to fix the problem. In many cases, employees don't go from being productive one day to being unproductive the next. Rather, the change happens gradually and may be a function of what is occurring in their personal lives. Employee counseling attempts to assist employees in getting help to resolve whatever is bothering them.

The premise behind employee counseling is fairly simple: It is beneficial to both the organization and the employee. Just as it is costly to have a worker quit shortly after being hired, it is costly to fire someone. The time spent recruiting and selecting, orienting, training, and developing employees translates into money. If, however, an organization can help employees overcome personal problems and get them back on the job quickly, it can avoid these costs. But make no mistake about it, employee counseling is not intended to lessen the effect of an employee's poor performance, nor is it intended to reduce his or her responsibility to change inappropriate work behavior. If the employee can't or won't accept help, then disciplinary actions must be taken.

Compensation and Benefits

You open the newspaper and the following job advertisement grabs your attention: "Wanted: Hard-working individual who is willing to work 60 hours a week in a less-than-ideal environment." The job pays no money but gives you the opportunity to say "I've done that." Sound intriguing to you? Probably not. Although there are exceptions, most of us work for money. What our jobs pay and what benefits we get fall under the heading of compensation and benefits. Determining what these will be is by no means easy.

HOW ARE PAY LEVELS DETERMINED?

How does management decide who gets paid $12.65 an hour and who receives $325,000 a year? The answer lies in compensation administration. The goals of **compensation administration** are to design a cost-effective pay structure that will attract and retain competent employees and to provide an incentive for these individuals to exert high energy levels at work. Compensation administration also attempts to ensure that pay levels, once determined, will be perceived as fair by all employees. Fairness means that the established pay levels are adequate and consistent for the demands and requirements of the job. Therefore, the primary determination of pay is the kind of job an employee performs. Different jobs require different kinds and levels of skills, knowledge, and abilities, and these vary in their value to the organization.[33] So, too, do the responsibility and authority of various positions. In short, the higher the skills, knowledge, and abilities—and the greater the authority and responsibility—the higher the pay.

compensation administration
The process of determining a cost-effective pay structure that will attract and retain competent employees, provide an incentive for them to work hard, and ensure that pay levels will be perceived as fair

Although skills, abilities, and the like directly affect pay levels, other factors may come into play. Pay levels may be influenced by the kind of business, the environment surrounding the job, geographic location, and employee performance levels and seniority. For example, private-sector jobs typically provide higher rates of pay than comparable positions in public and not-for-profit jobs. Employees who work under hazardous conditions (say, bridge builders operating 200 feet in the air), work unusual hours (e.g., the midnight shift), or work in geographic areas where the cost of living is higher (e.g., New York City rather than Tucson, Arizona) are typically more highly compensated. Employees who have been with an organization for a long time may have had a salary increase each year.

Irrespective of the factors mentioned above, there is one other most critical factor—management's compensation philosophy. Some organizations, for instance, don't pay employees any more than they have to. In the absence of a union contract that stipulates wage levels, those organizations only have to pay minimum wage for most of their jobs. On the other hand, some organizations are committed to a compensation philosophy of paying their employees at or above area wage levels in order to emphasize that they want to attract and keep the best pool of talent.

Teams at Saturn find that they can increase their wages by meeting and exceeding production and quality goals. Moreover, by putting some of their own pay at risk, they can earn up to 10 percent extra based on how well their entire team performs.

WHY DO ORGANIZATIONS OFFER EMPLOYEE BENEFITS?

When an organization designs its overall compensation package, it has to look further than just an hourly wage or annual salary. It has to take into account another element, employee benefits. **Employee benefits** are nonfinancial rewards designed to enrich employees' lives. They have grown in importance and variety over the past several decades. Once viewed as "fringes," today's benefit packages reflect a considered effort to provide something that each employee values.

employee benefits
Nonfinancial rewards designed to enrich employees' lives

The benefits offered by an organization will vary widely in scope. Most organizations are legally required to provide Social Security and workers' and unemployment compensations, but organizations also provide an array of benefits such as paid time off from work, life and disability insurance, retirement programs, and health insurance. The costs of some of these, such as retirement and health insurance benefits, are often borne by both the employer and the employee.

Current Issues in Human Resources Management

We'll conclude this chapter by looking at several human resource issues facing today's managers—workforce diversity, sexual harassment, family-friendly benefits, labor-management cooperation, employee violence, and layoff-survivor sickness.

HOW CAN WORKFORCE DIVERSITY BE MANAGED?

We have discussed the changing makeup of the workforce in several places in this book. Let's now consider how workforce diversity will affect such basic HRM concerns as recruitment, selection, and orientation.

Improving workforce diversity requires managers to widen their recruiting net. For example, the popular practice of relying on current employee referrals as a source of new job applicants tends to produce candidates who have similar characteristics to those of present employees. So managers have to look for applicants in places where they haven't typically looked before. To increase diversity, managers are increasingly turning to nontraditional recruitment sources such as women's job networks, over-50 clubs, urban job banks, disabled people's training centers, ethnic newspapers, and gay rights organizations. This type of outreach should enable the organization to broaden its pool of applicants.

Once a diverse set of applicants exists, efforts must be made to ensure that the selection process does not discriminate. Moreover, applicants need to be made comfortable with the organization's culture and be made aware of management's desire to accommodate their needs. For instance, at Microsoft Corporation, only a small number of women apply for its technical jobs, but the company makes every effort to hire a high percentage of the female applicants and strives to make sure that these women have a successful experience once they are on the job.[34]

Finally, orientation is often difficult for women and minorities. Many organizations today, such as Lotus and Hewlett-Packard, provide special workshops to raise diversity consciousness among current employees as well as programs for new employees that focus on diversity issues. The thrust of these efforts is to increase individual understanding of the differences each of us brings to the workplace. For example, at Kraft's cheese manufacturing plant in Missouri, managers have put together an ambitious diversity program that reflects the increased values the organization has placed on incorporating diverse perspectives. One thing they did was to reward "diversity champions," individual employees who supported and promoted the benefits of diversity. They also added diversity goals to employee evaluations, encouraged nontraditional promotions, sponsored ethnic-meal days, and trained over half the plant's employees in diversity issues.[35] A number of companies also have special mentoring programs to deal with the reality that lower-level female and minority managers have few role models with whom to identify.[36]

WHAT IS SEXUAL HARASSMENT?

Sexual harassment is a serious issue in both public and private sector organizations. More than 16,000 complaints are filed with the Equal Employment Opportunity Commission (EEOC) each year.[37] Data indicate that almost all Fortune 500 companies in the United States have had complaints lodged by employees, and about a third of them have been sued.[38] Not only were the settlements in these cases very costly for the companies in terms of litigation, it is estimated that it costs a "typical *Fortune* 500 company $6.7 million per year in absenteeism, low productivity, and turnover."[39] That amounts to more than $3 billion annually. Sexual harassment, however, is not just a U.S. phenomenon. It's a global issue. For instance, sexual harassment charges have been filed against employers in such countries as Japan, Australia, the Netherlands, Belgium, New Zealand, Sweden, Ireland, and Mexico.[40] Even though discussions of sexual harassment cases oftentimes focus on the large awards granted by a court, there are other concerns for employers. Sexual harassment creates an unpleasant work environment and undermines workers' ability to perform their job. But just what is sexual harassment?

sexual harassment
Sexually suggestive remarks, unwanted touching and sexual advances, requests for sexual favors, or other verbal and physical conduct of a sexual nature

Sexual harassment is defined as any unwanted activity of a sexual nature that affects an individual's employment. It can occur between members of the opposite sex or of the same sex. Although such activity is generally covered under employment discrimination laws, in recent years this problem has gained more recognition. By most accounts, prior to the mid-1980s this problem was generally viewed as an isolated incident, with the individual at fault being solely responsible (if at all) for his or her actions.[41] Yet charges of sexual harassment continue to appear in the headlines on a regular basis.

Much of the problem associated with sexual harassment is determining exactly what constitutes this illegal behavior. The EEOC cites three situations in which sexual harassment can occur. These are instances in which verbal or physical conduct toward an individual: (1) creates an intimidating, offensive, or hostile environment; (2) unreasonably interferes with an individual's work; or (3) adversely affects an employee's employment opportunities. For many organizations, it's the offensive or hostile environment issue that is problematic. Just what constitutes such an environment? Victims of hostile environment situations gained much support from the Supreme Court case of *Meritor Savings Bank v. Vinson*.[42] Ms. Vinson initially refused the sexual advances of her boss, but out of fear of losing her job, she ultimately conceded. The harassment did not stop there. Vinson's boss also "fondled Vinson in front of other employees, followed her into the restroom, and exposed himself to her on various occasions."[43] In addition to supporting hostile environment claims, the *Meritor* case also clarified the extent of employer liability: That is, an organization can be held liable for sexual harassment by its management team, employees, and even its customers.[44] What is the critical aspect of the *Meritor* case? The point is that we all must be attuned to what makes fellow employees uncomfortable—and if we don't know, then we should ask![45] Organizational success in the new millennium will, in part, reflect how sensitive each employee is toward others in the company.[46]

Like this police officer, former Long Beach California police officer Melissa Clerkin was one tough cop. But her toughness couldn't withstand the sexual harassment she encountered at the hands of her former boyfriend and sergeant, and fellow officers. After complaining to police officials about the harassment, Clerkin found herself in situations where she needed backup, and no one would come to her aid. Additionally, she was subjected to being called crude names, as well as getting offensive messages on her patrol car's computer. Although her sexual harassment case was finally settled and she was awarded about $900,000, Clerkin is saddened that the thing she valued most—being a police officer—was taken from her!

If sexual harassment carries with it potential costs to the organization, what can a company do to protect itself?[47] The courts want to know two things: Did the organization know about, or should it have known about, the alleged behavior? What did management do to stop it? With the number and dollar amounts of the awards against organizations today increasing, there is a greater need for management to educate all employees on sexual harassment matters and have mechanisms available to monitor employees.

Furthermore, in June 1998, the Supreme Court ruled that sexual harassment may have occurred even if the employee had not experienced any negative job repercussions.[48] In this case, Kimberly Ellerth, a marketing assistant at Burlington Industries, filed harassment charges against her boss because he "touched her, suggested she wear shorter skirts, and told her during a business trip that he could make her job 'very hard or very easy.'" When Ellerth refused, the harasser never "punished" her. In fact, she even received a promotion during the time of the harassment. The Supreme Court's decision in this case indicated that "harassment is defined by the ugly behavior of the manager, not by what happened to the worker subsequently."[49]

Before we leave the topic of sexual harassment, we'd be remiss not to mention the case of *Jerold Mackenzie vs. Miller Brewing,* and its implications.[50] In this case, Mackenzie allegedly made inappropriate comments to a female employee similar to those made on an an episode of the *Seinfeld* television show. In investigating the case, Miller officials determined that Mackenzie acted inappropriately, and his actions constituted sexual harassment of a female employee. Consequently, acting in what they believed was good faith, they fired Mackenzie, but he challenged his firing, filing suit for wrongful termination. In the end, he was awarded $18 million in punitive damages and $8.2 million in compensatory damages. And $1.5 million of the total award was to be personally paid by the woman who filed the harassment complaint.[51] Needless to say, this case has left some companies wondering just what to do.

What *Mackenzie* tells us is that the harasser has rights, too. No action should be taken against someone until a thorough investigation has been conducted. Furthermore, the results of the investigation should be reviewed by an independent and objective individual before any action against the alleged harasser is taken. The harasser should be given an opportunity to respond to the allegation and have a disciplinary hearing if desired. Additionally, an avenue for appeal should also exist for the alleged harasser—an appeal to be heard by someone in a higher level of management who is not associated with the case. There's no doubt the Mackenzie case adds new dimensions to sexual harassment issues. And given this precedent-setting case, it's well worth the time, effort, and money for HRM to make sure it protects everyone involved in the controversy.

HOW CAN ORGANIZATIONS BE FAMILY FRIENDLY?

family-friendly benefits

A wide range of work and family programs to help employees; includes on-site day care, child and elder care, flexible work hours, job sharing, part-time employment, relocation programs, adoption benefits, parental leave, and other programs

Another major trend affecting managers today is the push for benefits that fall under the category of **family-friendly benefits.** Family-friendly benefits are so named because they are supportive of caring for one's family.[52] These would include such benefits as flextime, child care, part-time employment, relocation programs, summer camp for employees' children, parental leave, and adoption benefits.[53] Companies such as CompUSA, Excalibur Hotel, Barnes & Noble, and Summit Systems currently offer such benefits.[54] At the heart of such programs are increasing child- and elder-care benefits. Today's working parents and people caring for elderly relatives are eagerly seeking ways of having quality child and elder care near their place of work, especially in organizations that operate staggered shifts or around the clock.

Family-friendly benefits also address the issue of parents who can't (and won't) leave their family concerns behind when they go to work. When an organization hires employees, they not only get their special skills, they also get their feelings, personal problems, and family commitments. Although management cannot be sympathetic to every detail of employees' lives, we are seeing that organizations are becoming more considerate of family issues. For instance, summer can be a difficult time for employees because the children are out of school. Stratco—a Leawood, Kansas-based chemical engineering organization—permits employees to bring their children to work and infants are permitted to spend the entire day at the workplace.[55] At Johnson & Johnson, employees' children are transported to a summer camp after parents bring them to work.

Another concern arises with the large number of dual-career couples—couples in which both partners have a professional, managerial, or administrative occupation.[56] An organization's human resource management policies need to reflect the special needs this situation creates. For instance, special attention needs to be given to an organization's policies regarding nepotism, relocations, transfers, and conflicts of interest.

CAN UNIONS AND MANAGEMENT COOPERATE?

Historically, the relationship between a labor union and management was based on conflict. The interests of labor and management were basically at odds—each treated the other as the opposition. But times have changed somewhat. Management has become increasingly aware that successful efforts to increase productivity, improve quality, and lower costs require employee involvement and commitment. Similarly, some labor unions have come to recognize that they can help their members more by cooperating with management rather than fighting it.[57]

Unfortunately, current U.S. labor laws, passed in an era of mistrust and antagonism between labor and management, may be a barrier to both parties becoming cooperative partners. As a case in point, the National Labor Relations Act was passed to encourage collective bargaining and to balance workers' power against that of management.[58] That legislation also sought to eliminate the then-widespread practice of firms setting up company unions for the sole purpose of undermining the efforts of outside unions to organize their employees. So the law prohibits employers from creating or supporting a "labor organization." Ironically, labor laws—like the National Labor Relations Act—may have also presented a minor roadblock to management and labor cooperation. For instance, the National Labor Relations Board ruled in the *Electromation Inc.* case that it was an unfair labor practice for the employer to set up employee committees in "order to impose its own unilateral form of bargaining on employees."[59] Furthermore, Electromation's actions were also viewed as a means of thwarting a Teamsters union organizing campaign that began in its Elkhart, Indiana, plant. The *Electromation* case, and a few others indicated that companies must ensure that their quality circle programs, quality of work life, and other employee involvement programs operate under federal labor laws.[60]

Although this issue has been the subject of Congressional debate,[61] the current legal environment doesn't prohibit employee-involvement programs in the United States. Rather, to comply with the law, management is required to give its employee-involvement programs independence. When such programs become dominated by management, they're likely to be interpreted as performing some functions of labor unions but really controlled by management. What kinds of actions would indicate that an employee-involvement program is not dominated by management? Some examples might include choosing program members through secret-ballot elections, giving program members wide latitude in deciding what issues to deal with, permitting members to meet apart from management, and specifying that program members are not susceptible to dissolution by management whim. The key theme labor laws appear to be conveying is that where employee-involvement programs are introduced, members must have the power to make decisions and act independently of management.

CAN MANAGERS PREVENT WORKPLACE VIOLENCE?

Inasmuch as there is growing concern for job safety, a much greater emphasis is placed on the increasing violence that has erupted on the job.[62] No organization is immune from such happenstance, and the problem appears to be getting worse. Shootings at a local U.S. post office by a recently disciplined employee, an upset purchasing manager who stabs his boss because they disagreed over how some paperwork was to be completed, a disgruntled significant other who enters the workplace and shoots his mate[63]—incidents like these have become all too prevalent. Consider the following statistics. Twenty employees are murdered each week at work. Homicide has become the number-two cause of work-related death in the United States.[64] For women, it's the number-one cause of work-related death.[65] In the United States more than one million employees are attacked each year, and more than six million threatened with bodily harm.[66] But this is not just a U.S. phenomenon. For instance, in Great Britain, there were more than 135,000 violent acts against employees in retail stores alone.[67]

Critics have noted that in U.S. cities, violent behaviors are spilling over into the workplace.[68] And we're talking about much more here than homicides committed during the commission of a crime—those horrendous events happening to cab drivers or to clerks at retail stores.[69] Two factors have contributed greatly to this trend—domestic violence and disgruntled employees.[70] The issue for companies, then, is how to prevent the violence from occurring on the job and to reduce their liability should an unfortunate event occur.[71]

Because the circumstances of each incident are different, a specific plan of action for companies is difficult to detail. However, several suggestions can be made.[72] First, the organization must develop a plan to deal with the issue.[73] This may mean reviewing all corporate policies to ensure that they are not adversely affecting employees. In fact, in many cases, violent individuals who caused mayhem in an office setting complained that they were not treated with respect or dignity. They were laid off without any warning, or they perceived they were treated too harshly in the discipline process. Sound HRM practices can help to ensure respect and dignity for employees, even in the most difficult of issues like terminations.

Organizations must also train their management personnel to identify troubled employees before the problem results in violence.[74] Employee assistance programs (EAPs) can be designed specifically to help these individuals. Rarely does an individual go from being happy to committing some act of violence overnight. Furthermore, if managers are better able to spot the types of demonstrated behaviors that may lead

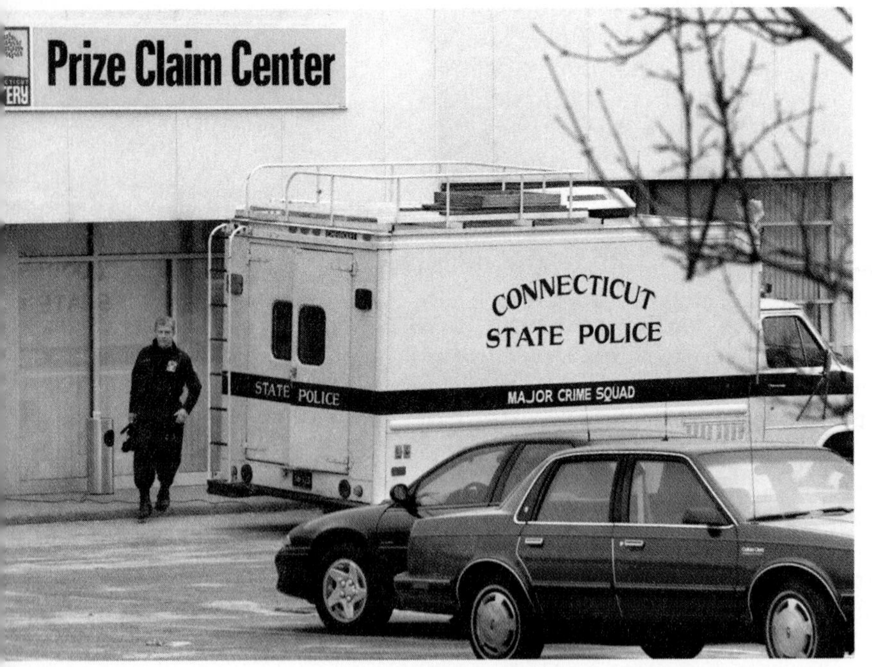

No matter what an organization does to ensure the safety of its employees, some events just happen. At the Connecticut State Lottery Agency, troubled employee Matthew Beck returned from work after a four-month "stress" leave of absence, with pay. A few short days after his return, he shot three Lottery officials before turning the gun on himself.

to violence, then those who cannot be helped through the EAP can be removed from the organization before others are harmed. Organizations should also implement stronger security measures. For example, many women are killed at work after a domestic dispute by someone who didn't belong on company premises. These individuals as well as their weapons must be kept away from the facilities.

No matter how careful the organization is and how much it attempts to prevent workplace violence, some will still occur. In those cases, the organization must be prepared to deal with the situation.[75] As one researcher has stated, we need to "teach managers what to do when someone goes berserk,"[76] and we need to be prepared to offer whatever assistance we can to deal with the aftermath.

HOW DO "SURVIVORS" RESPOND TO LAYOFFS?

As we discussed in Chapter 2, one of the significant trends we witnessed was organizational downsizing. Because downsizing typically involves shrinking the organization's workforce, it is an issue in human resource management that needs to be addressed.

Many organizations have done a fairly good job of helping layoff victims by offering a variety of job-help services, psychological counseling, support groups, severance pay, extended health insurance benefits, and detailed communications. Although some individuals react very negatively to being laid off (the worst cases involve returning to the former organization and committing a violent act), the assistance offered reveals that the organization does care about its former employees. Unfortunately, very little has been done for those who retain their jobs and have the task of keeping the organization going or even of revitalizing it.

It may surprise you to learn that both victims and survivors experience feelings of frustration, anxiety, and loss.[77] But layoff victims get to start over with a clean slate and a clear conscience. Survivors don't. As one author suggested, "The terms could be reversed: Those who leave become survivors, and those who stay become victims."[78] A new syndrome seems to be popping up in more and more organizations: **layoff-survivor sickness,** a set of attitudes, perceptions, and behaviors of employees who survive involuntary staff reductions.[79] Symptoms include job insecurity, perceptions of unfairness, guilt, depression, stress from increased workload, fear of change, loss of loyalty and commitment, reduced effort, and an unwillingness to do anything beyond the required minimum.

layoff-survivor sickness
A set of attitudes, perceptions, and behaviors of employees who remain after involuntary employee reductions; include security, guilt, depression, stress, fear, loss of loyalty, and reduced effort

To address this survivor syndrome, managers may want to provide opportunities for employees to talk to counselors about their guilt, anger, and anxiety. Group discussions can also provide an opportunity for the survivors to vent their feelings. Some organizations have used downsizing as the spark to implement increased employee participation programs such as empowerment and self-managed work teams. In short, to keep morale and productivity high, every attempt should be made to ensure that those individuals who are still working in the organization know that they are valuable and much-needed resources.

PHLIP Companion Web Site

We invite you to visit the Robbins/DeCenzo companion Web site at *www.prenhall.com/robbins* for this chapter's Internet resources.

Chapter Summary

How will you know if you have fulfilled the Learning Outcomes on page 183? You will have fulfilled the Learning Outcomes if you are able to:

1 *Describe the human resource management process.*
The human resource management process seeks to staff the organization and to sustain high employee performance through strategic human resource planning, recruitment or downsizing, selection, orientation, training, performance appraisal, compensation and benefits, safety and health, and by dealing with contemporary issues in HRM.

2 *Discuss the influence of government regulations on human resource decisions.*
Since the mid-1960s, the U.S. government has greatly expanded its influence over HRM decisions by enacting new laws and regulations. Because of the government's effort to provide equal employment opportunities, management must ensure that key HRM decisions—recruitment, selection, training, promotions, and terminations—are made without regard to race, sex, religion, age, color, national origin, or disability. Financial penalties can be imposed on organizations that fail to follow these laws and regulations.

3 *Differentiate between job descriptions and job specifications.*
A job description is a written statement of what a jobholder does, how it is done, and why it is done. A job specification states the minimum acceptable qualifications that a potential employee must possess to successfully perform a given job.

4 *Contrast recruitment and downsizing options.*
Recruitment seeks to develop a pool of potential job candidates. Typical sources include an internal search, advertisements, employee referrals, employment agencies, school placement centers, and temporary services. Downsizing typically reduces the labor supply within an organization through options such as firing, layoffs, attrition, transfers, reduced workweeks, early retirements, and job sharing.

5 *Explain the importance of validity and reliability in selection.*
All HRM decisions must be based on factors or criteria that are both reliable and valid. If a selection device is not reliable, then it cannot be assumed to measure consistently. If a device is not valid, then no proven relationship exists between it and relevant job criteria.

6 *Describe the selection devices that work best with various kinds of jobs.*
Selection devices must match the job in question. Work sampling works best with low-level jobs; assessment centers work best for managerial positions. The validity of the interview as a selection device increases at progressively higher levels of management.

7 *Identify various training methods.*
Employee training can be on the job or off the job. Popular on-the-job methods include job rotation, understudying, and apprenticeships. The more popular off-the-job methods are lectures, films, and simulation exercises.

8 *Explain the various techniques managers can use in evaluating employee performance.*
Managers can use several techniques in evaluating employee performance such as

comparing employee performance against some set performance standard, comparing employees with one another, or measuring performance on the basis of preset objectives. One of the newer performance evaluation methods used in contemporary organizations is the 360-degree evaluation, whereby an employee is evaluated by bosses, peers, direct reports, if any, and possibly customers.

9 *Describe the goals of compensation administration and factors that affect wage structures.*
Compensation administration attempts to ensure that pay levels will be perceived as fair by all employees. Fairness means that the established levels of pay are adequate and consistent for the demands and requirements of the job. Therefore, the primary determination of pay is the kind of job an employee performs.

10 *Explain what is meant by the terms sexual harassment, family-friendly benefits, labor-management cooperation, workplace violence, and layoff-survivor sickness.*
Sexual harassment encompasses sexually suggestive remarks, unwanted touching and sexual advances, requests for sexual favors, or other verbal and physical conduct of a sexual nature. Labor-management cooperation involves mutual efforts on the part of a labor union and the management of an organization. Family-friendly benefits are benefits offered to employees that are supportive of caring for one's family. These include flextime, child care, part-time employment, relocation programs, summer camp for employees' children, parental leave, and adoption benefits. The layoff-survivor sickness represents the set of attitudes, perceptions, and behaviors of employees who remain after involuntary staff reductions.

Review and Application Questions

READING FOR COMPREHENSION

1. How does HRM affect all managers?
2. Contrast reject errors and accept errors. Which are most likely to open an employer to charges of discrimination? Why?
3. What are the major problems of the interview as a selection device?
4. What is the relationship between selection, recruitment, and job analysis?
5. How are orientation and employee training alike? How are they different?

LINKING CONCEPTS TO PRACTICE

1. Should an employer have the right to choose employees without government interference into the hiring process? Explain your position.
2. Do you think there are moral limits on how far a prospective employer should delve into an applicant's life by means of interviews, tests, and background investigations? Explain your position.
3. What constitutes sexual harassment? Describe how companies can minimize sexual harassment in the workplace?
4. Why should managers be concerned with diversity in the workplace? What special HRM issues does diversity raise?

5 "Victims of downsizing are not those employees who were let go. Rather, the victims are the ones who have kept their jobs." Do you agree or disagree with this statement? Defend your position.

6 "Workplace violence is indicative of the violence that exists in our society. Accordingly, no amount of prevention can eliminate all workplace violence occurrences." Do you agree or disagree with the statement? Explain.

Management Workshop

Team Skill-Building Exercise

Laying Off Workers

Every manager, at some point in his or her career, is likely to be faced with the difficult task of laying off employees. Assume that you are the manager in the accounting department of a 6,500-member corporation. You have been notified by top management that you must permanently reduce your staff by two individuals. Below are some data about your five employees.

Jasmine Connor: African-American female, age 36. Jasmine has been employed with your company for five years, all in the accounting department. Her evaluations over the past three years have been outstanding, above average, and outstanding. Jasmine has an MBA from a top-25 business school. She has been on short-term disability for the past few weeks because of the birth of her second child and is expected to return to work in 20 weeks.

George Ericson: White male, age 49. George has been with you for four months and has 11 years of experience in the company in Payroll. He has an associate's degree in business administration and bachelor's and master's degrees in accounting. He's also a CPA. George's evaluations over the past three years in Payroll have been average, but he did save the company $150,000 on a suggestion he made regarding using electronic time sheets.

Raul Fernandez: Hispanic male, age 31. Raul has been with the company almost four years. His evaluations over the past three years in your department have been outstanding. He is committed to getting the job done and devoting whatever it takes. He has also shown initiative by taking job assignments that no one else wanted, and he has recovered a number of overdue and uncollected accounts that you had simply thought should be written off as a loss.

Connie Wilson: White female, age 35. Connie has been with your company seven years. Four years ago, Connie was in an automobile accident while traveling on business to a customer's location. As a result of the accident, she was disabled and is wheelchair-bound. Rumors have it that she is about to receive several million dollars from the insurance company of the driver that hit her. Her performance during the past two years has been above average. She has a bachelor's degree in accounting and specializes in computer information systems.

Chuck Smith: African-American male, age 43. Chuck just completed his joint masters degree in taxation and law and recently passed the Bar exam. He has been with your department for four years. His evaluations have been good to above average. Five years ago, Chuck won a lawsuit against your company for discriminating against him in a promotion to a supervisory position. Rumors have it that now, with his new degree, Chuck is actively pursuing another job outside the company.

Given these five brief descriptions, which two employees should be laid off? Discuss any other options that can be used to meet the requirement of downsizing by two employees without resorting to layoffs. Discuss what you will do to assist the two individuals who have been let go and to assist the remaining three employees. Then, in a group of three to five students, seek consensus on the questions posed above. Be prepared to defend your actions.

Developing Your Interviewing Skill

Interviewing Job Applicants

ABOUT THE SKILL

Every manager needs to develop his or her interviewing skills. The following discussion highlights the key behaviors associated with this skill.

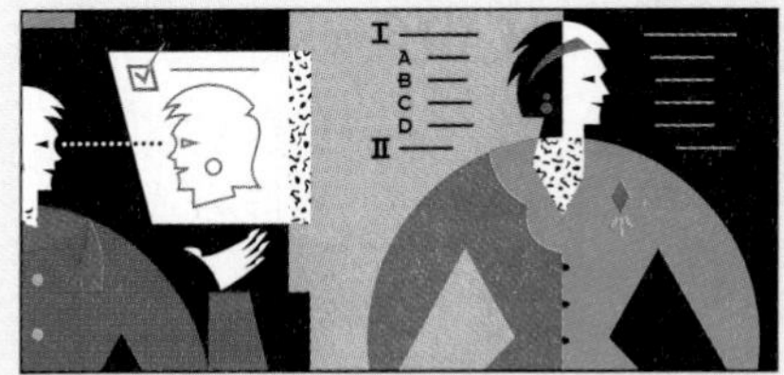

By opening with small talk (e.g., the weather) you give the candidate time to adjust to the interview setting. By providing a preview of topics to come, you are giving the candidate an agenda that helps the candidate to begin framing what he or she will say in response to your questions.

STEPS IN PRACTICING THE SKILL

- **Review the job description and job specification.** Reviewing pertinent information about the job provides valuable information about what you will assess the candidate on. Furthermore, relevant job requirements help to eliminate interview bias.
- **Prepare a structured set of questions to ask all applicants for the job.** By having a set of prepared questions, you ensure that the information you wish to elicit is attainable. Furthermore, if you ask them all similar questions, you are able to better compare all candidates' answers against a common base.
- **Before meeting a candidate, review his or her application form and résumé.** Doing so helps you to create a complete picture of the candidate in terms of what is represented on the résumé or application and what the job requires. You will also begin to identify areas to explore in the interview. That is, areas that are not clearly defined on the résumé or application but that are essential for the job will become a focal point of your discussion with the candidate.
- **Open the interview by putting the applicant at ease and by providing a brief preview of the topics to be discussed.** Interviews are stressful for job candidates.
- **Ask your questions and listen carefully to the applicant's answers.** Select follow-up questions that naturally flow from the answers given. Focus on the responses as they relate to information you need to ensure that the candidate meets your job requirements. Any uncertainty you may still have requires a follow-up question to probe further for the information.
- **Close the interview by telling the applicant what is going to happen next.** Applicants are anxious about the status of your hiring decision. Be honest with the candidate regarding others who will be interviewed and the remaining steps in the hiring process. If you plan to make a decision in two weeks or so, let the candidate know what you intend to do. In addition, tell the applicant how you will let him or her know about your decision.
- **Write your evaluation of the applicant while the interview is still fresh in your mind.** Don't wait until the end of your day, after interviewing several candidates, to write your analysis of a candidate. Memory can fail you. The sooner you complete your write-up after an interview, the better chance you have for accurately recording what occurred in the interview.

Practicing the Skill

INTERVIEWING

Review and update your résumé. Then have several friends critique it who are employed in management-level positions or in management-training programs. Ask them to explain their comments, and make any changes to your résumé that they think will improve it.

Now inventory your interpersonal and technical skills and any practical experiences that do not show up in your résumé. Draft a set of leading questions that you would like to be asked in an interview that would give you a chance to discuss the unique qualities and attributes you could bring to the job.

A Case Application

Developing Your Diagnostic and Analytical Skills

CONNECTICUT STATE LOTTERY

Whenever you put a group of employees together, disagreements and conflicts may arise. Still, no one possibly could have anticipated the events that occurred at the headquarters of the Connecticut State Lottery (CSL) office in Newington, Connecticut, at the hands of one employee, Matthew Beck.[80]

Matthew Beck worked in the accounting office of CSL. For the major part of his tenure at CSL, he had been a successful performer. Yet sometime in 1997, problems arose for Beck. He had been questioning his pay. He didn't feel that his boss or other CSL officials were adequately compensating him for all the extra hours he had worked. Beck challenged company officials, following policies and protocols as expected. He even had the support of his employees' association, which helped him in his dispute. But to no avail—Beck was unsuccessful in his challenge. Upset over the decisions, Beck became stressed, unhappy, and had difficulty concentrating on his job. Nothing his boss did could ease Beck's feeling that he was being wronged. Finally, these feelings overwhelmed Beck, and company officials decided that he needed a stress leave. For the next several months, Beck was away from work, with pay, to regain his composure and put this issue behind him. Four months later, he seemed fine, in good spirits, and ready to resume his job. And his boss welcomed him back to CSL.

For most of his first week back, everything appeared normal. Beck was discharging his assigned duties, and everything about him appeared ordinary. What happened that frightful Friday, March 6, 1998, however, may never be explained. Beck arrived at work and headed to the executive offices. Inside the building, he produced a weapon and shot his boss and two other CSL officials. Hearing the commotion and recognizing the threat to all employees, the president of CSL attempted to get everyone out of the building. Confident that he had removed employees from the immediate threat, the president ran from the building. In hot pursuit was Matthew Beck. With police officers arriving in the parking lot, the president tripped and fell to the ground. In spite of pleas from the president not to kill him, Beck twice fired his 9-mm weapon. Moments later, Beck shot again—a self-inflicted wound that ended the horror. We all know that there are no guarantees in life. Yet going to work should not be a game of chance. That frightful day in March proved that things do unexpectedly transpire—three CSL officials and Matthew Beck died at the scene.

QUESTIONS

1 Do you believe the tragedy at the Connecticut State Lottery office could have been prevented? Why or why not? Defend your position.

2 Stress interviews are designed to see how a job applicant reacts when faced with a pressure situation. Do you believe that stress interviews can help identify future employees who may have a potential for violence? Explain.

3 Matthew Beck's manager appeared to handle the situation properly. Beck had an opportunity to have his complaint heard, was suspended with pay for a period of time to "re-collect" himself, and was welcomed back as a contributing member of the lottery team. In this instance, however, something went wrong. What would you recommend management of the Lottery office do differently to avoid this tragedy happening again?

Developing Your Investigative Skills

Using the Internet

Visit *www.prenhall.com/robbins* for updated Internet Exercises.

Enhancing Your Writing Skills

Communicating Effectively

1 Visit your campus career center and make an appointment with a career counselor. During your meeting, ask the counselor for advice about how to succeed in interviews. Focus specifically on the kinds of things campus recruiters looking for today, how you should prepare for the interview, and what kinds of questions you can expect to get in the interview. Once your appointment is completed, provide a three- to five-page summary of the interview, highlighting how the information can be useful for you in a future job search.

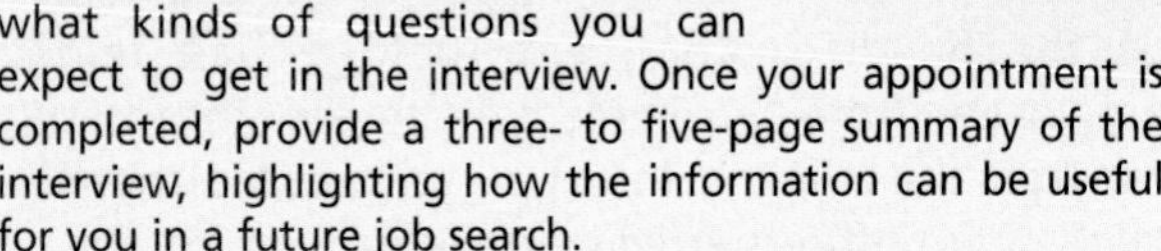

2 College faculty are frequently evaluated by their peers, their department chair, their students, and oftentimes, other academic administrators. Do you believe this process is reflective of a 360-degree appraisal? Discuss and support your position. Are there other constituents that you believe should be part of a faculty member's appraisal? Explain.

3 Go to the EEOC's Web site <www.eeoc.gov>. Research the procedure one must follow to file an EEOC charge. Also, review the sexual harassment data and summary statistics the EEOC collects. Ascertain the number of cases filed during the past three years for which data have been kept, how many cases were settled, and the amount of the monetary benefits awarded.

Career Module

Introduction

The term *career* has a number of meanings. In popular usage, it can mean advancement ("his career is progressing nicely"), a profession ("she has chosen a career in medicine"), or a lifelong sequence of jobs ("his career has included 15 jobs in 6 organizations"). For our purposes, we choose the third definition and define a **career** as the sequence of positions occupied by a person during the course of a lifetime.[1] From this definition, it is apparent that we all have, or will have, a career. Moreover, the concept is as relevant to transient, unskilled laborers as it is to engineers or physicians.

career
The sequence of positions occupied by a person during the course of a lifetime

Although career development has been an important topic in management-related courses for the past three decades, we have witnessed some drastic changes in recent years. Twenty years ago, career development programs were designed to assist employees in advancing their work lives, to provide the information and assessment needed to help realize career goals. Career development was also a way for the organization to attract and retain highly talented personnel, but those concerns are all but disappearing in today's organizations. Downsizing, restructuring, reengineering, and the like have reshaped the organization's role in career development. Today, the individual—not the organization—is responsible for his or her own career.[2] Millions of employees have learned this the hard way over the past few years.[3] You, therefore, must be prepared to take responsibility for managing your career.[4]

Making a Career Decision

The best career is whatever offers the best match between what you want out of life and what you need. Good career choices should result in a series of positions that give you an opportunity to be a good performer, make you want to maintain your commitment to your career, lead to highly satisfying work, and give you the proper balance between work and personal life. A good career match, then, is one in which you are able to develop a positive self-concept, to do work that you think is important, and to lead the kind of life you desire.[5] Creating that balance is referred to as career planning.

Career planning is designed to assist you in becoming more knowledgeable of your needs, values, and personal goals. This knowledge can be achieved through a three-step, self-assessment process:[6]

1. Identify and organize your skills, interests, work-related needs, and values. The best place to begin is by drawing up a profile of your educational record. List each school attended from high school on. What courses do you remember liking most and least? In what courses did you score highest and lowest? In what extracurricular activities did you participate? Are there any specific skills that you acquired? Are there other skills in which you have gained proficiency? Next, begin to assess your occupational experience. List each job you have held, the organization you worked for, your overall level of satisfaction, what you liked most and least about the job, and why you left. It's important to be honest in covering each of these points.
2. Convert this information into general career fields and specific job goals. Step 1 should have provided some insights into your interests and abilities. Now you need to look at how they can be converted into the kind of organizational setting or field of endeavor with which you will be a good match. Then you can become specific and identify distinct job goals.

   What fields are available? In business? In government? In nonprofit organizations? Your answer can be broken down further into areas such as education, financial, manufacturing, social services, or health services. Identifying areas of interest is usually far easier than pinpointing specific occupations. When you are able to identify a limited set of occupations that interest you, you can start to align them with your abilities and skills. Will certain jobs require you to move? If so, would the location be compatible with your geographic preferences? Do you have the educational requirements necessary for the job? If not, what additional schooling will be needed? Does the job offer the status and earning potential that you aspire to? What is the long-term outlook for jobs in this field? Does the field suffer from cyclical employment? Because no job is without its drawbacks, have you seriously considered all the negative aspects? When you have fully answered questions such as these, you should have a relatively short list of specific job goals.
3. Test your career possibilities against the realities of the organization or the job market by talking with knowledgeable people in the fields, organizations, or jobs you desire. These informational interviews should provide reliable feedback as to the accuracy of your self-assessment and the opportunities available in the fields and jobs that interest you.

Getting into the Organization

In Chapter 6 we introduced you to the recruiting and selection processes. When recruiters make a decision to hire employees, information is often sent out announcing the job. If you see that announcement and think there's a potential match between what you can offer and what the organization wants, you need to throw your hat into the hiring ring.

One of the more stressful situations you will face is the job application process because there are no specific guidelines to success. However, several tips may increase your chances of finding employment. Even getting an interview opportunity requires hard work. You should view getting a job as your job at the moment.[7]

Competition for most jobs today is fierce.[8] You can't wait until the last minute to enter the job market: Your job hunt must start well in advance of when you plan to start work. Seniors in college who plan to graduate in May, for instance, should start a job search around the previous September. Why is starting in the fall helpful? There are two advantages. First, it shows that you are taking an interest in your career and that you're not waiting until the last minute to begin planning. This reflects favorably on you. Second, starting in the fall coincides with many companies' recruiting cycles. If you wait until March to begin the process, some job openings are likely to already have been filled. For specific information regarding the company recruiting cycles in your area, visit your college's career development center.

WHERE CAN I FIND JOBS ADVERTISED ON THE INTERNET?

Over the past few years, there has been a proliferation of Web sites that provide job searchers with information about job openings. Listed below are some of the more popular sites that have been shown to help individuals in their job searches.[9] As you begin your job search, we recommend you surf some of these Web sites for valuable information.

Site	Web Address
America's Job Bank	www.ajb.dni.us
Boldface Jobs	www.boldfacejobs.com
Career Resource Center	www.careers.org
Career Path	www.careerpath.com
CareerMosaic	www.careermosaic.com
Careers and Jobs	www.starthere.com/jobs
Emory Colossal List	www.emory.edu/CAREER/Links.html
Federal Jobs	fedworld.gov//jobs/jobsearch/html
High Tech Careers	www.hitechcareer.com/hitech
JobWeb	www.jobweb.org
NationJob Network	www.nationjob.com
Online Career Center	www.careers.org
The Riley Guide	www.jobtrack.com/jobguide
The Monster Board	www.monster.com

HOW DO I PREPARE MY RÉSUMÉ?

All job applicants need to circulate information that reflects positively on their strengths. That information should be sent to prospective employers in a format that is understandable and consistent with the organization's hiring practices. In most instances, this is done through the résumé.

No matter who you are or where you are in your career, you need a current résumé, which is typically the only information source that a recruiter will use in determining whether to grant you an interview. Therefore, your résumé must be a sales tool; it must give key information that supports your candidacy, highlights your strengths, and differentiates you from other job applicants. An example of the type of information that should be included is shown in Exhibit CM-1. Notice, too, that volunteer experience is noted on the résumé. It shows that you are well rounded, committed to your community, and willing to help others. Anything that distinguishes you from other applicants should be included.

Exhibit CM-1 A Sample Résumé

Résumé of:	Dana Brown 1690 West Road Knoxville, TN 55555
CAREER OBJECTIVE:	Seeking employment in an investment firm that provides a challenging opportunity to combine exceptional interpersonal and computer skills.
EDUCATION:	Knoxville Community College A.A., Business Administration (May 1999) University of Tennessee B.S., Finance (May 2001)
EXPERIENCE:	University of Tennessee
12/99 to present	Campus Bookstore, Assistance Bookkeeper Primary Duties: Responsible for coordinating book purchases with academic departments; placing orders with publishers; invoicing, receiving inventory, pricing, and stocking shelves. Supervised four student employees. Managed annual budget of $25,000.
9/97 to 9/99	Knoxville Community College Student Assistant, Business Administration Primary Duties: Responsible for routine administrative matters in an academic department—including answering phones, word processing faculty materials, and answering student questions.
10/95 to 6/97	Volunteer High School Yearbook Staff Primary Duties: Responsible for coordinating marketing efforts in local community. Involved in fund raising through contacts with community organizations.
SPECIAL SKILLS:	Experienced in Microsoft Excel and Word, Netscape, D-Base, and Powerpoint presentations software. Fluent Spanish (spoken and written). Certified in CPR.
SERVICE ACTIVITIES:	Vice-president, Student Government Association Volunteer, Meals-on-Wheels Volunteer, United Way
REFERENCES:	Available on request.

It is important to pinpoint a few key themes regarding résumés that may seem like common sense but are frequently ignored. First, copies of your résumé must be printed on a quality printer. The font should be easy to read (e.g., Courier or Times New Roman font). Avoid any style that may be hard on the eyes, such as a script or italic font. A recruiter who must review 100 or more résumés a day is not going to look favorably at pages that are difficult to read. So use an easy-to-read font and make the recruiter's job easier.

It is also important to note that many companies today are using computer scanners to make the first pass through résumés. They scan each résumé for specific information such as key job elements, experience, work history, education, or technical expertise.[10] The use of scanners, then, emphasizes two important aspects of résumé writing.[11] The computer matches key words to a job description. Thus, when you are creating a résumé, use typical job description phraseology. The font used should be easily read by the scanner. If the scanner can't read it, your résumé may be put in the rejection file.

Your résumé should be copied on good-quality white or off-white paper (no off-the-wall colors). There are certain types of jobs—a creative artist, for example—where this suggestion may be inappropriate, but these are the exceptions. You can't go wrong using a bond paper that has some cotton content (about 20 percent). By all means, don't use standard duplicating paper—you don't want to seem to be mass-mailing résumés (even if you are).

Much of what we just stated also holds true if you are producing an electronic résumé. That is, the style should be similar; fonts should be easy to read, and the like. Many of today's technology-rich companies are requiring electronic résumés. That means that rather than mailing a printed version of your résumé to the company, you are asked to e-mail it in an attached file to the organization. Accordingly, you'll need to be able to e-mail an attachment, ensure that your electronically attached résumé is properly formatted, and that it is sent in a word-processing format that is readable. Whether the electronic résumé is required will often be specified in the advertisement you've read or be part of the directions in the Internet recruiting sites that list the job opening.

Our last point regarding résumés—irrespective of whether it's a paper copy or an electronic version—relates to proofreading. Because the résumé is the only representation of you the recruiter has, errors can be deadly. If your résumé contains misspelled words or is grammatically incorrect, your chances for an interview will be significantly reduced. Proofread your résumé, and, if possible, let others proofread it too.

To accompany your résumé, you need a cover letter. Your cover letter should tell the recruiter why you should be considered for the job. You need to describe why you are a good candidate in a cover letter that highlights your greatest strengths and indicates how these strengths can be useful to the company. Your cover letter should also explain why the organization getting your résumé is of interest to you. Cover letters should be carefully tailored to each organization. This shows that you've taken some time and given some thought to the job you're applying for.

Cover letters should be addressed to a real person. Don't send anything to "To Whom It May Concern." Such salutations frequently tell the recruiter that you are on a fishing expedition or mass-mailing résumés in hopes of generating some positive response. This technique seldom works in job hunting. You may not always know the recruiter's name and title, but with some work you can get it. Telephone the company and ask for it; most receptionists in an employment office will tell you the recruiter's name and title. If you can't get a name, go to the reference section of a library (you may also find this information on the Internet) and look at a copy of a publication such as the *Standard and Poor's Register Manual,* or *Moody's.* These publications usually list the names and titles of officers in the organization. If everything else fails, send your résumé to one of the officers, preferably the officer in charge of employment or administration, or even to the president of the organization.

Like the résumé, the cover letter should be error free—whether it's in a paper version or an electronic one. Proofread this as carefully as you do the résumé. Finally, if you're using a paper version, sign each cover letter individually.

ARE THERE WAYS TO EXCEL AT AN INTERVIEW?

Once you've made it through the initial screening process, you're likely to be called in for an interview. Interviews play a critical role in determining whether you will get the job. Up to now, all the recruiter has seen is your well-polished cover letter and résumé. Remember, however, what was said in Chapter 6 regarding hiring. Few individuals, if any, get a job without an interview. No matter how qualified you are for a position, if you perform poorly in the interview, you're not likely to be hired.

The reason interviews are so popular is that they help the recruiter determine if you are a good fit for the organization in terms of your level of motivation and interpersonal skills.[12] Popularity aside, however, how interviews are conducted can be problematic. We presented a summary of the research on interviews on pages 192–195. Although interviewer mistakes or bias shouldn't be part of your interview, it's important for you to understand that they may exist. Why is this knowledge important? If you know how the interviewer may react in the hiring process, it can help you to avoid making a costly mistake.

impression management
A technique that attempts to project the sort of image that will result in a favorable outcome

Many of the biases that may exist in the interview can be overcome through a technique called **impression management.** Impression management attempts to project an image that will result in a favorable outcome.[13] For example, if you can say or do something that is viewed favorably by the interviewer, then you may create a more favorable impression of yourself. Suppose that you find out in the early moments of the interview that your interviewer values workers who are capable of balancing work and personal responsibilities. Stating that you like to work hard but also reserve time to spend with family and friends may create a positive impression. You need to understand, too, that interviewers generally have short and inaccurate memories. Research has shown that most only remember about half of what you say. Although taking notes can help them remember more, what they remember most will be the impression you make—both favorable and unfavorable.[14] Given this background information on interviews and interviewers, what can you do to increase your chances of excelling in the interview?

First, do some homework. Go to your library—or do a search for the company on the Internet—and get as much information as possible on the organization. Develop a solid grounding in the company, its history, markets, financial situation, and the industry in which it competes.

The night before the interview, get a good night's rest. Eat a good breakfast to build up your energy level, as the day's events will be grueling. As you prepare for the interview, keep in mind that your appearance is going to be the first impression you make. Dress appropriately. Even though appearance is not supposed to enter into the hiring decision, incorrect attire can result in a negative impression. In fact, one study suggests that 80 percent of the interviewer's perception of you in the interview is drawn from his or her initial perception of you, based primarily on your appearance and body language.[15] Therefore, dress appropriately and be meticulous in your attire. In getting to the interview location, arrive early—about 30 minutes before your appointment. It is better to wait than to have to contend with something unexpected, like a traffic jam, that could make you late. Arriving early also gives you an opportunity to survey the office environment and possibly gather some clues about the organization. Use any clues you do pick up to increase your chances of making a favorable impression.

As you meet the recruiter, give him or her a firm handshake. Make eye contact and maintain it throughout the interview. Remember, your body language may be giving away secrets about you that you don't want an interviewer to notice. Sit erect and maintain good posture. At this point, you are probably as nervous as you have ever been. Although this is natural, try your best to relax. Recruiters know that you'll be anxious, and a good one will try to put you at ease. Being prepared for an interview can also help build confidence and reduce nervousness.

You can start by reviewing a set of questions most frequently asked by interviewers. You can usually get a copy of these from the career center at your college. Because you know that you may be asked these questions, you should develop responses beforehand. But let's add a word of caution here. The best advice is to be yourself. Don't go into an interview with a prepared text and recite it from memory. Have an idea of what you would like to say, but don't rely on verbatim responses. Experienced interviewers will see through this over-preparedness and downgrade their evaluation.

You should also try to arrange several practice interviews if possible. Universities often have career days on campus, during which recruiters from companies are on site to interview students. Take advantage of them. Even if the job does not appeal to you, the process will at least serve to help you become more skilled at dealing with interviewers. You can also practice with family, friends, career counselors, student groups to which you belong, or your faculty advisor.

When the interview ends, thank the interviewer for his or her time and for giving you this opportunity to talk about your qualifications, but don't think that selling yourself has stopped there. As soon as you get home, send a thank-you letter to the recruiter for giving you the opportunity to discuss your job candidacy. You'd be amazed at how many people fail to do this. This little act of courtesy has a positive effect—use it to your advantage.

WHAT ARE SOME SUGGESTIONS FOR DEVELOPING A SUCCESSFUL MANAGEMENT CAREER?

If you choose a career in management, there are certain keys to success you should consider (see Exhibit CM-2). The following suggestions are based on proven tactics that managers have used to advance their careers.[16]

Select your first job judiciously All first jobs are not alike. Where managers begin in the organization has an important effect on their subsequent career. Specifically, evidence suggests that if you have a choice, you should select a powerful department as the place to start your management career.[17] A power department is one in which crucial and important organizational decisions are made. If you start out in departments that are high in power within the organization, you're more likely to advance rapidly.

Participate in an internship Although it's currently a seller's market, and unemployment rates are relatively low in the United States, the competition for the select positions in an organization is tremendous. Companies often want individuals who have some experience and who show some initiative. One of the better ways of demonstrating these attributes is through an internship.

Many universities today not only offer internships as part of their curriculum, many require some type of job experience to fulfill their degree prerequisites. Internships offer you a chance to see what the work is really like, to get a better understanding of an organization's culture, and to see if you fit well into the organization. And although no guarantees are given, many organizations use internships as a means of developing their applicant pool—often extending job offers to outstanding interns.

Even if a job offer at the end of an internship is not available, the internship is not wasted. The work experience the intern gets and the realistic preview of his or her profession of choice is invaluable. Furthermore, internship experience also enables an individual to list work experience on a résumé—something that recruiters view very favorably.

Exhibit CM-2
Steps of a Successful Management Career

Develop a network

Acquire and continue upgrading your skills

Participate in an internship

Think laterally

Stay mobile

Support your boss

Find a mentor

Don't stay too long

Stay visible

Gain control of organizational resources

Learn the power structure

Present the right image

Do good work

Select your job judiciously

If an internship is not possible, consider part-time employment in your field of choice while you pursue your education. Like internships, part-time work in entry-level positions provides you with a sound foundation that reflects well on you when you seek full-time employment in the near future.

Do good work Good work performance is a necessary (but not sufficient) condition for managerial success. The marginal performer may be rewarded in the short term, but his or her weaknesses are bound to surface eventually and cut off career advancement. Your good work performance is no guarantee of success, but without it, a successful management career is unlikely.

Present the right image Assuming that your work performance is in line with that of other successful managers, the ability to align your image with that sought by the organization is certain to be interpreted positively. You should assess the organization's culture so that you can determine what the organization wants and values. Then you need to project that image in terms of style of dress, organizational relationships that you do and do not cultivate, risk-taking or risk-averse stance, leadership style, attitude toward conflict, the importance of getting along well with others, and so forth.

Learn the power structure The authority relationships defined by the organization's formal structure as shown by an organizational chart explain only part of the influence patterns within an organization. It's of equal or greater importance to know and understand the organization's power structure. You need to learn who's really in charge, who has the goods on whom, what are the major debts and dependencies—all things that won't be reflected in neat boxes on the organizational chart. Once you have this knowledge, you can work within the power structure with more skill and ease.[18]

Gain control of organizational resources The control of scarce and important organizational resources is a source of power. Knowledge and expertise are particularly effective resources to control. They make you more valuable to the organization and therefore more likely to gain job security and advancement.

Stay visible Because the evaluation of managerial effectiveness can be very subjective, it's important that your boss and those in power in the organization be made aware of your contributions. If you're fortunate enough to have a job that brings your accomplishments to the attention of others, taking direct measures to increase your visibility might not be needed. But your job may require you to handle activities that are low in visibility, or your specific contribution may be indistinguishable because you're part of a group endeavor. In such cases, without creating the image of a braggart, you'll want to call attention to yourself by giving progress reports to your boss and others. Other tactics include being seen at social functions, being active in your professional associations, and developing powerful allies who speak positively of you.

Don't stay too long in your first job Evidence has shown that given a choice between staying in your first management job until you've "really made a difference" or accepting an early transfer to a new job assignment, you should go for the early transfer.[19] By moving quickly through different jobs, you signal to others that you're on the fast track. This, then, often becomes a self-fulfilling prophecy. Start fast by seeking early transfers or promotions from your first management job.

Find a mentor It has become increasingly clear over the years that employees who aspire to higher management levels in organizations often need the assistance and advocacy of someone higher up in the organization.[20] These career progressions often require the favor of the dominant in-group that sets corporate goals, priorities, and standards.[21]

When a senior employee takes an active role in guiding another individual, we refer to this activity as mentoring. The effective mentor directs, advises, criticizes, and suggests in an attempt to aid the employee's growth.[22] These individuals offer to assist certain junior employees by providing a support system. This system, in part, is likened to the passing of the proverbial baton—that is, the senior employee shares his or her experiences with the protégé, providing guidance on how to make it in the organization.[23] In organizations such as The Washington Post, J&L Peaberry's Coffee & Tea Company, Prudential, and Wal-Mart that promote from within, employees who aspire to succeed must have the corporate support system[24] in their favor. This support system, guided by a mentor, vouches for the candidate, answers for the candidate in the highest circles within the organization, makes appropriate introductions, and advises and guides the candidate on how to effectively move through the system. In one study, this effort generated significant outcomes.[25] For example, these researchers found that where a significant mentoring relationship existed, those protégés had more favorable and frequent promotions, were paid significantly more than those who were not mentored,[26] had a greater level of commitment to the organization, and eventually had greater career success.[27]

Support your boss Your immediate future is in the hands of your current boss. He or she evaluates your performance, and you are unlikely to have enough power to successfully challenge this manager. Therefore, you should make the effort to help your boss succeed, be supportive if your boss is under siege from other organizational members, and find out how he or she will be assessing your work effectiveness. Don't undermine your boss or speak negatively of your boss to others. If your boss is competent and visible and possesses a power base, he or she is likely to be on the way up in the organization. If you are perceived as supportive, you might find yourself pulled along, too. If your boss's performance is poor and his or her power is negligible, you need to transfer to another unit. A mentor may be able to help you arrange a transfer. It's hard to have your competence recognized or your positive performance evaluation taken seriously if your boss is perceived as incompetent.

Stay mobile You're likely to advance more rapidly if you indicate your willingness to move to different geographical locations and across functional lines within the organization. Career advancement may also be facilitated by your willingness to change organizations. Working in a slow-growth, stagnant, or declining organization should make mobility even more important to you.

Think laterally Lateral thinking acknowledges the changing world of management. Because of organizational restructurings and downsizings, there are fewer rungs on the promotion ladder in many large organizations. To survive in this environment, you should think in terms of lateral career moves.[28] It's important to recognize that lateral movers in the 1960s and 1970s were presumed to be mediocre performers. That presumption doesn't hold today. Lateral shifts are now a viable career consideration. They give you a wider range of experiences, which enhances your long-term mobility. In addition, these moves can energize you by making your work more interesting and satisfying. So if you're not moving ahead in your organization, consider a lateral move internally or a lateral shift to another organization.

Keep your skills current Organizations need employees who can readily adapt to the demands of the rapidly changing marketplace. Focusing on skills that you currently have and continuing to learn new skills can establish your value to the organization. It's the employees who don't add value to an organization whose jobs (and career advancement) are in jeopardy. College graduation is not an end. Rather, it's the beginning of a continued life-long learning journey. And remember, it's your responsibility to manage your career.

Develop a network Our final suggestion is based on the recognition that a network of friends, colleagues, neighbors, customers, suppliers, and so on can be a useful tool for career development.[29] If you spend some time cultivating relationships and contacts throughout your industry and community, you'll be prepared if your current job is eliminated. Even if your job is in no danger of being cut, a network can prove beneficial in getting things done.

Seven

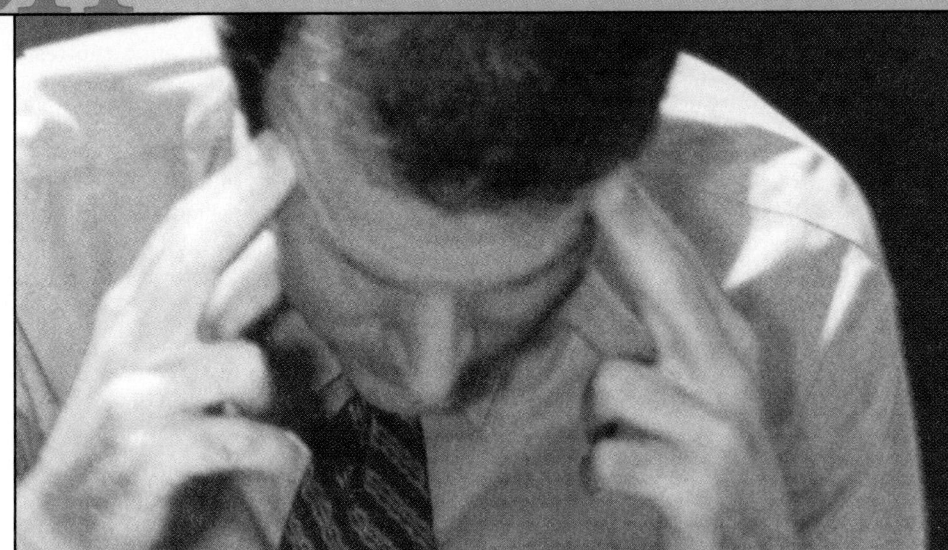

Managing Change and Innovation

LEARNING OUTCOMES After reading this chapter, I will be able to:

1. Describe what change variables are within a manager's control.
2. Identify external and internal forces for change.
3. Explain how managers can serve as change agents.
4. Contrast the "calm waters" and "white-water rapids" metaphors for change.
5. Explain why people are likely to resist change.
6. Describe techniques for reducing resistance to change.
7. Identify what is meant by the term *organization development* and specify four popular OD techniques.
8. Explain the causes and symptoms of stress.
9. Differentiate between creativity and innovation.
10. Explain how organizations can stimulate innovation.

In July 1995, Michael Volkema was promoted to CEO at the Zeeland, Michigan, office furniture manufacturer, Herman Miller. Volkema, just 39 years old at the time, was selected because of his record of successfully managing the company's profitable file cabinet division.[1]

Shortly after assuming his new job duties, Volkema sat down to review the problems he faced. The company had built its reputation by producing premium office furniture. It justified its high prices on the grounds that the furniture paid for itself in higher employee productivity. That strategy worked fine in the 1970s and the 1980s, but it wasn't working in the 1990s because businesses were cutting costs and downsizing their staffs. In 1992, for instance, Herman Miller's sales dropped from $879 million in 1991 to $804 million. Its earnings dropped from $37 million to $17 million. The company's expenses were also growing faster than its sales. Additionally, competitors like Steelcase were successfully attacking Herman Miller's argument that better designs were equated to productivity gains. Compared to Herman Miller, competitors were developing more new designs, more choices, and greater style options. Customers found these attributes more appealing than the claim that employees would be more productive simply because they had "better" furniture.

One of the few bright spots in the company was a small division that built a less expensive line of furniture. The SQA (Simple, Quick, and Affordable) division had grown from nothing to annual revenues of $200 million in just under six years. Revenues in this division were growing 30 percent a year. What was the appeal of SQA? Many small businesses knew the Herman Miller name and wanted to buy furniture, but the cost of the traditional Herman Miller line was too high. A fully furnished Herman Miller cubicle costs $10,400, but SQA could provide comparable quality—of course, with fewer frills and fabric choices—for $8,300. It also prided itself on using technology to provide rapid delivery. Sales representatives were given laptop computers with sophisticated software so that they could design the furniture layout in 3-D at the customer's location. Then, with just a keystroke, the sales rep could submit the work order to the factory, place the order into Herman Miller's manufacturing process, and prompt an invoice for the customer. The order in the manufacturing process prompts suppliers to deliver supplies on an as-needed basis. Customers receive their furniture in as little as two weeks—sometimes in two days—compared to the industry average lead time of five weeks. With this system, Herman Miller's SQA on-time delivery has increased to 99 percent, and the increased efficiencies in manufacturing and decreased inventory has led to a $56 million cut in production costs. As a result, Volkema has been able to pass on significant savings to customers.

The problems faced by Michael Volkema are not unique. Big companies, small businesses, universities, state and city governments, hospitals, and even the military are being forced to significantly change the way they do things. Although change has always been a part of the manager's job, it has become more so in recent years. We discuss why in this chapter as well as discuss ways in which managers can stimulate innovation and increase their organization's adaptability.

What Is Change?

change
An alteration of an organization's environment, structure, technology, or people

Change is an alteration of an organization's environment, structure, technology, or people. If it weren't for change, the manager's job would be relatively easy. Planning would be simple because tomorrow would be no different from today. The issue of organization design would be solved. Because the environment would be free from uncertainty, there would be no need to adapt. All organizations would be tightly structured. Similarly, decision making would be dramatically simplified because the outcome of each alternative could be predicted with almost pinpoint accuracy. It would, indeed, simplify the manager's job if, for example, competitors did not introduce new products or services, if customers did not make new demands, if government regulations were never modified, if technology never advanced, or if employees' needs always remained the same.

However, change is an organizational reality. Handling change is an integral part of every manager's job. But what can a manager change? The manager's options essentially fall into one of three categories: altering structure, technology, or people (see Exhibit 7-1). We look at these three areas of change later in this chapter.

FORCES FOR CHANGE

In Chapter 2, we pointed out that there are both external and internal forces that constrain managers. These same forces also bring about the need for change. Let's briefly look at these factors.

WHAT EXTERNAL FORCES CREATE A NEED FOR CHANGE?

The external forces that create the need for change come from various sources. In recent years, the marketplace has affected firms such as Bell Atlantic and Domino's by introducing new competition. Bell Atlantic, for example, is experiencing competition from cable companies to provide local phone service. Domino's, too, must now contend with a host of new competitors such as Pizza Hut and Little Caesar's, which also moved into the home-delivery market. Government laws and regulations are also an impetus for change. In 1990 for example, the passage of the Americans with Disabilities Act required thousands of businesses to widen doorways, reconfigure restrooms, add ramps, and take other actions to improve accessibility.

Technology also creates the need for change. In the new millennium, the Internet and e-commerce have changed the way we get information and how products are sold. As we discussed in Chapter 3, recent developments in sophisticated equipment have created significant economies of scale for many organizations. New technology and competition from discount brokerage houses caused Merrill Lynch (the brokerage firm) to offer its clients the opportunity to make trades over the Internet without a broker. The assembly line in many industries is also undergoing dramatic change as employers continue to replace human labor with technologically advanced mechanical robots, and the fluctuation in labor markets is forcing managers to initiate changes. For instance, the shortage of software developers has required many software firms to redesign jobs and to alter their reward and benefit packages.

Economic changes, of course, affect almost all organizations. The dramatic decreases in interest rates in the late 1990s fostered significant growth in the housing market. This meant more jobs, more employees hired, and significant increases in sales of other businesses that support the building industry.

Structure		Technology		People
Authority relationships Coordinating mechanisms Job redesign Spans of control	+	Work processes Work methods Equipment	+	Attitudes Expectations Perceptions Behavior

Exhibit 7-1
Three Categories of Change

WHAT INTERNAL FORCES CREATE A NEED FOR CHANGE?

In addition to the external forces noted previously, internal forces can also stimulate the need for change. These internal forces tend to originate primarily from the internal operations of the organization or from the impact of external changes.

When management redefines or modifies its strategy, it often introduces a host of changes. For example, when Oracle developed a new strategy of competing more aggressively in Internet e-commerce markets, organizational members had to change how they performed their jobs—marketing efforts shifted dramatically, and sales reps now sell a full array of Oracle products rather than specializing in a particular product line.[2] The introduction of new equipment represents another internal force for change. Employees may have their jobs redesigned, need to undergo training to operate the new equipment, or be required to establish new interaction patterns within their formal group. An organization's workforce is rarely static. Its composition changes in terms of age, education, gender, nationality, and so forth. In a stable organization in which managers have been in their positions for years, there might be a need to restructure jobs in order to retain more ambitious employees by affording them some upward mobility. The compensation and benefits systems might also need to be reworked to reflect the needs of a diverse workforce and market forces in which certain skills are in short in supply. Employee attitudes, such as increased job dissatisfaction, may lead to increased absenteeism, resignations, and even strikes. Such events will, in turn, often lead to changes in management policies and practices.

HOW CAN A MANAGER SERVE AS A CHANGE AGENT?

change agent
A person who initiates and assumes the responsibility for managing a change in an organization

Changes within an organization need a catalyst. People who act as catalysts and assume the responsibility for managing the change process are called **change agents.**[3]

Any manager can be a change agent. As we review the topic of change, we assume that it is initiated and carried out by a manager within the organization. However, the change agent can be a nonmanager—for example, an internal staff specialist or outside consultant whose expertise is in change implementation. For major systemwide changes, internal management will often hire outside consultants to provide advice and assistance. Because these consultants are from the outside, they often can offer an objective perspective that insiders usually lack. However, outside consultants may have an inadequate understanding of the organization's history, culture, operating procedures, and personnel. They are also prone to initiate more drastic changes than insiders—which can be either a benefit or a disadvantage—because they do not have to live with the repercussions after the change is implemented. In contrast, internal managers who act as change agents may be more thoughtful (and possibly more cautious) because they must live with the consequences of their actions.[4]

Change within an organization needs a catalyst—someone who's responsible for managing the process.

TWO VIEWS OF THE CHANGE PROCESS

"calm waters" metaphor
A description of traditional practices in and theories about organizations that likens the organization to a large ship making a predictable trip across a calm sea and experiencing an occasional storm

We often use two metaphors to clarify the change process.[5] The **"calm waters" metaphor** envisions the organization as a large ship crossing a calm sea. The ship's captain and crew know exactly where they are going because they have made the trip many times before. Change surfaces as the occasional storm, a brief distraction in an otherwise calm and predictable trip. In the **"white-water rapids" metaphor,** the organization is seen as a small raft navigating a raging river with uninterrupted white-water rapids. Aboard the raft are half a dozen people who have never worked together before, who are totally unfamiliar with the river, who are unsure of their eventual destination, and who, as if things weren't bad enough, are traveling in the pitch-dark night. In the white-water rapids metaphor, change is a natural state and managing change is a continual process.

"white-water rapids" metaphor
A description of the organization as a small raft navigating a raging river

These two metaphors present very different approaches to understanding and responding to change. Let's take a closer look at each one.

WHAT IS THE CALM WATERS METAPHOR?

Until very recently, the calm waters metaphor dominated the thinking of practicing managers and academics. The prevailing model for handling change in calm waters is best illustrated in Kurt Lewin's three-step description of the change process[6] (see Exhibit 7-2).

According to Lewin, successful change requires unfreezing the status quo, changing to a new state, and refreezing the new change to make it permanent. The status quo can be considered an equilibrium state. Unfreezing is necessary to move from this equilibrium. It can be achieved in one of three ways:

- The driving forces, which direct behavior away from the status quo, can be increased.
- The restraining forces, which hinder movement from the existing equilibrium, can be decreased.
- The two approaches can be combined.

Once unfreezing has been accomplished, the change itself can be implemented. However, the mere introduction of change does not ensure that it will take hold. The new situation, therefore, needs to be refrozen so that it can be sustained over time. Unless this last step is attended to, there is a strong chance that the change will be short lived and employees will revert to the previous equilibrium state. The objective of refreezing, then, is to stabilize the new situation by balancing the driving and restraining forces.

Note how Lewin's three-step process treats change as a break in the organization's equilibrium state. The status quo has been disturbed, and change is necessary to establish a new equilibrium state. This view might have been appropriate to the relatively calm environment that most organizations faced in the 1950s, 1960s, and early 1970s, but the calm waters metaphor is increasingly obsolete as a description of the kind of seas that current managers have to navigate.

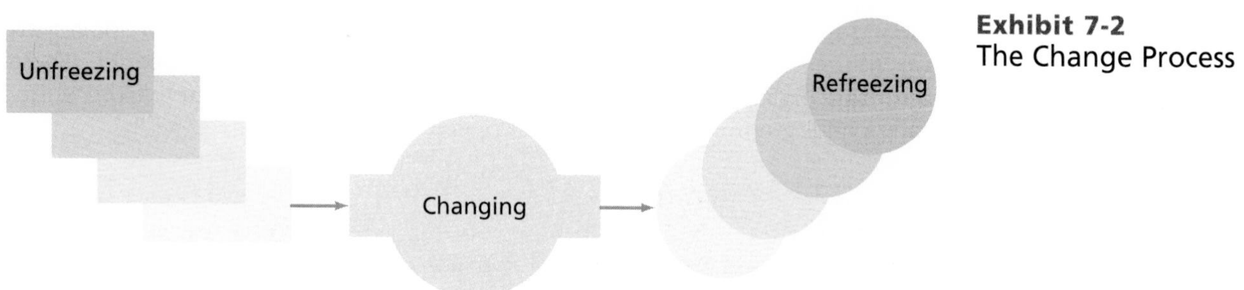

Exhibit 7-2
The Change Process

Change in a dynamic environment is typically filled with uncertainty. Just as white-water rafters have to continuously maneuver their raft to make it successfully through the rapids, a manager, too, must be prepared to deal with unexpected events.

WHAT IS THE WHITE-WATER RAPIDS METAPHOR?

This metaphor takes into consideration the fact that environments are both uncertain and dynamic. To get a feeling for what managing change might be like when you have to continually maneuver in uninterrupted rapids, imagine attending a college in which courses vary in length, so when you sign up, you don't know whether a course will last for 2 weeks or 30 weeks. Furthermore, the instructor can end a course any time he or she wants, with no prior warning. If that isn't bad enough, the length of the class session changes each time—sometimes it lasts 20 minutes, other times it runs for 3 hours—and the time of the next class meeting is set by the instructor during the previous class. Oh yes, there's one more thing. The exams are all unannounced, so you have to be ready for a test at any time. To succeed in this college, you would have to be incredibly flexible and be able to respond quickly to every changing condition. Students who were too structured or slow on their feet would not survive.

A growing number of managers are coming to accept that their job is much like what a student would face in such a college. The stability and predictability of the calm waters do not exist. Disruptions in the status quo are not occasional and temporary, to be followed by a return to calm waters. Many of today's managers never get out of the rapids. They face constant change, bordering on chaos. These managers are being forced to play a game they have never played before that is governed by rules created as the game progresses.[7]

Is the white-water rapids metaphor merely an overstatement? No! Take the case of Converse, Inc., of North Reading, Massachusetts.[8] In the intensely competitive athletic shoe business, a company has to be prepared for any possibility. Younger shoe wearers (a major target market for athletic shoes) are no longer content with athletic shoe styles that are updated every few years. They want new and unique styles more frequently. Large mega-retailers who sell shoes are demanding that manufacturers hold more inventory, replenish supplies faster, and help find ways to sell more shoes. And competition in the industry is hot. Industry leaders Nike and Reebok are far ahead of their competitors. Converse's management knew that if they wanted to remain competitive, they had to change the way they do business. Company managers made a series of changes, from reviving their once-popular Chuck Taylor line of canvas basketball shoes to signing new spokespersons to implementing a company-wide continuous improvement program. These significant organizational changes are essential if Converse is to survive the white-water rapids environment in which it operates.

DOES EVERY MANAGER FACE A WORLD OF CONSTANT AND CHAOTIC CHANGE?

Not every manager faces a world of constant and chaotic change, but the set of managers who don't is dwindling rapidly.[9]

Managers in such businesses as women's fashion apparel and computer software have long confronted a world of white-water rapids. They used to envy their counterparts in industries such as auto manufacturing, oil exploration, banking, publishing, telecommunications, and air transportation, who historically faced a stable and predictable environment. That might have been true in the 1960s but not today.

Few organizations can treat change as the occasional disturbance in an otherwise peaceful world. Even those few do so at great risk. Too much is changing too fast for any organization or its managers to be complacent.[10] Most competitive advantages last less than 18 months. A firm such as People Express—a no-frills, no-reservations airline—was described in business periodicals as the model "new-look" firm; it went bankrupt a short time later. Southwest Airlines, and USAirways Metrojet, however, use this no-frills model extensively and are quite successful. As management writer Tom Peters has aptly noted, the old saying "If it ain't broke, don't fix it" no longer applies. He suggests "If it ain't broke, you just haven't looked hard enough. Fix it anyway."[11] Of course, what Peters is saying is consistent with current process engineering trends. Recall in our discussion of process engineering in Chapter 2, we noted that management needs to rethink all of the activities and processes in its organization. The quantum change that is required to remain competitive in today's global marketplace cannot be overstated.

"If it ain't broke, you just haven't looked hard enough. Fix it anyway."

Organizational Change and Member Resistance

Managers should be motivated to initiate change because they are concerned with improving their organization's effectiveness.[12] However, change can be a threat to managers and nonmanagerial personnel as well. Organizations, and people within them, can build up inertia that propels them to resist any change even if that change might be beneficial (see Details on a Management Classic). In this section, we review why people in organizations resist change and what can be done to lessen that resistance.

WHY DO PEOPLE RESIST CHANGE?

It has been said that most people hate any change that doesn't jingle in their pockets. This resistance to change is well documented.[13] But why do people resist change? An individual is likely to resist change for three reasons: uncertainty, concern over personal loss, and the belief that the change is not in the organization's best interest[14] (see Exhibit 7-3).

Changes substitute ambiguity and uncertainty for the known. No matter how much students may dislike some of the work associated with attending college, at least they know the ropes. They understand what is expected of them. When they leave college and venture out into the world of full-time employment, regardless of how eager they are to get out of college, they will have to trade the known for the unknown. Employees in organizations often hold the same dislike for uncertainty. For example, the introduction in manufacturing plants of six sigma processes means that employees will have to learn these new methods. Some employees who have been accustomed to their work routines or who have inadequate math and statistics backgrounds, may fear that they will be unable to meet the six sigma demands. They may, therefore, develop a negative attitude toward this methodology or behave dysfunctionally if required to use the process.

Coch and French: Resistance to Change

One of the most famous studies on organizational change took place in the late 1940s at a Harwood Manufacturing Company plant, where pajamas were made.[15] The plant employed about 500 people and had a long history of disruptions every time changes were made in the way work progressed. Although the changes were typically minor—for example, workers who had formerly folded the tops that went with pre-folded bottoms would be required to fold the bottoms as well—the employees resisted. They would complain bitterly and refuse to make the changes. Production decreased and grievances, absenteeism, and job turnover increased.

Harwood's management usually made these changes autocratically. Management would make the decision and then announce the changes to employees at a group meeting. The changes would be implemented immediately. Then, as mentioned, the employees would rebel. So Harwood's executives brought in a consultant as a change agent to help with their problem. As an experiment, the consultant arranged for the next change to be conducted in three groups, using three different methods. In the control group, the change was initiated in the usual manner—autocratically. The second group involved employee participation through selected representatives. These representatives, with management, worked out the details of the change, then tried the new methods and trained others in the new procedures. In the third group, all employees shared in the designing of the new methods with management.

The change agent gathered data over a 40-day period. What he found strongly supported the value of participation. In the control group, resistance occurred as before. Seventeen percent of the employees quit during the 40-day period, and grievances and absenteeism increased. However, in the representative and full-participation groups, there were no resignations, only one grievance, and no absenteeism. Moreover, participation was positively related to productivity. In the control group, output actually dropped from an average of 60 units per hour to 48 during the experimental period. The participation group generated 68 units per hour, and the total-participation group averaged 73 units per hour.

The Coch and French study still holds a major key for today's organizational change. That is, for permanent change to occur without extensive resistance, employees must be involved. Without employee involvement in matters that directly affect their work, companies run the risk of negating any possible gain a change can bring about or, worse, making the problem more serious than it was originally.

The second cause of resistance is the fear of losing what one already possesses. Change threatens the investment in the status quo. The more people have invested in the current system, the more they resist change. Why? They fear the loss of their position, money, authority, friendships, personal convenience, or other benefits that they value. That is why senior employees resist change more than do relatively new employees. Senior employees generally have invested more in the current system and, therefore, have more to lose by adapting to a change.

Exhibit 7-3
Why People Resist Change

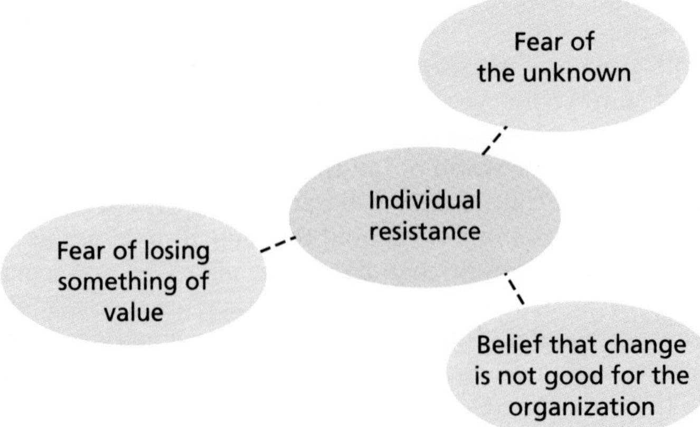

A final cause of resistance is a person's belief that the change is incompatible with the goals and best interests of the organization. If an employee believes that a new job procedure proposed by a change agent will reduce productivity or product quality, that employee can be expected to resist the change. If the employee expresses his or her resistance positively (clearly expressing it to the change agent, along with substantiation), this form of resistance can be beneficial to the organization.

WHAT ARE SOME TECHNIQUES FOR REDUCING RESISTANCE TO ORGANIZATIONAL CHANGE?

When management sees resistance to change as dysfunctional, what actions can it take? Several tactics have been suggested for use by managers or other change agents in dealing with resistance to change.[16] These include education and communication, participation, facilitation and support, negotiation, manipulation and cooptation, and coercion. These tactics are summarized here and described in Exhibit 7-4.

Education and communication can help reduce resistance to change by helping employees to see the logic of the change effort.[17] This technique, of course, assumes that much of the resistance lies in misinformation or poor communication. *Participation* involves bringing those individuals directly affected by the proposed change into the decision-making process. Their participation allows these individuals to express their feelings, increase the quality of the process, and increase employee commitment to the final decision. *Facilitation and support* involves helping employees deal with the fear and anxiety associated with the change effort. This help may include employee counseling, therapy, new skills training, or a short paid leave of absence. *Negotiation* involves a bargain: exchanging something of value for an agreement to lessen the resistance to the change effort. This resistance technique may be quite useful when the resistance comes

Exhibit 7-4 Techniques for Reducing Resistance to Change

Technique	When Used	Advantage	Disadvantages
Education and communication	When resistance is due to misinformation	Clear up misunderstandings	May not work where mutual trust and credibility are lacking
Participation	When resisters have the expertise to make a contribution	Increases involvement and acceptance	Time-consuming; has potential for a poor solution
Facilitation and support	When resisters are fearful and anxiety-ridden	Can facilitate needed adjustments	Expensive; no guarantee of success
Negotiation	Necessary when resistance comes from a powerful group	Can "buy" commitment	Potentially high cost; opens door for others to apply pressure, too
Manipulation and cooptation	When a powerful group's endorsement is needed	Inexpensive, easy way to gain support	Can backfire, causing change agent to lose credibility
Coercion	When a powerful group's endorsement is needed	Inexpensive, easy way to gain support	May be illegal; may undermine change agent's credibility

from a powerful source. *Manipulation and cooptation* refers to covert attempts to influence others about the change. It may involve twisting or distorting facts to make the change appear more attractive. Finally, *coercion* can be used to deal with resistance to change. Coercion involves the use of direct threats or force against the resisters.

Making Changes in the Organization

What can a manager change? The manager's options, as we mentioned at the beginning of this chapter, fall into one of three categories: structure, technology, or people. Let's look more closely at each of these three areas.

Changing *structure* includes any alteration in any authority relationships, coordination mechanisms, degree of centralization, job design, or similar organization structure variables. For instance, in our previous discussions we mentioned that process engineering, restructuring, and empowering result in decentralization, wider spans of control, reduced work specialization, and cross-functional teams. These structural components give employees the authority and means to implement process improvements. For instance, the creation of work teams that cut across departmental lines allows those people who understand a problem best to solve that problem. In addition, cross-functional work teams encourage cooperative problem solving rather than "us versus them" situations.

Changing *technology* encompasses modification in the way work is processed or the methods and equipment used. The primary focus on technological change in continuous improvement initiatives is directed at developing flexible processes to support better quality operations. Employees committed to continuous improvements are constantly looking for things to fix. Thus, work processes must be adaptable to continual change and fine-tuning. This adaptability requires an extensive commitment to educating and training workers. The organization must provide employees with skills training in problem solving, decision making, negotiation, statistical analysis, and team building.[18] For example, employees need to be able to analyze and act on data. At Amoco Oil, employees had to learn how to deal with the visibility and accountability fostered by the implementation of SAP R/3 software (a software program that integrates the information system of an organization).[19] The integrative nature of SAP meant that what any employee did on his or her computer automatically affected other computer systems on the internal network.

Changes in *people* refers to changes in employee attitudes, expectations, perceptions, or behaviors. The human dimension of change requires a workforce committed to the organization's objectives of quality and continuous improvement. Again, this dimension necessitates proper education and training. It also demands a performance evaluation and reward system that supports and encourages continuous improvements. For example, successful programs put quality objectives into bonus plans for executives and incentives for operating employees.[20]

HOW DO ORGANIZATIONS IMPLEMENT "PLANNED" CHANGES?

We know that most change that employees experience in an organization does not happen by chance. Often, management makes a concerted effort to alter some aspect of the organization. Whatever happens—in terms of structure or technology—however, ultimately affects organizational members. The effort to assist organizational members with a planned change is referred to as *organization development*.

WHAT IS ORGANIZATION DEVELOPMENT?

> *One of the fundamental issues behind OD is to foster an environment of communication and trust.*

Organization development (OD) facilitates long-term organization-wide changes. Its focus is to constructively change the attitudes and values of organizational members so that they can more readily adapt to and be more effective in achieving the new directions of the organization.[21] When OD efforts are planned, organization leaders are, in essence, attempting to change the organization's culture.[22] However, one of the fundamental issues of organization development is its reliance on employee participation to foster an environment in which open communication and trust exist.[23] Persons involved in OD efforts acknowledge that change can create stress for employees. Therefore, OD attempts to involve organizational members in changes that will affect their jobs and seeks their input about how the innovation is affecting them.

organization development (OD)
An activity designed to facilitate planned, long-term organization-wide change that focuses on the attitudes and values of organizational members; essentially an effort to change an organization's culture

ARE THERE TYPICAL OD TECHNIQUES?

Any organizational activity that assists with implementing planned change can be viewed as an OD technique (see Ethical Dilemma in Management). However, the more popular OD efforts in organizations rely heavily on group interactions and cooperation. These include survey feedback, process consultation, team building, and intergroup development.

Survey feedback efforts are designed to assess employee attitudes about and perceptions of the change they are encountering. Employees are generally asked to respond to a set of specific questions regarding how they view such organizational aspects as decision making, leadership, communication effectiveness, and satisfaction with their jobs, coworkers, and management. The data the change agent obtains are used to clarify problems that employees may be facing. As a result of this information, the change agent can take some action to remedy the problems.

survey feedback
A method of assessing employees' attitudes about and perceptions of a change they are encountering by asking specific questions

In **process consultation,** outside consultants help managers to "perceive, understand, and act upon process events" with which they must deal.[24] These might include, for example, workflow, informal relationships among unit members, and formal communications channels. Consultants give managers insight into what is going on. It is important to recognize that consultants are not there to solve these problems. Rather, they act as coaches to help managers diagnose the interpersonal processes that need improvement. If managers, with consultants' help, cannot solve the problem, consultants will often help managers locate experts who do have the requisite knowledge.

process consultation
The use of consultants from outside an organization to help change agents within the organization assess process events such as workflow, informal intraunit relationships, and formal communications channels

Organizations are made up of individuals working together to achieve some goals. Because organizational members are frequently required to interact with peers, a primary function of OD is to help them become a team. **Team building** is generally an activity that helps work groups set goals, develop positive interpersonal relationships, and clarify the role and responsibilities of each team member. There may be no need to address each area because the group may be in agreement and understand what is expected of it. Team building's primary focus is to increase each member's trust and openness toward one another.

team building
An activity that helps work groups set goals, develop positive interpersonal relationships, and clarify the role and responsibilities of each team member

Whereas team building focuses on helping a work group to become more cohesive, **intergroup development** attempts to achieve the same results among different work groups. That is, intergroup development attempts to change attitudes, stereotypes, and perceptions that one group may have toward another group. In doing so, better coordination among the various groups can be achieved.

intergroup development
An activity that attempts to make several work groups become more cohesive

Ethical Dilemma in Management

The OD Intervention

Organization development interventions often produce positive change results. Interventions that rely on participation of organizational members can create openness and trust among coworkers and respect for others. Interventions can also help employees understand that the company wants to promote risk taking and empowerment. "Living" these characteristics can lead to better organizational performance.

However, any change agent involved in an OD effort imposes his or her value system on those involved in the intervention, especially when the cause for that intervention is coworker mistrust. To deal with this problem, the change agent may bring all affected parties together to openly discuss their perceptions of the dilemma. Although many change agents are well versed in OD practices, sometimes they walk a very thin line between success and failure. For personal problems to be resolved in the workplace, participants must disclose private and, often, sensitive information. Even though an individual can refuse to divulge such information, doing so may carry negative ramifications. For example, it could lead to lower performance appraisals, fewer pay increases, or the perception that the employee is not a team member.

On the other hand, active participation can cause employees to speaking their minds, but that, too, carries some risks. That information might be used against them at a later time. For instance, imagine, in such a setting, that an employee questions a manager's competence. This employee fully believes that the manager's behavior is detrimental to the work unit, but his or her reward for being open and honest could be retaliation from the boss. Although, at the time, the manager might appear to be receptive to the feedback, he or she may retaliate later. In either case—participating or not—employees could be hurt. Even though the intent was to help overcome coworker mistrust, the result may be more back stabbing, more hurt feelings, and more mistrust (see Exhibit 7-5).

Do you think that coworkers can be too open and honest under this type of OD intervention? What do you think a change agent can do to ensure that employees' rights will be protected?

Stress: The Aftermath of Organizational Change

For many employees, change creates stress. A dynamic and uncertain environment characterized by restructurings, downsizings, empowerment, and the like, has caused large numbers of employees to feel overworked and "stressed out."[25] In this section, we will review specifically what is meant by the term *stress,* what causes stress, how to identify it, and what managers can do to reduce anxiety.

WHAT IS STRESS?

stress
A force or influence a person feels when he or she faces opportunities, constraints, or demands that he or she perceives to be both uncertain and important

Stress is a dynamic condition in which an individual is confronted with an opportunity, constraint, or demand related to what he or she desires, and for which the outcome is perceived to be both uncertain and important.[26] Stress is a complex issue, so let's look at it more closely. Stress can manifest itself in both a positive and a negative way. Stress is said to be positive when the situation offers an opportunity for one to gain something; for example, the "psyching-up" that an athlete goes through can be stressful but can lead to maximum performance.

Exhibit 7-5
Change, Dilbert Style

SOURCE: DILBERT reprinted by permission of United Feature Syndicate, Inc.

It is when constraints or demands are placed on us that stress can become negative. Let us explore these two features—constraints and demands.

Constraints are barriers that keep us from doing what we desire. Purchasing a sports utility vehicle (SUV) may be your desire, but if you cannot afford the $30,000 price, you are constrained from purchasing it. Accordingly, constraints take control of a situation out of your hands. If you cannot afford the SUV, you cannot get it. Demands, on the other hand, may cause you to give up something you desire. If you wish to go to a movie with friends on Tuesday night but have a major exam on Wednesday, the exam may take precedence. Thus, demands preoccupy your time and force you to shift priorities.

Constraints and demands can lead to potential stress. When they are coupled with uncertainty about the outcome and importance of the outcome, potential stress becomes actual stress.[27] Regardless of the situation, if you remove the uncertainty or the importance, you remove stress. For instance, you may have been constrained from purchasing the SUV because of your budget, but if you win one in McDonald's Monopoly game, the uncertainty element is significantly reduced. Furthermore, if you are only auditing a class, the importance of the major exam is essentially nil. However, when constraints or demands have an effect on an important event and the outcome is unknown, pressure is added—pressure resulting in stress.

While we are not attempting to minimize the impact of stress in people's lives, it is important to recognize that both good and bad personal factors may cause stress. Of course, when you consider the changes, such as restructuring, that are occurring in U.S. companies, it is little wonder that stress is so rampant today. Just how rampant? A Northwestern National Life Insurance study reported that more than 60 percent of workers surveyed experienced significant job stress[28]—resulting in more than $150 billion in lost time and productivity.[29] And stress on the job knows no boundaries.

In Japan, worker stress has been identified in 70 percent of the workers by a Fukoku Life Insurance Company study.[30] In fact, there is a Japanese term, **karoshi,** which means death from overworking, for employees who die after working more than 3,000 hours the previous year. Over 2,300 individuals who die each year have karoshi listed as their cause of death.[31] Many Japanese employees literally work themselves to death—one in six Japanese employees work more than 3,100 hours annually.[32] Employees in Germany and Britain, too, have suffered the ill effects of stress—costing their organizations more than DM 100 billion and £7 billion ($65 billion and $11.4 billion, respectively).[33]

karoshi
A Japanese term that refers to a sudden death caused by overworking

In Japan, more than 2,300 individuals die annually from overwork.

ARE THERE COMMON CAUSES OF STRESS?

Stress can be caused by a number of factors called **stressors.** Factors that create stress can be grouped into two major categories—organizational and personal (see Exhibit 7-6)—that directly affect employees and, ultimately, their jobs.

stressors
A factor that causes stress

There is no shortage of factors within the organization that can cause stress. Pressures to avoid errors or complete tasks in a limited time period, a demanding supervisor, and unpleasant coworkers are a few examples. The discussion that follows organizes stress factors into five categories: task demands, role demands, interpersonal demands, organization structure, and organizational leadership.[34]

Task demands are related to an employee's job. They include the design of the person's job (autonomy, task variety, degree of automation), working conditions,

Exhibit 7-6
Major Stressors

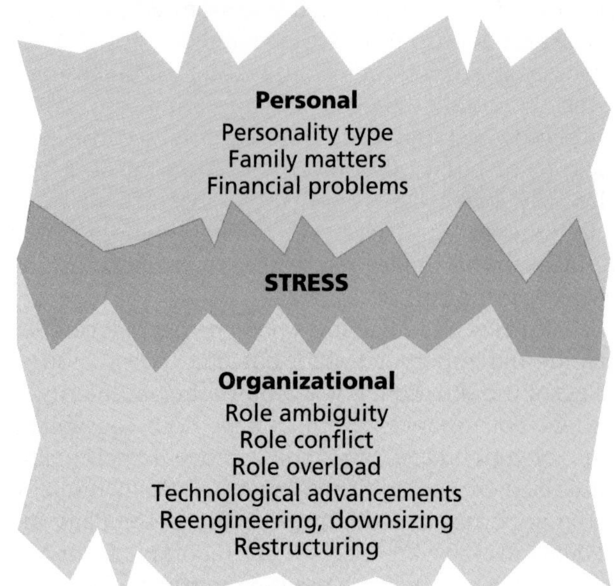

and the physical layout. Work quotas can put pressure on employees when they are perceived as excessive. The more interdependence existing between an employee's tasks and the tasks of others, the more potential stress there is. *Autonomy,* on the other hand, tends to lessen stress. Jobs at which temperatures, noise, or other working conditions are dangerous or undesirable can increase anxiety. So, too, working in an overcrowded room or in a visible location at which interruptions are constant can cause stress.

Role demands are pressures placed on an employee as a function of the particular role he or she plays in the organization. *Role conflicts* create expectations that may be hard to reconcile or satisfy. *Role overload* is experienced when the employee is expected to do more than time permits. *Role ambiguity* is created when role expectations are not clearly understood and the employee is not sure what he or she is to do.

Interpersonal demands are pressures created by other employees. Lack of social support from colleagues and poor interpersonal relationships can cause considerable stress, especially among employees with a high social need.

Organization structure can increase stress. Excessive rules and an employee's lack of opportunity to participate in decisions that affect him or her are structural variables that might be potential sources of stress.

Organizational leadership represents the supervisory style of the organization's officials. Some managers create a culture characterized by tension, fear, and anxiety. They establish unrealistic pressures to perform in the short run, impose excessively tight controls, and routinely fire employees who don't measure up. This style of leadership flows down through the organization to affect all employees.

Personal factors that can create stress include family issues, personal economic problems, and inherent personality characteristics.[35] Because employees bring their personal problems to work with them, a full understanding of employee stress requires a manager to be understanding of these personal factors. There is also evidence that employee's personalities have an effect on how susceptible they are to stress. The most commonly used description of some basic personality traits is called Type A–Type B dichotomy.

Type A behavior is characterized by a chronic sense of urgency, an excessive competitive drive, and difficulty in accepting and enjoying leisure time. The opposite of such behavior is **Type B behavior.** Type Bs never suffer from urgency or impatience. Until quite recently, it was believed that Type As were more likely to experience stress on and off the job. A closer analysis of the evidence, however, has indicated that only the hostility and anger associated with Type A behavior are actually associated with the negative effects of stress. And Type Bs are just as susceptible to these same anxiety-producing elements. For managers, it is important to recognize that Type A employees are more likely to show symptoms of stress even if organizational and personal stressors are low.

The stress associated with an auto accident can be overwhelming. Aside from potential injuries, the aftermath of repairing a damaged vehicle (or buying a new one) can be more frustrating than the accident itself. As a result, physiological, psychological, and behavioral symptoms of stress can occur.

WHAT ARE THE SYMPTOMS OF STRESS?

What signs indicate that an employee's stress level might be too high? There are three general ways that stress reveals itself: physiological, psychological, and behavioral symptoms.

Most of the early interest over stress focused heavily on health-related or *physiological concerns*.[36] This was attributed to the realization that high stress levels result in changes in metabolism, increased heart and breathing rates, increased blood pressure, headaches, and increased risk of heart attacks. Because detecting many of these signs requires the skills of trained medical personnel, their immediate and direct relevance to HRM is negligible.

type A personality type
People who have a chronic sense of urgency and an excessive competitive drive

type B personality type
People who are relaxed and easygoing and accept change easily

Of greater importance to managers are psychological and behavioral symptoms of stress that can be witnessed in the employee. The *psychological symptoms* can be manifested as increased tension and anxiety, boredom, and procrastination, which can all lead to productivity decreases. So, too, can the *behaviorally related symptoms*—changes in eating habits, increased smoking or substance consumption, rapid speech, or sleep disorders.

HOW CAN STRESS BE REDUCED?

Reducing stress presents a dilemma for managers. Some stress in organizations is absolutely necessary. Without it, there's no energy. Accordingly, whenever one considers stress reduction, what is at issue is the reduction of its dysfunctional aspects.

One of the first means of reducing stress is to make sure that employees are properly matched to their jobs and that they understand the extent of their authority. Furthermore, by letting employees know precisely what is expected of them, role conflict and ambiguity can be reduced. Redesigning jobs can also help ease stressors related to overwork. Employees should also have some input in redesigns that affect them. Their involvement and participation have been found to lessen their stress.[37]

As a manager, you must recognize that no matter what is done to eliminate organizational stressors, some employees will still be stressed out. You simply have little or no control over the personal factors. You also face an ethical issue if personal factors are causing stress. That is, just how far can you intrude on an employee's personal life? To help deal with this issue, many companies have started employee assistance and wellness programs to assist employees in areas such as financial planning, legal matters, health, fitness, stress, and the like when they are having difficulties.

employee assistance programs (EAPs)
Programs offered by organizations to help their employees overcome personal and health-related problems

Contemporary **employee assistance programs (EAPs)** are extensions of programs that had their start in U.S. companies in the 1940s. Companies such as DuPont, Standard Oil, and Kodak recognized that a number of their employees were experiencing problems with alcohol.[38] Formal programs were implemented on the company's site to educate these workers about the dangers of alcohol and to help them overcome their addiction.[39] The rationale for these programs, which still holds today, is getting a productive employee back on the job as swiftly as possible. And there can be a benefit to the organization in terms of a return on investment. It is estimated that U.S. companies spend almost $1 billion each year on EAP programs.[40] Studies suggest that most of these companies save up to $5.00 for every EAP dollar spent.[41]

Since their early focus on alcoholic employees, EAPs have ventured into new areas. One of the most notable areas is the use of EAPs to help control rising health insurance premiums, especially in the areas of mental health and substance abuse services.[42] For example, at the Campbell's Soup Company, the company's EAP program is the first stop for individuals seeking psychiatric or substance abuse help. By doing this, Campbell's has been able to trim insurance

One Manager's Perspective

Angela L. Schwers Vice President, Human Resources, Pearson Education

Pearson Education is a large worldwide publisher of textbooks in all academic areas. In 1992 its human resource managers realized that employees were struggling to manage both their personal lives and their work lives. The struggle had become a source of stress for many, which detracted from their performance on the job. As Angela L. Schwers recalls, the company's Employee Assistance Program (EAP), as well as other work-life programs, was begun to help employees "navigate their lives a little better."

As the EAP was designed, managers can recommend the program to employees but cannot require them to take part in it. Every part of the program is voluntary. Employees access the programs by calling an 800 number, and from there they can take advantage of counseling, wellness seminars, informational materials, and crisis management. Schwers finds that all the program offerings are equally popular among employees, and that about seven percent of the Pearson workforce uses the programs nationwide.

In addition to the expected benefits of the EAP—employees' improved ability to handle stress-related issues before they become a real problem—Schwers notes another benefit of the programs: the company has lowered the cost of the mental health benefits it offers its employees.

claims by 28 percent.[43] These cost savings accrue from such measures as reducing inpatients' length of stay, outpatients' treatment days, disability days, and stress-related claims.[44]

A **wellness program** is designed to keep employees healthy. These programs may cover smoking cessation, weight control, stress management,[45] physical fitness, nutrition education, blood-pressure control, violence protection, or work team problem intervention.[46] Wellness programs are designed to help cut employer health costs[47] and to lower absenteeism and turnover by preventing health-related problems.[48] For instance, it is estimated that over a 10-year period, the Coors Brewing Company's wellness program saved the firm almost $2 million in decreased medical premium payments, reduced sick leave, and increased productivity.[49] For Coors, that represents a greater than $6.00 return for every $1.00 spent on wellness.[50] Although savings like those achieved at Coors are not often calculated, there is evidence that the effects on health-care premiums and productivity are positive.[51]

wellness programs
Programs offered by organizations to help their employees prevent health problems

Stimulating Innovation

"Innovate or die!" These harsh words are increasingly becoming the rallying cry of today's managers. In the dynamic world of global competition, organizations must create new products and services and adopt state-of-the-art technology if they are to compete successfully.[52] The standard of innovation toward which many organizations strive is that achieved by such companies as DuPont, Sharp, Eastman Chemical, and the 3M Company.[53] Management at 3M, for example, has developed a reputation for being able to stimulate innovation over a long period of time. One of its stated objectives is that 25 percent of each division's profits are to come from products less than five years old. Toward that end, 3M typically launches more than 200 new products each year. During one recent five-year period, 3M generated better than 30 percent of its $13 billion in revenues from products introduced during that period.[54]

What's the secret to 3M's success? What, if anything, can other managers do to make their organizations more innovative? In the following pages, we will try to answer those questions as we discuss the factors behind innovation.

HOW ARE CREATIVITY AND INNOVATION RELATED?

In general usage, **creativity** means the ability to combine ideas in a unique way or to make unusual associations between ideas.[55] For example, when Nolan Bushnell thought that combining television and playing games might be of interest to the American public, he turned his idea into a $100 million video invention.[56] An organization that stimulates creativity develops novel approaches to things or unique solutions to problems.[57] At Kellogg, for example, company officials have created the Institute for Food and Nutritional Research; that is, employees are encouraged to spend approximately 15 percent of their time at work coming up with new products.[58]

creativity
The ability to combine ideas in a unique way or to make unusual connections

Innovation is the process of taking a creative idea and turning it into a useful product, service, or method of operation.[59] Custom Foot, a Connecticut-based shoe manufacturer, has combined mass production with customized fit. As a result, they are able to offer customized shoes at a reduced cost and have translated this ability into a $10 million business.[60] At Novo Nordisk, a biotechnology company in Denmark, scientists found ways of replacing manufactured chemicals by natural

innovation
The process of taking a creative idea and turning it into a useful product, service, or method of operation

How can you make the mundane appear exciting? Innovations at Custom Foot have combined mass production with tailored customer service. Through the use of electronics, a customer's precise foot measurements are calculated, transferred to a computer database, and used to make the perfect shoe based on what the customer wants.

substances. For instance, they uncovered "an enzyme found in soil that helps turn starch into soil, and one from a bug that removes protein stains."[61]

The innovative organization is characterized by the ability to channel its creative juices into useful outcomes. When managers talk about changing an organization to make it more creative, they usually mean that they want to stimulate innovation.[62] The 3M Company is aptly described as innovative because it has taken novel ideas and turned them into profitable products such as cellophane tape, Scotchgard protective coatings, Post-It notepads, and diapers with elastic waistbands. So, too, is the highly successful microchip manufacturer Intel. It leads all chip manufacturers in miniaturization, and the success of its Pentium II and III chips gives the company a 75 percent share of the microprocessor market for IBM-compatible PCs. With \$5 billion a year in sales, Intel's commitment to staying ahead of the competition by introducing a stream of new and more powerful products is supported by annual expenditures of \$1.2 billion for its plant and equipment and \$800 million for research and development.

WHAT IS INVOLVED IN INNOVATION?

Some people believe that creativity is inborn; others believe that with training, anyone can be creative.[63] The latter group views creativity as a fourfold process consisting of perception, incubation, inspiration, and innovation.[64]

Perception involves the way you see things. Being creative means seeing things from a unique perspective. An employee may see solutions to a problem that others cannot or will not see at all. The movement from perception to reality, however, doesn't occur instantaneously. Instead, ideas go though a process of *incubation*. Sometimes, employees need to "sit" on their ideas. This doesn't mean sitting and doing nothing. Rather, during this incubation period, employees should collect massive amounts of data that are stored, retrieved, studied, reshaped, and finally molded into something new. During this period, it is common for years to pass.

Think for a moment about a time you struggled for an answer on a test. Although you tried hard to jog your memory, nothing worked. Then suddenly, like a flash of light, the answer popped into your head. You found it! *Inspiration* in the creative process is similar. Inspiration is the moment when all your efforts successfully come together.

Although inspiration leads to euphoria, the creative work is not complete. It requires an innovative effort. *Innovation* involves taking that inspiration and turning it into a useful product, service, or way of doing things. Thomas Edison is often credited with saying that "Creativity is 1 percent inspiration and 99 percent perspiration." That 99 percent, or the innovation, involves testing, evaluating, and retesting what the inspiration found (see Developing Your Skill at Creativity, p. 251). It is usually at this stage that an individual involves others more in what he or she had been working on. That involvement is critical because even the greatest invention may be delayed, or lost, if an individual cannot effectively deal with others in communicating and achieving what the creative idea is supposed to do.

HOW CAN A MANAGER FOSTER INNOVATION?

Three sets of variables have been found to stimulate innovation. They pertain to the organization's structure, culture, and human resource practices.

How do structural variables affect innovation? On the basis of extensive research, we can make three statements regarding the effect of structural variables on innovation.[65] First, organic structures positively influence innovation because they have less work specialization and fewer rules and are more decentralized than mechanistic structures. They facilitate the flexibility, adaptation, and cross-fertilization that make the adoption of innovations easier.[66] Second, easy availability of plentiful resources is a key building block for innovation. An abundance of resources allows management to purchase innovations, bear the cost of instituting innovations, and absorb failures. Finally, frequent interunit communication helps to break down possible barriers to innovation by facilitating interaction across departmental lines.[67] 3M, for instance, is highly decentralized and takes on many of the characteristics of small, organic organizations. The company also has the deep pockets needed to support its policy of allowing scientists and engineers to use up to 15 percent of their time on projects of their own choosing. Of course, none of three innovation stimulants can exist unless top management is committed to them.[68]

How does an organization's culture affect innovation? Innovative organizations tend to have similar cultures.[69] They encourage experimentation. They reward both successes and failures. They celebrate mistakes. For example, at Sony, employees are encouraged to experiment and rewarded for experimenting with new products in the marketplace. Unlike other organizations, Sony "sends a lot of products into the market knowing not all will be successful."[70] Its culture, therefore, promotes this risk-taking behavior. Had it not, the Sony Walkman would probably never have made it into stores. An innovative culture is likely to have the following seven characteristics:

- **Acceptance of ambiguity** Too much emphasis on objectivity and specificity constrains creativity.
- **Tolerance of the impractical** Individuals who offer impractical, even foolish, answers to what-if questions are not stifled. What seems impractical at first might lead to innovative solutions.
- **Low external controls** Rules, regulations, policies, and similar controls are kept to a minimum.
- **Tolerance of risk** Employees are encouraged to experiment without fear of consequences should they fail. Mistakes are treated as learning opportunities.
- **Tolerance of conflict** Diversity of opinions is encouraged. Harmony and agreement between individuals or units are not assumed to be evidence of high performance.

- **Focus on ends rather than on means** Goals are made clear, and individuals are encouraged to consider alternative routes toward their attainment. Focusing on ends suggests that there might be several right answers to any given problem.
- **Open systems focus** The organization closely monitors the environment and responds rapidly to changes as they occur.

What human resource variables affect innovation? Within the human resources category, we find that innovative organizations actively promote the training and development of their members so that their knowledge remains current, offer their employees high job security to reduce the fear of getting fired for making mistakes, and encourage individuals to become champions of change. Once a new idea is developed, champions of change actively and enthusiastically promote the idea, build support, overcome resistance, and ensure that the innovation is implemented. Research finds that champions have common personality characteristics: extremely high self-confidence, persistence, energy, and a tendency to take risks. Champions also display characteristics associated with dynamic leadership. They inspire and energize others with their vision of the potential of an innovation and through their strong personal conviction in their mission. They are also good at gaining the commitment of others to support their mission. In addition, champions have jobs that provide considerable decision-making discretion. This autonomy helps them introduce and implement innovations.[71]

PHLIP Companion Web Site

We invite you to visit the Robbins/DeCenzo companion Web site at *www.prenhall.com/robbins* for this chapter's Internet resources.

Chapter Summary

How will you know if you fulfilled the Learning Outcomes on page 229? You will have fulfilled the Learning Outcomes if you are able to:

1 *Describe what change variables are within a manager's control.*
Managers can change the organization's structure by altering work specialization, rules and regulations, or centralization variables or by redesigning jobs; they can change the organization's technology by altering work processes, methods, and equipment, or they can change people by altering attitudes, expectations, perceptions, or behavior.

2 *Identify external and internal forces for change.*
External forces for change include the marketplace, government laws and regulations, technology, labor markets, and economic changes. Internal forces of change include organizational strategy, equipment, the workforce, and employee attitudes.

3 *Explain how managers can serve as change agents.*
Managers can serve as change agents by becoming the catalysts for change in their units and by managing the change process.

4 *Contrast the calm waters and white-water rapids metaphors for change.*
The calm waters metaphor views change as a break in the organization's equilibrium state. Organizations are seen as stable and predictable, disturbed by only an occasional crisis. The white-water rapids metaphor views change as continual and unpredictable. Managers must deal with ongoing and almost chaotic change.

5 *Explain why people are likely to resist change.*
People resist change because of the uncertainty it creates, fear of personal loss, and conviction that it might not be in the organization's best interest.

6 *Describe techniques for reducing resistance to change.*
Six tactics have been proposed for reducing the resistance to change. They are education and communication, participation, facilitation and support, negotiation, manipulation and cooptation, and coercion.

7 *Identify what is meant by the term* organization development *and specify four popular OD techniques.*
Organization development is an organizational activity designed to facilitate long-term organization-wide changes. Its focus is to constructively change the attitudes and values of organizational members so that they can more readily adapt to and be more effective in achieving the new directions of the organization. The more popular OD efforts in organizations rely heavily on group interactions and cooperation and include survey feedback, process consultation, team building, and intergroup development.

8 *Explain the causes and symptoms of stress.*
Stress is the tension that individuals feel when they face opportunities, constraints, or demands that they perceive to be both uncertain and important. It can be caused by organizational factors, such as work overload, role conflict, and role ambiguity. Personal factors can also contribute to stress—a serious illness, death of a family member, divorce, financial difficulties, or personality type.

9 *Differentiate between creativity and innovation.*
Creativity is the ability to combine ideas in a unique way or to make unusual associations between ideas. Innovation is the process of taking creative ideas and turning them into a useful product, service, or method of operation.

10 *Explain how organizations can stimulate innovation.*
Organizations that stimulate innovation will have flexible structures, easy access to resources, and fluid communication; a culture that is relaxed, supportive of new ideas, and encourages monitoring of the environment; and creative people who are well trained, current in their fields, and secure in their jobs.

Review and Application Questions

READING FOR COMPREHENSION

1 Why is handling change an integral part of every manager's job?

2 Describe Lewin's three-step change process. How is it different from the change process needed in the white-water rapids metaphor of change?

3 How do work overload, role conflict, and role ambiguity contribute to employee stress?

4 How do creativity and innovation differ? Give an example of each.

5 How does an innovative culture make an organization more effective. Do you think an innovative culture could ever make an organization less effective? Why or why not?

LINKING CONCEPTS TO PRACTICE

1 Who are change agents? Do you think that a low-level employee could act as a change agent? Explain.

2 Why is organization development planned change? Explain how planned change is important for organizations in today's dynamic environment.

3 Which organization—IBM or Intel—do you believe would have more difficulty changing its culture? Explain your position.

4 "Managers have a responsibility to their employees who are suffering serious ill effects of work-related stress?" Do you agree or disagree with the statement? Support your position.

5 Do you think changes can occur in an organization without a champion to foster new and innovative ways of doing things? Explain.

Management Workshop

Team Skill-Building Exercise

The Celestial Aerospace Company

OBJECTIVES

1 To illustrate how forces for change and stability must be managed in organizations.
2 To illustrate the effects of alternative change techniques on the relative strength of forces for change and forces for stability.

THE SITUATION

The marketing division of the Celestial Aerospace Company (CAP) has gone through two major reorganizations in the past seven years. Initially, the structure changed from a functional to a matrix form, which did not satisfy some functional managers nor did it lead to organizational improvements. The managers complained that the structure confused the authority and responsibility relationships. In reaction to these complaints, senior management returned to the functional form, which maintained market and project teams that were managed by project managers with a few general staff personnel. No functional specialists were assigned to these groups. After the change, some problems began to surface. Project managers complained that they could not obtain the necessary assistance from functional staffs. It not only took more time to obtain necessary assistance but also created problems in establishing stable relationships with functional staff members. Because these problems affected customer services, project managers demanded a change in the organizational structure. Faced with these complaints and demands from project managers, senior management is pondering yet another reorganization for the division. They have requested an outside consultant (you) to help them in their reorganization plan—one that will provide some stability in the structure, address their issues, and help the organization achieve its strategic goals.

PROCEDURE

1 Divide into groups of five to seven and take the role of consultants.
2 Each group should identify the forces necessitating the change and the resistance to that change in the company.
3 Each group should develop a set of strategies for dealing with the resistance to change and for implementing those strategies.
4 Reassemble the class and hear each group's recommendations and explanations.
5 After each group has presented, the other consulting groups should pose probing questions about the presenting group's recommendations.

Developing Your Skill at Creativity

Becoming More Creative

ABOUT THE SKILL

Creativity is a frame of mind. You need to open your mind up to new ideas. Every individual has the ability to be creative. But many people simply don't try to develop that ability. In contemporary organizations, those people may have difficulty being successful. Dynamic environments and managerial chaos require that managers look for new and innovative ways to attain their goals as well as those of the organization.

STEPS IN BECOMING MORE CREATIVE[72]

1 **Think of yourself as creative.** Although this is a simple suggestion, research shows that if you think you can't be creative, you won't be. Believing in yourself is the first step in becoming more creative.
2 **Pay attention to your intuition.** Every individual's subconscious mind works well. Sometimes answers

come to you when least expected. For example, when you are about to go sleep, your relaxed mind sometimes whispers a solution to a problem you're facing. Listen to that voice. In fact, most creative people keep a notepad near their bed and write down those "great" ideas when they occur. That way, they don't forget them.

3 **Move away from your comfort zone.** Every individual has a comfort zone in which certainty exists. But creativity and the known often do not mix. To be creative, you need to move away from the status quo and focus your mind on something new.

4 **Engage in activities that put you outside your comfort zone.** You not only must think differently; you need to do things differently and, thus, challenge yourself. Learning to play a musical instrument or learning a foreign language, for example, opens your mind up to a new challenge.

5 **Seek a change of scenery.** People are often creatures of habit. Creative people force themselves out of their habits by changing their scenery. That may mean going into a quiet and serene area where you can be alone with your thoughts.

6 **Find several right answers.** In the discussion of bounded rationality (Chapter 4), we said that people seek solutions that are good enough. Being creative means continuing to look for other solutions even when you think you have solved the problem. A better, more creative solution just might be found.

7 **Play your own devil's advocate.** Challenging yourself to defend your solutions helps you to develop confidence in your creative efforts. Second guessing yourself may also help you to find more creative solutions.

8 **Believe in finding a workable solution.** Like believing in yourself, you also need to believe in your ideas. If you don't think you can find a solution, you probably won't.

9 **Brainstorm with others.** Being creative is not a solitary activity. Bouncing ideas off of others creates a synergistic effect.

10 **Turn creative ideas into action.** Coming up with ideas is only half of the process. Once the ideas are generated, they must be implemented. Keeping great ideas in your mind or on paper that no one will read does little to expand your creative abilities.

Practicing the Skill

CREATIVITY

How many words can you make using the letters in the word *Brainstorm?* There are at least 95.

A Case Application

Developing Your Diagnostic and Analytical Skills

CHANGING MITSUBISHI

Mitsubishi Motor's Corporation president, Katsuhiko Kawasoe, was the bearer of bad news. In the fiscal year 1997, his company had lost more than $800 million. Mitsubishi, the fourth largest automaker in Japan, was suffering from weak truck and bus markets at home. Additionally, the company had been slow to take on Toyota and Honda in the hot minivan and sport-utility sectors.[73]

Closer analysis suggests that Kawasoe's problems involve a lot more than its product line. The major problem lies in the roots of the larger system of which it is part. Mitsubishi Corporation, the super-conglomerate, owns Mitsubishi Motors, Bank of Tokyo (the world's largest bank), Mitsubishi Heavy Industries, and dozens of other businesses. The group's annual revenues of $370 billion equaled 10 percent of Japan's gross domestic product.

Much of the Mitsubishi empire is isolated in many ways from the real world of competition. Mitsubishi companies do things the way they've been doing them for more than a century. Long and close relationships with customers and suppliers preclude dropping loss-making product lines. Executives, for the most part, pay little attention to the market, and the organization's culture focuses on the past. New recruits, for example, are told about the company's special place in history and duty to country. When a reporter asked a senior Mitsubishi executive why his company didn't follow such U.S. management practices as downsizing, the executive sternly replied, "Employment is more important than profits! We are not concerned with return on equity. . . . If foreign investors don't see merit on our stock they can sell it." Mitsubishi executives believe that it would be un-Japanese to fire anyone or close plants. And these same executives seem to lack incentives to respond to the sort of market pressures that might make their counterparts in North America or Europe change.

QUESTIONS

1 What effect is the century-old organizational culture at Mitsubishi having on the company?

2 What role do you believe the crisis of losing nearly a billion dollars annually will have on fostering change at Mitsubishi? Do you see this issue as one that will promote calm-water or white-water rapids forces of change? Explain.

3 Using the seven characteristics of organizational culture and innovation (pp. 247–248), describe how each of the seven elements is affecting innovation and creativity at Mitsubishi.

Developing Your Investigative Skills

Using the Internet

Visit *www.prenhall.com/robbins* for updated Internet Exercises.

Enhancing Your Writing Skills

Communicating Effectively

1 Describe a significant change event you experienced (like going from high school to college, changing jobs, etc.). How did you prepare for the change? What fears did you encounter and how did you overcome those fears? Knowing what you know now about the change, what would you do differently today that you didn't do then? How can you apply these "should-haves" to changes you'll face in the future?

2 Go to the employee assistance programs provider Interlock's Web site at <http://www.interlock.org>. Research the following information: What are the components of an EAP, and how does Interlock evaluate an EAP's program success? Also identify how Interlock recommends implementing an EAP in an organization. Provide a three- to five-page summary of your findings.

3 Business programs have traditionally focused on developing rationality, not creativity. That may be a mistake. In two or three pages, describe how you would change the business curriculum to promote student creativity. Specify the kinds of courses or activities that you think should be included in business school classes that would foster creativity and innovation.

Part Four Leading

Eight

Foundations of Individual and Group Behavior

LEARNING OUTCOMES After reading this chapter, I will be able to:

1 Define the focus and goals of organizational behavior.
2 Identify and describe the three components of attitudes.
3 Explain cognitive dissonance.
4 Describe the Myers-Briggs personality type framework and its use in organizations.
5 Define *perception* and describe the factors that can shape or distort perception.
6 Explain how managers can shape employee behavior.
7 Contrast formal and informal groups.
8 Explain why people join groups.
9 State how roles and norms influence employees' behavior.
10 Describe how group size affects group behavior.

In today's dynamic organization, we continue to hear about management's need to be sensitive to others and treat employees with kid gloves, but not all managers follow this model. For some, showing sensitivity to others and respecting them is simply not part of their personality. One such manager is Linda Wachner, CEO of Warnaco and Authentic Fitness, makers of sports and intimate apparel (e.g., Christian Dior, Chaps, Olga, and Speedo).[1]

Linda Wachner was one of the first women to become a Fortune 500 CEO. Ask others to describe her, and you'll hear less-than-flattering descriptions. She is characterized as a screaming, combative, ruthless taskmaster who always gets her way. She is known for humiliating employees in front of their peers. She simply doesn't take any lip from anyone, and she dismisses attacks on how she treats organizational members by one simple motto: "You can't run a company efficiently with a 'bunch of babies.' If you don't like it, leave. This is not a prison." As for advice to other senior managers, she lives by two simple words: Be tough. She advises them from the beginning to show employees they are serious. How? By firing a few employees to set an example.

In spite of people's reactions toward her, Wachner is smart and an efficient manager—one who only rewards performance. Her record at Warnaco has been nothing short of stellar. Since she led a leveraged buyout and became head of the company in 1986, profits and company stock prices have skyrocketed. Warnaco stock, for example, continually outperforms others in the industry and the Standard & Poor's 500. Wachner's strong management skills have made money for her stockholders and for herself—turning her original $3 million investment into something worth more than $100 million today.

How does Wachner see herself? As effective and good, with an excellent record. You don't achieve that without focus, strategy, and having people do it your way. When she earned the title from *Fortune* magazine as one of the seven toughest bosses in the United States, she made no apologies. Although she recognized that the article didn't present her in the best light, she simply stated that "if you're going to run a company and improve the results and the image, you're not going to come out being a darling."

Insights into her personality construct can help people who work with Linda Wachner understand and predict her behavior, but this is true for everyone because personality goes a long way in shaping behavior. In this chapter, we look at four psychological concepts—attitudes, personality, perception, and learning—and demonstrate how these concepts can help managers understand the behavior of those people with whom they have to work.

Toward Explaining and Predicting Behavior

organizational behavior
The study of the actions of people at work

The material in this and the following four chapters draws heavily on the field of study known as organizational behavior. Although it is concerned with the general area of behavior—that is, the actions of people—**organizational behavior (OB)** is concerned specifically with the actions of people at work.

One of the challenges of understanding organizational behavior is that it addresses some issues that are not obvious. Like an iceberg, a lot of organizational behavior is not visible to the naked eye (see Exhibit 8-1). What we tend to see when we look at organizations are their formal aspects—strategies, objectives, policies and procedures, structure, technology, formal authority, and chains of command. But, just under the surface, lie informal elements that managers need to understand. OB provides managers with considerable insight into these important but hidden aspects of the organization.

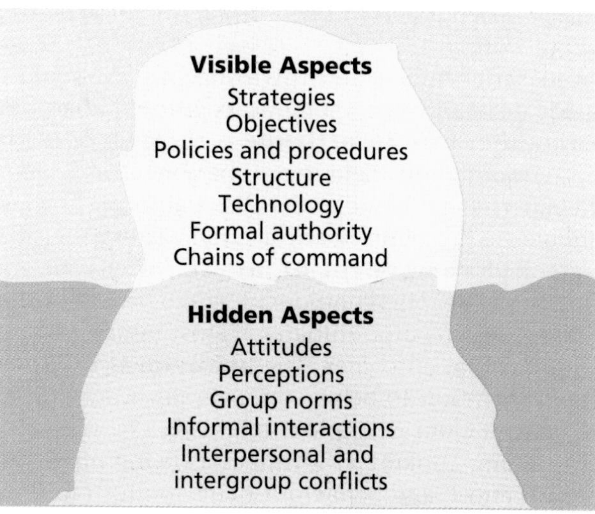

Exhibit 8-1
The Organization as an Iceberg Metaphor

WHAT IS THE FOCUS OF ORGANIZATIONAL BEHAVIOR?

Organizational behavior focuses primarily on two major areas. First, OB looks at individual behavior. Based predominantly on contributions from psychologists, this area includes such topics as personality, perception, learning, and motivation. Second, OB is concerned with group behavior, which includes norms, roles, team building, and conflict. Our knowledge about groups comes basically from the work of sociologists and social psychologists. Unfortunately, the behavior of a group of employees cannot be understood by merely summing up the actions of the individuals, because individuals in groups behave differently from individuals acting alone. You see this difference when individuals engage in some risk-taking behavior like bungee jumping. The individuals might never engage in such behavior if they were to act alone. Put them together, add peer pressure, and they act differently. Therefore, because employees in an organization are both individuals and members of groups, we need to study them at two levels. This chapter provides the foundation for understanding individual and group behavior. In the next chapter, we will introduce basic concepts related to special cases of group behavior—when individuals come together as a work team.

WHAT ARE THE GOALS OF ORGANIZATIONAL BEHAVIOR?

The goals of OB are to explain and to predict behavior. Why do managers need this skill? Simply, in order to manage their employees' behavior. We know that a manager's success depends on getting things done through other people. The manager needs to be able to explain why employees engage in some behaviors rather than others and to predict how employees will respond to various actions the manager might take.

The employee behaviors we are specifically concerned about are employee productivity, absenteeism, and turnover.[2] In addition, we will look at job satisfaction. Although job satisfaction is not a "behavior," it is an outcome with which many managers are concerned.

In the following pages, we address how an understanding of employee personality, perception, and learning can help us to predict and explain employee productivity, absence and turnover rates, and job satisfaction.

attitudes
Valuative statements concerning objects, people, or events

Attitudes are valuative statements, either favorable or unfavorable, concerning objects, people, or events. They reflect how an individual feels about something. When a person says, "I like my job," he or she is expressing an attitude about work.

cognitive component of an attitude
The beliefs, opinions, knowledge, and information held by a person

affective component of an attitude
The emotional, or feeling, segment of an attitude

behavioral component of an attitude
An intention to behave in a certain way toward someone or something

To better understand this concept, we should look at an attitude as being made up of three components: cognition, affect, and behavior.[3] The **cognitive component of an attitude** is made up of the beliefs, opinions, knowledge, and information held by a person. For example Sid Wing, president of Datametrics in Woodland Hills, California, believes that only one employee should be "recognized" at a time.[4] This belief illustrates Sid's cognition. The **affective component of an attitude** is the emotional, or feeling, segment of an attitude. This component would be reflected in the statement, "I don't like Eric because he discriminates against minorities." Cognition and affect can lead to behavioral outcomes. The **behavioral component of an attitude** refers to an intention to behave in a certain way toward someone or something. So, to continue our example, I might choose to avoid Eric because of my feelings about him. Looking at attitudes as being made up of three components—cognition, affect, and behavior—helps to illustrate the complexity of attitudes. For the sake of clarity, keep in mind that the term usually refers only to the affective component.

Naturally, managers are not interested in every attitude an employee might hold. Rather, they are specifically interested in job-related attitudes. The three most important and most studied are job satisfaction, job involvement, and organizational commitment.[5] *Job satisfaction* is an employee's general attitude toward his or her job. When people speak of employee attitudes, more often than not they mean job satisfaction. *Job involvement* is the degree to which an employee identifies with his or her job, actively participates in it, and considers his or her job performance important to his or her self-worth. Finally, *organizational com-*

One Manager's Perspective

Anders Grondstedt President, The Gronstedt Group

As president of a small and growing marketing and communications consulting and training firm, Anders Gronstedt spends most of his time meeting with clients and holding training programs in marketing and communications, as well as writing articles and a book.

Because the firm is still young and small, there are no quantitative measures set up for the performance of its four employees. Top performance by everybody is a must. Grondstedt selects employees who already share the company's values and point of view on marketing. He screens potential hires for what he describes as an "almost obsessive" focus on the client.

Grondstedt has individual discussions with employees every three months to discuss their progress and set personal development goals. If he sees points that need correction or improvement, he deals with them immediately instead of saving them up for the scheduled meetings.

The most reliable measure of success for Grondstedt is the feedback his firm receives from clients about his employees' performance. As for the most important way he has of shaping their attitudes, that's "setting a good personal example at work."

Ethical Dilemma in Management

Must Attitudes and Behaviors Align?

You work for a large international organization that manufactures and sells computer hard drives. In your position as a recruiter, you have the primary responsibility to hire individuals to fill entry-level positions in your company. Your organization prefers to hire recent college graduates for these entry-level manufacturing and marketing positions. It gets an opportunity to hire individuals who have the latest knowledge in their fields at a discounted price.

Your job requires you to travel extensively. In fact, over the past several years, you have averaged visits to 35 colleges on three different continents during a semester. Your performance evaluation rests primarily on one factor—how many people you have hired.

Over the past several months, you have noticed a surge in open positions. These are not new positions but replacements for employees who have quit. A little investigating on your part finds that, after about three years with your firm, entry-level employees quit. There is no upward mobility for them, and they burn out after working up to 12 hours a day, 6 days a week. Furthermore, you know that the benefits for entry-level employees—especially vacation and sick leave—aren't competitive with those offered by similar firms in your industry. So you think you know why these employees quit. On the other hand, almost everyone who has quit has gone on to a bigger, better job with more responsibility and greater pay. To get the most productivity out of these employees, your company invested heavily in their training. Almost all workers in these positions receive over 40 hours of specialized training each year and have jobs that offer excellent learning experiences but little advancement opportunity. Top management believes it is better to hire new people than to pay the higher salaries that seniority and experience demand. Although you don't totally agree with management's treatment of these employees, you recognize that the company is giving many of them a great start in their career.

Should you disclose to college recruits during interviews that the jobs they are being considered for are dead-end jobs in the organization? Why or why not? Would your response change if you were evaluated not only on how many people you hired but also on how long they stay with the organization? Defend your position.

mitment represents an employee's orientation toward the organization in terms of his or her loyalty to, identification with, and involvement in the organization.[6]

DO AN INDIVIDUAL'S ATTITUDE AND BEHAVIOR NEED TO BE CONSISTENT?

Did you ever notice how people change what they say so that it doesn't contradict what they do? Perhaps a friend of yours had consistently argued that American-manufactured cars were poorly built and that he'd never own anything but a foreign import. Then his parents gave him a late-model American-made car, and suddenly they weren't so bad. Or, when going through sorority rush, a new freshman believes that sororities are good and that pledging a sorority is important. If she fails to make a sorority, however, she may say, "I recognized that sorority life isn't all it's cracked up to be, anyway."

Research has generally concluded that people seek consistency among their attitudes and between their attitudes and their behavior.[7] Individuals try to reconcile differing attitudes and align their attitudes and behavior so that they appear rational and consistent. When there is an inconsistency, individuals will take steps to correct it (see Ethical Dilemma in Management). They can correct it by altering either the attitudes or the behavior or by developing a rationalization for the discrepancy.

WHAT IS COGNITIVE DISSONANCE THEORY?

Can we assume from this consistency principle that an individual's behavior can always be predicted if we know his or her opinion on a subject? The answer, unfortunately, cannot simply be a yes or a no.

cognitive dissonance
Any incompatibility between two or more attitudes or between behavior and attitudes

Leon Festinger, in the late 1950s, proposed the theory of **cognitive dissonance** to explain the relationship between attitude and behavior.[8] Dissonance in this case means inconsistency. Cognitive dissonance refers to any incompatibility that an individual might perceive between two or more of his or her attitudes or between his or her behavior and attitude. Festinger argued that any form of inconsistency is uncomfortable and that individuals will attempt to reduce the dissonance and, hence, the discomfort. Therefore, individuals will seek a stable state with a minimum of dissonance.

Of course, no individual can completely avoid dissonance. You know that cheating on your income tax is wrong, but you may fudge the numbers a bit every year and hope you won't be audited. Or you tell your children to brush after every meal even though you might not. So how do people cope? Festinger proposed that the desire to reduce dissonance is determined by the importance of the elements creating the dissonance, the degree of influence the individual believes he or she has over the elements, and the rewards that may be involved.[9] Let's look at some examples of cognitive dissonance.

Suppose that the factors creating the dissonance are relatively unimportant. In this case, the pressure to correct the imbalance would be low. However, say that a corporate manager, Jane Bradley, believes strongly that no company should lay off employees. Unfortunately, Bradley is placed in the position of having to make decisions that would trade off her company's strategic direction against her convictions on layoffs. She knows that, because of restructuring in the company, some jobs may no longer be needed, and the layoffs are in the best economic interest of her firm. What will she do? Undoubtedly, Jane is experiencing a high degree of cognitive dissonance. Because of the importance of the issues in this example, we cannot expect Bradley to ignore the inconsistency. There are several paths that she can follow to deal with her dilemma. She can change her behavior (lay off employees). Or she can reduce dissonance by concluding that the dissonant behavior is not so important after all ("I've got to make a living, and in my role as a decision maker, I often have to place the good of my company above that of individual organizational members"). A third alternative would be for Jane Bradley to change her attitude ("There is nothing wrong in laying off employees"). Still another choice would be to seek out more consonant elements to outweigh the dissonant ones ("The long-term benefits to the surviving employees from our restructuring more than offset the costs associated with the retrenchment effort").

The degree of influence that individuals like Jane Bradley believe they have over the elements also will have an impact on how they will react to the dissonance. If they perceive the dissonance to be uncontrollable—something about which they have no choice—they are less likely to feel a need for an attitude change. If, for example, the dissonance-producing behavior were required by the boss's directive, the pressure to reduce dissonance would be less than if the behavior were performed voluntarily. Dissonance would exist but it could be rationalized and justified. Rewards also influence the degree to which individuals are motivated to reduce dissonance. High dissonance, when accompanied by high rewards, tends to reduce the tension inherent in the dissonance. The reward reduces dissonance by adding to the consistency side of the individual's balance sheet.

These moderating factors suggest that just because individuals experience dissonance, they will not necessarily move directly toward consistency, that is, toward reduction of the dissonance. If the issues underlying the dissonance are of minimal importance, if an individual perceives that the dissonance is externally imposed and is substantially uncontrollable, or if rewards are significant enough to offset the dissonance, the individual will not be under great tension to reduce the dissonance.

HOW CAN AN UNDERSTANDING OF ATTITUDES HELP MANAGERS BE MORE EFFECTIVE?

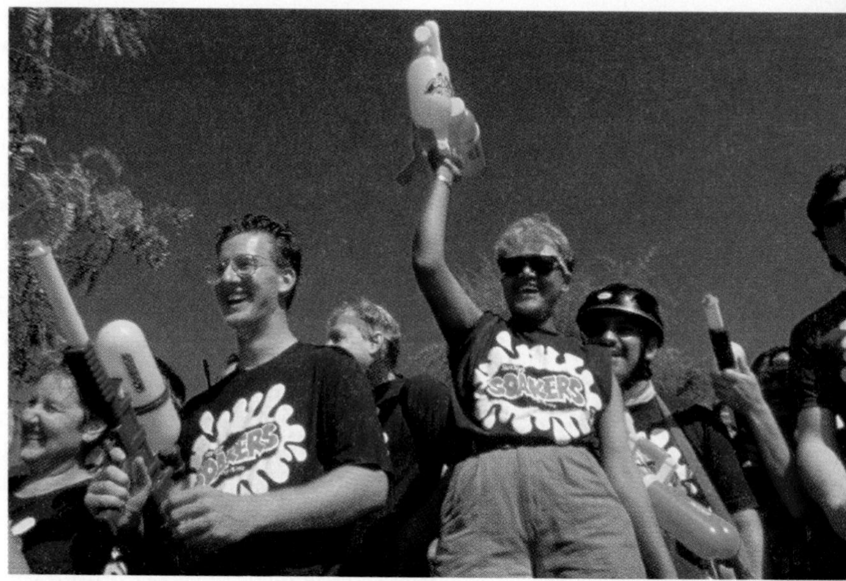

Employees at this company are benefitting from their management's belief that satisfied employees are happy employees. By offering these employees a "fun" day, management is helping to create a caring environment, which will lead to greater productivity at work.

We know that employees can be expected to try to reduce dissonance. Therefore, not surprisingly, there is relatively strong evidence that committed and satisfied employees have low rates of turnover and absenteeism.[10] Because most managers want to minimize the number of resignations and absences—especially among their more productive employees—they should do those things that will generate positive job attitudes. Dissonance can be managed. If employees are required to engage in activities that appear inconsistent to them or that are at odds with their attitudes, managers should remember that pressure to reduce the dissonance is lessened when the dissonance is perceived as externally imposed and uncontrollable. The pressure is also lessened if rewards are significant enough to offset the dissonance.

But let's not confuse satisfied workers with productive workers. We need to be aware of a debate that has lasted almost seven decades: Are happy workers more productive? Several research studies in the past have important implications for managers.[11] They suggested that making employees satisfied would lead to high productivity. That suggestion, in part, explains why in the 1930s, 1940s, and 1950s, management spent considerable time doing things that would create a caring environment. For instance, company bowling teams, picnics, and credit unions all gave something to employees and made them happy, but their effect on productivity was questioned.[12] As a result, most researchers perceived that managers would get better results by directing their attention primarily to what would help employees become more productive.[13] Successful job performance should then lead to feelings of accomplishment, increased pay, promotions, and other rewards—all desirable outcomes—which then lead to satisfaction with the job. Research in the early 1990s, however, provided renewed support for the original premise that happy workers are productive workers.[14] However, in this recent research, satisfaction and productivity data were gathered for entire organizations as opposed to individual employees. Organizations with satisfied employees were more effective than organizations with less satisfied employees.

Personality

Some people are quiet and passive. Some, like Linda Wachner, are loud and aggressive. When we describe people in terms such as quiet, passive, loud, aggressive, ambitious, extroverted, loyal, tense, or sociable, we are categorizing them in terms of personality traits. An individual's *personality* is the combination of the psychological traits we use to classify that person.[15]

CAN PERSONALITY PREDICT BEHAVIOR?

Literally dozens of traits are used to describe an individual's behavior. The more common traits include shyness, aggressiveness, submissiveness, laziness, ambitiousness, loyalty, and timidness. These characteristics, when exhibited consistently in a large number of situations, are called personality traits.[16] Through the years, researchers attempted to focus specifically on which traits would identify sources of one's personality. Two of these efforts have been widely recognized—the Myers-Briggs Type Indicator and the five-factor model of personality.

Myers-Briggs Type Indicator
A method of identifying personality types

What is the Myers-Briggs Type Indicator? One of the more widely used methods of identifying personalities is the **Myers-Briggs Type Indicator (MBTI).** The MBTI uses four dimensions of personality to identify 16 different personality types based on the responses to an approximately 100-item questionnaire (see Exhibit 8-2). More than two million individuals each year in the United States alone take the MBTI. And it's used in such companies as Apple Computer, AT&T, Exxon, 3M, as well as many hospitals, educational institutions, and the U.S. Armed Forces.[17]

The 16 personality types are based on the four dimensions noted in Exhibit 8-2. That is, the MBTI dimensions include *extroversion* versus *introversion* (EI), *sensing* versus *intuitive* (SN), *thinking* versus *feeling* (TF), and *judging* versus *perceiving* (JP). The EI dimension measures an individual's orientation toward the inner world of ideas (I) or the external world of the environment (E). The sensing-intuitive dimension indicates an individual's reliance on information gathered from the external world (S) or from the world of ideas (N). Thinking-feeling reflects one's preference of evaluating information in an analytical manner (T) or on the basis of values and beliefs (F). The judging-perceiving index reflects an attitude toward the external world that is either task completion oriented (J) or information seeking (P).[18]

How could the MBTI help managers? Proponents of the instrument believe that it's important to know these personality types because they influence the way people interact and solve problems. For example, if your boss is an intuitor and you are a sensor, you will gather information in different ways. An intuitor prefers gut reactions, whereas a sensor prefers facts. To work well with your boss, you have to present more than just facts about a situation and discuss how you feel. Also, the MBTI has been used to help managers match employees with jobs. For instance, a marketing position that requires extensive interaction with outsiders would be best filled by someone who has extroverted tendencies.

big-five model
Five-factor model of personality that includes extroversion, agreeableness, conscientiousness, emotional stability, and openness to experience

What is the big-five model of personality? Although the MBTI is very popular, it suffers from one major criticism: It lacks evidence to support its validity. That same criticism, however, cannot be imposed on the five-factor model of personality—more typically called the **Big-Five model.**[19] The Big-Five factors are:

1. **Extroversion** A personality dimension that describes the degree to which someone is sociable, talkative, and assertive.
2. **Agreeableness** A personality dimension that describes the degree to which someone is good-natured, cooperative, and trusting.
3. **Conscientiousness** A personality dimension that describes the degree to which someone is responsible, dependable, persistent, and achievement oriented.

Exhibit 8-2 Characteristics Frequently Associated with Myers-Briggs Types

ISTJ Quiet, serious, dependable, practical, matter of fact. Value traditions and loyalty.	**ISFJ** Quiet, friendly, responsible, thorough, considerate. Strive to create order and harmony.	**INFJ** Seek meaning and connection in ideas. Committed to firm values. Organized and decisive in implementing vision.	**INTJ** Have original minds and great drive for their ideas. Skeptical and independent. Have high standards of competence for self and others.
ISTP Tolerant and flexible. Interested in cause and effect. Value efficiency.	**ISFP** Quiet, friendly, sensitive. Like own space. Dislike disagreements and conflicts.	**INFP** Idealistic, loyal to their values. Seek to understand people and help them fulfill their potential.	**INTP** Seek logical explanations. Theoretical and abstract over social interactions. Skeptical, sometimes critical. Analytical.
ESTP Flexible and tolerant. Focus on here and now. Enjoy material comforts. Learn best by doing.	**ISFP** Outgoing, friendly. Enjoy working with others. Spontaneous. Learn best by trying a new skill with other people.	**ENFP** Enthusiastic, imaginative. Want a lot of affirmation. Rely on verbal fluency and ability to improvise.	**ENTP** Quick, ingenious, stimulating. Adept at generating conceptual possibilities and analyzing them strategically. Bored by routine.
ESTJ Practical, realistic, matter of fact, decisive. Focus on getting efficient results. Forceful in implementing plans.	**ESFJ** Warmhearted, cooperative. Want to be appreciated for who they are and for what they contribute.	**ENFJ** Warm, responsive, responsible. Attuned to needs of others. Sociable, facilitate others, provide inspirational leadership.	**ENTJ** Frank, decisive, assumes leadership. Enjoy long-term planning and goal setting. Forceful in presenting ideas.

SOURCE: Modified and reproduced by special permission of the publisher, Consulting Psychologists Press, Inc., Palo Alto, CA 94303, from *Introduction to Type,* 6th Edition by Isabel Myers Briggs, Katherine C. Briggs. Copyright 1998 by Consulting Psychologists Press, Inc. All rights reserved. Further reproduction is prohibited without publisher's written consent. *Introduction to Type* is a trademark of Consulting Psychologists Press, Inc. (The Myers-Briggs Type Indicator and MBTI are registered trademarks of Consulting Psychologists Press, Inc.)

4 **Emotional stability** A personality dimension that describes the degree to which someone is calm, enthusiastic, and secure (positive) or tense, nervous, depressed, and insecure (negative).

5 **Openness to experience** A personality dimension that describes the degree to which someone is imaginative, artistically sensitive, and intellectual.

The Big Five provide more than just a personality framework. Research has shown that important relationships exist between these personality dimensions and job performance.[20] For example, one study reviewed five categories of occupations: *professionals* (e.g., engineers, architects, attorneys), *police, managers, sales,* and *semiskilled and skilled employees.*[21] Job performance was defined in terms of employee performance ratings, training competency, and personnel data such as salary level. The results of the study showed that conscientiousness predicted job performance for all five occupational groups. Predictions for the other personality dimensions depended on the situation and the occupational group. For example, extroversion predicted performance in managerial and sales positions, in which high social interaction is necessary. Openness to experience was found to be important in predicting training competency. Ironically, emotional security was not positively related to job performance. Although it would appear logical that calm and secure workers would be better performers, that wasn't the case. Perhaps that result is a function of the likelihood that emotionally stable workers often keep their jobs and emotionally unstable people may not. Given that all those participating in the study were employed, the variance on that dimension was probably small.

What is emotional intelligence? People who understand their own emotions and are good at reading others' emotions may be more effective in their jobs. That, in essence, is the theme of the underlying research on *emotional intelligence*.[22]

emotional intelligence (EI)
An assortment of noncognitive skills, capabilities, and competencies that influence a person's ability to cope with environmental demands and pressures

Emotional intelligence (EI) refers to an assortment of noncognitive skills, capabilities, and competencies that influence a person's ability to cope with environmental demands and pressures. It's composed of five dimensions:

1. **Self-awareness** Being aware of what you're feeling.
2. **Self-management** The ability to manage your own emotions and impulses.
3. **Self-motivation** The ability to persist in the face of setbacks and failures.
4. **Empathy** The ability to sense how others are feeling.
5. **Social skills** The ability to handle the emotions of others.

Several studies suggest EI may play an important role in job performance. For instance, one study looked at the characteristics of the Bell Lab engineers who were rated as stars by their peers. The scientists concluded that these stars were better at relating to others. That is, it was EI, not academic IQ that characterized high performers. A second study of Air Force recruiters generated similar findings: Top-performing recruiters exhibited high levels of EI. Using these findings, the Air Force revamped its selection criteria. A follow-up investigation found that future hires who had high EI scores were 2.6 times more successful than those with low scores. A recent poll of human resource managers asked this question: How important is it for your workers to demonstrate EI to move up the corporate ladder? Forty percent of the managers replied "very important." Another 16 percent said "moderately important."

CAN PERSONALITY TRAITS PREDICT PRACTICAL WORK-RELATED BEHAVIORS?

Five specific personality traits have proven most powerful in explaining individual behavior in organizations. These are locus of control, Machiavellianism, self-esteem, self-monitoring, and risk propensity.

Who has control over an individual's behavior? Some people, like Charles Wang of Computer Associates International, Inc., of Islandia, New York, believe that they control their own fate.[23] After nearly 20 years of struggling, Computer Associates has grown into the second largest independent software company in the world (after Microsoft), has more than $3.5 billion in annual revenues, and has had more than 18 quarters of double-digit growth.

locus of control
A personality attribute that measures the degree to which people believe that they are masters of their own fate

Others see themselves as pawns of fate, believing that what happens to them in their lives is due to luck or chance. The **locus of control** in the first case is internal; people like Wang believe that they control their destiny. In the second case, it is external; these people believe that their lives are controlled by outside forces.[24] A manager might also expect to find that "externals" blame a poor performance evaluation on their boss's prejudice, their coworkers, or other events outside their control, whereas "internals" explain the same evaluation in terms of their own action.

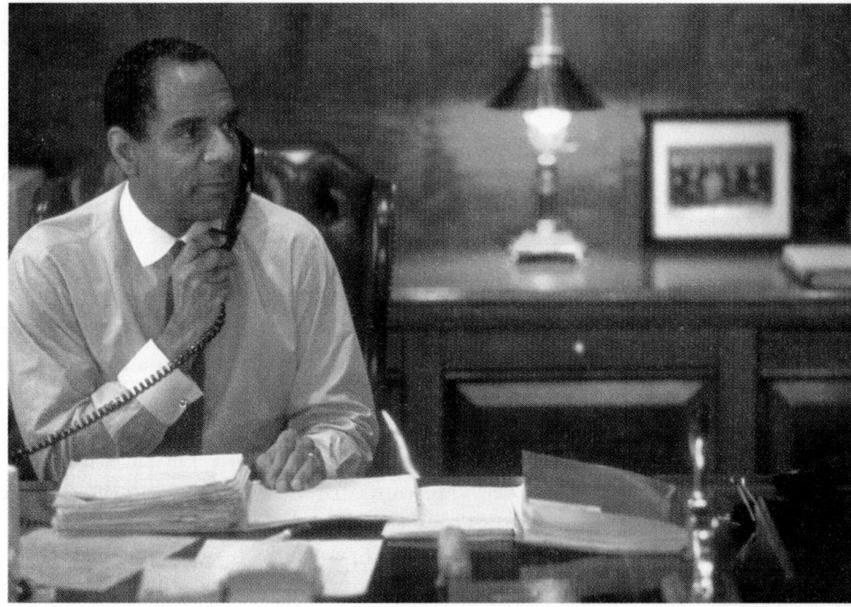

What personality characteristics does Ken Chenault, president and COO of American Express, have? The Big-Five Model states that individuals like Chenault possess such characteristics as extroversion, agreeableness, conscientiousness, emotional stability, and openness to experience.

The second characteristic is called **Machiavellianism ("Mach")** after Niccolo Machiavelli, who provided instruction in the sixteenth century on how to gain and manipulate power. An individual who is high in Machiavellianism is pragmatic, maintains emotional distance, and believes that ends can justify means.[25] "If it works, use it" is consistent with a high-Mach perspective. Do high Machs make good employees? That answer depends on the type of job and whether you consider ethical implications in evaluating performance. In jobs that require bargaining skills (a labor negotiator) or that have substantial rewards for winning (a commissioned salesperson), high Machs are productive. In jobs in which ends do not justify the means or that lack absolute standards of performance, it is difficult to predict the performance of high Machs.

Machiavellianism
A measure of the degree to which people are pragmatic, maintain emotional distance, and believe that ends can justify means

People differ in the degree to which they like or dislike themselves. This trait is called **self-esteem (SE).**[26] The research on SE offers some interesting insights into organizational behavior. For example, SE is directly related to expectations for success. High SEs believe that they possess the ability to succeed at work. Individuals with high SE will take more risks in job selection and are more likely to choose unconventional jobs than are people with low SE.[27]

self-esteem
An individual's degree of like or dislike for him- or herself

The most common finding on self-esteem is that low SEs are more susceptible to external influence than are high SEs. Low SEs are dependent on positive evaluations from others.[28] As a result, they are more likely to seek approval from others and more prone to conform to the beliefs and behaviors of those they respect than are high SEs. In managerial positions, low SEs will tend to be concerned with pleasing others and, therefore, will be less likely to take unpopular stands than will high SEs. Not surprisingly, self-esteem has also been found to be related to job satisfaction. A number of studies confirm that high SEs are more satisfied with their jobs than are low SEs.

Another personality trait that has recently received increased attention is called **self-monitoring.**[29] It refers to an individual's ability to adjust his or her behavior to external, situational factors. Individuals high in self-monitoring can show considerable adaptability in adjusting their behavior to external, situational factors. They are highly sensitive to external cues and can behave differently in different situations. High self-monitors are capable of presenting striking contradictions between their public persona and their private selves. Low self-monitors

self-monitoring
A measure of an individual's ability to adjust his or her behavior to external, situational factors

can't alter their behavior. They tend to display their true dispositions and attitudes in every situation; hence, there is high behavioral consistency between who they are and what they do.

The research on self-monitoring is in its infancy, so predictions are hard to make. Preliminary evidence suggests, however, that high self-monitors tend to pay closer attention to the behavior of others and are more capable of conforming than are low self-monitors.[30] We might also hypothesize that high self-monitors will be more successful in managerial positions that require individuals to play multiple, and even contradicting, roles. The high self-monitor is capable of putting on different faces for different audiences.[31]

The final personality trait influencing worker behavior reflects the willingness to take chances—the propensity for *risk taking*. A preference to assume or avoid risk has been shown to have an impact on how long it takes individuals to make a decision and how much information they require before making their choice. For instance, in one classic study 79 managers worked on a simulated human resource management exercise that required them to make hiring decisions.[32] High-risk-taking managers made more rapid decisions and used less information in making their choices than did the low-risk-taking managers. Interestingly, the decision accuracy was the same for both groups.

Although it is generally correct to conclude that managers in organizations are risk aversive,[33] there are still individual differences on this dimension.[34] As a result, it makes sense to recognize these differences and even to consider aligning risk-taking propensity with specific job demands. For instance, a high-risk-taking propensity may lead to effective performance for a stock trader in a brokerage firm. This type of job demands rapid decision making. On the other hand, this personality characteristic might prove a major obstacle to accountants performing auditing activities, which might be better done by someone with a low-risk-taking propensity.

HOW DO WE MATCH PERSONALITIES AND JOBS?

Obviously, individual personalities differ. So, too, do jobs. Following this logic, efforts have been made to match the proper personalities with the proper jobs. The best-documented personality-job fit theory has been developed by psychologist John Holland.[35] His theory states that an employee's satisfaction with his or her job as well as his or her propensity to leave that job depends on the degree to which the individual's personality matches his or her occupational environment. Holland has identified six basic employee personality types. Exhibit 8-3 describes each of the six types, their personality characteristics, and examples of congruent occupations.

Holland's research strongly supports the hexagonal diagram in Exhibit 8-4.[36] This exhibit shows that the closer two fields or orientations are in the hexagon, the more compatible they are. For instance, Realistic and Social are opposite each other in the diagram. A person with a Realistic preference wants to work with objects, not people. A person with a Social preference wants to work with people, no matter what else they do. Therefore, they have opposing preferences about working alone or with others. Investigative and Enterprising are opposing themes as are Artistic and Conventional preferences. An example of mutually reinforcing themes is the Social-Enterprising-Conventional (SEC) vocational preference structure. Sally, for example, likes working with people, being successful, and following established rules. That combination is perfect for someone who's going to suc-

Exhibit 8-3 Holland's Typology of Personality and Sample Occupations

Type	Personality Characteristics	Sample Occupations
Realistic Prefers physical activities that require skill, strength, and coordination	Shy, genuine, persistent, stable, conforming, practical	Mechanic, drill press operator, assembly-line worker, farmer
Investigative Prefers activities involving thinking, organizing, and understanding	Analytical, original, curious, independent	Biologist, economist, mathematician, reporter
Social Prefers activities that involve helping and developing others	Sociable, friendly, cooperative, understanding	Social worker, teacher, counselor, clinical psychologist
Conventional Prefers rule-regulated, orderly, and unambiguous activities	Conforming, efficient, practical, unimaginative, inflexible	Accountant, corporate manager, bank teller, file clerk
Enterprising Prefers verbal activities where there are opportunities to influence others and attain power	Self-confident, ambitious, energetic, domineering	Lawyer, real estate agent, public relations specialist, small business manager
Artistic Prefers ambiguous and unsystematic activities that allow creative expression	Imaginative, disorderly, idealistic, emotional, impractical	Painter, musician, writer, interior decorator

SOURCE: Reproduced by special permission of the publisher, Psychological Assessment Resources, Inc., *Making Vocational Choices,* Third Edition, copyright 1973, 1985, 1992, 1997 by Psychological Assessment Resources, Inc. All rights reserved.

ceed in a bureaucracy. But let's look at another employee, Bob. He's Realistic-Investigative-Artistic, preferring solitary work to large groups, asking questions to answering them, and making his own rules instead of following someone else's. How would Bob fit into Sally's bureaucracy? Probably not very well. In fact, his preferred actions could be viewed as trouble making. Where then would Bob bet-

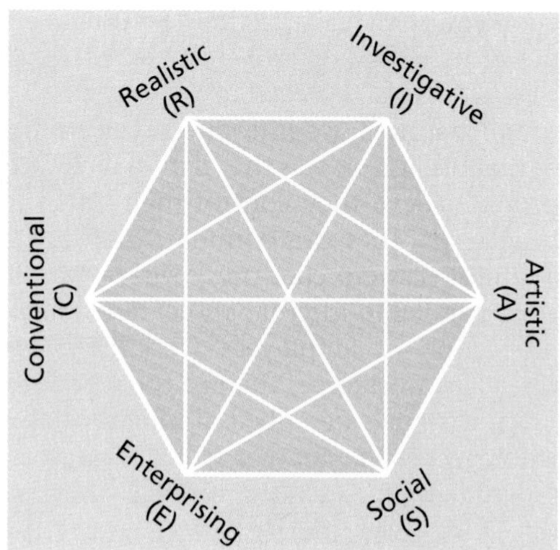

Exhibit 8-4 Relationships among Occupational Personality Types

SOURCE: Reproduced by special permission of the publisher, Psychological Assessment Resources, Inc., *Making Vocational Choices,* Third Edition, copyright 1973, 1985, 1992, 1997 by Psychological Assessment Resources, Inc. All rights reserved.

ter fit? Possibly in a research lab? Both the preference of the scientist and the environment of the research lab are characterized by a lack of human interruptions and a concentration on factual material. That's consistent with the Realistic-Investigative-Artistic profile.

What does all this mean? The theory argues that satisfaction is highest and turnover lowest when personality and occupation are in agreement.[37] Social individuals should be in social jobs, conventional people in conventional jobs, and so forth. A realistic person in a realistic job is in a more congruent situation than is a realistic person in an investigative job. A realistic person in a social job is in the most incongruent situation possible. The key points of this model are:

1 there do appear to be intrinsic differences in personality among individuals;
2 there are different types of jobs; and
3 people in job environments congruent with their personality types should be more satisfied and less likely to resign voluntarily than people in incongruent jobs.

HOW CAN AN UNDERSTANDING OF PERSONALITY HELP MANAGERS BE MORE EFFECTIVE?

The major value of a manager's understanding personality differences probably lies in employee selection. Managers are likely to have higher-performing and more satisfied employees if personality types are matched to compatible jobs. In addition, there may be other benefits. By recognizing that people approach problem solving, decision making, and job interactions differently, a manager can better understand why, for instance, an employee is uncomfortable with making quick decisions or why an employee insists on gathering as much information as possible before addressing a problem. Or, for instance, managers can expect that individuals with an external locus of control may be less satisfied with their jobs than those with an internal locus and also that they may be less willing to accept responsibility for their actions.

DO PERSONALITY ATTRIBUTES DIFFER ACROSS NATIONAL CULTURES?

There certainly are no dominant personality types within a given country. You can, for instance, find high risk takers and low risk takers in almost any culture, yet a country's culture should influence the dominant personality characteristics of its population. We can see this influence by looking at the locus of control.

In Chapter 2, we introduced you to the issues of national cultures. One point of that discussion was that national cultures differ in terms of the degree to which people believe they control their environment. North Americans, for example, believe that they can dominate their environment, whereas other societies, such as Middle Eastern countries, believe that life is essentially preordained. Notice the close parallel to internal and external locus of control. We should expect a larger proportion of employees who have internal loci in the United States and Canadian workforces than in the workforces of Saudi Arabia or Iran.

As we have described throughout this section, personality traits influence employees' behavior. For global managers, understanding how personality traits differ takes on added significance when we adopt the perspective of national culture.

Perception is a process by which individuals organize and interpret their sensory impressions in order to give meaning to their environment. Research on perception consistently demonstrates that several individuals may look at the same thing, yet perceive it differently. One manager, for instance, can interpret the fact that her assistant regularly takes several days to make important decisions as evidence that the assistant is slow, disorganized, and afraid to make decisions. Another manager, with the same assistant, might interpret the same approach as evidence that the assistant is thoughtful, thorough, and deliberate. The first manager would probably evaluate her assistant negatively, and the second manager would probably evaluate the person positively. The point is that none of us actually sees reality. We interpret what we see and call it reality. And, of course, as the preceding example illustrates, we act according to our perceptions.

perception
The process of organizing and interpreting sensory impressions in order to give meaning to the environment

WHAT INFLUENCES PERCEPTION?

How do we explain the fact that Brian, a marketing supervisor for a large commercial petroleum products organization, 45, noticed Rhonda's nose ring during her employment interview and Sean, a human resources recruiter, 22, didn't? A number of factors operate to shape and sometimes distort perception. These factors can reside in the perceiver, in the object or target being perceived, or in the context of the situation in which the perception is made.

When an individual looks at a target and attempts to interpret what he or she sees, that individual's personal characteristics will heavily influence the interpretation.[38] These personal characteristics include attitudes, personality, motives, interests, past experiences, and expectations. The characteristics of the target being observed can also affect what is perceived. Loud people are more likely than quiet people to be noticed in a group. So, too, are extremely attractive or unattractive individuals. Because targets are not looked at in isolation, the relationship of a target to its background also influences perception (see Exhibit 8-5 for an example) as does our tendency to group close things and similar things together.

The context in which we see objects or events is also important. The time at which an object or event is seen can influence attention, as can location, lighting, temperature, and any number of other situational factors.

HOW DO MANAGERS JUDGE EMPLOYEES?

Much of the research on perception is directed at inanimate objects. Managers, though, are more concerned with human beings. Our perceptions of people differ from our perceptions of such inanimate objects as computers, robots, or build-

Exhibit 8-5
Perceptual Challenges: What Do You See?

Old woman or young woman?

Two faces or an urn?

A knight on a horse?

ings because we make inferences about the actions of people that we don't, of course, make about inanimate objects. When we observe people, we attempt to develop explanations of why they behave in certain ways. Our perception and judgment of a person's actions, therefore, will be significantly influenced by the assumptions we make about the person's internal state. Many of these assumptions have led researchers to develop attribution theory.

Quick, what's your perception of this individual? What if he were applying for a computer job at your company? Careful! The person you see is Jaron Lanier, the individual who's credited with developing the software that has made virtual reality commonplace in our society. His client list includes Xerox, Kodak, American Express, and the Department of Defense.

What is attribution theory? **Attribution theory** has been proposed to develop explanations of how we judge people differently depending on what meaning we attribute to a given behavior.[39] Basically, the theory suggests that when we observe an individual's behavior, we attempt to determine whether it was internally or externally caused. Internally caused behavior is believed to be under the control of the individual. Externally caused behavior results from outside causes; that is, the person is seen as having been forced into the behavior by the situation. That determination, however, depends on three factors: distinctiveness, consensus, and consistency.

Distinctiveness refers to whether an individual displays a behavior in many situations or whether it is particular to one situation. Is the employee who arrived late to work today also the person coworkers see as a goof-off? What we want to know is whether this behavior is unusual. If it is, the observer is likely to give the behavior an external attribution. If this action is not unique, it will probably be judged as internal.

If everyone who is faced with a similar situation responds in the same way, we can say the behavior shows *consensus*. Our tardy employee's behavior would meet this criterion if all employees who took the same route to work today were also late. If consensus is high, you would be expected to give an external attribution to the employee's tardiness, whereas if other employees who took the same route made it to work on time, your conclusion for the reason would be internal.

attribution theory
A theory based on the premise that we judge people differently depending on the meaning we attribute to a given behavior

Finally, a manager looks for *consistency* in an employee's actions. Does the individual engage in the behaviors regularly and consistently? Does the employee respond the same way over time? Coming in 10 minutes late for work is not perceived in the same way if, for one employee, it represents an unusual case (she hasn't been late for several months), but for another it is part of a routine pattern (he is late two or three times a week). The more consistent the behavior, the more the observer is inclined to attribute it to internal causes.

Exhibit 8-6 summarizes the key elements in attribution theory. It would tell us, for instance, that if an employee, Mr. Rice, generally performs at about the same level on other related tasks as he does on his current task (low distinctiveness), if other employees frequently perform differently—better or worse—than Mr. Rice does on that current task (low consensus), and if Mr. Rice's performance on this current task is consistent over time (high consistency), his manager or anyone else who is judging Mr. Rice's work is likely to hold him primarily responsible for his task performance (internal attribution).

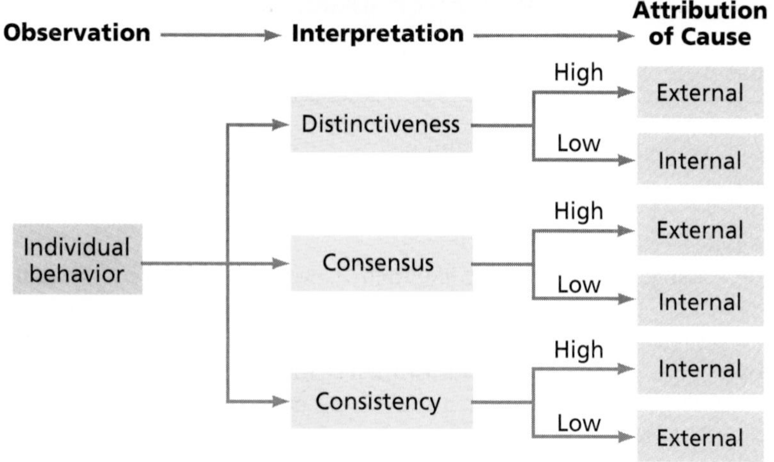

Exhibit 8-6
The Process of Attribution Theory

Can attributions be distorted? One of the more interesting findings drawn from attribution theory is that errors or biases distort attributions. For instance, there is substantial evidence to support the hypothesis that when we make judgments about the behavior of other people, we have a tendency to underestimate the influence of external factors and overestimate the influence of internal or personal factors.[40] This is the **fundamental attribution error,** which can explain why a sales manager may be prone to attribute the poor performance of her sales agents to laziness rather than to the innovative product line introduced by a competitor. Individuals also tend to attribute their own successes to internal factors such as ability or effort while putting the blame for failure on external factors such as luck. This is called the **self-serving bias** and suggests that feedback provided to employees in performance reviews will be predictably distorted by them, whether it is positive or negative.

fundamental attribution error
The tendency to underestimate the influence of external factors and overestimate the influence of internal or personal factors when making judgments about the behavior of others

self-serving bias
The tendency for individuals to attribute their own successes to internal factors while putting the blame for failures on external factors

WHAT SHORTCUTS DO MANAGERS USE IN JUDGING OTHERS?

Managers use a number of shortcuts to judge others. Perceiving and interpreting what others do are burdensome processes. As a result, individuals develop techniques for making the task more manageable. These techniques are frequently valuable; they allow us to make accurate perceptions rapidly and provide valid data for making predictions. However, they are not foolproof. They can and do get us into trouble. An understanding of these shortcuts can help us determine when they can result in significant distortions (see Exhibit 8-7).

Individuals cannot assimilate all they observe, so they are *selective.* They absorb bits and pieces. These bits and pieces are not chosen randomly; rather, they are selectively chosen depending on the interests, background, experience, and attitudes of the observer. Selective perception allows us to "speed read" others but not without the risk of drawing an inaccurate picture.[41]

It is easy to judge others if we assume that they are similar to us. In *assumed similarity,* or the "like-me" effect, the observer's perception of others is influenced more by the observer's own characteristics than by those of the person observed.

Exhibit 8-7 Distortions in Shortcut Methods in Judging Others

Shortcut	What It Is	Distortion
Selectivity	People assimilate certain bits and pieces of what they observe depending on their interests, background, experience, and attitudes	"Speed reading" others may result in an inaccurate picture of them
Assumed similarity	People assume that others are like them	May fail to take into account individual differences, resulting in incorrect similarities
Stereotyping	People judge others on the basis of their perception of a group to which the others belong	May result in distorted judgments because many stereotypes have no factual foundation
Halo effect	People form an impression of others on the basis of a single trait	Fails to take into account the total picture of what an individual has done
Self-fulfilling prophecy	People perceive others in a certain way, and, in turn, those others behave in ways that are consistent with the perception	May result in getting the behavior expected, not the true behavior of individuals

For example, if you want challenge and responsibility in your job, you will assume that others want the same. People who assume that others are like them can, of course, be proven right, but most of the time they're wrong.

When we judge someone on the basis of our perception of a group to which he or she belongs, we are using the shortcut of *stereotyping*. "Most women won't relocate for a promotion" and "older workers are less productive" are examples of stereotyping. If someone holds such stereotypes, that is what he or she will perceive—whether or not they're accurate. When stereotypes have no foundation, they distort judgments.

When we form a general impression about an individual on the basis of a single characteristic such as intelligence, sociability, or appearance, we are being influenced by the *halo effect*. This effect frequently occurs, for instance, when students evaluate their classroom instructor. Students may isolate a single trait such as enthusiasm and allow their entire evaluation to be tainted by their perception of this one trait. An instructor might be assured, knowledgeable, and highly qualified, but if he or she lacks zeal, he or she may be rated lower on a number of other characteristics.

A final shortcut in judging others involves a manager's expectations of employees. It is the *self-fulfilling prophecy* (or the Pygmalion effect).[42] The self-fulfilling prophecy involves how a manager perceives others and how they, in turn, behave in ways that are consistent with the manager's expectations. For example, if a manager expects outstanding performance from his employees, they are not likely to disappoint him. They will work (or be perceived to work) up to the manager's expectations. On the other hand, if this same manager believes that he is supervising a group of underachievers, his employees will respond accordingly. As a result, the manager's expectations will become a reality as the employees work in such a way as to meet his low expectations.

HOW CAN AN UNDERSTANDING OF PERCEPTIONS HELP MANAGERS BE MORE EFFECTIVE?

Managers need to recognize that their employees react to perceptions, not to reality. Whether a manager's appraisal of an employee is actually objective and unbiased or whether the organization's wage levels are actually among the highest in the industry is less relevant than what employees perceive. If employees perceive appraisals to be biased or wage levels as low, they will behave as if those conditions actually existed. Employees organize and interpret what they see, creating the potential for perceptual distortion.

The message to managers should be clear. Pay close attention to how employees perceive both their jobs and management practices. Remember, the valuable employee who quits because of an inaccurate perception is just as great a loss to an organization as the valuable employee who quits for a valid reason.

Learning

The last individual-behavior concept we introduce in this chapter is learning. It is included for the obvious reason that almost all complex behavior is learned. If we want to explain and predict behavior, we need to understand how people learn. What is learning? A psychologist's definition is considerably broader than the layperson's view that "it's what we did when we went to school." In actuality, each of us is continually going to school. Learning occurs all the time. We constantly learn from our experiences. A workable definition here of **learning** is, therefore, any relatively permanent change in behavior that occurs as a result of experience.

Learning is any relatively permanent change in behavior that occurs as a result of experience.

How do we learn? Two popular theories explain the process by which we acquire patterns of behavior: operant conditioning and social learning theory.

learning
Any relatively permanent change in behavior that occurs as a result of experience

WHAT IS OPERANT CONDITIONING?

Operant conditioning argues that behavior is a function of its consequences. People learn to behave so as to get something they want or to avoid something they don't want. Operant behavior is voluntary or learned rather than reflexive or unlearned behavior. The tendency to repeat such behavior is influenced by the reinforcement or lack of reinforcement brought about by the consequences of the behavior. Reinforcement, therefore, strengthens a behavior and increases the likelihood that it will be repeated.

operant conditioning
A behavioral theory that argues that voluntary, or learned, behavior is a function of its consequences

Building on earlier work in the field, the late Harvard psychologist B. F. Skinner extensively expanded our knowledge of operant conditioning.[43] Even his staunchest critics, who represent a sizable group, admit that his operant concepts work.

Behavior is assumed to be determined from without (learned) rather than from within (reflexive, or unlearned). Skinner argued that causing pleasing consequences to follow a specific form of behavior will increase the frequency of that behavior. People are most likely to engage in desired behaviors if they are positively reinforced for doing so. Rewards, for example, are most effective if they immediately follow the desired response. In addition, behavior that is not rewarded or is punished is less likely to be repeated.

You see illustrations of operant conditioning everywhere. For example, any situation in which it is either explicitly stated or implicitly suggested that reinforcements are contingent on some action on your part involves operant learning. Your instructor asserts that if you want a high grade in the course, you must supply correct answers on the test. A real estate agent finds that high income is contingent on generating many home listings and sales in his or her territory. Of course, the linkage can also teach the individual to engage in behaviors that work against the best interests of the organization. Assume that your boss tells you that if you will work overtime during the next three-week-long busy season, you will be compensated for it at the next performance appraisal. However, when performance appraisal time comes, you are given no positive reinforcement for your overtime work. The next time your boss asks you to work overtime, what will you do? You may decline. Your behavior can be explained by operant conditioning: If a behavior fails to be positively reinforced, the probability that the behavior will be repeated declines.

WHAT IS SOCIAL LEARNING THEORY?

Individuals can also learn by observing what happens to other people and by being told about something as well as by direct experience. For example, much of what we have learned comes from watching models—parents, teachers, peers, television and movie performers, bosses, and so forth. This view that we can learn through both observation and direct experience has been called **social learning theory.**[44]

social learning theory
The theory that people can learn through observation and direct experience

Social learning theory is an extension of operant conditioning—that is, it assumes that behavior is a function of consequences—but it also acknowledges the existence of observational learning and the importance of perception in learning. People respond to the way that they perceive and define consequences, not to the objective consequences themselves.

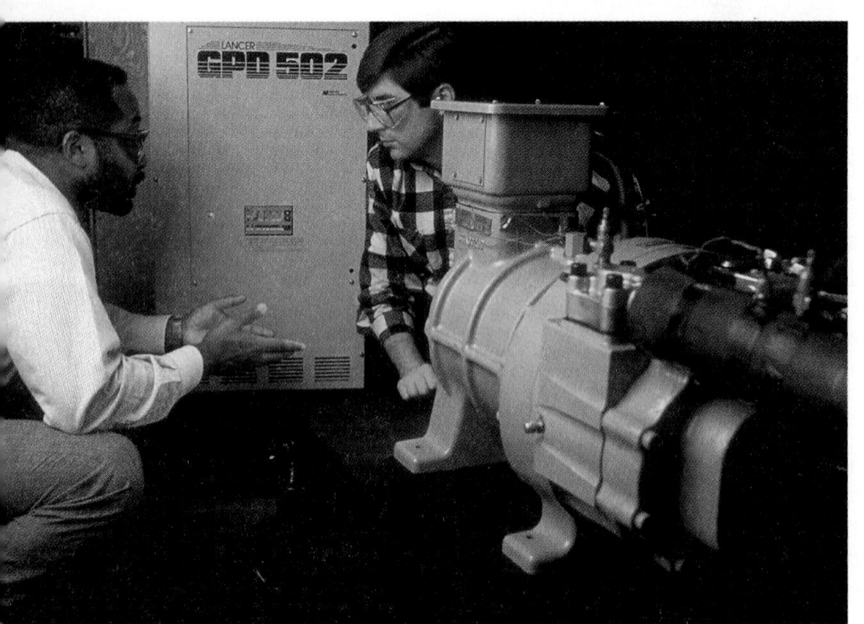

Employees learn their jobs in different ways. Here, this supervisor uses social learning theory to help this apprentice learn his job. This process bases learning on both observation and direct, hands-on experience.

The influence of models is central to the social learning viewpoint. Four processes determine the influence that a model will have on an individual:

1. **Attentional processes** People learn from a model only when they recognize and pay attention to its critical features. We tend to be most influenced by repeatedly available models, which we think are attractive, important, or similar to us.
2. **Retention processes** A model's influence will depend on how well the individual remembers the model's action, even after the model is no longer readily available.
3. **Motor reproduction processes** After a person has seen a new behavior by observing the model, watching must be converted to doing. This process demonstrates that the individual can perform the modeled activities.

4 Reinforcement processes Individuals will be motivated to exhibit the modeled behavior if positive incentives or rewards are provided. Behaviors that are reinforced will be given more attention, learned better, and performed more often than will behaviors that are not reinforced.

HOW CAN MANAGERS SHAPE BEHAVIOR?

Managers should be concerned with how they can teach employees to behave in ways that most benefit the organization. Thus, managers will often attempt to mold individuals by guiding their learning in graduated steps. This process is called **shaping behavior** (see Developing Your Skill at Shaping Behavior, p. 284).

shaping behavior
Systematically reinforcing each successive step that moves an individual closer to a desired behavior

Consider the situation in which an employee's behavior is significantly different from that desired by management. If management reinforced the individual only when he or she showed desirable responses, there might be very little reinforcement.

We shape behavior by systematically reinforcing each successive step that moves the individual closer to the desired response. If an employee who has chronically been 30 minutes late for work arrives only 20 minutes late, we can reinforce this improvement. Reinforcement would increase as responses more closely approximate the desired behavior.

There are four ways in which to shape behavior: positive reinforcement, negative reinforcement, punishment, or extinction. When a response is followed with something pleasant, such as when a manager praises an employee for a job well done, it is called *positive reinforcement.* Rewarding a response with the termination or withdrawal of something pleasant is called *negative reinforcement.* Managers who habitually criticize their employees for taking extended coffee breaks are using negative reinforcement. The only way these employees can stop the criticism is to shorten their breaks. Punishment penalizes undesirable behavior. Suspending an employee for two days without pay for showing up drunk is an example of *punishment.* Eliminating any reinforcement that is maintaining a behavior is called *extinction.* When a behavior isn't reinforced, it gradually disappears. Managers who wish to discourage employees from continually asking distracting or irrelevant questions in meetings can eliminate that behavior by ignoring those employees when they raise their hands to speak. Soon, the behavior will be diminished.

Both positive and negative reinforcement result in learning. They strengthen a desired response and increase the probability of repetition. Both punishment and extinction also result in learning; however, they weaken behavior and tend to decrease its subsequent frequency.

HOW CAN AN UNDERSTANDING OF LEARNING HELP MANAGERS BE MORE EFFECTIVE?

Managers can undoubtedly benefit from understanding the learning process. Because employees must continually learn on the job, the only issue is whether managers are going to let employee learning occur randomly or whether they are going to manage learning through the rewards they allocate and the examples they set. If marginal employees are rewarded with pay raises and promotions, they will have little reason to change their behavior. If managers want a certain type of behavior but reward a different type of behavior, it shouldn't surprise them to find that employees are learning to engage in the latter. Similarly, managers should expect that employees will look to them as models. Managers who are constantly late to work, take two hours for lunch, or help themselves to company office supplies for personal use should expect employees to read the message they are sending and model their behavior accordingly.

Foundations of Group Behavior

The behavior of individuals in groups is not the same as the sum total of all the individuals' behavior. Individuals act differently in groups than they do when they are alone. Therefore, if we want to understand organizational behavior more fully, we need to study groups.

WHAT IS A GROUP?

group
Two or more interacting and interdependent individuals who come together to achieve particular objectives

A **group** is two or more interacting and interdependent individuals who come together to achieve particular objectives. Groups can be either formal or informal. Formal groups are work groups established by the organization that have designated assignments and established tasks. Behaviors are stipulated by and directed toward organizational goals.

In contrast, informal groups are of a social nature. These groups are natural formations that appear in the work environment in response to the need for social contact. Informal groups tend to form around friendships and common interests.

WHY DO PEOPLE JOIN GROUPS?

There is no single reason why individuals join groups. Because most people belong to a number of groups, it's obvious that different groups provide different benefits to their members. Most people join a group out of needs for security, status, self-esteem, affiliation, power, or goal achievement (see Exhibit 8-8).

Security reflects a strength in numbers. By joining a group, individuals can reduce the insecurity of standing alone. The group helps the individual to feel stronger, have fewer self-doubts, and be more resistant to threats. *Status* indicates a prestige that comes from belonging to a particular group. Inclusion in a group

Exhibit 8-8 Reasons Why People Join Groups

Reason	Perceived Benefit
Security	Gaining strength in numbers; reducing the insecurity of standing alone
Status	Achieving some level of prestige from belonging to a particular group
Self-esteem	Enhancing one's feeling of self-worth—especially membership in a highly valued group
Affiliation	Satisfying one's social needs through social interaction
Power	Achieving something through a group action not possible individually; protecting group members from unreasonable demands of others
Goal achievement	Providing an opportunity to accomplish a particular task when it takes more than one person's talents, knowledge, or power to complete the job

that others view as important provides recognition and status for its members. *Self-esteem* conveys people's feelings of self-worth. That is, in addition to conveying status to those outside the group, membership can also raise feelings of self-esteem—being accepted into a highly valued group.

Affiliation with groups can fulfill one's social needs. People enjoy the regular interaction that comes with group membership. For many people, on-the-job interactions are their primary means of fulfilling their need for affiliation. For almost all people, work groups significantly contribute to fulfilling their need for friendships and social relations. One of the appealing aspects of groups is that they represent power. What often cannot be achieved individually becomes possible through group action. Of course, this power might not be sought to make demands on others; it might be desired merely as a countermeasure. To protect themselves from unreasonable demands by management, individuals may align with others. Informal groups additionally provide opportunities for individuals to exercise power over others. For individuals who desire to influence others, groups can offer power without a formal position of authority in the organization. As a group leader, you might be able to make requests of group members and obtain compliance without any of the responsibilities that traditionally go with formal managerial positions. For people with a high power need, groups can be a vehicle for fulfillment. Finally, people may join a group for *goal achievement.* There are times when it takes more than one person to accomplish a particular task; there is a need to pool talents, knowledge, or power in order to get a job completed. In such instances, management will rely on the use of a formal group.

WHAT ARE THE BASIC CONCEPTS OF GROUP BEHAVIOR?

The basic foundation for understanding group behavior includes roles, norms and conformity, status systems, and group cohesiveness. Let's take a closer look at each of those concepts.

What are roles? We introduced the concept of roles in Chapter 1 when we discussed what managers do. Of course, managers are not the only individuals in an organization who have roles. The concept of roles applies to all employees in organizations and to their lives outside the organization as well.

A **role** refers to a set of expected behavior patterns attributed to someone who occupies a given position in a social unit. Individuals play multiple roles, adjusting their roles to the group to which they belong at the time. In an organization, employees attempt to determine what behaviors are expected of them. They read their job descriptions, get suggestions from their boss, and watch what their coworkers do. An individual who is confronted by divergent role expectations experiences role conflict. Employees in organizations often face such role conflicts. The credit manager expects her credit analysts to process a minimum of 30 applications a week, but the work group pressures members to restrict output to 20 applications a week so that everyone has work to do and no one gets laid off. A newly hired college instructor's colleagues want him to give out very few high grades in order to maintain the department's high-standards reputation, whereas students want him to give out lots of high grades to enhance their grade-point averages. To the degree that the instructor sincerely seeks to satisfy the expectations of both his colleagues and his students, he faces role conflict.

role
A set of expected behavior patterns attributed to someone who occupies a given position in a social unit

norm
Acceptable standards shared by the members of a group

How do norms and conformity affect group behavior? All groups have established **norms,** acceptable standards that are shared by the group's members. Norms dictate output levels, absenteeism rates, promptness or tardiness, the amount of socializing allowed on the job, etc.

Norms, for example, dictate the dress code of customer service representatives at one credit-card processing company. Most workers who have little direct customer contact come to work dressed very casually. However, on occasion, a newly hired employee will come to work dressed in a suit. Those who do are often teased and pressured until their dress conforms to the group's standard.

Although each group will have its own unique set of norms, common classes of norms appear in most organizations. These focus on effort and performance, dress, and loyalty. Probably the most widespread norms are related to levels of effort and performance. Work groups typically provide their members with very explicit cues on how hard to work, what level of output to have, when to look busy, when it's acceptable to goof off, and the like. These norms are extremely powerful in affecting an individual employee's performance. They are so powerful that performance predictions that are based solely on an employee's ability and level of personal motivation often prove wrong.

Some organizations have formal dress codes—even describing what is considered acceptable for corporate casual dress. However, even in their absence, norms frequently develop to dictate the kind of clothing that should be worn to work. College seniors, when interviewing for their first postgraduate job, pick up this norm quickly. Every spring, on college campuses throughout the country, the students who are interviewing for jobs can be spotted; they are the ones walking around in the dark gray or blue pinstriped suits. They are enacting the dress norms that they have learned are expected in professional positions. Of course, acceptable dress in one organization may be very different from the norms of another.

Why are these employees not wearing suits to work? The reason is that the norm in the organization is one that supports casual attire. Dressing "out of the ordinary" would go against the grain of this company's norm. Accordingly, norms help to promote conformity in an organization.

Few managers appreciate employees who ridicule the organization. Similarly, professional employees and those in the executive ranks recognize that most employers view persons who actively look for another job unfavorably. People who are unhappy know that they should keep their job searches secret. These examples demonstrate that loyalty norms are widespread in organizations. This concern for demonstrating loyalty, by the way, often explains why ambitious aspirants to top management positions willingly take work home at night, come in on weekends, and accept transfers to cities in which they would otherwise not prefer to live.

Because individuals desire acceptance by the groups to which they belong, they are susceptible to conformity pressures. The impact of group pressures for conformity on an individual member's judgment and attitudes was demonstrated in the classic studies by Solomon

Asch[45] (see Details on a Management Classic). Asch's results suggest that group norms press us toward conformity. We desire to be one of the group and to avoid being visibly different. We can generalize this finding to say that when an individual's opinion of objective data differs significantly from that of others in the group, he or she feels extensive pressure to align his or her opinion to conform with those of the others (see also groupthink, p. 130).

What is status and why is it important? **Status** is a prestige grading, position, or rank within a group. As far back as scientists have been able to trace human groupings, they have found status hierarchies: tribal chiefs and their followers, nobles and peasants, the Haves and the Have-nots. Status systems are important factors in understanding behavior. Status is a significant motivator that has behavioral consequences when individuals see a disparity between what they perceive their status to be and what others perceive it to be.

status
A prestige grading, position, or rank within a group

Status may be informally conferred by characteristics such as education, age, skill, or experience. Anything can have status value if others in the group admire it. Of course, just because status is informal does not mean that it is unimportant or that there is disagreement on who has it or who does not. Members of groups

Details on a Management Classic

Solomon Asch and Group Conformity

Does the desire to be accepted as part of a group leave one susceptible to conforming to the group's norms? Will the group exert pressure that is strong enough to change a member's attitude and behavior? According to the research by Solomon Asch, the answer appears to be yes.

Asch's study involved groups of seven or eight people who sat in a classroom and were asked to compare two cards held by an investigator.[46] One card had one line; the other had three lines of varying length. As shown in Exhibit 8-9, one of the lines on the three-line card was identical to the line on the one-line card. The difference in line length was quite obvious; under ordinary conditions, subjects made fewer than 1 percent errors. The object was to announce aloud which of the three lines matched the single line. But what happens if all the members in the group begin to give incorrect answers? Will the pressures to conform cause the unsuspecting subject (USS) to alter his or her answers to align with those of the others? That was what Asch wanted to know. He arranged the group so that only the USS was unaware that the experiment was fixed. The seating was prearranged so that the USS was the last to announce his or her decision.

The experiment began with two sets of matching exercises. All the subjects gave the right answers. On the third set, however, the first subject gave an obviously wrong answer—for example, saying *C* in Exhibit 8-9. The next subject gave the same wrong answer, and so did the others, until it was the unsuspecting subject's turn. He knew that *B* was the same as *X*, but everyone else had said *C*. The decision confronting the USS was this: Do you publicly state a perception that differs from the preannounced position of the others? Or do you give an answer that you strongly believe to be incorrect in order to have your response agree with the other group members? Asch's subjects conformed in about 35 percent of many experiments and many trials. That is, the subjects gave answers that they knew were wrong but were consistent with the replies of other group members.

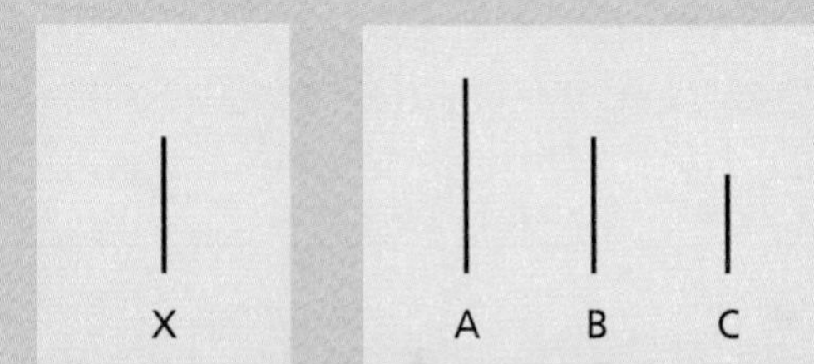

Exhibit 8-9
Examples of Cards Used in Asch Study

For managers, the Asch study provides considerable insight into group behaviors. The tendency, as Asch showed, is for individual members to go along with the pack. To diminish the negative aspects of conformity, managers should create a climate of openness in which employees are free to discuss problems without fear of retaliation.

have no problem placing people into status categories, and they usually agree about who is high, low, and in the middle.

It is important for employees to believe that the organization's formal status system is congruent. That is, there should be equity between the perceived ranking of an individual and the status symbols he or she is given by the organization. For instance, incongruence may occur when a supervisor earns less than his or her employees or when a desirable office is occupied by a lower-ranking individual. Employees may view such cases as a disruption to the general pattern of order and consistency in the organization.

Does group size affect group behavior? The size of a group affects the group's behavior. However, that effect depends on what criteria you are looking at.[47]

The evidence indicates, for instance, that small groups complete tasks faster than larger ones do. However, if the group is engaged in problem solving, large groups consistently get better marks than their smaller counterparts. Translating these results into specific numbers is a bit more hazardous, but we can offer some parameters. Large groups—with a dozen or more members—are good for gaining diverse input. Thus, if the goal of the group is to find facts, larger groups should be more effective. On the other hand, smaller groups are better at doing something productive with those facts. Groups of approximately five to seven members tend to act more effectively.

Large groups are good for gaining diverse input; smaller groups are better for taking action.

One of the more disturbing findings is that, as groups get incrementally larger, the contribution of individual members often tends to lessen.[48] That is, although the total productivity of a group of four is generally greater than that of a group of three, the individual productivity of each group member declines as the group expands. Thus, a group of four will tend to produce at a level of less than four times the average individual performance. The best explanation for this reduction of effort is that dispersion of responsibility encourages individuals to slack off; this behavior is referred to as **social loafing.** When the results of the group cannot be attributed to any single person, the relationship between an individual's input and the group's output is clouded. In such situations, individuals may be tempted to become "free riders" and coast on the group's efforts. In other words, there will be a reduction in efficiency when individuals think that their contributions cannot be measured. The obvious conclusion from this finding is that managers who use work teams should also provide a means by which individual efforts can be identified.

social loafing
The tendency of an individual in a group to decrease his or her effort because responsibility and individual achievement cannot be measured

Are cohesive groups more effective? Intuitively, it makes sense that groups in which there is a lot of internal disagreement and lack of cooperation are less effective than are groups in which individuals generally agree, cooperate, and like each other. Research on this position has focused on **group cohesiveness,** the degree to which members are attracted to one another and share the group's goals. The more the members are attracted to one another and the more the group's goals align with their individual goals, the greater the group's cohesiveness.

group cohesiveness
The degree to which members of a group are attracted to each other and share goals

Research has generally shown that very cohesive groups are more effective than are those with less cohesiveness,[49] but the relationship between cohesiveness and effectiveness is more complex. A key moderating variable is the degree to which

		Cohesiveness: High	Cohesiveness: Low
Alignment of Group and Organizational Goals	High	Strong increase in productivity	Moderate increase in productivity
	Low	Decrease in productivity	No significant effect on productivity

Exhibit 8-10
The Relationship Between Group Cohesiveness and Productivity

the group's attitude aligns with its formal goals or those of the larger organization.[50] The more cohesive a group is, the more its members will follow its goals. If these goals are favorable (for instance, high output, quality work, cooperation with individuals outside the group), a cohesive group is more productive than a less cohesive group. But if cohesiveness is high and attitudes are unfavorable, productivity decreases. If cohesiveness is low and goals are supported, productivity increases but not as much as when both cohesiveness and support are high. When cohesiveness is low and goals are not supported, cohesiveness has no significant effect upon productivity. These conclusions are summarized in Exhibit 8-10.

PHLIP Companion Web Site

We invite you to visit the Robbins/DeCenzo companion Web site at *www.prenhall.com/robbins* for this chapter's Internet resources.

Chapter Summary

How will you know if you fulfilled the Learning Outcomes on page 255? You will have fulfilled the Learning Outcomes if you are able to:

1 *Define the focus and goals of organizational behavior.*
The field of organizational behavior is concerned with the actions of people—managers and operatives alike—in organizations. By focusing on individual- and group-level concepts, OB seeks to explain and predict behavior. Because they get things done through other people, managers will be more effective leaders if they have an understanding of behavior.

2 *Identify and describe the three components of attitudes.*
Attitudes are made up of three components. The cognitive component involves the beliefs, opinions, knowledge, or information held by the person. The affective component is the emotional or feeling side of the individual. And the behavioral component of an attitude is one's intention to behave in a certain manner toward someone or something.

3 *Explain cognitive dissonance.*
Cognitive dissonance explains the relationship of attitudes and behavior. Cognitive dissonance refers to any incompatibility that an individual might perceive between two or more attitudes or between behavior and attitudes. Cognitive dissonance recognizes that any form of inconsistency is uncomfortable and that an individual will attempt to reduce the dissonance and the associated discomfort.

4 *Describe the Myers-Briggs personality type framework and its use in organizations.*
The Myers-Briggs Type Indicator (MBTI) is a personality assessment test that asks individuals how they usually act or feel in different situations. The way the individual responds to the questions reveals one of 16 different personality types. The MBTI can help managers understand and predict employees' behaviors.

5 *Define* perception *and describe the factors that can shape or distort perception.*
Perception is the process of organizing and interpreting sensory impressions in order to give meaning to the environment. Several factors operate to shape and sometimes distort perceptions. These factors can reside in the perceiver, in the target being perceived, or in the context of the situation in which the perception is being made.

6 *Explain how managers can shape employee behavior.*
Managers can shape or mold employee behavior by systematically reinforcing each successive step that moves the employee closer to the desired response. Shaping employee behavior can be aided through positive reinforcement (providing a reward the employee desires), negative reinforcement (terminating or withdrawing something that an employee finds pleasant), punishment (penalizing undesirable behavior), or extinction (eliminating any reinforcement).

7 *Contrast formal and informal groups.*
Formal groups are defined by the organization's structure, with designated work assignments establishing tasks. Informal groups are social alliances that are neither structured nor organizationally determined.

8 *Explain why people join groups.*
People join groups because of their need for security (strength in numbers), status (a prestige that comes from belonging to a specific group), self-esteem (feelings of self-worth), affiliation (fulfilling one's social needs), power (achieving goals through a group), and goal achievement (if it takes more than one person's time and talents to accomplish some task).

9 *State how roles and norms influence employees' behavior.*
A role refers to a set of behavior patterns expected of someone occupying a given position in a social unit. At any given time, employees adjust their role behaviors to the group of which they are a part. Norms are standards shared by group members. They informally convey to employees which behaviors are acceptable and which are unacceptable.

10 *Describe how group size affects group behavior.*
Group size affects group behavior in a number of ways. Smaller groups are generally faster at completing tasks than larger ones are. However, larger groups are frequently better at fact finding because of their diversified input. As a result, larger groups are generally better at problem solving.

Review and Application Questions

READING FOR COMPREHENSION

1 How is an organization like an iceberg? Use the iceberg metaphor to describe the field of organizational behavior.

2 What role does role consistency play in one's attitude?

3 Clarify how individuals reconcile inconsistencies between attitudes and behaviors.

4 Name five different shortcuts used in judging others. What effect does each have on perception?

5 What is the most effective size for a group?

LINKING CONCEPTS TO PRACTICE

1 What behavioral predictions might you make if you knew that an employee had (a) an external locus of control? (b) a low Mach score? (c) low self-esteem? (d) high self-monitoring tendencies?

2 How might a manager might use personality traits to improve employee selection in his department? Discuss.

3 Describe the implications of social learning theory for managing people at work.

4 "Informal groups in an organization can be detrimental to management." Do you agree or disagree with that statement? Explain your position.

5 Discuss the organizational implications drawn from Asch's conformity studies.

Management Workshop

Team Skill-Building Exercise

Salary Increase Request[51]

OBJECTIVES

1 To illustrate how perceptions can influence decisions.

2 To illustrate the effects of shortcuts used in evaluating others.

THE SITUATION

Your instructor will give you a scenario involving an employee's salary increase request. You are to read it and make a recommendation (either favorable or unfavorable) about the raise.

PROCEDURE

1 Divide into groups of five to seven and take the role of a manager making the decision.

2 Each group should identify their perceptions about the employee's work habits and other factors in support of its decision.

3 Reassemble the class and hear each group's recommendations and explanations.

Developing Your Skill at Shaping Behavior

Shaping Others' Behaviors

ABOUT THE SKILL

In today's dynamic work environments, learning is continual. But this learning shouldn't be done in isolation or without any guidance. Most employees need to be shown what is expected of them on the job. As a manager, you must teach your employees the behaviors that are most critical to their, and the organization's, success.

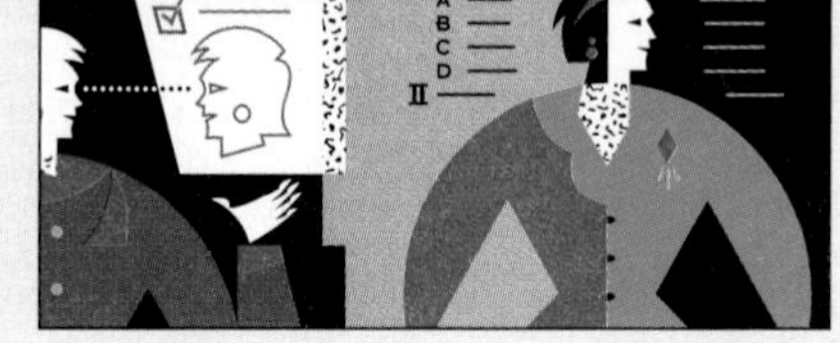

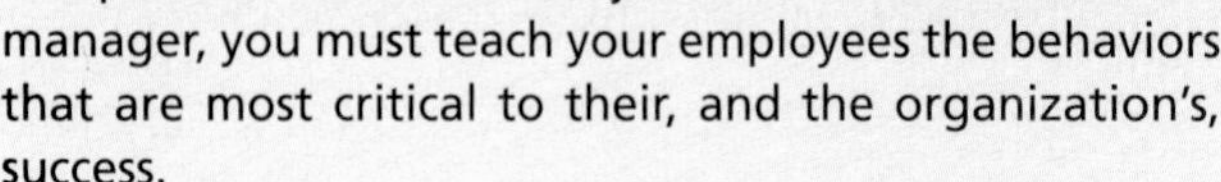

STEPS IN SHAPING BEHAVIOR SKILL

1 **Identify the critical behaviors that have a significant impact on an employee's performance.** Not everything employees do on the job is equally important in terms of performance outcomes. A few critical behaviors may, in fact, account for the majority of one's results. These high-impact behaviors need to be identified.

2 **Establish a baseline of performance.** This is obtained by determining the number of times the identified behaviors occur under the employee's present job conditions.

3 **Analyze the contributing factors to performance and their consequences.** A number of factors, such as the norms of a group, may be contributing to the baseline performance. Identify these factors and their effect on performance.

4 **Develop a shaping strategy.** The change that may occur will entail changing some element of performance—structure, processes, technology, groups, or the task. The purpose of the strategy is to strengthen the desirable behaviors and weaken the undesirable ones.

5 **Apply the appropriate strategy.** Once the strategy has been developed, it needs to be implemented. In this step, the intervention occurs.

6 **Measure the change that has occurred.** The intervention should produce the desired results in performance behaviors. Evaluate the number of times the identified behaviors now occur. Compare these with the baseline evaluation in step 2.

7 **Reinforce desired behaviors.** If the intervention has been successful and the new behaviors are producing the desired results, maintain these behaviors through reinforcement mechanisms.

Practicing the Skill

Shaping Behavior

Imagine that your assistant is ideal in all respects but one—he or she is hopeless at taking phone messages for you when you are not in the office. Since you are often in training sessions and the calls are sales leads you are anxious to follow up, you have identified taking accurate messages as a high-impact behavior for your assistant.

Focus on steps 3 and 4, and devise a way to shape your assistant's behavior. Identify some factors that might contribute to his or her failure to take messages—these could range from a heavy workload to a poor understanding of the task's importance (you can rule out insubordination). Then develop a shaping strategy by determining what you can change—the available technology, the task itself, the structure of the job, or some other element of performance.

Now plan your intervention, a brief meeting with your assistant in which you explain the change you expect. Recruit a friend to help you role play your intervention. Do you think you would succeed in a real situation?

A Case Application

Developing Your Diagnostic and Analytical Skills

ANNE BEILER AT AUNTIE ANNE'S

What makes a person change his or her attitude toward a chosen career? Is it the dissonance between the ideals one possesses and the reality of making them come true? Is it a matter of chance? Or can it be strong personality traits that take an individual in other directions? For Anne Beiler, founder of Auntie Anne's Hand-Rolled Soft Pretzels, it's probably a combination of all three.[52]

Anne Beiler grew up in Gap, Pennsylvania, a town with a population of 2,000. Her early childhood was rooted in the Mennonite traditions of this Amish town. Family values were the centerpiece of her early life—including working hard on the family farm, marrying young, and raising a family of her own. Those were elements of certainty for Mennonites. And for the first 38 years of her life, she followed the traditional path precisely. In 1987, however, Beiler—somewhat restless after raising two children and in need of some extra cash—decided to earn an income. She took a job managing a food stand some two hours away from her home. While there, she began to get a feel for the business and recognized that hand-rolled pretzels were the best-selling item. At $.55 each, they were quite profitable for the food stand owner, as pretzels cost less than $.07 each to make. Although she had never had a formal business course, Anne realized that selling pretzels could be very lucrative. Nearly a year later—tiring of the two-hour commute—Anne opened her own pretzel stand in the farmer's market in the heart of Gap.

Anne's goal was to make her pretzel stand a successful business at which she and her family could work together. As in any new business start-up, the early times were difficult. But what she didn't expect was how quickly success would be thrust on her. Several weeks into the operation, business proved to be so good that Anne opened a second stall across town. Several months later, her brother paid Anne $2,500 for her pretzel recipe and the right to use the Auntie Anne's name to start a pretzel shop in the next town. Weeks later, she sold an additional 10 franchises to family and friends, generating almost $50,000 in revenues. In 1991, she sold another 43 to strangers who were willing to pay $15,000 for the right to use Anne's pretzel recipe.

Anne Beiler took a chance that paid off in order to have some control of her life. Today, Auntie Anne's franchises sell for about $30,000 each—and she gets nearly 500 requests for franchises each month. There are now 550 stores spread out over 42 states—pretzel shops that sell 10 varieties of pretzels each for under two bucks. Auntie Anne's annual revenues are surpassing the $160 million mark. And the company's rated as one of the top 500 women-owned business in the United States.

Yet, even with this much success, Anne's traditions haven't changed much. She is still family oriented, donates more than $150,000 annually to charities, and underwrites a Family Information Center, a not-for-profit counseling facility in Lancaster, Pennsylvania.

QUESTIONS

1 Using locus of control, Machiavellianism, self-esteem, and risk propensity, rate Anne Beiler on each dimension and discuss how it affects her management style.

2 What role do you think perception plays in getting franchisers to believe in Beiler's concept? Discuss.

3 Describe how Anne Beiler is shaping her community's behavior by being active and supporting community efforts.

Developing Your Investigative Skills

Using the Internet

Visit *www.prenhall.com/robbins* for updated Internet Exercises.

Enhancing Your Writing Skills

Communicating Effectively

1 There's been a lengthy debate about the following two viewpoints in management: "Happy employees are productive employees" versus "Productive employees are happy employees." Which one of the two statements do you support? Explain and defend your position. Use examples to support your viewpoint.

2 Visit your college's career center and take the Myers-Briggs Type Indicator. Identify and describe your profile. What are the implications of this profile for your career choices?

3 Each semester students are typically asked to evaluate their professors. In completing the evaluations, students typically use shortcuts in judging the effectiveness of their instructor. Using the information contained in Exhibit 8-7 (page 272), describe how each of these shortcuts may be applicable to a student evaluation of a professor. Then describe how specific distortions may exist.

Nine

Understanding Work Teams

LEARNING OUTCOMES After reading this chapter, I will be able to:

1. Explain the growing popularity of work teams in organizations.
2. Describe the five stages of team development.
3. Contrast work groups with work teams.
4. Identify four common types of work teams.
5. List the characteristics of high-performing work teams.
6. Discuss how organizations can create team players.
7. Explain how managers can keep teams from becoming stagnant.
8. Describe the role of teams in continuous process improvement programs.

Tape Resources, Inc., is what many people would consider a classic small company. Headquartered in Virginia Beach, Virginia, Tape Resources sells blank videotapes and audiotapes to businesses such as television stations and production companies. Its most popular tapes—from manufacturers such as Sony, BASF, and Panasonic—carry price tags ranging from $10 to $25. The company doesn't try to compete on price. Rather, its strategy is to offer superior service to its customers. For many of its customers, this means that Tape Resources provides a guaranteed in-stock program and speedy delivery.

The company has fewer than 15 employees, with annual sales approaching the $5 million mark, but Tape Resources is growing fast. Sales for their most recent year increased 70 percent from the previous year.[1] The company's owner, Seph Barnard, wanted that trend to continue. So, he implemented a plan that he thought would excite his six-person sales staff and promote teamwork among them. Salespeople at Tape Resources fill orders from repeat customers as well as from new ones who contact the company as a result of direct-mail campaigns and trade-magazine advertising. Once the sale is completed, it goes to the shipping department for packaging and delivery. Barnard added a commission incentive on top of the sales staff's salaries, but the new program was met with almost immediate resistance in the company. "Tensions appeared in the office that we'd never had before," says Barnard. These salespeople worked in the same offices as everyone else, primarily over the phone; however, they now had an opportunity to make much more money than the other employees—especially those in shipping. Employees who had been excluded from the incentive program felt resentful.

Somewhat surprisingly, even the salespeople who would benefit from the added income started to have difficulties. Salespeople who once cooperated with one another became reluctant to spend time away from the phones or to help fellow employees on other tasks. They would no longer pitch in to help in the shipping department if problems arose. They also didn't like it when another salesperson served a customer they had helped earlier—thereby taking away the commission. As a result of Barnard's "great idea," nearly all of the company's employees had become territorial and began looking out for themselves. Within six months, Barnard realized he had made a mistake. All he wanted to do was to increase sales. Instead, his incentive plan undermined employee morale and drastically increased resentment among organizational members. Or did it?

Was the sales incentive system flawed? Were employees not part of a team? Ironically, something happened at the same time as the implementation of the new sales commission program that made Barnard think that maybe the problem wasn't with incentives. Over a three-month period, several Tape Resources employees formed a team to win a sales contest sponsored by BASF. The prize was a trip to Cancun, Mexico. The employees came together as a unified group to achieve that goal.

Like Seph Barnard, managers today believe that the use of teams will allow them to increase sales or produce better products faster and at lower costs. Although the effort to create teams isn't always successful, well-planned teams can reinvigorate productivity and better position an organization to deal with a rapidly changing environment.

The Popularity of Teams

More than two decades ago, when companies such as Toyota, General Foods, and Volvo introduced teams, they made news because no one else was doing it. Today, it's just the opposite: It's the organization that doesn't use some form of team that is noteworthy. Pick up almost any business publication, and you will read how teams have become an essential part of work in companies such as Honeywell,

Boeing, General Electric, Saab, John Deere, Imperial Oil, Australian Airlines, Honda, Florida Power and Light, Shiseido, and Federal Express. In fact, about 80 percent of all Fortune 500 companies are using teams in some part of their organizations.[2]

How do we explain the current popularity of teams? The evidence suggests that teams typically outperform individuals when tasks require multiple skills, judgment, and experience.[3] At BP Amoco, for example, work teams have helped the oil company improve productivity and saved the company more than $700 million in 1998.[4]

As organizations restructure themselves to compete more effectively and efficiently, they are turning to teams as a better way to utilize employee talents. Management has found that teams are more flexible and responsive to a changing environment than traditional departments or other forms of permanent work groupings.[5] Teams also can be quickly assembled, deployed, refocused, and disbanded.

Finally, teams may offer more than just increased efficiency and enhanced performance for the organization: They can serve as a source of job satisfaction.[6] Because team members are frequently empowered to handle many of the things that directly affect their work, teams serve as an effective means for management to enhance employee involvement, increase employee morale, and promote workforce diversity.[7]

WHAT ARE THE STAGES OF TEAM DEVELOPMENT?

Team development is a dynamic process. Most teams find themselves in a continual state of change. But even though teams probably never reach stability, there's a general pattern to most teams' evolution. The five stages of team development, shown in Exhibit 9-1, are forming, storming, norming, performing, and adjourning.[8]

The first stage, **forming,** is characterized by a great deal of uncertainty about the group's purpose, structure, and leadership. Members are testing the waters to determine what types of behaviors are acceptable. This stage is complete when members have begun to think of themselves as part of a team.

forming
The first stage of work team development, characterized by uncertainty about purpose, structure, and leadership

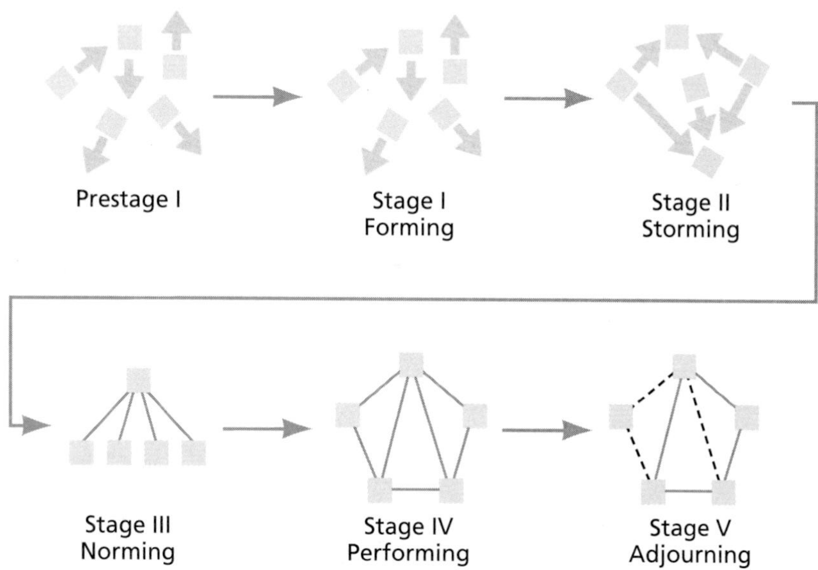

Exhibit 9-1
Stages of Team Development

storming
The second stage of work team development, characterized by intragroup conflict

norming
The third stage of work team development, in which close relationships develop and members begin to demonstrate cohesiveness

performing
The fourth stage of work team development, in which the structure is fully functional and accepted by team members

adjourning
The fifth and final stage of the development of temporary work teams, in which the team prepares for its disbandment

The **storming** stage is one of intragroup conflict. Members accept the existence of the team but resist the control that the group imposes on individuality. Further, there is conflict over who will control the team. When Stage II is complete, there will be relatively clear leadership within the team.

The third stage is one in which close relationships develop and members begin to demonstrate cohesiveness. There is now a stronger sense of team identity and camaraderie. This **norming** stage is complete when the team structure solidifies and members have assimilated a common set of expectations of appropriate work behavior. The fourth stage is **performing.** The structure is fully functional and accepted by team members. Their energy is diverted from getting to know and understand each other to performing the necessary tasks. For permanent teams, performing is the last stage of their development. For temporary teams—those that have a limited task to perform—there is an **adjourning** stage. In this stage, the team prepares for its disbandment. A high level of task performance is no longer the members' top priority. Instead, their attention is directed toward wrapping-up activities.

Recognizing that teams progress through these stages, one can pose an obvious question: Do they become more effective as they progress through each stage? Some researchers argue that the effectiveness of work units does increase at advanced stages, but it's not that simple.[9] Although that assumption may be generally true, what makes a team effective is complex. Under some conditions, high levels of conflict are conducive to high levels of group performance.[10] We might expect, then, to find situations in which teams in Stage II outperform those in Stages III or IV. Similarly, teams do not always proceed clearly from one stage to the next. Sometimes, in fact, several stages are going on simultaneously—as when teams are storming and performing at the same time. Therefore, one should not always assume that all teams precisely follow this developmental process or that Stage IV is always most preferable. Instead, it is better to think of these stages as a general framework, which should remind you that teams are dynamic entities and can help you better understand what issues may surface in a team's life.

AREN'T WORK GROUPS AND WORK TEAMS THE SAME?

At this point, you may be asking yourself where this discussion is going. Aren't teams really just groups of people? And don't they come together in the same way any grouping of individuals does? If you're asking those questions, you are making a logical connection, but *groups* and *teams* are not the same thing. In this section, we define and clarify the difference between a work group and a work team.[11]

work group
A group that interacts primarily to share information and to make decisions that will help each member perform within his or her area of responsibility

work team
A group that engages in collective work that requires joint effort and generates a positive synergy

In the last chapter, we defined a group as two or more individuals who have come together to achieve certain objectives. A **work group** interacts primarily to share information and to make decisions that will help each group member perform within his or her area of responsibility. Work groups have no need or opportunity to engage in collective work that requires joint effort. Consequently, their performance is merely the summation of all the group members' individual contributions. There is no positive synergy that would create an overall level of performance greater than the sum of the inputs.

A **work team,** on the other hand, generates positive synergy through a coordinated effort. Their individual efforts result in a level of performance that is greater than the sum of those individual inputs.[12] Exhibit 9-2 highlights the main differences between work groups and work teams.

These descriptions should help to clarify why so many organizations have restructured work processes around teams. Management is looking for that posi-

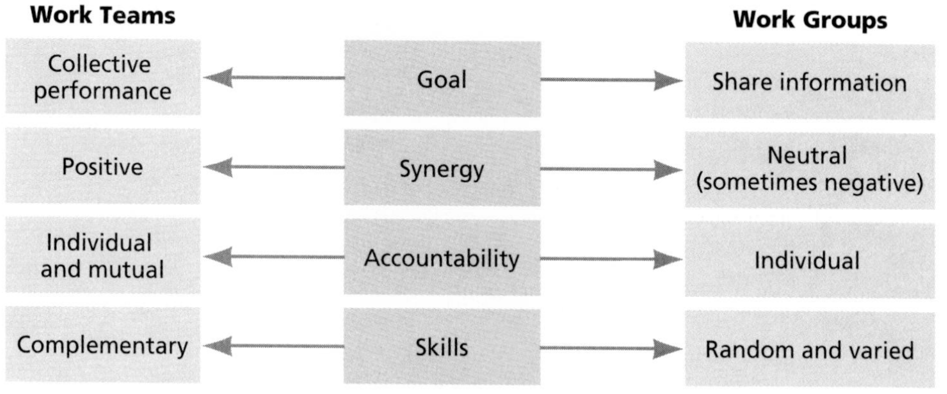

Exhibit 9-2
Comparing Work Teams and Work Groups

tive synergy that will allow the organization to increase performance. The extensive use of teams creates the potential for an organization to generate greater outputs with no increase in (or even fewer) inputs. For example, at the Dayton, Ohio-based Monarch Marking Systems company (makers of labeling and identification materials), teams reduced late shipments by 90 percent, and identified more than 1,400 inefficient areas of operations. As a result, the company was able to reduce the assembly area square footage by nearly 70 percent.[13]

Notice, however, that such increases are simply "potential." Nothing inherently magical in the creation of work teams guarantees that this positive synergy and its accompanying productivity will occur. Accordingly, merely calling a group a team doesn't automatically increase its performance.[14] As we show later in this chapter, successful or high-performing work teams have certain common characteristics. If management hopes to gain increases in organizational performance—like those at Monarch Marking—it will need to ensure that its teams possess those characteristics.

Types of Work Teams

Work teams can be classified on the basis of their objectives. The four most common forms of teams in an organization are functional teams, problem-solving teams, self-managed teams, and cross-functional teams (see Exhibit 9-3). A new type of team, the virtual team, will also be discussed.

WHAT IS A FUNCTIONAL TEAM?

Functional teams are composed of a manager and the employees in his or her unit. Within this functional team, issues such as authority, decision making, leadership, and interactions are relatively simple and clear. Functional teams are often involved in efforts to improve work activities or to solve specific problems within a particular functional unit. For example, at the California headquarters of Birkenstock Footprint Sandals, employees in sales, credit, production, warehousing, and other functional areas now work in independent teams to complete tasks and solve customer problems.[15]

functional teams
A work team composed of a manager and the employees in his or her unit and involved in efforts to improve work activities or to solve specific problems within the particular functional unit

HOW DOES A PROBLEM-SOLVING TEAM OPERATE?

Almost 20 years ago, teams were just beginning to grow in popularity, and the form they took was strikingly similar. These teams typically were composed of 5

Exhibit 9-3
Types of Work Teams

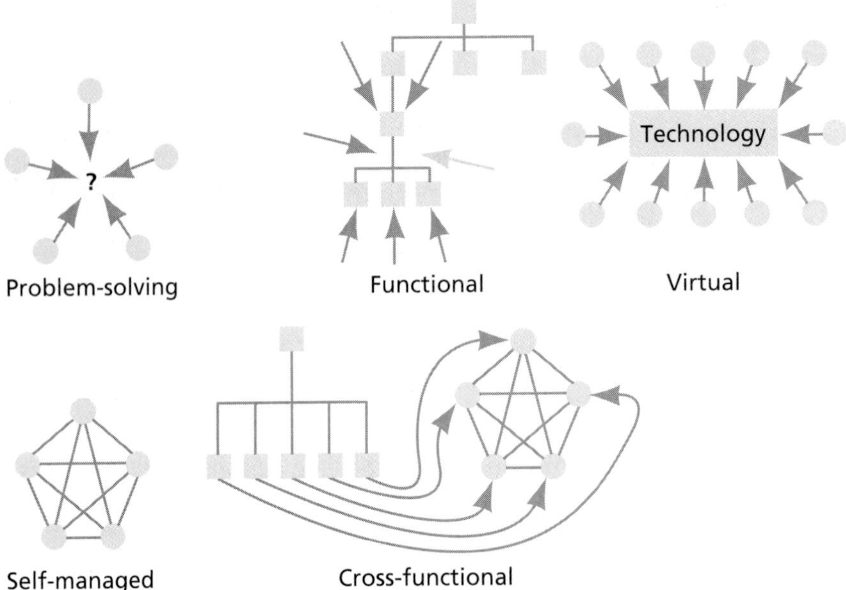

to 12 hourly employees from the same department who met for a few hours each week to discuss ways of improving quality, efficiency, and the work environment.[16] We call these **problem-solving teams.**

problem-solving teams
Work teams typically composed of 5 to 12 hourly employees from the same department who meet each week to discuss ways of improving quality, efficiency, and the work environment

In problem-solving teams, members share ideas or offer suggestions on how work processes and methods can be improved. Some of the most widely practiced applications of problem-solving teams witnessed during the 1980s were **quality circles,** work teams of 8 to 10 employees and supervisors who share an area of responsibility. They meet regularly to discuss their quality problems, investigate causes of the problems, recommend solutions, and take corrective actions. They assume responsibility for solving quality problems, and they generate and evaluate their own feedback. Rarely, however, are these teams given the authority to unilaterally implement any of their suggestions. Instead, they make a recommendation to management, which usually makes the decision about the implementation of recommended solutions. Honda Motor Company recognized that the costs of producing the Honda Civic were increasing and put together a quality circle to investigate the reasons for the increases and to make recommendations about how the car could be built cheaper.[17] After 18 months of work, the team made recommendations that, after being implemented, reduced the price of the Honda Civic by more than 3 percent.

quality circles
Work teams composed of 8 to 10 employees and supervisors who share an area of responsibility and who meet regularly to discuss quality problems, investigate the causes of the problesm, recommend solutions, and take corrective actions but who have no authority

WHAT IS A SELF-MANAGED WORK TEAM?

Another type of team commonly being used in organizations is the self-directed or self-managed team. A **self-managed work team** is a formal group of employees that operates without a manager and is responsible for a complete work process or segment that delivers a product or service to an external or internal customer.[18] Typically, this kind of team has control over its work pace, determines work assignments and when breaks are taken, and inspects its own work. Fully self-managed work teams even select their own members and have the members evaluate each other's performance.[19] As a result, supervisory positions take on decreased importance and may even be eliminated. For example, at L-S Electrogalvanizing Company in Cleveland, Ohio, the entire plant is run by self-managed teams. They

self-managed work teams
A formal group of employees that operates without a manager and is responsible for a complete work process or segment that delivers a product or service to an external or internal customer

do their own hiring and scheduling, rotate jobs on their own, establish production targets, set pay scales that are linked to skills, and fire coworkers whenever necessary.[20] Xerox, General Motors, Coors Brewing, Tokyo String Quartet, U.S. Navy Seals, Stanadyne Automotive Corporation, Massachusetts General Hospital, Hewlett-Packard, and Textron are just a few of the many organizations that have implemented self-managed work teams.[21]

Self-directed work teams just don't pop up out of thin air. They're the result of major changes that occur in an organization in how work gets done. This team at Unisys, the Medium-Speed Configuration Team, recognized that it takes a lot of care and an organization culture change to give teams the opportunity to manage themselves. For these Unisys workers, that meant company management working with their union to carefully plan and implement the transition to teams.

HOW DO CROSS-FUNCTIONAL TEAMS OPERATE?

The last type of team we will identify is the **cross-functional work team,** which consists of employees from about the same hierarchical level but from different work areas in the organization. Workers are brought together to accomplish a particular task.[22]

cross-functional work team
A team composed of employees from about the same hierarchical level but from differed work areas in an organization who are brought together to accomplish a particular task

Many organizations have used cross-functional teams for years. For example, in the 1960s, IBM created a large team made up of employees from across departments in the company to develop the highly successful System 360. However, the popularity of cross-functional work teams exploded in the late 1980s. All the major automobile manufacturers—including Toyota, DaimlerChrysler, Nissan, General Motors, Ford, Honda, and BMW—have turned to this form of team in order to coordinate complex projects. For example, DaimlerChrysler has used cross-functional teams to get such popular models as the subcompact Neon, the full-size Ram pickup, and the sporty Viper to market. And with cross-functional teams, DaimlerChrysler is getting closer to the industry leader, Toyota, in terms of the time it takes to assemble a car and in terms of quality.[23]

Cross-functional teams are also an effective way to allow employees from diverse areas within an organization to exchange information, develop new ideas, solve problems, and coordinate complex tasks.[24] But cross-functional teams can be difficult to manage.[25] The early stages of development (e.g., storming) are very often time-consuming as members learn to work with diversity and complexity. This difficulty with diversity, however, can be turned into an advantage. For example, remember our discussion of group decision making in Chapter 4. One of the tenets of that process was that groups provided more complete information and were more creative than individuals. The diversity of a work team can help identify creative or unique solutions. Furthermore, the lack of a common perspective caused by diversity usually means that team members will spend more time discussing relevant issues, which decreases the likelihood that a weak solution will be selected. However, keep in mind that the contribution that diversity makes to teams probably will decline over time. As team members become more familiar with one another, they form a more cohesive group, but the positive aspect of this decline in diversity is that a team bond is built. It takes time to build trust and teamwork. Later in this chapter we present ways managers can help facilitate and build trust among team members.

Can virtual teams really work? At VeriFone, a virtual team quickly assembled to assist one of its sales representatives in Greece helped land a major sales order. The team members, in Greece, the United States, and Hong Kong, did their part so effectively that it impressed the client. Without the work of this virtual team, thousands of dollars in this sale would have been lost.

ARE VIRTUAL TEAMS A REALITY TODAY?

A **virtual team** is an extension of the electronic meetings we discussed in Chapter 4. A virtual team allows groups to meet without concern for space or time and enables organizations to link workers together in a way that would have been impossible in the past.[26] Team members use technological advances like conference calls, video conferencing, or e-mail to solve problems even though they may be geographically dispersed or several time zones away. VeriFone, a California-based manufacturer of in-store credit card authorization terminals, provides a glimpse of the possibilities of virtual teams.[27] VeriFone uses virtual teams in every aspect of its operations—from groups of facility managers who determine how to reduce toxins in their offices, to manufacturing or purchasing groups that seek hard-to-find semiconductors, to marketing and development groups that brainstorm new products. Virtual teams are also used to solve problems and enhance sales success. Let's look at how a virtual team can function.

virtual team
An electronic meeting team; allows groups to meet without concern for space or time

One VeriFone sales rep in Greece knew he was in big trouble when he left the offices of an Athens bank at 4:30 P.M. A competitor had challenged VeriFone's ability to deliver a new payment service technology. The sales rep knew his company was the main supplier of this technology in the United States and in many other countries, but the technology was unproven in Greece. The rep needed to convince bank executives that this technology would work, but he had no details on its effectiveness by users in other countries. So what did this VeriFone rep do? He created a virtual team. He found the nearest phone and hooked up to his laptop computer. Then he sent an emergency e-mail to all VeriFone sales, marketing, and technical support staff worldwide.

In San Francisco, an international marketing staffer who was on duty to monitor such distress calls got the message at home when he checked his e-mail at 6:30 A.M. He organized a conference call with two other marketing staffers, one in Atlanta and one in Hong Kong, where it was 9:30 A.M. and 10:30 P.M., respectively. A few hours later, the two U.S. team members spoke on the phone again while they used the company's wide area network to fine tune a sales presentation. Before leaving for the day, the leader passed the presentation on to the Hong Kong team member so he could add Asian information to the detailed account of experiences and references when he arrived at work.

The Greek sales rep awakened a few hours later. He retrieved the presentation from the network, got to the bank before 8:00 A.M., and showed the customer the data. Impressed by the speedy and informative response, the customer's apprehensions about VeriFone's technology were alleviated. As a result, the sales rep got the order.

Characteristics of High-Performance Work Teams

Teams are not automatic productivity enhancers. We know, as we saw in the Tape Resources case, that they can also be disappointments for management. What common characteristics, then, do effective teams have? Research provides some

Exhibit 9-4
Characteristics of High-Performing Work Teams

insight into the primary characteristics associated with high-performance work teams.[28] Let's take a look at these characteristics as summarized in Exhibit 9-4.

High-performance work teams have both a *clear understanding* of the goal and a belief that the goal embodies a worthwhile or important result.[29] Moreover, the importance of these goals encourages individuals to redirect energy away from personal concerns and toward team goals. In high-performing work teams, members are committed to the team's goals, know what they are expected to accomplish, and understand how they will work together to achieve those goals. Effective teams are composed of competent individuals. They have the *relevant* technical *skills* and abilities to achieve the desired goals and the personal characteristics required to achieve excellence while working well with others. These same individuals are also capable of readjusting their work skills—called *job-morphing*—to fit the needs of the team.[30] It's important not to overlook the personal characteristics. Not everyone who is technically competent has the skills to work well as a team member. High-performing team members possess both technical and interpersonal skills.

Effective teams are characterized by *high mutual trust* among members. That is, members believe in the integrity, character, and ability of one another.[31] But, as you probably know from your own personal relationships, trust is fragile. We'll look at the issue of trust in more detail in Chapter 11. Members of an effective team exhibit intense loyalty and dedication to the team. They are willing to do anything that has to be done to help their team succeed. We call this loyalty and dedication *unified commitment.* Studies of successful teams have found that members identify with their teams.[32] Members redefine themselves to include membership in the team as an important aspect of the self. Unified commitment, then, is characterized by dedication to the team's goals and a willingness to expend extraordinary amounts of energy to achieve them.

Not surprisingly, effective teams are characterized by *good communication.* Members are able to convey messages in a form that is readily and clearly understood. This includes nonverbal as well as spoken messages. Good communication is characterized by a healthy dose of feedback from team members and management.[33] This helps to guide team members and to correct misunderstandings. Like two individuals who have been together for many years, members on high-performing teams are able to quickly and efficiently share ideas and feelings.

When jobs are designed around individuals, job descriptions, rules and procedures, and other types of formalized documentation clarify employee roles. Effective teams, on the other hand, tend to be flexible and continually make adjustments, so team members must possess adequate *negotiating skills.* Because problems and relationships are regularly changing in teams, the members have to be able to confront and reconcile differences.

Effective leaders can motivate a team to follow them through the most difficult situations. How? Leaders help clarify goals. They demonstrate that change is possible by overcoming inertia. And they increase the self-confidence of team members, helping them to realize their potential more fully. The best leaders are not necessarily directive or controlling. Increasingly, effective team leaders are taking the roles of coach and facilitator (see Developing Your Coaching Skill, p. 307). They help guide and support the team, but they don't control it. This description obviously applies to self-managed teams, but it also increasingly applies to problem-solving and cross-functional teams in which the members themselves are empowered. For some traditional managers, changing their role from boss to facilitator—from giving orders to working for the team—is a difficult transition. Although most managers relish the new-found shared authority or come to understand its advantages through leadership training, some hard-nosed dictatorial managers are just ill suited to the team concept and must be transferred or replaced.

One Manager's Perspective

James Fripp Field Staffing Manager, Taco Bell Corp.

What makes a good team? According to James Fripp, field staffing manager for Taco Bell in Omaha, Nebraska, there are several characteristics: "First and foremost," he says, "is ensuring that everyone on the team clearly knows and understands what the goals and expectations are. Second is that everyone knows and understands what their specific role is on the team. Third is allowing input from the team members (whenever possible) on how to achieve the goal." Allowing input, Fripp believes, is a way to foster "ownership,"—another key ingredient of an effective team. "Last, but by no means least," he concludes, "is ensuring that all team members understand they will be held accountable for the outcome of the team."

In his role at Taco Bell, Fripp evaluates staffing needs for 178 units, analyzes turnover, and handles recruiting events. He also recruits and interviews potential employees. His expert "people skills" have given him insight into managing conflicts on work teams.

The main one, which he communicates to his teams early and often, is that no matter what happens, all team members treat each other with respect and dignity. With that understanding, he brings individuals together to share their own sides of the issue and then asks for their help in resolving the conflict.

The final condition for an effective team is a *supportive climate*. Internally, the team should be provided with a sound infrastructure. This includes proper training, an understandable measurement system with which team members can evaluate their overall performance, an incentive program that recognizes and rewards team activities, and a supportive human resource system. The infrastructure should support members and reinforce behaviors that lead to high levels of performance. Externally, management should provide the team with the resources needed to get the job done.

Turning Individuals into Team Players

So far, we have made a strong case for the value and growing popularity of work teams, but not every worker is inherently a team player.[34] Some individuals prefer to be recognized for their individual achievements. In some organizations, too, work environments are such that only the strong survive. Creating teams in such an environment may meet some resistance. Finally, as we mentioned in Chapter 2, countries differ in terms of how conducive they are to individualism and collectivism. Teams fit well with countries that score high on *collectivism*. But what if an organization wants to introduce teams into a highly individualistic society (like that of the United States)? As one writer stated regarding teams in the United States, "Americans don't grow up learning how to function in teams. In school they don't get a team report card, or learn the names of the team of sailors who traveled with Columbus to America."[35] This limitation apparently would apply to Canadians, British, Australians, and others from highly individualistic societies.

WHAT ARE THE MANAGEMENT CHALLENGES OF CREATING TEAM PLAYERS?

The points raised are meant to dramatize that one substantial barrier to work teams is the individual resistance that may exist. Employees' success, when they are part of teams, is no longer defined in terms of individual performance. Instead, success is a function of how well the team as a whole performs. To perform well as team members, individuals must be able to communicate openly and honestly with one another, to confront differences and resolve conflicts, and to place lower priority on personal goals for the good of the team. For many employees, these are difficult—and sometimes impossible—assignments.

The challenge of creating team players will be greatest where the national culture is highly individualistic and the teams are being introduced into an established organization that has historically valued individual achievement.[36] This describes, for instance, the environment that faced managers at AT&T, Ford, Motorola, and other large U.S. companies. These firms prospered by hiring and rewarding corporate stars, and they bred a competitive work climate that encouraged individual achievement and recognition—similar to what Seph Barnard at Tape Resources found. Employees in these types of organizations can experience culture shock caused by a sudden shift to the importance of teamwork.[37] For example, one employee in a large organization who had been well rewarded for working independently for more than 20 years found himself having serious difficulty working as a team player. This difficulty was reflected in his performance evaluation—the first negative evaluation of his career.[38]

In contrast, the challenge for management is less demanding when teams are introduced in places in which employees have strong collectivist values—such as

Teams are nothing new at Saturn. From the beginning the company grouped its employees into teams. Accordingly, when individuals apply for jobs at Saturn, they understand that they will be assigned to a team, and that being a team player is a prerequisite for successful job performance.

in Japan or Mexico. The challenge of forming teams will also be less in new organizations that use teams as their initial form of structuring work. Saturn Corporation, for instance, is an American organization. Although owned by General Motors, the company was designed around teams from its start. Everyone at Saturn was hired on the understanding that they would be working in teams, and the ability to be a good team player was a hiring prerequisite.

WHAT ROLES DO TEAM MEMBERS PLAY?

High-performing work teams carefully match people to various roles. One stream of research has identified nine potential roles that work team members often can play: creator-innovator, explorer-promoter, assessor-developer, thruster-organizer, concluder-producer, controller-inspector, upholder-maintainer, reporter-adviser, and linker[39] (see Exhibit 9-5). Let's briefly review each team role.

Creator-innovators are usually imaginative and good at initiating ideas or concepts. They are typically very independent and prefer to work at their own pace in their own way—and very often on their own time. *Explorer-promoters* like to

Exhibit 9-5
Team Member Roles
SOURCE: Based on C. Margerison and D. McCann, *Team Management: Practical New Approaches* (London: Mercury Books, 1990).

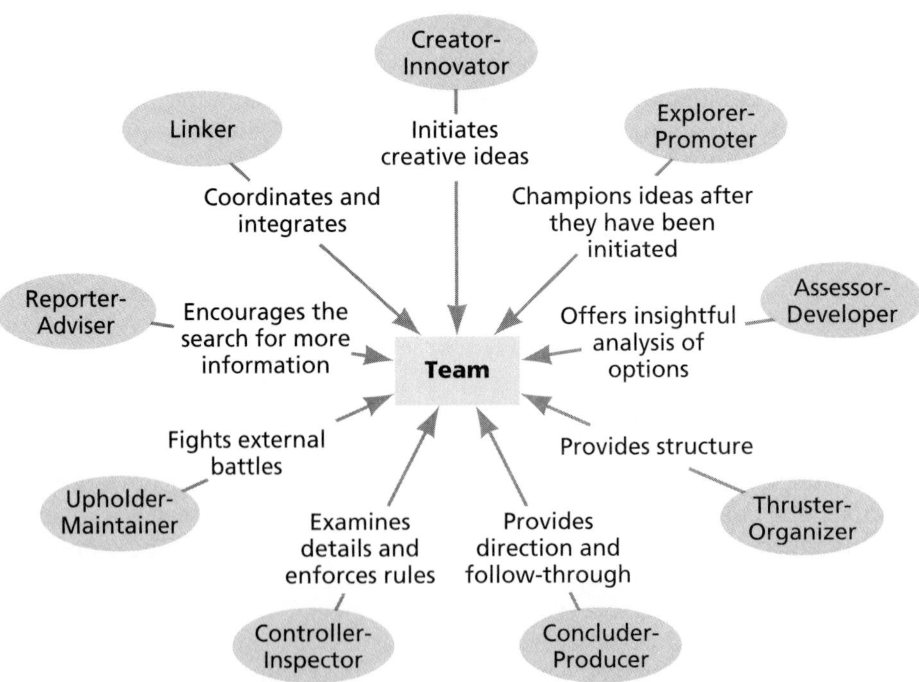

take new ideas and champion their cause. These individuals are good at picking up ideas from the creator-innovators and finding the resources to promote those ideas. However, they often lack the patience and control skills to ensure that the ideas are followed through in detail. *Assessor-developers* have strong analytical skills. They're at their best when given several different options to evaluate and analyze before a decision is made. *Thruster-organizers* like to set up operating procedures to turn ideas into reality and get things done. They set goals, establish plans, organize people, and establish systems to ensure that deadlines are met. And, somewhat like thruster-organizers, *concluder-producers* are concerned with results. Only their role focuses on keeping to deadlines and ensuring that all commitments are followed through. Concluder-producers take pride in producing a regular output to a standard.

Controller-inspectors have a high concern for establishing and enforcing rules and policies. They are good at examining details and making sure that inaccuracies are avoided. They want to check all the facts and figures to make sure they're complete. *Upholder-maintainers* hold strong convictions about the way things should be done. They will defend the team and fight its battles with outsiders while, at the same time, strongly supporting fellow team members. Accordingly, these individuals provide team stability. *Reporter-advisers* are good listeners and don't tend to press their point of view on others. They tend to favor getting more information before making decisions. As such, they perform an important role in encouraging the team to seek additional information before making decisions and discouraging the team from making hasty decisions.

The last role—*the linkers*—overlaps the others. This role can be assumed by any actors of the previous eight roles. Linkers try to understand all views. They are coordinators and integrators. They dislike extremism and try to build cooperation among all team members. They also recognize the various contributions that other team members make and try to integrate people and activities despite differences that might exist.

If forced to, most individuals can perform any of these roles. However, most have two or three they strongly prefer. Managers need to understand the strengths that each individual can bring to a team, select team members on the basis of an appropriate mix of individual strengths, and allocate work assignments that fit each member's preferred style. By matching individual preferences with team role demand, managers increase the likelihood that the team members will work well together. Unsuccessful teams may have an unbalanced portfolio of individual talents, with too much energy being expended in one area and not enough in other areas.

HOW CAN A MANAGER SHAPE TEAM BEHAVIOR?

There are several options available for managers who are trying to turn individuals into team players (see Ethical Dilemma in Management). The three most popular ways include proper selection, employee training, and rewarding the appropriate team behaviors. Let's look at each of these.

What role does selection play? Some individuals already possess the interpersonal skills to be effective team players. When hiring team members, in addition to checking on the technical skills required to successfully perform the job, the organization should ensure that applicants can fulfill their team roles.

As we have mentioned before, some applicants have been socialized around individual contributions and, consequently, lack team skills as might some current employees who are restructuring into teams. When faced with such candidates, a

Ethical Dilemma in Management

Must Employees Work on a Team?

After earning her bachelor's degree in business administration from the University of South Florida, Jennifer Singleton took a job with Cable News Network (CNN) in its Paris bureau. After several years at CNN, Jennifer decided to return to the United States and earn a master's degree. She applied to and was accepted at the University of South Carolina's business school. Two years later, Jennifer graduated in the top 10 percent of her class and accepted a job from PSINet doing market research.

After about four months on the job, Jennifer was told she was being assigned to a cross-functional team that would look at ways the company could reduce inventory costs. This cross-functional team was to be a permanent structure and would include individuals from cost accounting, production, supplier relations, and marketing. Jennifer was not happy about her new assignment; she felt that she was not a team player. In fact, she even bragged at times about being a loner. Although she knew she could work well with others, she didn't like the "added" time it took to get things done. She preferred to just jump in and do things without discussing them. And, although she prided herself on being an outstanding performer, she didn't like the idea of having her performance dependent on the actions of others.[40] As she said, "I know I won't shirk my responsibilities, but I can't be so sure of the others."

Do you think that Jennifer's boss should have allowed her to decide whether she would join the team? Do you think that everyone should be expected to be a team player, given the trends that we're seeing as we enter the twenty-first century?

manager can do several things. First, and most obvious, if team skills are woefully lacking, don't hire that candidate. If successful performance requires team interaction, rejecting such a candidate is appropriate. On the other hand, a candidate who has only some basic team skills can be hired on a probationary basis and required to undergo training to shape him or her into a team player. If the skills aren't learned or practiced, the individual may have to be separated from the company for failing to achieve the skills necessary for performing successfully on the job.

Can we train individuals to be team players? Performing well in a team involves a set of behaviors. As we discussed in the preceding chapter, new behaviors can be learned. Even a large portion of people who were raised on the importance of individual accomplishment can be trained to become team players. Training specialists can conduct exercises that allow employees to experience the satisfaction that teamwork can provide. The workshops usually cover such topics as team problem solving, communications, negotiations, conflict resolution, and coaching skills. It's not unusual, too, for these individuals to be exposed to the five stages of team development we discussed earlier. At Bell Atlantic, for example, trainers focus on how a team goes through various stages before it gels. And employees are reminded of the importance of patience, because teams take longer to do some things—such as make decisions—than do employees acting alone.[41] Emerson Electric's Specialty Motor Division in Missouri was remarkably successful in getting its 650-member workforce to not only accept but to welcome team training.[42] Outside consultants provide a learning environment in which workers can gain practical skills for working in teams. And, after less than one year, employees enthusiastically accepted the value of teamwork.

What role do rewards play in shaping team players? The organization's reward system needs to encourage cooperative efforts rather than competitive ones. For instance, Lockheed Martin's Space Launch Systems has organized its 1,000+ employees into teams. Rewards are structured to return a percentage increase in the bottom line to the team members on the basis of achievement of the team's performance goals.

Promotions, pay raises, and other forms of recognition should be given to employees who are effective collaborative team members. This doesn't mean that individual contribution is ignored but rather that it is balanced with selfless contributions to the team. Examples of behaviors that should be rewarded include training new colleagues, sharing information with teammates, helping resolve team conflicts, and mastering new skills in which the team is deficient. Finally, managers cannot forget the inherent rewards that employees can receive from teamwork. Work teams provide camaraderie. It's exciting and satisfying to be an integral part of a successful team. The opportunity to engage in personal development and to help teammates grow can be a very satisfying and rewarding experience for employees.[43]

Can rewards shape team members' behaviors? That depends on the rewards offered. At Lockheed Martin's Space Launch operations, employees are rewarded based on how well they achieve their performance goals.

HOW CAN A MANAGER REINVIGORATE A MATURE TEAM?

Just because a team is performing well at any given point in time is no assurance that it will continue to do so.[44] Effective teams can become stagnant. Initial enthusiasm can give way to apathy. Time can diminish the positive value from diverse perspectives as cohesiveness increases. In terms of the five-stage development model, teams don't automatically stay at the performing stage. Familiarity and team success can lead to contentment and complacency. And, as that happens, the team may become less open to novel ideas and innovative solutions. Mature teams, also, are particularly prone to suffer from groupthink (see Chapter 4), as team members begin to believe they can read everyone's mind and assume that they know what the others are thinking. Consequently, team members become reluctant to express their thoughts and are less likely to challenge one another.

Another source of problems for mature teams is that their early successes are often due to having taken on easy tasks. It's normal for new teams to begin by taking on those issues and problems they can most easily handle. But as time passes, the easy problems are solved, and the team has to begin to tackle the more difficult issues. At this point, the team has frequently established its processes and routines, and team members are often reluctant to change the workable system they have developed. When that happens, problems arise. Internal team processes no longer work smoothly. Communication bogs down, and conflict increases because problems are less likely to have obvious solutions. All in all, team performance may dramatically drop.

What can a manager do to reinvigorate mature teams—especially ones that are encountering the problems described above? We offer the following suggestions

Exhibit 9-6
How to Reinvigorate Mature Teams

1. Prepare members to deal with the problems of maturity.
2. Offer refresher training.
3. Offer advanced training.
4. Encourage teams to treat their development as a constant learning experience.

(see Exhibit 9-6). Prepare team members to deal with the problems of team maturity. Remind them that they are not unique. All successful teams eventually have to address maturity issues: Members shouldn't feel let down or lose their confidence in the team concept when the initial excitement subsides and conflicts begin to surface. When teams get into ruts, it may help to provide them with refresher training in communication, conflict resolution, team processes, and similar skills. This training can help team members regain their confidence and trust in each other. Offer advanced training. The skills that worked well with easy problems may be insufficient for some of the more difficult problems the team is addressing. Mature teams can often benefit from advanced training to help members develop stronger problem-solving, interpersonal, and technical skills. Encourage teams to treat their development as a constant learning experience. Just as organizations use continuous improvement programs, teams should approach their own development as part of a search for continuous improvement. Teams should look for ways to improve, to confront member fears and frustrations, and to use conflict as a learning opportunity.

Contemporary Team Issues

As we close this chapter, we will address two issues related to managing teams—continuous process improvement programs and diversity in teams.

WHY ARE TEAMS CENTRAL TO CONTINUOUS PROCESS IMPROVEMENT PROGRAMS?

One of the central characteristics of continuous process improvement programs is the use of teams. Why teams? The essence of continuous improvement is process improvement, and employee participation is the linchpin of process improvement. In other words, continuous improvement requires management to encourage employees to share ideas and to act on what the employees suggest. As one author put it, "None of the various processes and techniques will catch on and be applied except in work teams. All such techniques and processes require high levels of communication and contact, response, adaption, and coordination and sequencing. They require, in short, the environment that can be supplied only by superior work teams."[45]

Teams provide the natural vehicle for employees to share ideas and implement improvements. As stated by a continuous improvement specialist at McDonnell-Douglas: "When your measurement system tells you your process is out of control, you need teamwork for structured problem-solving. Not everyone needs to know how to do all kinds of fancy control charts for performance tracking, but everybody does need to know where their process stands so they can judge if it is improving."[46] Examples from Ford Motor Company and Allegiance HealthCare Corporation illustrate how teams are being used in continuous improvement programs.[47]

Ford began its continuous improvement efforts in the early 1980s, with teams as the primary organizing mechanism. "Because this business is so complex, you can't make an impact on it without using a team approach," noted one Ford manager. In designing the quality problem-solving teams, Ford's management identified five goals. The teams should (1) be small enough to be efficient and effective, (2) be properly trained in the skills their members will need, (3) be allocated enough time to work on the problems they plan to address, (4) be given the authority to resolve the problems and implement corrective action, and (5) have a designated "champion" whose job it is to help the team get around roadblocks.

Teams at Allegiance HealthCare have earned the respect of their peers by being named one of America's best plant operations. How have they worked to achieve that honor? Part of their success is that each team sets its goals, which are critically linked to the organization's strategic plan. Furthermore, the Allegiance HealthCare teams have cut costs and have reduced workplace accidents.

At Allegiance HealthCare, teams made up of people from different levels within the company develop goals and objectives that are linked to the organization's strategic initiatives and deal with quality problems that cut across various functional areas. Allegiance claims that these teams have improved the organization in a number of ways. For example, sales in the company are up 61 percent in the five years since teams have been implemented; cycle time has been reduced by 91 percent; hazardous waste disposal has been reduced 98 percent, and employee accidents have been reduced by 88 percent.[48]

HOW DOES WORKFORCE DIVERSITY AFFECT TEAMS?

Managing diversity on teams is a balancing act. Diversity typically provides fresh perspectives on issues, but it makes it more difficult to unify the team and reach agreements.

The strongest case for diversity on work teams arises when these teams are engaged in problem-solving and decision-making tasks. Heterogeneous teams bring multiple perspectives to the discussion, thus increasing the likelihood that the team will identify creative or unique solutions.[49] Additionally, the lack of a common perspective usually means diverse teams spend more time discussing issues, which decreases the chances that a weak alternative will be chosen. However, keep in mind that the positive contribution that diversity makes to decision-making teams undoubtedly declines over time. As we pointed out in the previous chapter, diverse groups have more difficulty working together and solving problems, but this problem dissipates with time.[50] Expect the value-added component of diverse teams to increase as members become more familiar with each other and the team becomes more cohesive.

Studies tell us that members of cohesive teams have greater satisfaction, lower absenteeism, and lower attrition from the group.[51] Yet cohesiveness is likely to be lower on diverse teams.[52] So here is a potential negative of diversity: It is detrimental to group cohesiveness.[53] But again, referring to the previous chapter, the relationship between cohesiveness and group productivity is moderated by performance-related norms. We suggest that if the norms of the team are supportive of diversity, a team can maximize the value of heterogeneity while achieving the benefits of high cohesiveness.[54] This makes a strong case for having team members participate in diversity training.

Cohesive teams have greater satisfaction, lower absenteeism, and lower attrition.

PHLIP Companion Web Site

We invite you to visit the Robbins/DeCenzo companion Web site at *www.prenhall.com/robbins* for this chapter's Internet resources.

Chapter Summary

How will you know if you fulfilled the Learning Outcomes on page 287? You will have fulfilled the Learning Outcomes if you are able to:

1 *Explain the growing popularity of work teams in organizations.*
Teams have become increasingly popular in organizations because they typically outperform individuals when the tasks require multiple skills, judgment, and experience. Teams are also more flexible and responsive to a changing environment. Teams may serve as an effective means for management to enhance employee involvement, increase employee morale, and promote workforce diversity.

2 *Describe the five stages of team development.*
The five stages of team development are forming, storming, norming, performing, and adjourning. In forming, people join the team and define the team's purpose, structure, and leadership. Storming is a stage of intragroup conflict over control issues. During the norming stage, close relationships develop and the team demonstrates cohesiveness. Performing is the stage at which the team is doing the task at hand. Finally, adjourning is the stage when teams with a limited task to perform prepare to be disbanded.

3 *Contrast work groups with work teams.*
A work group interacts primarily to share information and to make decisions to help each member perform within his or her area of responsibility. Work groups have no need nor opportunity to engage in collective work that requires joint effort. Consequently, their performance is merely the summation of all the group members' individual contributions. There is no positive synergy that would create an overall level of performance greater than the sum of the inputs. A work team, on the other hand, generates positive synergy through a coordinated effort. Individual efforts result in a level of performance that is greater than the sum of those individual inputs.

4 *Identify four common types of work teams.*
The four most popular types of teams are functional teams (a manager and the employees in his or her unit), problem-solving teams (typically 5 to 12 hourly employees from the same department who meet for a few hours each week to discuss ways of improving quality, efficiency, and the work environment), self-managed teams (a formal group of employees that operates without a manager and is responsible for a complete work process or segment that delivers a product or service to an external or internal customer), and cross-functional teams (employees from about the same hierarchical level but from different work areas in the organization, brought together to accomplish a particular task).

5 *List the characteristics of high-performing work teams.*
High-performing work teams are characterized by clear goals, unified commitment, good communications, mutual trust, effective leadership, external support, internal support, negotiating skills, and relevant skills.

6 *Discuss how organizations can create team players.*
Organizations can create team players by selecting individuals with the interpersonal skills to be effective team players, providing training to develop teamwork skills, and rewarding individuals for cooperative efforts.

7 *Explain how managers can keep teams from becoming stagnant.*
As teams mature, they can become complacent. Managers need to support mature teams with advice, guidance, and training if these teams are to continue to improve.

8 *Describe the role of teams in continuous process improvement programs.*
Continuous process improvement programs provide a natural vehicle for employees to share ideas and to implement improvements as part of the process. Teams are particularly effective for resolving complex problems.

Review and Application Questions

READING FOR COMPREHENSION

1 Contrast (1) self-managed and cross-functional teams and (2) virtual and face-to-face teams.

2 What problems might surface on teams during each of the five stages of team development?

3 How do virtual teams enhance productivity?

4. In what ways can management invigorate stagnant teams?
5. Why do you believe mutual respect is important to developing high-performing work teams?

LINKING CONCEPTS TO PRACTICE

1. How do you explain the rapidly increasing popularity of work teams in countries, such as the United States and Canada, whose national cultures place a high value on individualism?
2. "All work teams are work groups, but not all work groups are work teams." Do you agree or disagree with the statement? Discuss.
3. Would you prefer to work alone or as part of a team? Why?
4. Describe a situation in which individuals, acting independently, outperform teams in an organization.
5. Contrast the pros and cons of diverse teams.

Management Workshop

Team Skill-Building Exercise

Building Effective Work Teams

OBJECTIVE

This exercise is designed to allow class members to (a) experience working together as a team on a specific task and (b) analyze this experience.

TIME

Teams will have 90 minutes to engage in steps 2 and 3. Another 45–60 minutes of class time will be used to critique and evaluate the exercise.

PROCEDURE

1 Class members are assigned to teams of about six people.

2 Each team is required to:

a. Determine a team name
b. Compose a team song

3 Each team is to try to find the following items on its scavenger hunt:

a. A picture of a team
b. A newspaper article about a group or team
c. A piece of apparel with the college name or logo
d. A drinking straw
e. A ball of cotton
f. A piece of stationery from a college department
g. A Post-It pad
h. A 3.5″ floppy disk
i. A beverage cup from McDonald's
j. A pet leash
k. A book by Ernest Hemingway
l. An ad brochure for a Ford product
m. A test tube
n. A pack of gum
o. A college catalog

4 After 90 minutes, all teams are to be back in the classroom. (A penalty, determined by the instructor, will be imposed on late teams.) The team with the most items on the list will be declared the winner. The class and instructor will determine whether the items meet the requirements of the exercise.

5 Debriefing of the exercise will begin by having each team engage in self-evaluation. Specifically, each should answer the following:

a. What was the team's strategy?
b. What roles did individual members perform?
c. How effective was the team?
d. What could the team have done to be more effective?

6 Full class discussion will focus on issues such as:

a. What differentiated the more effective teams from the less effective teams?
b. What did you learn from this experience that is relevant to the design of effective teams?

SOURCE: Adapted from M. R. Manning and P. J. Schmidt, "Building Effective Work Teams: A Quick Exercise Based on a Scavenger Hunt," *Journal of Management Education,* August 1995, pp. 392–98. © 1995. Reprinted by permission of Sage Publications, Inc.

Developing Your Coaching Skill

Coaching Others

ABOUT THE SKILL

Effective managers are increasingly being described as coaches rather than bosses. Just like coaches, they're expected to provide instruction, guidance, advice, and encouragement to help team members improve their job performance.

STEPS IN THE COACHING SKILL

1 Analyze ways to improve the team's performance and capabilities. A coach looks for opportunities for team members to expand their capabilities and improve performance. How? You can use the following behaviors. Observe your team members' behavior on a day-to-day basis. Ask questions of them: Why do you do a task this way? Can it be improved? What other approaches might be used? Show genuine interest in team members as individuals, not merely as employees. Respect them individually. Listen to each employee.

2 **Create a supportive climate.** It's the coach's responsibility to reduce barriers to development and to facilitate a climate that encourages personal performance improvement. How? You can use the following behaviors. Create a climate that contributes to a free and open exchange of ideas. Offer help and assistance. Give guidance and advice when asked. Encourage your team. Be positive and upbeat. Don't use threats. Ask "What did we learn from this that can help us in the future?" Reduce obstacles. Assure team members that you value their contribution to the team's goals. Take personal responsibility for the outcome, but don't rob team members of their full responsibility. Validate the team members' efforts when they succeed. Point to what was missing when they fail. Never blame team members for poor results.

3 **Influence team members to change their behavior.** The ultimate test of coaching effectiveness is whether an employee's performance improves. You must encourage ongoing growth and development. How can you do this? Try the following behaviors. Recognize and reward small improvements and treat coaching as a way of helping employees to continually work toward improvement. Use a collaborative style by allowing team members to participate in identifying and choosing among improvement ideas. Break difficult tasks down into simpler ones. Model the qualities that you expect from your team. If you want openness, dedication, commitment, and responsibility from your team members, you must demonstrate these qualities yourself.

Practicing the Skill

COACHING SKILLS

Collaborative efforts are more successful when every member of the group or team contributes a specific role or task toward the completion of the goal. To improve your skill at nurturing team effort, choose two of the following activities and break each one into at least six to eight separate tasks or steps. Be sure to indicate which steps are sequential, and which can be done simultaneously with others. What do you think is the ideal team size for each activity you chose?

1 Making an omelet

2 Washing the car

3 Creating a computerized mailing list

4 Designing an advertising poster

5 Planning a ski trip

6 Restocking a supermarket's produce department

A Case Application

Developing Your Diagnostic and Analytical Skills

DISTRIBUTION AT HEWLETT-PACKARD

Even well-managed organizations don't always work as efficiently and effectively as management would like. At Hewlett-Packard (HP), billions of dollars of products are being shipped—from computers and diagnostic devices to toner cartridges—each year. Customer orders come in 24 hours a day, 365 days a year.[55] Nearly 16,000 different products are requested daily and have to be shipped from six different warehouses—oftentimes located 30 or more miles apart. It oftentimes takes weeks to get the products into the customer's hand. This is a serious problem if customers have contracts with HP stating deliveries are to be made in four hours or less. That means that from the time a customer calls the HP customer service line, they will have their replacement part and be back in operation within four hours no matter where that customer is located.

One of the characteristics that distinguishes an outstanding organization is the ability to know when problems need to be addressed and then proceed to do something about it. The job of getting the deliveries made on time fell on the shoulders of HP's distribution manager, Loretta Wilson.

Wilson quickly assembled a team of experts from within and outside the organization. These included logistics, systems, and operations experts. They quickly assessed the situation and established their goals. In essence, the team wanted to "find smarter and simpler ways to handle parts fewer times at several points in the distribution channel." They concluded that a new, high-tech facility was needed—one in which the distribution process could maximize efficiencies. The team designed a 405,000-square-foot facility and specified the precise equipment and layout of the operation. For example, the distribution facility now has over a mile of conveyor belts that run constantly. New sorting machines are capable of sorting over 45 pieces a minute, enabling the company to process over 60,000 products each day. Inventory is stocked within minutes after it's received in the warehouse—rather than the nearly eight days it previously took. Packing and creating are done with the assistance of robotics. Work stations for employees have been redesigned to reduce product handling. And a special shipping dock is equipped so that shipments can be held and their weight determined right up to the moment that Federal Express backs up to the dock. The cargo is then immediately placed into the trucks and the drivers are sent to the airport. Then, as the FedEx drivers head to the airport, they call in the cargo's weight on their cell phones and drive to a waiting aircraft—and send the cargo off to the customer.

Was Wilson's team successful? Yes. The new distribution facility is getting its orders filled within the four-hour limit as contractually required. Additionally, after consolidating the previous six independent facilities into one operation, productivity has risen by more that 33 percent.

QUESTIONS

1. Why do you think a team was needed for the design of a complex project like the distribution center for HP? How would you classify this team?
2. Do you believe that the advantages accrued from specialization (see Chapter 5) are lost or diminished when individuals from different specialities are put together on a team? Discuss.
3. Do you think Loretta Wilson's team achieved its objective? Explain.
4. Using the nine characteristics of a high-performing work team (Exhibit 9-4), describe each of the nine elements as they relate to the case. Use examples where appropriate. If a characteristic was not specifically cited in the case, describe how it may have been witnessed in this project.

Developing Your Investigative Skills

Using the Internet

Visit *www.prenhall.com/robbins* for updated Internet Exercises.

Enhancing Your Writing Skills

Communicating Effectively

1 "Teams create conflict among its members and conflict can lead to lower productivity. Management, then, should not support the concept of teams." Build one argument to support this statement and another to show why the statement is false. Then, take a position on one side of the controversy and support your opinion.

2 Describe why work teams are more acceptable in Japan than in the United States or Canada. Explain how Japanese firms in the United States can still use teams even though the cultural dimensions are different.

3 In two to three pages, explain whether you would prefer to work alone or as part of a team. What does your response indicate in terms of organizational cultures in which you might work? Explain.

Ten

Motivating and Rewarding Employees

LEARNING OUTCOMES After reading this chapter, I will be able to:

1. Describe the motivation process.
2. Define *needs.*
3. Explain the hierarchy of needs theory.
4. Differentiate Theory X from Theory Y.
5. Explain the motivational implications of the motivation-hygiene theory.
6. Describe the motivational implications of equity theory.
7. Explain the key relationships in expectancy theory.
8. Describe how managers can design individual jobs to maximize employee performance.
9. Describe the effect of workforce diversity on motivational practices.

"Incentives are dangerous. They can keep people from doing the right thing!" These are harsh words from Pat Lancaster, founder and CEO of the Louisville, Kentucky, packaging machinery manufacturer, Lantech, Inc.[1]

Starting the company in 1972, Lancaster always had an infinity for incentive plans that would help increase employee productivity. One of his first ventures in incentives was permitting employees to rate one another's job performance and distributing bonuses based on the evaluations. However, this program caused too much employee anxiety, and Lancaster decided to stop it. In its place, he set up another incentive plan. This time each of the five divisions of the company were evaluated on their profits. Based on the profits earned, employees could receive as much as an additional 10 percent of their salary. Although in theory the plan sounded good, getting work out the door required many interdependent activities from each of the five divisions. Accordingly, it became nearly impossible to sort out which division was responsible for the profits. For example, one division built a standard packaging machine, and another division was responsible for customizing the standard machine to customer specifications. Both departments relied heavily on the engineering division and on the division that was responsible for ordering and inventorying parts. The uncertainty of who added what value led to excessive secrecy in the organization and to a lot of politicking when it came time to figure out the bonus awards. Moreover, division members clashed with other division employees, each trying to lay claim to the profits while shifting the costs to the other. It got so bad that arguments occurred over how management should allocate toilet paper costs to each division. As a result, Pat Lancaster was spending more than 95 percent of his time refereeing the conflicts—taking considerable time away from attending to his customers and growing the business. Again, Lancaster abandoned the incentive plan.

Nevertheless, that's not where this story ends. Lancaster, always looking for ways to motivate employees, felt that a workable plan could be found. Still, any plan had to reflect employee performance and link to the organization's strategic direction. Moreover, the plan had to be fair to all employees and promote teamwork. To achieve this goal, Lancaster coupled his new incentive plan with a continuous improvement program. He also placed employees on teams that were independent of divisional affiliation. He then linked incentives to the company's end-of-year profits, with all employees sharing in the rewards. The response to this simple formula has been just short of remarkable.

Employee productivity has nearly doubled over the past five years. A company that had $45 million in revenues and 330 employees at the end of 1998 now has 310 employees and revenues over $70 million. Furthermore, shipping time has decreased from the norm of five weeks in the early 1990s to something less than five hours today. And defective products have been reduced by more than 50 percent.

As for the employees, all 310 of them are averaging an additional five weeks of pay each year as a bonus. More importantly, to them and to Lancaster, employees feel involved, empowered, and part of the decision-making team. They believe they have a personal stake in making sure the company does well. For them, the company-wide incentive plan has created a sense of ownership for them and significantly increased their commitment and loyalty to the company.

As Pat Lancaster learned, incentive plans can play a key role in affecting employee productivity and their motivation. The way employees behave at work and why they do so are of interest to all managers. In this chapter, we provide some insight into how to maximize employee behavior—which we classify under the heading of motivation. Let's begin this chapter by defining motivation.

Motivation and Individual Needs

To understand what motivation is, let us begin by pointing out what motivation *isn't.* Why? Because many people incorrectly view motivation as a personal trait—

that is, they think that some have it and others don't. In practice, this attitude would characterize the manager who labels a certain employee as unmotivated. Our knowledge of motivation, though, tells us that people can't be labeled in this way. We know that motivation is the result of the interaction between the individual and the situation. Certainly, individuals differ in motivational drive, but an individual's motivation varies from situation to situation. As we analyze the concept of motivation, keep in mind that level of motivation varies both among individuals and within individuals at different times.

We define **motivation** as the willingness to exert high levels of effort to reach organizational goals, conditioned by the effort's ability to satisfy some individual need. Although general motivation refers to effort toward any goal, here it refers to organizational goals because our focus is on work-related behavior. The three key elements in our definition are effort, organizational goals, and needs.

motivation
The willingness to exert high levels of effort to reach organizational goals, conditioned by the effort's ability to satisfy some individual need

The *effort* element is a measure of intensity. When someone is motivated, he or she tries hard. However, high levels of effort are unlikely to lead to favorable job performance outcomes unless the effort is channeled in a direction that benefits the organization.[2] Therefore, we must consider the quality of the effort as well as its intensity. Effort that is directed toward and consistent with the organization's goals is the kind of effort that we should be seeking. Finally, we treat motivation as a need-satisfying process. This is depicted in Exhibit 10-1.

A **need,** in our terminology, is some internal state that makes certain outcomes appear attractive. An unsatisfied need creates tension that stimulates drives within an individual. These drives generate a search behavior to find particular goals that, if attained, will satisfy the need and reduce the tension.

need
An internal state that makes certain outcomes appear attractive

We can say that motivated employees are in a state of tension. To relieve this tension, they exert effort. The greater the tension, the higher the effort level. If this effort successfully leads to the satisfaction of the need, it reduces tension. Because we are interested in work behavior, this tension-reduction effort must also be directed toward organizational goals. Therefore, inherent in our definition of motivation is the requirement that the individual's needs be compatible and consistent with the organization's goals. When they aren't, individuals may exert high levels of effort that run counter to the interests of the organization. Incidentally, this situation is not so unusual. Some employees regularly spend a lot of time talking with friends at work—or surf their favorite Web sites and chat rooms—in order to satisfy their social needs. There is a high level of effort, but it's being unproductively directed.

Early Theories of Motivation

The 1950s were a fruitful time for the development of motivation concepts. Three specific theories were formulated during this period that, although heavily

Exhibit 10-1 The Motivation Process

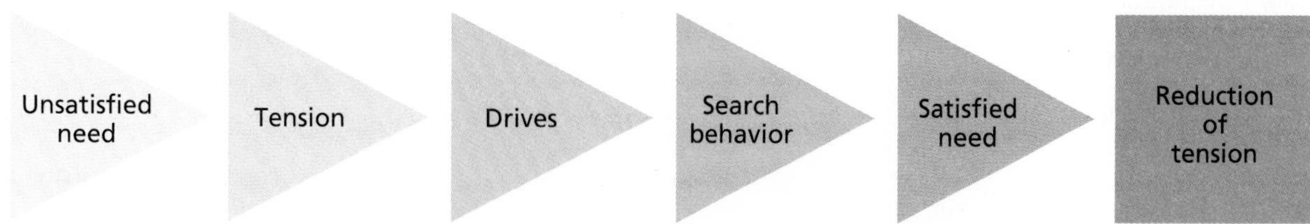

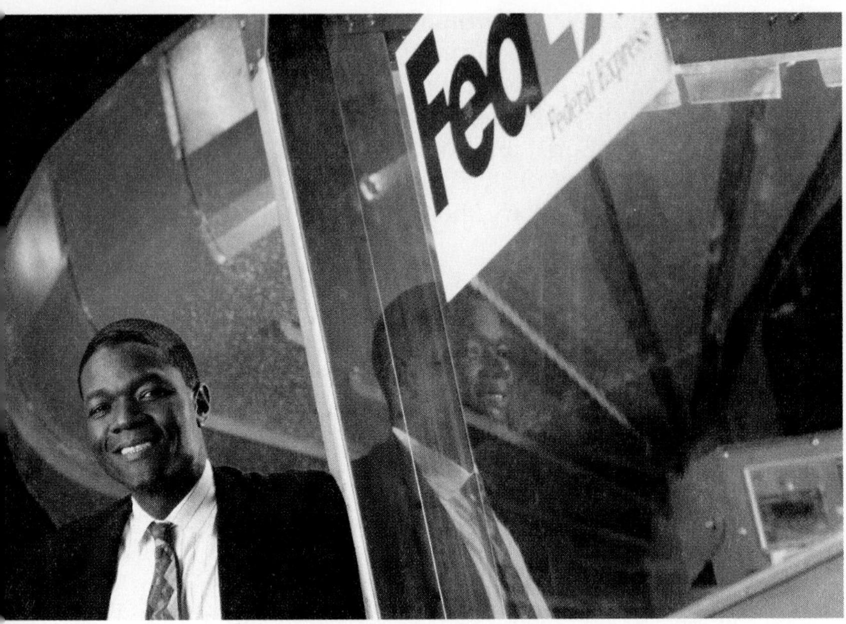

Is there support for Maslow's hierarchy of needs theory of motivation in business today? That depends on who you talk to. Although rigorous empirical research in academe has been unable to support the theory, people like David Kirby, a service-assurance manager at FedEx believes in it. As Kirby puts it, "working for a winner, and industry leader gives me a great deal of pride." Under Maslow's theory, we can conclude that Kirby is expressing fulfillment of a self-esteem need.

attacked and now considered questionable, are probably still the best-known explanations of employee motivation. These are the hierarchy of needs theory, Theories X and Y, and the motivation-hygiene theory. Although more valid explanations of motivation have been developed, you should know these theories for at least two reasons: (1) They represent the foundation from which contemporary theories grew and (2) practicing managers regularly use these theories and their terminology in explaining employee motivation.

WHAT IS MASLOW'S HIERARCHY OF NEEDS THEORY?

The best-known theory of motivation is probably psychologist Abraham Maslow's **hierarchy of needs theory.**[3] He stated that within every human being exists a hierarchy of five types of needs:

1 **Physiological needs** Food, drink, shelter, sexual satisfaction, and other bodily requirements

2 **Safety needs** Security and protection from physical and emotional harm

3 **Social needs** Affection, belongingness, acceptance, and friendship

4 **Esteem needs** Internal esteem factors such as self-respect, autonomy, and achievement and external esteem factors such as status, recognition, and attention

5 **Self-actualization needs** Growth, achieving one's potential, and self-fulfillment; the drive to become what one is capable of becoming

heirarchy of needs theory
Maslow's theory that there is a hierarchy of five human needs: physiological, safety, social, esteem, and self-actualization; as each need becomes satisfied, the next need becomes dominant

As each level of need is substantially satisfied, the next need becomes dominant. As shown in Exhibit 10-2, the individual moves up the hierarchy. From a motivation viewpoint, the theory says that, although no need is ever fully grati-

Exhibit 10-2
Maslow's Hierarchy of Needs

SOURCE: *Motivation and Personality,* 2nd ed., by A. H. Maslow, 1970. Reprinted by permission of Prentice Hall, Inc., Upper Saddle River, New Jersey.

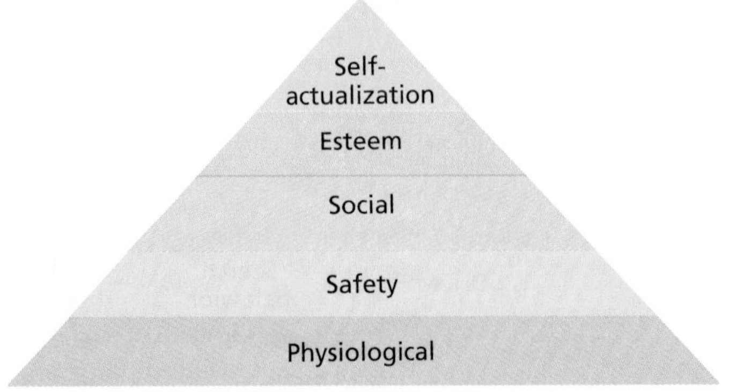

fied, a substantially satisfied need no longer motivates. If you want to motivate someone, according to Maslow, you need to understand where that person is in the hierarchy and focus on satisfying needs at or above that level.

Maslow's need theory has received wide recognition, particularly among practicing managers.[4] Its popularity can be attributed to the theory's intuitive logic and ease of understanding. Unfortunately, however, research does not generally validate the theory. Maslow provided no empirical substantiation for his theory, and several studies that sought to validate it found no support.[5]

WHAT IS McGREGOR'S THEORY X AND THEORY Y?

Douglas McGregor proposed two distinct views of the nature of human beings: a basically negative view, labeled **Theory X,** and a basically positive view, labeled **Theory Y.**[6] After viewing the way managers dealt with employees, McGregor concluded that a manager's view of human nature is based on a group of assumptions, either positive or negative (see Exhibit 10-3), and that the manager molds his or her behavior toward employees according to these suppositions.

Theory X
McGregor's term for the assumption that employees dislike work, are lazy, seek to avoid responsibility, and must be coerced to perform

Theory Y
McGregor's term for the assumption that employees are creative, seek responsibility, and can exercise self-direction

What does McGregor's analysis imply about motivation? The answer is best expressed in the framework presented by Maslow. Theory X assumes that physiological and safety needs dominate the individual. Theory Y assumes that social and esteem needs are dominant.[7] McGregor himself held to the belief that the assumptions of Theory Y were more valid than those of Theory X. Therefore, he proposed that participation in decision making, responsible and challenging jobs, and good group relations would maximize work effort.

Unfortunately, there is no evidence to confirm that either set of assumptions is valid or that accepting Theory Y assumptions and altering one's actions accordingly will make one's employees more motivated. In the real world, effective man-

Exhibit 10-3 Theory X and Theory Y Premises

Theory X: A manager who views employees from a Theory X (negative) perspective believes:

1. Employees inherently dislike work and, whenever possible, will attempt to avoid it
2. Because employees dislike work, they must be coerced, controlled, or threatened with punishment to achieve desired goals
3. Employees will shirk responsibilities and seek formal direction whenever possible
4. Most workers place security above all other factors associated with work and will display little ambition

Theory Y: A manager who views employees from a Theory Y (positive) perspective believes:

1. Employees can view work as being as natural as rest or play
2. Men and women will exercise self-direction and self-control if they are committed to the objectives
3. The average person can learn to accept, even seek, responsibility
4. The ability to make good decisions is widely dispersed throughout the population and is not necessarily the sole province of managers

agers do make Theory X assumptions. For instance, Bob McCurry, vice president of Toyota's U.S. marketing operations, essentially follows Theory X. He drives his staff hard and uses a "crack-the-whip" style, yet he has been extremely successful at increasing Toyota's market share in a highly competitive environment.

WHAT IS HERZBERG'S MOTIVATION-HYGIENE THEORY?

motivation-hygiene theory
Herzberg's theory that intrinsic factors are related to job satisfaction and extrinsic factors are related to job dissatisfaction

The **motivation-hygiene theory** was proposed by psychologist Frederick Herzberg.[8] Believing that an individual's attitude toward his or her work can very well determine success or failure, Herzberg investigated the question of what people want from their jobs. He asked people to describe in detail situations in which they felt exceptionally good or bad about their jobs. Their responses were then tabulated and categorized. Exhibit 10-4 represents Herzberg's findings.

After analyzing the responses, Herzberg concluded that the replies of people who felt good about their jobs were significantly different from the replies they gave when they disliked their jobs. As seen in Exhibit 10-4, certain characteristics were consistently related to job satisfaction (on the left side of the figure) and others to job dissatisfaction (on the right side of the figure). *Intrinsic factors* such as achievement, recognition, and responsibility were related to job satisfaction. When the people questioned felt good about their work, they tended to attribute these characteristics to themselves.[9] On the other hand, when they were dissatisfied, they tended to cite *extrinsic factors* such as company policy and administration, supervision, interpersonal relationships, and working conditions.[10]

The data suggest, said Herzberg, that the opposite of satisfaction is not dissatisfaction, as was traditionally believed. Removing dissatisfying characteristics from a job does not necessarily make the job satisfying. As illustrated in Exhibit 10-5, Herzberg proposed that his findings indicate that the opposite of "satisfaction" is "no satisfaction" and the opposite of "dissatisfaction" is "no dissatisfaction."

hygiene factors
Herzberg's term for factors, such as working conditions and salary, that, when adequate, may eliminate job dissatisfaction but do not necessarily increase job satisfaction

According to Herzberg, the factors that lead to job satisfaction are separate and distinct from those that lead to job dissatisfaction. Therefore, managers who seek to eliminate factors that create job dissatisfaction can bring about peace but not necessarily motivation: They are placating their workforce rather than motivating it. Because they don't motivate employees, the factors that eliminate job dissatisfaction were characterized by Herzberg as **hygiene factors.** When these factors are adequate, people will not be dissatisfied, but neither will they be satisfied. To

Exhibit 10-4
Herzberg's Motivation-Hygiene Theory

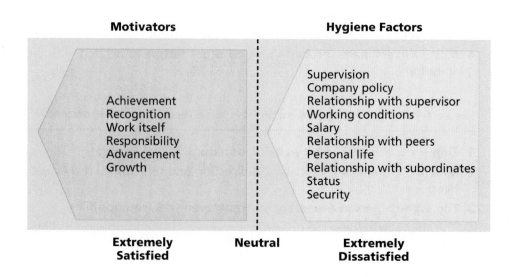

Motivators	Hygiene Factors
Achievement Recognition Work itself Responsibility Advancement Growth	Supervision Company policy Relationship with supervisor Working conditions Salary Relationship with peers Personal life Relationship with subordinates Status Security

Extremely Satisfied — Neutral — Extremely Dissatisfied

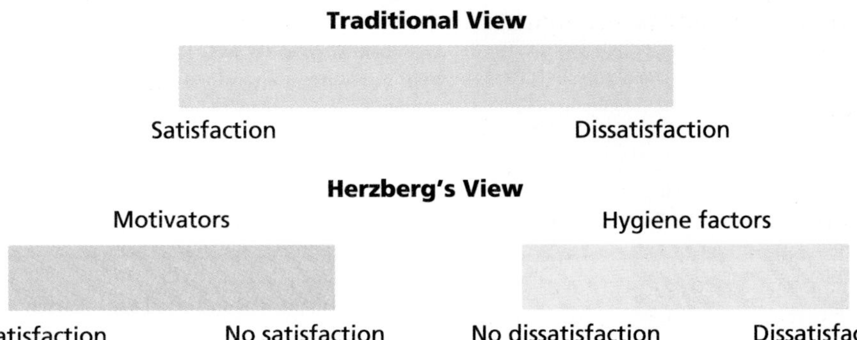

Exhibit 10-5
Contrasting Views of Satisfaction-Dissatisfaction

motivate people on their jobs, Herzberg suggested emphasizing **motivators,** those factors that increase job satisfaction.

motivators
Herzberg's term for factors, such as recognition and growth, that increase job satisfaction

The motivation-hygiene theory is not without its detractors, who criticize, for example, the methodology Herzberg used to collect data and his failure to account for situational variables.[11] Regardless of any criticism, Herzberg's theory has been widely popularized, and few managers are unfamiliar with his recommendations. Much of the enthusiasm for enriching jobs—that is, making them more challenging and giving more autonomy to work—can be attributed to Herzberg's findings and recommendations.

Contemporary Theories of Motivation

Although the previous theories are well known, they unfortunately have not held up well under close examination. However, all is not lost. There are contemporary theories that all have reasonable degrees of valid supporting documentation. The following theories represent the current state-of-the-art explanations of employee motivation.

WHAT IS McCLELLAND'S THREE-NEEDS THEORY?

David McClelland and others have proposed the **three-needs theory,** which maintains that there are three major relevant motives or needs in work situations:

- **Need for achievement (nAch)** The drive to excel, to achieve in relation to a set of standards, to strive to succeed;
- **Need for power (nPow)** The need to make others behave in a way that they would not have behaved otherwise;
- **Need for affiliation (nAff)** The desire for friendly and close interpersonal relationships.[12]

three-needs theory
McClelland's theory that the needs for achievement, power, and affiliation are major motives in work

need for achievement
The drive to excel, to achieve in relation to a set of standards, and to strive to succeed

need for power
The need to make others behave in a way that they would not have behaved otherwise

need for affiliation
The desire for friendly and close interpersonal relationships

Some people have a compelling drive to succeed, but they are striving for personal achievement rather than for the rewards of success per se *(nAch)*. They have a desire to do something better or more efficiently than it has been done before. This drive is the need for achievement. From his research on the achievement need, McClelland concluded that high achievers differentiate themselves by their desire to do things better.[13] They seek situations in which they can assume personal responsibility for finding solutions to problems, in which they can receive rapid and unambiguous feedback on their performance in order to tell whether they are improving, and in which they can set moderately challenging goals (see Details on a Management Classic, p. 319). High achievers are not gamblers; they

Marc Whalen and Lisa Chacon, research scientists at Corning gleefully describe their organization as human-centered. In this type of environment, McClelland's need for affiliation plays an integral role. Those desiring a friendly and close interpersonal work relationship would fit nicely into Corning's corporate culture.

dislike succeeding by chance. They prefer the challenge of working at a problem and accepting the personal responsibility for success or failure rather than leaving the outcome to chance or the actions of others. An important point is that they avoid what they perceive to be very easy or very difficult tasks.[14]

The need for power *(nPow)* is the desire to have impact and to be influential. Individuals high in nPow enjoy being in charge, strive for influence over others, and prefer to be in competitive and status-oriented situations. The third need isolated by McClelland is affiliation *(nAff),* which is the desire to be liked and accepted by others. This need has received the least attention from researchers. Individuals with high nAff strive for friendships, prefer cooperative situations rather than competitive ones, and desire relationships involving a high degree of mutual understanding.

HOW DO INPUTS AND OUTCOMES INFLUENCE MOTIVATION?

Employees don't work in a vacuum. They make comparisons. If someone offered you $85,000 a year on your first job upon graduation from college, you would probably grab the offer and report to work enthusiastic and certainly satisfied with your pay. But how would you react if you found out a month or so into the job that a coworker—another recent graduate, your age, with comparable grades from a comparable college—was getting $95,000 a year? You probably would be upset. Even though, in absolute terms, $85,000 is a lot of money for a new graduate to make (and you know it!), that suddenly would not be the issue. The issue would now center on relative rewards and what you believe is fair. There is considerable evidence that employees make comparisons of their job inputs and outcomes relative to others and that inequities influence the degree of effort that employees exert.[15]

equity theory
Adams's theory that employees perceive what they get from a job situation (outcomes) in relation to what they put into it (inputs) and then compare their input-outcome ratio with the input-outcome ratios of relevant others

referent
In equity theory, the other persons, the systems, or the personal experiences against which individuals compare themselves to assess equity

Developed by J. Stacey Adams, **equity theory** says that employees perceive what they get from a job situation (outcomes) in relation to what they put into it (inputs) and then compare their input-outcome ratio with the input-outcome ratios of relevant others. This relationship is shown in Exhibit 10-6. If workers perceive their ratio to be equal to those of the relevant others with whom they compare themselves, a state of equity exists. They perceive that their situation is fair—that justice prevails. If the ratios are unequal, inequity exists; that is, workers view themselves as underrewarded or overrewarded. When inequities occur, employees attempt to correct them.

The **referent** with whom employees choose to compare themselves is an important variable in equity theory.[16] The three referent categories have been classified as "other," "system," and "self." The *other* category includes individuals

Details on a Management Classic

David McClelland and the Three-Needs Theory

David McClelland helped to understand motivation in organizational settings by focusing on aspects of personality characteristics. Much of his research centered on achievement, power, and affiliation orientations. McClelland found that some people have a compelling drive to succeed for personal achievement rather than for the rewards of success per se. The questions then are: How do you find out if someone is, for instance, a high achiever? What effect can that person's need for achievement have on an organization?

In his research, McClelland used a projective test in which subjects responded to a set of pictures. Each picture was briefly shown to a subject, who then wrote a story based on the picture. The responses were then classified by McClelland as focusing on a need for achievement, power, or affiliation. Subjects who had a high need for achievement, however, shared some similar attributes.

High achievers perform best when they perceive their probability of success as being about 50 percent—that is, when they estimate they have a 50–50 chance of success. They dislike gambling when the odds are high because they get no satisfaction from happenstance success. Similarly, they dislike low odds (high probability of success) because then there is no challenge to their skills. They like to set goals that require stretching themselves a little. When there is an approximately equal chance of success or failure, there is optimum opportunity to feel successful and satisfied.

On the basis of extensive research, some reasonably well-supported predictions can be made about the relationship of the achievement need and job performance. Though less research has been done on power and affiliation needs, there are consistent findings in those areas, too. First, individuals with a high need to achieve prefer job situations with personal responsibility, feedback, and an intermediate degree of risk. When these characteristics are prevalent, high achievers are strongly motivated. The evidence consistently demonstrates, for instance, that high achievers are successful in entrepreneurial activities such as running their own business, managing a self-contained unit within a large organization, and in many sales positions.[17] Second, a high need to achieve does not necessarily indicate that someone is a good manager, especially in large organizations. A high nAch salesperson at Hitachi Ltd. does not necessarily make a good sales manager, and good managers in large organizations such as General Electric, Glaxo Wellcome, or Unilever do not necessarily have a high need to achieve.[18] Third, the needs for affiliation and power are closely related to managerial success.[19] The best managers are high in the need for power and low in the need for affiliation. Last, employees can be trained to stimulate their achievement need.[20] If a job calls for a high achiever, management can select a person with a high nAch or develop its own candidate through achievement training.

with similar jobs in the same organization and friends, neighbors, or professional associates. On the basis of information through word of mouth, newspapers, and magazine articles on issues such as executive salaries or a recent union contract, employees compare their pay with that of others.

The *system* category considers organizational pay policies and procedures and the administration of that system. It considers organization-wide pay policies,

Exhibit 10-6
Equity Theory Relationships

Perceived Ratio Comparison*	Employee's Assessment
$\frac{\text{Outcomes A}}{\text{Inputs A}} < \frac{\text{Outcomes B}}{\text{Inputs B}}$	Inequity (underrewarded)
$\frac{\text{Outcomes A}}{\text{Inputs A}} = \frac{\text{Outcomes B}}{\text{Inputs B}}$	Equity
$\frac{\text{Outcomes A}}{\text{Inputs A}} > \frac{\text{Outcomes B}}{\text{Inputs B}}$	Inequity (overrewarded)

*Person A is the employee, and Person B is a relevant other or referent.

both implied and explicit. Patterns by the organization in terms of allocation of pay are major determinants in this category.

The *self* category refers to input-outcome ratios that are unique to the individual. It reflects personal experiences and contacts. This category is influenced by criteria such as previous jobs or family commitments.

The choice of a particular set of referents is related to the information available about referents as well as to the perceived relevance.[21] On the basis of equity theory, when employees perceive an inequity, they might (1) distort either their own or others' inputs or outcomes, (2) behave so as to induce others to change their inputs or outcomes, (3) behave so as to change their own inputs or outcomes, (4) choose a different comparison referent, and/or (5) quit their job.

Equity theory recognizes that individuals are concerned not only with the absolute rewards they receive for their efforts but also with the relationship of those rewards to what others receive. They make judgments concerning the relationship between their inputs and outcomes and the inputs and outcomes of others. On the basis of one's inputs, such as effort, experience, education, and competence, one compares outcomes such as salary levels, raises, recognition, and other factors. When people perceive an imbalance in their input-outcome ratio relative to those of others, they experience tension. This tension provides the basis for motivation as people strive for what they perceive to be equity and fairness.

The theory establishes four propositions relating to inequitable pay, listed in Exhibit 10-7, that have generally proven to be correct.[22] Research consistently confirms the equity thesis: Employee motivation is influenced significantly by relative rewards as well as by absolute rewards. Whenever employees perceive inequity, they will act to correct the situation.[23] The result might be lower or higher productivity, improved or reduced quality of output, increased absenteeism, or voluntary resignation.

Exhibit 10-7
Equity Theory Propositions

1. **If paid according to time, overrewarded employees will produce more than equitably paid employees.** Hourly and salaried employees will generate a high quantity or quality of production in order to increase the input side of the ratio and bring about equity.
2. **If paid according to quantity of production, overrewarded employees will produce fewer but higher-quality units than equitably paid employees.** Individuals paid on a piece-rate basis will increase their effort to achieve equity, which can result in greater quality or quantity. However, increases in quantity will only increase inequity, because every unit produced results in further overpayment. Therefore, effort is directed toward increasing quality rather than quantity.
3. **If paid according to time, underrewarded employees will produce less or poorer-quality output.** Effort will be decreased, which will bring about lower productivity or poorer-quality output than equitably paid subjects produce.
4. **If paid according to quantity of production, underrewarded employees will produce a large number of low-quality units in comparison with equitably paid employees.** Employees on piece-rate pay plans can bring about equity because trading off quality of output for quantity will increase in rewards with little or no increase in contributions.

From the preceding discussion, however, we should not conclude that equity theory is without problems. The theory leaves some key issues still unclear.[24] For instance, how do employees define inputs and outcomes? How do they combine and weigh their inputs and outcomes to arrive at totals? When and how do the factors change over time? Regardless of these problems, equity theory has an impressive amount of research support and offers us some important insights into employee motivation.

DOES JOB DESIGN INFLUENCE MOTIVATION?

What differentiates one job from another? We know that a traveling salesperson's job is different from that of an emergency-room nurse. And we know that both of those jobs have little in common with the job of an editor in a newsroom or that of a component assembler on a production line. But what is it that allows us to draw these distinctions? Currently, the best answer is something called the **job characteristics model (JCM)** developed by J. Richard Hackman and Greg R. Oldham.[25]

job characteristics model (JCM)
Hackman and Oldham's job description model: The five core job dimensions are skill variety, task identity, task significance, autonomy, and feedback

According to Hackman and Oldham, any job can be described in terms of the following five core job dimensions:

1. **Skill variety** The degree to which the job requires a variety of activities so the worker can use a number of different skills and talents
2. **Task identity** The degree to which the job requires completion of a whole and identifiable piece of work
3. **Task significance** The degree to which the job affects the lives or work of other people
4. **Autonomy** The degree to which the job provides freedom, independence, and discretion to the individual in scheduling the work and in determining the procedures to be used in carrying it out
5. **Feedback** The degree to which carrying out the work activities required by the job results in the individual's obtaining direct and clear information about the effectiveness of his or her performance

The core dimensions can be combined into a single index called the **Motivating Potential Score (MPS).** The MPS is calculated as follows:

Motivating Potential Score (MPS)
The core job dimensions combined into one index

$$\frac{[\text{skill variety} + \text{task identity} + \text{task significance}]}{3} \times \text{autonomy} \times \text{feedback}$$

Exhibit 10-8 offers examples of job activities that rate high and low for each characteristic. As the model in Exhibit 10-9 shows, the links between the job dimensions and the outcomes are moderated or adjusted by the strength of the individual's growth need; that is, by the employee's desire for self-esteem and self-actualization. This means that individuals with a high growth need are more likely to experience the expected psychological states when their jobs are enriched than are their counterparts with a low growth need. Moreover, they will respond more positively to the psychological states when they are present than will low-growth-need individuals.

Research on the JCM has found that the first three dimensions—skill variety, task identity, and task significance—combine to create meaningful work. That is, if these three characteristics exist in a job, we can predict that the person will view his or her job as important, valuable, and worthwhile. Autonomy gives the worker a feeling of personal responsibility for the results, and feedback lets the employee know how effectively he or she is performing.

Exhibit 10-8 Examples of High and Low Job Characteristics

JOB CHARACTERISTIC	EXAMPLE JOB
Skill Variety	
High variety	The owner-operator of a garage who does electrical repair, rebuilds engines, does body work, and interacts with customers
Low variety	A body shop worker who sprays paint eight hours a day
Task Identity	
High identity	A cabinetmaker who designs a piece of furniture, selects the wood, builds the object, and finishes it to perfection
Low identity	A worker in a furniture factory who operates a lathe solely to make table legs
Task Significance	
High significance	Nursing the sick in a hospital intensive-care unit
Low significance	Sweeping hospital floors
Autonomy	
High autonomy	A police detective who schedules his or her own work for the day, makes contacts without supervision, and decides on the most effective techniques for solving a case
Low autonomy	A police telephone dispatcher who must handle calls as they come according to a routine, highly specified procedure
Feedback	
High feedback	An electronics factory worker who assembles a modem and then tests it to determine if it operates properly
Low feedback	An electronics factory worker who assembles a modem and then routes it to a quality control inspector who tests it for proper operation and makes needed adjustments

SOURCE: Adapted from G. Johns, *Organizational Behavior: Understanding and Managing Life at Work,* 4th ed. p. 204. © 1996 Addison Wesley Longman, Inc. Reprinted by permission of Addison Wesley Longman.

From a motivational standpoint, the JCM says that internal rewards are obtained when one learns (knowledge of results) that one personally (experienced responsibility) has performed well on a task that one cares about (experienced meaningfulness).[26] The more these three conditions are present, the greater will be the employee's motivation, performance, and satisfaction.[27]

What does the JCM tell us? Jobs score high on motivating potential if they are high on at least one of the three factors that lead to experiencing meaningfulness (skill variety, task identity, or task significance). They must also be high on both autonomy and feedback. Creating jobs that meet these requirements can result in a high score. In doing so, motivation, performance, and satisfaction will be positively affected, and the likelihood of absenteeism and turnover will be decreased.[28]

The job characteristics model has been well researched. Most of the evidence supports the general framework of the theory—that is, there is a set of multiple job characteristics, and these characteristics affect behavioral outcomes.[29] However, there is still considerable debate about the five specific core dimensions in the JCM and the validity of growth-need strength as a moderating variable.

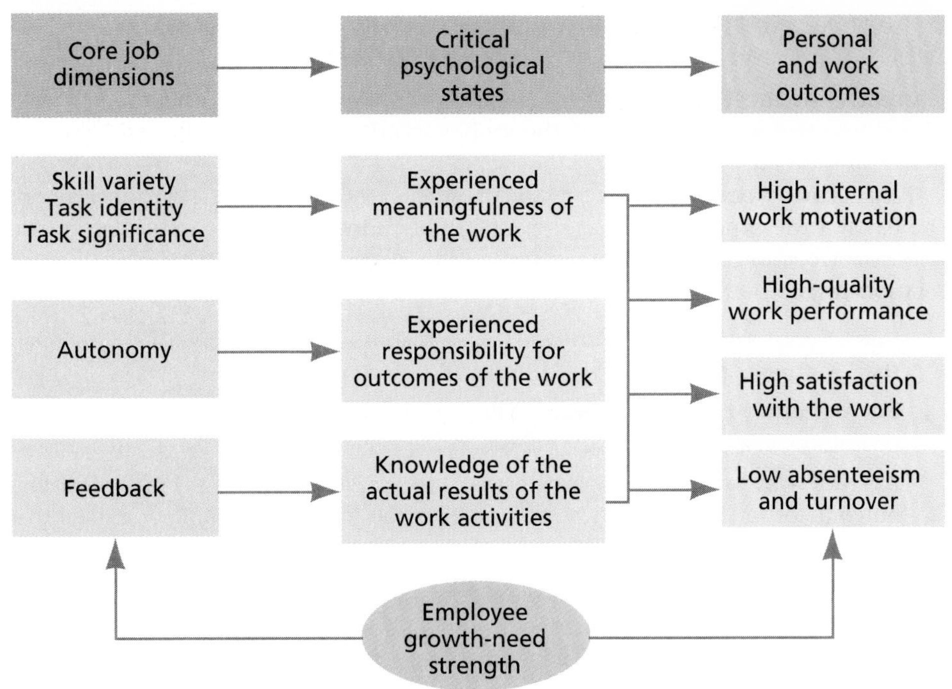

Exhibit 10-9
The Job Characteristics Model

SOURCE: J. R. Hackman, "Work Design," in J. R. Hackman and J. L. Suttle, eds., *Improving Life at Work* (Glenview, IL: Scott, Foresman, 1977), p. 129.

There is some question as to whether task identity adds to the model's predictive ability,[30] and evidence suggests that skill variety may be redundant if autonomy is present.[31] In addition, the strength of an individual's growth needs as a meaningful moderating variable has recently been called into question.[32] Other variables such as the presence or absence of social cues, perceived equity with comparison groups, and likelihood of integrating work experience[33] may be more valid in moderating the job characteristics–outcome relationship. Given the current state of research on moderating variables, one should be cautious about unequivocally accepting growth-need strength as originally included in the JCM.

What is it that will make this electrical engineer at Inter-Tel, a telecommunications equipment manufacturer in Chandler, Arizona, have meaningful work? According to the JCM, three dimensions—skill variety, task identity, and task significance—combine to provide the main elements of motivation. In addition, this employee's ability to work autonomously and receive proper feedback assist in creating a meaningful and productive work setting.

Where does this leave us? We can make the following statements with relative confidence: (1) The JCM provides a reasonably valid framework for defining the core characteristics in a cross section of jobs, (2) People who work on jobs with high core job dimensions are generally more motivated, satisfied, and productive than are those who do not, (3) Job dimensions operate through the psychological states in influencing personal and work outcome variables rather than influencing them directly.[34]

WHY IS EXPECTANCY THEORY CONSIDERED A COMPREHENSIVE THEORY OF MOTIVATION?

Currently the most comprehensive explanation of motivation is Victor Vroom's expectancy theory.[35] Though the theory has its critics,[36] most of the research evidence supports it.[37]

expectancy theory
Vroom's theory that an individual tends to act in a certain way in the expectation that the act will be followed by a given outcome and according to the attractiveness of that outcome

Expectancy theory states that an individual tends to act in a certain way on the basis of the expectation that the act will be followed by a given outcome and the attractiveness of that outcome to the individual. It includes three variables or relationships:

1. **Effort-performance linkage** The probability perceived by the individual that exerting a given amount of effort will lead to performance;
2. **Performance-reward linkage** The degree to which the individual believes that performing at a particular level will lead to the attainment of a desired outcome;
3. **Attractiveness** The importance that the individual places on the potential outcome or reward that can be achieved on the job. This variable considers the goals and needs of the individual.[38]

Although this might sound complex, it really is not that difficult to visualize. The theory can be summed up in the following questions: How hard do I have to work to achieve a certain level of performance, and can I actually achieve that level? What reward will performing at that level get me? How attractive is this reward to me, and does it help achieve my goals? Whether one has the desire to produce at any given time depends on one's particular goals and one's perception of the relative worth of performance as a path to the attainment of those goals.[39]

How does expectancy theory work?

Exhibit 10-10 illustrates a very simple version of expectancy theory that expresses its major contentions. The strength of a person's motivation to perform (effort) depends on how strongly that individual believes that he or she can achieve what is being attempted. If this goal is achieved (performance), will he or she be adequately rewarded by the organization? If so, will the reward satisfy his or her individual goals? Let us consider the four steps inherent in the theory and then attempt to apply it.

First, what perceived outcomes does the job offer the employee? Outcomes may be positive: pay, security, companionship, trust, employee benefits, a chance to use talent or skills, or congenial relationships. On the other hand, an employee may view the outcomes as negative: fatigue, boredom, frustration, anxiety, harsh supervision, or threat of dismissal. Reality is not relevant here: The critical issue is what the employee perceives the outcome to be, regardless of whether his or her perceptions are accurate.

Exhibit 10-10 Simplified Expectancy Theory

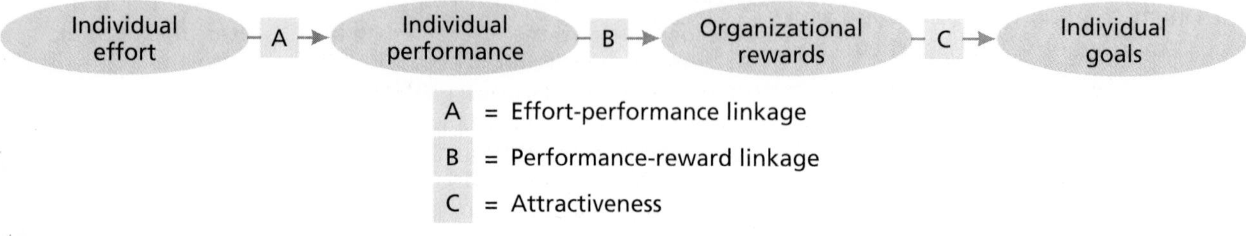

Ethical Dilemma in Management

Rewarding Appropriate Behavior

You have just been hired as a customer service representative at the Barnett World Travel Agency in San Diego, California. Customers call you to arrange travel plans. You look up airline flights, times, and fares on your computer and help your customers make travel reservations that work best for them. You also provide assistance in reserving rental cars, finding suitable hotel accommodations, and booking tours and cruises.

Most car rental agencies and hotels frequently run contests for the customer service representative who reserves the most cars for a particular firm or books the most clients for a specific hotel chain. The rewards for doing so are very attractive. For instance, one car rental firm offers to place your name in a monthly drawing to win $2,500 if you book just 20 reservations. Book 100 in the same amount of time, and you will be eligible for a $10,000 prize. And, if you book 200 clients, you will receive an all-expenses-paid, four-day Caribbean vacation for two. So the incentives are attractive enough for you to steer customers toward those companies even though it might not be the best arrangement or the cheapest for them. Your supervisor doesn't discourage your participation in these programs. In fact, the programs are viewed as a bonus for your hard work.

Is there anything wrong with doing business with those car rental and hotel firms that offer kickbacks to you? How could your organization design a performance reward system that would encourage you to high levels of bookings if it could not be certain that you gave highest priority to customer satisfaction?

Second, how attractive does an employee consider these outcomes to be? Are they valued positively, negatively, or neutrally? This obviously is an internal issue and takes into account the individual's personal attitudes, personality, and needs. The individual who finds a particular outcome attractive—that is, values it positively—would rather attain it than not attain it. Others may find it negative and, therefore, prefer not attaining it to attaining it. Still others may be neutral.

Third, what kind of behavior must the employee exhibit to achieve these outcomes? The outcomes are not likely to have any effect on an employee's performance unless the employee knows, clearly and unambiguously, what he or she must do to achieve them[40] (see Ethical Dilemma in Management). For example, what does "doing well" mean in terms of performance appraisal? What criteria will be used to judge the employee's performance?

Fourth and last, how does the employee view his or her chances of doing what is asked? After the employee has considered his or her own competencies and ability to control those variables that will determine success, what probability does he or she assign to successful attainment?[41]

How can expectancy theory be applied? Let's use a classroom analogy as an illustration of how one can use expectancy theory to explain motivation.

Most students prefer an instructor to tell them what is expected in the course. They want to know what the assignments and examinations will be like, when they are due or have to be taken, and how much weight each carries in the final term grade. They also like to think that the amount of effort they exert in attending classes, taking notes, and studying will be reasonably related to the grade they will earn in the course. Let's assume that you, as a student, feel this way. Consider that five weeks into a class you are really enjoying (we'll call it MNGT 301), an examination is returned to you. You studied hard for this examination, and you have consistently made A's and B's on examinations in other courses in which you have expended similar effort. The reason you work so hard is to make top grades, which you believe are important for getting a good job upon graduation. Also, although you are not sure, you might want to go on to graduate school, and you think grades are important if you are going to get into a good graduate school.

Well, the results of that first examination are in. The class average was 76. Ten percent of the class scored an 88 or higher and got an A. Your grade was 54; the minimum passing mark was 60. You're mad. You're frustrated. Even more, you're perplexed. How could you possibly have done so poorly on the examination when you usually score in the top range in other classes by preparing as you did for this one?

Several interesting things are immediately evident in your behavior. Suddenly, you may no longer be driven to attend MNGT 301 classes regularly. You may find several reasons why you don't want to study for the course either. When you do attend classes, you may find yourself daydreaming—the result is an empty notebook instead of several pages of notes. One would probably be correct in saying that you lack motivation in MNGT 301. Why did your motivation level change? You know and we know, but let's explain it in expectancy terms.

If we use Exhibit 10-10 to understand this situation, we might say the following: Studying for MNGT 301 (effort) is conditioned by the correct answers on the examination (performance), which will produce a high grade (reward), which will lead, in turn, to the security, prestige, and other benefits that accrue from obtaining a good job (individual goal).

The attractiveness of the outcome, a good grade, is high. But what about the performance-reward linkage? Do you feel that the grade you received truly reflects your knowledge of the material? In other words, did the test fairly measure what you know? If it did, then this linkage is strong. If you think it didn't, then at least part of the reason for your reduced motivational level is your belief that the test was not a fair measure of your performance. If the test was an essay type, maybe you believe that the instructor's grading method was poor. Was too much weight placed on a question that you thought was trivial? Maybe the instructor does not like you and was biased in grading your paper. These are examples of perceptions that influence the performance-reward linkage and your level of motivation.

Another possible demotivating force may be the effort-performance relationship. If, after you took the examination, you believe that you could not have passed it regardless of the amount of preparation you had done, then your desire to study may drop. Possibly, the instructor assumed that you had a considerably broader background in the subject matter. Maybe the course had several prerequisites that you did not know about, or possibly you had the prerequisites but took those courses several years ago. The result is the same: You place a low value on your effort leading to answering the examination questions correctly; hence, your motivational level decreases, and you reduce your effort.

Can we relate this classroom analogy to a work setting? What does expectancy theory say that can help us motivate our employees? Let's summarize some of the issues surrounding the theory. First, expectancy theory emphasizes payoffs or rewards. As a result, managers have to believe that the rewards they offer will align with what the employee wants. As such, it is a theory based on self-interest, wherein each individual seeks to maximize his or her expected satisfaction.[42] Second, expectancy theory stresses that managers understand why employees view certain outcomes as attractive or unattractive. They will want to reward individuals with those things they value positively. Third, the expectancy theory emphasizes expected behaviors. Do individuals know what is expected of them and how they

Expectancy theory is filled with perceptions—relevant or not. The individual's perception of the outcome will determine the effort expended.

will be appraised? Unless employees see this connection between performance and rewards, organizational goals may not be met. Finally, the theory is concerned with perceptions. The facts are irrelevant. An individual's own perceptions of performance, reward, and goal satisfaction will determine his or her level of effort, not the objective outcomes themselves. Accordingly, there must be continuous feedback to align perceptions with reality.

HOW CAN WE INTEGRATE THE CONTEMPORARY THEORIES OF MOTIVATION?

There is a tendency to view the motivation theories in this chapter independently. Doing so is a mistake. Many of the ideas underlying the theories are complementary, and your understanding of how to motivate people is maximized when you see how the theories fit together.[43]

Exhibit 10-11 visually integrates much of what we know about motivation. Its basic foundation is the simplified expectancy model in Exhibit 10-10. Let's work through Exhibit 10-11, beginning at the left.

The individual effort box has an arrow leading into it. This arrow flows out of the individual's goals. This goals-effort loop reminds us that goals direct behavior. Expectancy theory predicts that an employee will exert a high level of effort if he or she perceives a strong relationship between effort and performance, performance and rewards, and rewards and satisfaction of personal goals. Each of these relationships, in turn, is influenced by certain factors. If effort is to lead to good performance, the individual must have the requisite ability to perform, and the performance-evaluation system that measures the individual's performance must be perceived as fair and objective. The performance-reward relationship will be strong if the individual perceives that performance (rather than seniority, per-

Exhibit 10-11 Integrating Theories of Motivation

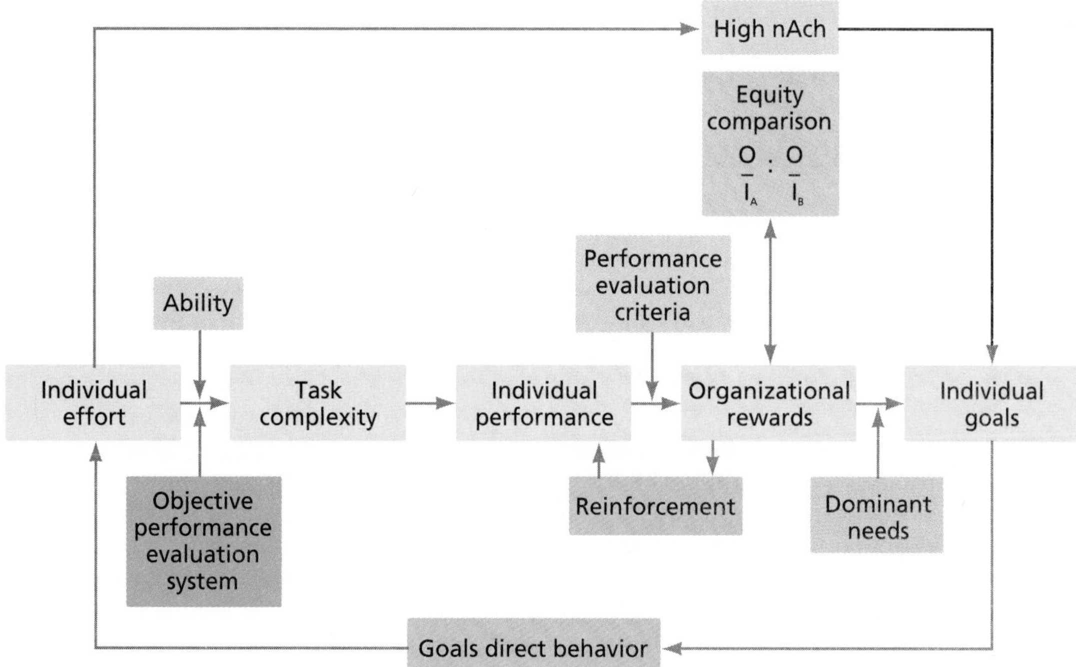

sonal favorites, or other criteria) is rewarded. Thus, if management has designed a reward system that is seen by employees as paying off for good performance, the rewards will reinforce and encourage continued good performance. The final link in expectancy theory is the rewards-goals relationship. Need theories come into play at this point. Motivation is high to the degree that the rewards an individual received for his or her high performance satisfy the dominant needs consistent with his or her individual goals.

A closer look at Exhibit 10-11 will also reveal that the model considers the need for achievement, equity, and the job characteristics model theories. The high achiever is not motivated by the organization's assessment of his or her performance or organizational rewards, hence the jump from effort to individual goals for those with a high nAch. Remember that high achievers are internally driven as long as the jobs they are doing provide them with personal responsibility, feedback, and moderate risks. They are not concerned with the effort-performance, performance-rewards, or rewards-goal linkages. Rewards also play the key part in equity theory. Individuals will compare the rewards (outcomes) they receive from the inputs they make with the input-outcome ratio of relevant others, and inequities may influence the effort expended.

Finally, we can see the JCM in this exhibit. Task characteristics (job design) influence job motivation at two places. First, jobs that score high in motivating potential are likely to lead to higher actual job performance because the employee's motivation is stimulated by the job itself.[44] So jobs that are high in complexity (that is, have motivating potential) increase the linkage between effort and performance. Second, jobs that score high in motivating potential also increase an employee's control over key elements in his or her work. Therefore, jobs that offer autonomy, feedback, and similar complex task characteristics help to satisfy the individual goals of those employees who desire greater control over their work.[45]

If you were a manager concerned with motivating your employees, what specific recommendations could you draw from this integration? Although there is no simple, all-encompassing set of guidelines, we offer the following suggestions, which draw on the essence of what these theories have taught us about motivating employees (see Developing Your Skill at Motivating Employees, p. 338).

Contemporary Issues in Motivation

In this final section, we address some contemporary motivation issues facing today's managers. These include motivating a diversified workforce, pay-for-performance programs, motivating minimum-wage employees, motivating professional and technical employees, and flexible work schedule options.

WHAT IS THE KEY TO MOTIVATING A DIVERSE WORKFORCE?

To maximize motivation among today's diversified workforce, management needs to think in terms of flexibility.[46] For instance, studies tell us that men place considerably more importance on autonomy in their jobs than do women. In contrast, the opportunity to learn, convenient work hours, and good interpersonal relations are more important to women than to men.[47] Managers need to recognize that the motivation of a single mother with two dependent children who is working full time to support her family may be very different from the needs of a young, single, part-time worker or the needs of the older employee who is working to supplement his or her pension income. Employees have different personal needs and goals that they're hoping to satisfy through their job. The offer of various types of rewards to meet their diverse needs can be highly motivating.[48]

How do organizations like Wal-Mart respond to diversity in the organization in an attempt to create a motivating work environment? Wal-Mart managers recognize that each employee is unique, and accordingly has different needs to fulfill. This flexibility in dealing with employees has proven to be a big winner!

Motivating a diverse workforce also means that managers must be flexible enough to accommodate cultural differences. The theories of motivation we have been studying were developed largely by U.S. psychologists and were validated in studies of American workers. Therefore, these theories need to be modified for different cultures.[49] For instance, the self-interest concept is consistent with capitalism and the extremely high value placed on individualism in countries such as the United States. Because almost all the motivation theories presented in this chapter are based on the self-interest motive, they should be applicable to employees in countries such as Great Britain and Australia, where capitalism and individualism are highly valued. In less individualistic nations such as Venezuela, Singapore, Japan, and Mexico the link to the organization is the worker's loyalty to the organization or society rather than his or her self-interest. Employees in such cultures should be more receptive to team-based job design, group goals, and group-performance evaluations. Reliance on the fear of being fired in such cultures is likely to be less effective even if the laws in the respective countries allow managers to fire employees.

The need-for-achievement concept is another aspect of a motivation theory with a U.S. bias. The view that a high need for achievement acts as an internal motivator presupposes the existence of two cultural characteristics: a willingness to accept a moderate degree of risk and a concern with performance. These characteristics would exclude countries with high uncertainty-avoidance scores and high quality-of-life ratings. The remaining countries are, predictably, such countries as New Zealand, South Africa, Ireland, the United States, and Canada that have large populations influenced by British and U.S. cultural norms.

Results, however, of several recent studies among employees in other countries indicate that some aspects of motivation theory are transferable.[50] For instance, the motivational techniques presented earlier in this chapter were shown to be effective in changing performance-related behaviors of Russian textile mill workers. However, we should not assume that motivation concepts are universally applicable. Managers must change their motivational techniques to fit the culture.[51] The technique used by a large department store in Xian, China—singling out and embarrassing the worst sales clerks by giving them awards—may be effective in China,[52] but humiliating employees isn't likely to work in North America or Western Europe.

SHOULD EMPLOYEES BE PAID FOR PERFORMANCE OR TIME ON THE JOB?

What's in it for me? That's a question every person consciously or unconsciously asks before engaging in any form of behavior. Our knowledge of motivation tells us that people act in order to satisfy some need. Before they do anything, therefore, they look for a payoff or reward. Although many different rewards may be offered by organizations, most of us are concerned with earning an amount of money that allows us to satisfy our needs and wants. Because pay is an important variable in motivation, we need to look at how we can use pay to motivate high levels of employee performance. This concern explains the logic behind pay-for-performance programs.

pay-for-performance
Compensation plans such as piece-rate plans, profit sharing, and the like that pay employees on the basis of some performance measure

Pay-for-performance programs pay employees on the basis of some performance measure.[53] Piece-rate plans, gainsharing, wage-incentive plans, profit sharing, and lump-sum bonuses are examples of pay-for-performance programs.[54] What differentiates these forms of pay from the more traditional compensation plans is that instead of paying an employee for time on the job, his or her pay is adjusted to reflect some performance measures. These performance measures might include such things as individual productivity, team or work group productivity, departmental productivity, or the overall organization's profits for a given period.[55]

Performance-based compensation is probably most compatible with expectancy theory. That is, employees should perceive a strong relationship between their performance and the rewards they receive if motivation is to be maximized. If rewards are allocated solely on nonperformance factors—such as seniority, job title, or across-the-board cost-of-living raises—then employees are likely to reduce their efforts.[56]

Pay-for-performance programs are gaining in popularity in organizations. One survey of 1,000 companies found that almost 80 percent of firms surveyed were providing some form of pay-for-performance for salaried employees.[57] The growing popularity can be explained in terms of both motivation and cost control.[58] From a motivation perspective, making some or all of a worker's pay conditional on performance measures focuses his or her attention and effort on that measure, then reinforces the continuation of that effort with rewards. However, if the employee, team, or the organization's performance declines, so, too, does the reward.[59] Thus, there is an incentive to keep efforts and motivation strong. For instance, employees at Hallmark Cards, Inc., in Kansas City, have up to 10 percent of their pay at risk. Depending on their productivity on such performance measures as customer satisfaction, retail sales, and profits, employees can turn that 10 percent into rewards as high as 25 percent.[60] However, failure to reach the performance measures can result in the forfeiture of that 10 percent of salary placed at risk. Companies such as Saturn, Steelcase, TRW, Hewlett-Packard, DuPont, and Ameritech use similar formulas, in which employee compensation is composed of base and reward pay.[61] On the cost-savings side, performance-based bonuses and other incentive rewards avoid the fixed expense of permanent—and often annual—salary increases. The bonuses typically do not accrue to base salary, which means that the amount is not compounded in future years. As a result, they save the company money.

competency-based compensation
A program that pays and rewards employees on the basis of skills, knowledge, or behaviors they possess

A recent extension of the pay-for-performance concept, **competency-based compensation,** is used in such organizations as Amoco Corporation and Champion International.[62] A competency-based compensation program pays and rewards employees on the basis of the skills, knowledge, or behaviors they possess.[63] These competencies may include such behaviors and skills as leadership, problem solving, decision making, or strategic planning. Pay levels are established on the basis of the degree to which these competencies exist. Pay increases in a competency-based system are awarded for growth in personal competencies as well as for the contributions one makes to the overall organization.[64] Accordingly, an employee's rewards are tied directly to how capable he or she is of contributing to the achievement of the organization's goals and objectives.

HOW CAN MANAGERS MOTIVATE MINIMUM-WAGE EMPLOYEES?

Imagine for a moment that your first managerial job after graduating from college involves overseeing a group of minimum-wage employees. Offering more pay to these employees for high levels of performance is out of the question. Your company just can't afford it. What are your motivational options at this point?[65] One of the toughest motivational challenges facing many managers today is how to achieve high performance levels among minimum-wage workers.

One trap many managers fall into is thinking that employees are motivated only by money. Although money is important as a motivator,[66] it's not the only reward that people seek and that managers can use.[67] What are some other types of rewards that managers can use? Many companies use employee recognition programs such as employee of the month, quarterly employee-performance award ceremonies, or other celebrations of employee accomplishment.[68] For instance, at many fast-food restaurants such as McDonald's and Wendy's, you'll often see plaques hanging in prominent places that feature the "Crew Member of the Month." These types of programs highlight employees whose performance has been of the type and level the organization wants to encourage. Many managers also recognize the power of praise, but you need to be sure that these "pats on the back" are sincere and done for the right reasons; otherwise, employees can interpret such actions as manipulative. However, we know from the motivation theories presented earlier that rewards are only part of the motivation equation. We can look to job design and expectancy theories for additional insights. In service industries such as travel and hospitality, retail sales, child care, and maintenance, where pay for front-line employees generally doesn't get much above the minimum-wage level, successful companies are empowering these front-line employees with more authority to address customers' problems. If we use the JCM to examine this change, we can see that this type of job redesign provides enhanced motivating potential because employees now experience increased skill variety, task identity, task significance, autonomy, and feedback. For instance, Marriott International is redesigning almost every job in its hotels to place more workers in contact with more guests more of the time.[69] These employees are now able to take care of customer complaints and requests that formerly were referred to a supervisor or another department. In addition, employees have at least part of their pay tied to customer satisfaction, so there is a clear link between level of performance and reward (a key linkage from expectancy theory). So, even though motivating minimum-wage employees may be more of a challenge, we can still use what we know about employee motivation to help us come up with some answers.

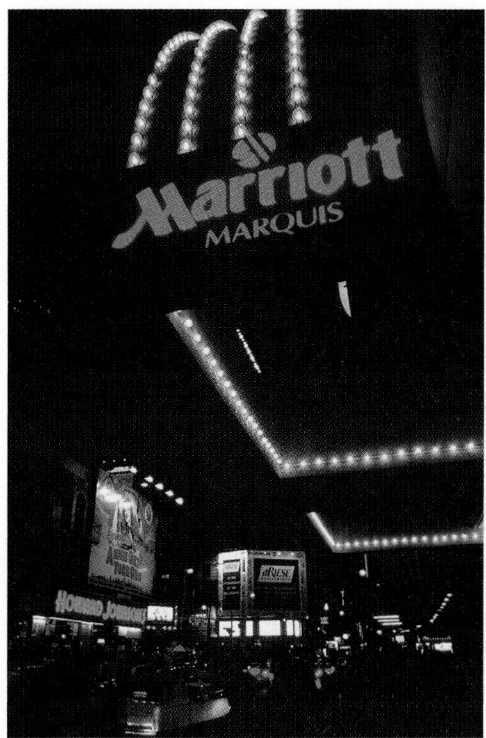

Can an organization attract, hire, and retain low-wage service workers effectively? If you're Marriott Hotels, you can. They've done this by assisting employees in matters that, in some cases, are very personal. For example, they've helped employees learn basic skills, trained them in a variety of jobs, and helped some deal with domestic abuse problems. As a result of their efforts, Marriott employees have a loyalty to the organization, and turnover in the hotel is significantly less than that in comparable companies.

WHAT'S DIFFERENT IN MOTIVATING PROFESSIONAL AND TECHNICAL EMPLOYEES?

Professional and technical employees are typically different from nonprofessionals. They have a strong and long-term commitment to their field of expertise. Their loyalty, however, is more often to their profession than to their employer. To keep current in their field, they need to regularly update their knowledge, and their commitment to their profession or technical field means they rarely define their workweek in terms of 9 to 5 or 5 days a week.

So what motivates these types of employees? Money and promotions into management typically are low on their priority list. Why? They tend to be well paid, and they enjoy what they do. In contrast, job challenge tends to be ranked high. They like to tackle problems and find solutions. Their chief reward is the work itself. Professional and technical employees generally also value support. They want others to think that what they are working on is important.[70]

The above points imply that managers should provide professional and technical employees with new assignments and challenging projects. Give them autonomy to follow their interests and allow them to structure their work in ways they find productive. Reward them with educational opportunities—training, workshops, conferences—that allow them to keep current in their field and to network with their peers. Also reward them with recognition. Managers should ask questions and engage in other actions that demonstrate to their professional and technical employees that they're sincerely interested in what they're doing.

One Manager's Perspective

Michelle Albert Senior Director of Special Marketing, Columbia Records/Sony Music Entertainment, Inc.

Managers often worry about how to motivate the people who report to them. They have, of course, the traditional "carrots" of increased pay, added responsibility, special bonuses, praise, perks, and so on. But how does a manager motivate people over whom he or she has no authority?

Michelle Albert has found some useful answers to this question. At Columbia Records/Sony Music, Inc. she is responsible for marshaling the resources of the firm—including the art director, publicist, radio promotion staff, salespeople, video production crew, and new technology group—on behalf of the new artists she champions. Although none of these professionals report to her, Albert must find ways to keep them focused on the tasks that matter to her (among all other tasks for which they have responsibility).

She's found that "My peers react to me positively and quickly and will go the extra mile in helping an artist on my roster. I believe this is due to my fostering very solid professional relationships based on positive reinforcement and mutual respect."

Persistence and persuasion pay off, too, and so does being a team player. Says Albert, "Others know that I will do whatever I can to pitch in and help, and I receive the same from them."

Because professional and technical employees often work long hours, they frequently have limited time to do typical household chores and errands. As a result, they put a high value on organizational efforts to simplify their nonwork lives. Employees at Wilton Connor Packaging in Charlotte, North Carolina, can take their laundry to work and have it washed, dried and folded courtesy of the company. In addition to on-site laundry service, Wilton Connor has a handyman on staff who does free minor household repairs for employees while they're at work.[71]

An increasing number of companies are creating alternative career paths for these employees—especially companies in highly technical fields such as IT. These allow employees to earn more money and status without assuming managerial responsibilities. At Merck & Co., IBM, and AT&T, the best scientists, engineers, and researchers earn titles such as fellow and senior scientist. Their pay and prestige are comparable to those of managers but without the corresponding authority.[72]

HOW CAN FLEXIBLE WORK OPTIONS INFLUENCE MOTIVATION?

Barry Cunningham is the classic "morning person." He rises each day at 5 A.M. sharp, full of energy. On the other hand, as he puts it, "I'm usually ready for bed right after the 7 P.M. news."

Barry's work schedule as a claims processor at Chubb Insurance is flexible. It allows him some degree of freedom as to when he comes to work and when he leaves. His office opens at 6 A.M. and closes at 7 P.M. It's up to him how he schedules his eight-hour day within this thirteen-hour period. Because Barry is a morning person, shares childcare responsibility with his wife, who works the evening shift at a local food-processing plant, and has a seven-year-old son who gets out of school at 3 P.M., a flexible schedule motivates him. He's at the job when he's most alert and can be home to take care of his son after he gets out of school.

Many employees continue to work an eight-hour day, five days a week. They are full-time employees who report to a fixed organizational location and start and leave at a fixed time. But, consistent with managers' attempts to increase their organizations' flexibility, a number of scheduling options have been introduced to give management and employees more flexibility.[73] In addition to an increased use of temporary workers, an idea that has been around for a long time, these include compressed workweeks, flextime, job sharing, and telecommuting.

What is a compressed workweek? A compressed workweek consists of four ten-hour days (a 4-40 program). Proponents claim that 4-40 programs have a favorable effect on employee absenteeism, job satisfaction, and productivity.[74] A new twist to compressed workweeks is a 9-80 schedule, which started as a way to limit pollution from commuters' cars. For example, at Texaco's headquarters in Harrison, New York, employees work nine hours every Monday through Thursday, eight hours on Friday, and zero hours the next Friday. The flexible schedule provides employees with time off for errands, hobbies, or family matters.[75] Historical studies of organizations that use compressed workweeks, however, have shown such drawbacks as a decrease in workers' productivity near the end of their longer workday, a decrease in service to customers or clients, and unwillingness to work even longer days if a deadline needs to be met, and underutilization of equipment.[76] Because the compressed workweek does have its problems for employees and managers, many organizations have tried a different approach to giving workers increased freedom—flexible work hours.

How does flextime work? Flextime is a scheduling option that allows employees, within specific parameters, to decide when to go to work. Barry Cunningham's work schedule at Chubb Insurance is an example of flextime. But what specifically is it?

Flextime is short for flexible work hours. Employees have to work a specific number of hours a week, but they are free to vary the hours of work within certain limits. Each day consists of a common core, usually six hours, with a flexibility band surrounding the core. For example, exclusive of a one-hour lunch break, the core may be 9:00 A.M. to 3:00 P.M., with the office actually opening at 6:00 A.M. and closing at 6:00 P.M. All employees are required to be at their jobs during the common core period, but they are allowed to schedule their other two hours before or after the core time. Some flextime programs allow extra hours to be accumulated and turned into a free day off each month. Flextime has become an extremely popular scheduling option. For instance, a recent study of Fortune 500 firms found that 77 percent offered employees some form of flextime.[77]

The potential benefits from flextime are numerous. They include improved employee motivation and morale, reduced absenteeism as a result of enabling employees to better balance work and family responsibilities, and the ability of the organization to recruit higher-quality and more diverse employees.[78]

Flextime's major drawback is that it is not applicable to every job. It works well with clerical tasks in which an employee's interaction with people outside his or her department is limited. It is not a viable option when key people must be available during standard hours, when workflow requires tightly determined scheduling, or when specialists are called upon to maintain coverage of all functions in a unit.[79]

Flextime enables employees to better balance work and family responsibilities.

job sharing
A type of part-time work that allows two or more workers to split a traditional 40-hour-a-week job

Can employees share jobs? **Job sharing** is a special type of part-time work. It allows two or more individuals to split a traditional 40-hour-a-week job. So, for example, one person might perform the job from 8 A.M. to noon while another performs the same job from 1 P.M. to 5 P.M., or both could work full, but alternate, days.

Job sharing is growing in popularity, but it is less widespread than flextime. Only about 30 percent of large organizations offer job sharing.[80] Xerox is one such organization. Laura Meier and Lori Meagher share a sales management position at Xerox.[81] Both are mothers of preschoolers and wanted greater flexibility, but they did not want to give up their managerial careers at Xerox. So now Laura oversees their eight sales reps on Thursdays and Fridays; Lori has the job on Mondays and Tuesdays, and the two women work alternate Wednesdays.

Job sharing allows the organization to draw upon the talents of more than one individual for a given job. A bank manager who oversees two job sharers describes it as an opportunity to get two heads while paying for one.[82] It also opens up the opportunity to acquire skilled workers—for instance, women with young children and retirees—who might not be available on a full-time basis.[83] The major drawback, from management's perspective, is finding compatible pairs of employees who can successfully coordinate the intricacies of one job.[84]

telecommuting
A system of working at home on a computer that is linked to the office

What is telecommuting? It might be close to the ideal job for many people. No commuting, flexible hours, freedom to dress as you please, and little or no interruptions from colleagues. **Telecommuting** employees do their work at home on a computer that is linked to their office.[85] Currently, about 16 million people work at home in the United States taking orders over the phone, filling out reports and other forms, and processing or analyzing information.[86] It is presently the fastest-growing trend in work scheduling and is found in such varied organizations as Levi Strauss, Pacific Bell, AT&T, IBM, Johnson & Johnson, American Express, and JC Penney.[87]

For employees, the two big advantages of telecommuting are the decrease in time and stress of commuting in congested areas and the increase in flexibility in coping with family demands. But it may have some potential drawbacks. For instance, will telecommuting employees miss the social contact that a formal office provides? Will they be less likely to be considered for salary increases and promotions? Is being out of sight equivalent to being out of mind? Will non-work-related distractions such as children, neighbors, and the proximity of the refrigerator significantly reduce productivity for those without superior willpower and discipline? Answers to these questions are central in determining whether telecommuting will continue to expand in the future.

PHLIP Companion Web Site

We invite you to visit the Robbins/DeCenzo companion Web site at *www.prenhall.com/robbins* for this chapter's Internet resources.

Chapter Summary

How will you know if you fulfilled the Learning Outcomes on page 311? You will have fulfilled the Learning Outcomes if you are able to:

1 *Describe the motivation process.*
Motivation is the willingness to exert high levels of effort toward organizational goals, conditioned by the effort's ability to satisfy some individual need. The motivation process begins with an unsatisfied need, which creates tension and drives an individual to search for goals that, if attained, will satisfy the need and reduce the tension.

2 *Define* needs.
Needs are internal states that make certain outcomes appear attractive. Because needs may be unfulfilled, people attempt to do something. That "something" is behavior designed to satisfy an unfulfilled need.

3 *Explain the hierarchy of needs theory.*
The hierarchy of needs theory states that there are five needs—physiological (food, water, shelter), safety (freedom from emotion and physical harm), social (affection, belongingness, friendship), esteem (self-respect, autonomy, achievement), and self-actualization (achieving's one's potential)—that individuals attempt to satisfy in a step-like progression. A substantially satisfied need no longer motivates.

4 *Differentiate Theory X from Theory Y.*
Theory X is basically a negative view of human nature, assuming that employees dislike work, are lazy, seek to avoid responsibility, and must be coerced to perform. A Theory X employee is motivated by fear of losing job security. Theory Y is basically positive, assuming that employees are creative, seek responsibility, and can exercise self-direction. A Theory Y employee is motivated by challenging work and empowerment.

5 *Explain the implications of the motivation-hygiene theory.*
The motivation-hygiene theory states that not all job factors can motivate employees. The presence or absence of certain job characteristics or hygiene factors can only placate employees but do not lead to satisfaction or motivation. Factors that people find intrinsically rewarding such as achievement, recognition, responsibility, and growth act as motivators and produce job satisfaction.

6 *Describe the motivational implications of equity theory.*
In equity theory, individuals compare their job's input-outcome ratio with those of relevant others. If they perceive that they are underrewarded, their motivation declines. They may adjust the quantity and quality of their work, leave the organization, or simply compare themselves to another relevant other. When individuals perceive that they are overrewarded, they often are motivated to work harder in order to justify their pay. Oftentimes both quality and quantity of work will increase.

7 *Explain the key relationships in expectancy theory.*
The expectancy theory states that an individual tends to act in a certain way based on the expectation that the act will be followed by a given outcome and on the attractiveness of that outcome to the individual. The theory's prime components are the relationships between effort and performance, performance and rewards, and rewards and individual goals.

8 *Describe how managers can design individual jobs to maximize employee performance.*
Managers can design individual jobs to maximize employee performance by combining tasks, creating natural work units, establishing client relationships, expanding jobs vertically, and opening feedback channels.

9 *Describe the effect of workforce diversity on motivational practices.*
Maximizing motivation in contemporary organizations requires that managers be flexible in their practices. They must recognize that employees have different personal needs and goals that they are attempting to satisfy through work. Managers must also recognize that cultural differences may play a role, too. Various types of rewards must be developed to meet and motivate these diverse needs.

Review and Application Questions

READING FOR COMPREHENSION

1 How do needs affect motivation?

2 Contrast lower-order and higher-order needs in Maslow's needs hierarchy.

3 Describe the three needs in the three-needs theory.

4 What are some of the possible consequences of employees' perceiving an inequity between their inputs and outcomes and those of others?

5 What are some advantages of using pay-for-performance to motivate employee performance? Are there drawbacks? Explain.

LINKING CONCEPTS TO PRACTICE

1 What role would money play in (a) the hierarchy of needs theory, (b) motivation-hygiene theory, (c) equity theory, (d) expectancy theory, and (e) motivating employees with a high nAch?

2 If you accept Theory Y assumptions, how would you be likely to motivate employees?

3 Would an individual with a high nAch be a good candidate for a management position? Explain.

4 What difficulties do you think workforce diversity causes for managers who are trying to use equity theory?

5 Describe several means that you might use to motivate (1) a minimum-wage employee or (2) professional and technical employees. Which of your suggestions do you think is best? Support your position.

Management Workshop

Team Skill-Building Exercise

How Can You Motivate Others?

This exercise is designed to help increase your awareness of how and why you motivate others and to help focus on the needs of those you are attempting to motivate.

STEP 1

Break into groups of five to seven people. Each group member is to individually respond to the following:

Situation 1: You are the owner and president of a 50-employee organization. Your goal is to motivate all 50 employees to their highest effort level.

Task 1: On a separate piece of paper, list the factors you would use to motivate your employees. Avoid general statements such as "give them a raise." Rather, be as specific as possible.

Task 2: Rank (from highest to lowest) all the factors listed in Task 1 above.

Situation 2: Consider now that you are one of the 50 employees who have been given insight as to what motivates you.

Task 3: As an employee, list those factors that would most effectively motivate you. Again, be as specific as possible.

Task 4: Rank (from highest to lowest) all the factors listed in Task 3.

STEP 2

Each member should share his or her prioritized lists (the lists from Tasks 2 and 4) with the other members of the group.

STEP 3

After each member has presented his or her lists, the group should respond to the following questions:

1 Are each individual's lists (Task 2 and Task 4) similar or dissimilar? What do the differences or similarities suggest to you?

2 What have you learned about how and why to motivate others, and how can you apply these data?

Developing Your Skill at Motivating Employees

Maximizing Employee Effort

ABOUT THE SKILL

There is no simple, all-encompassing set of motivational guidelines, but the following suggestions draw on the essence of what we know about motivating employees.

STEPS IN DEVELOPING A SKILL AT MOTIVATING EMPLOYEES[88]

- **Recognize individual differences.** Almost every contemporary motivation theory recognizes that employees are not homogeneous. They have different needs. They also differ in terms of attitudes, personality, and other important individual variables.
- **Match people to jobs.** There is a great deal of evidence showing the motivational benefits of carefully matching people to jobs. People who lack the necessary skills to perform successfully will be disadvantaged.
- **Use goals.** You should ensure that employees have hard, specific goals and feedback on how well they are doing in pursuit of those goals. In many cases, these goals should be participatively set.
- **Ensure that goals are perceived as attainable.** Regardless of whether goals are actually attainable, employees who see goals as unattainable will reduce their effort. Be sure, therefore, that employees feel

confident that increased efforts can lead to achieving performance goals.

- **Individualize rewards.** Because employees have different needs, what acts as a reinforcer for one may not do so for another. Use your knowledge of employee differences to individualize the rewards over which you have control. Some of the more obvious rewards that you can allocate include pay, promotions, autonomy, and the opportunity to participate in goal setting and decision making.
- **Link rewards to performance.** You need to make rewards contingent on performance. Rewarding factors other than performance will only reinforce the importance of those other factors. Key rewards such as pay increases and promotions should be given for the attainment of employees' specific goals.
- **Check the system for equity.** Employees should perceive that rewards or outcomes are equal to the inputs given. On a simplistic level, experience, ability, effort, and other obvious inputs should explain differences in pay, responsibility, and other obvious outcomes.
- **Don't ignore money.** It's easy to get so caught up in setting goals, creating interesting jobs, and providing opportunities for participation that you forget that money is a major reason why most people work. Thus, the allocation of performance-based wage increases, piecework bonuses, employee stock ownership plans, and other pay incentives are important in determining employee motivation.

Practicing the Skill

MOTIVATION

Employees at Zero-Knowledge Systems in Montreal can get their laundry washed, dried, and folded for them at work. At Gymboree Corp.'s California headquarters the benefits include free cookies and mild and daily breaks for "recess." Arcnet, a New Jersey architectural firm, gives the use of a BMW to employees who stay more than a year. The firm believes the car makes a more lasting impression on employees than cash.

All of the following traditional and offbeat benefits are currently offered at various U.S. firms. Rank order them for yourself, putting those that are most likely to motivate you at the top of your list. Now look at your top five choices. How do you think you will rank them in 10 years? Why?

Flextime
Telecommuting
Dental insurance
Tuition refund
Matching gift plan
Vision insurance
Health club
Life insurance
On-site day care
Employee assistance program
Laundry/dry cleaning service
Company car
Subsidized cafeteria
Paid vacation
Profit sharing
Stock purchase plan
Ability to keep frequent flier miles
Pets at work
Management program
Daily naptime
Free snacks/candy
Year-end bonus
Clothing allowance
Flexible spending plan
Free lunch
Retirement plan
Paid sick days
Children's college tuition
Annual birthday gift
Non-work-related courses
Company-sponsored sports team
Free uniform
Transportation voucher
Family picnics and parties
Child and elder care referral services
Benefits for unmarried domestic partners

SOURCES: Kim Clark, "Perking Up the Office," *U.S. News & World Report,* November 22, 1999, p. 73; Lynn Brenner, "Perks that Work," *Business Week Frontier,* October 11, 1999, p. F22–40.

A Case Application

Developing Your Diagnostic and Analytical Skills

INVOLVING FAMILY MEMBERS IN INCENTIVE PROGRAMS

Build a better mousetrap. If you do, the rewards will be yours. That's the cry of the American way of business—looking for the competitive edge that makes your product or service stand out. Richard Gaeta, President of Premier Incentives in Marblehead, Massachusetts, may have just found that edge.[89]

Gaeta recognizes that in today's dynamic organizations, family values play an important role. He clearly understands the connection between a happy family life and high job performance, but he feels that many organizations have overlooked the opportunities their family-oriented programs could offer. Although a variety of family-oriented benefits (flexible work schedules, company-sponsored family events like annual summer picnics, and so forth) are offered, no one has attempted to link them to productivity. Gaeta concluded that such family value programs could drive performance, especially of those in sales positions. Gaeta believes that most organizational incentive programs fail to reach the spouses and that companies should spend money promoting the incentive program to spouses by, for example, mailing home glossy brochures and letting the spouses review them. Then, according to Gaeta, the spouse could become a second boss, "pushing the other spouse" to reach a goal.

Anil Vazirani, a sales manager for Bruce Wilcox Insurance (a division of Mutual of Omaha Insurance), knows exactly what Gaeta is saying. He, too, works in an organization in which his boss believes that family values can and do drive sales performance. At Bruce Wilcox, management promotes a program called "Summer Fun." Insurance agents are rewarded with "Bruce Bucks" for exceeding their sales goals—one Bruce Buck for every dollar of commission earned. The Bruce Bucks are then used in an annual auction to bid for merchandise at the company's annual end-of-summer picnic. With spouses and children rooting them on, agents bid for sporting goods, electronics, camping equipment, and other desirable items with the incentive dollars they've earned. As Vazirani indicates, with the family "lighting a fire under you, there's a desire to win at the auction." And that comes simply by having more Bruce Bucks than another agent.

QUESTIONS

1. What's your reaction to this incentive plan at Bruce Wilcox Insurance? Explain your position.
2. Do you believe that such incentives as the one described at Bruce Wilcox Insurance can be successfully used at other companies? Why or why not? Do special conditions have to exist for such a system to work? Explain.
3. What issues do you see in this case for (a) the Wilcox sales people, (b) their spouses and family members, (c) Anil Vazirani, and (d) Richard Gaeta?
4. What ethical issues, if any, do you believe surface in this case?

Developing Your Investigative Skills

Using the Internet

Visit *www.prenhall.com/robbins* for updated Internet Exercises.

Enhancing Your Writing Skills

Communicating Effectively

1 Develop a two- to three-page response to the following questions. "What motivates me? What rewards can an employer provide that will make me give the extra effort? How realistic is it that I will find such an organization?"

2 Randomly contact 25 fellow students on your campus. Ask them to identify the top three rewards they want from an employer. Keep a log of these responses. Provide a two- to three-page report about your findings. What did the sample respondents indicate they wanted most? Given the responses, which of the motivation theories discussed in this chapter appear to be best supported? Explain your reasoning.

3 Go to *http://www.chartcourse.com* and visit the Web site *Free Articles.* Review two articles in particular: "Build Work Force Using Pride" and "How To Attract, Keep and Motivate Your Workforce." Summarize the key concepts of these articles and relate the premises of both to motivating minimum-wage and technical-service workers.

Eleven

Leadership and Trust

LEARNING OUTCOMES After reading this chapter, I will be able to:

1 Define *leader* and explain the difference between managers and leaders.

2 Summarize the conclusions of trait theories of leadership.

3 Describe the Fiedler contingency model.

4 Summarize the path-goal model of leadership.

5 Explain situational leadership.

6 Identify the qualities that characterize charismatic leaders.

7 Describe the skills that visionary leaders exhibit.

8 Explain the four specific roles of effective team leaders.

9 Identify the five dimensions of trust.

D.L. Rogers Corp., based in Bedford, Texas, owns and operates 54 franchises of Sonic Corp., a chain of fast-food drive-in restaurants. Jack Hartnett, Rogers's president, leads by combining ingredients from both the Stone Age and the New Age.[1]

Hartnett prides himself on knowing everything about his employees—both at work and at home. If they have marital problems or credit-card debt, he wants to know. And he thinks nothing of using that information if he thinks he can help. For instance, how many executives do you know who counsel employees on their sex life? When a wife of one of his managers called Hartnett to say her husband was impotent and didn't know what to do, Hartnett had an answer. He met with the couple in a motel room, where he prodded the fellow to confess to an affair and to beg for forgiveness.

Is Hartnett's style intrusive. Yes! But neither he nor his employees consider it a problem. "There are no secrets here," he says. No subject is too delicate for his ears. And his defense? He's merely doing what any good friend might do. Also, he believes that the more he knows about his workers, the more he can help them stay focused at work and happy at home.

Hartnett plays golf with his managers, sends them personally signed birthday cards, and drops by their homes to take them to dinner. But if you think he's "Mr. Nice Guy," think again. He badmouths academic theories that propose that leaders need to persuade workers to buy in to the leader's vision. Hartnett instructs his employees to "do it the way we tell you to do it." He's perfectly comfortable using the authority in his position to make rules and dish out punishments. One of Hartnett's basic rules is "I will only tell you something once." Break one of his rules twice and he'll fire you.

The managers who work for Hartnett are well compensated for meeting his demanding requirements. His unit managers and regional managers earn an average of $65,000 and $150,000, respectively. This compares with industry averages of $30,000 and $52,700. Moreover, Hartnett's managers are eligible for upwards of a 15 percent bonus program as well as an opportunity to own 25 percent of the company.

Does Hartnett seem inconsistent? Maybe. He believes in openness, integrity, and honesty, but he expects as much as he gives. It's not an option. So he's "your best friend," and, at the same time, he's rigid and autocratic. He admits to purposely keeping everybody slightly off balance "so they'll work harder."

Hartnett's approach to leadership seems to be effective. His per-store revenues are nearly 18 percent higher than the chain's average, and profits are 25 percent above the norm. Moreover, people seem to like working for him. In an industry known for high turnover, Hartnett's managers stay about nine years, compared with an industry average of less than two.

Jack Hartnett's story tells us something about leadership. On one hand, it's the leaders in organizations who make things happen. However, the ways that they do this may differ widely.

Managers Versus Leaders

Let's begin by clarifying the distinction between managers and leaders. Writers frequently use the two terms synonymously. However, they aren't necessarily the same.

Managers are appointed. They have legitimate power that allows them to reward and punish. Their ability to influence is based on the formal authority inherent in their positions. In contrast, leaders may either be appointed or emerge from within a group. Leaders can influence others to perform beyond the actions dictated by formal authority.[2]

Should all managers be leaders? Conversely, should all leaders be managers? Because no one yet has been able to demonstrate through research or logical argument that leadership ability is a handicap to a manager, we can state that all managers should ideally be leaders. However, not all leaders necessarily have capabilities in other managerial functions, and thus not all should hold managerial positions.[3] The fact that an individual can influence others does not mean that he or she can also plan, organize, and control. Given (if only ideally) that all managers should be leaders, we can pursue the subject from a managerial perspective. Therefore, by **leaders** we mean those who are able to influence others and who possess managerial authority.

Not all leaders are managers, nor are all managers leaders.

Trait Theories of Leadership

leaders
People who are able to influence others and who possess managerial authority

trait theories of leadership
Theories that isolate characteristics that differentiate leaders from nonleaders

Ask the average person on the street what comes to mind when he or she thinks of leadership. You're likely to get a list of qualities such as intelligence, charisma, decisiveness, enthusiasm, strength, bravery, integrity, and self-confidence. These responses represent, in essence, **trait theories of leadership.** The search for traits or characteristics that differentiate leaders from nonleaders, though done in a more sophisticated manner than our on-the-street survey, dominated the early research efforts in the study of leadership.

Is it possible to isolate one or more traits in individuals who are generally acknowledged to be leaders—for instance, Herb Kelleher, Cheong Choong Kong, Governor Whitman of New Jersey, Nelson Mandela, or Katherine Graham—that nonleaders do not possess? We may agree that these individuals meet our definition of a leader, but they have utterly different characteristics. If the concept of traits were to prove valid, all leaders would have to possess specific characteristics.

Research efforts at isolating these traits resulted in a number of dead ends. Attempts failed to identify a set of traits that would always differentiate leaders from followers and effective leaders from ineffective leaders. Perhaps it was a bit optimistic to believe that a set of consistent and unique personality traits could apply across the board to all effective leaders, whether they were in charge of the Carolina Panthers Football Team, Nortel, Cedars-Sinai Hospital, Volvo, Bombardier, United Way, or Outback Steakhouse.

However, attempts to identify traits consistently associated with leadership have been more successful. Six traits on which leaders are seen to differ from nonleaders include drive, the desire to lead, honesty and integrity, self-confidence, intelligence, and job-relevant knowledge.[4] These traits are briefly described in Exhibit 11-1.

Yet traits alone do not sufficiently explain leadership. Explanations based solely on traits ignore situational factors. Possessing the appropriate traits only makes it more likely that an individual will be an effective leader. He or she still has to take the right actions. And what is right in one situation is not necessarily right for a different situation. So, although there has been some resurgent interest in traits during the past decade, a major movement away from trait theories began as early as the 1940s. Leadership research from the late 1940s through the mid-1960s emphasized the preferred behavioral styles that leaders demonstrated.

Behavioral Theories of Leadership

The inability to explain leadership solely from traits led researchers to look at the behavior of specific leaders. Researchers wondered whether there was something

Exhibit 11-1 Six Traits That Differentiate Leaders from Nonleaders

1 **Drive** Leaders exhibit a high effort level. They have a relatively high desire for achievement, they're ambitious, they have a lot of energy, they're tirelessly persistent in their activities, and they show initiative.

2 **Desire to lead** Leaders have a strong desire to influence and lead others. They demonstrate the willingness to take responsibility.

3 **Honesty and integrity** Leaders build trusting relationships between themselves and followers by being truthful or nondeceitful and by showing high consistency between word and deed.

4 **Self-confidence** Followers look to leaders for an absence of self-doubt. Leaders, therefore, need to show self-confidence in order to convince followers of the rightness of goals and decisions.

5 **Intelligence** Leaders need to be intelligent enough to gather, synthesize, and interpret large amounts of information and to be able to create visions, solve problems, and make correct decisions.

6 **Job-relevant knowledge** Effective leaders have a high degree of knowledge about the company, industry, and technical matters. In-depth knowledge allows leaders to make well-informed decisions and to understand the implications of those decisions.

SOURCE: Reprinted from "Leadership: Do Traits Really Matter?" by S. A. Kirkpatrick and E. A. Locke by permission of Academy of Management Executive, May 1991, pp. 48–60. © 1991 by Academy of Management Executive.

unique in the behavior of effective leaders. For example, do leaders tend to be more democratic than autocratic?

behavioral theories of leadership
Theories that isolate behaviors that differentiate effective leaders from ineffective leaders

It was hoped that the **behavioral theories of leadership approach** would not only provide more definitive answers about the nature of leadership but, if successful, also have practical implications quite different from those of the trait approach. If trait research had been successful, it would have provided a basis for selecting the right people to assume formal positions in organizations requiring leadership.[5] In contrast, if behavioral studies were to turn up critical behavioral determinants of leadership, we could train people to be leaders.[6] That's precisely the premise behind the management development programs at, for example, Sun Microsystems, the U.S. Postal System, Ernst and Young, Sonoco, and Sears.[7]

A number of studies looked at behavioral styles. We shall briefly review three of the most popular studies: Kurt Lewin's studies at the University of Iowa, the Ohio State group, and the University of Michigan studies. Then we shall see how the concepts that those studies developed could be used to create a grid for appraising leadership styles.

autocratic style of leadership
The term used to describe a leader who centralizes authority, dictates work methods, makes unilateral decisions, and limits employee participation

democratic style of leadership
The term used to describe a leader who involves employees in decision making, delegates authority, encourages participation in deciding work methods and goals, and uses feedback to coach employees

ARE THERE IDENTIFIABLE LEADERSHIP BEHAVIORS?

One of the first studies of leadership behavior was done by Kurt Lewin and his associates at the University of Iowa.[8] In their studies, the researchers explored three leadership behaviors or styles: autocratic, democratic, and laissez-faire. An **autocratic style** is that of a leader who typically tends to centralize authority, dictate work methods, make unilateral decisions, and limit employee participation. A leader with a **democratic style** tends to involve employees in decision making, delegates authority, encourages participation in deciding work methods and goals, and uses feedback as an opportunity to coach employees. The democratic style can be further classified in two ways: consultative and participative. A *democratic-consultative leader* seeks input and hears the concerns and issues of employees but makes the final decision him- or herself. In this capacity, the democratic-consultative leader is using the input as an information-seeking exercise. A *democratic-participative leader* often allows employees to have a say in what's decided. Here, decisions are made by the group, with the leader providing one input to that group. Finally, the **laissez-faire** leader generally gives his or her employees complete freedom to make decisions and to complete their work in whatever way they see fit. A laissez-faire leader might simply provide necessary materials and answer questions.

What traits characterize leaders like Cheong Choong Kong, CEO of Singapore Airlines? Research has identified six: drive, the desire to lead, honesty and integrity, self-confidence, intelligence, and job-relevant knowledge. Using these traits to the best of his ability has made Kong Asia's Businessman of the Year for 1999.

Lewin and his associates wondered which one of the three leadership styles was most effective. On the basis of their studies of leaders from boys' clubs, they concluded that the laissez-faire style was ineffective on every performance criterion when compared with both democratic and autocratic styles. Quantity of work done was equal in groups with democratic and autocratic leaders, but work quality and group satisfaction were higher in democratic groups. The results suggest that a democratic leadership style could contribute to both good quantity and high quality of work.

laissez-faire style of leadership
The term used to describe a leader who gives employees complete freedom to make decisions and to decide on work methods

Later studies of autocratic and democratic styles of leadership showed mixed results. For example, democratic leadership styles sometimes produced higher performance levels than autocratic styles, but at other times they produced group performance that was lower than or equal to that of autocratic styles. Nonetheless, more consistent results were generated when a measure of employee satisfaction was used.

Group members' satisfaction levels were generally higher under a democratic leader than under an autocratic one.[9] Did this mean that managers should always exhibit a democratic style of leadership? Two researchers, Robert Tannenbaum and Warren Schmidt, attempted to provide that answer.[10]

Tannenbaum and Schmidt developed a continuum of leader behaviors (see Exhibit 11-2). The continuum illustrates that a range of leadership behaviors, all the way from boss centered (autocratic) on the left side of the model to employee centered (laissez-faire) on the right side of the model, is possible. In deciding which leader behavior from the continuum to use, Tannenbaum and Schmidt proposed that managers look at forces within themselves (such as comfort level with the chosen leadership style), forces within the employees (such as readiness to assume responsibility), and forces within the situation (such as time pressures). They suggested that managers should move toward more employee-centered styles in the long run because such behavior would increase employees' motivation, decision quality, teamwork, morale, and development.

Exhibit 11-2 Continuum of Leader Behavior

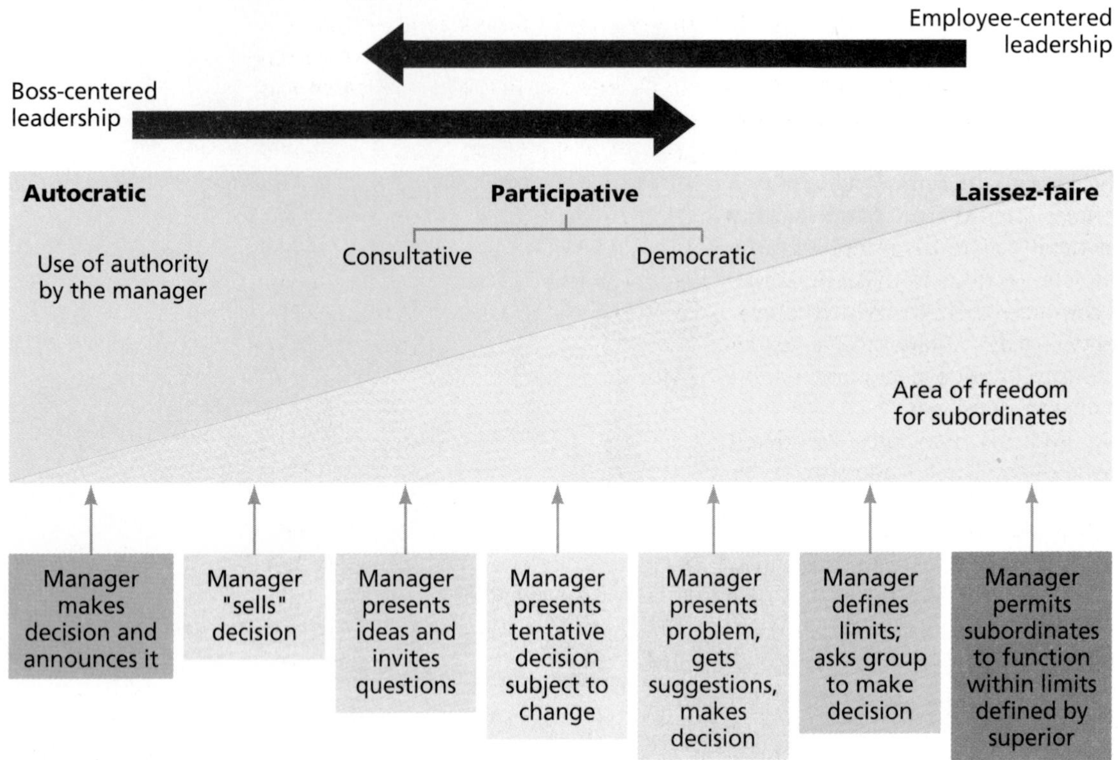

SOURCE: Adapted and reprinted by permission of the Harvard Business Review. An Exhibit from "How to Choose a Leadership Pattern" by R. Tannenbaum and W. Schmidt, May–June 1973. Copyright © 1973 by the President and Fellows of Harvard College; all rights reserved.

This dual nature of leader behaviors—that is, focusing on the work to be done and focusing on the employees—is also a key characteristic of the Ohio State and University of Michigan studies.

WHY WERE THE OHIO STATE STUDIES IMPORTANT?

The most comprehensive and replicated of the behavioral theories resulted from research that began at Ohio State University in the late 1940s.[11] These studies sought to identify independent dimensions of leader behavior. Beginning with over 1,000 dimensions, the researchers eventually narrowed the list down to two categories that accounted for most of the leadership behavior described by employees. They called these two dimensions initiating structure and consideration.

initiating structure
The extent to which a leader defines and structures his or her role and the roles of employees to attain goals

consideration
The extent to which a leader has job relationships characterized by mutual trust, respect for employees' ideas, and regard for their feelings

Initiating structure refers to the extent to which a leader is likely to define and structure his or her role and those of employees in the search for goal attainment. It includes behavior that attempts to organize work, work relationships, and goals. For example, the leader who is characterized as high in initiating structure assigns group members to particular tasks, expects workers to maintain definite standards of performance, and emphasizes the meeting of deadlines.

Consideration is defined as the extent to which a leader has job relationships characterized by mutual trust and respect for employees' ideas and feelings. A leader who is high in consideration helps employees with personal problems, is friendly and approachable, and treats all employees as equals. He or she shows concern for his or her followers' comfort, well-being, status, and satisfaction.

Extensive research based on these definitions found that a leader who is high in initiating structure and consideration (a "high-high" leader) achieved high employee performance and satisfaction more frequently than one who rated low on either consideration, initiating structure, or both. However, the high-high style did not always yield positive results. For example, leader behavior characterized as high on initiating structure led to greater rates of grievances, absenteeism, and turnover and lower levels of job satisfaction for workers performing routine tasks. Other studies found that high consideration was negatively related to performance ratings of the leader by his or her manager. In conclusion, the Ohio State studies suggested that the high-high style generally produced positive outcomes, but enough exceptions were found to indicate that situational factors needed to be integrated into the theory.

WHAT WERE THE LEADERSHIP DIMENSIONS OF THE UNIVERSITY OF MICHIGAN STUDIES?

Leadership studies undertaken at the University of Michigan's Survey Research Center, at about the same time as those being done at Ohio State, had similar research objectives: to locate the behavioral characteristics of leaders that were related to performance effectiveness. The Michigan group also came up with two dimensions of leadership behavior, which they labeled employee oriented and production oriented.[12] Leaders who were **employee oriented** emphasized interpersonal relations; they took a personal interest in the needs of their employees and accepted individual differences among members. The **production-oriented** leaders, in contrast, tended to emphasize the technical or task aspects of the job, were concerned mainly with accomplishing their group's tasks, and regarded group members as a means to that end.

The conclusions of the Michigan researchers strongly favored leaders who were employee oriented. Employee-oriented leaders were associated with higher group productivity and higher job satisfaction. Production-oriented leaders were associated with lower group productivity and lower worker satisfaction.

employee oriented
The term used to describe a leader who emphasizes interpersonal relations, takes a personal interest in the needs of employees, and accepts individual differences

production oriented
The term used to describe a leader who emphasizes the technical or task aspects of a job, is concerned mainly with accomplishing tasks, and regards group members as a means to accomplishing goals

WHAT IS THE MANAGERIAL GRID?

The **managerial grid** is a two-dimensional view of leadership style developed by Robert Blake and Jane Mouton.[13] They proposed a managerial grid based on the styles of "concern for people" and "concern for production," which essentially represent the Ohio State dimensions of consideration and initiating structure and the Michigan dimensions of employee orientation and production orientation.

The grid, depicted in Exhibit 11-3, has nine possible positions along each axis, creating 81 different positions into which a leader's style may fall. The grid does not show the results but rather the dominating factors in a leader's thinking in regard to getting the results. That is, although there are 81 positions on the grid, the five key positions identified by Blake and Mouton focus on the four corners of the grid and a middle-ground area.

Blake and Mouton concluded that managers perform best using a 9,9 style. Unfortunately, the grid offers no answers to the question of what makes an effective leader but only a framework for conceptualizing leadership style. In fact, there is little substantive evidence to support the conclusion that a 9,9 style is most effective in all situations.[14]

managerial grid
A two-dimensional view of leadership style that is based on concern for people versus concern for production

Exhibit 11-3
The Managerial Grid

SOURCE: Adapted and reprinted by permission of the Harvard Business Review. An Exhibit from "Breakthrough in Organization Development" by R. R. Blake, J. A. Mouton, L. B. Barnes & L. E. Greiner November–December 1964, p. 136. Copyright © 1964 by the President and Fellows of Harvard College; all rights reserved.

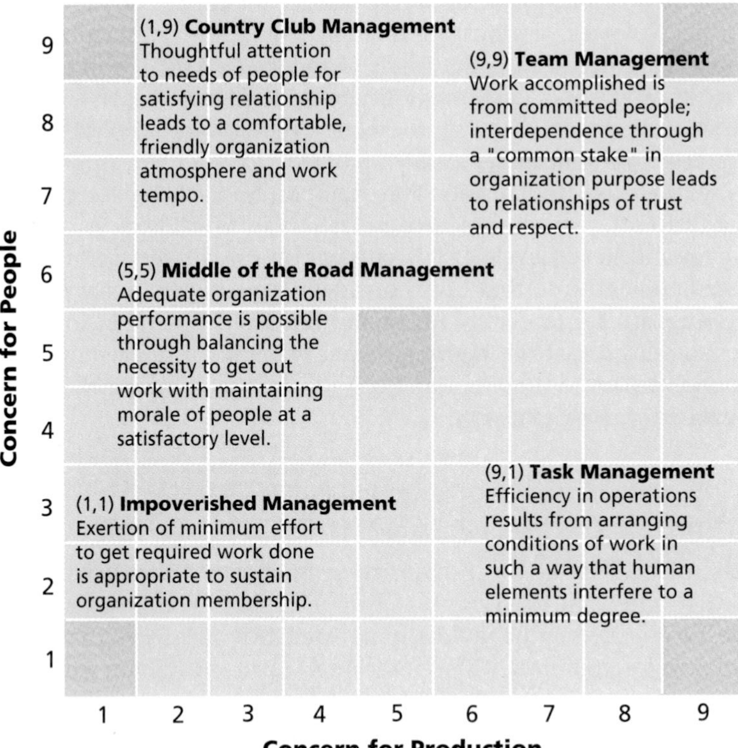

(1,9) Country Club Management
Thoughtful attention to needs of people for satisfying relationship leads to a comfortable, friendly organization atmosphere and work tempo.
(9,9) Team Management
Work accomplished is from committed people; interdependence through a "common stake" in organization purpose leads to relationships of trust and respect.
(5,5) Middle of the Road Management
Adequate organization performance is possible through balancing the necessity to get out work with maintaining morale of people at a satisfactory level.
(1,1) Impoverished Management
Exertion of minimum effort to get required work done is appropriate to sustain organization membership.
(9,1) Task Management
Efficiency in operations results from arranging conditions of work in such a way that human elements interfere to a minimum degree.
Concern for People
9 8 7 6 5 4 3 2 1
1 2 3 4 5 6 7 8 9
Concern for Production

WHAT DID THE BEHAVIORAL THEORIES TEACH US ABOUT LEADERSHIP?

We have described the most popular and important attempts to explain leadership in terms of behavior. There have been other efforts,[15] but they faced the same problem that confronted the early behavioral researchers: They had very little success in identifying consistent relationships between patterns of leadership behavior and successful performance. General statements could not be made because results would vary over different ranges of circumstances. What was missing was a consideration of the situational factors that influence success or failure. For example, would Mother Teresa have been a great leader of the poor at the turn of the century? Would Ralph Nader have risen to lead a consumer activist group had he been born in 1834 rather than in 1934 or in Costa Rica rather than in Connecticut? It seems quite unlikely, yet the behavioral approaches we have described could not clarify such situational factors. These uncertainties the efficacy of certain leadership styles in all situations led researchers to try to better understand the effect of the situation on effective leadership styles.

Contingency Theories of Leadership

It became increasingly clear to students of the leadership phenomenon that predicting leadership success was more complex than isolating a few traits or preferable behaviors. The failure to obtain consistent results led to a new focus on situational influences. The relationship between leadership style and effectiveness suggested that under condition *a,* style X would be appropriate, whereas style Y would be more suitable for condition *b,* and style Z for condition *c.* But what were the conditions *a, b, c,* and so forth? It was one thing to say that leadership effectiveness depended on the situation and another to be able to isolate situational conditions.

Several approaches to isolating key situational variables have proved more successful than others and, as a result, have gained wider recognition. We shall consider four: the Fiedler model, path-goal theory, the leader-participation model, and Hersey and Blanchard's situational leadership theory.

Are Navy Seals born leaders? Probably not. Members of this elite group of the military become leaders in their field by learning what to do and how to do it. Behavioral leadership theorists would say, then, that they are trained in knowing when to focus on results and when to take into account a people orientation.

WHAT IS THE FIEDLER MODEL?

The first comprehensive contingency model for leadership was developed by Fred Fiedler.[16] His model proposes that effective group performance depends on the proper match between the leader's style of interacting with his or her subordinates and the degree to which the situation gives control and influence to the leader.

Fiedler developed an instrument, which he called the **least-preferred coworker (LPC) questionnaire,** that purports to measure the leader's behavioral orientation—either task oriented or relationship oriented. Then, he isolated three situational criteria—leader-member relations, task structure, and position power—that could be manipulated so as to create the proper match with the behavioral orientation of the leader. In a sense, the **Fiedler contingency leadership model** is an outgrowth of trait theory, because the LPC questionnaire is a simple psychological test. Fiedler, however, went significantly beyond trait and behavioral approaches in attempting to isolate situations, relating his personality measure to his situational classification and then predicting leadership effectiveness as a function of the two. This description of the Fiedler model is somewhat abstract. Let's look at it more closely.

least-preferred co-worker (LPC) questionnaire
A questionnaire that measures whether a person is task or relationship oriented

Fiedler contingency model
The theory that effective group performance depends on the proper match between the leader's style of interacting with employees and the degree to which the situation gives control and influence to the leader

Fiedler believed that an individual's basic leadership style is a key factor in leadership success, so he began by trying to find out the leader's basic style using the LPC questionnaire, which contains 16 contrasting adjectives (such as pleasant-unpleasant, efficient-inefficient, open-guarded, supportive-hostile). The questionnaire asks the respondent to think of all the coworkers he or she has ever had and to describe the one person he or she *least enjoyed* working with by rating that person on a scale of 1 to 8 for each of the 16 sets of contrasting adjectives. Fiedler believed that, on the basis of the answers to this LPC questionnaire, he could determine a respondent's basic leadership style. His premise was that what you say about others tells more about you than it tells about the person you're describing. If the least-preferred coworker was described in relatively positive terms (a high LPC score), then the respondent was primarily interested in good personal relations with coworkers. That is, if you essentially described the person you are least able to work with in favorable terms, Fiedler would label you relationship oriented. In contrast, if the least-preferred coworker is seen in relatively unfavorable terms (a low LPC score), the respondent is primarily interested in productivity and thus would be labeled task oriented. Notice that Fiedler assumed that an individual's leadership style is fixed, that is, either relationship oriented or task oriented. This assumption is important because it means that if a situation requires a task-oriented leader and the person in that leadership position is relationship oriented, either the situation has to be modified or the leader replaced for optimum effectiveness. Fiedler argued that leadership style is innate to a person—you *can't* change your style to fit changing situations.

After an individual's basic leadership style has been assessed through the LPC, it is necessary to match the leader with the situation. The three situational factors or contingency dimensions identified by Fiedler are defined as follows:

- **Leader-member relations** The degree of confidence, trust, and respect subordinates have in their leader
- **Task structure** The degree to which the job assignments of subordinates are structured or unstructured
- **Position power** The degree of influence a leader has over power variables such as hiring, firing, discipline, promotions, and salary increases

So, the next step in the Fiedler model is to evaluate the situation in terms of these three contingency variables. Leader-member relations are either good or poor, task structure either high or low, and position power either strong or weak. Fiedler stated that the better the leader-member relations, the more highly structured the job, and the stronger the position power, the more control or influence the leader has. For example, a very favorable situation (in which the leader has a great deal of control) might involve a payroll manager who is well respected and whose subordinates have confidence in him or her (good leader-member relations), where the activities to be done—such as wage computation, check writing, report filing—are specific and clear (high task structure), and the job provides considerable freedom to reward and punish subordinates (strong position power). On the other hand, an unfavorable situation might be that of the disliked chairman of a voluntary United Way fund-raising team. In this job, the leader has very little control. Altogether, by mixing the three contingency variables, there are potentially eight different situations or categories in which a leader could find himself or herself (see Details on a Management Classic). Fiedler concluded that task-oriented leaders perform best in situations that are very favorable or very unfavorable to them. A moderately favorable situation, however, is best handled through relationship-oriented leadership.

path-goal theory
The theory that it is a leader's job to assist followers in attaining their goals and to provide the necessary direction and support

HOW DOES PATH-GOAL THEORY OPERATE?

Currently, one of the most respected approaches to leadership is **path-goal theory.** Developed by Robert House, path-goal theory is a contingency model of leadership that extracts key elements from the Ohio State leadership research and the expectancy theory of motivation (see Chapter 12).[17]

A leader's job is to assist his or her followers in attaining their goals.

The essence of the theory is that it is the leader's job to assist his or her followers in attaining their goals and to provide the necessary direction and support to ensure that their goals are compatible with the overall objectives of the group or organization. The term "path-goal" is derived from the belief that effective leaders clarify the path to help

Details on a Management Classic

Fred Fiedler and the Fiedler Contingency Model of Leadership

The Fiedler contingency model of leadership proposes matching an individual's LPC score and an assessment of the three contingency variables to achieve maximum leadership effectiveness. In his studies of over 1,200 groups, in which he compared relationship- versus task-oriented leadership styles in each of the eight situational categories, Fiedler concluded that task-oriented leaders tend to perform best in situations that are either very favorable or very unfavorable to them (see Exhibit 11-4). Fiedler predicted that, when faced with a category I, II, III, VII, or VIII situation, task-oriented leaders would perform well. Relationship-oriented leaders, however, perform best in moderately favorable situations—categories IV through VI.

Remember that, according to Fiedler, an individual's leadership style is fixed. Therefore, there are really only two ways in which to improve leader effectiveness. First, you can change the leader to fit the situation. For example, if a group situation rates as highly unfavorable to the leader but is currently led by a relationship-oriented manager, the group's performance could be improved by replacing that manager with one who is task oriented. The second alternative would be to change the situation to fit the leader by restructuring tasks or increasing or by decreasing the power that the leader has to control factors such as salary increases, promotions, and disciplinary actions.

As a whole, the major studies undertaken to test the overall validity of the Fiedler model show there is considerable evidence to support it.[18] Even though Fiedler may not have identified all the situational variables that affect leadership, the ones he did identify do appear to contribute substantially to our understanding of situational factors.[19]

Exhibit 11-4 The Findings of the Fiedler Model

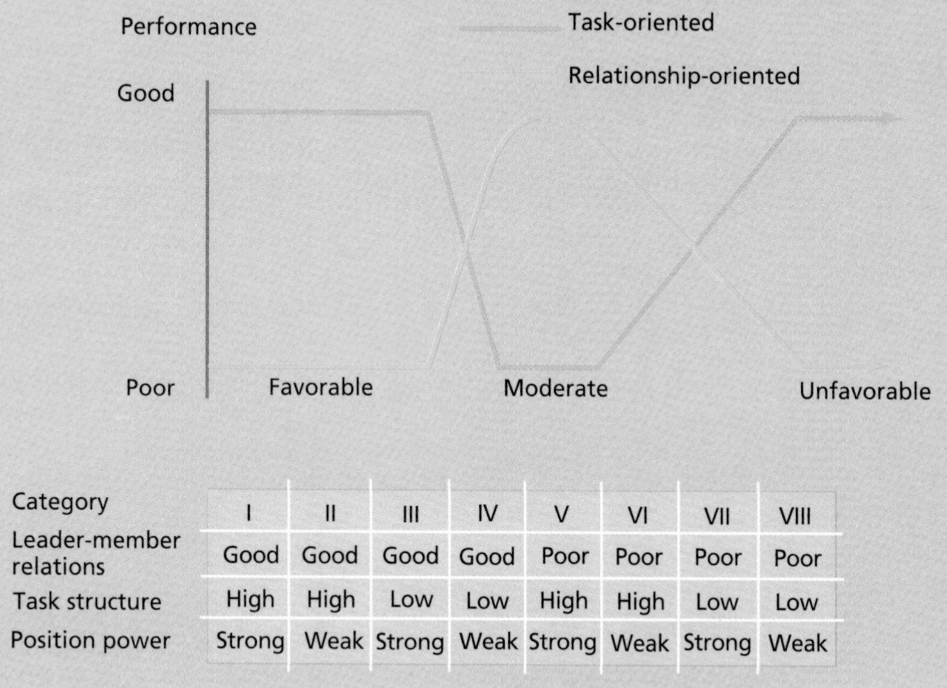

Category	I	II	III	IV	V	VI	VII	VIII
Leader-member relations	Good	Good	Good	Good	Poor	Poor	Poor	Poor
Task structure	High	High	Low	Low	High	High	Low	Low
Position power	Strong	Weak	Strong	Weak	Strong	Weak	Strong	Weak

their followers get from where they are to the achievement of their work goals and make the journey along the path easier by reducing roadblocks and pitfalls.

According to path-goal theory, a leader's behavior is acceptable to the degree that employees view it as an immediate source of satisfaction or as a means of future satisfaction. A leader's behavior is motivational to the degree that it (1) makes employee need satisfaction contingent on effective performance and

Oprah Winfrey, the highly successful talk show host and one of America's leading businesswomen, confirms the path-goal theory of leadership in that a person's leadership is to assist followers in attaining their goals. As a directive leader, Oprah Winfrey lets her staff know precisely what is expected of them, works her employees hard in understanding how to do their jobs, and gives them specific guidance as to how to accomplish their task of being an award-winning entertainment company.

(2) provides the coaching, guidance, support, and rewards that are necessary for effective performance. To test these statements, House identified four leadership behaviors. The *directive leader* lets employees know what is expected of them, schedules work to be done, and gives specific guidance as to how to accomplish tasks. This type of leadership closely parallels the Ohio State dimension of initiating structure. The *supportive leader* is friendly and shows concern for the needs of employees. This type of leadership is essentially synonymous with the Ohio State dimension of consideration. The *participative leader* (à la Lewin's democratic-consultative style) consults with employees and uses their suggestions before making a decision. The *achievement-oriented leader* sets challenging goals and expects employees to perform at their highest level. In contrast to Fiedler's view of a leader's behavior, House assumes that leaders are flexible. Path-goal theory implies that the same leader can display any or all of these leadership styles depending on the situation.[20]

As Exhibit 11-5 illustrates, path-goal theory proposes two classes of situational or contingency variables that moderate the leadership behavior–outcome rela-

Exhibit 11-5
Path-Goal Theory

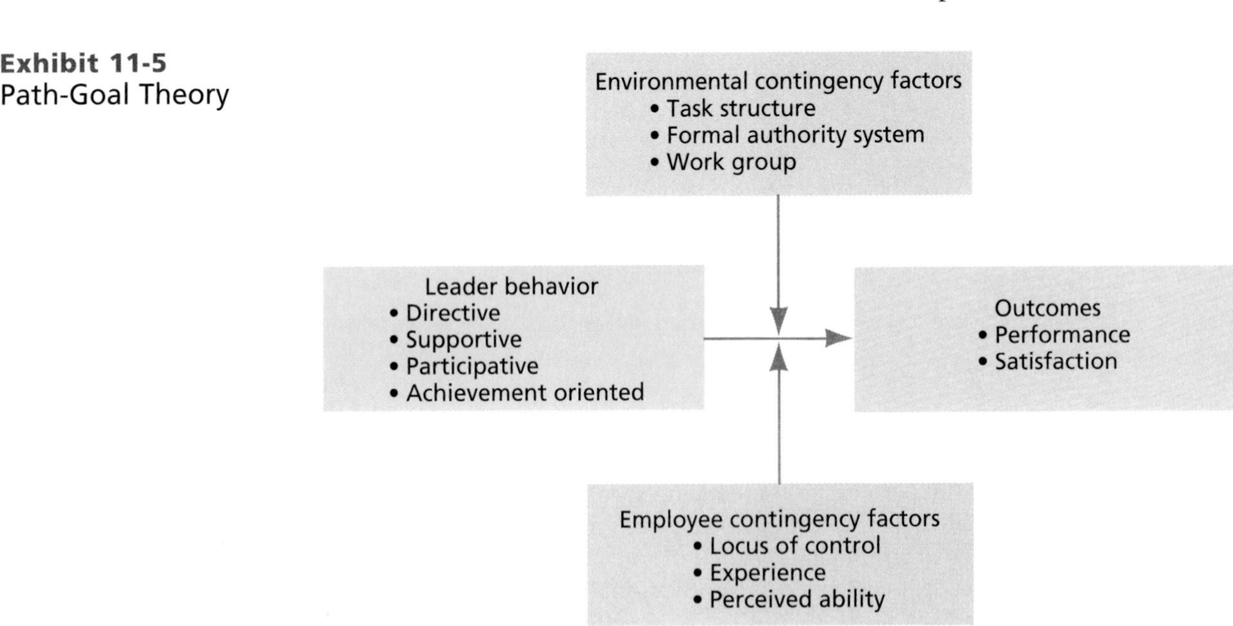

tionship—environmental variables that are outside the control of the employee (task structure, the formal authority system, and the work group) and variables that are part of the personal characteristics of the employee (locus of control, experience, and perceived ability). Environmental factors determine the type of leader behavior required if employee outcomes are to be maximized, and personal characteristics of the employee determine how the environment and leader behavior are interpreted. The theory proposes that leader behavior will be ineffective when it is redundant to sources of environmental structure or incongruent with subordinate characteristics.

Research to validate path-goal predictions has been generally encouraging although not every study found positive support.[21] However, the majority of the evidence supports the logic underlying the theory. That is, employee performance and satisfaction are likely to be positively influenced when the leader compensates for shortcomings with the employee or the work setting. But if the leader spends time explaining tasks when those tasks are already understood or the employee has the ability and experience to handle them without interference, the employee is likely to see such directive behavior as redundant or even insulting.

WHAT IS THE LEADER-PARTICIPATION MODEL?

Back in 1973, Victor Vroom and Phillip Yetton developed a **leader-participation model** that related leadership behavior and participation to decision making.[22] Recognizing that task structures have varying demands for routine and nonroutine activities, these researchers argued that leader behavior must adjust to reflect the task structure. Vroom and Yetton's model was normative. That is, it provided a sequential set of rules to be followed in determining the form and amount of participation in decision making in different types of situations. The model was a decision tree incorporating seven contingencies (whose relevance could be identified by making yes-or-no choices) and five alternative leadership styles.

leader-participation model
A leadership theory that provides a sequential set of rules for determining the form and amount of participation a leader should exercise in decision making according to different types of situations

More recent work by Vroom and Arthur Jago has revised that model.[23] The new model retains the same five alternative leadership styles but expands the contingency variables to twelve—from the leader's making the decision completely by him- or herself to sharing the problem with the group and developing a consensus decision. These variables are listed in Exhibit 11-6.

Research testing the original leader-participation model was very encouraging.[24] But, unfortunately, the model is far too complex for the typical manager to use regularly. In fact, Vroom and Jago have developed a computer program to guide managers through all the decision branches in the revised model. Although we obviously cannot do justice to this model's sophistication in this discussion, the model has provided us with some solid, empirically supported insights into key contingency variables related to leadership effectiveness. Moreover, the leader-participation model confirms that leadership research should be directed at the situation rather than at the person. That is, it probably makes more sense to talk about autocratic and participative situations rather than autocratic and participative leaders. As did House in his path-goal theory, Vroom, Yetton, and Jago argue against the notion that leader behavior is inflexible. The leader-participation model assumes that the leader can adapt his or her style to different situations.[25]

HOW DOES SITUATIONAL LEADERSHIP OPERATE?

Paul Hersey and Kenneth Blanchard's leadership model has gained a strong following among management development specialists. Called **situational leadership theory (SLT),** it shows how a leader should adjust his or her leadership

situational leadership
A model of leadership behavior that reflects how a leader should adjust his or her leadership style in accordance with the readiness of followers

Exhibit 11-6
Contingency Variables in the Revised Leader-Participation Model

SOURCE: V. H. Vroom and A. G. Jago, *The New Leadership: Managing Participation in Organizations* (Upper Saddle River, NJ: Prentice Hall, 1988), pp. 111–12. Reprinted by permission of Prentice Hall, Inc., Upper Saddle River, New Jersey.

QR: Quality Requirement:	How important is the technical quality of this decision?
CR: Commitment Requirement:	How important is employee commitment to the decision?
LI: Leader Information:	Do you have sufficient information to make a high-quality decision?
ST: Problem Structure:	Is the problem well structured?
CP: Commitment Probability:	If you were to make this decision by yourself, is it reasonably certain that your employees would be committed to the decision?
GC: Goal Congruence:	Do employees share the organizational goals to be attained in solving this problem?
CO: Employee Conflict:	Is conflict among employees over preferred solutions likely?
SI: Employee Information:	Do employees have sufficient information to make a high-quality decision?
TC: Time Constraint:	Does a critically severe time constraint limit your ability to involve employees?
GD: Geographical Dispersion:	Are the costs involved in bringing together geographically dispersed employees prohibitive?
MT: Motivation Time:	How important is it to you to minimize the time it takes to make the decision?
MD: Motivation-Development:	How important is it to you to maximize the opportunities for employee development?

style to reflect what followers want.[26] This model has been incorporated into leadership training programs at over 400 of the Fortune 500 companies, and over one million managers a year from a wide variety of organizations are learning its basic elements.[27]

Situational leadership is a contingency theory that focuses on the followers. Successful leadership is achieved by selecting the right leadership style, which Hersey and Blanchard argue is contingent on the follower's level of readiness. Before we proceed, let's clarify two points: Why focus on the *followers?* And what is meant by the term *readiness?*

readiness
The situational leadership model term for a follower's ability and willingness to perform

The emphasis on the followers in leadership effectiveness reflects the reality that it is the followers who accept or reject the leader. Regardless of what the leader does, effectiveness depends on the actions of his or her followers. This important dimension has often been overlooked or underemphasized in most leadership theories. **Readiness,** as defined by Hersey and Blanchard, refers to the extent which people have the ability and the willingness to accomplish a specific task.

Essentially, SLT views the leader-follower relationship as analogous to that of a parent and a child. Just as a parent needs to relinquish control as a child becomes more mature and responsible, so, too, should leaders. Hersey and Blanchard identify four specific behaviors—from highly directive to highly laissez-faire (see Exhibit 11-7). The most effective behavior depends on a follower's ability and motivations. So SLT says if a follower is unable and unwilling, the leader needs to display high task orientation to compensate for the follower's lack of ability and high relationship orientation to get the follower to buy into the leader's desires.

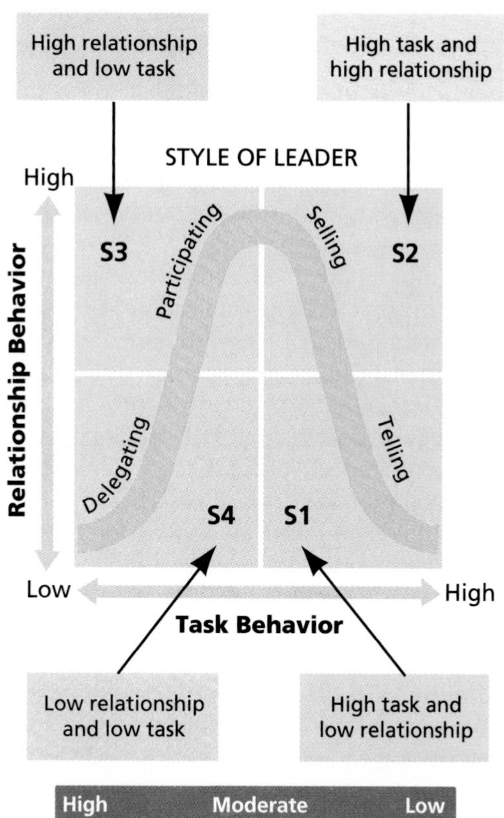

Exhibit 11-7
Hersey and Blanchard's Situational Leadership Model

SOURCE: Reprinted with permission from the Center for Leadership Studies. Situational Leadership® is a registered trademark of the Center for Leadership Studies, Escondido, California. All rights reserved.

At the other end of the readiness spectrum, if followers are able and willing, the leader doesn't need to do much.

SLT has an intuitive appeal. It acknowledges the importance of followers and builds on the idea that leaders can compensate for the lack of ability and motivation of their followers. Yet research efforts to test and support the theory have generally been disappointing.[28] Why? Possible explanations include internal ambiguities and inconsistencies of the model itself as well as problems with research methodology in tests of the theory. So in spite of its intuitive appeal and wide popularity, at least at this point in time, any endorsement of SLT has to be guarded.[29]

Emerging Approaches to Leadership

We'll conclude our review of leadership theories by presenting three emerging approaches to the subject: charismatic leadership, visionary leadership, and transactional versus transformational leadership. If there is one theme that underlies these approaches, it is that they take a more practical view of leadership than previous theories have (with the exception of trait theories, of course). That is, these approaches look at leadership the way the average person on the street does.

WHAT IS CHARISMATIC LEADERSHIP THEORY?

charismatic leadership theory
The theory that followers make attributions of heroic or extraordinary leadership abilities when they observe certain behaviors

In Chapter 10, we discussed attribution theory in relation to perception. **Charismatic leadership theory** is an extension of that theory. It says that followers make attributions of heroic or extraordinary leadership abilities when they observe certain behaviors.[30] Studies on charismatic leadership have, for the most part, attempted to identify those behaviors that differentiate charismatic leaders—the Jack Welches, Elizabeth Doles, and Colin Powells of the world—from their noncharismatic counterparts.[31]

Several authors have attempted to identify personal characteristics of the charismatic leader. Robert House (of path-goal fame) has identified three: extremely high confidence, dominance, and strong convictions.[32] Warren Bennis, after studying 90 of the most effective and successful leaders in the United States, found that they had four common competencies: They had a compelling vision or sense of purpose; they could communicate that vision in clear terms that their followers could readily identify with; they demonstrated consistency and focus in the pursuit of their vision; and they knew their own strengths and capitalized on them.[33] The most comprehensive analysis, however, has been completed by Jay Conger and Rabindra Kanungo at McGill University.[34] They concluded that charismatic leaders have an idealized goal that they want to achieve and a strong personal commitment to that goal, are perceived as unconventional, are assertive and self-confident, and are perceived as agents of radical change rather than as managers of the status quo. Exhibit 11-8 summarizes the key characteristics that appear to differentiate charismatic leaders from noncharismatic ones.

What leadership traits does retired four-star general Colin Powell possess that helped him become the head of the Joint Chiefs of Staff under the George Bush administration? Warren Bennis would state that Powell's traits include his compelling vision, the consistency of his actions, his ability to communicate his vision to others, and the ability to capitalize on his personal strengths.

What can we say about the charismatic leader's effect on his or her followers? There is an increasing body of research that shows impressive correlations between charismatic leadership and high performance and satisfaction among followers.[35] Compared with people working for noncharismatic leaders, people working for charismatic leaders are motivated to exert extra work effort and, because they like their leader, express greater satisfaction.[36] But charismatic leadership may not always be needed to achieve high levels of employee performance. It may be most appropriate when the follower's task has an ideological component.[37] This aspect may explain why charismatic leaders most often surface in politics, religion, or a business firm that is introducing a radically new product or facing a life-threatening crisis. Such conditions tend to involve ideological issues. Second, charismatic leaders may be ideal for pulling an organization through a crisis

1 **Self-confidence** Charismatic leaders have complete confidence in their judgment and ability.
2 **Vision** They have an idealized goal that proposes a future better than the status quo. The greater the disparity between this idealized goal and the status quo, the more likely that followers will attribute extraordinary vision to the leader.
3 **Ability to articulate the vision** They are able to clarify and state the vision in terms that are understandable to others. This articulation demonstrates an understanding of the followers' needs and, hence, acts as a motivating force.
4 **Strong convictions about the vision** Charismatic leaders are perceived as being strongly committed and willing to take on high personal risk, incur high costs, and engage in self-sacrifice to achieve their vision.
5 **Behavior that is out of the ordinary** They engage in behavior that is perceived as being novel, unconventional, and counter to norms. When successful, these behaviors evoke surprise and admiration in followers.
6 **Appearance as a change agent** Charismatic leaders are perceived as agents of radical change rather than as caretakers of the status quo.
7 **Environmental sensitivity** They are able to make realistic assessments of the environmental constraints and resources needed to bring about change.

Exhibit 11-8
Key Characteristics of Charismatic Leaders

SOURCE: Based on J. A. Conger and R. N. Kanungo, "Behavioral Dimensions of Charismatic Leadership," in J. A. Conger and R. N. Kanungo, *Charismatic Leadership* (San Francisco: Jossey-Bass, 1988), p. 91.

but become a liability to an organization once the crisis and the need for dramatic change subside.[38] Why? Because the charismatic leader's overwhelming self-confidence often becomes a problem. He or she is unable to listen to others, becomes uncomfortable when challenged by assertive employees, and begins to hold an unjustifiable belief in his or her "rightness" on issues.[39]

WHAT IS VISIONARY LEADERSHIP?

The term *vision* appeared in our previous discussion of charismatic leadership, but visionary leadership goes beyond charisma. In this section, we review recent revelations about the importance of visionary leadership.

Visionary leadership is the ability to create and articulate a realistic, credible, attractive vision of the future for an organization or organizational unit that grows out of and improves upon the present.[40] This vision, if properly selected and implemented, is so energizing that it "in effect jump-starts the future by calling forth the skills, talents, and resources to make it happen."[41]

visionary leadership
The ability to create and articulate a realistic, credible, attractive vision of the future that grows out of and improves upon the present

A review of various definitions finds that a vision differs from other forms of direction setting in several ways: "A vision has clear and compelling imagery that offers an innovative way to improve, which recognizes and draws on traditions, and connects to actions that people can take to realize change. Vision taps people's emotions and energy. Properly articulated, a vision creates the enthusiasm that people have for sporting events and other leisure-time activities, bringing this energy and commitment to the workplace."[42]

The key properties of a vision seem to be inspirational possibilities that are value centered, realizable, and have superior imagery and articulation.[43] Visions should be able to create possibilities that are inspirational, unique, and offer a new order that can produce organizational distinction. A vision is likely to fail if it doesn't offer a view of the future that is clearly and demonstrably better for the organization and its members. Desirable visions fit the times and circumstances and reflect the uniqueness of the organization. People in the organization must also believe that the vision is attainable. It should be perceived as challenging yet doable. Visions that have clear articulation and powerful imagery are more easily grasped and accepted.

A vision should create enthusiasm, bringing energy and commitment to the organization.

What are some examples of visions? Rupert Murdoch had a vision of the future of the communication industry that combined entertainment and media. Through his News Corporation, Murdoch has successfully integrated a broadcast network, TV stations, movie studio, publishing, and global satellite distribution. Mary Kay Ash's vision of women as entrepreneurs selling products that improved their self-image gave impetus to her cosmetics company. Michael Dell has created a vision of a business that allows Dell Computer to sell and deliver a finished PC directly to a customer in fewer than eight days.

What skills do visionary leaders exhibit? Once the vision is identified, these leaders appear to have three qualities that are related to effectiveness in their visionary roles.[44] First is the *ability to explain the vision* to others. The leader needs to make the vision clear in terms of required actions and aims through clear oral and written communication. Former President Ronald Reagan—the so-called "great communicator"—used his years of acting experience to help him articulate a simple vision for his presidency: a return to happier and more prosperous times through less government, lower taxes, and a strong military. Second is the ability to *express the vision* not just verbally but through the leader's behavior. This requires behaving in ways that continually convey and reinforce the vision. Herb Kelleher at Southwest Airlines lives and breathes his commitment to customer service. He's famous within the company for jumping in, when needed, to help check in passengers, load baggage, fill in for flight attendants or do anything else to make the customer's experience more pleasant. The third skill is the ability to *extend the vision* to different leadership contexts. This is the ability to sequence activities so the vision can be applied in a variety of situations. For instance, the vision has to be as meaningful to the people in accounting as to those in marketing and to employees in Prague as well as in Pittsburgh.[45]

HOW DO TRANSACTIONAL LEADERS DIFFER FROM TRANSFORMATIONAL LEADERS?

transactional leaders
Leaders who guide or motivate their followers toward established goals by clarifying role and task requirements

transformational leaders
Leaders who inspire followers to transcend their own self-interests for the good of the organization and are capable of having a profound and extraordinary effect on followers

The third area we touch on is the continuing interest in differentiating transformational leaders from transactional leaders.[46] As you will see, because transformational leaders are also charismatic, there is some overlap between this topic and our discussion on charismatic leadership.

Most of the leadership theories presented in this chapter—for instance, the Ohio State studies, Fiedler's model, path-goal theory, the leader-participation model, and Hersey and Blanchard's situational leadership model—address the issue of **transactional leaders.** These leaders guide or motivate their followers in the direction of established goals by clarifying role and task requirements, but another type of leader inspires followers to transcend their own self-interests for the good of the organization and is capable of having a profound and extraordinary effect on his or her followers. **Transformational leaders** include such individuals as Orit Gadiesh of Bain & Company, Peter Neff of Rhone-Poulenc, and Jim Clark of Netscape.[47] They pay attention to the concerns and developmental needs of individual followers; they change followers' awareness of issues by helping those followers to look at old problems in new ways, and they are able to excite, arouse, and inspire followers to put out extra effort to achieve group goals.[48]

Transactional and transformational leadership should not be viewed as opposing approaches to getting things done.[49] Transformational leadership is built on transactional leadership. Transformational leadership produces levels of employee effort and performance that go beyond what would occur with a transactional approach alone.[50] Moreover, transformational leadership is more than charisma. "The purely charismatic [leader] may want followers to adopt the charismatic's world view and go no further; the transformational leader will attempt to instill in followers the ability to question not only established views but eventually those established by the leader."[51]

What is it that makes Jim Clark, founder of Netscape, a charismatic leader? Research tells us that he pays attention to the concerns and development needs of his employees; helps his employees look at problems in new ways; and excites, arouses, and inspires employees to put out extra effort to achieve group goals. Given the success of Netscape over the past few years, Clark's results illustrate the benefits that can be achieved by a charismatic leader.

The evidence supporting the superiority of transformational leadership over the transactional variety is overwhelmingly impressive. For instance, a number of studies with U.S., Canadian, and German military officers found, at every level, that transformational leaders were evaluated as more effective than their transactional counterparts.[52] Managers at Federal Express who were rated by their followers as transformational leaders were evaluated by their immediate supervisors as the highest performers and most promotable.[53] In summary, the overall evidence indicates that transformational, as compared with transactional, leadership is more strongly correlated with lower turnover rates, higher productivity, and higher employee satisfaction.[54]

Contemporary Leadership Issues

As you may have deduced from the preceding discussions on the various theories, models, and roles of leadership, the concept of effective leadership is continually being refined as researchers continue to study leadership in organizations (see Ethical Dilemma in Management, p. 362). Let's take a closer look at some of the contemporary issues in leadership: team leadership, leadership and national culture, and the relevance of leadership.

WHAT IS TEAM LEADERSHIP?

Leadership increasingly exists within a team context. As teams grow in popularity, the role of the team leader takes on heightened importance.[55] This role is different from the traditional leadership role performed by first-line supervisors. J. D. Bryant, a supervisor at Texas Instruments' Forest Lane plant in Dallas, found that out.[56] One day he was happily overseeing a staff of 15 circuit-board assemblers. The next day he was informed that the company was moving to teams and that

Ethical Dilemma in Management

Gender Differences in Leadership

Are there gender differences in leadership styles? Are men more effective leaders, or does that honor belong to women? Even asking those questions is certain to evoke emotions on both sides of the debate.

The evidence indicates that the two sexes are more alike than different in the ways that they lead.[57] Much of this similarity is based on the fact that leaders, regardless of gender, perform similar activities in influencing others. That's their job, and the two sexes do it equally well. The same is also true in other professions. For instance, although the stereotypical nurse is a woman, men are equally effective and successful in this career.

Saying the sexes are more alike than different still means the two are not exactly the same. The most common difference lies in leadership styles. Women tend to use a more democratic style. They encourage participation of their followers and are willing to share their positional power with others. In addition, women tend to influence others best through their "charisma, expertise, contacts, and their interpersonal skills.[58] Men, on the other hand, tend to typically use a task-centered leadership style—such as directing activities and relying on their positional power to control the organization's activities." But surprisingly, even this difference is blurred. All things considered, when a woman is a leader in a traditionally male-dominated job (such as that of a police officer), she tends to lead in a manner that is more task centered.[59]

Further compounding this issue are the changing roles of leaders in today's organizations. With an increased emphasis on teams, employee involvement, and interpersonal skills, democratic leadership styles are more in demand. Leaders need to be more sensitive to their followers' needs, be more open in their communications, and build more trusting relationships. And, many of these are behaviors that women have typically grown up developing.

So what do you think? Is there a difference between the sexes in terms of leadership styles? Do men or women make better leaders? Would you prefer to work for a man or a woman? Explain.

he was to become a "facilitator." "I'm supposed to teach the teams everything I know and then let them make their own decisions," he said. Confused about his new role, he admitted "there was no clear plan on what I was supposed to do." In this section, we consider the challenge of being a team leader, review the new roles that team leaders take on, and offer some tips on how to perform effectively in this position.

Many leaders are not equipped to handle the change to teams. As one prominent consultant noted, "even the most capable managers have trouble making the transition because all the command-and-control type things they were encouraged to do before are no longer appropriate. There's no reason to have any skill or sense of this."[60] This same consultant estimated that "probably 15 percent of managers are natural team leaders; another 15 percent could never lead a team because it runs counter to their personality. [They're unable to sublimate their dominating style for the good of the team.] Then there's that huge group in the middle: Team leadership doesn't come naturally to them, but they can learn it."[61]

The challenge for most managers, then, is to become an effective team leader. They have to learn the patience to share information, the ability to trust others and to give up authority, and the understanding of when to intervene. Effective leaders have mastered the difficult balancing act of knowing when to leave their teams alone and when to intercede. New team leaders may try to retain too much control at a time when team members need more autonomy, or they may abandon their teams at times when the teams need support and help.[62]

A study of 20 organizations that had reorganized themselves around teams found certain common responsibilities that all leaders had to assume. These included coaching, facilitating, handling disciplinary problems, reviewing team/individual performance, training, and communication.[63] Many of these responsibilities apply to managers in general. A more meaningful way to describe

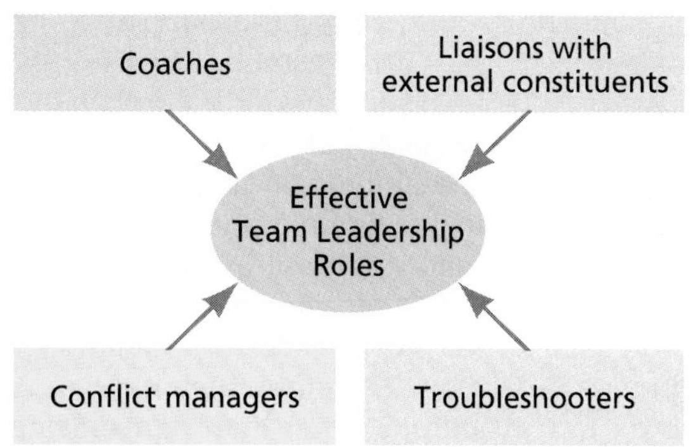

Exhibit 11-9
Team Leader Roles

the team leader's job is to focus on two priorities: managing the team's external boundary and facilitating the team process.[64] We've broken these priorities down into four specific roles (see Exhibit 11-9).

First, team leaders are *liaisons with external constituencies*. These include upper management, other internal teams, customers, and suppliers. The leader represents the team to other constituencies, secures needed resources, clarifies others' expectations of the team, gathers information from the outside, and shares this information with team members.

Second, team leaders are *troubleshooters*. When the team has problems and asks for assistance, team leaders sit in on meetings and help to resolve the problems. This rarely relates to technical or operational issues because the team members typically know more about the tasks than does the team leader. The leader is most likely to contribute by asking penetrating questions, helping the team talk through problems, and getting needed resources from external constituencies. For instance, when a team in an aerospace firm found itself short-handed, its team leader took responsibility for getting more staff. He presented the team's case to upper management and got approval through the company's human resources department.

Third, team leaders are *conflict managers*. When disagreements surface, they help process the conflict. What's the source of the conflict? Who is involved? What are the issues? What resolution options are available? What are the advantages and disadvantages of each? By getting team members to address questions such as these, the leader minimizes the disruptive aspects of intrateam conflicts.

Finally, team leaders are *coaches*. They clarify expectations and roles, teach, offer support, cheerlead, and whatever else is necessary to help team members improve their work performance.

DOES NATIONAL CULTURE AFFECT LEADERSHIP?

We've learned in this chapter that leaders don't use any single style. They adjust their style to the situation.[65] Although not mentioned explicitly in any of the theories we presented, certainly national culture is an important situational factor determining which leadership style will be most effective.[66] We propose that you consider it as another contingency variable. It can help explain, for instance, why executives at the highly successful Asia Department Store in central China blatantly brag about practicing "heartless" management, require new employees to undergo two to four weeks of military training with units of the People's Liberation Army in order to increase their obedience, and conduct the store's in-house training sessions in a public place at which employees can openly suffer embarrassment from their mistakes.[67]

National culture affects leadership style because leaders cannot choose their styles at will: They are constrained by the cultural conditions that their followers have come to expect. Consider the following: Korean leaders are expected to be paternalistic toward employees.[68] Arab leaders who show kindness or generosity without being asked to do so are seen by other Arabs as weak.[69] Japanese leaders are expected to be humble and speak infrequently.[70] And Scandinavian and Dutch leaders who single out individuals for public praise are likely to embarrass those individuals rather than energize them.[71]

Remember that most leadership theories were developed in the United States, using U.S. subjects. Therefore, they have an American bias. They emphasize follower responsibilities rather than rights; assume hedonism rather than commitment to duty or altruistic motivation; assume centrality of work and democratic value orientation; and stress rationality rather than spirituality, religion, or superstition.[72]

As a guide for adjusting your leadership style, you might consider the value dimensions of national culture presented in Chapter 2. For example, a manipulative or autocratic style is compatible with high power distance, and we find high power distance scores in Arab, Far Eastern, and Latin countries. Power distance rankings should also be good indicators of employee willingness to accept participative leadership. Participation is likely to be most effective in such low power distance cultures such as Norway, Finland, Denmark, and Sweden. Not incidentally, this may explain (a) why a number of leadership theories (the more obvious being ones like the University of Michigan behavioral studies and the leader-participation model) implicitly favor the use of a participative or people-oriented style, (b) the emergence of development-oriented leader behavior found by Scandinavian researchers, and (c) the recent enthusiasm in North America for empowerment.

IS LEADERSHIP ALWAYS IMPORTANT?

In keeping with the contingency spirit, we conclude this section by offering this opinion: The belief that a particular leadership style will always be effective regardless of the situation may not be true. Leadership may not always be important. Data from numerous studies demonstrate that, in many situations, any behaviors a leader exhibits are irrelevant. Certain individual, job, and organizational variables can act as "substitutes for leadership," negating the influence of the leader.[73]

For instance, characteristics of employees such as experience, training, professional orientation, or need for independence can neutralize the effect of leadership. These characteristics can replace the need for a leader's support or ability to create structure and reduce task ambiguity. Similarly, jobs that are inherently unambiguous and routine or that are intrinsically satisfying may place fewer demands on the leadership variable. Finally, such organizational characteristics as explicit formalized goals, rigid rules and procedures, or cohesive work groups can act in the place of formal leadership.

Building Trust: The Essence of Leadership

Trust, or lack of trust, is an increasingly important issue in today's organizations. We briefly introduced you to trust in Chapter 9 in our discussion of high-performing work teams. In this chapter, we want to further explore this issue of trust by defining what trust is and show you how trust is a vital component of effective leadership.

WHAT IS TRUST?

Imagine you're the new CEO of a multi-billion dollar corporation. You're succeeding the founder's son-in-law who held the position for more than 33 years—growing it to the company that it is today. Your predecessor was dynamic. You're considered mellow and laid back. And he's not really leaving, just going to the position of Chairman of the Board to "keep an eye" on things. How would you feel and what should you do? Well, that's exactly what Robert E. Brown, CEO of Bombardier, the Canadian-based manufacturer of such products as snowmobiles, rail cars, and aircraft had to ask. His answer is *trust*. By building trust with his employees—focusing on his integrity, competence, consistency, loyalty, and openness—his transition will be made that much easier.

Trust is a positive expectation that another will not—through words, actions, or decisions—act opportunistically.[74] Most important, trust implies familiarity and risk.

The phrase *positive expectation* in our definition assumes knowledge of and familiarity with the other party. Trust is a history-dependent process based on relevant but limited samples of experience.[75] It takes time to form, building incrementally and accumulating (see Developing Your Trust-Building Skill, p. 372). Most of us find it hard, if not impossible, to trust someone immediately if we don't know anything about them. At the extreme, in the case of total ignorance, we can gamble but we can't trust.[76] But as we get to know someone and the relationship matures, we gain confidence in our ability to make a positive expectation.

The word *opportunistically* refers to the inherent risk and vulnerability in any trusting relationship. Trust involves making oneself vulnerable as when, for example, we disclose intimate information or rely on another's promises.[77] By its very nature, trust provides the opportunity to be disappointed or to be taken advantage of.[78] But trust is not taking risk per se; rather it is a *willingness* to take risk.[79] So when we trust someone, we expect that they will not take advantage of us. This willingness to take risks is common to all trust situations.[80]

trust
The belief in the integrity, character, and ability of a leader

What are the key dimensions that underlie the concept of trust? Recent evidence has identified five: integrity, competence, consistency, loyalty, and openness[81] (see Exhibit 11-10).

Integrity refers to honesty, conscientiousness, and truthfulness.[82] Of all five dimensions, this one seems to be most critical. "Without a perception of the other's 'moral character' and 'basic honesty,' other dimensions of trust [are] meaningless."[83]

Exhibit 11-10
Five Dimensions of Trust

■ Integrity	Honesty and truthfulness
■ Competence	Technical and interpersonal knowledge and skills
■ Consistency	Reliability, predictability, and good judgment
■ Loyalty	Willingness to protect and save face for a person
■ Openness	Willingness to share ideas and information freely

Source: Adapted and reproduced with permission of publisher from: Butler, J. K., Jr. and Cantrell, R. S. "A Behavioral Decision Theory Approach to Modeling Dyadic Trust in Superiors and Subordinates."

Competence encompasses an individual's technical and interpersonal knowledge and skills. Does the person know what he or she is talking about? You're unlikely to listen to or depend upon someone whose abilities you don't respect. You need to believe that a person has the skills and abilities to carry out what he or she says they will do.

Consistency relates to an individual's reliability, predictability, and good judgment in handling situations. "Inconsistencies between words and action decrease trust."[84] This dimension is particularly relevant for managers. "Nothing is noticed more quickly . . . than a discrepancy between what executives preach and what they expect their associates to practice."[85]

Loyalty is the willingness to protect and save face for another person. Trust requires that you can depend on someone not to act opportunistically.

The final dimension of trust is *openness*. Can you rely on the person to give you the full truth?

WHY IS TRUST ONE FOUNDATION OF LEADERSHIP?

Trust appears to be a primary attribute associated with leadership. In fact, if you look back at our discussion of leadership traits, honesty and integrity were found to be among the six traits consistently associated with leadership.

As one author noted: "Part of the leader's task has been, and continues to be, working with people to find and solve problems, but whether leaders gain access to the knowledge and creative thinking they need to solve problems depends on how much people trust them. Trust and trust-worthiness modulate the leader's access to knowledge and cooperation."[86]

When followers trust a leader, they are willing to be vulnerable to the leader's actions—confident that their rights and interests will not be abused.[87] People are unlikely to look up to or follow someone who they perceive as dishonest or who is likely to take advantage of them. Honesty, for instance, consistently ranks at the top of most lists of characteristics admired in leaders. "Honesty is absolutely essential to leadership. If people are going to follow someone willingly, whether it be into battle or into the boardroom, they first want to assure themselves that the person is worthy of their trust."[88]

Now, more than ever, managerial and leadership effectiveness depends on the ability to gain the trust of followers.[89] For instance, work process engineering, downsizing, and the increased use of temporary employees have undermined a lot of employees' trust in management. A recent survey of employees by a firm in Chicago found 40 percent agreed with the statement: "I often don't believe what management says."[90] In times of change and instability, people turn to personal relationships for guidance, and the quality of these relationships are largely determined by level of trust. Moreover, contemporary management practices such as empowerment and the use of work teams require trust to be effective.

WHAT ARE THE THREE TYPES OF TRUST?

There are three types of trust in organizational relationships: *deterrence*-based, *knowledge*-based, and *identification*-based.[91] Let's briefly look at each of these.

deterrence-based trust
Trust based on fear of reprisal if the trust is violated

Deterrence-based trust The most fragile relationships are based on **deterrence-based trust.** One violation or inconsistency can destroy the relationship. This form of trust is based on fear of reprisal if the trust is violated. Individuals who are in this type of relationship act because they fear the consequences of not following through on their obligations.

One Manager's Perspective

Betsy Reifsnider Executive Director, Friends of the River

Friends of the River, in Sacramento, California, is a conservation group staffed by both paid professionals and unpaid volunteers. Its many projects are dependent on a strong fundraising program. Betsy Reifsnider's primary responsibility is setting the budget and ensuring it is met, as well as working with the conservation director to develop new programs.

A low-key manager, Reifsnider allows her staff a great deal of autonomy, which she feels contributes to high morale, productivity, and creativity as well as creating a team environment of mutual commitment and trust. She intervenes with direction or authority as little as possible; one result is that when she does require specific action, her team knows she is serious about it. In weekly meetings with her more senior managers Betsy discusses budget, personnel, and management issues, but she also encourages all staff members to come to her with any problems. Trust is reinforced by the confidentiality in which she holds these conversations. She has a simple rule: "I do not violate their confidences."

Reifsnider also stops at people's desks during the day to chat with them about their work. Keeping up to date also earns the trust of employees, who know from her quiet interest that she shares a stake in their success.

Deterrence-based trust will work only to the degree that punishment is possible, consequences are clear, and the punishment is actually imposed if the trust is violated. To be sustained, the potential loss of future interaction with the other party must outweigh the profit potential that comes from violating expectations. Moreover, the potentially harmed party must be willing to introduce harm (for example, I have no qualms about speaking badly of you if you betray my trust) to the person acting distrustingly.

Most new relationships begin on a base of deterrence. Take, as an illustration, a situation of selling your car to a friend of a friend. You don't know the buyer. You might be motivated to refrain from telling this buyer about all the problems that you know the car has. Such behavior would increase your chances of selling the car and securing the highest price. However, you don't withhold information; you openly share the car's flaws. Why? Probably because of fear of reprisal. If the buyer later thinks you deceived him, he is likely to share this with your mutual friend. If you knew that the buyer would never say anything to the mutual friend, you might be tempted to take advantage of the opportunity. If it's clear that the buyer would tell and that your mutual friend would think considerably less of you for taking advantage of this buyer-friend, your honesty could be explained in deterrence terms.

Another example of deterrence-based trust is a new manager-employee relationship. As an employee, you typically trust a new boss even though there is little experience to base that trust on. The bond that creates this trust lies in the authority held by the boss and the punishment he or she can impose if you fail to fulfill your job-related obligations.

knowledge-based trust Trust based on the behavioral predictability that comes from a history of interaction

Knowledge-based trust Most organizational relationships are rooted in **knowledge-based trust.** That is, trust is based on the behavioral predictability that comes from a history of interaction. It exists when you understand someone well enough to be able to accurately predict his or her behavior.

Knowledge-based trust relies on information rather than deterrence. Knowledge of the other party and predictability of his or her behavior replaces the contracts, penalties, and legal arrangements more typical of deterrence-based trust. This knowledge develops over time, largely as a function of experience that builds confidence of trustworthiness and predictability. The better you know someone, the more accurately you can predict what he or she will do. Predictability enhances trust even if the other person is predictably untrustworthy because the ways that the other will violate the trust can be predicted. The more communication and regular interaction you have with someone, the more this form of trust can be developed and depended upon.

Interestingly, at the knowledge-based level, trust is not necessarily broken by inconsistent behavior. If you believe you can adequately explain or understand another's apparent violation, you can accept it, forgive the person, and move on in the relationship. However, the same inconsistency at the deterrence level is likely to irrevocably break the trust.

In an organizational context, most manager-employee relationships are knowledge based. Both parties have enough experience working with each other to know what to expect. A long history of consistently open and honest interactions, for instance, is not likely to be permanently destroyed by a single violation.

Identification-based trust The highest level of trust is achieved when there is an emotional connection between the parties. It allows one party to act as an agent for the other and substitute for that person in interpersonal transactions. This is called **identification-based trust.** Trust exists because the parties understand each other's intentions and appreciate the other's wants and desires. This mutual understanding is developed to the point that each can effectively act for the other.

identification-based trust
Trust based on an emotional connection between the parties

Controls are minimal at this level. You don't need to monitor the other party because unquestioned loyalty exists.

The best example of identification-based trust is a long-term, happily married couple. A spouse comes to learn what's important to his or her partner and anticipates those actions. The partner, in turn, takes this for granted. Increased identification enables each to think like the other, feel like the other, and respond like the other.

You see identification-based trust occasionally in organizations among people who have worked together for long periods of time and have a depth of experience that allows them to know each other inside and out. This is also the type of trust that managers ideally seek in teams. Team members are so comfortable and trusting of each other that they can anticipate each other and freely act in each's absence. Realistically, in the current work world, most large corporations have broken the bonds of identification trust they may have built with long-term employees. Broken promises have led to a breakdown in what was, at one time, a bond of unquestioned loyalty. It's likely to have been replaced with knowledge-based trust.

PHLIP Companion Web Site

We invite you to visit the Robbins/DeCenzo companion Web site at *www.prenhall.com/robbins* for this chapter's Internet resources.

Chapter Summary

How will you know if you fulfilled the Learning Outcomes on page 343? You will have fulfilled the Learning Outcomes if you are able to:

1 *Define* leader *and explain the difference between managers and leaders.*
A leader is able to influence others. Managers are appointed. They have legitimate power that allows them to reward and punish, and their ability to influence is founded upon the formal authority inherent in their positions. Leaders may either be appointed or emerge from within a group. Leaders can influence others to perform beyond the actions dictated by formal authority.

2 *Summarize the conclusions of trait theories of leadership.*
Six traits have been found on which leaders differ from nonleaders—drive (exerting high energy levels), the desire to lead (wanting to influence others and willingness to take responsibility), honesty and integrity (being truthful and nondeceitful, and being consistent in one's actions), self-confidence (an absence of self-doubt), intelligence (ability to gather, synthesize, and interpret large amounts of information), and job-relevant knowledge (knowledge about the company and the industry to assist in making well-informed decisions). Yet possession of these traits is no guarantee of leadership because one can't ignore situational factors.

3 *Describe the Fiedler contingency model.*
Fiedler's contingency model of leadership focuses on the belief that an individual's basic leadership style is a key factor in leadership success. To determine one's basic style, Fiedler created the least-preferred coworker questionnaire—containing 16 contrasting adjectives. Fiedler's contingency model identifies three situational variables: leader-member relations, task structure, and position power. In situations that are highly favorable or highly unfavorable, task-oriented leaders tend to perform best. In moderately favorable or unfavorable situations, relations-oriented leaders are preferred.

4 *Summarize the path-goal model of leadership.*
The path-goal model proposes two classes of contingency variables—those in the environment and those that are part of the personal characteristics of the subordinate. Leaders select a specific type of behavior—directive, supportive, participative, or achievement oriented—that is congruent with the demands of the environment and the characteristics of the subordinate.

5 *Explain situational leadership.*
Situational leadership theory, developed by Hersey and Blanchard, proposes four leadership styles—telling, selling, participating, and delegating. Which style a leader chooses to use depends on the followers' readiness—their willingness and

ability to do the job. As followers reach higher levels of readiness, the leader responds by reducing control over and involvement with the employee.

6 *Identify the qualities that characterize charismatic leaders.*
Charismatic leaders are self-confident (assured of their actions), possess a vision of a better future (have an idealized goal for a better future), articulate the vision (clearly state the vision to others in understandable terms), have a strong belief in that vision (willing to take high personal risk to achieve the vision), engage in unconventional behaviors (focus on behaviors that are novel, unconventional, and counter to norms), are perceived as agents of radical change (don't accept the status quo), and are sensitive to the environment around them (make realistic assessments of the constraints they'll face and the resources they'll need to achieve their vision).

7 *Describe the skills that visionary leaders exhibit.*
Several skills are associated with visionary leaders. Although possessing these skills is not a guarantee that someone will be a visionary leader, visionary leaders typically exhibit them frequently. The skills include: (1) having the ability to explain, both orally and in writing, the vision to others in a way that is clear in terms of required actions; (2) having the ability to express the vision through one's behavior so it reinforces to organizational members the importance of the vision; and (3) being able to extend the vision to different leadership contexts, gaining commitment and understanding from organizational members regardless of their department affiliation or their location.

8 *Explain the four specific roles of effective team leaders.*
Team leaders oftentimes have a variety of responsibilities. To be effective in their jobs, team leaders need to be involved in four specific roles. These are liaisons with external constituencies (representing the team to other constituencies, both internal and external to the organization), troubleshooters (sitting in on meetings to assist in resolving problems that arise for team members), conflict managers (helping to process the disagreement that surface among team members), and coaches (clarifying expectations and roles, teaching, cheerleading, and offering support to team members).

9 *Identify the five dimensions of trust.*
The five dimensions of trust include integrity, competence, consistency, loyalty, and openness. *Integrity* refers to one's honesty and truthfulness. *Competence* involves an individual's technical and interpersonal knowledge and skills. *Consistency* relates to an individual's reliability, predictability, and good judgement in handling situations. *Loyalty* is an individual's willingness to protect and save face for another person. *Openness* means that you can rely on the individual to give you the whole truth.

Review and Application Questions

READING FOR COMPREHENSION

1. Discuss the strengths and weaknesses of the trait theory of leadership.
2. What is the managerial grid? Contrast this approach to leadership with that developed by the Ohio State and Michigan groups.

3 How is a least-preferred coworker determined? What is the importance of one's LPC for the Fiedler theory of leadership?

4 What are the contingencies of the path-goal theory of leadership?

5 What similarities, if any, can you find among Fiedler's model, path-goal theory, and Hersey and Blanchard's situational leadership?

6 How might leadership in Japan contrast with leadership in the United States or Canada?

LINKING CONCEPTS TO PRACTICE

1 "All managers should be leaders, but not all leaders should be managers." Do you agree or disagree with that statement? Support your position.

2 Do you think trust evolves out of an individual's personal characteristics or out of specific situations? Explain.

3 "Charismatic leadership is always appropriate in organizations." Do you agree or disagree? Support your position.

4 Contrast the three types of trust. Relate them to your experience in personal relationships.

5 When might leaders be irrelevant?

Team Skill-Building Exercise

The Pre-Post Leadership Assessment

OBJECTIVE

To compare characteristics intuitively related to leadership with leadership characteristics found in leadership theory.

PROCEDURE

Identify three people (e.g., friends, relatives, previous boss, public figures, etc.) whom you consider to be outstanding leaders. List why you feel each individual is a good leader. Compare your lists of the three individuals. Which traits, if any, are common to all three? Your instructor will lead the class in a discussion of leadership characteristics based on your lists. Students will call out what they identified, and your instructor will write the traits on the chalkboard. When all students have shared their lists, class discussion will focus on the following:

1. What characteristics consistently appeared on students' lists?
2. Were these characteristics more trait oriented or behavior oriented?
3. Under what situations were these characteristics useful?
4. What, if anything, does this exercise suggest about leadership attributes?

Developing Your Trust-Building Skill

Building Trust

ABOUT THE SKILL

Given the importance trust plays in the leadership equation, today's leaders should actively seek to build trust with their followers. Here are some suggestions for achieving that goal.[92]

STEPS IN THE TRUST-BUILDING SKILL

- **Practice openness** Mistrust comes as much from what people don't know as from what they do know. Openness leads to confidence and trust. So keep people informed; make clear the criteria on how decisions are made; explain the rationale for your decisions; be candid about problems; and fully disclose relevant information.
- **Be fair** Before making decisions or taking actions, consider how others will perceive them in terms of objectivity and fairness. Give credit where credit is due; be objective and impartial in performance appraisals; and pay attention to equity perceptions in reward distributions.
- **Speak your feelings** Leaders who convey only hard facts come across as cold and distant. When you share your feelings, others will see you as real and human. They will know who you are and their respect for you will increase.
- **Tell the truth** If honesty is critical to credibility, you must be perceived as someone who tells the truth. Followers are more tolerant of being told something they "don't want to hear" than of finding out that their leader lied to them.
- **Be consistent** People want predictability. Mistrust comes from not knowing what to expect. Take the time to think about your values and beliefs. Then let them consistently guide your decisions. When you know your central purpose, your actions will follow accordingly, and you will project a consistency that earns trust.
- **Fulfill your promises** Trust requires that people believe that you are dependable. So you need to keep your word. Promises made must be promises kept.

- **Maintain confidences** You trust those whom you believe to be discrete and whom you can rely on. If people make themselves vulnerable by telling you something in confidence, they need to feel assured that you won't discuss it with others or betray that confidence. If people perceive you as someone who leaks personal confidences or someone who can't be depended on, you won't be perceived as trustworthy.
- **Demonstrate confidence** Develop the admiration and respect of others by demonstrating technical and professional ability. Pay particular attention to developing and displaying your communication, negotiating, and other interpersonal skills.

Practicing the Skill

TRUST BUILDING

You are a new manager. Your predecessor, who was very popular and who is still with your firm, concealed from your team how far behind they are on their goals this quarter. As a result, your team members are looking forward to a promised day off that they are not entitled to and will not be getting.

It's your job to tell them the bad news. How will you do it?

A Case Application

Developing Your Diagnostic and Analytical Skills

HIROSKI OKUDA AT TOYOTA

Hiroski Okuda isn't afraid to speak his mind nor impose radical change in an organization. And because of these traits, he sticks out in Toyota, where he is the chairman of the board. Prior to becoming chairman, Okuda served as Toyota's president—the first nonfamily member in over 30 years to head the company. He also sticks out in his executive circles, because in Japan executives are suppose to be unseen. Okuda justifies his outspoken and aggressive style as necessary to change a company that has become lethargic and overly bureaucratic.[93]

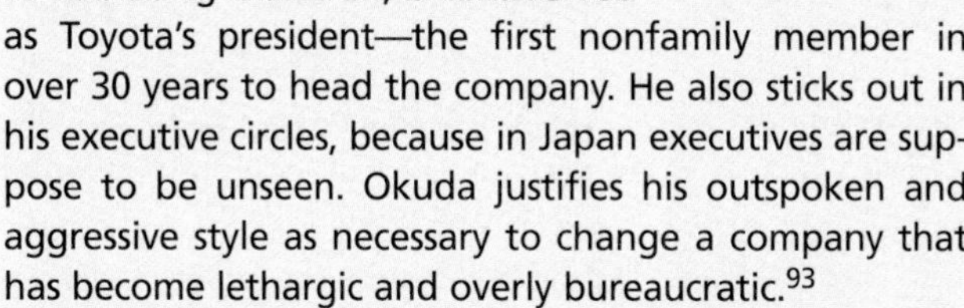

Okuda moved ahead at Toyota by taking jobs that other employees didn't want. For example, in the early 1980s, the company was trying to build a plant in Taiwan, but the Taiwanese government's demands for high local content, technology transfer, and guaranteed exports convinced many at Toyota that the project should be scrapped. Okuda thought differently. He successfully lobbied for the plant in the company, and it's now very profitable for the organization. As Okuda has noted, "Everyone wanted to give up. But I restarted the project and led it to success." His drive and ability to overcome obstacles were central to his rise in the company's hierarchy.

When Okuda ascended to the presidency of Toyota in early 1995, the company was losing market share in Japan to both Mitsubishi and Honda. Okuda attributed this problem to several factors. Toyota had been losing touch with customers in Japan for several years. For example, when engineers redesigned the Corolla in 1991, they made it too big and too expensive for the Japanese tastes. Then, four years later, they stripped out so many of the costs in the car that the Corolla looked too cheap. Competitors, on the other hand, had also done a much better job at identifying the boom in recreational vehicles—especially the sports utility market. Toyota's burdensome bureaucracy also bothered Okuda. A decision that took only five minutes to filter through the company at Suzuki Motor Corporation took upwards of three weeks at Toyota.

In his first 18 months on the job, Okuda implemented some drastic changes. In a country in which lifetime employment is consistent with the culture, he replaced nearly one third of Toyota's highest-ranking executives. He revamped Toyota's long-standing promotion system based on seniority, adding performance as a factor. Some outstanding performers were also moved up several levels in management at one time—something unheard of in the history of the company.

Okuda also worked with vehicle designers to increase the speed at which a vehicle went from concept to market. What once took 27 months was shortened to 18. Finally, he is using the visibility of his job to address larger societal issues facing all Japanese businesses. He recently accused Japan's Finance Ministry of trying to destroy the auto industry by driving up the yen. And he has been an audible voice in the country, condemning the lax lending practices that force Japanese banks to write off billions of dollars in bad loans and that led, in part, to the economic crisis in the country.

Unfortunately, some of Okuda's actions may have backfired. Speculation that he overstepped his boundary at times by his "blunt demands for change and his refusal to bail out other members of the Toyota keiretsu," may have offended the founding Toyoda family—leading to his removal as president of the company in June 1999. However, his strategic leadership and the good he's done for the company didn't go unnoticed—they helped him ascend to the chairman's job.

QUESTIONS

1 How would you describe Hiroski Okuda's leadership style? Cite specifics where appropriate.

2 When a company is in a crisis, do you believe that a radical change in leadership is required to turn the company around? Support your position.

3 Would you describe Okuda's leadership style to be (a) charismatic, (b) visionary, and (c) culturally consistent with the practices in Japan? Explain.

Developing Your Investigative Skills

Using the Internet

Visit *www.prenhall.com/robbins* for updated Internet Exercises.

Enhancing Your Writing Skills

Communicating Effectively

1 Think about a person in your life (a parent, a supervisor, a teacher, etc.) who has influenced you to the extent that you enthusiastically gave 110 percent. Describe the characteristics of this individual. Pick one of the contemporary leadership theories in this chapter and relate your list to the model, explaining how your leader demonstrated the attributes of your selected theory.

2 Develop a two- to three-page discussion when responding to the following questions. What kind of activities could a full-time college student pursue that might lead to the perception that he or she is a charismatic leader? In pursuing those activities, what might the student do to enhance this perception of being charismatic?

3 Visit the Southwest Airlines Web site <http://www.southwest.com>. Surf through the various Web pages of this airline. Using two of the skills of a visionary leader, locate examples of how Herb Kelleher has demonstrated these attributes. Specifically, show (1) how Kelleher's vision is clearly explained in terms of what's expected from Southwest employees and (2) how Kelleher's behavior reinforces to organizational members the importance of his vision.

Twelve

Communication and Interpersonal Skills

LEARNING OUTCOMES After reading this chapter, I will be able to:

1 Define *communication* and explain why it is important to managers.

2 Describe the communication process.

3 List techniques for overcoming communication barriers.

4 Identify behaviors related to effective active listening.

5 Explain what behaviors are necessary for providing effective feedback.

6 Describe the contingency factors influencing delegation.

7 Identify behaviors related to effective delegating.

8 Describe the steps in analyzing and resolving conflict.

9 Explain why a manager might stimulate conflict.

10 Contrast distributive and integrative bargaining.

George Cohon, a Canadian, made history when he opened the first McDonald's restaurant near Moscow's Red Square in the former Soviet Union, but it took him nearly 14 years to pull off his achievement.[1]

Getting the McDonald's operating took many years of battling red tape and cultural as well as economic obstacles. Discussions with individuals at several levels of the Soviet government at times appeared to be going in circles. When an agreement finally appeared within reach, the negotiations became even more intense. The Soviet delegates, for instance, flatly demanded his consent on such issues as rents for land and the percentage of sales that were to be paid to Cohon's Canadian company. Although Cohon found negotiating in a foreign language to be difficult, it was nothing compared to dealing with a totalitarian government as a prospective partner. As Cohon states, "this was a communications challenge straight from hell."

Once the agreement had been reached, a new set of obstacles had to be overcome. Suppliers had to be found, and, at the time, the agricultural industry in the former Soviet Union was dismal, marred by constant crop failures and poor management. Moreover, staff had to be hired, trained, introduced to McDonald's unique corporate culture focusing on quality, cleanliness, and consistency. Could this culture be adapted to Russian workers? As Cohon stated, "When we began our training, most of our crew and our Soviet managers had never actually tasted a hamburger, much less made or served one." So to help facilitate this training, Soviet managers were flown to Toronto and schooled at the Canadian Institute of Hamburgerology. Taking the information they learned in Toronto, the Soviet managers began training employees on site.

On the first day of operation, Moscow McDonald's served over 30,000 people. Since then, the chain has expanded throughout Russia. It was a major accomplishment that George Cohon pulled off. He managed to create a reliable system of suppliers, overcome government bureaucracy, and train employees to function at the high level demanded by McDonald's. And he did all of this in a country that was going through one of its greatest periods of upheaval. This was a major victory for Cohon and demonstrated that effective communication is fundamentally linked to successful performance.[2]

In this chapter, we present basic concepts in interpersonal communication and explain the communication process, methods of communicating, barriers to effective communication, and ways to overcome those barriers. In addition, we review several communication-based interpersonal skills—active listening, providing feedback, delegating, managing conflict, and negotiating—that managers must be proficient in in order to manage effectively in today's organizations.

Understanding Communication

The importance of effective communication for managers cannot be overemphasized for one specific reason: Everything a manager does involves communicating. Not *some* things but *everything!* A manager can't make a decision without information. That information has to be communicated. Once a decision is made, communication must again take place. Otherwise, no one will know that a decision has been made. The best idea, the most creative suggestion, or the finest plan cannot take form without communication. Managers, therefore, need effective communication skills. We are not suggesting, of course, that good communication skills alone make a successful manager. We can say, however, that ineffective communication skills can lead to a continuous stream of problems for the manager.

HOW DOES THE COMMUNICATION PROCESS WORK?

Communication can be thought of as a process or flow. Communication problems occur when there are deviations or blockages in that flow. Before communication can take place, a purpose, expressed as a message to be conveyed, is needed. It passes between a source (the sender) and a receiver. The message is encoded (converted to symbolic form) and is passed by way of some medium (channel) to the receiver, who retranslates (decodes) the message initiated by the sender. The result is a transference of meaning from one person to another.[3]

Exhibit 12-1 depicts the **communication process.** This model is made up of seven parts: (1) the communication source, (2) encoding, (3) the message, (4) the channel, (5) decoding, (6) the receiver, and (7) feedback.

communication process
The transferring and understanding of meaning

The source initiates a message by **encoding** a thought. Four conditions affect the encoded message: skill, attitudes, knowledge, and the social-cultural system.

encoding
The conversion of a message into some symbolic form

Our message in our communication to you is dependent upon our writing skills; if the authors of textbooks are without the requisite writing skills, their messages will not reach students in the form desired. One's total communicative success includes speaking, reading, listening, and reasoning skills as well. As we discussed in Chapter 8, our attitudes influence our behavior. We hold predisposed ideas on numerous topics, and our communications are affected by these attitudes. Furthermore, we are restricted in our communicative activity by the extent of our knowledge of the particular topic. We cannot communicate what we don't know, and should our knowledge be too extensive, it's possible that our receiver will not understand our message. Clearly, the amount of knowledge the source holds about his or her subject will affect the message he or she seeks to transfer. And, finally, just as attitudes influence our behavior, so does our position in the social-cultural system in which we exist. Your beliefs and values, all part of your culture, act to influence you as a communicative source.

The **message** is the actual physical product from the source. "When we speak, the speech is the message. When we write, the writing is the message. When we paint, the picture is the message. When we gesture, the movements of our arms, the expressions on our face are the message."[4] Our message is affected by the code or group of symbols we use to transfer meaning, the content of the message itself, and the decisions that we make in selecting and arranging both codes and content.

message
A purpose to be conveyed

The **channel** is the medium through which the message travels. It is selected by the source, who must determine which channel is formal and which one is

channel
The medium by which a message travels

Exhibit 12-1 The Communication Process

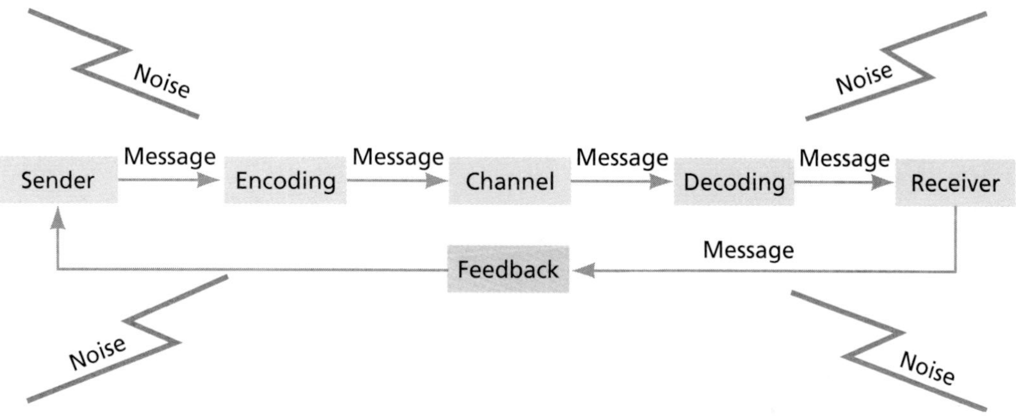

informal. Formal channels are established by the organization and transmit messages that pertain to the job-related activities of members. They traditionally follow the authority network within the organization. Other forms of messages, such as personal or social, follow the informal channels in the organization.

decoding
A receiver's translation of a sender's message

The receiver is the person to whom the message is directed. However, before the message can be received, the symbols in it must be translated into a form that can be understood by the receiver. This is the **decoding** of the message. Just as the encoder was limited by his or her skills, attitudes, knowledge, and social-cultural system, the receiver is equally restricted. Accordingly, the source must be skillful in writing or speaking; the receiver must be skillful in reading or listening, and both must be able to reason. One's knowledge, attitudes, and cultural background influence one's ability to receive, just as they do the ability to send.

feedback
The degree to which carrying out the work activities required by a job results in the individual's obtaining direct and clear information about the effectiveness of his or her performance

The final link in the communication process is a feedback loop. "If a communication source decodes the message that he encodes, if the message is put back into his system, we have feedback."[5] **Feedback** is the check on how successful we have been in transferring our messages as originally intended. It determines whether understanding has been achieved.

ARE WRITTEN COMMUNICATIONS MORE EFFECTIVE THAN VERBAL ONES?

Written communications include memos, letters, e-mail, organizational periodicals, bulletin boards, or any other device that transmits written words or symbols. Why would a sender choose to use written communications? Because they are tangible, verifiable, and more permanent than the oral variety. Typically, both sender and receiver have a record of the communication. The message can be stored for an indefinite period of time. If there are questions about the content of the message, it is physically available for later reference. This feature is particularly important for complex or lengthy communications. For example, the marketing plan for a new product is likely to contain a number of tasks spread out over several months. By putting it in writing, those who have to initiate the plan can readily refer to the document over the life of the plan. A final benefit of written communication comes from the process itself. Except in rare instances, such as when presenting a formal speech, more care is taken with the written word than with the oral word. Having to put something in writing forces a person to think more carefully about what he or she wants to convey. Therefore, written communications are more likely to be well thought out, logical, and clear.

The main purpose of communication is to get a message from a sender to a receiver the way the sender intended it to be understood. International symbols transfer meaning and understanding. The red circle, for example, means "No," such as no drinking, no dogs, no biking, or no skating.

Of course, written messages have their drawbacks. Writing may be more precise, but it also consumes a great deal of time. You could convey far more information to your college instructor in a one-hour oral exam than in a one-hour written exam. In fact, you could probably say in 10 to 15 minutes what takes you an hour to write. The other major disadvantage is feedback or, rather, lack of it. Oral communications allow the receivers to respond rapidly to what they think they hear. However, written communications don't have a built-in feedback mechanism. Sending a memo is no assurance that it will be received; if it is received, there is no guarantee that the recipient will interpret it as the sender meant. The latter point is also relevant in oral communiques, but it's easier in such cases merely to ask the receiver to summarize what you have said. An accurate summary presents feedback evidence that the message has been received and understood.

IS THE GRAPEVINE AN EFFECTIVE WAY TO COMMUNICATE?

The **grapevine** is the unofficial way that communications take place in an organization. It is neither authorized nor supported by the organization. Rather, information is spread by word of mouth—and even through electronic means. Ironically this is a two-way process—good information passes among us rapidly; bad information, even faster.[6] The grapevine gets information out to organizational members as quickly as possible.

grapevine
An unofficial channel of communication

> *The grapevine motto: good information passes among people fairly rapidly—bad information, even faster!*

The biggest question raised about grapevines, however, focuses on the accuracy of the rumors. Research on this topic has found somewhat mixed results. In an organization characterized by openness, the grapevine may be extremely accurate. In an authoritative culture, the rumor mill may not be accurate. But even then, although the information flowing is inaccurate, it still contains some element of truth. Rumors about major layoffs, plant closings, and the like may be filled with inaccurate information regarding who will be affected or when it may occur. Nonetheless, the reports that something is about to happen are probably on target.

HOW DO NONVERBAL CUES AFFECT COMMUNICATIONS?

Some of the most meaningful communications are neither spoken nor written. These are nonverbal communications. A loud siren or a red light at an intersection tells you something without words. A college instructor doesn't need words to know that students are bored; their eyes get glassy or they begin to read the school newspaper during class. Similarly, when papers start to rustle and notebooks begin to close, the message is clear: Class time is about over. The size of a person's office and desk or the clothes he or she wears also convey messages to others. However, the best-known areas of nonverbal communication are body language and verbal intonation.

Body language refers to gestures, facial configurations, and other movements of the body.[7] A snarl, for example, says something different from a smile. Hand motions, facial expressions, and other gestures can communicate emotions or temperaments such as aggression, fear, shyness, arrogance, joy, and anger. **Verbal intonation** refers to the emphasis someone gives to words or phrases. To illustrate how intonations can change the meaning of a message, consider the student who asks the instructor a question. The instructor replies, "What do you mean by that?" The student's reaction will vary, depending on the tone of the instructor's response. A soft, smooth tone creates a different meaning from one that is abrasive with a strong emphasis on the last word. Most of us would view the first intonation as coming from someone who sincerely sought clarification, whereas the second suggests that the person is aggressive or defensive.

body language
Nonverbal communication cues such as facial expressions, gestures, and other body movements

verbal intonation
An emphasis given to words or phrases that conveys meaning

The fact that every oral communication also has a nonverbal message cannot be overemphasized. Why? Because the nonverbal component is likely to carry the greatest impact.[8] One researcher found that 55 percent of an oral message is derived from facial expression and physical posture, 38 percent from verbal intonation, and only 7 percent from the actual words used.[9] Most of us know that animals respond to how we say something rather than to what we say. Apparently, people aren't much different.

IS THE WAVE OF COMMUNICATION'S FUTURE IN ELECTRONIC MEDIA?

Today we rely on a number of sophisticated electronic devices to carry our interpersonal communications. We have closed-circuit television, voice-activated computers, cellular phones, fax machines, pagers, and e-mail. For example, e-mail allows us to instantaneously transmit written messages on computers that are linked together with the appropriate software. Today, it's one of the most widely used ways for organizational members to communicate. E-mail is fast, convenient, cheap, and you can send the same message to dozens of people at the same time. But it's also public information and, as such, should not be used to discuss sensitive issues like performance appraisals, disciplinary issues, or other confidential topics.[10] Interestingly, e-mail has taken on its own vocabulary and verbal intonation. Acronyms like IMO [in my opinion] and FWIW [for what it's worth] have found their ways into e-mail to create shortcuts for both the sender and the receiver. Emotions can also be displayed in e-mails. For instance, something typed in all caps means that you're yelling at the other person. A colon and a closing parenthesis typed together implies that someone is happy [:)].

WHAT BARRIERS EXIST TO EFFECTIVE COMMUNICATION?

filtering
The deliberate manipulation of information to make it appear more favorable to the receiver

A number of interpersonal and intrapersonal barriers help to explain why the message decoded by a receiver is often different than that which the sender intended. We summarize the more prominent barriers to effective communication in Exhibit 12-2 and briefly describe them here.

Filtering refers to the way that a sender manipulates information so that it will be seen more favorably by the receiver. For example, when a manager tells his

Exhibit 12-2
Barriers to Effective Communication

Filtering	The deliberate manipulation of information to make it appear more favorable to the receiver.
Selective Perception	Receiving communications on the basis of what one selectively sees and hears depending on his or her needs, motivation, experience, background, and other personal characteristics.
Information Overload	When the amount of information one has to work with exceeds one's processing capacity.
Emotions	Messages will often be interpreted differently depending on how happy or sad one is when the message is being communicated.
Language	Words have different meanings to different people. Receivers will use their definition of words communicated, which may be different from what the sender intended.
Communication Apprehension	Undue anxiety when one is required to interact face to face.

boss what he feels that boss wants to hear, he is filtering information. Does this happen much in organizations? Sure it does. As information is passed up to senior executives, it has to be condensed and synthesized by underlings so upper management doesn't become overloaded with information. The personal interests and perceptions of what is important by those doing the synthesizing are going to cause filtering. As a former group vice president of GM described it, the filtering of communications through levels at GM made it impossible for senior managers to get objective information because "lower-level specialists provided information in such a way that they would get the answer they wanted. I know. I used to be down below and do it."[11]

Filtering is most likely to occur in organizations in which there is emphasis on status differences and among employees with strong career mobility aspirations.[12] Additionally, large organizations, because they typically have more vertical levels, create more opportunities for filtering to occur. So expect to see more filtering taking place in large corporations than in small business firms.

The second barrier is *selective perception.* We've mentioned selective perception before in this book. The term appears again here because the receivers in the communication process selectively see and hear based on their needs, motivations, experience, background, and other personal characteristics. Receivers also project their interests and expectations into communications as they decode them. The employment interviewer who expects a female job applicant to put her family ahead of her career is likely to see that tendency in female applicants, regardless of whether the applicants would do so or not. As we said in Chapter 8, we don't see reality; rather, we interpret what we see and call it reality.

information overload
The result of the situation of information exceeding processing capacity

Individuals have a finite capacity for processing data. For instance, research indicates that most of us have difficulty working with more than about seven pieces of information at one time.[13] When the information exceeds our processing capacity, the result is **information overload.** Today's typical executive frequently complains of information overload. The demands of keeping up with e-mail, phone calls, faxes, meetings, and professional reading create an onslaught of data that is nearly impossible to process and assimilate. What happens when individuals have more information than they can sort out and use? They tend to select out, ignore, pass over, or forget information. Or they may put off further processing until the overload situation is over. In any case, the result is lost information and less effective communication.

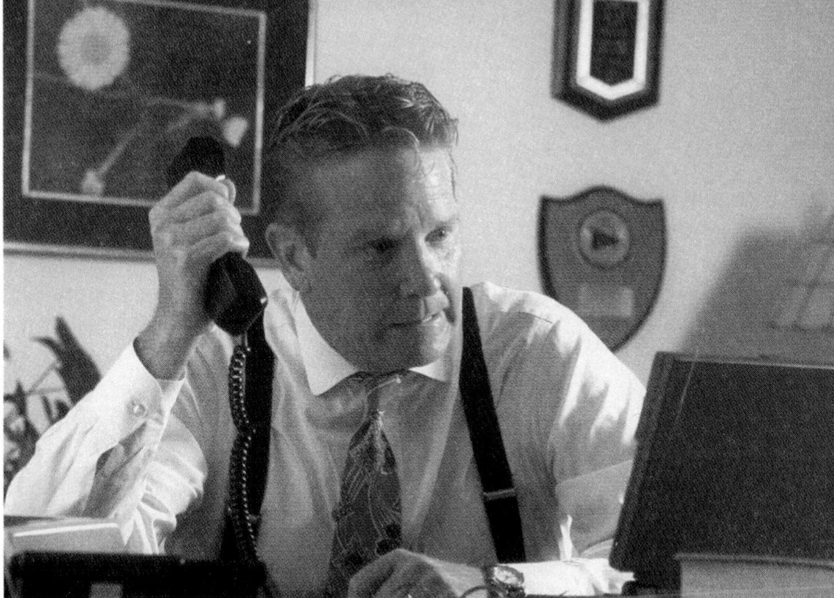

Technology and the fast-paced communications world has its benefits. We are able to communicate to others around the world almost instantaneously. But all this equipment and the bombardment of information can sometimes overload us. When this happens, communications may break down, and thus, information overload becomes a communication barrier.

When people feel threatened, they tend to react in ways that reduce their ability to achieve mutual understanding. That is, they become defensive—engaging in behaviors such as verbally attacking others, making sarcastic remarks, being overly judgmental, and questioning others' motives.[14] So when individuals interpret another's message as threatening, they often respond in ways that retard effective communication.

Words mean different things to different people. "The meanings of words are not in the words; they are in us."[15] Age, education, and cultural background are three of the more obvious variables that influence the language a person uses and the definitions he or she applies to words. Rap artist Snoop Doggy Dogg and columnist George F. Will both speak English. But the language one uses is vastly different from how the other speaks. In fact, the typical person on the street might have difficulty understanding both of these individuals' speech. As a case in point, do you have any idea what George Will meant when he recently said of Thomas Jefferson's defense of the French Revolution, "It is meretricious to treat an epistolary extravagance as an index of implacable conviction"?[16]

The meaning of words are not in the words; they are in us.

In an organization, employees usually come from diverse backgrounds and, therefore, have different patterns of speech. Additionally, the grouping of employees into departments creates specialists who develop their own **jargon** or technical language. In large organizations, members are also frequently widely dispersed geographically—even operating in different countries—and individuals in each locale will use terms and phrases that are unique to their area. And the existence of vertical levels can also cause language problems. The language of senior executives, for instance, can be mystifying to operative employees not familiar with management jargon.

jargon
Technical language

Our point is that although we speak a common language, our usage of that language is far from uniform.[17] If we knew how each of us modified the language, communication difficulties would be minimized. The problem is that members in an organization usually don't know how others with whom they interact have modified the language. Senders tend to assume that the words and terms they use have the same meaning for the receiver. This, of course, is often incorrect, thus creating communication difficulties.

Another major roadblock to effective communication is that some people—an estimated 5 percent to 20 percent of the population—suffer from debilitating **communication apprehension** or anxiety.[18] Although lots of people dread speaking in front of a group, communication apprehension is a more serious problem because it affects a whole category of communication techniques. People who suffer from it experience undue tension and anxiety in oral communication, written communication, or both.[19] For example, oral apprehensives may find it extremely difficult to talk with others face to face or become extremely anxious when they have to use the telephone. As a result, they may rely on memos or faxes to convey messages when a phone call would not only be faster but more appropriate.

communication apprehension
Communication anxiety

Studies demonstrate that oral-communication apprehensives avoid situations that require them to engage in oral communication.[20] We should expect to find some self-selection in jobs so that such individuals don't take positions, such as that of teacher, for which oral communication is a dominant requirement.[21] But almost all jobs require some oral communication. And of greater concern is the evidence that high oral-communication apprehensives distort the communication demands of their jobs in order to minimize the need for communication.[22] So we need to be aware that there is a set of people in organizations who severely limit their oral communication and rationalize this practice by telling themselves that more communication isn't necessary for them to do their job effectively.

Ethical Dilemma in Management

Purposefully Distorting Information

The issue of withholding information was introduced in Chapter 1. Since then, you've examined several dilemmas in other chapters to ponder and ample time to think about the issue of keeping quiet or stretching the truth. Because this is such a broad concern and so closely intertwined with interpersonal communication, this might be a good time to once again consider ethical dilemmas that managers face relating to the intentional distortion of information. Read through the following two incidents.

Incident 1: You've just seen your division's sales report for last month. Sales are down considerably. Your boss, who works 2,000 miles away in another city, is unlikely to see last month's sales figures. You're optimistic that sales will pick up this month and next so that your overall quarterly numbers will be right on target. You also know that your boss is the type of person who hates to hear bad news. You're having a phone conversation today with your boss. He happens to ask in passing, how last month's sales went. What do you tell him?

Incident 2: An employee asks you about a rumor she's heard that your department and all its employees will be transferred from New York to Baltimore. You know the rumor to be true, but you'd rather not let the information out just yet. You're fearful that it could hurt departmental morale and lead to premature resignations. What do you say to your employee?

These two incidents illustrate dilemmas that managers face related to evading the truth, distorting facts, or lying to others. And here's something else that makes the situation even more problematic: It might not always be in a manager's best interest or those of his or her unit to provide full and complete information. Keeping communications fuzzy can cut down on questions, permit faster decision making, minimize objections, reduce opposition, make it easier to deny one's earlier statements, preserve the freedom to change one's mind, permit one to say no diplomatically, help to avoid confrontation and anxiety, and provide other benefits to the manager.

Is it unethical to purposely distort communications to get a favorable outcome? What about "little white lies" that really don't hurt anybody? Are these ethical? What guidelines could you suggest for managers who want guidance in deciding whether distorting information is ethical or unethical?

HOW CAN MANAGERS OVERCOME COMMUNICATION BARRIERS?

Given these barriers to communication, what can managers do to overcome them? The following suggestions should help make communication more effective (see also Exhibit 12-3).

Why use feedback? Many communication problems can be directly attributed to misunderstandings and inaccuracies.[23] These problems are less likely to occur if the manager uses the feedback loop in the communication process. This feedback can be verbal or nonverbal.

Exhibit 12-3
Overcoming Barriers to Effective Communication

Use Feedback	Check the accuracy of what has been communicated—or what you think you heard.
Simplify Language	Use words that the intended audience understands.
Listen Actively	Listen for the full meaning of the message without making premature judgments or interpretations—or thinking about what you are going to say in response.
Constrain Emotions	Recognize when your emotions are running high. When they are, don't communicate until you have calmed down.
Watch Nonverbal Cues	Be aware that your actions speak louder than your words. Keep the two consistent.

If a manager asks a receiver, "Did you understand what I said?," the response represents feedback. Feedback should include more than yes and no answers.[24] The manager can ask a set of questions about a message in order to determine whether the message was received as intended. Better yet, the manager can ask the receiver to restate the message in his or her own words. If the manager then hears what was intended, understanding and accuracy should be enhanced. Feedback also includes subtler methods than direct questioning or the summarizing of messages. General comments can give a manager a sense of the receiver's reaction to a message. In addition, performance appraisals, salary reviews, and promotions represent important forms of feedback.

Of course, feedback does not have to be conveyed in words. Actions may speak louder than words. The sales manager who sends out a directive to his or her staff describing a new monthly sales report that all sales personnel will need to complete receives feedback if some of the salespeople fail to turn in the new report. This feedback suggests that the sales manager needs to clarify the initial directive. Similarly, when you give a speech to a group of people, you watch their eyes and look for other nonverbal clues to tell you whether they are getting your message.

Why should simplified language be used? Because language can be a barrier, managers should choose words and structure their messages in ways that will make those messages clear and understandable to the receiver (see Exhibit 12-4). The manager should consider the audience to whom the message is directed so that the language will be tailored to the receivers. Remember, communication is effective when a message is both received and understood. Understanding is improved by simplifying the language used to the intended audience. This means, for example, that a hospital administrator should always try to communicate in clear, easily understood terms and that the language used in messages to the surgical staff should be different from that used with office employees. Jargon can facilitate understanding when it is used within a group that knows what it means, but it can cause innumerable problems when used outside that group.

Why must we listen actively? When someone talks, we hear. But too often we don't listen. Listening is an active search for meaning, whereas hearing is passive. In listening, two people are thinking—the receiver and the sender.

Many of us are poor listeners. Why? Because listening is difficult, and it's usually more satisfying to be the talker. Listening, in fact, is often more tiring than talking. It demands intellectual effort. Unlike hearing, **active listening** demands total concentration. The average person speaks at a rate of about 150 words per minute, whereas we have the capacity to hear and process at the rate of nearly 1,000 words per minute.[25] The difference obviously leaves idle time for the brain and opportunities for the mind to wander.

active listening
Listening for full meaning without making premature judgments or interpretations

Active listening is enhanced by empathy with the sender—that is, by placing yourself in the sender's position. Because senders differ in attitudes, interests,

Exhibit 12-4
Using Simple Language?

SOURCE: DILBERT reprinted by permission of United Feature Syndicate, Inc.

needs, and expectations, empathy makes it easier to understand the actual content of a message. An empathic listener reserves judgment on the message's content and carefully listens to what is being said. The goal is to improve one's ability to receive the full meaning of a communication without having it distorted by premature judgments or interpretations. We'll return to active listening as an interpersonal skill shortly.

Why must we constrain emotions? It would be naive to assume that managers always communicate in a fully rational manner. We know that emotions can severely cloud and distort the transference of meaning. A manager who is emotionally upset over an issue is likely to misconstrue incoming messages and fail to express his or her outgoing messages clearly and accurately. What can the manager do? The simplest answer is to stop communicating until he or she has regained composure.

Why the emphasis on nonverbal cues? If actions speak louder than words, then it's important to watch your actions to make sure that they align with and reinforce the words that go along with them. We noted that nonverbal messages carry a great deal of weight. Given this fact, the effective communicator watches his or her nonverbal cues to ensure that they, too, convey the desired message.

International Insights into and Gender Issues in the Communication Process

Do men and women communicate in the same way? The answer is No. And the differences between men and women may lead to significant misunderstandings and misperceptions.[26]

Deborah Tannen's research on how men and women communicate has uncovered some interesting insights. She found that when men talk, they do so to emphasize status and independence; whereas women talk to create connections and intimacy. For instance, men frequently complain that women talk on and on about their problems. Women, however, criticize men for not listening. When a man hears a woman talking about a problem, he frequently asserts his desire for independence and control by providing solutions. Many women, in contrast, view conversing about a problem as a means of promoting closeness. The woman presents the problem to gain support and connection, not to get the man's advice.

Do men and women communicate differently? Research by Deborah Tannen suggests they do. Specifically she has found that men frequently complain that women talk on and on about most issues and that they speak from a desire to assert independence. Women on the other hand feel men don't listen and speak to gain support for others.

Effective communication between the sexes is important in all organizations if they are to meet organizational goals. But how can we manage the various differences in communication styles? To keep gender differences from becoming persistent barriers to effective communication requires acceptance, understanding, and a commitment to communicate adaptively with each other. Both men and women need to acknowledge that there are differences in communication styles, that one style isn't better than the other, and that it takes real effort to talk with each other successfully.

When men talk, they emphasize status and independence. Women talk to create connections and intimacy.

Beyond differences in gender communication styles, it's important to recognize that interpersonal communication isn't conducted in the same way around the world.[27] For example, compare countries that place a high value on individualism (such as the United States) with countries where the emphasis is on collectivism (such as Japan).[28]

Because of the emphasis on the individual in countries such as the United States, communication patterns are individual oriented and rather clearly spelled out. For instance, U.S. managers rely heavily on memoranda, announcements, position papers, and other formal forms of communication to stake out their positions in intraorganizational negotiations. Supervisors in the United States often hoard secret information in an attempt to promote their own advancement and to induce their employees to accept decisions and plans. For their own protection, lower-level employees also engage in this practice.

In collectivist countries such as Japan, there is more interaction for its own sake and a more informal manner of interpersonal contact. The Japanese manager, in contrast to U.S. managers, will engage in extensive verbal consultation over an issue first and only later will draw up a formal document to outline the agreement that was made. Face-to-face communication is encouraged. In addition, open communication is an inherent part of the Japanese work setting. Work spaces are open and crowded with individuals at different levels in the work hierarchy. U.S. organizations emphasize authority, hierarchy, and formal lines of communication.

Developing Interpersonal Skills

Would it surprise you to know that more managers are probably fired because of poor interpersonal skills than for a lack of technical ability?[29] A survey of 191 top executives at six *Fortune* 500 companies found that, according to these executives, the single biggest reason for failure was poor interpersonal skills.[30] The Center for Creative Leadership in North Carolina estimates that half of all managers and 30 percent of all senior managers have some type of difficulty in dealing with people. And a survey of senior managers in Canada's top 100 corporations showed that 32 percent of the respondents rated interpersonal skills as a top priority in hiring decisions.[31]

If you need any further evidence of the importance of interpersonal skills, we would point to a comprehensive study of people who hire students with undergraduate business degrees under the assumption that they will fill future management vacancies. The study found that the areas in which the graduates were most deficient were leadership and interpersonal skills.[32] Of course, these overall findings are consistent with our view of the manager's job. Because managers ultimately get things done through others, competencies in leadership, communication, and other interpersonal skills are prerequisites to managerial effectiveness. Therefore, the rest of this chapter focuses on key interpersonal skills that every manager needs.[33]

R. J. Heckman, Consultant Personnel Decisions International

What difference do good interpersonal skills make on the job? At Personnel Decisions International, a global human resources consulting firm headquartered in New York, these skills clearly differentiate those employees who are more motivated and more committed to their individual and team goals.

According to R. J. Heckman, consultant, the give-and-take relationships that interpersonal skills support create many benefits, both for individuals and for the firm. With everyone working to enhance understanding and mutual respect, the needs and feelings of others are acknowledged. Differences between employees can then be seen, not as stumbling blocks, but as necessary elements for building strong teams. That reduces conflict and allows employees to focus on the positive aspects of any conflicts that do arise.

The healthy environment needed for creativity is also dependent on interpersonal skills. As Heckman puts it, "Building relationships, managing conflict, valuing diversity, and leveraging networks foster personal and professional growth."

How exactly are interpersonal skills such as these developed in employees? At Personnel Decisions various strategies are used, among them both formal and informal feedback on performance and coaching, mentoring, on-the-job activities, and making skill improvement a personal goal. Although developing skill takes effort, in the case of interpersonal skills, the benefits are many.

WHY ARE ACTIVE LISTENING SKILLS IMPORTANT?

A few pages ago, we briefly mentioned that the ability to listen is too often taken for granted because we often confuse hearing with listening. Listening requires paying attention, interpreting, and remembering sound stimuli.

Effective listening is active rather than passive. In passive listening, you resemble a tape recorder. You absorb and remember the words spoken. If the speaker provides you with a clear message and makes his or her delivery interesting enough to keep your attention, you'll probably hear most of what the speaker is trying to communicate. Active listening requires you to get inside the speaker's mind to understand the communication from his or her point of view. As you will see, active listening is hard work.[34] You have to concentrate, and you have to want to fully understand what a speaker is saying. Students who use active listening techniques for an entire 75-minute lecture are as tired as their instructor when the lecture is over because they have put as much energy into listening as the instructor put into speaking.

There are four essential requirements for active listening: (1) intensity, (2) empathy, (3) acceptance, and (4) a willingness to take responsibility for completeness.[35] As noted, the human brain is capable of handling a speaking rate that is about six times as fast that of the average speaker. That leaves a lot of time for daydreaming. The active listener concentrates *intensely* on what the speaker is saying and tunes out the thousands of miscellaneous thoughts (about money, sex, vacation, parties, exams, and so on) that create distractions. What do active listeners do with their idle brain time? They summarize and integrate what has been said. They put each new bit of information into the context of what preceded it.

Empathy requires you to put yourself into the speaker's shoes. You try to understand what the speaker wants to communicate rather than what you want to hear.

Notice that empathy demands both knowledge of the speaker and flexibility on your part. You need to suspend your own thoughts and feelings and adjust what you see and feel to your speaker's world. In that way, you increase the likelihood that you'll interpret the message in the way the speaker intended.

An active listener demonstrates *acceptance*. He or she listens objectively without judging content. This is no easy task. It's natural to be distracted by what a speaker says, especially when we disagree with it. When we hear something we disagree with, we have a tendency to begin formulating our mental arguments to counter what is being said. Of course, in doing so, we miss the rest of the message. The challenge for the active listener is to absorb what's being said and withhold judgment on content until the speaker is finished.

The final ingredient of active listening is taking *responsibility for completeness*. That is, the listener does whatever is necessary to get the full intended meaning from the speaker's communication. Two widely used active listening techniques are listening for feeling as well as for content and asking questions to ensure understanding.

The biggest reason managers fail in their jobs is the lack of interpersonal skills.

Just how, though, can you develop effective listening skills? The literature on active listening emphasizes eight specific behaviors (see Developing Your Active Listening Skill, p. 407).[36] As you review these behaviors, ask yourself whether they describe your listening practices. If you're not currently using these techniques, there's no better time than right now to begin developing them.

WHY ARE FEEDBACK SKILLS IMPORTANT?

Ask a manager about the feedback he or she gives to employees, and you're likely to get a qualified answer. If the feedback is positive, it's likely to be given promptly and enthusiastically. Negative feedback is often treated very differently. Like most of us, managers don't particularly enjoy communicating bad news. They fear offending or having to deal with the receiver's defensiveness. The result is that negative feedback is often avoided, delayed, or substantially distorted.[37] The purposes of this section are to show you the importance of providing both positive and negative feedback and to identify specific techniques to help make your feedback more effective.

WHAT IS THE DIFFERENCE BETWEEN POSITIVE AND NEGATIVE FEEDBACK?

We know that managers treat positive and negative feedback differently. So, too, do receivers. You need to understand this fact and adjust your feedback style accordingly.

Positive feedback is more readily and accurately perceived than negative feedback. Furthermore, whereas positive feedback is almost always accepted, negative feedback often meets resistance.[38] Why? The logical answer appears to be that people want to hear good news and block out the rest. Positive feedback fits what most people wish to hear and already believe about themselves.

Does this mean, then, that you should avoid giving negative feedback? No! What it means is that you need to be aware of potential resistance and learn to use negative feedback in situations in which it's most likely to be accepted.[39] What are those situations? Research indicates that *negative feedback* is most likely to be accepted when it comes from a credible source or if it's objective. Subjective impressions carry weight only when they come from a person with high status and credibility.[40] This suggests that negative feedback that is supported by hard data—numbers, specific examples, and the like—is more likely to be accepted. Negative feedback that is subjective can be a meaningful tool for experienced managers, particularly those in upper levels of the organization who have built the trust and earned the respect of their employees. From less experienced managers, those in the lower ranks of the organization, and those whose reputations have not yet been established, negative feedback that is subjective in nature is not likely to be well received.

How do you give effective feedback? There are six specific suggestions that we can make to help you become more effective in providing feedback. We will discuss them below and summarize them in Exhibit 12-5.

- **Focus on specific behaviors** Feedback should be specific rather than general.[41] Avoid statements such as "You have a bad attitude" or "I'm really impressed with the good job you did." They are vague, and, although they provide information, they do not tell the receiver enough so that he or she can correct the "bad attitude" or on what basis you concluded that a "good job" has been done so the person knows what behaviors to repeat.
- **Keep feedback impersonal** Feedback, particularly the negative kind, should be descriptive rather than judgmental or evaluative.[42] No matter how upset you are, keep the feedback focused on job-related behaviors and never criticize someone personally because of an inappropriate action. Telling people they are incompetent, lazy, or the like is almost always counterproductive. It provokes such an emotional reaction that the performance deviation itself is apt to be overlooked. When you are criticizing, remember that you are censuring job-related behavior, not the person. You might be tempted to tell someone he or she is rude and insensitive (which might just be true); however, that is hardly impersonal. It's better to say something more specific like, "You've interrupted me three times with questions that weren't urgent when you knew I was talking long distance to a customer in Brazil."
- **Keep feedback goal oriented** Feedback should not be given primarily to "dump" or "unload" on another person.[43] If you have to say something negative, make sure it is directed toward the receiver's goals. Ask yourself whom the feedback is supposed to help. If the answer is essentially you ("I've got something I just want to get off my chest") bite your tongue and hold the comment. Such feedback undermines your credibility and lessens the meaning and influence of future feedback sessions.
- **Make feedback well timed** Feedback is most meaningful to a receiver when there is a very short interval between his or her behavior and the receipt of feedback about that behavior.[44] For example, a new employee who makes a mistake is more likely to respond to his or her manager's suggestions for

- Focus on specific behaviors
- Keep feedback impersonal
- Keep feedback goal oriented
- Make feedback well timed
- Ensure understanding
- Direct negative feedback toward behavior that the receiver can control

Exhibit 12-5
Suggestions for Effective Feedback

improving right after the mistake or at the end of the work day rather than during a performance review session six months from now. If you have to spend time recreating a situation and refreshing someone's memory of it, the feedback you are providing is likely to be ineffective.[45] Moreover, if you are particularly concerned with changing behavior, delays in providing timely feedback on the undesirable actions lessen the likelihood that the feedback will bring about the desired change.[46] Of course, making feedback prompt merely for promptness' sake can backfire if you have insufficient information or if you are upset. In such instances, "well timed" could mean "somewhat delayed."

- **Ensure understanding** Is your feedback concise and complete enough that the receiver clearly and fully understands your communication? Remember that every successful communication requires both transference and understanding of meaning. If feedback is to be effective, you need to ensure that the receiver understands it.[47] As suggested in our discussion of listening techniques, ask the receiver to rephrase the message to find out whether he or she fully captured the meaning you intended.
- **Direct negative feedback toward behavior that the receiver can control** There is little value in reminding a person of some shortcoming over which he or she has no control. Negative feedback should be directed toward behavior that the receiver can do something about.[48] For instance, criticizing an employee who's late for work because she forgot to set her alarm clock is valid. Criticizing her for being late for work when the subway she takes to work every day had a power failure, stranding her for 90 minutes, is pointless. There is nothing she could have done to correct what happened—short of finding a different means of traveling to work, which may be unrealistic. In addition, when negative feedback is given concerning something that the receiver can control, it might be a good idea to indicate specifically what can be done to improve the situation. Such suggestions take some of the sting out of the criticism and offer guidance to receivers who understand the problem but don't know how to resolve it.

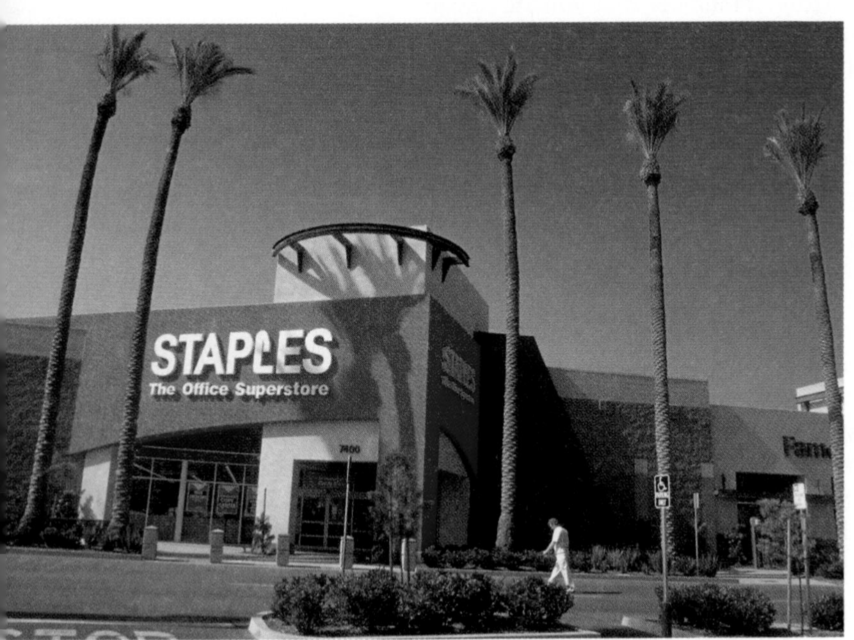

Empowering employees has a special meaning at Staples. Employees at all levels regularly attend staff meetings and are encouraged to "sound off" about ways to increase their sense of ownership in the company. Moreover, managers at Staples delegate much responsibility to their employees, letting those employees closest to the work find ways to improve the way work gets done.

WHAT ARE EMPOWERMENT SKILLS?

As we've described in various places throughout this text, managers are increasingly leading by empowering their employees. Millions of employees and teams of employees are making key operating decisions that directly affect their work. They're developing budgets, scheduling workloads, controlling inventories, solving quality problems, and engaging in activities that until recently were viewed exclusively as part of the manager's job.[49]

The increased use of empowerment is being driven by two forces. First is the need for quick decisions by those who are most knowledgeable about the issue. That requires moving decisions to lower levels. If organizations are to successfully compete in a dynamic global economy, they have to be able to make decisions and implement changes quickly. Second is the reality that the downsizing of organizations during the past two decades left many managers with considerably larger spans of control than they had previously. In order to cope with the demands of an increased load, managers had to empower their employees. Two aspects of this empowering effect are understanding the value of delegating and knowing how to do it.[50]

Delegation is the assignment of authority to another person to carry out specific activities. It allows an employee to make decisions—that is, it is a shift of decision-making authority from one organizational level to another, lower, one (see Exhibit 12-6).[51] Delegation, however, should not be confused with participation. In participative decision making, there is a sharing of authority. With delegation, employees make decisions on their own. That's why delegation is such a vital component of worker empowerment!

delegation
The assignment of authority to another person to carry out specific activities

Don't managers abdicate their responsibility when they delegate? When done properly, delegation is not abdication. The key word here is "properly." If you, as a manager, dump tasks on an employee without clarifying the exact job to be done, the range of the employee's discretion, the expected level of performance, the time frame in which the tasks are to be completed, and similar concerns, you are abdicating responsibility and inviting trouble.[52] Don't fall into the trap, however, of assuming that, to avoid the appearance of abdicating, you should minimize delegation. Unfortunately, that is how many new and inexperienced managers interpret the situation. Lacking confidence in their employees or fearful that they will be criticized for their employees' mistakes, these managers try to do everything themselves.

Exhibit 12-6
Effective Delegation

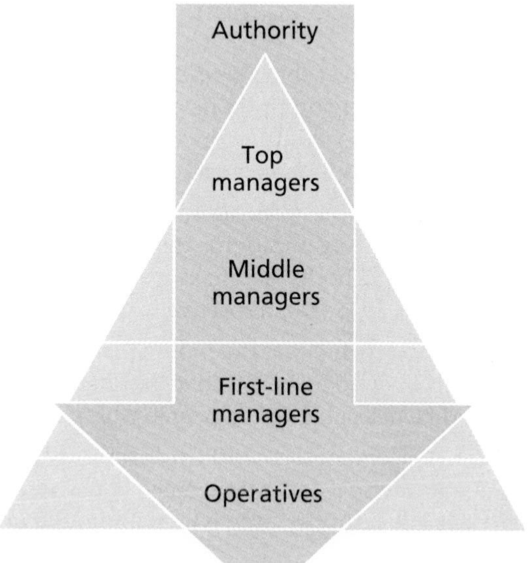

Effective delegation pushes authority down vertically through the ranks of an organization.

It might very well be true that you are capable of doing tasks better, faster, or with fewer mistakes. The catch is that your time and energy are scarce resources. It is not possible for you to do everything yourself. You need to delegate if you are going to be effective in your job.[53] This fact suggests two important points. First, you should expect and accept some mistakes by your employees. Mistakes are part of delegation. They are often good learning experiences for employees as long as their costs are not excessive. Second, to ensure that the costs of mistakes don't exceed the value of the learning, you need to put adequate controls in place. As we will discuss shortly, delegation without feedback controls that let you know where there are potentially serious problems is a form of abdication.

How much authority should a manager delegate? Should he or she keep authority centralized, delegating only the minimal amount to complete the delegated duties? What contingency factors should be considered in determining the degree to which authority is delegated? Exhibit 12-7 presents the most widely cited contingency factors to provide some guidance in making those determinations.

How do you delegate effectively? Assuming that delegation is in order, how do you delegate? A number of methods have been suggested for differentiating the effective from the ineffective delegator.[54]

- **Clarify the assignment** First determine what is to be delegated and to whom. You need to identify the person who is most capable of doing the task and then determine whether he or she has the time and motivation to do the job. Assuming that you have a willing employee, it is your responsibility to provide clear information on what is being delegated, the results you expect, and any time or performance expectations you hold. Unless there is an overriding need to adhere to specific methods, you should ask an employee only to provide the desired results. That is, get agreement on what is to be done and the results expected, but let the employee decide by which means the work is

Exhibit 12-7 Contingency Factors in Delegation

- **The size of the organization** The larger the organization, the greater the number of decisions that have to be made. Because top managers in an organization have only so much time and can obtain only so much information, in larger organizations they become increasingly dependent on the decision making of lower-level managers. Therefore, managers in large organizations resort to increased delegation.
- **The importance of the duty or decision** The more important a duty or decision (as expressed in terms of cost and impact on the future of an organization), the less likely it is to be delegated. For instance, a department head may be delegated authority to make expenditures up to $7,500, and division heads and vice presidents up to $50,000 and $125,000, respectively.
- **Task complexity** The more complex the task, the more difficult it is for top management to possess current and sufficient technical information to make effective decisions. Complex tasks require greater expertise, and decisions about them should be delegated to the people who have the necessary technical knowledge.
- **Organizational culture** If management has confidence and trust in employees, the culture will support a greater degree of delegation. However, if top management does not have confidence in the abilities of lower-level managers, it will delegate authority only when absolutely necessary. In such instances, as little authority as possible is delegated.
- **Qualities of employees** A final contingency consideration is the qualities of employees. Delegation requires employees with the skills, abilities, and motivation to accept authority and act on it. If these are lacking, top management will be reluctant to relinquish authority.

to be completed. By focusing on goals and allowing the employee the freedom to use her or her own judgment as to how those goals are to be achieved, you increase trust between you and the employee, improve the employee's motivation, and enhance accountability for results.

- **Specify employees' range of discretion** Every act of delegation comes with constraints. You are delegating authority to act but not unlimited authority. You are delegating the authority to act on certain issues within certain parameters. You need to specify what those parameters are so that employees know, in no uncertain terms, the range of their discretion. When those parameters have been successfully communicated, both you and employees will have the same idea of the limits to the latter's authority and how far they can go without further approval.
- **Allow employees to participate** One of the best ways to decide how much authority will be necessary is to allow employees who will be held accountable for the tasks to participate in that decision. Be aware, however, that participation can present its own set of potential problems as a result of employees' self-interest and biases in evaluating their own abilities. Some employees might be personally motivated to expand their authority beyond what they need and beyond what they are capable of handling. Allowing such people too much participation in deciding what tasks they should take on and how much authority they must have to complete those tasks can undermine the effectiveness of the delegation process.
- **Inform others that delegation has occurred** Delegation should not take place in a vacuum. Not only do you and your employees need to know specifically what has been delegated and how much authority has been granted, anyone else who is likely to be affected by the delegation act needs to be informed. This includes people outside the organization as well as inside it. Essentially, you need to convey what has been delegated (the task and amount of authority) and to whom. Failure to inform others makes conflict likely and decreases the chances that your employees will be able to accomplish the delegated act efficiently.
- **Establish feedback channels** To delegate without instituting feedback controls is inviting problems. There is always the possibility that employees will misuse the discretion they have been given. Controls to monitor employees' progress increase the likelihood that important problems will be identified early and that the task will be completed on time and to the desired specification. Ideally, these controls should be determined at the time of initial assignment. Agree on a specific time for completion of the task, and then set progress dates by which the employees will report on how well they are doing and on any major problems that have surfaced. These controls can be supplemented with periodic spot checks to ensure that authority guidelines are not being abused, organization policies are being followed, proper procedures are being met, and the like. Too much of a good thing can be dysfunctional. If the controls are too constraining, employees will be deprived of the opportunity to build self-confidence. As a result, much of the motivational aspect of delegation may be lost. A well-designed control system, which we will elaborate on in more detail in the next chapter, permits your employees to make small mistakes but quickly alerts you when big mistakes are imminent.

HOW DO YOU MANAGE CONFLICT?

The ability to manage conflict is undoubtedly one of the most important skills a manager needs to possess. A study of middle- and top-level executives by the

conflict
Perceived incompatible differences resulting in interference or opposition

traditional view of conflict
The view that all conflict is bad and must be avoided

human relations view of conflict
The view that conflict is natural and inevitable and has the potential to be a positive force

interactionist view of conflict
The view that some conflict is necessary for an organization to perform effectively

functional conflict
Conflicts that support an organization's goals

American Management Association revealed that the average manager spends approximately 20 percent of his or her time dealing with conflict.[55] The importance of conflict management is reinforced by a survey of the topics managers consider most important in management development programs; conflict management was rated as more important than decision making, leadership, or communication skills.[56]

What is conflict management? When we use the term **conflict,** we are referring to perceived incompatible differences resulting in some form of interference or opposition. Whether the differences are real is irrelevant. If people perceive differences, then a conflict state exists. In addition, our definition includes the extremes, from subtle, indirect, and highly controlled forms of interference to overt acts such as strikes, riots, and wars.

Over the years, three differing views have evolved toward conflict in organizations[57] (see Exhibit 12-8). One argues that conflict must be avoided, that it indicates a malfunctioning within the organization. We call this the **traditional view of conflict.** A second, the **human relations view of conflict,** argues that conflict is a natural and inevitable outcome in any organization and that it need not be evil but, rather, has the potential to be a positive force in contributing to an organization's performance. The third and most recent perspective proposes not only that conflict can be a positive force in an organization but also that some conflict is absolutely necessary for an organization or units within an organization to perform effectively. We label this third approach the **interactionist view of conflict.**

Can conflict be positive and negative? The interactionist view does not propose that all conflicts are good. Rather, some conflicts support the goals of the organization; these are **functional conflicts** of a constructive form. Other conflicts prevent an organization from achieving its goals; these are **dysfunctional conflicts** of a destructive form.

Exhibit 12-8 Three Views of Conflict

Traditional view	The early approach assumed that conflict was bad and would always have a negative impact on an organization. Conflict became synonymous with violence, destruction, and irrationality. Because conflict was harmful, it was to be avoided. Management had a responsibility to rid the organization of conflict. This traditional view dominated management literature during the late nineteenth century and continued until the mid-1940s.
Human relations view	The human relations position argued that conflict was a natural and inevitable occurrence in all organizations. Because conflict was inevitable, the human relations approach advocated acceptance of conflict. This approach rationalized the existence of conflict; conflict cannot be eliminated, and there are times when it may even benefit the organization. The human relations view dominated conflict thinking from the late 1940s through the mid-1970s.
Interactionist view	The current theoretical perspective on conflict is the interactionist approach. Although the human relations approach accepts conflict, the interactionist approach encourages conflict on the grounds that a harmonious, peaceful, tranquil, and cooperative organization is prone to become static, apathetic, and nonresponsive to needs for change and innovation. The major contribution of the interactionist approach, therefore, is that it encourages managers to maintain an ongoing minimum level of conflict—enough to keep units viable, self-critical, and creative.

Of course, it is one thing to argue that conflict can be valuable, but how does a manager tell whether a conflict is functional or dysfunctional? Unfortunately, the demarcation is neither clear nor precise. No one level of conflict can be adopted as acceptable or unacceptable under all conditions. The type and level of conflict that promote a healthy and positive involvement toward one department's goals may, in another department or in the same department at another time, be highly dysfunctional. Functionality or dysfunctionality, therefore, is a matter of judgment. Exhibit 12-9 illustrates the challenge facing managers. They want to create an environment within their organization or organizational unit in which conflict is healthy but not allowed to run to pathological extremes. Neither too little nor too much conflict is desirable. Managers should stimulate conflict to gain the full benefits of its functional properties yet reduce its level when it becomes a disruptive force. Because we have yet to devise a sophisticated measuring instrument for assessing whether a given conflict level is functional or dysfunctional, it remains for managers to make intelligent judgments concerning whether conflict levels in their units are optimal, too high, or too low.

dysfunctional conflict
Conflicts that prevent an organization from achieving its goals

If conflict is dysfunctional, what can a manager do? In the following sections, we review conflict-resolution skills. Essentially, you need to know your basic conflict-handling style as well as those of the conflicting parties to understand the situation that has created the conflict and to be aware of your options.

Exhibit 12-9
Conflict and Organizational Performance

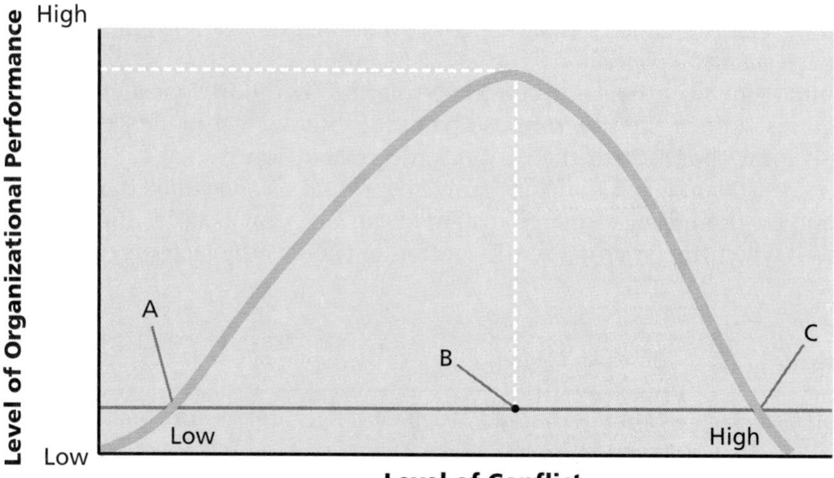

Situation	Level of Conflict	Type of Conflict	Organization's Internal Characteristics	Level of Organizational Performance
A	Low or none	Dysfunctional	Apathetic Stagnant Unresponsive to change Lack of new ideas	Low
B	Optimal	Functional	Viable Self-critical Innovative	High
C	High	Dysfunctional	Disruptive Chaotic Uncooperative	Low

What are the conflict-handling styles? Conflict in any organization is inevitable. Whenever you put people together and arrange them into some type of structure (formal or informal), there is a good probability that some individuals will perceive that others have negatively affected or are about to negatively affect something that they care about. How then do we deal with the conflict? The research of Kenneth W. Thomas has given us some insight.[58]

Thomas recognized that in these conflict-laden situations, one must first determine the intention of the other party. That is, one has to speculate about the other person's purpose for causing the conflict in order to respond to that behavior. Thomas concluded that one's response will depend on his or her cooperativeness or assertiveness. *Cooperativeness* is the degree to which an individual attempts to rectify the conflict by satisfying the other person's concerns. *Assertiveness* is the degree to which an individual will attempt to rectify the conflict to satisfy his or her own concerns. Using these two dimensions, Thomas was able to identify four distinct conflict-handling techniques plus one middle-of-the-road combination. These were competing (assertive but uncooperative), collaborating (assertive and cooperative), avoiding (unassertive and uncooperative), accommodating (unassertive but cooperative), and compromising (midrange on both assertiveness and cooperativeness). Managers essentially can draw on any of these five conflict-resolution options to reduce excessive conflict. Each has particular strengths and weaknesses, and no one option is ideal for every situation. Exhibit 12-10 describes when each is best used. You should consider each a tool in your conflict-management tool chest. You might be better at using some tools than others, but the skilled manager knows what each tool can do and when each is likely to be most effective.

Thomas recognized that one conflict-resolution method is not appropriate in all situations. Rather, the situation itself must dictate the technique. For instance, forcing is most appropriate when a quick, decisive action is vital or against people who take advantage of noncompetitive behaviors. *Collaboration* is appropriate when one is attempting to merge insights from different people, and *avoidance* works well when the potential for disruption outweighs the benefits of resolving

Exhibit 12-10
Conflict Management: What Works Best and When

Strategy	Best Used When
Avoidance	Conflict is trivial, when emotions are running high and time is needed to cool them down, or when the potential disruption from an assertive action outweighs the benefits of resolution
Accommodation	The issue under dispute isn't that important to you or when you want to build up credits for later issues
Forcing	You need a quick resolution on important issues that require unpopular actions to be taken and when commitment by others to your solution is not critical
Compromise	Conflicting parties are about equal in power, when it is desirable to achieve a temporary solution to a complex issue, or when time pressures demand an expedient solution
Collaboration	Time pressures are minimal, when all parties seriously want a win-win solution, and when the issue is too important to be compromised

the conflict. *Accommodation* can assist in issues that are more important to others than to you or when harmony and stability are important to you. Finally, *compromise* works well in achieving temporary settlements to complex issues or reaching a solution when time constraints dictate and parties are about equal in power.

Which conflicts do you handle? Not every conflict justifies your attention. Some might not be worth the effort; others might be unmanageable. Not every conflict is worth your time and effort to resolve. Avoidance might appear to be a cop-out, but it can sometimes be the most appropriate response. You can improve your overall management effectiveness and your conflict-management skills, in particular, by avoiding trivial conflicts. Choose your battles judiciously, saving your efforts for the ones that count.

Regardless of our desires, reality tells us that some conflicts are unmanageable.[59] When antagonisms are deeply rooted, when one or both parties wish to prolong a conflict, or when emotions run so high that constructive interaction is impossible, your efforts to manage the conflict are unlikely to meet with much success. Don't be lured into the naive belief that a good manager can resolve every conflict effectively. Some aren't worth the effort. Some are outside your realm of influence. Still others may be functional and, as such, are best left alone.

Who are the conflict players? If you choose to manage a conflict situation, it is important that you take the time to get to know the players. Who is involved in the conflict? What interests does each party represent? What are each player's values, personality, feelings, and resources? Your chances of success in managing a conflict will be greatly enhanced if you can view the conflict situation through the eyes of the conflicting parties.

What are the sources of the conflict? Conflicts don't pop out of thin air. They have causes. Because your approach to resolving a conflict is likely to be determined largely by its causes, you need to determine the source of the conflict. Research indicates that, although conflicts have varying causes, they can generally be separated into three categories: communication differences, structural differences, and personal differences.[60]

Communication differences are disagreements arising from semantic difficulties, misunderstandings, and noise in the communication channels. People are often quick to assume that most conflicts are caused by lack of communication, but, as one author has noted, there is usually plenty of communication going on in most conflicts.[61] As we pointed out at the beginning of this chapter, many people equate good communication with having others agree with their views. What might at first look like an interpersonal conflict based on poor communication is usually found, upon closer analysis, to be a disagreement caused by different role requirements, unit goals, personalities, value systems, or similar factors. As a source of conflict for managers, poor communication probably gets more attention than it deserves.

As we discussed in Chapter 5, organizations are horizontally and vertically differentiated. This *structural differentiation* creates problems of integration, which frequently cause conflicts. Individuals disagree over goals, decision alternatives, performance criteria, and resource allocations. These conflicts are not caused by poor communication or personal animosities. Rather, they are rooted in the structure of the organization itself.

The third conflict source is *personal differences*. Conflicts can evolve out of individual idiosyncrasies and personal value systems. The bad chemistry between some

Being a successful manager depends in part on knowing how to manage conflict. Resolving differences between employees who are likely to have diverse backgrounds (gender, age, culture) is not an easy task. But with proper training and an understanding of how to effectively manage conflict, success can be achieved.

people makes it hard for them to work together. Factors such as background, education, experience, and training mold each individual into a unique personality with a particular set of values. Thus, people may be perceived as abrasive, untrustworthy, or strange. These personal differences can create conflict.

How does a manager stimulate conflict? What about the other side of conflict management—situations that require managers to stimulate conflict? The notion of stimulating conflict is often difficult to accept. For almost all of us the term "conflict" has a negative connotation, and the idea of purposely creating conflict seems to be the antithesis of good management. Few of us enjoy being in conflict situations, yet evidence demonstrates that there are situations in which an increase in conflict is constructive.[62] Although there is no clear demarcation between functional and dysfunctional conflict, and there is no definitive method for assessing the need for more conflict, an affirmative answer to one or more of the following questions may suggest a need for conflict stimulation.[63]

- Are you surrounded by "yes people?"
- Are employees afraid to admit ignorance and uncertainties to you?
- Is there so much concentration by decision makers on reaching a compromise that they lose sight of values, long-term objectives, or the organization's welfare?
- Do managers believe that it is in their best interest to maintain the impression of peace and cooperation in their unit, regardless of the price?
- Are decision makers excessively concerned about hurting the feelings of others?
- Do managers believe that popularity is more important for obtaining organizational rewards than competence and high performance?
- Do managers put undue emphasis on obtaining consensus for their decisions?
- Do employees show unusually high resistance to change?
- Is there a lack of new ideas?

We know a lot more about resolving conflict than about stimulating it. That's only natural, because human beings have been concerned with the subject of conflict reduction for hundreds, maybe thousands, of years. The dearth of ideas on conflict-stimulation techniques reflects the very recent interest in the subject.[64] The following are some preliminary suggestions that managers might want to use.[65]

The initial step in stimulating functional conflict is for managers to convey to employees the message, supported by actions, that conflict has its legitimate place. This step may require changing the culture of the organization. Individuals who challenge the status quo, suggest innovative ideas, offer divergent opinions, and demonstrate original thinking need to be rewarded visibly with promotions, salary increases, and other positive reinforcers.

As far back as Franklin Roosevelt's administration, and probably before, the White House consistently has used communication to stimulate conflict. Senior officials plant possible decisions with the media through the infamous "reliable source" route. For example, the name of a prominent judge is leaked as a possible Supreme Court appointment. If the candidate survives the public scrutiny, his or her appointment will be announced by the president. However, if the candidate is found lacking by the media and the public, the president's press secretary or other high-level official may make a formal statement such as, "At no time was this candidate under consideration." Regardless of party affiliation, occupants of the White House have regularly used the reliable-source method as a conflict-stimulation technique. It is all the more popular because of its handy escape mechanism. If the conflict level gets too high, the source can be denied and eliminated.

Ambiguous or threatening messages also encourage conflict. Information that a plant might close, that a department is likely to be eliminated, or that a layoff is imminent can reduce apathy, stimulate new ideas, and force reevaluation—all positive outcomes of increased conflict.

Another widely used method for shaking up a stagnant unit or organization is to bring in outsiders either from outside or by internal transfer with backgrounds, values, attitudes, or managerial styles that differ from those of present members. Many large corporations have used this technique during the past decade to fill vacancies on their boards of directors. Women, minority-group members, consumer activists, and others whose backgrounds and interests differ significantly from those of the rest of the board have been selected to add a fresh perspective.

We also know that structural variables are a source of conflict. It is, therefore, only logical that managers look to structure as a conflict-stimulation device. Centralizing decisions, realigning work groups, increasing formalization, and increasing interdependencies between units are all structural devices that disrupt the status quo and increase conflict levels.

Finally, one can appoint a **devil's advocate,** a person who purposely presents arguments that run counter to those proposed by the majority or against current practices. He or she plays the role of the critic, even to the point of arguing against positions with which he or she actually agrees. A devil's advocate acts as a check against groupthink and practices that have no better justification than "that's the way we've always done it around here." When thoughtfully listened to, the advocate can improve the quality of group decision making. On the other hand, others in the group often view advocates as time wasters, and their appointment is almost certain to delay any decision process.

devil's advocate
A person who purposely presents arguments that run counter to those proposed by the majority or against current practices

WHAT ARE NEGOTIATION SKILLS?

We know that lawyers and auto salespeople spend a significant amount of time on their jobs negotiating. But so, too, do managers. They have to negotiate salaries for incoming employees, cut deals with their bosses, work out differences with their peers, and resolve conflicts with employees. Others like George Cohon have to negotiate to bring their company into a new area or make deals with others outside

Who is one of the best negotiators in the United States today? While there may be some debate about who's the best, Jesse Jackson's name should be on the list. Through his effective negotiation skills, he's been able to obtain the release of prisoners of war. What's Jackson's trick? He is a good listener, he prepares for the negotiations, and he gets to know what the other side wants.

their organizations. For our purposes, we will define **negotiation** as a process in which two or more parties who have different preferences must make a joint decision and come to an agreement. To achieve this goal, both parties typically use a bargaining strategy.[66]

How do bargaining strategies differ? There are two general approaches to negotiation—distributive bargaining and integrative bargaining.[67] Let's see what is involved in each.

You see a used car advertised for sale in the newspaper. It appears to be just what you've been looking for. You go out to see the car. It's great and you want it. The owner tells you the asking price. You don't want to pay that much. The two of you then negotiate over the price. The negotiating process you are engaging in is called **distributive bargaining.** Its most identifying feature is that it operates under *zero-sum* conditions. That is, any gain you make is at the expense of the other person and vice versa. Every dollar you can get the seller to cut from the price of the used car is a dollar you save. Conversely, every dollar more he or she can get from you comes at your expense. Thus, the essence of distributive bargaining is negotiating over who gets what share of a fixed pie. Probably the most widely cited examples of distributive bargaining are traditional labor-management negotiations over wages and benefits. Typically, labor's representatives come to the bargaining table determined to get as much as they can from management. Because every cent more that labor negotiates increases management's costs, each party bargains aggressively and often treats the other as an opponent who must be defeated. In distributive bargaining, each party has a target point that defines what he or she would like to achieve. Each also has a resistance point that marks the lowest acceptable outcome (see Exhibit 12-11). The area between their resistance points is the settlement range. As long as there is some overlap in their aspiration ranges, there exists a settlement area in which each one's aspirations can be met.

negotiation
A process in which two or more parties who have different preferences must make a joint decision and come to an agreement

distributive bargaining
Negotiation under zero-sum conditions, in which any gain made by one party invovles a loss to the other party

When engaged in distributive bargaining, you should try to get your opponent to agree to your specific target point or to get as close to it as possible.[68] Examples of such tactics are persuading your opponent of the impossibility of getting to his or her target point and the advisability of accepting a settlement near yours; arguing that your target is fair, but your opponent's isn't; and attempting to get your opponent to feel emotionally generous toward you and thus accept an outcome close to your target point.

A sales representative for a women's sportswear manufacturer has just closed a $25,000 order from an independent clothing retailer. The sales rep calls in the order to her firm's credit department. She is told that the firm can't approve credit

Exhibit 12-11 Determining the Bargaining Zone

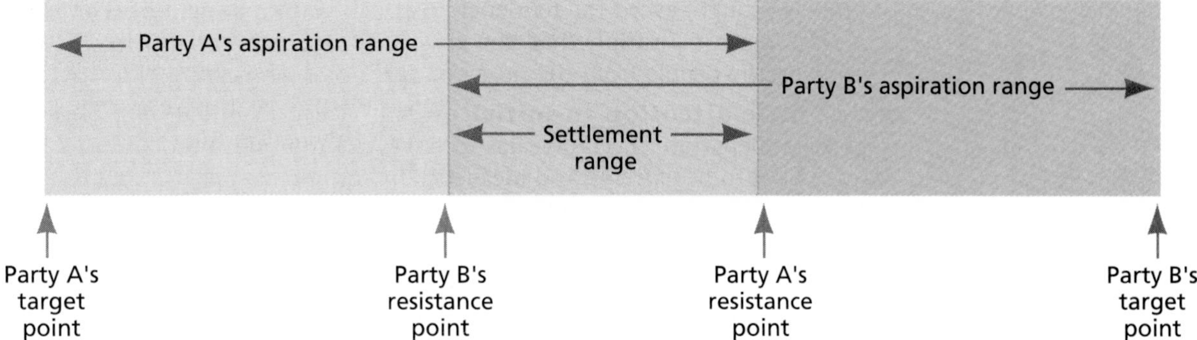

to this customer because of a past slow-pay record. The next day, the sales rep and the firm's credit manager meet to discuss the problem. The sales rep doesn't want to lose the business. Neither does the credit manager, but he also doesn't want to get stuck with an uncollectible debt. The two openly review their options. After considerable discussion, they agree on a solution that meets both their needs. The credit manager will approve the sale, but the clothing store's owner will provide a bank guarantee that will assure payment if the bill isn't paid within 60 days.

The sales-credit negotiation is an example of **integrative bargaining.** In contrast to distributive bargaining, integrative problem solving operates under the assumption that there is at least one settlement that can create a win-win solution. In general, integrative bargaining is preferable to distributive bargaining. Why? Because the former builds long-term relationships and facilitates working together in the future. It bonds negotiators and allows each to leave the bargaining table feeling that he or she has achieved a victory. Distributive bargaining, on the other hand, leaves one party a loser. It tends to build animosities and deepen divisions between people who have to work together on an ongoing basis.

integrative bargaining
Negotiation in which there is at least one settlement that involves no loss to either party

Why, then, don't we see more integrative bargaining in organizations? The answer lies in the conditions necessary for this type of negotiation to succeed. These conditions include openness with information and frankness between parties, a sensitivity by each party to the other's needs, the ability to trust one another, and a willingness by both parties to maintain flexibility.[69] Because many organizational cultures and intraorganizational relationships are not characterized by openness, trust, and flexibility, it isn't surprising that negotiations often take on a win-at-any-cost dynamic. With that in mind, let's look at some suggestions for negotiating successfully.

How do you develop effective negotiation skills? The essence of effective negotiation can be summarized in the following six recommendations.[70]

- **Research your opponent** Acquire as much information as you can about your opponent's interests and goals.[71] What people must he or she appease? What is his or her strategy? This information will help you to better understand your opponent's behavior, to predict his or her responses to your offers, and to frame solutions in terms of his or her interests.
- **Begin with a positive overture** Research shows that concessions tend to be reciprocated and lead to agreements. As a result, begin bargaining with a positive overture—perhaps a small concession—and then reciprocate your opponent's concessions.

- **Address problems, not personalities** Concentrate on the negotiation issues, not on the personal characteristics of your opponent. When negotiations get tough, avoid the tendency to attack your opponent. It is your opponent's ideas or position that you disagree with, not him or her personally. Separate the people from the problem, and don't personalize differences.
- **Pay little attention to initial offers** Treat an initial offer as merely a point of departure. Everyone has to have an initial position, and initial positions tend to be extreme and idealistic. Treat them as such.
- **Emphasize win-win solutions** If conditions are supportive, look for an integrative solution. Frame options in terms of your opponent's interests and look for solutions that can allow your opponent, as well as yourself, to declare a victory.
- **Be open to accepting third-party assistance** When stalemates are reached, consider the use of a neutral third party—a mediator, an arbitrator, or a conciliator. Mediators can help parties come to an agreement, but they don't impose a settlement. Arbitrators hear both sides of the dispute, then impose a solution. Conciliators are more informal and act as a communication conduit, passing information between the parties, interpreting messages, and clarifying misunderstandings.

WHAT IS AN EFFECTIVE PRESENTATION?

Most of us remember that first time in speech class when we were required to give a five-minute speech. It was typically a time of high anxiety—the realization that we'd have to get up in front of a group of people and talk. The nervousness, the excuses, the sweat rolling off the brow were all indicators that time was getting near. And then it was over, and many people hoped that they'd never have to get up an give a speech again. Comedian Jerry Seinfeld may have spoken for most of us when he said that "people prefer death over public speaking."[72]

The ability to deliver effective presentations is an important skill for career success. Unfortunately, organizations haven't spent much time helping students or employees.[73] But that's changing. Upper-level business courses are frequently requiring students to make group presentations. The same is true for businesses. More and more companies are offering training to their employees about how to make effective presentations.

Frightened about making a public speech? You're not alone. But research shows that it's one of the most needed skills for those seeking career advancement. So work through the apprehension, learn to speak publicly, and practice whenever you can. You'll look back one day and be thankful you developed sound presentation skills.

How do you make a presentation?

Although "podium fright" is not unusual—even for the most skilled speaker—research indicates the importance of presentation skills to your success in management.[74] So what can you do to enhance your presentation skills? Let's look at some suggestions.[75]

- **Prepare for the presentation** Singer Ethel Merman was once asked, just before a major performance, if she was nervous. Her answer: "Why should I be nervous? I know what I'm going to do! The audience should be nervous. They don't know what's going to happen!"

  What the Merman quote tells us is that when preparing for a presentation, you must identify the key issues you want to express. In essence, why are you making the presentation? You also need to know who will be in your audience so you can anticipate their needs and speak their language. The better you prepare and anticipate questions that may be thrown at you, the more comfortable you will be in the presentation.
- **Make your opening comments** The first few minutes of a presentation should be spent welcoming your audience, describing what you know about the issues your audience faces, citing your experience or credentials, and identifying your presentation's agenda. If you want your audience to do something at the end of your presentation—like approve your budget request, buy something, or so forth—tell them in your opening comments what you want them to do. By telling them ahead of time what you'd like at the end of your presentation, you frame the presentation and assist in having the audience actively listen to you.
- **Make your points** This is the heart of your presentation. It's where you'll discuss the pertinent elements of presentation. Here you justify why you should get funding or why your particular product or service should be purchased. In the discussion, you need to describe why your ideas are important and how they will benefit your listeners. Any supporting data you have should be presented at this time.
- **End the presentation** The end of a presentation includes nothing new. Rather, in the conclusion, you restate what you know about the issues facing your audience and what you recommended. If you had a request for action in the introductory part, you now come back to the action and seek closure on it. If the presentation is simply an information-sharing experience, there may not be a requested action of the audience.
- **Answer questions** In many cases, questions will be posed at the end of your presentation. However, questions may come at any point of the presentation and may even be invited by you at the beginning. Regardless of where questions are asked, there are a few simple rules to follow. First, clarify the question. This requires you to actively listen to the question. If you are not sure what the question was, ask for clarification. Don't assume you know what the questioner is asking. When you understand the question, answer it. Then go back to the questioner and make sure your response answered the question. If it didn't, you'll probably get another question. Handle it the same way.

What about delivery issues? The importance of delivering an effective presentation is open to debate. One side of the debate focuses on having a polished presentation, flashy multimedia support, and speaking without the irritating mannerisms that distract from a presentation. There's no doubt that overindulgence in any of these can decrease the effectiveness of a presentation.

But don't make the assumption that your speech has to be perfect. The other side of the debate promotes being natural in your presentation but ensuring that you address what's important. For example, the following passage appeared in an issue of *Forbes* magazine:

> A Canadian judge threw a case out of court because a witness was too boring. The case was originally reported in the *Forensic Accountant Newsletter.* The judge said the man was "beyond doubt the dullest witness I've ever had in court . . . [he] speaks in a monotonal voice . . . and uses language so drab and convoluted that even the court reporter cannot stay conscious." The judge said, "I've had it. Three solid days of this steady drone is enough. I cannot face the prospect of another 14 indictments. It's probably unethical, but I don't care."[76]

What's the message here? If your audience is interested in what you have to say, they'll listen. They'll overlook a casual "um" or "ah" and disregard your hand gestures. So, put your effort into presenting the material and meeting the audiences' needs. Any quirks in your mannerisms or your delivery will not matter greatly.

PHLIP Companion Web Site

We invite you to visit the Robbins/DeCenzo companion Web site at *www.prenhall.com/robbins* for this chapter's Internet resources.

Chapter Summary

How will you know if you fulfilled the Learning Outcomes on page 375? You will have fulfilled the Learning Outcomes if you are able to:

1 *Define communication and explain why it is important to managers.*
Communication is the transference and understanding of meaning. It is important because everything a manager does—making decisions, planning, leading, and all other activities—requires that information be communicated.

2 *Describe the communication process.*
The communication process begins with a communication sender (a source) who has a message to convey. The message is converted to symbolic form (encoding) and passed by way of a channel to the receiver, who decodes the message. To ensure accuracy, the receiver should provide the sender with feedback as a check on whether understanding has been achieved.

3 *List techniques for overcoming communication barriers.*
Some techniques for overcoming communication barriers include using feedback (ensuring that the message was, in fact received as intended), simplifying language (using language that is understood by your audience), listening actively (to capture the true meaning of the message being sent), constraining emotions (not allowing emotions to distort your ability to properly interpret the message), and watching nonverbal cues (aligning the nonverbal with the verbal).

4 *Identify behaviors related to effective active listening.*
Behaviors related to effective active listening are making eye contact, exhibiting affirmative nods and appropriate facial expressions, avoiding distracting actions

or gestures, asking questions, paraphrasing, avoiding interruption of the speaker, not overtalking, and making smooth transitions between the roles of speaker and listener.

5 *Explain what behaviors are necessary for providing effective feedback.*
In order to provide effective feedback, you must focus on specific behaviors; keep feedback impersonal, goal oriented, and well timed; ensure understanding; and direct negative feedback toward behavior that the recipient can control.

6 *Describe the contingency factors influencing delegation.*
Contingency factors guide managers in determining the degree to which authority should be delegated. These factors include the size of the organization (larger organizations are associated with increased delegation), the importance of the duty or decision (the more important a duty or decision is, the less likely it is to be delegated), task complexity (the more complex the task is, the more likely it is that decisions about the task will be delegated), organizational culture (confidence and trust in subordinates are associated with delegation), and qualities of subordinates (delegation requires subordinates with the skills, abilities, and motivation to accept authority and act on it).

7 *Identify behaviors related to effective delegating.*
Behaviors related to effective delegating are clarifying the assignment, specifying the employees' range of discretion, allowing the employee to participate, informing others that delegation has occurred, and establishing feedback controls.

8 *Describe the steps in analyzing and resolving conflict.*
The steps to be followed in analyzing and resolving conflict situations begin by finding out your underlying conflict-handling style. Then select only conflicts that are worth the effort and that can be managed. Third, evaluate the conflict players. Fourth, assess the source of the conflict. Finally, choose the conflict-resolution option that best reflects your style and the situation.

9 *Explain why a manager might stimulate conflict.*
A manager might want to stimulate conflict if his or her unit suffers from apathy, stagnation, a lack of new ideas, or unresponsiveness to change. A manager can stimulate conflict by changing the organization's culture through the use of communications, by bringing in outsiders, by restructuring the organization, or by appointing a devil's advocate.

10 *Contrast distributive and integrative bargaining.*
Distributive bargaining creates a win-lose situation because the object of negotiation is treated as fixed in amount. Integrative bargaining treats available resources as variable and hence creates the potential for win-win solutions.

Review and Application Questions

READING FOR COMPREHENSION

1 Which type of communication do you believe is most effective in a work setting? Why?

2 Why are effective interpersonal skills so important to a manager's success?

3 What is conflict?

4 Contrast the traditional, human relations, and interactionist views of conflict. Which of the three views do you think most managers have? Do you think this view is appropriate?

5 What are the five primary conflict-resolution techniques?

6 What can a manager do if he or she wants to be a more effective negotiator?

LINKING CONCEPTS TO PRACTICE

1 "Ineffective communication is the fault of the sender." Do you agree or disagree with this statement? Support your position.

2 Describe why effective communication isn't synonymous with agreement between the communicating parties?

3 How might a manager use the grapevine to his or her advantage? Support your response.

4 Using what you have learned about active listening in this chapter, would you describe yourself as a good listener? Are there any areas in which you are deficient? If so, how could you improve your listening skills?

5 Assume that you found an apartment that you wanted to rent and the ad had said: "$750/month, negotiable." What could you do to improve the likelihood that you would negotiate the lowest possible price?

Management Workshop

Team Skill-Building Exercise

Active Listening

PURPOSE

To reinforce the idea that good listening skills are necessary for managers and that as communicators we can motivate listeners to actively listen.

TIME REQUIRED

Approximately 30 minutes.

PROCEDURE

Most of us, if we would admit it, are at times pretty poor listeners. This is probably because active listening is very demanding. This exercise is specifically designed to dramatize how difficult it is to listen actively and to accurately interpret what is being said. It also points out how emotions can distort communication.

Your instructor will read you a story and ask you some follow-up questions. You will need a clean piece of paper and a pencil.

Developing Your Active Listening Skill

Listening More Effectively

ABOUT THE SKILL

Active listening requires you to concentrate on what is being said. It's more than just hearing the words. It involves a concerted effort to understand and interpret the speaker's message.

STEPS IN LISTENING ACTIVELY

- **Make eye contact.** How do you feel when somebody doesn't look at you when you're speaking? If you're like most people, you're likely to interpret this behavior as aloofness or disinterest. Making eye contact with the speaker focuses your attention, reduces the likelihood that you will become distracted, and encourages the speaker.
- **Exhibit affirmative nods and appropriate facial expressions.** The effective listener shows interest in what is being said through nonverbal signals. Affirmative nods and appropriate facial expressions, when added to good eye contact, convey to the speaker that you're listening.
- **Avoid distracting actions or gestures that suggest boredom.** In addition to showing interest, you must avoid actions that suggest that your mind is somewhere else. When listening, don't look at your watch, shuffle papers, play with your pencil, or engage in similar distractions. They make the speaker feel that you're bored or disinterested or indicate that you aren't fully attentive.
- **Ask questions.** The critical listener analyzes what he or she hears and asks questions. This behavior provides clarification, ensures understanding, and assures the speaker that you're listening.
- **Paraphrase using your own words.** The effective listener uses phrases such as: "What I hear you saying is . . ." or "Do you mean . . .?" Paraphrasing is an excellent control device to check on whether you're listening carefully and to verify that what you heard is accurate.
- **Avoid interrupting the speaker.** Let the speaker complete his or her thought before you try to respond. Don't try to second guess where the speaker's thoughts are going. When the speaker is finished, you'll know it.
- **Don't overtalk.** Most of us would rather express our own ideas than listen to what someone else says. Talking might be more fun and silence might be uncomfortable, but you can't talk and listen at the

same time. The good listener recognizes this fact and doesn't overtalk.

- **Make smooth transitions between the roles of speaker and listener.** The effective listener makes transitions smoothly from speaker to listener and back to speaker. From a listening perspective, this means concentrating on what a speaker has to say and practicing not thinking about what you're going to say as soon as you get your chance.

Practicing the Skill

ACTIVE LISTENING

Ask a friend to tell you about his or her day and listen without interrupting. When your friend has finished speaking, ask two or three questions if needed to obtain more clarity and detail. Listen carefully to the answers. Now summarize your friend's day in no more than five sentences.

How well did you do? Let your friend rate the accuracy of your paraphrase (and try not to interrupt).

A Case Application

Developing Your Diagnostic and Analytical Skills

KAREN VESPER READS THE SIGNALS

What do AT&T, the Men's Warehouse, and Doorway Rug Service, Inc., of Buffalo, New York, have in common? These organizations are teaching many of their employees—especially those in marketing and sales—to make decisions on the basis of nonverbal communication cues. For Karen Vesper, vice president of Doorway, focusing on nonverbal communications has become an important part of her interpersonal dealings.[77]

Several years ago, Karen became interested in how body movements and mannerisms truly reflect what an individual is saying. Continually reading in this area of study, Vesper has been able to make decisions about potential employees and potential customers by "reading" them. For example, Vesper believes that body language can give a person a competitive advantage. It can make the difference when closing the sale, or in Doorway's case, hiring new employees. For example, during interviews, Vesper pays constant attention to the job candidate's eye movements and mannerisms. Vesper believes that she can correctly predict if the job candidate will be an aggressive salesperson while simultaneously being personable and friendly. How does she do this? By looking at their eyes and the way that they present themselves. In one case, a hiring decision came down to two people. Candidate 1 was animated and made constant eye contact. Candidate 2 never looked Karen in the eye, leaned back in his chair, and crossed both his legs and arms. Candidate 1 demonstrated the communication skills that Vesper found aligned with successful performance in her organization.

Karen Vesper is convinced that nonverbal communications can play a significant role in helping her organization achieve its annual sales goals. Personally, she has found that it has helped her "qualify" customers. For instance, even though a potential customer says Yes, crossed arms and legs emphatically state No! Understanding this, Vesper is in a better position to probe further into the possible objections the customer has. She has found that, in many cases, she is able to steer the conversation in a direction that ultimately leads to successfully closing a sale. And that is a major competitive advantage.

QUESTIONS

1. Describe the communications process that Karen Vesper uses in her dealings with job candidates and employees.
2. What problems might Vesper encounter by her heavy reliance on the nonverbal communications?
3. What communication guidance would you give to Vesper and individuals like her who place an inordinately high value on body language? Explain your position.

Developing Your Investigative Skills

Using the Internet

Visit *www.prenhall.com/robbins* for updated Internet Exercises.

Enhancing Your Writing Skills

Communicating Effectively

1 Develop a two- to three-page report describing what you can do to improve the likelihood that your verbal communications will be received and understood as you intended them to be.

2 Do some research on male versus female communication styles. Provide a two- to three-page summary of what you've found. Do men and women communicate differently? If so, what are the implications of your findings for managers?

3 Search on the Internet for common communication shortcuts used by e-mail users. Identify 15 acronyms and describe what they mean. How should these acronyms be used? Describe any barriers these acronyms may cause a user. A receiver.

Thirteen

Foundations of Control

LEARNING OUTCOMES After reading this chapter, I will be able to:

1 Define *control.*
2 Describe three approaches to control.
3 Explain why control is important.
4 Describe the control process.
5 Distinguish among the three types of control.
6 Describe the qualities of an effective control system.
7 Identify the contingency factors in the control process.
8 Explain how controls can become dysfunctional.
9 Describe how national differences influence the control process.
10 Identify the ethical dilemmas in employee monitoring.

At the Port of New Orleans, the largest coffee port in the United States, one company is handling an old-fashioned product in a new-fashioned way. Frederico Pacorini's SiloCaf, a fully computerized bulk-coffee storage handling and processing facility, is a place where tradition meets technology and where control is taking on a new perspective.[1]

SiloCaf was founded in 1933 as a freight-forwarding company that moved products from one location to another. Today, however, the company primarily moves coffee, and the way that it controls and monitors its entire processing operations is about as technologically advanced as possible. Why has SiloCaf invested in technology for such a seemingly simple product? The primary reason is that consumers want the same flavor each time they purchase a can of coffee. However, coffee is a natural product, and coffee beans may vary from crop to crop. Getting consistent flavor is difficult without some way to control the coffee blend. That's crucial to a big company like Folgers that demands consistency in taste. Nearly one third of all coffee processed in the United States comes through the New Orleans facility. Without the technology, the company simply could not meet customer demands. As a result, SiloCaf is addressing these challenges by using information systems and computer technology.

Mossimo Toma is SiloCaf's systems and resources manager. He is responsible for overseeing the coffee-blending process. Each week, 10 million pounds of coffee beans come into SiloCaf's warehouse from all over the world. Once the coffee has been processed, it's loaded into bags or bulk containers and shipped to a coffee-roasting company. At any one time, SiloCaf has from 35 to 40 million pounds of coffee in its facility for processing. If you consider the price of a pound of coffee, SiloCaf has an extremely valuable resource in its possession. Actually, SiloCaf never owns the coffee. Rather, it's owned by the roasting company or the dealer who delivers the coffee to the roasting company.

All the mechanical parts in SiloCaf's New Orleans facility have been brought from Italy, where the company first developed its technology. Frederico Pacorini, the son of the founder and manager of the New Orleans facility, says that technology in a business like theirs is important because it allows them to make all the blends they need for the coffee roasters and to optimize the process of making the various coffee blends. SiloCaf's employees receive continually updated statistical reports for each one of the scales used to blend coffee. The reports enable them to check the consistency of the scale's performance, which is important for achieving the consistency that the coffee drinker wants. In addition, the technology also helps employees to oversee the cleaning, sorting, and bagging of raw coffee beans before they are shipped to roasters.

You might think that this high-tech control would be expensive. It's not! SiloCaf's solution to the blend-consistency challenge is to use technology that is relatively simple and inexpensive. In fact, the company's investment was a mere 1 percent of all plant investment expenditures.

The SiloCaf example illustrates how effective control systems can be instrumental in improving an organization's performance. As we show in this chapter, effective management requires a well-designed control system.

What Is Control?

control
The process of monitoring activities to ensure that they are being accomplished as planned and of correcting any significant deviations

Control is the process of monitoring activities to ensure that they are being accomplished as planned and correcting any significant deviations. Managers cannot really know whether their units are performing properly until they have evaluated what activities have been done and have compared the actual performance with the desired standard.[2] An effective control system ensures that activities are completed in ways that lead to the attainment of the organization's goals.

The effectiveness of a control system is determined by how well it facilitates goal achievement. The more it helps managers achieve their organization's goals, the better the control system.[3]

When we introduced organizations in Chapter 1, we stated that every organization attempts to effectively and efficiently reach its goals. Does that imply, however, that the control systems organizations use are identical? In other words, would Volvo, Bayer, France Telecom, and Wal-Mart all have the same type of control system? Probably not. Although similarities may exist, there are generally three different approaches to designing control systems. These are market, bureaucratic, and clan controls[4] as summarized in Exhibit 13-1.

Market control emphasizes the use of external market mechanisms. Controls are built around such criteria as price competition or market share. Organizations using a market control approach usually have clearly specified and distinct products and services and considerable competition. Under these conditions, the various divisions of the organization are typically turned into profit centers and evaluated by the percentage of total corporate profits each generates. For instance, at Matsushita, each of the various divisions—which produce such products as videos, home appliances, and industrial equipment—is evaluated according to its contribution to the company's total profits. Using these measures, managers make decisions about future resource allocations, strategic changes, and other work activities that may need attention.

market control
An approach to control that emphasizes the use of external market mechanisms such as price competition and market share

A second approach to control systems is **bureaucratic control,** a control approach that emphasizes authority and relies on administrative rules, regulations, procedures, and policies. This type of control depends on standardization of activities, well-defined job descriptions to direct employee work behavior, and other administrative mechanisms—such as budgets—to ensure that organizational members exhibit appropriate work behaviors and meet established performance standards. At British Petroleum, managers of various divisions are allowed considerable autonomy and freedom to run their units as they see fit. Yet they are expected to stick closely to their budgets and stay within corporate guidelines. And managers at AlliedSignal and Dana Corporation have taken the control sys-

bureaucratic control
An approach to control that emphasizes authority and relies on administrative rules, regulations, procedures, and policies

Exhibit 13-1
Characteristics of Three Approaches to Control Systems

Type of Control	Characteristics
Market	Uses external market mechanisms, such as price competition and relative market share, to establish standards used in system. Typically used by organizations with clearly specified and distinct products or services and that face considerable marketplace competition.
Bureaucratic	Emphasizes organizational authority. Relies on administrative and hierarchical mechanisms, such as rules, regulations, procedures, policies, standardization of activities, well-defined job descriptions, and budgets to ensure that employees exhibit appropriate behaviors and meet performance standards.
Clan	Regulates employee behavior by the shared values, norms, traditions, rituals, beliefs, and other aspects of the organization's culture. Often used by organizations in which teams are common and technology is changing rapidly.

What kind of control system is Dell Computer managers using in their dealings with employees? At Dell, it's clan control. Their approach is designed to control employee behaviors by regulating the shared values, norms, traditions, beliefs, and other aspects of the organization's culture. At Dell, such a system has had a profound effect—the computer manufacturer is one of the more successful companies in its industry.

tem one step further. They have imposed it on their suppliers in an attempt to control their company's production costs.[5]

Clan control is an approach to designing control systems in which employee behaviors are regulated by the shared values, norms, traditions, rituals, beliefs, and other aspects of the organization's culture. In contrast to bureaucratic control, which is based on strict hierarchical mechanisms, clan control depends on the individual and the group (the clan) to identify appropriate and expected work-related behaviors and performance measures. Clan control is typically found in organizations in which teams are widely used and technologies change often. For instance, organizational members at Dell Computer are aware of the company's obsession with customer service, speed, and flexibility. What's unique about the Dell culture? It—fostered by the company's founder, Michael Dell—conveys to employees what's really important in the organization. They are guided and controlled by the clan's culture rather than by prescribed administrative controls.

clan control
An approach to designing control systems in which employee behaviors are regulated by the shared values, norms, traditions, rituals, beliefs, and other aspects of the organization's culture

It is important to recognize that most organizations do not totally rely on just one of these three approaches to design an appropriate control system. Instead, an organization typically chooses to emphasize either bureaucratic or clan control and then add some market control measures. The key, however, in any of the approaches is to design an appropriate control system that helps the organization effectively and efficiently reach its goals.

The Importance of Control

Planning can be done; an organization structure can be created to efficiently facilitate the achievement of objectives, and employees can be directed and motivated. Still, there is no assurance that activities are going as planned and that the goals are, in fact, being attained. Control is the final link in the functional chain of management. However, the value of the control function lies predominantly in its relation to planning and delegating activities.

In Chapter 3, we described objectives as the foundation of planning. Objectives give specific direction to managers. However, just stating objectives or having employees accept your objectives is no guarantee that the necessary actions have been accomplished. The effective manager needs to follow up to ensure that the actions others are supposed to take and the objectives they are supposed to achieve are, in fact, being taken and achieved.

THE CONTROL PROCESS

The control process consists of three separate and distinct steps: (1) measuring actual performance, (2) comparing actual performance against a standard, and (3) taking managerial action to correct deviations or inadequate standards (see Exhibit 13-2). Before we consider each step in detail, you should be aware that the control process assumes that standards of performance already exist, having been created in the planning function. If managers use some variation of mutual goal setting, then the objectives set are, by definition, tangible, verifiable, and measurable. In such instances, those objectives are the standards against which progress is measured and compared. If goal setting is not practiced, then standards are the specific performance indicators that management uses. Our point is that these standards are developed in the planning function; planning must precede control.

WHAT IS MEASURING?

To determine actual performance, a manager must acquire information about it. The first step in control, then, is measuring. Let's consider how we measure and what we measure.

How do managers measure? Four common sources of information frequently used to measure actual performance are personal observation, statistical reports, oral reports, and written reports. Each has particular strengths and weak-

Exhibit 13-2 The Control Process

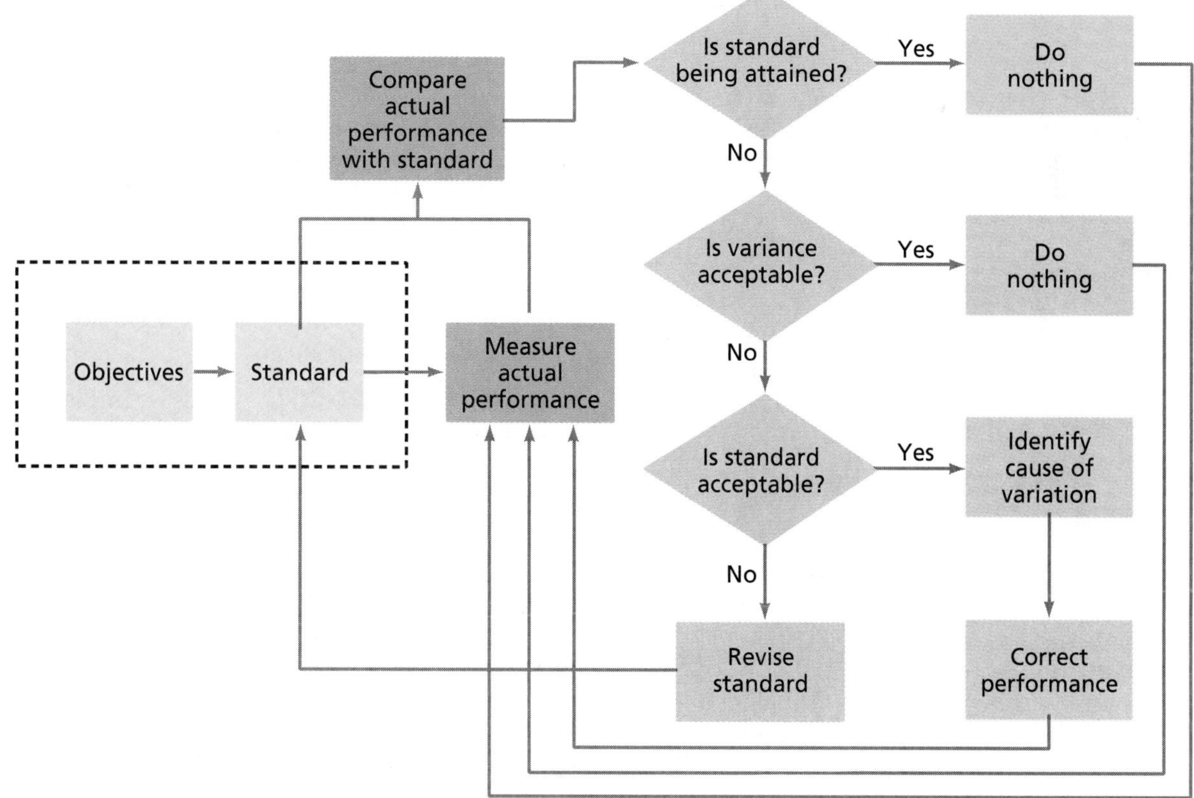

nesses; however, use of a combination of them increases both the number of input sources and the probability of receiving reliable information.

Personal observation provides first-hand, intimate knowledge of the actual activity—information that is not filtered through others. It permits intensive coverage because minor as well as major performance activities can be observed, and it provides opportunities for the manager to read between the lines. Management-by-walking-around can pick up omissions, facial expressions, and tones of voice that may be missed by other sources. Unfortunately, in a time when quantitative information suggests objectivity, personal observation is often considered an inferior information source. It is subject to perceptual biases; what one manager sees, another might not. Personal observation also consumes a good deal of time. Finally, this method suffers from obtrusiveness. Employees might interpret a manager's overt observation as a sign of a lack of confidence or of mistrust.

Computers and sophisticated software systems give managers realtime statistical reports for measuring actual performance.[6] Statistical reports, however, are not limited to computer printouts. They can also be presented as graphs, bar charts, or numerical displays of any form that managers can use for assessing performance. Although statistical information is easy to visualize and effective for showing relationships, it provides limited information about an activity. Statistics report on only a few key areas and may often ignore other important factors.

Information can also be acquired through oral reports—that is, through conferences, meetings, one-to-one conversations, or telephone calls. The advantages and disadvantages of this method of measuring performance are similar to those of personal observation. Although the information is filtered, it is fast, allows for feedback, and permits expression and tone of voice as well as words themselves to convey meaning. Historically, one of the major drawbacks of oral reports has been the problem of documenting information for later reference. However, our technological capabilities have progressed in the past couple of decades to the point where oral reports can be efficiently taped and become as permanent as if they were written.

Actual performance may also be measured by written reports. Like statistical reports, they are slower yet more formal than first- or second-hand oral measures. This formality also often gives them greater comprehensiveness and conciseness than is found in oral reports. In addition, written reports are usually easy to catalog and reference.

Given the varied advantages and disadvantages of each of these four measurement techniques, managers should use all four for comprehensive control efforts.

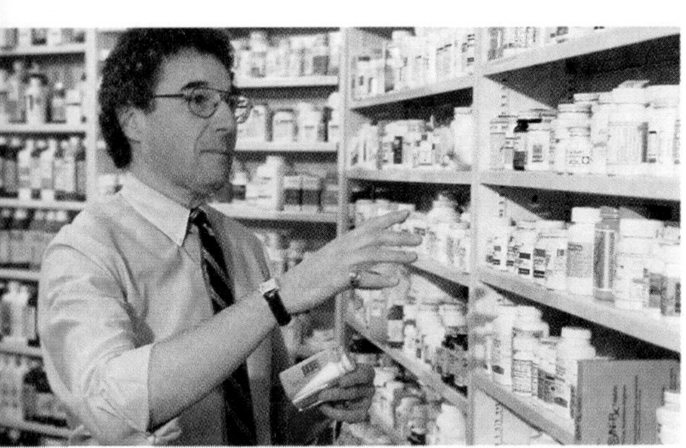

Baxter Pharmaceuticals uses a variety of controls to ensure that their business is operating effectively and that they are meeting customer's needs. These include ensuring adequate stock and helping customers lower their costs and increase their profits.

What do managers measure? What we measure is probably more critical to the control process than how we measure. The selection of the wrong criteria can result in serious dysfunctional consequences. Besides, what we measure determines, to a great extent, what people in the organization will attempt to excel at.[7] For example, assume that your instructor has required a total of 10 writing assignments from the exercises at the end of each textbook chapter. But, in the grade computation section of the syllabus, you notice that these assignments are not scored. In fact, when you ask your professor about this, she replies that these writing assignments are for your own enlightenment and do not affect your grade for the course; grades are solely a function of how well you perform on the three exams. We predict that you would, not surprisingly, exert most, if not all, of your effort toward doing well on the three exams.

For the most part, controls are directed at one of several areas: information, operations, finances, or people. Some control criteria, however, are applicable to any management situation. For instance, because all managers, by definition, direct the activities of others, criteria such as employee satisfaction or turnover and absenteeism rates can be measured. Most managers have budgets for their area of responsibility set in monetary units (dollars, pounds, francs, lire, and so on). Keeping costs within budget is, therefore, a fairly common control measure.[8] However, any comprehensive control system needs to recognize the diversity of activities among managers. A production manager in a manufacturing plant might use measures of the quantity of units produced per day, units produced per labor-hour, scrap per unit of output, or percentage of rejects or items returned by customers. The manager of an administrative unit in a government agency might use number of document pages produced per day, number of orders processed per hour, or average time required to process service calls. Marketing managers often use measures such as percentage of market captured, average dollar value per sale, or number of customer visits per salesperson.[9]

What we measure is probably more critical to the control process than how we measure. The selection of the wrong criteria can result in a seriously dysfunctional consequence.

The performance of some activities is difficult to measure in quantifiable terms. It is more difficult, for instance, for an administrator to measure the performance of a research chemist or an elementary school teacher than of a person who sells life insurance, but most activities can be broken down into objective segments that allow for measurement. The manager needs to determine what value a person, department, or unit contributes to the organization and then convert the contribution into standards.

Most jobs and activities can be expressed in tangible and measurable terms. When a performance indicator cannot be stated in quantifiable terms, managers should look for and use subjective measures. Certainly, subjective measures have significant limitations. Still, they are better than having no standards at all and ignoring the control function. If an activity is important, the excuse that it is difficult to measure is inadequate. In such cases, managers should use subjective performance criteria. Of course, any analysis or decisions made on the basis of subjective criteria should recognize the limitations of the data.

How do managers determine discrepancies between actual performance and planned goals? The comparing step determines the degree of discrepancy between actual performance and the standard. Some variation in performance can be expected in all activities; it is therefore critical to determine the acceptable **range of variation** (see Exhibit 13-3). Deviations in excess of this range become significant and receive the manager's attention. In the comparison stage, managers are particularly concerned with the size and direction of the variation. An example should help make this clearer.

range of variation
The acceptable parameters of variance between actual performance and the standard

Pat McFarlane is the sales manager for Mid-Western Distributors. The firm distributes imported beers in several states in the Midwest. McFarlane prepares a report during the first week of each month that summarizes sales for the previous month, classified by brand name. Exhibit 13-4 displays both the standard and actual sales figures (in hundreds of cases) for the month of July.

Exhibit 13-3
Defining an Acceptable Range of Variation

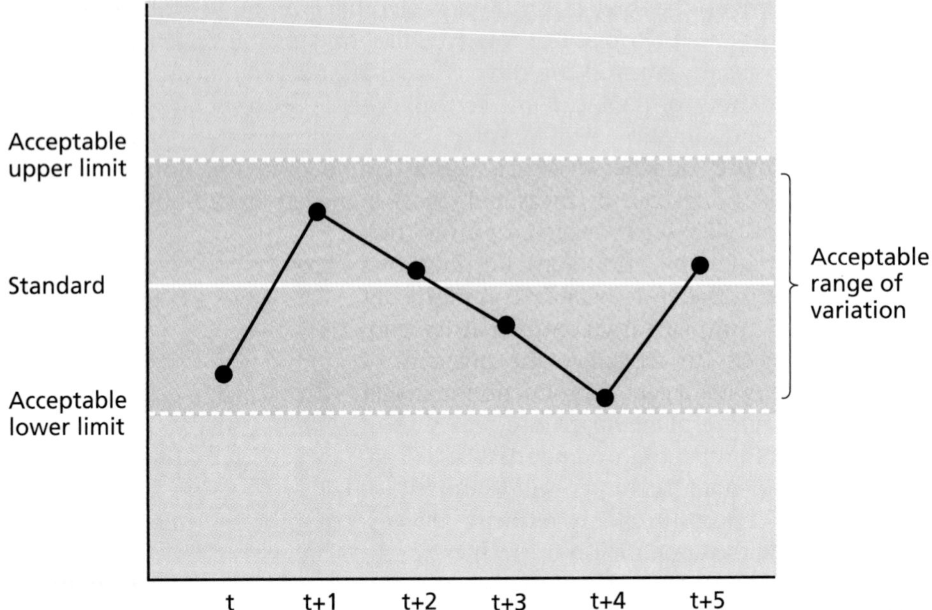

Should McFarlane be concerned about the July performance? Sales were a bit higher than he had originally targeted, but does that mean that there were no significant deviations? Even though overall performance was generally quite favorable, several brands might deserve the sales manager's attention. However, the number of brands that deserve attention depends on what Pat believes to be significant. How much variation should McFarlane allow before he takes corrective action?

The deviation on several brands is very small and undoubtedly not worthy of special attention. These include Molson, Moosehead, and Amstel Light. Are the shortages for Corona and Dos Equis brands significant? That's a judgment McFarlane must make. Heineken sales were 15 percent below the goal. This brand needs attention. McFarlane should look for a cause. In this case, he attributes the loss to aggressive advertising and promotion programs by the big domestic producers, Anheuser-Busch and Miller. Because Heineken is the best-selling import, it is most vulnerable to the promotion clout of the big domestic producers. If the

Exhibit 13-4
Mid-Western Distributors' Sales Performance for July (hundreds of cases)

Brand	Standard	Actual	Over (Under)
Heineken	1,075	913	(162)
Molson	630	634	4
Beck's	800	912	112
Moosehead	620	622	2
Labatt's	540	672	132
Corona	160	140	(20)
Amstel Light	225	220	(5)
Dos Equis	80	65	(15)
Tecate	170	286	116
Total cases	4,300	4,464	164

decline in Heineken is more than a temporary slump, McFarlane will need to reduce his orders with the brewery and reduce his inventory.

An error in understating sales can be as troublesome as an overstatement. For instance, is the surprising popularity of Tecate a one-month aberration, or is this brand increasing its market share? Our Mid-Western example illustrates that both overvariance and undervariance require managerial attention.

WHAT MANAGERIAL ACTION CAN BE TAKEN?

The third and final step in the control process is managerial action. Managers can choose among three courses of action: They can do nothing; they can correct the actual performance, or they can revise the standard. Because "doing nothing" is fairly self-explanatory, let's look more closely at the latter two choices.

If the source of the variation has been deficient performance, the manager will want to take corrective action. Examples of such corrective action might include changes in strategy, structure, compensation practices, or training programs; the redesign of jobs; or the replacement of personnel.

A manager who decides to correct actual performance has to make another decision: Should he or she take immediate or basic corrective action? **Immediate corrective action** corrects problems at once and gets performance back on track. **Basic corrective action** asks how and why performance has deviated and then proceeds to correct the source of deviation. It is not unusual for managers to rationalize that they do not have the time to take basic corrective action and therefore must be content to perpetually put out fires with immediate corrective action. Effective managers, however, analyze deviations and, when the benefits justify it, take the time to permanently correct significant variances between standard and actual performance.

immediate corrective action
Correcting a problem at once to get performance back on track

basic corrective action
Determining how and why performance has deviated and then correcting the source of deviation

To return to our example of Mid-Western Distributors, Pat McFarlane might take basic corrective action on the negative variance for Heineken. He might increase promotion efforts, increase the advertisement budget for this brand, or reduce future orders with the manufacturer. The action McFarlane takes will depend on his assessment of each brand's potential sales.

It is also possible that the variance was a result of an unrealistic standard—that is, the goal may have been too high or too low. In such cases the standard needs corrective attention, not the performance. In our example, the sales manager might need to raise the standard for Tecate to reflect its increasing popularity, much as, in sports, athletes adjust their performance goals upward during a season if they achieve their season goal early.

The more troublesome problem is revising of a performance standard downward. If an employee or unit falls significantly short of its target, the natural response is for the employee or unit to blame the standard. For instance, students who make a low grade on a test often attack the grade cutoff points as too high. Rather than accept the fact that their performance was inadequate, the students argue that the standards were unreasonable. Similarly, salespeople who fail to meet their monthly quota may attribute the failure to an unrealistic quota. It may be true that standards are too high, resulting in a significant variance and demotivating those employees being assessed against it. However, keep in mind that if employees or managers don't meet the standard, the first thing they are likely to attack is the standard itself. If you believe that the standard is realistic, hold your ground. Explain your position, reaffirm to the employee or manager that you expect future performance to improve, and then take the necessary corrective action to turn that expectation into reality.

Types of Control

Management can implement controls before an activity commences, while the activity is going on, or after the activity has been completed. The first type is called feedforward control; the second is concurrent control, and the last is feedback control (see Exhibit 13-5).

WHAT IS FEEDFORWARD CONTROL?

feedforward control
Control that prevents anticipated problems

The most desirable type of control—**feedforward control**—prevents anticipated problems because it takes place in advance of the actual activity. It's future directed.[10] For instance, managers at AlliedSignal may hire additional personnel as soon as the government announces that the firm has won a major defense contract. The hiring of personnel ahead of time prevents potential delays. The key to feedforward control, therefore, is taking managerial action before a problem occurs.

Feedforward controls allow management to prevent problems rather than having to cure them later. Unfortunately, these controls require timely and accurate information that is often difficult to develop. As a result, managers frequently have to use one of the other two types of control.

WHEN IS CONCURRENT CONTROL USED?

concurrent control
Control that takes place while an activity is in progress

Concurrent control, as its name implies, takes place while an activity is in progress. When control is enacted while the work is being performed, management can correct problems before they become too costly.

The best-known form of concurrent control is direct supervision. When a manager directly oversees the actions of an employee, the manager can concurrently monitor the employee's actions and correct problems as they occur. Although there is obviously some delay between the activity and the manager's corrective response, the delay is minimal. Technical equipment can be designed to include concurrent controls. Most computers, for instance, are programmed to provide operators with immediate response if an error is made. If you input the wrong command, the program's concurrent controls reject your command and may even tell you why it is wrong.

WHY IS FEEDBACK CONTROL SO POPULAR?

feedback control
Control that takes place after an action

The most popular type of control relies on feedback. The control takes place after the action. The control report that Pat McFarlane used for assessing beer sales is an example of a **feedback control.**

Exhibit 13-5
Types of Control

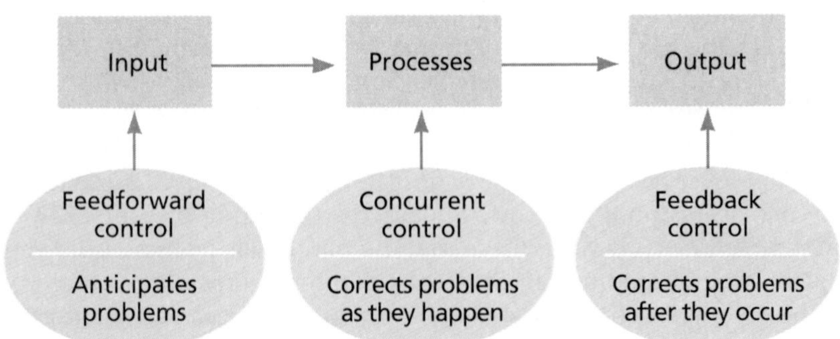

The major drawback of this type of control is that by the time the manager has the information the damage has already been done. It's analogous to closing the barn door after the horse has been stolen. But for many activities, feedback is the only viable type of control available. We should note that feedback has two advantages over feedforward and concurrent control.[11] First, feedback provides managers with meaningful information on how effective their planning effort was. Feedback that indicates little variance between standard and actual performance is evidence that planning was generally on target. If the deviation is great, a manager can use that information to make new plans more effective. Second, feedback control can enhance employee motivation. People want information on how well they have performed. Feedback control provides that information (see Developing Your Performance Feedback Skill, p. 433).

Through the use of sophisticated information systems, Boeing project managers are able to provide timely feedback to workers who assemble large freightliners. This feedback helps team members take any corrective measures necessary to ensure that quality standards are attained and the most efficient means of achieving it are used.

Qualities of an Effective Control System

Effective control systems tend to have certain qualities in common.[12] The importance of these qualities varies with the situation, but we can generalize that the following characteristics should make a control system effective.

- **Accuracy** A control system that generates inaccurate information can result in management's failing to take action when it should or responding to a problem that doesn't exist. An accurate control system is reliable and produces valid data.
- **Timeliness** Controls should call management's attention to variations in time to prevent serious infringement on a unit's performance. The best information has little value if it is dated. Therefore, an effective control system must provide timely information.
- **Economy** A control system must be economically reasonable. Any system of control has to justify the benefits that it gives in relation to the costs it incurs. To minimize costs, management should try to impose the least amount of control necessary to produce the desired results.
- **Flexibility** Controls must be flexible enough to adjust to problems or to take advantage of new opportunities. Few organizations face environments so stable that there is no need for flexibility. Even highly mechanistic structures require controls that can be adjusted as times and conditions change.
- **Understandability** Controls that cannot be understood have no value. It is sometimes necessary, therefore, to substitute less complex controls for sophisticated devices. A control system that is difficult to understand can cause unnecessary mistakes, frustrate employees, and eventually be ignored.

- **Reasonable criteria** Control standards must be reasonable and attainable. If they are too high or unreasonable, they no longer motivate. Because most employees don't want to risk being labeled incompetent by accusing superiors of asking too much, employees may resort to unethical or illegal shortcuts. Controls should, therefore, enforce standards that challenge and stretch people to reach higher performance levels without demotivating them or encouraging deception.
- **Strategic placement** Management can't control everything that goes on in an organization. Even if it could, the benefits couldn't justify the costs. As a result, managers should place controls on factors that are strategic to the organization's performance. Controls should cover the critical activities, operations, and events within the organization.[13] That is, they should focus on places at which variations from standard are most likely to occur or at which a variation would do the greatest harm. If a department's labor costs are $100,000 a month and postage costs are $150 a month, a 5 percent overrun in the former is more critical than a 20 percent overrun in the latter. Hence, we should establish controls for labor and a critical dollar allocation, whereas postage expenses would not appear to be critical.
- **Emphasis on the exception** Because managers can't control all activities, they should place their strategic control devices where those devices can call attention only to the exceptions. An exception system ensures that a manager is not overwhelmed by information on variations from standard. For instance, if management policy gives supervisors the authority to give annual raises up to $500 a month, approve individual expenses up to $1,500, and make capital expenditures up to $10,000, then only deviations above those amounts require approval from higher levels of management. These checkpoints become controls that are part of the authority constraints and free higher levels of management from reviewing routine expenditures.
- **Multiple criteria** Managers and employees alike will seek to look good on the criteria that are controlled. If management controls by using a single measure such as unit profit, effort will be focused only on looking good on that standard. Multiple measures of performance widen this narrow focus. Multiple criteria have a dual positive effect. Because they are more difficult to manipulate than a single measure, they can discourage employee efforts to merely look good. In addition, because performance can rarely be objectively evaluated from a single indicator, multiple criteria make possible more accurate assessments of performance.
- **Corrective action** An effective control system not only indicates when a significant deviation from standard occurs but also suggests what action should be taken to correct the deviation. That is, it ought to both point out the problem and specify the solution. This form of control is frequently accomplished by establishing if-then guidelines; for instance, if unit revenues drop more than 5 percent, then unit costs should be reduced by a similar amount.

Contingency Factors of Control

Although our generalizations about effective control systems provide guidelines, their validity is influenced by situational factors. These include size of the organization, one's position in the organization's hierarchy, degree of decentralization, organizational culture, and importance of an activity (see Exhibit 13-6).

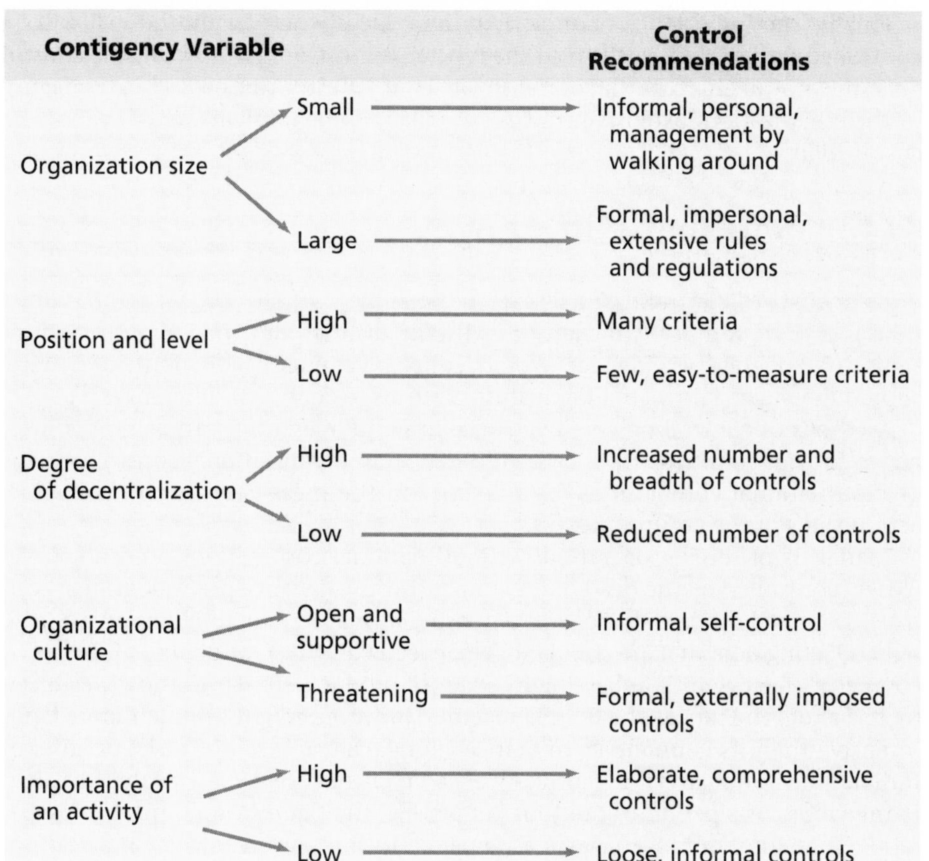

Exhibit 13-6
Contingency Factors in the Design of Control Systems

Control systems should vary according to the size of the organization. A small business relies on informal and more personal control devices. Concurrent control through direct supervision is probably most cost effective. As organizations increase in size, direct supervision is likely to be supported by an expanding formal system. Very large organizations will typically have highly formalized and impersonal feedforward and feedback controls.

The higher one moves in the organization's hierarchy, the greater the need for multiple sets of control criteria, tailored to the unit's goals. This reflects the increased ambiguity in measuring performance as a person moves up the hierarchy.[14] Conversely, lower-level jobs have clearer definitions of performance, which allow for a narrower interpretation of job performance.

The greater the degree of decentralization, the more managers will need feedback on the performance of their employees' decisions. Because managers who delegate authority are ultimately responsible for the actions of those to whom it is delegated, they will want proper assurances that their employees' decisions are both effective and efficient.

The organizational culture may be one of trust, autonomy, and openness or one of fear and reprisal. In the former, we can expect to find informal self-control and, in the latter, externally imposed and formal control systems to ensure that performance is within standards. As with leadership styles, motivation techniques, organizational structuring, conflict-management techniques, and the extent to which organizational members participate in decision making, the type and extent of controls should be consistent with the organization's culture.

Finally, the importance of an activity influences whether, and how, it will be controlled. If control is costly and the repercussions from error small, the control system is not likely to be elaborate. However, if an error can be highly damaging to the organization, extensive controls are likely to be implemented—even if the cost is high.

Adjusting Controls for National Differences

The concepts of control we've discussed are appropriate for organizational units that aren't geographically distant or culturally distinct. But what about organizations that operate worldwide? Would control systems be different, and what should managers know about adjusting controls for national differences?[15]

Methods of controlling employee behavior and operations can be quite different in foreign countries. In fact, the differences in organizational control systems of multinational corporations are primarily in the measurement and corrective action steps of the control process.

Managers of foreign operations of multinational corporations tend not to be closely controlled by the head office simply because distance precludes direct controls. The head office must rely on extensive formal reports to maintain control, but collecting data that are comparable between countries introduces problems. A company's factory in Bombay might produce products similar to those produced by its factory in France. The Bombay factory, however, might be much more labor intensive than its counterpart in France (to take advantage of low labor costs in India).[16] If headquarters' executives were to control costs by, for example, calculating labor costs per unit or output per worker, the figures would not be comparable. Therefore, distance creates a tendency to formalize controls, and technological differences often make control data incomparable.

One Manager's Perspective

Alan Pincus Manager, Deloitte Consulting

Alan Pincus brings vast experience to his position as a manager in the manufacturing practice of Deloitte Consulting. He started his career as a consultant at Anderson Consulting in New York. Pincus has worked in such diverse industries as financial services, manufacturing, telecommunications, utilities, and consumer business. At Deloitte, as in the preceding phases of his career, Pincus is responsible for diagnosing tough business and operational issues for his clients, and for identifying ways to address those issues or otherwise improve performance.

As a manager, Alan must also control the performance of his own employees and resources. He does this for each consulting project. Among the tools available to him to gauge performance are a formal employee appraisal system and reports about the profitability and resource use of each project. He uses period reports that allow him to monitor the financial and operational results of both internal and client-related activities.

Alan scans these reports for possible danger systems, like excess costs, that allow him to address trouble spots with his employees as soon as possible.

Technology's impact on control is most evident in comparisons of technologically advanced nations with more primitive countries. Organizations in technologically advanced nations such as the United States, Japan, Canada, Great Britain, Germany, and Australia use indirect control devices—particularly computer-related reports and analyses—in addition to standardized rules and direct supervision to ensure that activities are going as planned.[17] In less advanced countries, direct supervision and highly centralized decision making are the basic means of control. Constraints on managerial corrective action may also affect managers in foreign countries. For example, laws in some countries do not allow management the options of closing plants, laying off personnel, taking money out of the country, or bringing in a new management team from outside the country.

The Dysfunctional Side of Controls

Have you ever noticed that the people who work in the college registrar's office often don't seem to care much about students' problems? At times they appear to be so fixated on ensuring that every rule is followed that they lose sight of the fact that their job is to *serve* students not to *hassle* them.

At UPS, long a model of corporate efficiency, managers pushed employees to get even more productivity.[18] When it rolled out several new products and services—including computerized tracking systems, bulk discounts on large shipments, higher limits on package weights, and earlier guaranteed arrival times—employees were required to haul more packages and heavier loads, spend more time on complicated deliveries, and do all that without sacrificing their productivity. Although customers loved the changes, the company's highly unionized workers did not. They went out on strike.

This example illustrates what can happen when controls are inflexible or control standards are unreasonable. People lose sight of the organization's overall goals.[19] Instead of the organization running the controls, the controls can sometimes run the organization.

Because control systems don't monitor everything, problems can occur when individuals or organizational units attempt to look good exclusively on control measures. The result is dysfunctional. More often than not, this dysfunctionality is caused by incomplete measures of performance. If the control system evaluates only the quantity of output, people will ignore quality. Similarly, if the system measures activities rather than results, people will spend their time attempting to look good on the activity measures.

How does a Dana Corporation manager in the United States change control practices when dealing with employees at this Volkswagen plant in Resende, Brazil? According to research, control systems will change to reflect national differences. In this more labor-intensive location, more direct supervision, as well as other "people" controls, may be needed.

To avoid being reprimanded by managers, people may engage in behaviors that are designed solely to influence the information system's data output during a given control period. Rather than actually performing well, employees may manipulate measures to give the appearance that they are performing well. Evidence indicates that the manipulation of control data is not a random phenomenon. It depends on the importance of an activity. Organizationally important activities are likely to make a difference in a person's rewards; therefore, there is a great incentive to look good on those particular measures.[20] When rewards are at stake, individuals tend to manipulate data to appear in a favorable light by, for instance, distorting actual figures, emphasizing successes, and suppressing evidence of failures. On the other hand, only random errors occur when the distribution of rewards is unaffected.[21]

Our conclusion is that controls have both an upside and a downside. Failure to design flexibility into a control system can create problems more severe than those the controls were implemented to prevent.

Ethical Issues of Control

Even as managers design efficient and effective control systems (see Ethical Dilemma in Management), technological advances in computer hardware and software, for example, have made the process of controlling much easier. These advantages have also raised difficult questions regarding what managers have the right to know about employees and how far they can go in controlling employee behavior both on and off the job. Special attention needs to be given to the topic of employee monitoring.

In Chapter 2, we briefly discussed how technology is changing our organizations. Many of these improvements are allowing organizations to become more productive, to help members work smarter but not harder, and to bring efficiencies into the organization that weren't possible just a decade ago.[22] But technological advancements have also provided a means of sophisticated employee

Ethical Dilemma in Management

Control Systems and an Invasion of Privacy

When do management's efforts to control the actions of its employees become an invasion of privacy? Consider the following.[23]

You have been a loyal employee of a large hotel chain. You just found out that you and a friend have been secretly videotaped while in the restroom in the hotel lobby. Although you were discussing a private matter (in addition to using the lavatory), you feel as if the hotel doesn't trust you.

If you work for USAirways in telephone sales, your phone conversations may be monitored. The company monitors to determine how well you are doing and to identify where you may have areas for improvement. The monitoring could also be used to substantiate that you are not doing your job properly and could potentially lead to your dismissal.

At Olivetti, all employees are given a "smart badge." These identification devices permit your access to various parts of the company, but they can also be used to track your whereabouts. On one hand, knowing where you are assists in forwarding urgent messages to you. On the other, no matter where you are, Olivetti managers can track your location.

Do you believe any of these practices are an invasion of privacy? When does management's need for more information about employee performance cross over the line and interfere with a worker's right to privacy? Do you believe organizations should be permitted to monitor employee behavior off the job?

monitoring. Although most of this monitoring is designed to enhance worker productivity, it could be, and has been, a source of concern in regard to worker privacy.[24]

What can your employer find out about you and your work? You might be surprised by the answers. Employers can, among other things, read your e-mail (even confidential messages), tap your work telephone, monitor your activities by computer, and monitor you anywhere on company property.[25]

One area that has been a hot topic of debate over employee workplace privacy is e-mail communications.[26] The use of e-mail is flourishing throughout global organizations, and employees are concerned about whether they can be fired or disciplined for things they have written and sent. Many companies can and do monitor these electronic transmissions. For instance, a survey of more than 500 executives showed that 36 percent had reviewed employees' electronic files and mails.[27] E-mail communications is just one aspect of the concern over ethics of employees workplace privacy. Computer monitoring is another area in which ethical questions arise.

Computer monitoring can be an excellent control mechanism. Computer monitoring systems can be used to collect, process, and provide performance feedback information about employees' work that can help managers with performance improvement suggestions and employee development.[28] It has also been used to help managers identify employee work practices that might be unethical or costly. For example, many hospitals and other health care organizations use computer monitoring to control costs of medical procedures and access to controlled medications. Likewise, many business organizations use computer monitoring systems for controlling costs, employee work behavior, and a number of other areas of organizational activities. Telemarketing organizations often monitor the calls of their service operators. Other organizations monitor employees who deal with consumer complaints to ensure the complaints are being handled appropriately. Unfortunately, computer monitoring has a questionable reputation because of instances of overuse and abuse.

Just how far can an employer go in monitoring employees? Given the fear of corporate espionage, the law has provided companies a lot of latitude. They can legally read your e-mail or computer files; and they can even go so far as to film you while you are on company premises.

Many individuals perceive computer monitoring as nothing more than a technologically sophisticated form of eavesdropping or a surveillance technique to catch employees slacking off on the job. Critics also claim that these techniques lead to an increase in stress-related complaints from employees who feel pressured by constant surveillance.[29] Supporters argue, however, that computer monitoring can be an effective employee training device and a way to improve performance levels.

How can organizations benefit from the information provided by computer monitoring systems and yet minimize the potential behavioral and legal drawbacks?[30] Experts suggest that organizations do the following:

- Tell employees, both current and new, that they may be monitored.
- Have a written policy on monitoring that is posted where employees will see it and that is distributed to each employee. Have all employees acknowledge in writing that they have received a copy of the policy and that they understand it.
- Monitor only those situations in which a legitimate business purpose is at stake, such as training or evaluating workers or controlling costs.[31] When used in this manner, computer monitoring can be an effective and ethical managerial control tool.

The last area we look at in terms of ethical issues associated with control is that concerning employees' off-the-job behavior. Just how much control should a company have over the private lives of its employees? Where should an employer's rules and controls end? Does the boss have the right to dictate what you do on your own free time and in your own home? Could, in essence, your boss keep you from engaging in riding a motorcycle, skydiving, smoking, drinking alcohol, or eating junk food?[32] Again, the answers may surprise you. What's more, employer involvement in employees' off-work lives has been going on for decades. For instance, in the early 1900s, Ford Motor Company would send social workers to employees' homes to determine whether their off-the-job habits and finances were deserving of year-end bonuses. Other firms made sure employees regularly attended church services. Today, many organizations, in their quest to control safety and health insurance costs, are once again delving into their employees' private lives.

Although controlling employees' behaviors on and off the job may appear unjust or unfair, nothing in our legal system prevents employers from engaging in these practices. Rather, the law is based on the premise that "if employees don't like the rules, they have the option of quitting." But legally right doesn't make something ethically right.

PHLIP Companion Web Site

We invite you to visit the Robbins/DeCenzo companion Web site at *www.prenhall.com/robbins* for this chapter's Internet resources.

Chapter Summary

How will you know if you fulfilled the Learning Outcomes on page 411? You will have fulfilled the Learning Outcomes if you are able to:

1 *Define control.*
Control is a management function that focuses on the process of monitoring activities to ensure that they are being accomplished as planned. Control also includes correcting any significant deviations that may exist between goals and actual results.

2 *Describe three approaches to control.*
Three approaches to control are market control, bureaucratic control, and clan control. Market control emphasizes the use of external marketing mechanisms such as price competition and relative market share to establish standards used in the control system. Bureaucratic control emphasizes organizational authority and relies on administrative rules, regulations, procedures, and policies. Under clan control, employee behaviors are regulated by the shared values, norms, traditions, rituals, beliefs, and other aspects of organizational culture.

3 *Explain why control is important.*
Control is important because it monitors whether objectives are being accomplished as planned and whether delegated authority is being abused.

4 *Describe the control process.*
In the control process, management must first have standards of performance derived from the objectives it formed in the planning stage. Management must then measure actual performance and compare that performance against the standards. If a variance exists between standards and performance, management can adjust performance, adjust the standards, or do nothing, according to the situation.

5 *Distinguish among the three types of control.*
There are three types of control: feedforward, concurrent, and feedback control. Feedforward control is future directed and designed to prevent problems by anticipating them. Concurrent control takes place while an activity is in progress. Feedback control, the most frequently found in organizations, takes place after an activity or an event has occurred.

6 *Describe the qualities of an effective control system.*
An effective control system is accurate, timely, economical, flexible, and understandable. It uses reasonable criteria, has strategic placement, emphasizes the exception, uses multiple criteria, and suggests corrective action.

7 *Identify the contingency factors in the control process.*
A number of contingency factors in organizations affect the control process. The most frequent contingency factors in control systems include the size of the organization, the manager's level in the organization's hierarchy, the degree of decentralization, the organization's culture, and the importance of the activity.

8 *Explain how controls can become dysfunctional.*
Controls can be dysfunctional when they redirect behavior away from an organization's goals. This dysfunction can occur as a result of inflexibility or unreasonable standards. In addition, when rewards are at stake, individuals are likely to manipulate data so that their performance will be perceived positively.

9 *Describe how national differences influence the control process.*
Methods of controlling employee behavior and operations can be quite different according to the geographic location or cultural environment. As a result, control systems focus primarily on measurement and corrective action steps of the control process.

10 *Identify the ethical dilemmas in employee monitoring.*
The ethical dilemmas in employee monitoring revolve around the rights of employees versus the rights of employers. Employees are concerned with protecting their workplace privacy and intrusion into their personal lives. Employers, in contrast, are primarily concerned with enhancing productivity and controlling safety and health costs.

Review and Application Questions

READING FOR COMPREHENSION

1. What is the role of control in management?
2. Name four methods managers can use to acquire information about actual organizational performance.
3. Contrast immediate and basic corrective action.
4. What are the advantages and disadvantages of feedforward control?
5. What can management do to reduce the dysfunctionality of controls?

LINKING CONCEPTS TO PRACTICE

1. How are planning and control linked? Is the control function linked to the organizing and leading functions of management? Explain.
2. In Chapter 7 we discussed the white-water rapids view of change. Do you think it's possible to establish and maintain effective standards and controls in this type of atmosphere?
3. Why do you believe feedback control is the most popular type of control? Justify your response.
4. Why is what is measured probably more critical to the control process than how it is measured?
5. "Organizations have the right to monitor employees—both on and off the job." Build an argument supporting this statement and an argument disagreeing with the statement.

Management Workshop

Team Skill-Building Exercise

The Paper Plane Corporation

PURPOSES

1 To integrate the management functions.

2 To apply planning and control concepts specifically to improve organizational performance.

REQUIRED KNOWLEDGE

Planning, organizing, and controlling concepts.

TIME REQUIRED

Approximately one hour.

PROCEDURE

Any number of groups of six participants each are used in this exercise. These groups may be directed simultaneously in the same room. Each person should have assembly instructions (Exhibit 13-7) and a summary sheet, plus ample stacks of paper (8½ by 11 inches). The room should be large enough that each group of six can work without interference from other groups. A working space should be provided for each group.

The participants are doing an exercise in production methodology. Each group must work independently of the other groups. Each group will choose a manager and an inspector, and the remaining participants will be employees. The objective is to make paper airplanes in the most profitable manner possible. The facilitator will give the signal to start. This is a 10-minute, timed event involving competition among the groups. After the first round, each group should report its production and profits to the entire group. Each group reports the manner in which it planned, organized, and controlled for the production of the paper airplanes. This same procedure is followed for as many rounds as there is time.

Your group is the complete workforce for Paper Plane Corporation. Established in 1943, Paper Plane has led the market in paper plane production. Currently under new management, the company is contracting to make aircraft for the U.S. Air Force. You must establish a plan and organization to produce these aircraft. You must fulfill your contract with the Air Force under the following conditions:

1 The Air Force will pay $20,000 per airplane.

2 The aircraft must pass a strict inspection.

3 A penalty of $25,000 per airplane will be subtracted for failure to meet the production requirements (bid planes not made or defective planes).

4 Labor and other overhead will be computed at $300,000.

5 Cost of materials will be $3,000 per bid plane. If you bid for ten but make only eight, you must pay the cost of materials for those you failed to make or that did not pass inspection.

Exhibit 13-7 Paper Plane Data Sheet

Instructions for Aircraft Assembly

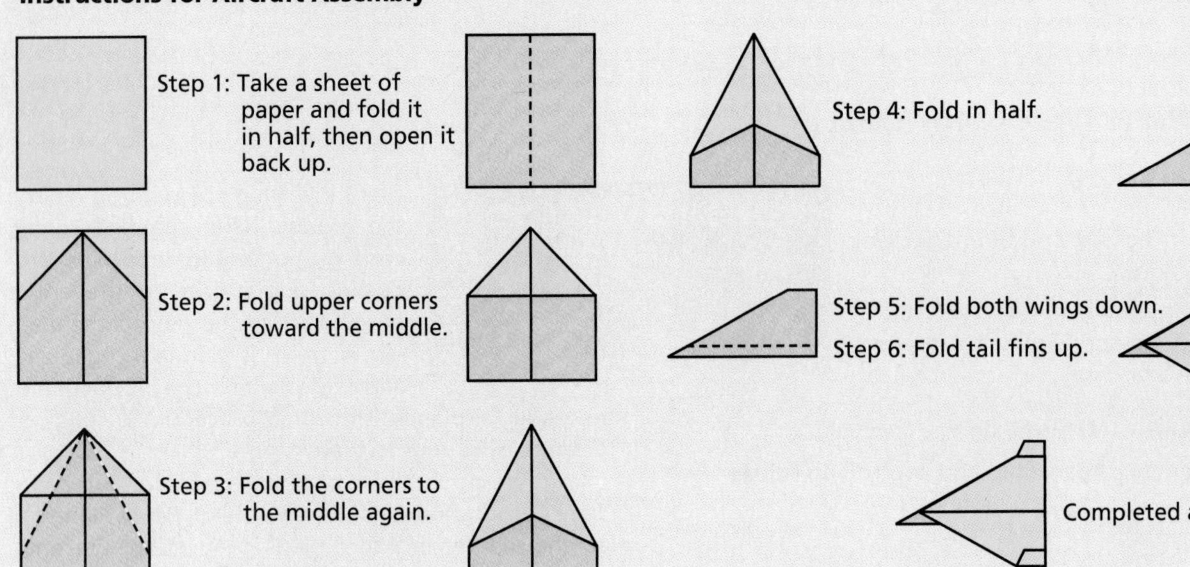

Step 1: Take a sheet of paper and fold it in half, then open it back up.
Step 2: Fold upper corners toward the middle.
Step 3: Fold the corners to the middle again.
Step 4: Fold in half.
Step 5: Fold both wings down.
Step 6: Fold tail fins up.
Completed aircraft

Round 1
Bid: [number of planes] x $20,000 per plane =
Result: [number of planes] x $20,000 per plane =
Less:
overhead = $300,000
[number of bid planes] x $3,000 cost of raw materials =
[number of unmade or defective planes] x $25,000 penalty =
Profit [result – (overhead + raw materials + penalty)]: =

Round 2
Bid: [number of planes] x $20,000 per plane =
Result: [number of planes] x $20,000 per plane =
Less:
overhead = $300,000
[number of bid planes] x $3,000 cost of raw materials =
[number of unmade or defective planes] x $25,000 penalty =
Profit [result – (overhead + raw materials + penalty)]: =

Round 3
Bid: [number of planes] x $20,000 per plane =
Result: [number of planes] x $20,000 per plane =
Less:
overhead = $300,000
[number of bid planes] x $3,000 cost of raw materials =
[number of unmade or defective planes] x $25,000 penalty =
Profit [result – (overhead + raw materials + penalty)]: =

SOURCE: Based on an exercise in J. H. Donnelly, Jr., J. L. Gibson, and J. M. Ivancevich, *Fundamentals of Management,* 8th ed. (Burr Ridge, IL: Irwin, 1992), pp. 285–89. With permission.

Developing Your Performance Feedback Skill

Providing Performance Feedback

ABOUT THE SKILL

In the last chapter, we introduced several suggestions for providing feedback. One of the more critical feedback sessions will occur when you, as a manager, are using feedback control to address performance issues.

STEPS IN THE PERFORMANCE FEEDBACK SKILL

- **Schedule the feedback session in advance and be prepared.** One of the biggest mistakes you can make is to treat feedback control lightly. Simply calling in an employee and giving feedback that is not well organized serves little purpose for you and your employee. For feedback to be effective, you must plan ahead. Identify the issues you wish to address and cite specific examples to reinforce what you are saying. Furthermore, set aside the time for the meeting with the employee. Make sure that what you do is done in private and can be completed without interruptions. That may mean closing your office door (if you have one), holding phone calls, and the like.
- **Put the employee at ease.** Regardless of how you feel about the feedback, you must create a supportive climate for the employee. Recognize that giving and getting this feedback can be an emotional event even when the feedback is positive. By putting your employee at ease, you begin to establish a supportive environment in which understanding can take place.
- **Make sure the employee knows the purpose of this feedback session.** What is the purpose of the meeting? That's something any employee will be wondering. Clarifying what you are going to do sets the appropriate stage for what is to come.
- **Focus on specific rather than general work behaviors.** Feedback should be specific rather than general. General statements are vague and provide little useful information—especially if you are attempting to correct a problem.
- **Keep comments impersonal and job related.** Feedback should be descriptive rather than judgmental or evaluative, especially when you are giving negative feedback. No matter how upset you are, keep the feedback job related and never criticize someone personally because of an inappropriate action. You are censuring job-related behavior, not the person.
- **Support feedback with hard data.** Tell your employee how you came to your conclusion on his or her performance. Hard data help your employees to identify with specific behaviors. Identify the "things" that were done correctly and provide a detailed critique. And, if you need to criticize, state the basis of your conclusion that a good job was not completed.
- **Direct the negative feedback toward work-related behavior that the employee controls.** Negative feedback should be directed toward work-related behavior that the employee can do something about. Indicate what he or she can do to improve the situation. This practice helps take the sting out of the criticism and offers guidance to an individual who understands the problem but doesn't know how to resolve it.
- **Let the employee speak.** Get the employee's perceptions of what you are saying, especially if you are addressing a problem. Of course, you're not looking for excuses, but you need to be empathetic to the employee. Get his or her side. Maybe there's something that has contributed to the issue. Letting the employee speak involves your employee and just might provide information you were unaware of.
- **Ensure that the employee has a clear and full understanding of the feedback.** Feedback must be concise and complete enough so that your employee clearly and fully understands what you have said. Consistent with active listening techniques, have your employee rephrase the content of your feedback to check whether it fully captures your meaning.
- **Detail a future plan of action.** Performing doesn't stop simply because feedback occurred. Good performance must be reinforced, and new performance goals set. However, when there are performance deficiencies, time must be devoted to helping your employee develop a detailed, step-by-step plan to correct the situation. This plan includes what has to be done, when, and how you will monitor the activities. Offer whatever assistance you can to help the employee, but make it clear that it is the employee, not you, who has to make the corrections.

Practicing the Skill

FEEDBACK

Think of a skill you would like to acquire or improve, or a habit you would like to break. Perhaps you would like to learn a foreign language, start exercising, quit smoking, ski better, or spend less. For the purpose of this exercise, assume you have three months to make a start on your project and all the necessary funds. Draft a plan of action that outlines what you need to do, when you need to do it, and how you will know that you have successfully completed each step of your plan. Be realistic, but don't set your sights too low either.

Review your plan. What outside help or resources will you require? How will you get them? Add these to your plan.

Could someone else follow the steps you've outlined to achieve the goal you set? What modifications would you have to make, if any?

A Case Application

Developing Your Diagnostic and Analytical Skills

SWAINE AND ADNEY

What do Queen Elizabeth, Prince Charles, and Swaine and Adney have in common? Each is a highly regarded symbol of aristocracy in the United Kingdom. For Swaine and Adney, this recognition stems from its production of leather goods, such as riding gear and buggy whips, and umbrellas. In fact, Swaine and Adney's products proudly display a "lion propping up a large gold crest, the equivalent of knighthood for inanimate objects." By all accounts, it's a symbol of "royal success."[33]

Swaine and Adney has been a tradition for nearly 250 years in England. Founded in the 1750s, it had been the Adney family's business. Back then, the company primarily focused on serving the monarchy—providing kings and queens, princes and princesses with top-quality products. For most of its existence, the company was on top of the world—exceptionally successful and profitable. It had an elite address on Piccadilly Street and catered to a distinguished clientele. In fact, its customer list read like a Who's Who in the world—with nearly every head of state of industrialized nations and the British aristocracy proudly displaying some Swaine and Adney product. The kings and queens of England were so proud of the Swaine and Adney tradition that they allowed the company to rent the property on Piccadilly Street for a small fraction of its true market value. Unfortunately, the good times didn't last forever.

Swaine and Adney managers assumed that the growth they were experiencing in the 1980s would be indefinitely sustainable. So they expanded their facilities—building new factories and consolidating all manufacturing operations under one roof. Swaine executives also significantly expanded their firm's retail space, even opening a site in San Francisco to process mail orders from the United States, but with this expansion came increased costs. The most notable of these was leaving the Picadilly Street location (and its low rent) for a facility a few blocks away at a cost nearly 100 times their previous expense.

The late 1980s ushered in significant changes that brought the decade of growth to an unexpected halt. The British pound weakened against the dollar, virtually halving Swaine and Adney's revenues in their mail-order business. Furthermore, consumers were beginning to change their taste and preferences for purchased goods. Luxury items—most of what Swaine produces—were no longer in demand. The events of the late 1980s led the company to the brink of financial disaster as annual losses began exceeding £3 million. In 1990 the Adney family, which had controlled Swaine and Adney for 240 years, sold out its interest to other investors, leaving England's pride and joy to be run by an impersonal corporation. For the next four years, the organization languished. Then John de Bruyne bought the firm.

What de Bruyne found when he took over the helm of Swaine and Adney in June 1994 was nothing short of chaos. Few if any control mechanisms were in place. No one really knew what was going on or how well plans were being met. He concluded that it was somewhat doubtful that standards were being set at all. De Bruyne knew he had to make some major changes if the organization were to survive.

One of the first things de Bruyne did was to focus on the firm's core business—making upscale leather goods—to recapture the firm's competitive advantage. He also reduced staff and moved the main production facility to a site that had much lower rent. He implemented production controls that would help increase output while simultaneously increasing the quality of each item. De Bruyne also implemented procedures to address current customer concerns, and he established plans and monitoring systems for capturing new business in locations such as Paris, New York, Moscow, and Hamburg.

What John de Bruyne did for Swaine and Adney was simply remarkable. In just over 12 months he helped the company earn more than £2 million in profit. Considering the previous losses, that's a £5 million turnaround!

QUESTIONS

1. Describe the type of control (market, bureaucratic, or clan) that John de Bruyne is using at Swaine and Adney. Cite specific example to support your selection.
2. Why do you think he has chosen this type of control system for the organization?
3. Describe how de Bruyne's emphasis on control at Swaine and Adney is helping the organization enhance organizational performance.
4. Given the fact that Swaine and Adney operates in different global locations, do you believe the company's control system should be different for each location? Explain your position.

Developing Your Investigative Skills

Using the Internet

Visit *www.prenhall.com/robbins* for updated Internet Exercises.

Enhancing Your Writing Skills

Communicating Effectively

1. "Controls have to be sophisticated for them to be effective." Present both sides of the argument (for and against) this statement. Conclude your paper with a persuasive statement of why you agree or disagree with the statement.
2. Describe how you can use the concepts of control in your own personal life. Be specific in your examples and think in terms of the feedforward, concurrent, and feedback controls that you use for different parts of your life.
3. Visit the Society of Human Resource Management's Web site <http://www.shrm.org/index.html> and research the latest information on privacy issues and employee monitoring. Describe the pros and cons of having employees monitored and the latest technology that is used to enhance monitoring activities for the organization.

Fourteen

Technology and Operations

LEARNING OUTCOMES After reading this chapter, I will be able to:

1 Describe the formula for calculating productivity.

2 Explain how technology can improve productivity.

3 Explain how information technology is providing managers with decision support.

4 Describe the advantages of computer-aided design.

5 Identify why management might consider introducing flexible manufacturing systems.

6 Define and describe the three key elements in work process engineering.

7 Describe what is meant by the term supply chain management.

8 Explain what is meant by the term just-in-time inventory systems.

9 Identify the steps in developing a PERT network.

Brenda French has used technology to totally reinvent her business.[1] Starting part time in 1978, French had built French Rags into a multi-million-dollar-a-year business of manufacturing women's knitwear. Her garments were being sold at leading department stores such as Neiman-Marcus, Bonwit Teller, and Bloomingdale's. From an outsider's perspective, the business looked healthy, but French knew otherwise. Retailers' slowness in paying for merchandise put pressures on her limited financial resources. In addition, she was frustrated by department store buyers who were often choosing to sell just a few of her styles, sizes, and colors. She felt that her knitwear product line was reaching only a small percentage of its potential market.

Her financial and distribution problems were solved, and her business completely reshaped by two isolated events in 1989. First, a friend introduced her to an expert in knitting equipment who just happened to have acquired a German-made Stoll computerized knitting machine. The sleek Stoll knitting machine uses thousands of precisely angled needles to do things the old-fashioned way—one stitch at a time—but it churns out garments at a breathtaking pace. This machine can produce as many as 24 garments for each one produced by a hand knitter. Second, French's cash crunch had forced her to cut back production and sell only to the few stores who were willing to pay COD (cash on delivery). One loyal customer, frustrated by not being able to buy her favored French Rags garments, called French on the phone. On learning of French's money problems, the customer said, "You bring your clothes to my house, and I know 20 people who'll buy them." Desperate, French went to the customer's home. To her surprise, she took an order for $80,000 worth of products (with a 50 percent deposit).

These two events—the availability of a knitting expert with a computerized knitting machine and access to a new marketing channel—led Brenda French to reinvent her business. Today, French Rags mass produces custom-made knitwear and sells it directly to customers. Her distribution system no longer includes retail stores. Her sales force is now composed of customers who sell her goods out of their homes. She supplies them with order forms, sample garments, and fabric snippets of 30 color choices. After customers select their style and color combinations, individual measurements are taken; a 50 percent down payment is secured, and the order form is faxed to the French Rags factory. It is at this point that French's high-tech operation kicks into gear.

French now owns 20 Stoll machines. Productivity in her business has doubled every year since 1990, and she now employs more than 100 people. Using custom software that produces knit-by-number templates for fast and easy switching from one garment to another and a Silicon Graphics work station for designing the knitwear—combined with the new, low-cost home-distribution system—French Rags is able to produce quality, custom-made knitwear and sell it at off-the-rack prices. For example, a software program on a personal computer produces portable templates with instructions about which color yarns should be loaded on which spools atop a knitting machine as the machine is about to knit a particular garment. An elaborate knit jacket that used to take a skilled craftsperson a day and a half to knit by hand can be produced on this equipment in less than an hour. Another jacket, in another style and color combination, can then be made in the following hour with a different knit-by-number template.

French can offer her customers more than 1.5 million style and color combinations, allowing them to wear custom-made outfits that fit perfectly and are exactly like no other. French ships her merchandise directly to customers, usually within four to six weeks. And best of all, for a business that had consistently had money problems, French no longer has to worry about carrying inventories or accounts receivables. "We have no inventory problems because we have no inventory," says French. "Everything we make is presold."

Technology has completely changed Brenda French's business, and it is having a similar impact on most organizations. In this chapter, we focus on the transformation process and productivity, the effect of technology on worker obsolescence, and how technology transfer, information, and operations technologies are influencing management and work processes. We also explore some of the current issues in operations management that are helping organizations to run at peak efficiencies as well as how managers can use scheduling techniques to maximize organizational productivity.

Transformation Process

All organizations produce goods or services through the **transformation process.** In a very simplified fashion, every organization has an operations system that creates value by transforming inputs into outputs. The system takes inputs—people, capital, equipment, materials—and transforms them into desired finished goods and services.

Does the transformation process apply to service organizations that now dominate work in the United States, Canada, Australia, and Western Europe? The answer is yes. A **service organization** produces nonphysical outputs such as educational, medical, or transportation services that are intangible, can't be stored in inventory, and incorporate the customer in the actual production process. For example, there's a transformation process operating in your college or university. University administrators bring together instructors, books, journals, multimedia materials, computer labs, and similar resources to transform unenlightened students into educated and skilled individuals. Our point is that the transformation process is as relevant to service organizations as it is to those in manufacturing. And, the study and application of this transformation process to organizations is called **operations management.**

tranformation process
The process through which an organization creates value by turning inputs (people, capital, equipment, materials) into outputs (goods or services)

service organization
An organization that produces nonphysical outputs such as educational, medical, or transportation services

Technology and Productivity

We briefly introduced the term "technology" in the Chapter 2 discussion of information processing. It is now time to focus on this phenomenon that is sweeping through companies. In its purest form, **technology** is how an organization transforms its inputs into outputs. In recent years, the term has become widely used by economists, managers, consultants, and business analysts to describe machinery and equipment that use sophisticated electronics and computers to produce those outputs.

All the new technologies in the workplace substitute machinery for human labor in transforming inputs into outputs. This substitution of capital for labor has been going on essentially nonstop since the Industrial Revolution in the mid-1800s. For instance, the introduction of electricity allowed textile factories to introduce mechanical looms that could produce cloth far faster and more cheaply than was previously possible when the looms were powered by individuals. But the computerization of equipment and machinery in the last quarter-century has been the prime mover in reshaping the twentieth-century workplace. Automated teller machines, for example, have replaced tens of thousands of human tellers in banks. Ninety-eight percent of the spot welds on new Ford Tauruses are performed by robots not by people. Many cars now come equipped with on-board computers that diagnose in seconds problems that mechanics used to take hours to diagnose. IBM has built a plant in Austin, Texas, that can produce laptop computers without a single worker. Everything from the time parts arrive at the IBM plant to the final packing of finished products is completely automated. An increasing number of companies, small and large alike, are turning to multimedia and interactive technology for employee training. And literally millions of organizations

operations management
The study and application of the transformation process

technology
How an organization transforms its inputs into outputs

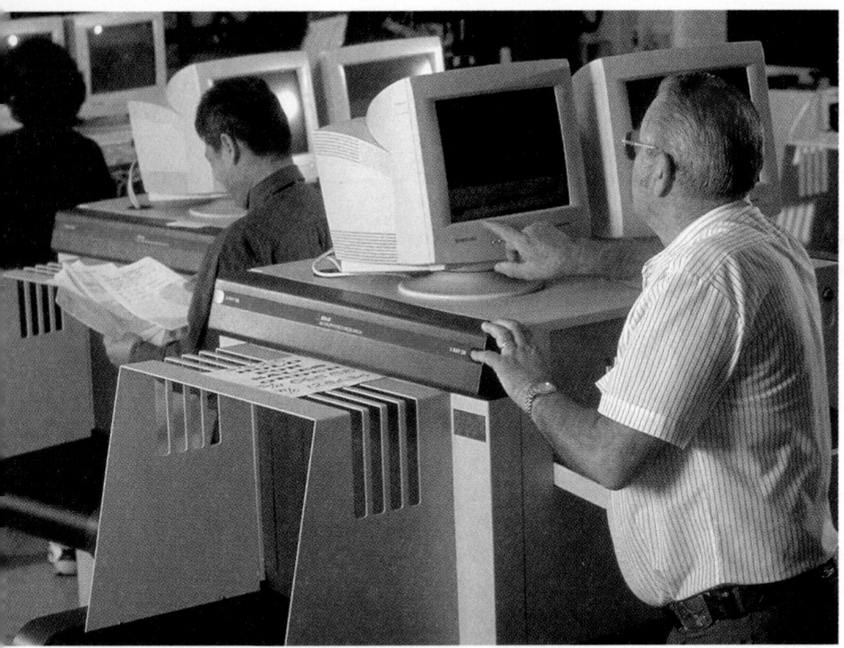

Technology means a lot of different things. For managers at EG&G Astrophysics plant in Long Beach, California (makers of x-ray screening systems), it has meant one simple thing—productivity. By investing in technology, they have seen their productivity leap by more than 300 percent in one year. They attribute this tremendous success to investments in cellular manufacturing and continuous improvement programs.

have utilized personal computers to decentralize decision making and generate enormous increases in productivity.

Productivity is the name of the game! It's technology's ability to significantly increase productivity that is driving the technology bandwagon. In its simplest form, productivity can be expressed in the following ratio:

Productivity = Outputs/
(Labor + Capital + Materials)

The above formula can be applied in its total form or broken down into subcategories.[2] For instance, output per labor-hour is perhaps the most common partial measure of productivity. Industrial engineers, who conduct time-and-motion studies in factories, are largely focused on generating increases in labor productivity. IBM's automated plant in Austin, Texas, is an example of how to increase productivity by substituting capital (i.e., machinery and equipment) for labor. Materials productivity is concerned with increasing the efficient use of material inputs and supplies. A meatpacking plant, as an illustrative case, improves its materials productivity when it finds uses for by-products that were previously treated as waste.

productivity
Outputs/(labor + capital + materials)

Productivity can also be applied at three different levels—the individual, the group, and the total organization. Word-processing software, fax machines, and e-mail have made administrative assistants more productive by allowing them to generate more output during their workday. The use of self-managed teams has increased the productivity of many work groups at companies such as Honeywell, Coors Brewing, and Aetna Life. And Southwest Airlines is overall a more productive organization than rivals such as American Airlines or USAirways because Southwest's cost per available seat-mile is 30 to 60 percent lower than theirs.

The above analysis brings us to the following conclusion. Because technology is the means by which inputs are turned into outputs, it is the primary focus of any management's efforts to improve productivity.[3]

Technology and Worker Obsolescence

Rob Hanc was in his late twenties when he came face to face with a new reality—his skills didn't match what employers needed.[4] Hanc graduated from high school and followed in his father's footsteps by taking a job at the Dofasco steel foundry in Hamilton, Ontario. His job? He was a heavy laborer—doing lifting and carrying. At 21, he was making $47,000 a year. But Dofasco couldn't compete while paying such high wages for unskilled labor. Hanc lost his job. "My biggest problem is lack of education," says Hanc. "Me and school don't go together. I need to work with my hands." However, as Hanc now knows, "heavy labor is a dying breed."

Glenna Cheney also has only a high school education.[5] But, unlike Rob Hanc, she has been changing with the times. Cheney went to work for Fingerhut Co., a Minneapolis-based catalog company, in 1965. She answered the telephone, took orders, and wrote customer orders and payment schedules on index cards. When Fingerhut replaced the index cards with a mainframe computer, Cheney learned about computers. She learned so well, in fact, that she was promoted to supervisor. When the mainframe system was recently replaced with a group of work stations, she enthusiastically took training classes to learn the new technology. She was recently promoted to a business analyst position, in which she advises Fingerhut's computer specialists on how to further develop the work stations to fit workers' needs.

Changes in technology have cut the shelf-life of most employees' skills. A factory worker or clerical employee in the 1950s could learn one job and be reasonably sure that his or her skills would be adequate to do that job for most of his or her work life. That certainly is no longer true. New technologies driven by computers, work process engineering, continuous improvement programs, and flexible manufacturing systems are changing the demands of jobs and the skills employees need to do them.

Repetitive tasks—such as those traditionally performed on assembly lines and by low-skilled office clerks—have nearly all been automated. A good number of jobs today have also been upgraded. For instance, as most managers and professionals take on the task of writing their own memos and reports using word-processing software, the traditional secretary's job will be upgraded to become more of an administrative assistant position. Those secretaries who are unable to perform in this expanded role will be displaced. In addition to secretaries, other white-collar jobs that are disappearing or being reshaped as a result of technology include bank teller, telephone operator, meter reader, and travel agent.

Work process engineering, as we previously noted, is significantly increasing employee productivity. The redesign of work processes is achieving higher output with fewer workers, and these reengineered jobs require different skills. Employees who are computer illiterate, have poor interpersonal skills, or can't work autonomously will increasingly find themselves ill prepared for the demands of new technologies.[6] Keep in mind that the obsolescence phenomenon does not exclude managers. Middle managers who merely acted as conduits in the chain of command between top management and the operating floor are being eliminated. Their role of processing information and sending it upward is being replaced by internal computer networks. And new skills—for example, coaching, negotiating, and building teams—are becoming absolute necessities for every manager.

> *As the world continues to change, employees will also need to change if they are to survive.*

Finally, software is changing the jobs of many professionals, including lawyers, doctors, accountants, financial planners, and librarians.[7] Software programs will allow laypeople to use specialized knowledge to solve routine problems themselves or opt for a software-armed paraprofessional. Particularly vulnerable are those professionals who do standardized jobs. A lot of legal work, for instance, consists of writing standard contracts and performing other routine activities. These tasks will be done inside law firms by computers or paralegals or by clients themselves, using software designed to prepare wills, trusts, incorporations, and partnerships. Software packages, such as Turbo Tax, will continue to take a lot of work away from professional accountants. And hospitals are using software to help doctors make their diagnoses. Punch in a patient's age, sex, lab results, and symptoms, answer a set of structured questions, and a $995 program called Iliad will draw on its knowledge of nine subspecialties of internal medicine to diagnose the patient's problem. These examples demonstrate that even the knowledge of highly trained professionals can become obsolete. As the world changes, professionals will also need to change if they are to survive.

Technology Transfer

Globe Silk, a Malaysian company that originally was in the clothing business, decided to diversify. One such project was to buy the technology from an Australian firm that would enable them to make crash helmets for cyclists. Globe Silk's management then added a feature to the helmets—a flashing light. By combining foreign technology with internal innovation, the company was able to create a highly successful and profitable new product.[8]

technology transfer
Transfer of knowledge from one country to another for the development of new products or for improvements in a production process

In today's global village, both countries and individual organizations are concerned with **technology transfer,** the transfer of knowledge from one country to another for the development of new products or for improvements in a production process.[9] For instance, Globe Silk's purchase of crash-helmet technology is an example of technology transfer for the purpose of creating a new product. When a manufacturer in Taiwan hires a Japanese firm to install state-of-the art robotic equipment in the Taiwanese manufacturing plant, you have an example of improvements in a production process. As a result, those organizations that have technology to transfer have found a globally competitive advantage.[10]

Developing countries have a vested interest in stimulating technology transfer. Why? Without it, a country can be stuck in labor-intensive industries—with low-paying jobs and modest growth potential. Where government policies have fostered technology transfer, economies have blossomed.[11] In Asia, Singapore is a model example of a country in which industrial development policies have encouraged foreign companies to settle and sow the seeds of technology transfer. When German industrial giant Siemens sought a site for its Asia-Pacific microelectronics design center, it looked at seven Asian cities. But Siemens's management settled on Singapore because of its supportive climate for foreign investments. To jump start its semiconductor industry, Singapore also provided Texas Instruments with tax incentives and an industrial infrastructure to establish the country's first water filtration plant. As competition heats up for new investments, countries like Singapore that provide a supportive climate for technology transfer are going to have faster growth rates and higher-paying jobs than countries that create technology transfer barriers.

Managers of companies, especially in developing countries, will be increasingly seeking strategies that will facilitate acquisition of new technologies. These will include mergers, joint ventures, contractual royalty agreements, hiring of foreign consultants, and sending staff to foreign markets to acquire new technological expertise. And they are likely to locate in those countries where government policies are most supportive.

Information Technology

Today's organizations are information-processing machines. With new technologies available, managers need to understand how to best use the information they provide and to ensure that organizational activities are proceeding as planned.[12] With a greater importance placed on efficiency, effectiveness, and productivity, managers must develop well-designed operating systems and tight controls to compete in a global economy.[13]

In this section, we highlight how technology is reshaping information systems and office workflows, changing the way internal communications are handled, and providing high-tech support for organizational decision making.

WHAT IS A MANAGEMENT INFORMATION SYSTEM (MIS)?

Although there is no universally agreed-upon definition for a **management information system (MIS),** we will define the term as a system used to provide management with needed information on a regular basis.[14] In theory, this system can be manual or computer based, although all current discussions, including ours, focus on computer-supported applications.

management information system (MIS)
A system used to provide management with needed information on a regular basis

The term system in MIS implies order, arrangement, and purpose. Further, an MIS focuses specifically on providing management with information, not merely data. These two points are important and require elaboration (see Developing Your Skill at Using MIS, p. 466).

data
Raw, unanalyzed facts, such as numbers, names, or quantities

information
Analyzed and processed data

A library is a good analogy. Although it can contain millions of volumes, a library doesn't do users much good if they can't find what they want quickly. That's why libraries spend a lot of time cataloging their collections and ensuring that volumes are returned to their proper locations. Organizations today are like well-stocked libraries: There is no lack of data. There is, however, a lack of ability to process that data so that the right information is available to the right person when he or she needs it.[15] A library is almost useless if it has the book you want, but you can't find it or it takes a week to retrieve it from storage. An MIS, on the other hand, has organized data in a meaningful way and can access the information in a reasonable amount of time. **Data** are raw, unanalyzed facts, such as numbers, names, or quantities. As data, these facts are relatively useless to managers. When data are analyzed and processed, they become **information.**

A library serves as a good analogy of the difference between data and information. A large library holding (the data) is useless unless the materials are readily accessible. When accessibility is enhanced, the data are able to be translated into useful information.

WHAT IS WORKFLOW AUTOMATION?

In the typical office, information spends most of its life moving from desk to desk.[16] For instance, consider the creation of a marketing plan. The marketing director approves the creation of the plan. A product manager is given responsibility for overseeing the plan's development. Staff marketing researchers gather the necessary data. A senior researcher then writes a first draft and sends it on to the product manager. This whole process requires documents to be passed along from one desk to another as the plan is developed, reviewed, edited, and rewritten until, eventually, a final document is agreed upon and approved. This process can take weeks or even months because the document can sit on someone's desk for days. One insurance company, for example, estimated that a life insurance application in its firm spent 22 days in process for only 17 minutes of actual work.[17] Workflow automation at Lockheed Martin has increased productivity nearly 40 percent over a 5-year period and cut costs by more than 38 percent.[18] Furthermore, it is estimated that gathering and transferring paper documents can take up as much as 90 percent of the time needed to finish typical office tasks.

workflow automation
A method of improving the process of creating and transferring documents by automating the flow of information

Workflow automation can solve much of this delay. It greatly improves the process of creating and transferring documents by automating the flow of information.[19] Workflow automation begins by examining how documents, business forms, and other information wind their way through an organization. It looks for bottlenecks and outdated procedures that slow things down and add to costs and finds creative solutions to them.[20] Once new routes are laid out, workflow software is installed on computer networks to instantly convey to the right desk all information, whether it's a digital image of an invoice or an e-mail question from a customer (see Ethical Dilemma in Management). This software makes the movement of documents automatic, eliminating the need for a human to figure out who should get the information next, collapsing the travel times, and avoiding misrouting. The system can also be programmed to send documents along different paths depending on content.

Exhibit 14-1 illustrates how workflow automation has improved one firm's information flow in the processing of an employee's expense reimbursement request. In Step 1, the employee fills out an expense form on her computer. The software then routes the form over a network to the appropriate decision maker for initial review (Step 2). The form's arrival triggers the retrieval of employee files that might be needed. In Step 3, the software recognizes that the transaction involves more than $5,000, so the form is automatically sent to an upper-level manager for special review. Upon final sign-off, in Step 4, the software sends a copy of the form to another computer, which processes payment; an electronic note is sent to notify the employee that her reimbursement check is ready (or that an automatic transfer of funds to her bank account has been completed). Then the form is automatically stored on an archival laser disk.

Exhibit 14-1 Workflow Automation Applied to an Expense Reimbursement

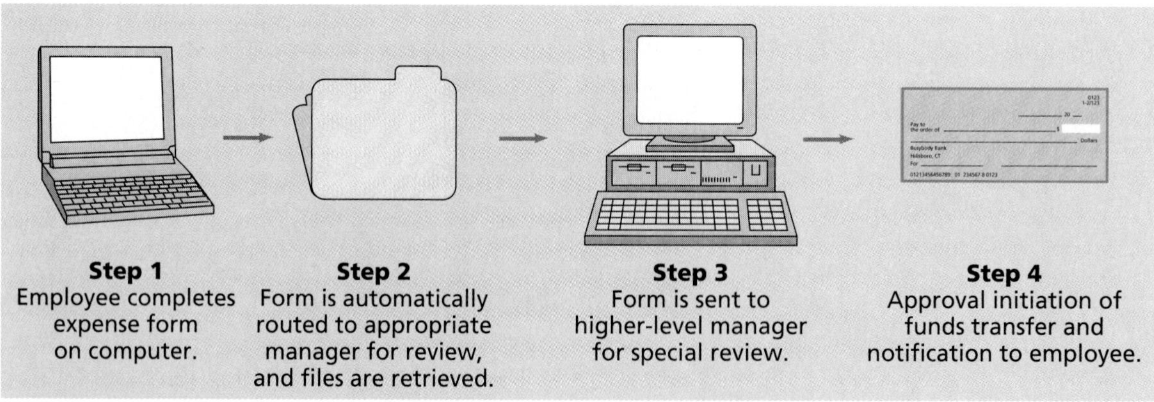

Step 1
Employee completes expense form on computer.
Step 2
Form is automatically routed to appropriate manager for review, and files are retrieved.
Step 3
Form is sent to higher-level manager for special review.
Step 4
Approval initiation of funds transfer and notification to employee.

SOURCE: Based on J. W. Verity, "Getting Work to Go with the Flow," Reprinted from the June 21, 1993 issue, p. 156, of *Business Week,* by special permission © 1993 by the McGraw-Hill Companies, Inc.

HOW DOES TECHNOLOGY ENHANCE INTERNAL COMMUNICATIONS?

Information technology is reshaping communications within organizations. For example, it is significantly improving management's ability to monitor organizational performance and is providing employees more complete information to make faster decisions. If we had to identify one of the most important developments in information technology in terms of its impact on internal organizational communications, it would probably be the wireless phenomenon.

Wireless products—such as personal pagers, cellular telephones, fax machines, and computers with modems—are making it possible for people in organizations to be fully accessible, at any time, regardless of where they are. Employees won't have to be at their desk with their computer turned on in order to communicate with others in the organization.

expert systems
Software programs to encode the relevant experience of an expert and allow a system to act like that expert in analyzing and solving ill-structured problems

IN WHAT WAYS DOES TECHNOLOGY ASSIST DECISION MAKING?

Information technology is providing managers with a wealth of decision-making support. These include expert systems, neural networks, groupware, and specific problem-solving software. **Expert systems** use software programs to encode the

Ethical Dilemma in Management

Is Sharing Software Okay?

Duplicating software programs for friends and coworkers has become a widespread practice. It has been estimated that nearly $250 billion worldwide is lost each year due to theft of intellectual property—including software piracy.[21] It affects all software companies such as Microsoft, Adobe Lotus, and McAfee. Microsoft alone lost more than $7 billion in 1998 to software piracy.[22] Yet almost all of these duplicated programs are protected by international copyright laws, and being caught for pirating software subjects the offender to fines of up to $100,000 and five years in jail.[23] How, then, has making illegal copies become such a common and accepted practice in people's homes as well as at their places of employment?

Part of the answer revolves around the issue that software isn't like other intellectual property. Intellectual property is attributable directly to intellectual processes. Software is different from a book in that anyone can easily copy it, and an exact replication is achievable. Cultural differences are also a factor. A lot of piracy occurs in places such as Brazil, Malaysia, Hong Kong, Pakistan, Mexico, and Singapore, where copyright laws don't apply and sharing rather than protecting creative work is the norm. Moreover, only seven countries have agreed to sign an agreement with the United States for protecting intellectual property rights.[24] But don't think that software piracy is just an overseas phenomenon. It has been estimated that in the United States, about 27 percent of all software used is pirated. In Canada, it's nearly 40 percent. This is "cheating these software developers out of billions of dollars in additional sales, reducing employment levels by more than 22,000 employees, and lessening tax collections by nearly a billion dollars."[25] In the United States, employees and managers who pirate software defend their behavior with such answers as: "Everybody does it," "I won't get caught," "The law isn't enforced," "No one really loses," or "Our departmental budget isn't large enough to handle buying dozens of copies of the same program."

Ask the same employees who copy software if it is acceptable to steal a book from the library or a tape from a video store. Most are quick to condemn such practices, but it seems as if they don't see copying as stealing. Some think that there's nothing wrong with checking out a video, making a copy, and returning it despite the copyright statement and the Interpol (the international policing agency) warning at the beginning of the tape that specifically states that the act of copying that tape is in violation of the law. Still, if they copy it, they can return the original to the store, no harm done.

Do you believe that reproducing copyrighted software is ever an acceptable practice? As a manager, what guidelines could you establish to direct your employees' behaviors regarding copying software?

relevant experience of an expert and allow a system to act like that expert in analyzing and solving ill-structured problems.[26] The essence of expert systems is that (1) they use specialized knowledge about a particular problem area rather than general knowledge that would apply to all problems, (2) they use qualitative reasoning rather than numerical calculations, and (3) they perform at a level of competence that is higher than that of nonexpert humans.[27] They guide users through problems by asking them a set of sequential questions about the situation and drawing conclusions based on the answers given. The conclusions are based on programmed rules that have been modeled on the actual reasoning processes of experts who have confronted similar problems before. Once in place, these systems are allowing employees and lower-level managers to make high-quality decisions that previously could have been made only by senior managers. Expert systems are being used in such diverse areas as medical diagnosis, mineral and oil explorations, equipment-fault locating, credit approvals, and financial planning.[28] For instance, IDS Financial Services has encoded the expertise of its best financial-planning account managers in an expert systems program. "Now even the worst of our 6,500 planners is better than our average planner used to be," said the company's chairman.[29]

neural networks
Networks that use computer software to imitate the structure of brain cells and connections among them

Neural networks are the next step beyond expert systems.[30] They use computer software to imitate the structure of brain cells and connections among them. Sophisticated robotics are using neural networks for their "intelligence."[31] Neural networks have the ability to distinguish patterns and trends too subtle or complex for human beings. For instance, people can't easily assimilate more than two or three variables at once, but neural networks can perceive correlations among hundreds of variables. As a result, they can perform many operations simultaneously, recognizing patterns, making associations, generalizing about problems they haven't been exposed to before, and learning through experience. For instance, Mellon Bank uses neural networks to flag potential credit card fraud.[32] The bank previously had an expert system to keep track of its 1.2 million Visa and MasterCard accounts, but this system could look at only a few factors, such as the size of a transaction. Thus, it would frequently generate as many as a thousand potential defrauding incidents a day, most of which were false positives. All these potential fraud cases were overwhelming Mellon's investigative staff. Since Mellon replaced its expert system with a neural network, it deals with only one tenth as many suspicious transactions, and they are much more likely to be actual cases of fraud. And, with the expert system, investigators usually did not get around to checking on a questionable transaction for a couple of days. With the new neural network system, investigators are on top of most problems in less than two hours.

How do robots like this get their intelligence? The answer to that lies in part to neural networks. Sophisticated software simulates the human brain and the connections it makes among its cells. This enables the robot to perform a variety of complex tasks and make connections among hundreds of different variables.

In Chapter 4, we introduced the concept of electronic meetings as one means of improving group decision making. When we envision group decision making, most of us typically picture a group of people sitting around a conference table sharing ideas, developing alternatives, analyzing those alternatives, debating differences, and finally reaching a consensus. This is a fairly accurate description of how group decision making took place until just a few years ago. However, technology, again, has changed that description. Today, groups are increasingly interacting electronically.[33]

Groupware is a term used to describe the many software programs that have developed to facilitate group interaction and decision making. For instance, groupware allows management to conduct electronic meetings in which people make decisions on computers that are networked together. Up to 50 people can sit around a table that is empty except for a series of computer terminals. Issues are presented to participants, and they type their response onto their computer screens. Individual comments, as well as aggregate votes, are then displayed on a projection screen in the room. These electronic meetings allow participants to be brutally honest and still maintain their anonymity.

groupware
Software programs developed to facilitate group interaction and decision making

Other applications of groupware include videoconferencing and on-line, realtime conferences. VeriFone, for instance, uses videoconferencing for group meetings, presentations, augmenting face-to-face customer visits, and even for preliminary interviews of job candidates.[34] Conferencing allows participants to communicate over networks or telephone lines with others at different locations at the same time.[35] If you have participated in chat-room sessions on the Internet or on one of the commercial on-line services, you are already familiar with conferencing.

The latest wrinkle in decision support software is the growing number of unique problem-solving programs to help managers do their jobs more effectively. Consider a few of the offerings: Forecast Pro analyzes data and enables managers with a minimal background in statistics to run simple forecasts. Business Insight helps managers brainstorm about "big-picture" issues such as strategic planning. Performance Now! provides a framework for managers to evaluate an employee's performance and then guides the manager through the steps in writing up a specific performance review. Negotiator Pro prepares a manager for any negotiation by preparing a psychological profile of the manager and the opponent and then helping the manager create a detailed negotiation plan.[36]

Operations Technology

High-tech manufacturing is going global. Satyan Pitroda, for instance, believes that developing countries, such as India and Mexico, can leapfrog into the upper ranks of high-tech manufacturing.[37] By importing technology developed elsewhere, these countries can bypass stages of development. To illustrate, Pitroda used an all-Indian team to design a phone switch suited to India's heat, humidity, dust, and frequent power failures. Inside the switch are chips from Motorola, Intel, and Texas Instruments, but Indian firms are designing and exporting the switches.

In this section, we look at key issues related to operations technology—design, production, customer service, distribution, continuous improvement processes, and work process engineering (see Exhibit 14-2).

HOW CAN PRODUCTS BE DESIGNED MORE EFFICIENTLY?

Technology continues to redefine how products are designed. For instance, computer-aided design is generating substantial improvements in design productivity,

Exhibit 14-2 Components of Operations Technology

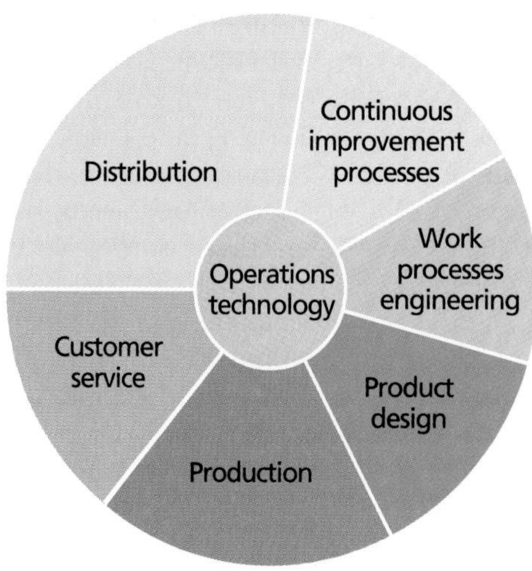

and sophisticated computer networks are allowing designers to collaborate as never before.

computer-aided design (CAD)
Computational and graphics software allows the geometry of a product or component to be graphically displayed and manipulated on video monitors

Computer-aided design (CAD) essentially has made manual drafting obsolete. Computational and graphics software allows the geometry of a product or component to be graphically displayed and manipulated on video monitors. At General Motors, for example, what used to take more than 20 feet of paper to display a drawing can now be displayed on a 17-inch computer monitor.[38] Alternative designs can also be created and evaluated quickly, and the cost of developing mockups and prototypes is often eliminated.[39] CAD enables engineers to develop new designs in as little as a third of the time required for manual drafting. Lucas Diesel Systems, for instance, used its CAD system to design a new engine in half the time it traditionally took.[40] This reduced design time is saving U.S. companies more than $40 billion annually—globally, more than $80 billion.[41]

The best CAD software lets engineers plan products, test them on-screen, and even design tools to make them. Designers at Caterpillar have one of the most sophisticated design systems anywhere. It's a virtual-reality proving ground where designers can test drive huge earthmoving machines before they are built.[42] It is a surround-screen, surround-sound cube about 10 feet on each side that creates the illusion of reality for anyone inside by projecting supercomputer-generated 3-D graphics onto the walls. Designers operate imaginary controls and make adjustments as needed. A recent Caterpillar backhoe and wheel loader incorporate visibility and performance improvements based on data from these virtual test drives.

IN WHAT WAYS CAN PRODUCTION PROCESSES BE ENHANCED?

Technological advances over the past 25 years have completely revolutionized the way products are manufactured. First there were robotics and specialized inventory systems. Today, as we saw with Brenda French, we have entered the stage of mass customization called flexible manufacturing systems. Of course, there have also been important breakthroughs in the basic technologies of manufacturing. For instance, consider the success Finarvedi Spa has had with its new sheet steel plant in Cremona, Italy.[43]

Traditional steelmaking uses a technology, hot and cold rolling, that wastes a lot of energy and floor space. Coils of steel about a twelfth of an inch thick are made by casting steel slabs, lugging them to giant ovens for reheating, and then flattening them out under a series of monstrous rollers that stretch for up to two miles. The whole process takes about three hours. The Cremona mill uses a revolutionary technology that gets the same results in 15 minutes, uses one third the energy, and requires a roller line that measures a little under 600 feet. The new technology allows the company to roll molten metal directly into thin steel. The mill employs only 400 people, compared with the 1,200 workers needed to generate comparable volume in a traditional plant. And not only does this new technology provide Finarvedi with a $25-a-ton advantage over its rivals, it can now produce steel to order. Management can guarantee delivery within three days, versus the industry norm of about three weeks.

What is robotics? Another means of assisting production in organizations has been the widespread use of robots. Robots are machines that act and see like human beings.[44] By the late 1970s, manufacturing firms began adding robots to assembly lines. General Dynamics uses robots to drill 500 holes in the tail fins of its F-16 jet fighter. The robot was able to do in 3 hours what previously had taken workers 24 hours![45] At the Stryker Corporation (makers of orthopedic implants and surgical instruments), robots now perform the more labor-intensive tasks, enabling workers to be retrained for jobs requiring more skills.[46] In the bakery industry, too, robots have been able to enhance productivity far beyond what is possible with human labor. For example, robots can handle from 1,000 to 15,000 products per minute, from wrapping to packaging. That's several orders of magnitude more productive than even the fastest human being.[47]

robotics
Computer-controlled machines that manipulate materials and perform complex functions

From those basic robots came industrial **robotics**—computer-controlled machines that manipulate materials and perform complex functions. Their sophistication has enabled them to perform a wide variety of complex tasks. As a result, they are used not only in manufacturing—for welding, painting, or lifting—but also wherever dangers may lie for humans.[48] For example, police agencies as well as the military are using robotics to assess circumstances (like a hostage situation) or to defuse bombs.[49] Sales of robotics in the United States have risen significantly over the past few years. It's estimated that nearly 100,000 robots are employed in American factories alone.[50]

Robotics have helped Stryker Corporation achieve many of its goals. By having robotics perform some of the more mundane tasks, Stryker employees are able to work on more challenging tasks. As a result, productivity per employee is up over 50 percent, market share for the company has increased 15 percent, and annual profits have increased more than 20 percent annually for the past 23 years!

What are flexible manufacturing systems? Flexible manufacturing systems look like something out of a science fiction movie in which remote-controlled carts deliver a basic casting to a computerized machining center. With robots positioning and repositioning the casting, the machining center calls upon its hundreds of tools to perform various operations that turn the casting into a finished part. Completed parts, each a bit different from the others, are finished at a rate of one every 90 seconds. Neither skilled machinists nor conventional machine tools are used, nor are there any costly delays for changing dies or tools in this factory. A single machine can make dozens or even hundreds of different parts in any order management wants. This is the world of **flexible manufacturing systems.**[51]

flexible manufacturing sytems
Systems that integrate computer-aided design, engineering, and manufacturing to produce low-volume products at a cost comparable to what had once only been possible through mass production

In a global economy, manufacturing organizations that can respond rapidly to change have a competitive advantage.[52] They can, for instance, meet the diverse needs of customers and deliver products faster than their competitors.[53] When customers were willing to accept standardized products, fixed assembly lines made sense. But nowadays, flexible technologies are increasingly necessary if a firm is to compete effectively.

The unique characteristic of flexible manufacturing systems is that, by integrating computer-aided design, engineering, and manufacturing, they can produce low-volume products for customers at a cost that had been previously possible only through mass production. Flexible manufacturing systems are, in effect, repealing the laws of economies of scale. Management no longer has to mass produce thousands of identical products to achieve low per-unit production costs. When management wants to produce a new part, it does not change machines—it just changes the computer program. So management is able to respond to each customer's unique taste, specifications, and budget.

Some automated plants can build a wide variety of flawless products and switch from one product to another on cue from a central computer. John Deere, for instance, has a $1.5 billion automated factory that can turn out ten basic tractor models with as many as 3,000 options without plant shutdowns for retooling. Andersen Corporation in Bayport Minnesota, makers of windows for houses, uses flexible manufacturing to produce any of over one million window variations for customers. In doing so, Andersen can provide customized windows at mass-produced prices.[54]

Flexible technologies are increasingly necessary to compete effectively in the global economy.

IN WHAT WAYS CAN CUSTOMER SERVICE BE IMPROVED?

In the midst of the Christmas rush, a frazzled customer came into Silverman's, a men's apparel chain in North and South Dakota.[55] "Do you know Benny Thompson?" she asked the saleswoman. "What does he like? What size does he wear? Help!" From a computer terminal on the sales floor, the saleswoman confidently checked Benny Thompson's record: He wears size large, looks best in Polo rugby shirts and Levi Dockers (items he looked at recently but didn't buy), works as a financial analyst, and enjoys boating. "No problem," the saleswoman said. "I can take care of this gift for you. Sit down and have a cup of coffee." A few minutes later the relieved customer left the store with her gift and the satisfaction of knowing that Benny Thompson was going to get a Christmas gift he wanted and in the right size.

Consistent with the quality movement, technology can be used to revitalize customer service.[56] It can identify and track individual customers, monitor service levels by company representatives, and assist customers in specifying, acquiring, fixing, or returning products.

Managers are using technology to improve their customer service strategies in three ways.[57] First, technology can personalize service that previously was standardized. It can allow management to individualize service for each customer's unique needs. For instance, if, as a previous customer of Domino's Pizza or L.L. Bean, you call to place an order, their computer system will already have data about your personal preferences recorded. This information enables the company to treat people as individuals rather than as objects, and it speeds the order-taking process.

Second, technology can provide the customer with additional support related to the acquisition or use of the product. Hertz used this strategy when it created its Gold Card service. Their computer system has your credit card number for billing, your car style and size preference, insurance data, and driver's license information. One short phone call makes your car reservation. When you arrive at your destination, an electronic sign with your name on it indicates where your car is located. The paperwork is already done, and your contract is sitting in your awaiting car. When your trip is complete and you drop the car off, you bypass the line at the checkout counter. All you have to do is hand the keys and contract to the lot attendant, who records the time, date, and mileage in his hand-held computer and prints you a receipt, and you're off to your next destination in a couple of minutes.

Third, technology can transform your business. That is, it can assist an organization to fundamentally develop new business practices and reinvent itself. Our discussion in Chapter 2 on electronic business and commerce is a clear indication of the effect that technology can have on a business. Technology is allowing companies—large and small—to enter markets that just a few short years ago were unapproachable.[58] For example, it's enabling companies to sell their goods on a global basis as well as fostering joint ventures, partnerships, and strategic alliances that were both improbable and impractical five years ago.[59]

HOW DOES TECHNOLOGY ENHANCE PRODUCT DISTRIBUTION?

Traditional distribution technology relied heavily on sales agents or brokers, wholesalers, and retailers. It was not unusual for a product to go through two or three intermediaries before getting into the consumer's hands. New technologies are increasingly cutting out those intermediaries—the process of disintermediation.[60] Management has been investing heavily in multiple-distribution technologies to get closer to the customer while cutting costs, providing quicker deliveries and better service, and better meeting the needs of a diverse customer base. The two most recent breakthroughs in distribution technology are home shopping through television and electronic shopping via the Internet. Each of these technologies allows manufacturers to reach customers directly.

Cable television channels such as the Home Shopping Network, Cable Value Network, and the QVC channel have created a multibillion-dollar industry. Most of the products sold on these channels are bought from manufacturers. As such, they merely create a new mechanism for manufacturers to reach customers. However, some manufacturers are paying the channels a commission for air time and using these channels to directly sell their products to customers. Joan Rivers, for example, can sell tens of thousands of dollars' worth of her jewelry products in a few minutes by appearing on one of these cable channels.

Infomercials are another vehicle by which manufacturers can directly take their product to the consumer. These programs—which typically last a half-hour and present product testimonials in an entertainment format—allow makers of products as diverse as car waxes, kitchen appliances, cosmetics, and self-help courses to sell merchandise without having to go through wholesalers or retailers.

The latest and potentially most exciting distribution method made possible by computer technology is the marketing of products directly to customers on the Internet.[61] Just about every major business firm, educational institution, and not-for-profit organization is setting up sites on the World Wide Web and creating a home page. Why? Because it's a relatively cheap way to reach over tens of millions of consumers.[62] If you want to learn about the latest offerings from General Motors and Dell Computer or review the latest exhibits at the Smithsonian Institute, you can merely tap into their Web site and review their home page. Toronto Dominion Bank, for instance, has turned its Web site into a one-stop financial shopping center. Its Web site contains 300 pages of general financial information about savings plans, mortgages, and other financial products and services.[63] And Amazon.com is selling more than $1.5 million worth of products every day through its Web site.[64]

IS CLOSE GOOD ENOUGH?

Continuous process improvement programs are designed so that variability is constantly reduced. When you eliminate variations, you increase the uniformity of the product or service. Uniformity, in turn, results in lower costs and higher quality. For instance, Advanced Filtration Systems Inc., of Champaign, Illinois, recently cut the number of product defects—as determined by a customer quality audit—from 26.5 per 1,000 units to zero over four years. And that occurred during a period when monthly unit production tripled and the number of workers declined by 20 percent.

Continuous improvement runs counter to the more typical American management approach of treating work projects as linear—with a beginning and an end. For example, American managers traditionally looked at cost cutting as a short-term project. They set a goal of cutting costs by 20 percent, achieved it, and then said: "Whew! Our cost cutting is over." The Japanese, on the other hand, regard cost control as something that never ends. The search for continuous improvement creates a race without a finish line.

The search for never-ending improvement requires a circular approach rather than a linear one as illustrated in the plan-do-check-act (PDCA) cycle in Exhibit 14-3.[65] Management plans a change, makes that change, checks the results, and, depending on the outcome, acts to standardize the change or begin the cycle of improvement again with new information. This cycle treats all organizational processes as being in a constant state of improvement.

Exhibit 14-3
The PDCA Cycle

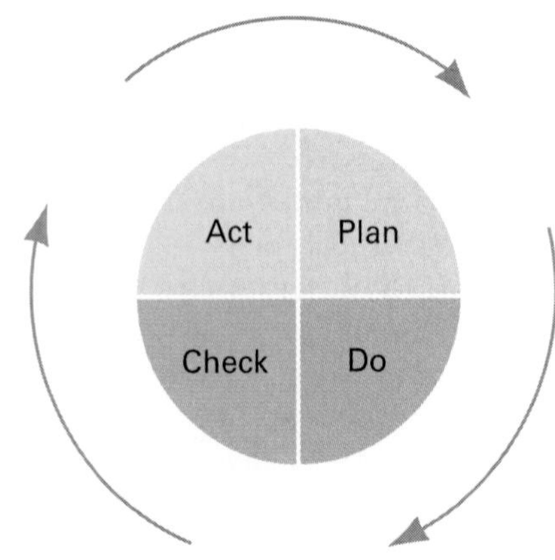

Dana Corporation's manufacturing plant in Stockton, California, has adopted the PDCA cycle. The plant builds truck chassis for only one customer—Toyota Motor Company. To win Toyota's business, Dana had to promise to shoot for a 2 percent price cut every year. This forced management to commit to constantly finding productivity gains.[66] To achieve these gains, management has taken some innovative steps. For example, it specifically hired welders with no experience, reasoning that unconditioned hands would be freer to explore new and improved ways of welding. Another technique for finding improvements has been demanding that every employee submit two improvement ideas in writing each month. Management considers no change too small. Surprisingly, 81 percent of these ideas have proved sufficiently worthwhile to implement.

HOW CAN PROCESS ENGINEERING ENHANCE WORK PROCESSES?

We also introduced work process engineering in Chapter 2. We described it as considering how things would be done if you could start all over from scratch. The term "work process engineering" comes from the historical process of taking apart an electronic product and designing a better version. Michael Hammer, who brought this concept to light, found companies using computers simply to automate outdated processes rather than finding fundamentally better ways of doing things and realized that the principles of work process engineering electronics products could be applied to business. So, as applied to organizations, work process engineering means starting with a clean sheet of paper, rethinking and redesigning the processes by which the organization creates value and does work, and eliminating operations that have become antiquated in the computer age.[67]

What are the key elements of work process engineering? Three key elements of work process engineering are identifying an organization's distinctive competencies, assessing core processes, and reorganizing horizontally by process (see Exhibit 14-4). As discussed in Chapter 3, an organization's distinctive competencies are the unique skills and resources that determine its competitive weapons. They are what the organization is better at than its competitors, such as superior store locations, a more efficient distribution system, higher-quality products, more knowledgeable sales personnel, or superior technical support. Why is identifying

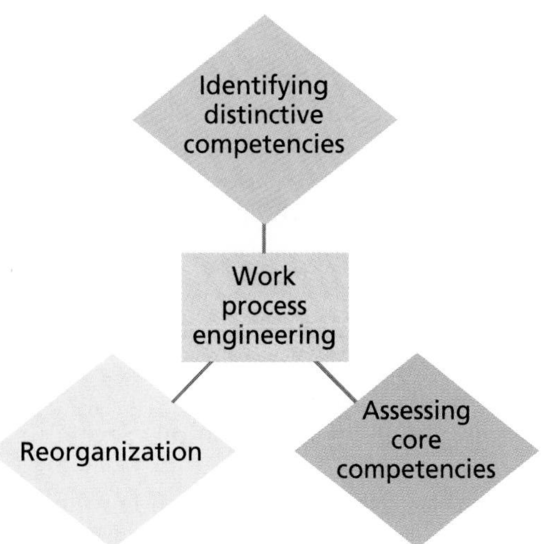

Exhibit 14-4
Key Elements of Work Process Engineering

distinctive competencies so important? Because it guides the decisions about which activities are crucial to the organization's success.

Management also needs to assess the core processes that clearly add value to the organization's distinctive competencies, the processes that transform materials, capital, information, and labor into products and services that the customer values. When the organization is viewed as a series of processes, ranging from strategic planning to after-sales customer support, management can determine to what degree each adds value. Not surprisingly, this **process value analysis** typically uncovers a whole lot of activities that add little or nothing of value and whose only justification is "we've always done it this way."

process value analysis
Analysis of the organization as a series of processes in order to determine to what degree each adds value

Work process engineering requires management to reorganize around horizontal processes using cross-functional and self-managed teams. It means focusing on processes rather than on functions. For instance, the vice president of marketing might become the "process owner of finding and keeping customers."[68] It also means cutting out levels of middle management. As Hammer points out, "Managers are not value-added. A customer never buys a product because of the caliber of management. Management is, by definition, indirect. So if possible, less is better. One of the goals of work process engineering is to minimize the necessary amount of management."[69]

Why use work process engineering now? Isn't reengineering something management should have been doing all along? Why didn't it become popular until the mid-1990s? The answers, according to Michael Hammer, are a changing global environment and organizational structures that had gotten top heavy.[70]

Traditional bureaucratic organizations worked fine in times of stable growth. Activities could be fragmented and specialized to gain economic efficiencies. That description fits the environment faced by most North American organizations in the 1950s, 1960s, and much of the 1970s. But most organizations today operate in a very different environment. Customers are much more informed and sophisticated than they were 30—or even 20—years ago. Moreover, markets, production, and capital can be moved all over the world. Investors in Australia, for example, can put their money into opportunities in Japan, Canada, or anywhere else in the world if they see better returns than they can get at home. Customers worldwide now demand quality, service, and low cost. If you can't provide it, they will get it from someone else.

Breaking up work into specialized tasks that were performed in narrowly defined functional departments drove down direct labor costs, but the bureaucracies they created had massive overhead costs. To coordinate all the fragmentation and specialization, the organization needed numerous levels of middle management. So, although bureaucracies drove down costs at the operating level, they required increasingly expensive coordinating systems. Those organizations that introduced teams, decentralized decisions, and flattened structures became more efficient and established a benchmark for the new way to do things.

Current Issues in Operations

This section focuses on the importance of efficiency and productivity in the operations side of the organization. Several current activities are allowing organizations to produce higher-quality products and services at prices that meet or beat those of their rivals. These include supply chain management, just-in-time inventory control, and quality control. Let's look at each of these.

WHAT IS SUPPLY CHAIN MANAGEMENT?

As we've already mentioned in this chapter, organizations operate to produce some product or service. In order to do this, they need to transform some raw material into a finished item. These raw materials frequently come from suppliers—even those in virtual organizations.[71] If these suppliers are late in providing the supplies or provide materials that are poor in quality, then the final product or service will suffer. As a result, some organizations like McDonald's, IBM, and the Dutch software producer, Baan, have implemented supply chain management principles.[72]

Supply chain management refers to the facilities, functions, and activities involved in producing and delivering a product or service, from suppliers (and their suppliers) to customers (and their customers).[73] It includes all activities from product planning to delivery. That is, supply chain management focuses on "estimating the demand for a product or service, planning and managing supply and demand; acquiring materials; producing and scheduling the product or service; warehousing, inventory control, and distribution; and delivery and customer service" to provide customers quality products at the lowest possible cost. Companies that successfully manage their supply chain have found such actions to be instrumental in creating a competitive competency.[74] Effective supply chain management, then, is contingent on the effective communications between suppliers and organizations.

supply chain management
Management of the facilities, functions, and activities involved in producing and delivering a product or service, from suppliers to customers

One of the ways that organizations have adapted in order to promote supply chain management is to vertically integrate their processes.[75] In this situation, a company owns or significantly controls their suppliers who provide vital materials for their finished product. For example, to ensure that a Big Mac in Moscow tastes exactly like it does in the United States, McDonald's has an exclusive arrangement with "a bakery, meat plant, chicken plant, lettuce plant, fish plant, and a distribution center." Each of these plants works solely for McDonald's and is required to supply food products that meet the precise standards McDonald's has established.[76]

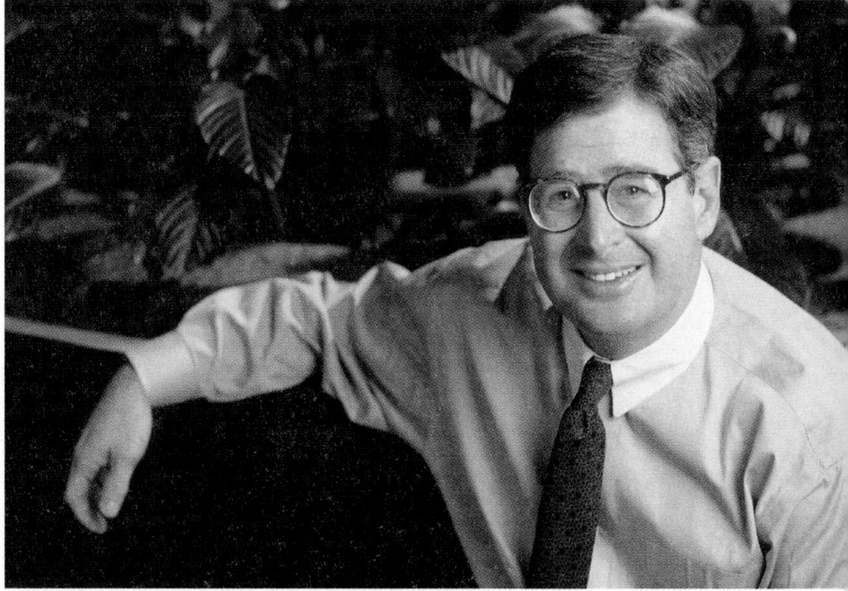
One of the events that has helped IBM regain its stature in the computer industry has been its work with supply chain management. By helping customers assess, plan, design, implement, and operate their supply chain technology, IBM has found a unique niche in the market. With the efforts of Sam Palmisano, IBM has been able to sell this concept to such companies as Merrill Lynch and Bank One.

A variation of supply chain management involves reducing the number of vendors an organization uses in order to oversee their operations. That is, instead of using 10 or 12 vendors and forcing them to compete to gain the organization's business, managers are using 3 or fewer vendors and working closely with them to improve efficiency and quality. Motorola, for instance, sends its design and manufacturing engineers to suppliers to help with any problems. Other firms now routinely send inspection teams to assess suppliers' production and delivery techniques, statistical process controls that identify causes of defects, and ability to handle data electronically. North American companies and many international firms are doing what has long been a tradition in Japan—developing long-term relationships with suppliers. As collaborators and partners rather than adversaries, firms are finding that they can achieve better quality of inputs, fewer defects, and lower costs. Furthermore, when problems arise with suppliers, open communication channels facilitate quick resolutions.

WHAT IS A JUST-IN-TIME INVENTORY PRACTICE?

just-in-time (JIT) inventory systems
Systems in which inventory items arrive when needed in the production process instead of being stored in stock

kanban
Japanese for "card" or "signal"; refers to a system of cards in shipping containers that uses the just-in-time concept (a card reorders a shipment when a container is opened)

Large companies such as Boeing, Toyota, and General Electric have billions of dollars tied up in inventories. It is not unusual for even small firms to have a million dollars or more tied up in inventories. So anything management can do to significantly reduce the size of its inventory will improve productivity. **Just-in-time (JIT) inventory systems** change the technology by which inventories are managed. Inventory items arrive when they are needed in the production process instead of being stored in stock.[77] With JIT, the ultimate goal is to have only enough inventory on hand to complete the day's work—thereby reducing a company's lead time, inventory, and its associated costs, to nearly zero.[78]

In Japan, JIT systems are called **kanban,** a word that gets to the essence of the just-in-time concept.[79] Kanban is Japanese for "card" or "signal." Japanese suppliers ship parts in containers. Each container has a card, or kanban, slipped into a side pocket. When a production worker at the manufacturing plant opens a container, he or she takes out the card and sends it back to the supplier. Receipt of the card initiates the shipping of a second container of parts that, ideally, reaches the production worker just as the last part in the first container is being used up.

An illustration of how JIT works in the United States can be seen in the relationship that has developed between Lemco-Miller Corporation (a manufacturer of precision custom-machine parts) and both Eaton and Northstar Steel and Aluminum.[80] Each of these companies reached an agreement on how many parts would be in inventory at Lemco-Miller for the manufacturing process. They established the volume, flow, and when to replenish the stock. Price for each raw material was also agreed upon. As a result of the kanban system, Lemco-Miller was able to increase productivity by more than 50 percent and cut its delivery time from 12 weeks to one or two days. And as a by-product of the system, Eaton, one of the suppliers, also was able to reduce its inventory holdings by more than 50 percent through a well-designed kanban system arrangement with Lemco-Miller.

As a result of the kanban system, Lemco-Miller was able to increase productivity by more than 50 percent and cut its delivery time from 12 weeks to one or two days.

The ultimate goal of a JIT inventory system is to eliminate raw material inventories by coordinating production and supply deliveries precisely. When the system works as designed, it results in a number of positive benefits for a manufacturer: reduced inventories, reduced setup time, better workflow, shorter manufacturing time, less space consumption, and even higher quality. Of course, suppliers who can be depended on to deliver quality materials on time must be found. Because there are no inventories, there is no slack in the system to compensate for defective materials or delays in shipments.

ARE CONTINUOUS IMPROVEMENT AND QUALITY CONTROL THE SAME THING?

We have discussed continuous improvement throughout this book, describing it as a comprehensive, customer-focused program to continuously improve the quality of the organization's processes, products, and services. Whereas continuous improvement programs emphasize actions to prevent mistakes, quality control emphasizes identifying mistakes that may have already occurred.

What do we mean by **quality control?** It refers to monitoring quality—weight, strength, consistency, color, taste, reliability, finish, or any one of myriad characteristics—to ensure that it meets some preestablished standard. Quality control will probably be needed at one or more points, beginning with the receipt of inputs. It will continue with work in process and all steps up to the final product. Assessments at intermediate stages of the transformation process typically are part of quality control. Early detection of a defective part or process can save the cost of further work on the item.

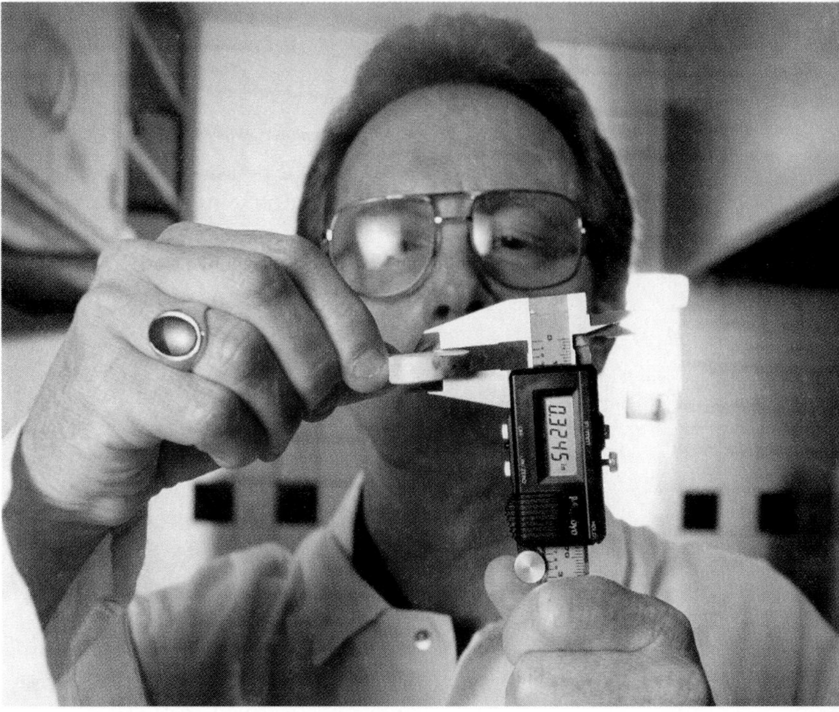

Quality control can involve a variety of activities. In their effort to better compete with Papa John's Pizza, Pizza Hut's focus has shifted to providing the highest-quality ingredients. Here, a Pizza Hut inspector tests the thickness of a mushroom to ensure consistency and quality control.

Before implementing any quality control measures, managers need to ask whether they expect to examine 100 percent of the items produced or only a sample. The inspection of every item makes sense if the cost of continuous evaluation is very low or if the consequences of a statistical error are very high (as in the manufacturing of a drug used in open-heart surgery). Statistical samples are usually less costly, and sometimes they're the only viable option. For example, if the quality test destroys the product as it does when testing flash bulbs, fireworks, or home pregnancy tests, then sampling has to be used.

quality control
Ensuring that what is produced meets some preestablished standard

Project Management and Control Tools

Managing a production department at DaimlerChrysler's Windsor, Ontario, minivan plant is different from managing a design team at DaimlerChrysler's Technology Center in Auburn Hills, Michigan. The former involves an ongoing process; the latter is an example of project management. In this section, we briefly describe project management, discuss why it has become so popular, and assess the challenges that project managers face. We then take a look at two popular scheduling tools used by project managers, the Gantt Chart and PERT.

project
One-time only set of activities with a definite beginning and ending point in time

WHAT IS PROJECT MANAGEMENT?

A **project** is a one-time-only set of activities with a definite beginning and ending point.[81] Projects vary in size and scope, from a NASA space shuttle launch to a wedding. **Project management** is the task of getting the activities done on time, within budget, and according to specifications.[82]

project management
Task of getting the activities done on time, within budget, and according to specifications

There is no shortage of project-management cheerleaders. For instance, William Dauphinais, a partner at PricewaterhouseCoopers, says: "Project management is going to be huge in the next decade."[83] Project management is "the wave of the future," according to a General Motors in-house newsletter.[84] "Project management is the way the business world is going," says Michael Strickland, a manager with Bell South.[85]

Project management has actually been around for a long time in industries such as construction and movie making, but now it has expanded into almost every type of business. For instance, Mortgage Association, which processes more than $1 billion in mortgage purchases every day, uses it. Says Fannie Mae's chief information officer, "Automation and empowerment take away the need to have managers oversee the day-to-day work. Everything has become projects. This is the way Fannie Mae does business today."[86]

What explains the growing popularity of project management? It fits well with a dynamic environment and the need for flexibility and rapid response. Organizations are increasingly undertaking projects that are somewhat unusual or unique, have specific deadlines, contain complex interrelated tasks requiring specialized skills, and are temporary in nature. These types of projects don't lend themselves well to the standardized operating procedures that guide routine and continuous organizational activities.

In the typical project, team members are temporarily assigned to and report to a project manager, who coordinates the project's activities with other departments and reports directly to a senior executive. The project is temporary: It exists only long enough to complete its specific objectives. Then it's wound down and closed up; members move on to other projects, return to their permanent departments, or leave the organization.

WHAT IS THE ROLE OF THE PROJECT MANAGER?

The temporary nature of projects makes managing them different from, say, overseeing a production line and preparing a weekly tally of costs on an ongoing basis. The one-shot nature of the work makes project managers the organizational equivalent of hired gunmen. There's a job to be done. It has to be defined in detail, with much haggling. And the project manager is responsible for how it's done.

In spite of the availability of sophisticated computerized scheduling programs and other project management tools, the role of project manager remains difficult because he or she is managing people who are still responsible to their permanent department. "You have to know how to work with people who have different priorities, who march to a different tune than you," says Ian Benson, a vice president with Chase Manhattan Bank.[87] Janine Coleman, a project manager for AT&T's global business communications systems that installs equipment for large corporate clients says, "The company tells the client, 'We assign you a project manager, and she's in charge.' If it fails, it's my fault. But does this put real authority there? No. If a VP won't go along, it's up to the project manager to get him to."[88] The only real influence project managers have is their power or persuasion. To make matters worse, team members seldom work on just one project. They're usually assigned two or three at any given time. So project managers often end up competing with each other to focus a worker's attention on his or her particular undertaking.[89]

WHAT ARE SOME POPULAR SCHEDULING TOOLS?

If you were to observe a group of supervisors or department managers for a few days, you would see them regularly detailing what activities have to be done, the

Chris Kartchner Aztec Technology Partners

Chris Kartchner has worked in a variety of industries including electronics distribution, home fashion, and electronic publishing. At Aztec, a web-focused software applications development firm, a very flat organizational structure allows Kartchner and other employees to handle simultaneously a number of tasks including consulting, project management, and sales and marketing functions. The result, says Kartchner, is both "chaotic and synergistic."

Aztec's project management methods reflect the flat and open structure of the firm. Once in place, most of the project team is dedicated to a particular project, and everyone has a say in all phases including the use of resources. The teams rely on many Microsoft tools for planning and communication within the group, but additional tools are welcome if they apply to present or future projects. A comprehensive internal quality check ensures that the finished software applications meet Aztec's high standards while maintaining tight production schedules.

Chris credits project management technology with much of Aztec's success in exceeding its clients' expectations. Improvements in the science of project management can only help, he feels, as good project managers strive to become outstanding ones.

order in which they are to be done, who is to do each, and when they are to be completed. The managers are doing what we call scheduling. The following discussion reviews some useful scheduling devices.

How do you use a Gantt chart? The **Gantt chart** is a planning tool developed around the turn of the century by Henry Gantt (see History Module). The idea behind the Gantt chart is relatively simple. It is essentially a bar graph, with time on the horizontal axis and the activities to be scheduled on the vertical axis. The bars show output, both planned and actual, over a period of time. The Gantt chart visually shows when tasks are supposed to be done and compares the assigned date with the actual progress on each. This simple but important device allows managers to detail easily what has yet to be done to complete a job or project and to assess whether it is ahead of, behind, or on schedule.

Gantt chart
A planning tool that shows in bar graph form when tasks are supposed to be done and compares that with the actual progress on each

Exhibit 14-5 shows a Gantt chart that was developed for book production by a manager in a publishing firm. Time is expressed in months across the top of the chart. Major activities are listed down the left side. The planning comes in deciding what activities need to be done to get the book finished, the order in which those activities need to be done, and the time that should be allocated to each activity. The gold shading represents actual progress made in completing each activity.

A Gantt chart, then, actually becomes a managerial control device as the manager looks for deviations from the plan. In this case, most activities were completed on time. However, if you look at the "print galley proofs" activity, you will notice that it actually took two weeks longer than planned to do this. Given this information, the manager might want to take some corrective action—either to make up the lost two weeks or to ensure that no further delays will occur. At this point, the manager can expect that the book will be published at least two weeks late if no corrective action is taken.

Exhibit 14-5
A Sample Gantt Chart

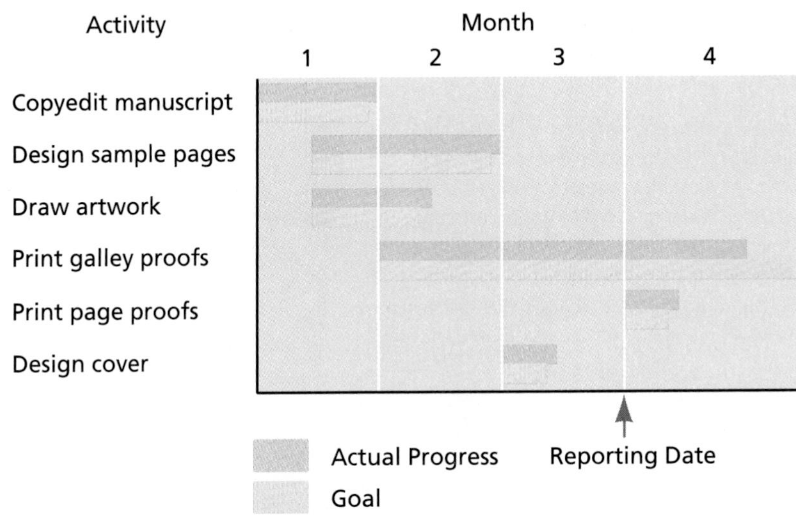

A modified version of the Gantt chart is a load chart. Instead of listing activities on the vertical axis, load charts list either whole departments or specific resources. This information allows managers to plan and control for capacity utilization. In other words, load charts schedule capacity by work stations. For example, Exhibit 14-6 shows a load chart for six production editors at the same publishing firm. Each editor supervises the design and production of several books. By reviewing the load chart, the executive editor who supervises the six production editors can see who is free to take on a new book. If everyone is fully scheduled, the executive editor might decide not to accept any new projects, to accept some new projects and delay others, to ask the editors to work overtime, or to employ more production editors.

What is a PERT network analysis? Gantt and load charts are helpful as long as the activities or projects being scheduled are few and independent of each other. But what if a manager had to plan a large project—such as a complex reorganization, the launching of a major cost-reduction campaign, or the development of a new product—that required coordinating inputs from marketing, pro-

Exhibit 14-6
A Sample Load Chart

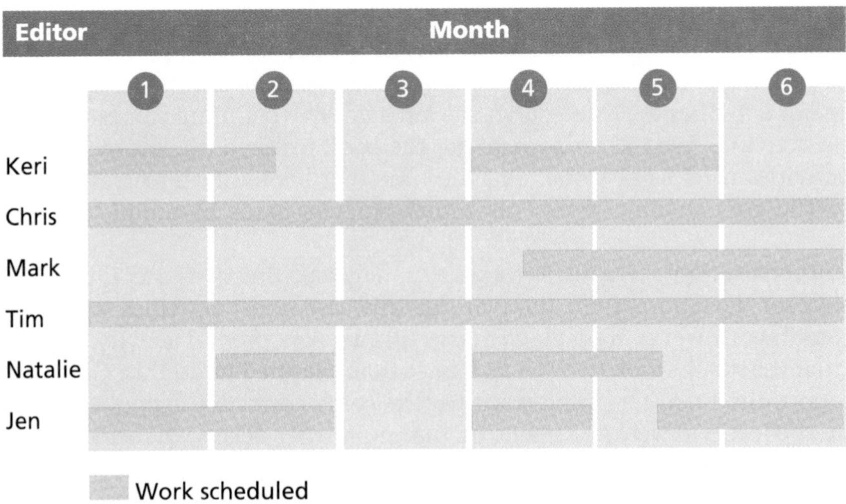

duction, and product design personnel? Such projects require coordinating hundreds or thousands of activities, some of which must be done simultaneously and some of which cannot begin until earlier activities have been completed. If you are constructing a shopping mall, you obviously cannot start erecting walls until the foundation has been laid. How, then, can you schedule such a complex project? You could use the program evaluation and review technique.

The **program evaluation and review technique**—usually just called **PERT,** or the PERT network analysis—was originally developed in the late 1950s for coordinating the more than 3,000 contractors and agencies working on the Polaris submarine weapon system.[90] This project was incredibly complicated, with hundreds of thousands of activities that had to be coordinated. PERT is reported to have cut two years off the completion date for the Polaris project.

program evaluation and review technique (PERT)
A flowchart-like diagram that depicts the sequence of activities needed to complete a project and the time or costs associated with each activity

A PERT network is a flowchart-like diagram that depicts the sequence of activities needed to complete a project and the time or costs associated with each activity. With a PERT network, a project manager must think through what has to be done, determine which events depend on one another, and identify potential trouble spots (see Exhibit 14-7). PERT also makes it easy to compare the effects alternative actions will have on scheduling and costs. PERT has been used to design and construct facilities, prepare environmental studies, conduct research

Exhibit 14-7
Developing PERT Charts

Developing a PERT network requires the manager to identify all key activities needed to complete a project, rank them in order of dependence, and estimate each activity's completion time. This procedure can be translated into five specific steps:

1. Identify every significant activity that must be achieved for a project to be completed. The accomplishment of each activity results in a set of events or outcomes.
2. Ascertain the order in which these events must be completed.
3. Diagram the flow of activities from start to finish, identifying each activity and its relationship to all other activities. Use circles to indicate events and arrows to represent activities. The result is a flowchart diagram that we call the PERT network.
4. Compute a time estimate for completeing each activity, using a weighted average that employs an optimistic time estimate (t_o) of how long the activity would take under ideal conditions, a most-likely estimate (t_m) of the time the activity normally should take, and a pessimistic estimate (t_p) that represents the time that an activity should take under the worst possible conditions. The formula for calculating the expected time (t_e) is then

$$t_e = \frac{t_o + 4t_m + t_p}{6}$$

5. Finally, using a network diagram that contains time estimates for each activity, the manager can determine a schedule for the start and finish dates of each activity and for the entire project. Any delays that occur along the critical path require the most attention because they delay the entire project. That is, the critical path has no slack in it; therefore, any delay along that path immediately translates into a delay in the final deadline for the completed project.

and development, design software, and even plan large conferences.[91] PERT allows managers to monitor a project's progress, identify possible bottlenecks, and shift resources as necessary to keep the project on schedule. NASA and its many contractors use PERT to schedule Space Shuttle flights and in the engineering design of NASA's space station. It is also used in product design activities at such companies as Samsung.[92]

What are the key components of PERT? To understand how to construct a PERT network, you need to know three terms: events, activities, and critical path. Let us define these terms, outline the steps in the PERT process, and then develop an example. **Events** are end points that represent the completion of major activities. Sometimes called milestones, events indicate that something significant has happened (such as receipt of purchased items) or an important component is finished. In PERT, events represent a point in time. **Activities,** on the other hand, are the actions that take place. Each activity consumes time, as determined on the basis of the time or resources required to progress from one event to another. The **critical path** is the longest or most time-consuming sequence of events and activities required to complete the project in the shortest amount of time. Let's apply PERT to a construction manager's task of building a 5,500-square-foot custom home.

events
End points that represent the completion of major activities

activities
Actions that take place

critical path
The longest or most time-consuming sequence of events and activities required to complete a project in the shortest amount of time

As a construction manager, you recognize that time really is money in your business. Delays can turn a profitable job into a money loser. Accordingly, you must determine how long it will take to complete the house. You have carefully dissected the entire project into activities and events. Exhibit 14-8 outlines the major events in the construction project and your estimate of the expected time

Exhibit 14-8
Major Activities in Building a Custom Home

Event	Description	Time (Weeks)	Predecessor Activity
A	Approve design and get permits	3	None
B	Perform excavation/lot clearing	1	A
C	Pour footers	1	B
D	Erect foundation walls	2	C
E	Frame house	4	D
F	Install windows	0.5	E
G	Shingle roof	0.5	E
H	Install brick front and siding	4	F, G
I	Install electrical, plumbing, and heating and A/C rough-ins	6	E
J	Install insulation	0.25	I
K	Install sheetrock	2	J
L	Finish and sand sheetrock	7	K
M	Install interior trim	2	L
N	Paint house (interior and exterior)	2	H, M
O	Install all cabinets	0.5	N
P	Install flooring	1	N
Q	Final touch-up and turn over house to homeowner	1	O, P

Exhibit 14-9 A PERT Network for Building a Custom Home

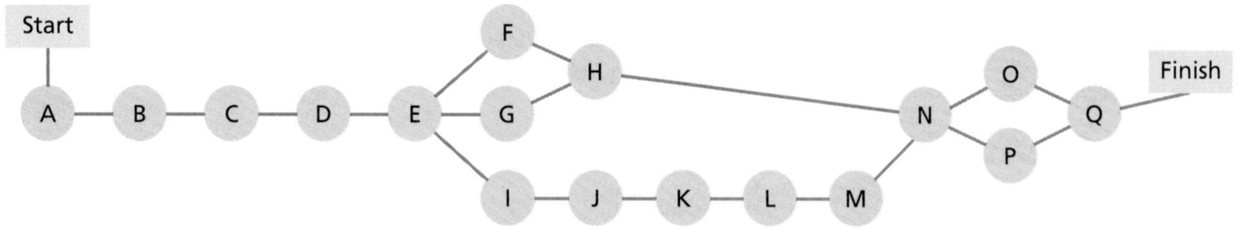

required to complete each activity. Exhibit 14-9 depicts the PERT network based on the data in Exhibit 14-8.

Your PERT network tells you that if everything goes as planned, it will take just over 32 weeks to build the house. This time is calculated by tracing the network's critical path: A-B-C-D-E-I-J-K-L-M-N-P-Q. Any delay in completing the events along this path will delay the completion of the entire project. For example, if it took six weeks instead of four to frame the house (event E), the entire project would be delayed by two weeks (or the time beyond that expected). But a one-week delay for installing the brick (event H) would have little effect because that event is not on the critical path. By using PERT, the construction manager would know that no corrective action would be needed. Further delays in installing the brick, however, could present problems—for such delays may, in actuality, result in a new critical path. Now back to our original critical path dilemma.

Notice that the critical path passes through activities N, P, and Q. Our PERT chart (Exhibit 14-8) tells us that these three activities take four weeks. Wouldn't path N-O-Q be faster? Yes. The PERT network shows that it takes only 3.5 weeks to complete that path. So why isn't N-O-Q on the critical path? Because activity Q cannot begin until both activities O and P are completed. Although activity O takes half a week, activity P takes one full week. So, the earliest we can begin Q is after one week. What happens to the difference between the critical activity (activity P) time and the noncritical activity (activity O) time? The difference, in this case half a week, becomes **slack time.** Slack time is the time difference between the critical path and all other paths. What use is there for slack? If the project manager notices some slippage on a critical activity, perhaps slack time from a noncritical activity can be borrowed and temporarily assigned to work on the critical one.

slack time
The time difference between the critical path and all other paths

How is PERT both a planning and a control tool? Not only does PERT help us to estimate the times associated with scheduling a project, it also gives us clues about where our controls should be placed. Because any event on the critical path that is delayed will delay the overall project (making us not only late but probably also over budget), our attention needs to be focused on the critical activities at all times. For example, if activity F (installing windows) is delayed by a week because supplies have not arrived, that is not a major issue. It's not on the critical path. But if activity P (installing flooring) is delayed from one week to two weeks, the entire project will be delayed by one week. Consequently, anything that has the immediate potential for delaying a project (critical activities) must be monitored very closely.

PHLIP Companion Web Site

We invite you to visit the Robbins/DeCenzo companion Web site at *www.prenhall.com/robbins* for this chapter's Internet resources.

Chapter Summary

How will you know if you fulfilled the Learning Outcomes on page 437? You will have fulfilled the Learning Outcomes if you are able to:

1 *Describe the formula for calculating productivity.*
In its simplest form, productivity can be expressed in terms of the following ratio: outputs divided by labor plus capital plus materials. Productivity can also be calculated for three different areas. These include the individual, a work group, and the total organization.

2 *Explain how technology can improve productivity.*
By substituting computerized equipment and machinery for human labor and traditional machinery, technology allows organizations to achieve increased levels of output with less labor, capital, and materials.

3 *Explain how information technology is providing managers with decision support.*
Expert systems, neural networks, groupware, and specific managerial problem-solving software are examples of information technologies that have been created to support and improve organizational decision making.

4 *Describe the advantages of computer-aided design.*
Computer-aided design has essentially made manual drafting obsolete. It allows designers to create and evaluate alternative designs quickly, and it dramatically cuts the costs of developing prototypes. CAD lets engineers plan products, test them on the computer screen, and design tools to make the product.

5 *Identify why management might consider introducing flexible manufacturing systems.*
Flexible manufacturing systems provide management with the technology to meet customers' unique demands by producing nonstandardized products with the efficiency associated with standardization.

6 *Define and describe the three key elements in work process engineering.*
The three key elements of work process engineering are: (1) identifying an organization's distinctive competencies—the unique skills and resources that determine an organization's competitive weapons, (2) assessing core processes—the processes that customers value, and (3) reorganizing horizontally by process—this requires flattening the structure and relying more on teams.

7 *Describe what is meant by the term* supply chain management.
Supply chain management refers to the facilities, functions, and activities involved in producing and delivering a product or service, from suppliers (and their suppliers) to customers (and their customers). It includes all activities from product plan-

ning to delivery—including estimating the demand for a product or service, planning and managing supply and demand; acquiring materials; producing and scheduling the product or service; warehousing, inventory control, and distribution; and delivery and customer service.

8 *Explain what is meant by the term just-in-time inventory systems.*
Just-in-time inventory systems change the technology with which inventories are managed. Inventory items arrive when they are needed in the production process instead of being stored in stock.

9 *Identify the steps in developing a PERT network.*
The five steps in developing a PERT network are: (1) identify every significant activity that must be achieved for a project to be completed, (2) determine the order in which those activities must be completed, (3) diagram the flow of activities in a project from start to finish, (4) estimate the time needed to complete each activity, and (5) use the network diagram to determine a schedule for start and finish dates of each activity for the entire project.

Review and Application Questions

READING FOR COMPREHENSION

1 Explain how supply chain management and just-in-time systems improve productivity.

2 Describe how technology can improve an organization's customer service.

3 Compare and contrast work process engineering and continuous improvement programs.

4 Why would technology transfer be relevant to a large, European-based global company?

5 In what ways is managing a project different from managing a department?

LINKING CONCEPTS TO PRACTICE

1 How do you think information technology will have reshaped the office by the year 2010?

2 What downside, if any, do you see for (a) the organization and (b) employees of replacing humans with computerized technology?

3 What are the implications of worker obsolescence on (a) society, (b) management practice, and (c) you, as an individual planning your career?

4 How is the Internet changing organizations and management practices?

5 In what ways could quality control be designed into an organization's operations systems.

Management Workshop

Team Skill-Building Exercise

Designing Your University

Break into groups of four or five students. Your team's task is to assess how you believe technology will change the way your college disseminates information to students a decade from now. Specifically, what do you believe the typical college's teaching technologies will look like in the year 2010. To assist you in this activity, here's some questions to consider:

1 Will there still be a need for a college campus spanning several hundred acres?

2 Do you believe every student will be required to have a laptop for classes?

3 Will there be computers in every classroom, coupled with hi-tech media technologies?

4 Do you believe students will be required to physically come to campus for their classes?

5 What role will distance learning and telecommuting have on classroom activities?

You have 30 minutes to discuss these issues and develop your responses. Appoint someone on your team to make a presentation to the class on your findings.

Developing Your Skill at Using the MIS

Getting the Most from Your MIS

ABOUT THE SKILL

Just as there is no universal definition of a management information system, there is no universally agreed-upon approach to how an MIS system is designed. However, the following steps represent the key elements in getting the most relevant information for a manager.

STEPS IN GETTING THE MOST FROM YOUR MIS

- **Analyze the decision system.** The decisions that you make should drive the information obtained in an MIS. Therefore, the first step is to identify all the management decisions for which information is needed. This analysis should encompass all the functions within the unit.
- **Analyze information requirements.** Once the decisions are isolated, you need to know the exact information required to effectively make those decisions. Because information needs differ according to managerial and unit functions, the MIS has to be designed to meet these varying needs.
- **Aggregate the decisions.** After your needs have been identified, request information that contains the least amount of duplication and that groups together similar decisions under a single report.
- **Design information processing.** In this step, internal technical specialists or outside consultants typically develop the actual system for collecting, storing, transmitting, and retrieving information. You should work with these individuals to understand how frequently your data will be available and how the data will be accessed.
- **Regularly evaluate the information you receive.** The information that you received last year may not be what's needed today. Your MIS should be viewed as an ongoing process. If it's to be valuable over time, the data you receive must be evaluated periodically and modified to adapt to your needs.

Practicing the Skill

GETTING THE MOST FROM AN MIS

You are the manager of a large independent music store, selling popular CDs, videotapes, DVDs, audiotapes, and accessories. Your comptetitor, a national chain, has just extended its weekend hours to 3 AM on Fridays and Saturdays. You need to decide whether to do the same.

Analyze your information needs for this decision. What do you need to know, and in what form do you want to receive the information?

A Case Application

Developing Your Diagnostic and Analytical Skills

VOLKSWAGEN FUTURISTIC FACTORY

It's being described as a revolution in the auto industry. It's likely to change the way cars will be built in the future all over the world. And it's being done by Volkswagen at its new Resende truck plant outside Rio de Janeiro, Brazil.[93]

Assembling vehicles has traditionally followed a conventional process. Many parts were put together on assembly lines. The parts used typically came from suppliers who brought them to the assembly plant's loading dock. From there, these parts were moved either manually or in some automated fashion to the appropriate place on the assembly line. Finally, employees assembled what parts they could, and robots frequently did the rest.

At Resende, Volkswagen has essentially outsourced the entire assembly of its vehicles to its suppliers. This $250 million plant, which assembles 7- to 35-ton trucks, uses hundreds of suppliers who channel their materials through just seven final assemblers. Each of these assemblers is responsible for putting together one of the seven modules that makes up a finished truck. German instrument maker VDO Kienzle, for example, starts with the steel shell of a truck cab. Up to 200 VDO employees install everything from seats to the instrument panels in the interior of the truck. Then, they attached the finished cab to the chassis moving down the assembly line through various suppliers' spaces. In total, more than 1,400 workers are involved in the assembly process. None of them are Volkswagen employees.

As a result of this supply chain management, Volkswagen saves money in a number of ways. It has fewer employees for which it is directly responsible. Suppliers pay their own employees as well as for their tools and fixtures. Suppliers are also responsible for incurring their own inventory costs—minimized, however, by a sophisticated just-in-time inventory system, in which parts arrive just one hour before they are needed. Finally, management seeks the advice and cooperation of its suppliers in cutting costs and boosting productivity. The net result is that Volkswagen expects the Resende plant to use 12 percent fewer labor-hours per truck than traditional truck assembly operations. And Volkswagen doesn't pay for or take delivery of the final product until all quality inspections have been completed and passed. The value of Volkswagen's approach is that it lets the company do what it believes it does best—designing and engineering vehicles, not assembling them, which others did better, faster, and cheaper!

Given some of the initial success of Volkswagen, other vehicle manufacturers are adopting VW's practices. For example, a strategic partnership between DaimlerChrysler and watchmaker SMH Swatch will be relying on a modular approach to build the Smart—a $10,000 urban car. The car is to be built in a new factory in western France, and the production run is divided into seven modules. Each of the seven completed modules will be finally assembled in the western France plant by the suppliers. And in the United States,

DaimlerChrysler is using this approach with its suppliers of the Dodge Dakota pickup truck.

QUESTIONS

1 Describe how elements of supply chain management and just-in-time inventory systems are demonstrated in this story.

2 Costs of producing vehicles in modules appears to have significant cost savings. Do you believe that quality is also enhanced by such a process? Why or why not?

3 "Both Volkswagen and DaimlerChrysler are European-based and culturally influenced companies. These same processes would not work in an organization and culture of a vehicle manufacturer like General Motors." Do you agree or disagree with the statement? Defend your position.

Developing Your Investigative Skills

Using the Internet

Visit *www.prenhall.com/robbins* for updated Internet Exercises.

Enhancing Your Writing Skills

Communicating Effectively

1 Describe how the Plan-Do-Check-Act (PDCA) cycle can be used by your college to implement a new required course for the business curriculum and assess its effectiveness.

2 In a two- to three-page report, discuss what you plan to do to ensure that the skills you're developing remain current and you won't suddenly finding yourself a victim of worker obsolescence.

3 Search the Internet for project management software programs currently on the market. Compare and contrast three different software packages. Evaluate the information presented in terms of stated ease of use, whether it's for beginners oradvanced project managers, and unique features. Given this information, if you were evaluating this information for a purchase, which software would you buy and why?

Notes

Chapter 1

1. W. Royal, "Made in Taiwan," *Industry Week,* February 15, 1999, pp. 68–70.
2. Adapted from *U.S. Bureau of the Census, Statistical Abstracts of the United States: 1997,* 117th ed. (Washington, D.C.: Government Printing Office, 1997), p. 406.
3. B. M. Case, "All in the Family," *Latin Trade,* September 1998, p. 36.
4. J. Kahn, "The World's Largest Corporations," *Fortune,* August 3, 1998, p. 134.
5. D. Brady, I. Sager, and J. Rae-Dupree, "Xerox," *Business Week,* April 12, 1999, p. 94.
6. J. Kahn, "The World's Largest Corporations," p. F-1.
7. See, for example, K. M. Kroll, "Good Management Pays Dividends," *Industry Week,* January 4, 1999, pp. 40–42; and J. Collins, "When Good Managers Manage Too Much," *Inc.,* April 1999, pp. 31–32.
8. H. Fayol, *Industrial and General Administration* (Paris: Dunod, 1916).
9. H. Koontz and C. O'Donnell, *Principles of Management: An Analysis of Managerial Functions* (New York: McGraw-Hill, 1955).
10. For a comprehensive review of this question, see C. P. Hales, "What Do Managers Do? A Critical Review of the Evidence," *Journal of Management Studies,* January 1986, pp. 88–115.
11. H. Mintzberg, *The Nature of Managerial Work* (New York: Harper & Row, 1973).
12. See, for example, H. Mintzberg, "Managing Government, Governing Management," *Harvard Business Review,* May/June 1996, pp. 75–85.
13. "Survey of Small Business Economic Trends: Monthly Report-January 1999," *Small Business Economic Trends,* January 1999, p. 1; and P. Davidsson, L. Lindmark, and C. Olofsson, "The Extent of Overestimation of Small Firm Job Creation—An Empirical Examination of the Regression Bias," *Small Business Economics,* August 1998, pp. 87–100.
14. W. Sengenberger, G. Loveman, and M. J. Piore, eds., *The Reemergence of Small Enterprises: Industrial Restructuring in Industrial Countries* (Geneva: International Institute of Labour Studies, 1990); and "Entrepreneurs Pop Up in China," *Wall Street Journal,* April 7, 1994, p. A10.
15. J. G. P. Paolillo, "The Manager's Self-Assessments of Managerial Roles: Small vs. Large Firms," *American Journal of Small Business,* January-March 1984, pp. 58–64.
16. See, for example, G. d'Amboise and M. Muldowney, "Management Theory for Small Business: Attempts and Requirements," *Academy of Management Review,* April 1988, pp. 226–40.
17. See for example, R. Calori and B. Dufour, "Management European Style," *Academy of Management Executive,* February 1995, pp. 61–71.
18. R. L. Katz, "Skills of an Effective Administrator," *Harvard Business Review,* September–October, 1974, pp. 90–102.
19. For an interesting overview of competencies, see C. A. Bartlett and S. Ghoshal, "The Myth of the Generic Manager: New Personal Competencies for New Management Roles," *California Management Review,* Fall 1997, pp. 92–116; and M. A. Verespej, "The Old Workforce," *Industry Week,* September 21, 1998, pp. 53–62.
20. The first three skills were originally proposed by R. L. Katz, "Skills of an Effective Administrator," *Harvard Business Review,* September–October, 1974, pp. 90–102. The fourth skill was added by C. M. Pavett and A. W. Lau, "Managerial Work: The Influence of Hierarchical Level and Functional Specialty," *Academy of Management Journal,* March 1983, pp. 170–77.
21. F. Luthans, R. M. Hodgetts, and S. A. Rosenkrantz, *Real Managers* (Cambridge, MA: Ballinger Publishing, 1988); and D. A. Gioia and C. O. Longnecker, "Delving into the Dark Side: The Politics of Executive Appraisal," *Organizational Dynamics,* Winter 1994, pp. 47–58.
22. J. J. Morse and F. R. Wagner, "Measuring the Process of Managerial Effectiveness," *Academy of Management Journal,* March 1978, pp. 23–35.
23. See, for example, S. B. Parry, "The Quest for Competencies," *Training,* July 1996, pp. 46–56; "The Challenges in Applying Competencies," *Compensation & Benefits Review,* March-April 1997, pp. 64–75; P. A. McLagan, "Just What Is a Competency?" *Training,* June 1998, pp. 58–64.
24. "Management Charter Initiative Issues Competence Standards," *Personnel Management,* October 1990, p. 17; "MCI Launches Standards for First Two Levels," *Personnel Management,* November 1990, p. 13; and L. Carrington, "Competent to Manage?" *International Management,* September 1994, p. 17.
25. G. Colvin, "It's a Banner Year for CEO Pay," *Fortune,* April 26, 1999, pp. 422–24.
26. Based on information presented in J. Reingold and R. Grover, "Executive Pay," *Business Week,* April 19, 1999, pp. 72–118.
27. Ibid., pp. 72–73.
28. L. Light, "Who Earned the Pay—and Who Didn't," *Business Week,* April 19, 1999, p. 75.
29. W. Grossman, and R. E. Hoskisson, "CEO Pay at the Crossroads of Wall Street and Main: Toward the Strategic Design of Executive Compensation," *The Academy of Management Executive,* February 1998, pp. 43–57; R. Dogar, "Nineteenth Annual Salary Report," *Working Woman,* February 1998, pp. 24–25; and John Mariotti, "How Much Is Too Much?" *Industry Week,* March 2, 1998, p. 68.
30. S. F. Marino, "Chief Executives Are Underpaid," *Industry Week,* April 20, 1998, p. 22.
31. The idea for this exercise came from B. Goza, "Graffiti Needs Assessment: Involving Students in the First Class Session," *Journal of Management Education* 17, No. 1, February 1993, pp. 99–106.
32. Information for this case is based on "Sustainability Consulting Service Promotes Partnership," *IIE Solutions,* April 1999, p. 16; B. Beyaztas, "Body Shop Eyes for Revival," *Marketing,* November 12, 1998, p. 14; J. Martin,

K. Knopoff, and C. Beckman, "An Alternative to Bureaucratic Impersonality and Emotional Labor: Bounded Emotionality at the Body Shop," *Administrative Science Quarterly,* June 1998, pp. 429–69; A. Sanders, "Success Secrets of the Successful, *Forbes,* November 2, 1998, pp. 22–24; C. P. Wallace, "Can the Body Shop Shape Up?" *Fortune,* April 15, 1996, pp. 118–20.

History Module

1. C. S. George Jr., *The History of Management Thought,* 2nd ed. (Upper Saddle River, NJ: Prentice Hall, 1972), p. 4.
2. W. E. Wallace, "Michelangelo, C.E.O.," *New York Times,* April 16, 1994, p. Y11.
3. A. Smith, *An Inquiry into the Nature and Causes of Wealth of Nations* (New York: Modern Library, 1937). Originally published in 1776.
4. F. W. Taylor, *The Principles of Scientific Management* (New York: Harper, 1911).
5. These facts about the dissemination of Taylor's ideas are from S. R. Barley and G. Kunda, "Design and Devotion: Surges of Rational and Normative Ideologies of Control in Managerial Discourse," *Administrative Science Quarterly,* September 1992, pp. 369–71. See also M. Banta, *Taylored Lives: Narrative Productions in the Age of Taylor, Veblen, and Ford* (Chicago: University of Chicago Press, 1993).
6. F. B. Gilbreth, *Motion Study* (New York: D. Van Nostrand, 1911); and F. B. Gilbreth and L. M. Gilbreth, *Fatigue Study* (New York: Sturgis and Walton, 1916).
7. Gilbreth, *Motion Study.*
8. H. Fayol, *Industrial and General Administration* (Paris: Dunod, 1916).
9. M. Weber, *The Theory of Social and Economic Organizations,* ed. T. Parsons, trans. A. M. Henderson and T. Parsons (New York: Free Press, 1947).
10. W. J. Duncan, *Great Ideas in Management* (San Francisco: Jossey-Bass, 1989), p. 137.
11. R. A. Owen, *A New View of Society* (New York: E. Bliss and White, 1825).
12. H. Munsterberg, *Psychology and Industrial Efficiency* (Boston: Houghton Mifflin, 1913).
13. M. P. Follett, *The New State: Group Organization the Solution of Popular Government* (London: Longmans, Green, 1918).
14. C. I. Barnard, *The Functions of the Executive* (Cambridge, Mass.: Harvard University Press, 1938).
15. E. Mayo, *The Human Problems of an Industrial Civilization* (New York: Macmillan, 1933); and F. J. Roethlisberger and W. J. Dickson, *Management and the Worker* (Cambridge, Mass.: Harvard University Press, 1939).
16. Mayo, *The Human Problems of an Industrial Civilization.*
17. A. Carey, "The Hawthorne Studies: A Radical Criticism," *American Sociological Review,* June 1967, pp. 403–16; R. H. Franke and J. Kaul, "The Hawthorne Experiments: First Statistical Interpretations," *American Sociological Review,* October 1978, pp. 623–43; B. Rice, "The Hawthorne Defect: Persistence of a Flawed Theory," *Psychology Today,* February 1982, pp. 70–74; J. A. Sonnenfeld, "Shedding Light on the Hawthorne Studies," *Journal of Occupational Behavior,* April 1985, pp. 111–30; S. R. G. Jones, "Worker Interdependence and Output: The Hawthorne Studies Reevaluated," *American Sociological Review,* April 1990, pp. 176–90; and S. R. G. Jones, "Was There a Hawthorne Effect?" *American Journal of Sociology,* November 1992, pp. 451–68.
18. D. Carnegie, *How to Win Friends and Influence People* (New York: Simon & Schuster, 1936).
19. D. Wren, *The Evolution of Management Thought,* 3rd ed. (New York: John Wiley & Sons, 1987), p. 422.
20. A. Maslow, "A Theory of Human Motivation," *Psychological Review,* July 1943, pp. 370–96. See also Maslow, Motivation and Personality (New York: Harper & Row, 1954).
21. M. T. Matteson, "Some Reported Thoughts on Significant Management Literature," *Academy of Management Journal,* June 1974, pp. 386–89.
22. J. B. Miner, *Theories of Organizational Behavior* (Hinsdale, IL: Dryden, 1980), p. 41.
23. D. McGregor, *The Human Side of Enterprise* (New York: McGraw-Hill, 1960).
24. Wren, *The Evolution of Management Thought,* 3rd ed., p. 127.
25. Matteson, "Some Reported Thoughts on Significant Management Literature."
26. M. Warner, "Organizational Behavior Revisited," *Human Relations,* October 1994, p. 1153.
27. Cited in E. Burack and R. B. D. Batlivala, "Operations Research: Recent Changes and Future Expectation in Business Operations," *Business Perspectives,* June 1972, pp. 15–22.
28. Wren, *The Evolution of Management Thought,* 3rd ed., p. 51.
29. H. Koontz, "The Management Theory Jungle," *Journal of the Academy of Management,* December 1961, pp. 174–88.
30. H. Koontz, ed., *Toward a Unified Theory of Management* (New York: McGraw-Hill, 1964).
31. See for example, W. J. Cook, "On Track in the Slowdown," *U.S. News & World Report,* May 29, 1995, pp. 47–52.
32. See, for example, L. W. Fry and D. A. Smith, "Congruence, Contingency, and Theory Building," *Academy of Management Review,* January 1987, pp. 117–32.

Chapter 2

1. E. Brown, "Selling to Customers: Amazon.com," *Fortune,* May 24, 1999, p. 123; M. Slovan, "Bound for the Internet," *Nation's Business,* March 1997, pp. 34–35; and M. Krantz, "Amazonian Challenge," *Time,* April 14, 1997, p. 71.
2. See for example, A. Toffler, *The Third Wave* (New York: Bantam Books, 1981).
3. P. F. Drucker, "The Age of Social Transformation," *The Atlantic Monthly,* November 1994, p. 56.
4. A. Fox, "Leaders Offer Insights on the Workforce of the 21st Century," *HRNews,* May 1999, p. 3.
5. See, for example, G. Epstein, "Economic Beat: The Economy Runs on Service Jobs (Not That There's Anything Wrong with That), *Barron's,* March 8, 1999, p. 40.
6. P. F. Drucker, "The Age of Social Transformation," p. 56.
7. Ibid.
8. M. A. Verespej, "Name That Salary," *Industry Week,* February 15, 1999, p. 33; and D. North, "Revenge of the Nerds," *Canadian Business,* December 1996, p. 39.

9. J. Martin, "Mercedes: Made in Alabama," *Fortune,* July 7, 1997, pp. 150–58.
10. See, for instance, P. Digh, "Shades of Gray in the Global Marketplace," *HRMagazine,* April 1997, pp. 91–98.
11. See J. Kahn, "The World's Most Admired Companies, *Fortune,* October 26, 1998, pp. 206–226; "Buying American," *Forbes,* July 28, 1997, pp. 218–220.
12. S. Perrin, "All It Takes Is Money," *Accountancy,* April 1999, pp. 52–53; and M. LeSeac'h and A. Klotz, "Corporate Translating: Handling with Care," *Business and Economic Review,* January–March 1999, pp. 12–14.
13. See T. A. Stewart, "A Way to Measure Worldwide Success," *Fortune,* March 15, 1999, p. 196.
14. For a review of strategic alliances, see H. Thomas, T. Pollock, and P. Gorman, "Global Strategic Analyses: Frameworks and Approaches," *Academy of Management Review,* February 1999, pp. 70–82.
15. R. L. Rose, "For Whirlpool, Asia Is the New Frontier," *Wall Street Journal,* April 25, 1996, p. B1.
16. See, for example, L. B. Pincus and James A. Belohlav, "Legal Issues in Multinational Business Strategy: To Play the Game You Have to Know the Rules," *Academy of Management Executive,* November 1996, pp. 52–60.
17. N. Adler, *International Dimensions of Organizational Behavior,* 3rd ed. (Boston: PWS-Kent, 1994), p. 11.
18. See, for example, C. Hampden-Turner and A. Trompenaars, *The Seven Cultures of Capitalism* (New York: Bantam Doubleday Dell Publishing Group, 1993).
19. Ibid., p. 347.
20. "Denty vs. SmithKline Beecham Corp. (DC EPA, No. 93-6978, November 6, 1995), in "ADEA Claim Is Not Applicable Overseas," *HRNews,* December 1995, p. 24.
21. G. Hofstede, *Culture's Consequences: International Differences in Work-Related Values* (Beverly Hills, Calif.: Sage Publications, 1980), pp. 25–26; and Hofstede, "The Cultural Relativity of Organizational Practices and Theories," *Journal of International Business Studies,* Fall 1983, pp. 75–89.
22. Hofstede called this last dimension masculinity-femininity. We have changed it because of the strong sexist connotation in his choice of terms. Also see C. C. Chen, X-P Chen, and J. R. Meindl, "How Can Cooperation Be Fostered? The Cultural Effects of Individualism-Collectivism," *Academy of Management Review,* April 1998, pp. 285–304.
23. See "Don't Be an Ugly-American Manager," *Fortune,* October 16, 1995, p. 225.
24. C. Johnson, "Cultural Sensitivity Adds up to Good Business Sense," *HRMagazine,* November 1995, pp. 82–85.
25. See, for example, J. C. Collins and J. I. Porras, "A Theory of Evolution," *Audacity,* Winter 1996, pp. 5–11.
26. J. H. Sheridan, "Betting on a Smart Mill," *Industry Week,* February 5, 1996, p. 39.
27. J. King and T. Hoffman, "The Next IT Generation," *Computerworld,* April 6, 1998, pp. 1, 101.
28. L. Zuckerman, "Do Computers Lift Productivity? It's Unclear, but Business Is Sold," *New York Times,* January 2, 1997, p. C–15.
29. See, for instance, G. Hasek, "Data's New Dimension," *Industry Week,* December 16, 1996, pp. 65–72.
30. See L. J. Bassi and M. E. VanBuren, "The 1999 ASTD State of the Industry Report" (Alexandria, VA: American Society for Training and Development, 1999); and V. Frazee, "ASTD Identifies Workplace Trends," *Workforce,* March 1997, pp. 25–28.
31. G. Colvin, "How To Be a Great CEO," *Fortune,* May 24, 1999, p. 105.
32. D. Kirkpatrick, "IBM from Big Blue Dinosaur to E-Business Animal," *Fortune,* April 26, 1999, p. 118.
33. B. Tucker, "Tommy Boy Can CD Future," Fast Company Web Page, <*http://www.fastcompany.com*> April 17, 1997.
34. B. Schlender, "Larry Ellison: Oracle at Web Speed," *Fortune,* May 24, 1999, pp. 128–36.
35. For an excellent overview of e-corporations, see G. Hamel and J. Sampler, "The E-Corporation, *Fortune,* December 1998, pp. 80–92.
36. W. W. Conhaim, "The Business-to-Business Marketplace," *Link-Up,* January–February 1999, p. 5; and W. Zellner, "Can EDS Catch up with the Net," *Business Week,* May 17, 1999, p. 46.
37. E. Brown, "9 Ways to Win on the Web," *Fortune,* May 24, 1999, p. 114.
38. E. Brown, "The E-Consultants," *Fortune,* April 12, 1999, p. 118.
39. Ibid., p. 82.
40. B. Schlender, "E-Business According to Gates," *Fortune,* April 12, 1999, p. 71.
41. G. Hamel and J. Sampler, "The E-Corporation," p. 82.
42. L. Grensing-Pophal, "Training Supervisors to Manage Teleworkers," *HRMagazine,* January 1999, pp. 67–72.
43. S. Paynter, "Workplace 2020," *Working Mother,* June 1999, p. 32.
44. S. E. O'Connell, "The Virtual Workplace Moves at Warp Speed," *HRMagazine,* March 1996, pp. 51–53; and "Managing the Reinvented Work Place Becomes a Hot Topic," *Wall Street Journal,* March 20, 1996, p. A1.
45. M. A. Berry and D. A. Rondinelli, "Proactive Corporate Environmental Management: A New Industrial Revolution," *Academy of Management Executive,* May 1998, pp. 38–50; W. H. Miller, "Cracks in the Green Wall," *Industry Week,* January 19, 1998, pp. 58–65.
46. See, for instance, G. Kinkead, "In the Future, People Like Me Will Go to Jail," *Fortune,* May 24, 1999, p. 190–200.
47. A. B. Carroll, "A Three-Dimensional Conceptual Model of Corporate Performance," *Academy of Management Review,* October 1979, p. 499.
48. For an interesting discussion on the "profit motive" of social responsibility, see A. Underwood, "Being Cruel to Be Kind," *Newsweek,* October 17, 1994, p. 51.
49. "Can Doing Good Be Good for Business?" *Fortune,* February 2, 1998, pp. 148[G]–148[J].
50. See, for example, R. A. Buchholz, *Essentials of Public Policy for Management,* 2nd ed. (Upper Saddle River, NJ: Prentice Hall, 1990).
51. See S. Prakash Sethi, "A Conceptual Framework for Environmental Analysis of Social Issues and Evaluation of Business Response Patterns," *Academy of Management Review,* January 1979, pp. 68–74.
52. See, for example, D. J. Wood, "Corporate Social Performance Revisited," *Academy of Management Review,* October 1991, pp. 703–708.
53. K. Davis and W. C. Frederick, *Business and Society: Management, Public Policy, Ethics,* 5th ed. (New York: McGraw-Hill, 1984), p. 76.

54. G. F. Cavanagh, D. J. Moberg, and M. Valasquez, "The Ethics of Organizational Politics," *Academy of Management Journal,* June 1981, pp. 363–74. See E. N. Brady, "Rules for Making Exceptions to Rules," *Academy of Management Review,* July 1987, pp. 436–44 for an argument that the theory of justice is redundant to the utilitarian and rights theories.
55. B. Dumaine, "Exporting Jobs and Ethics," *Fortune,* October 5, 1992, p. 10.
56. See, for example, M. C. Mathews, "Codes of Ethics: Organizational Behavior and Misbehavior," in W. C. Frederick and L. E. Preston, eds., *Business Ethics: Research Issues and Empirical Studies* (Greenwich, CT: JAI Press, 1990), pp. 99–122.
57. K. Walter, "Ethics Hot Lines Tap into More than Wrongdoing," *HRMagazine,* September 1995, pp. 79–81.
58. P. Richter, "Big Business Puts Ethics in Spotlight," *Los Angeles Times,* June 19, 1986, p. 29.
59. Cited in C. Fredman, "Nationwide Examination of Corporate Consciences," *Working Woman,* December 1991, p. 39.
60. J. S. McClenahen, "Your Employees Know Better," *Industry Week,* March 1, 1999, pp. 12–13.
61. See, for instance, G. R. Weaver, L. K. Trevino, and P. L. Cochran, "Corporate Ethics Programs as Control Systems: Influences of Executive Commitment and Environmental Factors," *Academy of Management Journal,* February 1999, pp. 41–57.
62. M. Selz, "Entrepreneurship in the U.S. Is Taking Off," *Wall Street Journal,* December 13, 1996, p. B-5.
63. See, for instance, S. A. Zahra, "The Changing Rules of Global Competitiveness in the 21st Century," *Academy of Management Executive,* February 1999, pp. 36–42; and C. Mellow, "Russia's Robber Barons," *Fortune,* March 3, 1997, pp. 120–26.
64. J. Useem, "The New Entrepreneurial Elite," *Inc.,* December 1997, p. 50.
65. A. Thomson, "Franchising Fever," *Latin Trade,* March 1998, pp. 36–40; and "Franchise Superstars: The Top 100 Fastest Growing Franchises," *Entrepreneur,* April 1996, pp. 150–53.
66. See, for instance, T. M. Begley and D. P. Boyd, "A Comparison of Entrepreneurs and Managers of Small Business Firms," *Journal of Management,* Spring 1987, pp. 99–108.
67. P. E. Drucker, *Innovation and Entrepreneurship* (New York: Harper & Row, 1985).
68. K. H. Vesper, *New Venture Strategies* (Upper Saddle River, NJ: Prentice Hall, 1980), p. 14.
69. I. Taylor, "Winning at Diversity," *Working Woman,* March 1999, p. 36; L. Urresta and J. Hickman, "The Diversity Elite," *Fortune,* August 3, 1998.
70. R. S. Johnson, "The 50 Best Companies for Asians, Blacks, and Hispanics," *Fortune,* August 3, 1998, p. 94.
71. R. LaGow, "Motorola Official Downplays Formal Cultural Audits," *HRNews,* December 1998, p. 3.
72. See, for instance, R. S. Johnson, "The 50 Best Companies for Asians, Blacks, and Hispanics," pp. 94–110; M. Evanstock, "Women and Children First," *Working Woman,* February 1999, pp. 28–29; J. K. Ford and S. Fisher, "The Role of Training in a Changing Workplace: New Perspectives and Approaches," and S. A. Lobel and E. E. Kossek, "Human Resource Strategies to Support Diversity in Work and Personal Lifestyles: Beyond the 'Family-Friendly' Organization," both in E. E. Kossek and S. A. Lobel (eds.), *Managing Diversity* (Cambridge, MA: Blackwell Publishers, 1996), pp. 164–93 and 221–44, respectively.
73. See for example, S. Branch, "The 100 Best Companies to Work for in America, *Fortune,* January 11, 1999, pp. 118–44.
74. J. Lynn, "Fathers Figure," *Entrepreneur,* March 1999, p. 33; and M. N. Martinez, "An Inside Look at Making the Grade," *HRMagazine,* March 1998.
75. F. J. Milliken, L. L. Martins, and H. Morgan, "Explaining Organizational Responsiveness to Work-Family Issues: The Role of Human Resource Executives as Issue Interpreters," *Academy of Management Journal,* October 1998, pp. 580–91; and R. W. Judy and C. D'Amico, *Workforce 2020* (Indianapolis, IN: Hudson Institute, 1997), p. 109.
76. A. Fisher, "The 100 Best Companies to Work for in America," *Fortune,* January 12, 1998, pp. 69–70; and L. Grant, "Happy Workers, High Returns," *Fortune,* January 12, 1998, p. 81.
77. M. Galen, "Work & Family," *Business Week,* June 28, 1993, p. 82.
78. See J. E. Ellis, "Monsanto's New Challenges: Keeping Minority Workers," *Business Week,* July 8, 1991, p. 61; and T. Cox Jr. and S. Blake, "Managing Cultural Diversity: Implications for Organizational Competitiveness," *Academy of Management Executive,* August 1991, pp. 45–56.
79. S. Leonard, "Love That Customer," *Management Review,* October 1987, pp. 36–39.
80. See J. Lorinc, "Now the Customer Is Job One," *Canadian Business,* July 1997, pp. 22–28; and J. DeYoung and G. Jidoun, "Service Is Alive and Well," *Working Woman,* November 1997, pp. 18–20.
81. A. V. Feigenbaum, quoted in *Boardroom Reports,* April 1, 1991, p. 16.
82. See, for example, B. Krone, "Total Quality Management: An American Odyssey," *Bureaucrat,* Fall 1990, pp. 35–38; A. Gabor, *The Man Who Discovered Quality* (New York: Random House, 1990); J. Clemmer, "How Total Is Your Quality Management?" *Canadian Business Review,* Spring 1991, pp. 38–41; and M. Sashkin and K. J. Kiser, *Total Quality Management* (Seabrook, MD: Ducochon Press, 1991).
83. For an excellent review of the theory of development and the implications of Deming's TQM, see J. W. Dean Jr. and D. E. Bowen, "Management Theory and Total Quality: Improving Research and Practice through Theory Development," *Academy of Management Review,* July 1994, pp. 392–418; and J. C. Anderson, M. Rungtusanatham, and R. G. Schroeder, "A Theory of Quality Management Underlying the Deming Management Method," *Academy of Management Review,* July 1994, pp. 472–509. See also, T. A. Stewart, "A Conversation with Joseph Juran," *Fortune,* January 11, 1999, pp. 168–70.
84. A. C. Hyde, "Rescuing Quality Management from TQM," *Bureaucrat,* Winter 1990–91, p. 16.
85. M. Hendricks, "Step by Step," *Entrepreneur,* March 1996, p. 70.

86. J. H. Sheridan, "Kaizen Blitz," *Industry Week,* September 1997, pp. 18–28.
87. See A. R. Korukonda, J. G. Watson, and T. M. Rajkumar, "Beyond Teams and Empowerment: A Counterpoint to Two Common Precepts in TQM," *SAM Advanced Management Journal,* Winter 1999, pp. 29–36; T. Y. Choi and O. C. Behling, "Top Managers and TQM Success: One More Look After All These Years," *Academy of Management Executive,* February 1997, pp. 37–46.
88. T. A. Stewart, "Reengineering: The Hot New Managing Tool," *Fortune,* August 23, 1993, pp. 41–48.
89. A. B. Shani and Y. Mitki, "Reengineering, Total Quality Management, and Sociotechnical Systems Approaches to Organizational Change: Towards an Eclectic Approach?" *Journal of Quality Management,* 1996, pp. 133–34; and M. Hammer and S. A. Stanton, *The Reengineering Revolution* (New York: Harper Business, 1995).
90. Hammer and Stanton, *The Reengineering Revolution,* pp. 41–43; B. S. Moskal, "Reengineering without Downsizing," *Industry Week,* February 19, 1996, p. 23; and material cited in *Training,* October 1996, p. 68.
91. Hammer and Stanton, *The Reengineering Revolution,* p. 42.
92. S. Hamm and M. Stepanek, "From Reengineering to E-Engineering," *Business Week,* March 22, 1999, pp. EB-13–EB-18.
93. See A. Bernstein, "Who Says Job Anxiety Is Easing?" *Business Week,* April 7, 1997, p. 38; and "Loser Layoffs," *U.S. News and World Report,* November 25, 1996, pp. 73–81; and "Happy Labor Day," *Time,* September 4, 1995, p. 21.
94. A. Taylor III, "New Ideas from Europe's Automakers," *Fortune,* March 21, 1994, p. 166; see also D. Woodruff, I. Katz, and K. Naughton, "VW's Factory of the Future," *Business Week,* October 7, 1996, pp. 52–54; and D. Woodruff, "Is VW Revving Too High," *Business Week,* March 30, 1998, pp. 48–49.
95. I. M. Kunii, E. Thornton, and J. Rae-Dupree, "Sony's Shakeup," *Business Week,* March 22, 1999, pp. 52–53.
96. See, for example, W. F. Casio, C. E. Young, and J. R. Morris, "Financial Consequences of Employment—Change Decisions in Major U.S. Corporations," *Academy of Management Journal,* October 1997, pp. 1175–89.
97. S. Leibs, "Outsourcing's No-Cure All," *Industry Week,* April 6, 1998, pp. 20–38.
98. C. Ansberry, "Workers Are Forced to Take More Jobs with Few Benefits," *Wall Street Journal,* March 11, 1993, p. A–1.
99. S. F. Cooper, "The Expanding Use of the Contingent Workforce in the American Economy: New Opportunities for Employers," *Employee Relations Law Journal,* Spring 1995, pp. 525–59.
100. A. Fisher, "Contract Work: Temp Jobs That Make Sense for Many," *Fortune,* May 24, 1999, p. 296; J. Templemann, M. Trinephi, and S. Toy, "A Contingent Swarming with Temps," *Business Week,* April 8, 1996, p. 54.
101. L. Helm, "Microsoft Testing Limits on Worker Use," *Los Angeles Times,* December 7, 1997, p. D–14.
102. See E. L. Andrews, "Only Employment for Many in Europe Is Part-Time Work," *New York Times,* September 1, 1997, pp. A-1; B-7.
103. Ibid.
104. L. Uchitelle, "Strike Points to Inequalities in a Two-Tier Job Market," *New York Times,* August 8, 1997, p. A-15.
105. See K. W. Thomas and B. A. Velthouse, "Cognitive Elements of Empowerment: An 'Interpretive' Model of Intrinsic Task Motivation," *Academy of Management Review,* October 1990, pp. 666–81.
106. See, for example, P. LaBarre, "Lighten Up," *Industry Week,* February 5, 1996.
107. A. Bennett, *The Death of the Organization Man* (New York: William Morrow, 1990), p. 205.
108. D. Peppers and M. Rogers, "Why Zane's Cycles Is Riding High," *Marketing 1-to-1,* <*http://www.1to1.com*> April 9, 1998, p. 1; and D. Fenn, "Leader of the Pack," *Inc.,* February 1996, pp. 31–38.

Chapter 3

1. "The Top 500 Women-Owned Businesses," *Working Woman,* June 1999, pp. 52–54.
2. H. Mintzberg, *The Rise and Fall of Strategic Planning* (New York: Free Press, 1994).
3. S. McKay, "A Paper Tiger in the Paperless World," *Canadian Business,* April 1996, pp. 25–26.
4. Mintzberg, *The Rise and Fall of Strategic Planning.*
5. Ibid.
6. G. Hamel and C. K. Prahalad, *Competing for the Future* (Boston: Harvard Business School Press, 1994).
7. J. Moore, "The Death of Competition," *Fortune,* April 15, 1996, pp. 142–43.
8. D. Miller, "The Architecture of Simplicity," *Academy of Management Review,* January 1993, pp. 116–38.
9. See, for example, J. A. Pearce II, K. K. Robbins, and R. B. Robinson Jr., "The Impact of Grand Strategy and Planning Formality on Financial Performance," *Strategic Management Journal,* March–April 1987, pp. 125–34; L. C. Rhyne, "Contrasting Planning Systems in High, Medium, and Low Performance Companies," *Journal of Management Studies,* July 1987, pp. 363–85; R. Brahm and C. B. Brahm, "Formal Planning and Organizational Performance: Assessing Emerging Empirical Research Trends," paper presented at the National Academy of Management Conference, New Orleans, August 1987; J. A. Pearce II, E. B. Freeman, and R. B. Robinson Jr., "The Tenuous Link between Formal Strategic Planning and Financial Performance," *Academy of Management Review,* October 1987, pp. 658–75; D. K. Sinha, "The Contribution of Formal Planning to Decisions," *Strategic Management Journal,* October 1990, pp. 479–92; N. Capon, J. U. Farley, and J. M. Hubert, "Strategic Planning and Financial Performance," *Journal of Management Studies,* January 1994, pp. 22–38; and C. C. Miller and L. B. Cardinal, "Strategic Planning and Firm Performance: A Synthesis of More Than Two Decades of Research," *Academy of Management Journal,* March 1994, pp. 1649–85.
10. W. H. Miller, "Vision Vanquisher, *Industry Week,* May 18, 1998, pp. 37–42; and G. McWilliams, S. Moshavi, and M. Shari, "Enron: Maybe Megadeals Mean Megarisk," *Business Week,* September 4, 1995, pp. 52–53.
11. R. Ackoff, "A Concept of Corporate Planning," *Long Range Planning,* September 1970, p. 3.
12. M. B. McCaskey, "A Contingency Approach to Planning: Planning with Goals and Planning without Goals," *Academy of Management Journal,* June 1974, pp. 281–91.

13. The concept is generally attributed to Peter F. Drucker, *The Practice of Management* (New York: Harper & Row, 1954).
14. See, for example, E. A. Locke, "Toward a Theory of Task Motivation and Incentives," *Organizational Behavior and Human Performance,* May 1968, pp. 157–89; E. A. Locke, K. N. Shaw, L. M. Saari, and G. P. Latham, "Goal Setting and Task Performance: 1969–1980," *Psychological Bulletin,* July 1981, pp. 125–52; M. E. Tubbs, "Goal Setting: A Meta-Analytic Examination of the Empirical Evidence," *Journal of Applied Psychology,* August 1986, pp. 474–83; A. J. Mento, R. P. Steel, and R. J. Karren, "A Meta-Analytic Study of the Effects of Goal Setting on Task Performance: 1966–1984," *Organizational Behavior and Human Decision Processes,* February 1987, pp. 52–83; and E. A. Locke and G. P. Latham, *A Theory of Goal Setting and Task Performance* (Upper Saddle River, NJ: Prentice Hall, 1990).
15. See, for example, G. P. Latham and L. M. Saari, "The Effects of Holding Goal Difficulty Constant on Assigned and Participatively Set Goals," *Academy of Management Journal,* March 1979, pp. 163–68; M. Erez, P. C. Earley, and C. L. Hulin, "The Impact of Participation on Goal Acceptance and Performance: A Two-Step Model," *Academy of Management Journal,* March 1985, pp. 50–66; and G. P. Latham, M. Erez, and E. A. Locke, "Resolving Scientific Disputes by the Joint Design of Crucial Experiments by the Antagonists: Application to the Erez-Latham Dispute Regarding Participation in Goal Setting," *Journal of Applied Psychology,* November 1988, pp. 753–72.
16. G. P. Latham, T. R. Mitchell, and D. L. Dossett, "Importance of Participative Goal Setting and Anticipated Rewards on Goal Difficulty and Job Performance," *Journal of Applied Psychology,* April 1978, pp. 163–71.
17. R. Rodgers and J. E. Hunter, "Impact of Management by Objectives on Organizational Productivity," *Journal of Applied Psychology,* April 1991, pp. 322–36.
18. W. E. Deming, *Out of Crisis* (Cambridge, MA: MIT Center for Advanced Engineering Study, 1986).
19. S. Kaufman, "Going for the Goals," *Success,* January 1988, pp. 38–41.
20. See, for instance, P. P. Carson, and K. D. Carson, "Deming versus Traditional Management Theorists on Goal Setting: Can Both Be Right?" *Business Horizons,* September–October 1993, pp. 79–84.
21. See for example, L. J. Rosenberg and C. D. Schewe, "Strategic Planning: Fulfilling the Promise," *Business Horizons,* July–August 1985, pp. 54–62; and W. Kiechel III, "Corporate Strategy for the 1990s," *Fortune,* February 28, 1989, pp. 34–42.
22. See, for example, S. Hart and C. Banbury, "How Strategy Making Processes Can Make a Difference," *Strategic Management Journal,* May 1994, pp. 251–69.
23. L. W. Rue, and N. A. Ibrahim, "The Relationship Between Planning sophistication and Performance in Small Businesses," *Journal of Small Business Management,* October 1998, pp. 24–32.
24. See, for example, J. H. Waterhouse, "Measuring Up," *CA Magazine,* March 1999, pp. 41–42; and C. C. Miller and L. B. Cardinal, "Strategic Planning and Firm Performance: A Synthesis of More Than Two Decades of Research," *Academy of Management Journal,* March 1994, pp. 16–61.
25. "Colleges Undergo Reassessment," *Time,* April 14, 1992, p. 18.
26. P. LaBarre, "Knowledge Brokers," *Industry Week,* April 1, 1996, p. 52.
27. N. Venkatraman and J. E. Prescott, "Environment-Strategy Coalignment: An Empirical Test of Its Performance Implications," *Strategic Management Journal,* January 1990, pp. 1–23.
28. J. Hyatt and J. Useem, "Competition: It's against Regulations," *Inc.,* April 1996, p. 57.
29. See, for example, D. Marline, B. T. Lamont, and J. J. Hoffman, "Choice Situation, Strategy, and Performance: A Reexamination," *Strategic Management Journal,* March 1994, pp. 229–39.
30. B. Dumaine, "Payoff from the New Management," *Fortune,* December 13, 1993, pp. 103–10.
31. M. Schuman, "Thin Is Out, Fat Is In," *Forbes,* May 9, 1994, pp. 92–94.
32. J. Diffenbach, "Corporate Environmental Analysis in Large U.S. Corporations," *Long Range Planning,* June 1983, pp. 107–16; S. C. Jain, "Environmental Scanning in U.S. Corporations," *Long Range Planning,* April 1984, pp. 117–28; L. M. Fuld, *Monitoring the Competition* (New York: John Wiley & Sons, 1988); and E. H. Burack and N. J. Mathys, "Environmental Scanning Improves Strategic Planning," *Personnel Administrator,* April 1989, pp. 82–87.
33. R. Subramanain, N. Fernandes, and E. Harper, "Environmental Scanning in U.S. Companies: Their Nature and Their Relationship to Performance," *Management International Review,* July 1993, pp. 271–86.
34. See note 32.
35. B. Gilad, "The Role of Organized Competitive Intelligence in Corporate Strategy," *Columbia Journal of World Business,* Winter 1989, pp. 29–35; B. D. Gelb, M. J. Saxton, G. M. Zinkhan, and N. D. Albers, "Competitive Intelligence: Insights from Executives," *Business Horizons,* January–February 1991, pp. 43–47; L. Fuld, "A Recipe for Business Intelligence," *Journal of Business Strategy,* January–February 1991, pp. 12–17; G. B. Roush, "A Program for Sharing Corporate Intelligence," *Journal of Business Strategy,* January–February 1991, pp. 4–7; and R. S. Teitelbaum, "The New Role for Intelligence," *Fortune,* November 2, 1992, pp. 104–107.
36. M. Robichaux, " 'Competitor Intelligence': A Grapevine to Rivals' Secrets," *Wall Street Journal,* April 12, 1989, p. B2.
37. W. H. Davidson, "The Role of Global Scanning in Business Planning," *Organizational Dynamics,* Winter 1991, pp. 5–16.
38. See, for example, W. J. Holstein, "Corporate Spy Wars," *U.S. News & World Report,* February 23, 1998, pp. 46–52; E. A. Robinson, "China's Spies Target Corporate America," *Fortune,* March 30, 1998, pp. 118–22; and A. Farnham, "Spy vs. Spy: Are Your Company Secrets Safe?" *Fortune,* February 17, 1997, p. 136.
39. W. J. Holstein, "Corporate Spy Wars," p. 46.
40. See S. E. Jackson and J. E. Dutton, "Discerning Threats and Opportunities," *Administrative Science Quarterly,* September 1988, pp. 370–87.
41. J. B. Barney, "Looking Inside for Competitive Advantage," *Academy of Management Executive,* February 1995, p. 49.
42. A. Taylor III, "New Ideas from Europe's Automakers," *Fortune,* March 21, 1994, pp. 159–72.
43. "Sounds Awful, Tastes Great," *Canadian Business,* December 1995, p. 79.

44. See, for example, J. B. Barney, "Organizational Culture: Can It Be a Source of Sustained Competitive Advantage?" *Academy of Management Review,* July 1986, pp. 656–65; C. Scholz, "Corporate Culture and Strategy—The Problem of Strategic Fit," *Long Range Planning,* August 1987, pp. 78–87; S. Green, "Understanding Corporate Culture and Its Relation to Strategy," *International Studies of Management and Organization,* Summer 1988, pp. 6–28; T. Kono, "Corporate Culture and Long-Range Planning," *Long Range Planning,* August 1990, pp. 9–19; and C. M. Fiol, "Managing Culture as a Competitive Resource: An Identity-Based View of Sustainable Competitive Advantage," *Journal of Management,* March 1991, pp. 191–211.
45. M. Maremount, "Kodak's New Focus," *Business Week,* January 30, 1995, p. 63.
46. See, W. J. Duncan, P. M. Ginter, and L. E. Swayne, "Competitive Advantage and Internal Organizational Assessment," *Academy of Management Executive,* August 1998, pp. 6–16.
47. "Bigger Is Better: Success Isn't Spelled S-M-A-L-L," *Industry Week,* April 1, 1996, p. 27.
48. A. Know, "From Also-Ran to Front-Runner, *Industry Week,* April 19, 1999, p. 28.
49. J. Flynn and L. Bongiorno, "IKEA's New Game Plan," *Business Week,* October 6, 1997, p. 99.
50. L. Nakarmi, K. Kelly, and L. Armstrong, "Look Out, World—Samsung Is Coming," *Business Week,* July 10, 1995, pp. 52–53.
51. K. Harris, "Edgar in Hollywood," *Fortune,* April 15, 1996, p. 102.
52. A. Barrett and G. DeGeorge, "Home Improvement at Black & Decker," *Business Week,* May 11, 1998, pp. 54–56.
53. P. Burrows, "Pennzoil Switches on Its Searchlight," *Business Week,* February 13, 1995, pp. 74–75.
54. See, for example, M. E. Porter, *Competitive Strategy: Techniques for Analyzing Industries and Competitors* (New York: Free Press, 1980); Porter, *Competitive Advantage: Creating and Sustaining Superior Performance* (New York: Free Press, 1985); "From Competitive Advantage to Corporate Strategy," *Harvard Business Review,* May–June 1987, pp. 43–59; Porter, "Know Your Place," *Inc.,* September 1991, pp. 90–93; G. G. Dess and P. S. Davis, "Porter's (1980) Generic Strategies as Determinants of Strategic Group Membership and Organizational Performance," *Academy of Management Journal,* September 1984, pp. 467–88; Dess and Davis, "Porter's (1980) Generic Strategies and Performance: An Empirical Examination with American Data. Part I: Testing Porter," *Organization Studies,* 1986, pp. 37–55; Dess and Davis, "Porter's (1980) Generic Strategies and Performance: An Empirical Examination with American Data. Part II: Performance Implications," *Organization Studies,* June 1986, pp. 255–61; A. I. Murray, "A Contingency View of Porter's 'Generic Strategies,'" *Academy of Management Review,* July 1988, pp. 390–400; C. W. L. Hill, "Differentiation versus Low Cost or Differentiation and Low Cost: A Contingency Framework," *Academy of Management Review,* July 1988, pp. 401–12; and I. Bamberger, "Developing Competitive Advantage in Small and Medium-Sized Firms," *Long Range Planning,* October 1989, pp. 80–88.
55. W. Zellner, "Back to 'Coffee, Tea, or Milk'?" *Business Week,* July 3, 1995, p. 52; and J. Loric, "Road Warriors," *Canadian Business,* October 1995, pp. 26–28.
56. K. Riley, "Patenting New Laser, Gas Process Lets Business Clean up in Computer Chips," *Washington Times,* January 29, 1996, pp. B17, B20.
57. R. T. King Jr., "Grapes of Wrath: Kendall-Jackson Sues Gallo Winery in a Battle over a Bottle," *Wall Street Journal,* April 5, 1996, p. B1.
58. G. Hamel, "Killer Strategies That Make Shareholders Rich," *Fortune,* June 23, 1997, p. 80.
59. See, for instance, R. M. Hodgetts, D. F. Kuratko, and J. S. Hornsby, "Quality Implementation in Small Business: Perspectives from the Baldrige Award Winners," *SAM Advanced Management Journal,* Winter 1999, pp. 37–48.
60. D. M. Schroeder and A. G. Robinson, "America's Most Successful Export to Japan: Continuous Improvement Programs," *Sloan Management Review,* Spring 1991, pp. 67–81; and R. J. Schonenberger, "Is Strategy Strategic? Impact of Total Quality Management on Strategy," *Academy of Management Executive,* August 1992, pp. 80–87.
61. See, for example, L. Goff, "Staying Power," *Working Woman,* April 1998, pp. 35–39.
62. M. Barrier, "Learning the Meaning of Measurement," *Nation's Business,* June 1994, pp. 72–74; and J. Case, "The Change Masters," *Inc.,* March 1992, p. 60.
63. L. McMillen, "To Boost Quality and Cut Costs, Oregon State University Adopts a Customer-Oriented Approach to Campus Services," *Chronicle of Higher Education,* February 6, 1991, p. A27.
64. This section is based on B. Brocka and M. S. Brocka, *Quality Management* (Homewood, Ill.: Business One Irwin, 1992), pp. 231–36; G. A. Weimer, "Benchmarking Maps the Route to Quality," *Industry Week,* July 20, 1992, pp. 54–55; J. Main, "How to Steal the Best Ideas Around," *Fortune,* October 19, 1992, pp. 102–106; and H. Rothman, "You Need Not Be Big to Benchmark," *Nation's Business,* December 1992, pp. 64–65.
65. O. Suris, "Honda Accord Pulls up Alongside Ford Taurus," *Wall Street Journal,* April 13, 1996, p. B1.
66. See, for example, R. Henkoff, "The Hot New Seal of Quality," *Fortune,* June 28, 1993, pp. 116–20; D. Fenn, "The Prevention Corrective-Action Report," *Inc.,* January 1996, pp. 67–69; J. Becker, "Passing the Quality Test," *Plant Engineering and Maintenance,* June 1994, p. 4; "Passenger Focus Keeps Railway on Track," *International Journal of Health Care Quality,* June 1995, p. 15; E. Kirschner, "Betz Laboratories—All or Nothing, Every Plant, Every Product," *Chemical Week,* April 28, 1993, p. 66; W. Ferguson, "EC Product and Service Standards," *Journal of Small Business,* October 1994, pp. 84–88; and Q. R. Skrabec Jr., "Maximizing the Benefits of Your ISO 9000 Campaign," *Industrial Engineering,* April 1995, pp. 34–38.
67. Henkoff, "The Hot New Seal of Quality," p. 116; and M. V. Uzumeri, "ISO 9000 and Other Metastandards: Principles for Management Practice," *Academy of Management Executive,* February 1997, pp. 21–36.
68. It is important to recognize that components of the ISO 9000 series focus on different areas. For example, ISO 9000 represents the guidelines to aid in selection and use of applying ISO standards. ISO 9001, the most comprehen-

sive standard, applies to organizations that research, design, manufacture, ship, or install service products. ISO 9002 are standards for organizations that manufacture and install products; 9003 is for organizations in the warehousing and distribution business. ISO 9004 covers quality management systems applications, and, with 9004–2, its guidelines. See, for examples, Skrabec, "Maximizing the Benefits of Your ISO 9000 Campaign," and Ferguson, "EC Product and Service Standards."

69. D. S. Holter, "Squeaky Clean: How Companies Prepare for ISO 14000," *Machine Design,* January 11, 1996, pp. 42–44.
70. M. Larson, "The Long Road Ahead: A Certification ISO Chronicle," *Quality,* January 1996, p. 34.
71. Green and black belts are terms used to designate individuals certified in six sigma methodologies. A green belt is an individual who has successfully completed a 40-hour six sigma training course as well as spent 40 hours in six sigma project work. In addition to the green belt requirements, black belts spend approximately four months in an intensive six sigma training program as well as apply their "tools" on at least two six sigma projects annually.
72. See, for example, C. A. Hendricks and R. L. Kelbaugh, "Implementing Six Sigma at GE," *The Journal for Quality and Participation,* July/August 1998, pp. 48–53; D. Harrold and F. J. Bartos, "Optimize Existing Processes to Achieve Six Sigma Capability," *Control Engineering,* May 1998, p. 87; and "Six Sigma Secrets," *Industry Week,* November 2, 1998, pp. 42–43.
73. D. Harrold and F. J. Bartos, "Optimize Existing Processes to Achieve Six Sigma Capability," p. 87.
74. Ibid.
75. "Is 99.9% Good Enough?" *Training,* March 1991, p. 38.
76. C. A. Hendricks and R. L. Kelbaugh, "Implementing Six Sigma at GE," p. 51.
77. "Using Six Sigma to Manage Suppliers," *Purchasing,* January 14, 1999, p. 90.
78. E. Schine, "This Woman's Place Is in the Hangar," *Business Week,* May 13, 1996, pp. ENT 16–ENT 18.
79. G. Williams, "2001: An Entrepreneurial Odyssey," *Entrepreneur,* April 1999, p. 106; W. Royal, "Vanishing Execs: Women," *Industry Week,* July 20, 1998, pp. 32–33; and "The Entrepreneurial Era," *Working Woman,* July/August 1998, pp. 31–36.
80. See, for example, J. B. Cunningham and J. Lischeron, "Defining Entrepreneurship," *Journal of Small Business Management,* January 1991, pp. 45–61.
81. G. D. Gallop, "The State of Small Black Business," *Black Enterprise,* November 1998, pp. 63–64.
82. Adapted from H. H. Stevenson, M. J. Roberts, and H. I. Grousbeck, *New Business Ventures and the Entrepreneur* (Homewood, IL: Irwin, 1989).
83. See, for instance, T. M. Begley and D. P. Boyd, "A Comparison of Entrepreneurs and Managers of Small Business Firms," *Journal of Management,* Spring 1987, pp. 99–108.
84. J. A. Hornaday, "Research about Living Entrepreneurs," in C. A. Kent, D. L. Sexton, and K. H. Vesper, eds., *Encyclopedia of Entrepreneurship* (Upper Saddle River, NJ: Prentice Hall, 1982), p. 28.
85. B. Bowers and U. Gupta, "New Entrepreneurs Offer a Simple Lesson in Building a Fortune," *Wall Street Journal,* October 19, 1994, p. A1.
86. R. H. Brockhaus Sr., "The Psychology of the Entrepreneur," in Kent, Sexton, and Vesper, eds., *Encyclopedia of Entrepreneurship,* pp. 41–49.
87. It's important to note that business plans may go by other names, including loan proposal or venture prospectus.
88. M. J. Dollinger, *Entrepreneurship: Strategies and Resources* (Upper Saddle River, NJ: Prentice-Hall, Inc., 1999), p. 132.
89. M. Frese, W. Kring, A. Soose, and J. Zemple, "Personal Initiative at Work: Differences between East and West Germany," *Academy of Management Journal,* January 1996, p. 37.
90. Adapted from M. J. Dollinger, *Entrepreneurship: Strategies and Resources* (Upper Saddle River, NJ: Prentice-Hall, Inc., 1999), pp. 137–49.
91. Ibid., p. 142.
92. Based on StockMaster News, "Watson Pharmaceuticals Announces First Quarter 1999 results," *<http://news.stockmaster.com>* April 30, 1999; StockMaster News, "Watson Pharmaceuticals Reorganizes Research & Development," *<http://news.stockmaster.com>* April 30, 1999; "Watson Pharmaceuticals to Acquire TheraTech for 7.0 Times Revenue," Weekly Corporate Growth Report, November 2, 1998, p. 9863; Watson Pharmaceuticals to Acquire TheraTech," *Chemical Market Reporter,* November 2, 1998, p. 16; and D. Darlin, "Still Running Scared," *Forbes,* September 26, 1994, pp. 127–28.

Chapter 4

1. Opening vignette based on J. Edgerton, "Can Nike Still Play above the Rim?" *Money,* May 1999, p. 48; A. Murdoch, "Just Doing It," *Accountancy,* March 1999, pp. 30–31; and "Adidas Takes on Nike with Global Glitz," *Marketing Week,* February 11, 1999, p. 9.
2. See, for example, J. W. Dean Jr. and M. P. Sharfman, "Does Decision Process Matter? A Study of Strategic Decision-Making Effectiveness," *Academy of Management Journal,* March 1996, pp. 368–96.
3. W. Pounds, "The Process of Problem Finding," *Industrial Management Review,* Fall 1969, pp. 1–19.
4. R. J. Volkema, "Problem Formulation: Its Portrayal in the Texts," *Organizational Behavior Teaching Review,* 1986–87, pp. 113–26.
5. See H. A. Simon, "Rationality in Psychology and Economics," *Journal of Business,* October 1986, pp. 209–24; and A. Langley, "In Search of Rationality: The Purposes Behind the Use of Formal Analysis in Organizations," *Administrative Science Quarterly,* December 1989, pp. 598–631.
6. See, for instance, G. McNamara and P. Bromley, "Decision Making in an Organizational Setting: Cognitive and Organizational Influences on Risk Assessment in Commercial Lending," *Academy of Management Journal,* October 1997, pp. 1063–88.
7. F. A. Shull Jr., A. L. Delbecq, and L. L. Cummings, *Organizational Decision Making* (New York: McGraw-Hill, 1970), p. 151.
8. See, for example, J. G. March, *A Primer on Decision Making* (New York: Free Press, 1994), pp. 8–25; and A. Langley, H. Mintzberg, P. Pitcher, E. Posada, and J. Saint-Macary, "Opening up Decision Making: The View from the Black

Stool," *Organizational Science,* May–June, 1995, pp. 260–79.

9. J. G. March, "Decision-Making Perspective: Decisions in Organizations and Theories of Choice," in A. H. Van de Ven and W. F. Joyce, eds., *Perspectives on Organization Design and Behavior* (New York: Wiley-Interscience, 1981), pp. 232–33.
10. H. A. Simon, *Administrative Behavior,* 3rd ed. (New York: Free Press, 1976).
11. See, for example, P. Bromiley, "Debating Rationality: Nonrational Aspects of Organizational Decision Making/Rational Choice Theory and Organizational Theory: A Critique," *Academy of Management Review,* January 1999, pp. 157–59.
12. See N. McK. Agnew and J. L. Brown, "Bounded Rationality: Fallible Decisions in Unbounded Decision Space," *Behavioral Science,* July 1986, pp. 148–61; B. E. Kaufman, "A New Theory of Satisficing," *Journal of Behavioral Economics,* Spring 1990, pp. 35–51; and D. R. A. Skidd, "Revisiting Bounded Rationality," *Journal of Management Inquiry,* December 1992, pp. 343–47.
13. See I. Yaniv, "Weighting and Trimming: Heuristics for Aggregating Judgements under Uncertainty," *Organizational Behavior and Human Decision Processes,* March 1997, pp. 237–49; and D. A. Duchon, and K. J. Donde-Dunegan, "Avoid Decision Making Disaster by Considering Psychological Biases," *Review of Business,* Summer/Fall 1991, pp. 13–18.
14. See for example, B. M. Staw, "The Escalation of Commitment to a Course of Action," *Academy of Management Review,* October 1981, pp. 577–87; and D. R. Bobocel and J. P. Meyer, "Escalating Commitment to a Failing Course of Action: Separating the Roles of Choice and Justification," *Journal of Applied Psychology,* June 1994, pp. 360–63.
15. M. R. Beschloss, "Fateful Presidential Decisions," *Forbes FYI,* vol. 1, 1995, pp. 171–72.
16. S. McKay, "When Good People Make Bad Choices," *Canadian Business,* February 1994, pp. 52–55.
17. G. White, "Escalating Commitment to a Course of Action: A Reinterpretation," *Academy of Management Review,* April 1986, pp. 311–21.
18. Based on J. Hancock, "Made in the Shade No Longer," *The Sun: Business,* January 26, 1996, pp. E1, E2; see also, W. E. Hopkins and S. A. Hopkins, "The Ethics of Downsizing: Perception of Rights and Responsibilities," *Journal of Business Ethics,* January 1999, pp. 145–56.
19. R. A. Melcher, "Fighting off Depression at Eli Lilly," *Business Week,* May 24, 1999, pp. 77–78.
20. A. J. Rowe, J. D. Boulgarides, and M. R. McGrath, *Managerial Decision Making: Modules in Management Series* (Chicago: SRA, 1994), pp. 18–22.
21. L. W. Busenitz and J. B. Barney, "Biases and Heuristics in Strategic Decision Making: Differences between Entrepreneurs and Managers in Large Organizations," in D. P. Moore, ed., *Academy of Management Best Papers Proceedings,* August 14–17, 1994, pp. 85–89.
22. S. Wally and J. R. Baum, "Personal and Structural Determinants of the Pace of Strategic Decision Making," *Academy of Management Journal,* June 1994, pp. 932–56.
23. "Meaningful Meetings," *Inc.,* September 1994, p. 122.
24. See, for example, J. Howe, "Share and Share Alike," *Psychology Today,* May/June 1999, p. 15; and J. R. Hollenbeck, D. R. Ilgen, J. A. LePine, J. A. Colquitt, and J. Hedlund, "Extending the Multilevel Theory of Team Decision Making: Effects of Feedback and Experience in Hierarchical Teams," *Academy of Management Journal,* June 1998, pp. 269–82.
25. I. L. Janis, *Groupthink* (Boston: Houghton Mifflin, 1982); C. R. Leana, "A Partial Test of Janis' Groupthink Model: Effects of Group Cohesiveness and Leader Behavior on Defective Decision Making," *Journal of Management,* Spring 1985, pp. 5–17; and G. Morehead and J. R. Montanari, "An Empirical Investigation of the Groupthink Phenomenon," *Human Relations,* May 1986, pp. 399–410.
26. See, for example, T. W. Costello and S. S. Zalkind, eds., *Psychology in Administration: A Research Orientation* (Upper Saddle River, NJ: Prentice Hall, 1963), pp. 429–30; R. A. Cooke and J. A. Kernaghan, "Estimating the Difference between Group versus Individual Performance on Problem-Solving Tasks," *Group and Organization Studies,* September 1987, pp. 319–42; and L. K. Michaelsen, W. E. Watson, and R. H. Black, "A Realistic Test of Individual versus Group Consensus Decision Making," *Journal of Applied Psychology,* October 1989, pp. 834–39.
27. See, for example, L. K. Michaelsen, W. E. Watson, and R. H. Black, "A Realistic Test of Individual vs. Group Consensus Decision Making," *Journal of Applied Psychology,* June 1989, pp. 834–39; P. W. Pease, M. Beiser, and M. E. Tubbs, "Framing Effects and Choice Shifts in Group Decision Making," *Organizational Behavior and Human Decision Processes,* October 1993, pp. 149–65; and S. Strauss and J. E. McGrath, "Does the Medium Matter? The Interaction of Task Type and Technology on Group Performance and Member Reactions," *Journal of Applied Psychology,* February 1994, pp. 87–97.
28. A. L. Delbecq, A. H. Van de Ven, and D. H. Gustafson, *Group Techniques for Program Planning and a Guide to Nominal and Delphi Processes* (Glenview, IL: Scott, Foresman, 1975).
29. Shull, Delbecq, and Cummings, *Organizational Decision Making,* p. 151.
30. A. E. Osborn, *Applied Imagination: Principles and Procedures of Creative Thinking* (New York: Scribners, 1941).
31. The following discussion is based on Delbecq, Van de Ven, and Gustafson, *Group Techniques for Program Planning and a Guide to Nominal and Delphi Processes.*
32. See A. R. Dennis, J. E. George, L. M. Jessup, J. E. Nunamaker Jr., and D. R. Vogel, "Information Technology to Support Group Work," *MIS Quarterly,* December 1988, pp. 591–619; D. W. Straub and R. A. Beauclair, "Current and Future Uses of Group Decision Support System Technology: Report on a Recent Empirical Study," *Journal of Management Information Systems,* Summer 1988, pp. 101–16; J. Bartimo, "At These Shouting Matches, No One Says a Word," *Business Week,* June 11, 1990, p. 78; and M. S. Poole, M. Holmes, and G. DeSanctis, "Conflict Management in a Computer-Supported Meeting Environment," *Management Science,* August 1991, pp. 926–53.
33. See W. M. Bulkeley, " 'Computerizing' Dull Meetings Is Touted as an Antidote to the Mouth That Bored," *Wall Street Journal,* January 28, 1992, p. B1.

34. "Picture Tel Fights to Stay in the Picture," *Business Week,* October 26, 1996, p. 168.
35. See, for example, E. F. Jackofsky, J. W. Slocum Jr., and S. J. McQuaid, "Cultural Values and the CEO: Alluring Companions?" *Academy of Management Executive,* February 1988, pp. 39–49; S. P. Robbins, *Organizational Behavior: Concepts, Controversies, Applications,* 8th ed. (Upper Saddle River, NJ: Prentice Hall, 1998), pp. 116–17; N. Sumihara, "A Case Study of Cross-Cultural Interaction in a Japanese Multinational Corporation Operating in the United States: Decision-Making Processes and Practices," in R. R. Sims and R. F. Dennehy, eds., *Diversity and Differences in Organizations: An Agenda for Answers and Questions* (Westport, CT: Quorum Books, 1993), pp. 135–47, S. J. Vitell, S. L. Nwachukwu, and J. H. Barnes, "The Effects of Culture on Ethical Decision-Making: An Application of Hofstede's Typology," *Journal of Business Ethics,* October 1993, pp. 753–60; R. M. Hodgetts and F. Luthans, *International Management,* 2nd ed. (New York: McGraw-Hill, 1994), pp. 214–15; and S. P. Robbins, *Organizational Behavior, Controversies, and Applications,* 8th ed (Upper Saddle River, NJ: Prentice-Hall, Inc., 1998), pp. 116–17.
36. Jackofsky, Slocum, and McQuaid, "Cultural Values and the CEO."
37. See, for example, P. M. Elsass and L. M. Graves, "Demographic Diversity in Decision-Making Groups: The Experiences of Women and People of Color," *Academy of Management Review,* October 1997, pp. 946–73.
38. This case is based on information contained in C. M. Jones, "TLC Sells Beverage Biz," *Black Enterprise,* October 1998, p. 20; L. Davis, "TLC Beatrice International: Loida Nicolas Lewis," *Working Woman,* May 1998, p. 60; D. T. Dingle, "TLC Beatrice Sells off Major Food Division, Black Enterprise, December 1997, pp. 19–20; and "TLC Beatrice International Announces Fourth Quarter and 1998 Results,"*http://biz.yahoo.com/bw/990324/ny_tlc_bea_1.html,* March 24, 1999, p. 1.

Quantitative Module

1. See, for example, S. Stiansen, "Breaking Even," *Success,* November 1988, p. 16.
2. S. E. Barndt and D. W. Carvey, *Essentials of Operations Management* (Upper Saddle River, NJ: Prentice Hall, 1982), p. 134.
3. We like to acknowledge and thank Professor Jeff Storm of Virginia Western Community College for his assistance in this example.

Chapter 5

1. This opening vignette is based on N. Austin, "Tear Down the Walls," *Inc.,* April 1999, pp. 68–76.
2. See, for instance, B. S. Moskal, "Supervisors, Begone!" *Industry Week,* June 20, 1988, p. 32; and G. A. Patterson, "Auto Assembly Lines Enter a New Era," *Wall Street Journal,* December 28, 1988, p. A2.
3. See, for example, R. Roher, "Keep the Right Hand Informed," *Supervision,* October 1995, pp. 3–5. See also W. Vastino, "A Chart Does Not an Organization Make," *National Petroleum News,* September 1995, p. 58.
4. The matrix organization is an obvious example of an organization design that breaks the chain of command. See also M. Hickins, "Managing Inside-Out," *Management Review,* November 1998, p. 7.
5. L. Urwick, *The Elements of Administration* (New York: Harper & Row, 1944), pp. 52–53.
6. J. S. McClenahen, "Managing More People in the '90s," *Industry Week,* March 20, 1989, p. 30. See also A. Bernstein, S. Jackson, and J. Byrne, "Jack Cracks the Whip Again," *Business Week,* December 15, 1997, pp. 34–35.
7. G. M. Spreitzer, "Social Structural Characteristics of Psychological Empowerment," *Academy of Management Journal,* April 1996, pp. 483–504.
8. D. Van Fleet, "Span of Management Research and Issues," *Academy of Management Journal,* September 1983, pp. 546–52.
9. B. S. Moskal, "A Shadow between Values and Reality," *Industry Week,* May 16, 1994, pp. 23–26.
10. Stanley Milgram, *Obedience to Authority* (New York: Harper & Row, 1974).
11. See, for instance, D. Kipnis, *The Powerholders* (Chicago: University of Chicago Press, 1976); J. Pfeffer, *Power in Organizations* (Marshfield, MA: Pitman Publishing, 1981); H. Mintzberg, *Power in and around Organizations* (Upper Saddle River, NJ: Prentice Hall, 1983); and D. W. Ewing, "Do It My Way or You're Fired." *Employee Rights and the Changing Role of Management Prerogatives* (New York: John Wiley, 1983).
12. T. A. Stewart, "Get with the New Power Game," *Fortune,* January 13, 1997, pp. 58–62.
13. See J. R. P. French and B. Raven, "The Bases of Social Power," in D. Cartwright and A. F. Zander, eds., *Group Dynamics: Research and Theory* (New York: Harper & Row, 1960), pp. 607–23; P. M. Podsakoff and C. A. Schriesheim, "Field Studies of French and Raven's Bases of Power: Critique, Reanalysis, and Suggestions for Future Research," *Psychological Bulletin,* May 1985, pp. 387–411; R. K. Shukla, "Influence of Power Bases in Organizational Decision Making: A Contingency Model," *Decision Sciences,* July 1982, pp. 450–70; D. E. Frost and A. J. Stahelski, "The Systematic Measurement of French and Raven's Bases of Social Power in Workgroups," *Journal of Applied Social Psychology,* April 1988, pp. 375–89; and T. R. Hinkin and C. A. Schriesheim, "Development and Application of New Scales to Measure the French and Raven (1959) Bases of Social Power," *Journal of Applied Psychology,* August 1989, pp. 561–67.
14. Henri Fayol, *General and Industrial Management,* trans. C. Storrs (London: Pitman Publishing, 1949), pp. 19–42.
15. R. E. Daft, *Management,* 3rd ed. (Fort Worth: Dryden Press, 1994), p. 298.
16. K. Kelly, "Who Says Big Companies Are Dinosaurs?" *Business Week,* July 25, 1994, p. 14.
17. J. H. Sheridan, "What's Your Story?" *Industry Week,* May 20, 1996, p. 118; and N. Brodsky and B. Burlingham, "Necessary Losses," *Inc.,* December 1997, pp. 117–23.
18. J. Teresko, "A Supplier on a Roll," *Industry Week,* March 2, 1998, p. 49.
19. S. Wetlaufer, "Organizing for Empowerment: An Interview with AES's Roger Sant and Dennis Bakke," *Harvard Business Review,* January/February 1999, pp. 110–23.

20. C. Joinson, "Teams at Work," *HRMagazine,* May 1999, p. 30.
21. T. Burns and G. M. Stalker, *The Management of Innovation* (London: Tavistock, 1961).
22. A. D. Chandler Jr., *Strategy and Structure: Chapters in the History of the Industrial Enterprise* (Cambridge, MA: MIT Press, 1962).
23. See, for instance, R. E. Miles and C. C. Snow, *Organizational Strategy, Structure, and Process* (New York: McGraw-Hill, 1978); and H. L. Boschken, "Strategy and Structure: Reconceiving the Relationship," *Journal of Management,* March 1990, pp. 135–50.
24. See, for instance, P. M. Blau and R. A. Schoenherr, *The Structure of Organizations* (New York: Basic Books, 1971); D. S. Pugh, "The Aston Program of Research: Retrospect and Prospect," in A. H. Van de Ven and W. F. Joyce, eds., *Perspectives on Organization Design and Behavior* (New York: John Wiley, 1981), pp. 135–66; and R. Z. Gooding and J. A. Wagner III, "A Meta-Analytic Review of the Relationship between Size and Performance: The Productivity and Efficiency of Organizations and Their Subunits," *Administrative Science Quarterly,* December 1985, pp. 462–81.
25. C. C. Miller, W. H. Glick, Y. D. Wang, and G. Huber, "Understanding Technology-Structure Relationships: Theory Development and Meta-Analytic Theory Testing," *Academy of Management Journal,* June 1991, pp. 370–99.
26. J. Woodward, *Industrial Organization: Theory and Practice* (London: Oxford University Press, 1965); and C. Perrow, *Organizational Analysis: A Sociological Perspective* (Belmont, CA: Wadsworth, 1970).
27. D. Gerwin, "Relationships between Structure and Technology," in P. C. Nystrom and W. H. Starbuck, eds., *Handbook of Organizational Design,* vol. 2 (New York: Oxford University Press, 1981), pp. 3–38; and D. M. Rousseau and R. A. Cooke, "Technology and Structure: The Concrete, Abstract, and Activity Systems of Organizations," *Journal of Management,* (Fall/Winter 1984), pp. 345–61.
28. See, for example, H. M. O'Neill, "Restructuring, Reengineering and Rightsizing: Do the Metaphors Make Sense?" *Academy of Management Executive* 8, No. 4 (1994), pp. 9–30; and R. K. Reger, J. V. Mullane, L. T. Gustafson, and S. M. DeMarie, "Creating Earthquakes to Change Organizational Mindsets," *Academy of Management Executive* 8, No. 4 (1994), pp. 31–46.
29. S. Lubove, "It Ain't Broke, but Fix It Anyway," *Forbes,* August 1, 1994, p. 56.
30. H. Mintzberg, *Structure in Fives: Designing Effective Organizations* (Upper Saddle River, NJ: Prentice Hall, 1983), p. 157.
31. See, for instance, J. Galbraith, "Matrix Organization Designs: How to Combine Functional and Project Forms," *Business Horizons,* February 1971, pp. 29–40; and L. R. Burns, "Matrix Management in Hospitals: Testing Theories of Structure and Development," *Administrative Science Quarterly,* September 1989, pp. 349–68.
32. S. G. Turner, D. Utley, and J. D. Westbrook, "Project Managers and Functional Managers: A Case Study of Job Satisfaction in a Matrix Organization," *Project Management Journal,* September 1998, pp. 11–19.
33. J. Brikinghaw, "Encouraging Entrepreneurial Activity in Multinational Corporations," *Business Horizons,* May–June 1995, pp. 32–38; and J. C. Spender and E. H. Kessler, "Managing the Uncertainties of Innovation," *Human Relations,* January 1995, pp. 35–56.
34. See, for example, H. Rothman, "The Power of Empowerment," *Nation's Business,* June 1993, pp. 49–52; and L. Grant, "New Jewel in the Crown," *U.S. News & World Report,* February 28, 1994, pp. 55–57.
35. B. Dumaine, "Payoff from the New Management," *Fortune,* December 13, 1993, pp. 103–10.
36. See, for example, G. G. Dess, A. M. A. Rasheed, K. J. McLaughlin, and R. L. Priem, "The New Corporate Architecture," *Academy of Management Executive* 9, No. 3 (1995), pp. 7–20.
37. For additional readings on boundaryless organizations, see "The Boundaryless Organization: Break the Chains of Organizational Structures," *HR Focus,* April 1996, p. 21; R. M. Hodgetts, "A Conversation with Steve Kerr," *Organizational Dynamics,* Spring 1996, pp. 68–79; J. Gebhardt, "The Boundaryless Organization," *Sloan Management Review,* Winter 1996, pp. 117–19. For another view of boundaryless organizations, see B. Victor, "The Dark Side of the New Organizational Forms: An Editorial Essay," *Organization Science,* November 1994, pp. 479–82.
38. See, for example, N. A. Wishart, J. J. Elam, and D. Robey, "Redrawing the Portrait of a Learning Organization: Inside Knight-Ridder, Inc.," *Academy of Management Executive* 10, No. 1 (1996), pp. 7–20; G. G. Dess, A. M. A. Rasheed, K. J. McLaughlin, and R. L. Priem, "The New Corporate Architecture," *Academy of Management Executive* 9, No. 3 (1995), pp. 7–20; J. C. Hyatt, "GE's Chairman's Annual Letter Notes Strides by 'Stretch' of the Imagination," *Wall Street Journal,* March 8, 1994, p. B6; and J. Lipnack and J. Stamps, "The Best of Both Worlds," Inc., March 1994, p. 33; and R. Keidel, "Rethinking Organizational Design," *Academy of Management Executive,* November 1994, pp. 12–27.
39. G. G. Dess, A. M. A. Rasheed, K. L. McLaughlin, and R. L. Priem, "The New Corporate Architecture," *Academy of Management Executive,* July 1995, pp. 7–20.
40. R. T. Golembiewski, "The Boundaryless Organization: Breaking the Chains of Organizational Structure," *International Journal of Organizational Analysis,* July 1998, pp. 267–70; and J. B. Nelson, "The Boundaryless Organization: Implications for Job analysis, Recruitment and Selection," *Human Resource Planning,* October 1997, pp. 39–49.
41. R. Jacob, "The Struggle to Create an Organization for the 21st Century," *Fortune,* April 3, 1995, pp. 98–99. See also R. P. Vecchio, "A Cross National Comparison of the Influence of Span of Control," *International Journal of Management,* September 1995, pp. 261–70.
42. T. A. Stewart, "Welcome to the Revolution," *Fortune,* December 13, 1993, p. 66; and N. M. Tichey, "Revolutionize Your Company," *Fortune,* December 13, 1993, pp. 114–18.
43. "A Master Class of Radical Change," *Fortune,* December 13, 1993, p. 83; and Byrne, "The Horizontal Corporation," p.

78. For an excellent discussion of the Horizontal Organization, see F. Ostroff, *The Horizontal Organization* (New York: Oxford University Press, 1999).
44. See, A. M. Townsend, S. M. DeMarie, and A. R. Hendrickson, "Virtual Technology and the Workplace of the Future," *Academy of Management Executive,* August 1998, pp. 17–28.
45. W. R. Pape, "The Fewer the Merrier," *Inc. Tech,* No. 4, 1998, p. 33.
46. L. Smircich, "Concepts of Culture and Organizational Analysis," *Administrative Science Quarterly,* September 1983, p. 339; and J. H. Sheridan, "Culture-Change Lessons, *Industry Week,* February 17, 1997, p. 20.
47. A. M. Sapienza, "Believing Is Seeing: How Culture Influences the Decisions Top Managers Make," in R. H. Kilmann et al., eds., *Gaining Control of the Corporate Culture* (San Francisco: Jossey-Bass, 1985), p. 68.
48. Based on G. Hofstede, B. Neuijen, D. D. Ohayv, and G. Sanders, "Measuring Organizational Culture: A Qualitative and Quantitative Study across Twenty Cases," *Administrative Science Quarterly,* June 1990, pp. 286–316; and C. A. O'Reilly III, J. Chatman, and D. F. Caldwell, "People and Organizational Culture: A Profile Comparison Approach to Assessing Person-Organization Fit," *Academy of Management Journal,* September 1991, pp. 487–516.
49. D. C. Hambrick and S. Finkelstein, "Managerial Discretion: A Bridge between Polar Views of Organizational Outcomes," in L. L. Cummings and B. M. Staw, eds., *Research in Organizational Behavior* (Greenwich, CT: JAI Press, 1987), pp. 384–85.
50. L. Hays, "Blue Period: Gerstner Is Struggling as He Tries to Change Ingrained IBM Culture," *Wall Street Journal,* May 13, 1994, p. A1.
51. Ibid., p. A8.
52. L. Sartain, "Why and How Southwest Airlines Uses Consultants," *Journal of Management Consulting,* November 1998, p. 12; and "The Cult(ure) of Herb," *Air Transport World,* October 1997, p. 43.
53. J. Case, "Corporate Culture," *Inc.,* November 1996, pp. 42–44.
54. See, for example, P. M. Senge, "Beyond the Bottleneck," *Executive Excellence,* May 1999, p. 20.
55. See, for example, D. Benton, *Applied Human Relations: An Organizational Approach,* 6th ed. (Upper Saddle River, NJ: Prentice Hall, 1998); and A. J. DuBrin, *Human Relations: A Job-Oriented Approach,* 7th ed. (Upper Saddle River, NJ: Prentice Hall, 1998).
56. See, for example, H. Lancaster, "When Your Boss Doesn't Like You, It's Detente or Departure," *Wall Street Journal,* August 15, 1995, p. B1.
57. Case is based on information in "Merger to Make New Powerhouse," *ENR,* April 5, 1999, p. 15; M. deVries, "Charisma in Action: The Transformation Abilities of Virgin's Richard Branson and ABB's Percy Barnevik," *Organizational Dynamics,* Winter 1998, pp. 6–21; O. Krzysztof and H. Thomas, "Transforming Former State-Owned Companies into Market Competitors in Poland: The ABB Experience," *European Management Journal,* August 1998, pp. 390–99; J. Main, "Globe-Zilla," *Working Woman,* October 1998, p. 63; and "Asea Brown Boveri, *Global Finance,* October 1998, p. 46.

Chapter 6

1. K. A. Goeldner, "Professional Employee Organizations—Opportunities and Considerations," *CPCU Journal,* Spring 1999, pp. 17–21, M. Cody, "Serving Small Firms Pays Off Big for HR Tech," *The Columbia Flyer,* December 3, 1998, p. 26; J. J. Occhiogrosso, "Professional Employers for Small Companies," *Management Accounting,* December 1998, pp. 38–42; K. Fleming, "Columbia Entrepreneurs Honored," *The Business Monthly,* August 1998, p. 17; "Largest Private Sector Employers in the Baltimore Area," *Baltimore Business Journal,* August 28, 1998, p. 22; and "HR Tech's Leaders of the Pack," *The Proemp Journal,* May 1998, pp. 76–79.
2. B. Roberts, "HR's Link to the Corporate Big Picture," *HRMagazine,* April 1999, pp. 103–10.
3. P. Digh, "Religion in the Workplace," *HRMagazine,* December 1998, p. 88.
4. S. Ang, S. Slaughter, and K. Y. Ng, "Determinants of Compensation for Information Technology (IT) Professionals: Modeling Cross-Level Interactions," *Proceedings of the Fifty-Eighth Annual Meeting of the Academy of Management,* S. J. Havlovic, ed., August 7–12, 1998, pp. HRC1–HRC4.
5. See, for example, D. A. DeCenzo and S. P. Robbins, *Human Resource Management,* 6th ed. (New York: John Wiley & Sons, Inc., 1999), Chapter 6.
6. See, for example, T. A. Stewart, "In Search of Elusive Tech Workers," *Fortune,* February 16, 1998, p. 171; A. Bargerstock and H. Engle, "Six Ways to Boost Employee Referral Programs," *HRMagazine,* December 1994; and L. Greenhalgh, A. T. Lawrence, and R. I. Sutton, "Determinants of Work Force Reduction Strategies in Declining Organizations," *Academy of Management Review,* April 1988, pp. 241–54.
7. C. Johnson, "Is After Hire Testing the Best Solution?" *HRMagazine,* July 1997, p. 120; A. Loftin and R. Hastings, "Research Helps to Avoid Testing-Related Problems," *HR News,* February 1997; and R. L. Dipboye, *Selection Interviews: Process Perspectives* (Cincinnati: South-Western Publishing, 1992), p. 6.
8. See, for instance, J. A. Parnel, "Improving the Fit Between Organizations and Employees," *SAM Advanced Management Journal,* Winter 1998, pp. 35–42; R. D. Arvey and J. E. Campion, "The Employment Interview: A Summary and Review of Recent Research," *Personnel Psychology,* Summer 1982, pp. 281–322; and M. M. Harris, "Reconsidering the Employment Interview: A Review of Recent Literature and Suggestions for Future Research," *Personnel Psychology,* Winter 1989, pp. 691–726.
9. J. A. Segal, "Take Applicants for a Test Drive," *HRMagazine,* December 1996, pp. 120–22.
10. Dipboye, *Selection Interviews,* p. 180.
11. See, for instance, H. G. Baker and M. S. Spier, "The Employment Interview: Guaranteed Improvement in Reliability," *Public Personnel Management,* Spring 1990, pp. 85–87; and Dipboye, *Selection Interviews,* pp. 6–9.
12. P. Taylor, "Providing Structure to Interviews and Reference Checks," *Workforce,* May 1999, pp. 7–10; W. G. Kirkwood and S. M. Ralston, "Inviting Meaningful Applicant Performance in Employment Interviews," *The Journal of Business Communications,* January 1999, pp. 55–76; "What

Personnel Offices Really Stress in Hiring," *Wall Street Journal,* March 6, 1991, p. A1.
13. This vignette was influenced by Stephen M. Pollan and Mark Levine, "How to Ace a Tough Interview," *Working Woman* (July 1994), p. 49. See also, D. V. Robinson, "Behavioral Interviewing at CIGNA," *HR Focus,* December 1998, p. 6.
14. See, for example, C. Foster and L. Godkin, "Employment Selection in Health Care: The Case for Structured Interviewing," *Health Care Management Review,* Winter 1998, p. 46; and C. K. Stevens, "Effects of Preinterview Beliefs on Applicants' Reaction of Campus Interviews," *Academy of Management Journal,* August 1997, pp. 947–66.
15. See, for example, S. L. Premack and J. P. Wanous, "A Meta-Analysis of Realistic Job Preview Experiments," *Journal of Applied Psychology,* November 1985, pp. 706–20.
16. B. Leonard, "Cover Story," *HRMagazine,* July 1996, pp. 75–82; and J. S. DeMatteo, G. H. Dobbins, and K. M. Luindby, "The Effects of Accountability on Training Effectiveness," in D. P. Moore, ed., *Academy of Management Best Papers Proceedings,* August 14–17, 1994, p. 122.
17. M. P. Cronin, "Training: Asking Workers What They Want," *Inc.,* August 1994, p. 103.
18. L. J. Bassi and M. E. VanBuren, *The 1999 ASTD State of the Industry Report* (Alexandria, VA: American Society for Training and Development, 1999), p. 5.
19. R. Henkoff, "Companies That Train Best," *Fortune* (March 22, 1993), p. 62; and Commerce Clearing House, "Quality Challenge for HR: Linking Training to Quality Program Goals," *1994 SHRM/CCH Survey* (June 22, 1994), p. 1.
20. L. Grant, "A School for Success," *U.S. News & World Report* (May 22, 1995), p. 53.
21. See, for example, R. E. Catalano and D. L. Kirkpatrick, "Evaluating Training Programs—The State of the Art," *Training and Development Journal* (May 1968), pp. 2–9.
22. See, for example, D. A. DeCenzo and S. P. Robbins, *Human Resource Management,* 6th ed. (New York: John Wiley & Sons, Inc., 1999), pp. 293–302.
23. See R. H. Woods, M Sciarini, and D. Breiter, "Performance Appraisals in Hotels," *Cornell Hotel and Restaurant Administration Quarterly,* April 1998, pp. 25–29.
24. J. Maiorca, "How to Construct Behaviorally Anchored Rating Scales (BARS) for Employee Evaluations," *Supervision,* August 1997, pp. 15–18.
25. R. Lepsinger and A. D. Lucia, "360 Degree Feedback and Performance Appraisal," *Training* (September 1997), pp. 62–70; M. R. Edwards and A. J. Ewen, "Moving Multisource Assessment beyond Development," *ACA Journal* (Winter 1995), pp. 82–93; and J. F. Milliman, R. A. Zawacki, C. Norman, L. Powell, and J. Kirksey, "Companies Evaluate Employees from All Perspectives," *Personnel Journal* (November 1994), p. 99.
26. G. D. Huet-Cox, T. M. Nielson, and E. Sundstrom, "Getting the Most From 360-Degree Feedback: Put It on the Internet," *HRMagazine,* May 1999, pp. 92–1003; L. Atwater and D. Waldman, "Accountability in 360 Degree Feedback," *HRMagazine* (May 1998), p. 96; R. Hoffman, "Ten Reasons You Should Be Using 360-Degree Feedback," *HRMagazine* (April 1995), p. 82; and "Companies Where Employees Rate Executives," *Fortune* (December 27, 1993), p. 128.
27. P. Brotherton, "Candid Feedback Spurs Changes in Culture," *HRMagazine* (May 1996), pp. 47–52.
28. R. Bookman, "Tools for Cultivating Constructive Feedback," *Association Management,* February 1999, pp. 73–79.
29. B. O'Reilly, "360 Feedback Can Change Your Life," *Fortune* (October 17, 1994), p. 96.
30. Ibid.
31. S. Brutus, "The Power of 360 Degree Feedback: How to Leverage Performance Evaluations for Top Productivity," *Personnel Psychology,* Spring 1999, pp. 235–38; See, for example, H. Lancaster, "Performance Reviews Are More Valuable When More Join in," *The Wall Street Journal* (July 9, 1996), p. B1; D. Nilsen, "Self-Observer Rating Discrepancies: Once an Over-rater, Always an Overrater," *Human Resource Management* (Fall 1993), pp. 265–82; W. W. Turnow, "Perceptions or Reality: Is Multi-Perspective Measurement a Means or an End?" *Human Resource Management* (Fall 1993), pp. 221–30; M. London and R. W. Beatty, "360-Degree Feedback as a Competitive Advantage," *Human Resource Management* (Fall 1993), pp. 353–73; and R. E. Kaplan, "360-Degree Feedback PLUS: Boosting the Power of Co-Worker Rating for Executives," *Human Resource Management* (Fall 1993), pp. 299–315.
32. R. D. Bretz Jr., G. T. Milkovich, and W. Read, "The Current State of Performance Appraisal Research and Practice: Concerns, Directions, and Implications," *Journal of Management,* June 1992, p. 331.
33. See, for example, J. Alley, "Where the Jobs Are," *Fortune,* September 18, 1995, pp. 53–55.
34. Interview with Bill Gates, "Bill Gates on Rewiring the Power Structure," *Working Woman,* April 1994, p. 62.
35. R. Leger, "Linked by Differences," *Springfield News-Leader,* December 31, 1993, p. B6.
36. B. R. Ragins and T. A. Scandura, "Gender and the Termination of Mentoring Relationships," in Moore, ed., *Academy of Management Best Papers Proceedings,* August 14–17, 1994, pp. 361–65.
37. P. Brimelow, "Is Sexual Harassment Getting Worse?" *Forbes,* April 19, 1999, p. 92.
38. A. B. Fisher, "Sexual Harassment, What to Do," *Fortune* (August 23, 1993), pp. 84–88.
39. P. M. Buhler, "The Manager's Role in Preventing Sexual Harassment," *Supervision,* April 1999, p. 18; and C. M. Koen, Jr., p. 88; and "Cost of Sexual Harassment in the U.S.," *Manpower Argus* (January 1997), p. 5.
40. E. Thornton, "Make Way for Women with Welding Guns," *Business Week,* April 19, 1999, p. 54; "Mexico: Sexual Harassment in the Workplace," *Manpower Argus* (March 1997), p. 8; S. Webb, *The Webb Report: A Newsletter on Sexual Harassment* (Seattle, WA: Premier Publishing, Ltd., January 1994), pp. 4–7; and (April 1994), pp. 2–5.
41. Although the male gender was referred to in this case, it is important to note that sexual harassment may involve persons of either sex sexually harassing others or a person of the same sex harassing another individual. (See, for instance, *Oncale v. Sundowner Offshore Service Inc.,* 118 S. Ct. 998.)
42. *Meritor Savings Bank v. Vinson,* U.S. Supreme Court 106, Docket No. 2399 (1986).

43. C. M. Koen, Jr., "Sexual Harassment Claims Stem from a Hostile Work Environment," *Personnel Journal* (August 1990), p. 89.
44. Ibid. See also, D. L. Deadrick, S. W. Kezman, and B. McAfee, "Harassment by Nonemployees: How Should Employers Respond," *HRMagazine* (December 1996), p. 108; F. Clancy, "When Customer Service Crosses the Line," *Working Woman* (December 1994), pp. 36–39; 77; and L. A. Winokur, "Harassment of Workers by 'Third Parties' Can Lead into Maze of Legal, Moral Issues," *Wall Street Journal* (October 26, 1992), p. B-1. Also, if an organization investigates the matter and takes immediate action, it may be held not liable for the action.
45. A. Fisher, "After All This Time, Why Don't People Know What Sexual Harassment Means?" *Fortune* (January 12, 1998), p. 68.
46. A. Field, "Trial by Hire," *Working Woman* (April 1998), p. 66.
47. See K. A. Hess, and D. R. M. Ehrens, "Sexual Harassment—Affirmative Defense to Employer Liability, *Benefits Quarterly,* Second Quarter 1999, p. 57; J. A. Segal, "The Catch-22s of Remedying Sexual Harassment Complaints," *HRMagazine* (October 1997), pp. 111–17; S. C. Bahls and J. E. Bahls, "Hand-Off Policy," *Entrepreneur* (July 1997), pp. 74–76; J. A. Segal, "Where Are We Now?" *HRMagazine* (October 1996), pp. 69–73; B. McAfee and D. L. Deadrick, "Teach Employees to Just Say No," *HRMagazine* (February 1996), pp. 86–89; G. D. Bloch, "Avoiding Liability for Sexual Harassment," *HRMagazine* (April 1995), pp. 91–97; and J. A. Segal, "Stop Making Plaintiffs' Lawyers Rich," *HRMagazine* (April 1995), pp. 31–35. Also, it should be noted here that under the Title VII and the Civil Rights Act of 1991, the maximum award that can be given, under the Federal Act, is $300,000. However, many cases are tried under state laws that permit unlimited punitive damages, such as the $7.1 million Rena Weeks received in her trial based on California statutes.
48. A. Sullivan, "Harassment on Trial," *Working Woman* (June 1998), p. 18.
49. G. Flynn, "Sexual Harassment Interpretations Give New Cause for Concerns," *Workforce,* May 1999, pp. 105–106; J. Salters, "Sexual Harassment: Responding to Changing Legal Guidelines," *Employment Relations Today,* Spring 1999, pp. 80–97; W. M. Lavelle, "The New Rules of Sexual Harassment," *U.S. News and World Report* (July 6, 1998), pp. 30–31.
50. M. H. Tanick, "No Rhyme or Reason for 'Seinfeld' Firing," *The National Law Journal* (August 18, 1997), p. A-19.
51. Dateline, NBC, "Dateline Follow-Up," *NBC News* (August 4, 1997).
52. See for example, P. Ingram and T. Simons, "Institutional and Resource Dependence Determinants of Responsiveness to Work-Family Issues," *Academy of Management Journal* 38, No. 5 (1995), pp. 1446–82.
53. F. J. Milliken, L. L. Martins, and H. Morgan, "Explaining Organizational Responsiveness to Work-Family Issues: The Role of Human Resource Executives as Issue Interpreters," *Academy of Management Journal,* October 1998, p. 585.
54. K. H. Hammond, and A. T. Palmer, "The Daddy Trap," *Business Week,* September 21, 1998, pp. 56–64.
55. S. Nelton, "A Flexible Style of Management," *Nation's Business,* December 1993, pp. 24–31; and A. Saltzman, "Family-Friendliness," *U.S. News & World Report,* February 22, 1993, pp. 59–66.
56. M. G. Harvey and M. R. Buckley, "The Process for Developing an International Program for Dual-Career Couples," *Human Resource Management Review,* Spring 1998, pp. 99–123; and C. A. Higgins, L. E. Duxburey, and R. H. Irving, "Work-Family Conflict in the Dual Career Family," *Organizational Behavior and Human Decision Process,* January 1992, pp. 51–75.
57. G. R. Gray, D. W. Meyers, and P. S. Meyers, "Cooperative Provisions in Labor Agreements: A New Paradigm," *Monthly Labor Review,* January 1999, pp. 29–45; M. M. Perline, "Union Views of Managerial Prerogatives Revisited: The Prospects for Labor-Management Cooperation," *Journal of Labor Research,* Winter 1999, pp. 147–54; T. J. Loney, "TQM and Labor-Management Cooperation-A Noble Experiment for the Public Sector," *International Journal of Public Administration* (October 1996), p. 1845; and B. Vlasic, "The Saginaw Solution," *Business Week* (July 15, 1996), pp. 78–80.
58. M. H. LeRoy, "Are Employers Constrained in the Use of Employee Participation Groups by Section 8(a)(2) of the National Labor Relations Act?," *Journal of Labor Research,* Winter 1999, pp. 53–71; "Teamwork for Employees and Managers (TEAM) Act," *HR Legislative Fact Sheet* (June 1996), pp. 28–29; and R. Hanson, R. I. Porterfield, and K. Ames, "Employee Empowerment at Risk: Effects of Recent NLRB Rulings," *Academy of Management Executive,* Vol. 9, No. 2 (1995), pp. 45–56.
59. B. S. Murphy, W. E. Barlow, and D. D. Hatch, "NLRB Decides Labor-Management Committees Case," *Personnel Journal* (February 1993), p. 20.
60. Ibid. and "Team Act," *The Journal for Quality and Participation* (January/February 1998), p. 7.
61. Legislation, referred to as the "Teamwork For Employees and Managers (TEAM) Act," was proposed in both the House of Representatives and the Senate. The Act was designed to "permit employers and employees to establish and maintain employee involvement programs—including various approaches to problem-solving, communication enhancement, productivity improvement programs." In May 1996, the Act was passed in the House and sent to the Senate for approval. By a vote of 53 to 46, the Senate approved the Act in principle but did not agree to some of its language. ["Teamwork for Employees and Managers (TEAM) Act," *HR Legislative Fact Sheet* (June 1996), pp. 28–29.]
62. J. A. Segal, "When Norman Bates and Baby Jane Act Out at Work," *HRMagazine* (February 1996), p. 31.
63. A. Toufexis, "Workers Who Fight Firing with Fire," *Time* (April 25, 1994), p. 35–36; and *L.A. Times* (April 9, 1994), p. A-31.
64. J. K. Sage, "Attack on Violence," *Industry Week* (February 15, 1997), p. 16. See also D. Harbrecht, "Talk about Murder, Inc.," *Business Week* (July 11, 1994), p. 8.
65. Ibid.; A. M. O'Leary-Kelly, R. W. Griffin, and D. J. Glew, "Organization-Motivated Aggression: A Research Framework," *Academy of Management Review,* Vol. 21, No. 1 (February 1996), p. 225; and T. Dunkel, "Danger Zone," *Working Woman* (August 1994), pp. 39–40.

66. F. Jossi, "Defusing Workplace Violence," *Business and Health,* February 1999, pp. 34–39; and "Self-Defense," *Entrepreneur* (March 1997), p. 38.
67. J. Welch, "Rising Violence Puts Focus on Staff Protection Policy," *People Management,* May 6, 1999, p. 17.
68. B. Pulley, "Crime Becomes Occupational Hazard of Deliverers," *Wall Street Journal* (March 7, 1994), p. B-1; and J. D. Thompson, "Employers Should Take Measures to Minimize Potential for Workplace Violence," *Commerce Clearing House: Ideas and Trends* (December 20, 1993), pp. 201–203; 208.
69. L. Micco, "Night Retailers Take Stock of Workers' Safety," *HRMagazine* (June 1997), p. 79.
70. J. A. Kinney, "When Domestic Violence Strikes the Workplace," *HRMagazine* (August 1995), pp. 74–78; and J. D. Thompson, "Employers Should Take Measures to Minimize Potential for Workplace Violence," *Commerce Clearing House: Ideas and Trends* (December 20, 1993), pp. 201–203; 208.
71. E. Unsworth, "Workplace Violence Risk Growing, Speakers Warn," *Business Insurance,* April 26, 1999, p. 12; E. Felsenthal, "Potentially Violent Employees Present Bosses with a Catch-22," *Wall Street Journal* (April 5, 1995), pp. B-1; B-5.
72. Ibid.
73. "Workplace Security: Preventing On-the-Job Violence," *Inc.* (June 1996), p. 116.
74. See, for example, K. Walter, "Are Your Employees on the Brink?" *HRMagazine* (June 1997), pp. 57–63; M. P. Coco, Jr., "The New War Zone: The Workplace," *SAM Advanced Management Journal* (Winter 1997), pp. 15–20; J. Lynn, "Striking Back," *Entrepreneur* (June 1995), p. 56; D. L. Johnson, J. G. Kurutz, and J. B. Kiehlbauch, "Scenario for Supervisors," *HRMagazine* (February 1995), p. 63; and Commerce Clearing House, "Workplace Violence: Strategies Start with Awareness," *Human Resources Management: Ideas and Trends* (July 11, 1994), p. 109.
75. J. K. Sage, "Attack on Violence," *Industry Week* (February 17, 1997), p. 18; R. M. Yandrick, "Long-Term Follow-up Urged after Workplace Disasters," *HR News* (December 1996), p. 6; and K. Menda, "Defusing Workplace Violence," *HRMagazine* (October 1994), p. 113.
76. Harbrecht, p. 8.
77. See, for instance, D. M. Noer, *Healing the Wounds* (San Francisco: Jossey-Bass, 1993).
78. S. P. Robbins, "Layoff-Survivor Sickness: A Missing Topic in Organizational Behavior," *Journal of Management Accounting,* February 1999, pp. 118–20.
79. Ibid.
80. This case is based on the Associated Press article "Connecticut Lottery Office Swept Clean of Traces of Gunman," *The Sun* (March 11, 1998), p. 9A; and F. Jossi, "Defusing Workplace Violence," *Business and Health,* February 1999, p. 12.

Career Module

1. D. E. Super and D. T. Hall, "Career Development: Exploration and Planning," in M. R. Rosenzweig and L. W. Porter, eds., *Annual Review of Psychology,* vol. 29 (Palo Alto, CA: Annual Reviews, 1978), p. 334.
2. See also A. Faircloth, "How To Recover from a Firing," *Fortune,* December 7, 1998, pp. 239–40.
3. R. W. Thompson, "Bigger Is Not Always Better, Report Says," *HRMagazine,* May 1999, p. 12; and B. Kenny, "Beyond Downsizing: Staffing and Workforce Management," *Employment Relations Today,* Spring 1999, pp. 29–36.
4. A. Grove, "Andy Grove on Navigating Your Career," *Fortune,* March 29, 1999, pp. 187–98.
5. D. E. Super, "A Life-Span Life Space Approach to Career Development," *Journal of Vocational Behavior* 16 (Spring 1980), pp. 282–98; see also pp. 99–131 in E. P. Cook and M. Arthur, *Career Theory Handbook* (Upper Saddle River, NJ: Prentice Hall, 1991); and L. S. Richman, "The New Worker Elite," *Fortune,* August 22, 1994, pp. 56–66.
6. I. R. Schwartz, "Self-Assessment and Career Planning: Matching Individuals and Organizational Goals," *Personnel,* January–February 1979, p. 48.
7. See, for instance, R. D. Clarke, "Getting a Job! . . . After College," *Black Enterprise* (February 1998), pp. 135–38.
8. N. Munk, "Finished at Forty," *Fortune,* February 1999, pp. 50–64.
9. Information for these Web addresses has been provided from J. Martin, "Changing Jobs? Try the Net," *Fortune,* March 2, 1998, pp. 205–208; L. Touby, "Finding a Job Online," *Working Mother* (April 1998), p. 20; "Careers: www.getajobyoulazybum.org," *Men's Health* (April 1997), p. 58; M. Frost, HR Cyberspace," *HRMagazine* (April 1997), pp. 34–35; and B. Fryer, "Job Hunting, the Electronic Way," *Working Woman* (March 1995), pp. 59, 78.
10. See, for example, J. Lawlor, "Scanning Resumes: The Impersonal Touch," *USA Today* (October 7, 1991), p. 7B.
11. T. Mullins, "How to Land a Job," *Psychology Today* (September/October 1994), pp. 12–13.
12. For a discussion on fit and its appropriateness to the interviewing process, see "The Right Fit," *Small Business Reports* (April 1993), p. 28.
13. For a more detailed discussion of impression management, see A. L. Kristof and C. K. Stevens, "Applicant Impression Management Tactics: Effects on Interviewer Evaluations and Interview Outcomes," Moore (ed.), *Academy of Management Best Papers Proceedings,* D. P. (August 14–17, 1994), pp. 127–31.
14. Reported in R. E. Carlson, P. W. Thayer, E. C. Mayfield, and D. A. Peterson, "Improvements in the Selection Interview," *Personnel Journal* (April 1971), p. 272.
15. K. Schabacker, "Tips on Making a Great First Impression," *Working Woman* (February 1992), p. 55.
16. A. N. Schoonmaker, *Executive Career Strategy* (New York: American Management Association, 1971); A. J. DuBrin, *Fundamentals of Organizational Behavior: An Applied Perspective,* 2nd ed. (Elmsford, NY: Pergamon Press, 1978), Chapter 5; E. E. Jennings, "Success Chess," *Management of Personnel Quarterly,* Fall 1980, pp. 2–8; and R. Henkoff, "Winning the New Career Game," *Fortune,* July 12, 1993, pp. 46–49.
17. J. E. Sheridan, J. W. Slocum Jr., R. Buda, and R. C. Thompson, "Effects of Corporate Sponsorship and Departmental Power on Career Tournaments," *Academy of Management Journal,* September 1990, pp. 578–602.

18. C. Perrow, *Complex Organizations: A Critical Essay* (Glenwood, IL: Scott, Foresman, 1972), p. 43.
19. Sheridan et al., "Effects of Corporate Sponsorship and Departmental Power on Career Tournaments."
20. E. O. Wells, "The Mentors," *Inc.,* June 1998, pp. 49–61; B. J. Tepper, "Upward Maintenance Tactics in Supervisory Mentoring and Nonmentoring Relationships," *Academy of Management Journal,* Vol. 38, No. 4 (May 1995), p. 1191; P. S. Estess, "A Few Good Mentors," *Entrepreneur* (September 1995), p. 83; and Commerce Clearing House, "Should Your Company Encourage Mentoring?" *Human Resources Management: Ideas and Trends* (July 20, 1994), p. 122.
21. S. Shellenbarger, "Corporate America Grooms Women Execs," *Working Woman* (October 1993), pp. 13–14.
22. See, for example, B. Rose Ragins and J. Cotton, "Mentoring Functions and Outcomes: A Comparison of Men and Women in Formal and Informal Mentoring Relationships," *Proceedings of the Fifty-Eighth Annual Meeting of the Academy of Management,* August 7–12, 1998, p. CAR-A1; J. A. Wilson and N. S. Elman, "Organizational Benefits of Mentoring," *Academy of Management Executive,* Vol. 4, No. 4 (November 1990), pp. 88–94.
23. Ibid.
24. "Work/Family Balance: News, Opinion, Child Care," *Working Woman,* April 1999, p. 8; and E. O. Wells, "The Mentors," p. 52; and M. N. Martinez, *HRMagazine,* Vol. 36, No. 6 (June 1991), p. 46.
25. G. F. Dreher and R. A. Ash, "A Comparative Study of Mentoring Among Men and Women in Managerial Professional, and Technical Positions," *Journal of Applied Psychology,* Vol. 75, No. 5 (October 1990), pp. 539–46.
26. For an excellent discussion of these issues, see W. Whitely, T. W. Dougherty, and G. F. Dreher, "Relationship of Career Mentoring and Socioeconomic Origin to Managers' and Professionals' Early Career Progress," *Academy of Management Journal,* Vol. 34, No. 5 (June 1991), pp. 331–51.
27. D. B. Turban and T. W. Dougherty, "Protege Personality, Mentoring, and Career Success," in J. L. Wall and L. R. Jauch (eds.), *Academy of Management Best Papers Proceedings 1992,* Las Vegas, Nevada (August 9–12, 1992), p. 419.
28. See, for example, D. Kirkpatrick, "Is Your Career on Track?" *Fortune,* June 2, 1990, pp. 38–48; A. Saltzman, "Sidestepping Your Way to the Top," *U.S. News & World Report,* October 17, 1990, pp. 60–61; and B. Nussbaum, "I'm Worried about My Job," *Business Week,* October 7, 1991, pp. 94–97.
29. J. Connelly, "Career Survival Guide," *Working Woman,* April 1999, p. 61; and P. R. Brotherton, "Network with Confidence," *Working Mother,* November 18, 1998, p. 18.

Chapter 7

1. Based on L. Estell, "Unchained Profits," *Sales and Marketing Management,* February 1999, pp. 62–67; C. L. Dannhauser, "Who's in the Home Office," *American Demographics,* June 1999, p. 52; B. Upbin, "A Touch of Schizophrenia," *Forbes,* July 7, 1997, pp. 57–59; and S. Avery, "Technology Transforms New Designs," *Purchasing,* April 22, 1999, p. 63.
2. B. Schlender, "L. Ellison: Oracle at Web Speed," *Fortune,* May 24, 1999, p. 136.
3. See, for instance, D. Buchanan, "Politics and Organizational Change: The Lived Experience," *Human Relations,* May 1999, pp. 609–29; and D. Buchanan, T. Claydon, and M. Doyle, "Organization Development and Change: The Legacy of the Nineties," *Human Resource Management Journal,* February 1999, pp. 20–37.
4. For a good discussion on internal versus external change agent issues, see A. Molinsky, "Sanding Down the Edges: Paradoxical Impediments to Organizational Change," *The Journal of Applied Behavioral Science,* March 1999, pp. 8–24.
5. The idea for these metaphors came from P. Vaill, *Managing as a Performing Art: New Ideas for a World of Chaotic Change* (San Francisco: Jossey-Bass, 1989).
6. K. Lewin, *Field Theory in Social Science* (New York: Harper & Row, 1951).
7. See, for instance, T. Peters, *Thriving on Chaos* (New York: Alfred A. Knopf, 1987).
8. M. Davids, "Wanted: Strategic Planners," *Journal of Business Strategy,* May–June 1995, pp. 30–38.
9. J. C. McCune, "The Change Makers," *Management Review,* May 1999, p. 16–22; S. F. Marino, "The Challenge of Change," *Industry Week,* January 19, 1998, p. 26; and P. F. Drucker, "Change Leaders," *Inc.,* June 1999, pp. 65–72.
10. Peters, *Thriving on Chaos,* p. 3.
11. Ibid.
12. J. O'Toole, "Lead Change Effectively," *Executive Excellence,* April 1999, p. 18.
13. See, for example, D. K. Denton, "9 Ways to Create an Atmosphere for Change," *HRMagazine,* October 1996, pp. 76–80; C. M. Lau and R. Woodman, "Understanding Organizational Change: A Schematic Perspective," *Academy of Management Journal* 38, No. 2 (1995), pp. 537–54; A. B. Fisher, "Making Change Stick," *Fortune,* April 17, 1995, pp. 121–31; and B. M. Staw, "Counterforces to Change," in P. S. Goodman and Associates, eds., *Change in Organizations* (San Francisco: Jossey-Bass, 1982), pp. 87–121.
14. L. G. Bolman and T. E. Deal, "4 Steps to Keeping Change Efforts Heading in the Right Direction," *The Journal for Quality and Participation,* May/June 1999, pp. 6–11; and J. P. Kotter and L. A. Schlesinger, "Choosing Strategies for Change," *Harvard Business Review,* March–April 1979, pp. 107–109.
15. L. Coch and J. R. P. French Jr., "Overcoming Resistance to Change," *Human Relations,* November 1948, pp. 512–32.
16. J. P. Kotler and L. A. Schlesinger, "Choosing Strategies for Change," *Harvard Business Review,* March–April 1979, pp. 106–14.
17. J. P. Daly, "Explaining Changes to Employees: The Influence of Justifications and Change Outcomes on Employees' Fairness Judgements," *Journal of Applied Behavioral Sciences,* December 1995, pp. 415–28.
18. D. Ciampa, *Total Quality: A User's Guide for Implementation* (Reading, MA: Addison-Wesley, 1992), pp. 100–104.
19. J. Jesitus, "Change Management: Energy to the People," *Industry Week,* September 1, 1997, pp. 37, 40.
20. K. H. Hammonds, "Where Did We Go Wrong?" *Business Week,* Quality 1991 Special Issue, p. 38.
21. F. J. Barrett, G. Fann Thomas, and S. P. Hocevar, "The Central Role of Discourse in Large-Scale Change: A Social Construction Perspective," *Journal of Applied Behavioral Science,* September 1995, p. 370.

22. See, for example, L. Light, "The Fall and Rise of HarperCollins," *Business Week,* June 14, 1999, pp. 74–78; T. Galpin, "Connecting Culture to Organizational Change," *HRMagazine,* March 1996, pp. 84–90.
23. C. Wild, N. Horney, and R. Koonce, "Cascading Communications Creates Momentum for Change," *HRMagazine,* December 1996, pp. 95–100; R. W. Boss and R. T. Golembiewski, "Do You Have to Start at the Top? The Chief Executive Officer's Role in Successful Organization Development Efforts," *Journal of Applied Behavioral Science,* September 1995, pp. 259–77; and R. T. Golembiewski, *Organization Development: Ideas and Issues* (New Brunswick, NJ: Transaction Books, Rutgers University, 1989).
24. E. H. Schein, *Process Consultation: Its Role in Organizational Development* (Reading, Mass.: Addison-Wesley, 1969), p. 9.
25. See, for instance, "Workplace Stress Is Rampant, Especially with the Recession," *Wall Street Journal,* May 5, 1992, p. A1; and C. L. Cordes and T. W. Dougherty, "A Review and an Integration of Research on Job Burnout," *Academy of Management Review,* October 1993, pp. 621–56.
26. Adapted from R. S. Schuler, "Definition and Conceptualization of Stress in Organizations," *Organizational Behavior and Human Performance,* April 1980, p. 189.
27. Ibid., p. 191.
28. "Workplace Stress Is Rampant, Especially with the Recession," *Wall Street Journal,* May 5, 1992, p. A-1.
29. K. Lynch, "Humor Can Beat Stress," *Industry Week,* May 4, 1998, p. 55.
30. This information is adapted from a newswire report by M. Yamaguchi as cited in "Stress in Japanese Business," *Audio Human Resource Report,* Vol. 2, No. 2, March 1991, pp. 6–7.
31. "Work-Related Deaths Are on the Rise in Japan," *Manpower Argus,* April 1997, p. 11.
32. "Huge Payout by Japanese Firm for 'Karoshi,'" *Manpower Argus,* September 1996, p. 8.
33. "Stress on the Job in Germany," and "Workplace Stress Is Biggest Health Hazard in Britain," *Manpower Argus,* February 1997, p. 7.
34. Also see J. H. Harris and L. A. Arendt, "Stress Reduction and the Small Business: Increasing Employee and Customer, Satisfaction," *SAM Advanced Management Journal,* Winter 1997, pp. 27–34.
35. For an interesting overview of this topic, see V. J. Doby and R. D. Caplan, "Organizational Stress as Threat to Reputation: Effects on Anxiety at Work and at Home," *Academy of Management Journal,* September 1995, pp. 1105–123.
36. See, for instance, J. Schaubroeck and D. E. Merritt, "Divergent Effects of Job Control on Coping with Work Stressors: The Key Role of Self-Efficacy," *Academy of Management Journal,* June 1997, pp. 738–54.
37. A. A. Brott, "New Approaches to Job Stress," *Nation's Business,* May 1994, pp. 81–82; and C. J. Bacher, "Workers Take Leave of Job Stress," *Personnel Journal,* January 1995, pp. 38–48.
38. Ibid.
39. Ibid.
40. Feldman, p. 3.
41. See G. Nicholas, "How to Make Employee Assistance Programs More Productive," *Supervision,* July 1991, pp. 3–6; and "EAPs to the Rescue," *Employee Benefit Plan Review,* February 1991, pp. 26–27.
42. "EAPs Evolve to Health Plan Gatekeeper," *Employee Benefit Plan Review,* February 1992, p. 18.
43. E. Stetzer, "Bringing Sanity to Mental Health Costs," *Business and Health,* February 1992, p. 72.
44. See M. Bryant, "Testing EAPs for Coordination," *Business and Health,* August 1991, pp. 20–24.
45. S. L. Hyland, "Health Care Benefits Show Cost-Containment Strategies," *Monthly Labor Review,* February 1992, p. 42.
46. R. M. Yandrick, "EAPs Explore Boundaries of Evolving Profession," *HR News,* August 1995, p. 1.
47. S. Campbell, "Better Than the Company Gym," *HRMagazine,* June 1995, pp. 108–10.
48. L. Ingram, "Many Healthy Returns," *Entrepreneur,* September 1994, p. 84.
49. Shari Caudron, "The Wellness Payoff," *Personal Journal,* July 1990, p. 56.
50. Ibid.
51. J. E. Riedel and A. Frank, "Corporate Health Promotion: Marketing Studies Show Who Buys and Who Succeeds," *Employee Benefits Journal,* Vol. 15, No. 2, June 1990, p. 29.
52. "Creativity Counts," *HR Focus,* May 1999, p. 4; and M. Moeller, S. Hamm, and T. J. Mullaney, "Remaking Microsoft," *Business Week,* May 17, 1999, p. 106.
53. See, for example, W. Royal, AFinding Sharp's Focus," *Industry Week,* May 3, 1999, pp. 32–38; T. Stevens, "Converting Ideas into Profits," *Industry Week,* June 3, 1996, p. 21; T. Stewart, "3M Fights Back," *Fortune,* February 5, 1996, pp. 94–99; K. Kelly, "3M Run Scared? Forget About It," *Business Week,* September 16, 1991, pp. 59–62; and R. Mitchell, "Masters of Innovation," *Business Week,* April 10, 1989, p. 58.
54. J. C. Collins and J. I. Porras, "A Theory of Evolution," *Audacity,* Winter 1996, pp. 5–11.
55. These definitions are based on T. M. Amabile, "A Model of Creativity and Innovation in Organizations," in B. M. Staw and L. L. Cummings, eds., *Research in Organizational Behavior* (Greenwich, CT: JAI Press, 1988), p. 126.
56. J. Calano and J. Salzman, "Ten Ways to Fire up Your Creativity," *Working Woman,* July 1989, p. 94.
57. T. DeSalvo, "Unleash the Creativity in Your Organization," *HRMagazine,* June 1999, pp. 154–58; and G. Taninecz, "Following the Muse," *Industry Week,* August 19, 1996, pp. 111–13.
58. A. Taylor, III, "Kellogg Cranks up Its Idea Machine," *Fortune,* July 5, 1999, p. 181.
59. T. Stevens, "A Modern-Day Ben Franklin," *Industry Week,* March 1, 1999, pp. 20–25.
60. J. Martin, "Give 'Em Exactly What They Want," *Fortune,* November 19, 1997, p. 283.
61. J. Flynn, Z. Schiller, J. Carey, and R. Coxeter, "Novo Nordisk's Mean Green Machine," *Business Week,* November 14, 1994, p. 72.
62. See, for example, G. R. Oldham and A. Cummings, "Employee Creativity: Personal and Contextual Factors at Work," *Academy of Management Journal* 39, No. 3 (1996), pp. 607–34; and T. M. Amabile, R. Conti, H. Coon, J. Lazenby, and M. Herron, "Assessing the Work Environment for Creativity," *Academy of Management Journal,* October 1996, pp. 1154–84.

63. "Be Creative Now: Companies Try to Inspire Creativity in a Leaner Work Place," *Wall Street Journal,* June 13, 1996, p. A1; and S. G. Scott and R. A. Bruce, "Determinants of Innovative Behavior: A Path Model of Individual Innovation in the Workplace," *Academy of Management Journal* 37, No. 3 (1994), pp. 580–607.
64. E. Glassman, "Creative Problem Solving," *Supervisory Management,* January 1989, pp. 21–22.
65. F. Damanpour, "Organizational Innovation: A Meta-Analysis of Effects of Determinants and Moderators," *Academy of Management Journal,* September 1991, pp. 555–90.
66. Stevens, "A Modern-Day Ben Franklin," p. 20.
67. P. R. Monge, M. D. Cozzens, and N. S. Contractor, "Communication and Motivation Predictors of the Dynamics of Organizational Innovation," *Organizational Science,* September 1991, pp. 250–74.
68. See, for example, T. S. Schoenecker, U. S. Daellenbach, and A. M. McCarthy, "Factors Affecting a Firm's Commitment to Innovation," in D. Perrin More, ed., *Best Paper Proceedings: Fifty-Fifth Annual Meeting of the Academy of Management,* August 6–9, 1996, pp. 52–56.
69. See, for instance, J. Myerson, "*Management Today* Innovation Awards," *Management Today,* May 1999, p. 86; T. M. Amabile, "A Model of Creativity and Innovation in Organizations," p. 147; M. Tushman and D. Nadler, "Organizing for Innovation," *California Management Review,* Spring 1986, pp. 74–92; R. Moss Kanter, "When a Thousand Flowers Bloom: Structure, Collective, and Social Conditions for Innovation in Organizations," in Staw and Cummings, *Research in Organizational Behavior,* pp. 169–211; and G. Morgan, "Endangered Species: New Ideas," *Business Month,* April 1989, pp. 75–77; S. G. Scott and R. A. Bruce, "Determinants of Innovative People in the Work Place," *Academy of Management Journal,* June 1994, pp. 580–607; Loeb, "Ten Commandments for Managing Creative People"; and T. Stevens, "Creativity Killers," *Industry Week,* January 23, 1995, pp. 63, 126.
70. Stevens, "A Modern-Day Ben Franklin," p. 21.
71. J. M. Howell, and C. A. Higgins, "Champions of Change," *Business Quarterly,* Spring 1990, pp. 31–32.
72. Adapted from E. Brown, "A Day at Innovation U," *Fortune,* April 12, 1999, pp. 163–66; M. Henricks, "Good Thinking," *Entrepreneur,* May 1996, pp. 70–73; M. Loeb, "Ten Commandments for Managing Creative People," *Fortune,* January 16, 1995, p. 16.
73. N. Weinberg, "A Setting Sun," *Forbes,* April 20, 1998, pp. 118–24.

Chapter 8

1. R. Quick, "Warnaco to Acquire Authentic Fitness for $14 Million in a Sweetened Offer," *Wall Street Journal,* November 17, 1999, p. A-1; "Warnaco Group Inc.: Chairman Wachner Has $11.1 Million Pay Package," *Wall Street Journal,* April 10, 1998, p. A-1; C. Pappas, "The Top 20 Best-paid Women in Corporate America," *Working Woman,* February 1998, p. 26; and "Linda Wachner," *Working Woman,* December 1996, pp. 107-108.
2. See, for instance, A. D. Stajkovic and F. Luthans, "A Meta-Analysis of the Effects of Organizational Behavioral Modification on Task Performance, 1975-95," *Academy of Management Journal,* October 1997, pp. 1122–49.
3. S. J. Becker, "Empirical Validation of Affect, Behavior, and Cognition as Distinct Components of Behavior," *Journal of Personality and Social Psychology,* May 1984, pp. 1191–205.
4. R. McGarvey, "Power of One," *Entrepreneur,* April 1995, p. 76.
5. P. P. Brooke Jr., D. W. Russell, and J. L. Price, "Discriminant Validation of Measures of Job Satisfaction, Job Involvement, and Organizational Commitment," *Journal of Applied Psychology,* May 1988, pp. 139–45.
6. J. W. Dean, Jr., P. Brandes, and R. Dharwadkar, "Organizational Cynicism," *Academy of Management Review,* April 1998, pp. 341–52.
7. I. Ajzen and M. Fishbein, *Understanding Attitudes and Predicting Behavior* (Upper Saddle River, NJ: Prentice Hall, 1980).
8. L. Festinger, *A Theory of Cognitive Dissonance* (Stanford, CA: Stanford University Press, 1957).
9. See, for example, R. C. Thompson and J. G. Hunt, "Inside the Black Box of Alpha, Beta, and Gamma Change: Using Cognitive Processing Model to Assess Attitude Structure," *Academy of Management Review,* October 1996, pp. 655–90.
10. J. B. Rotter, "Generalized Expectancies for Internal versus External Control of Reinforcement," *Psychological Monographs* 80, No. 609 (1966). See also, T. E. Becker, R. S. Billings, D. M. Eveleth, and N. L. Gilbert, "Foci and Bases of Employee Commitment: Implications for Job Performance," *Academy of Management Journal* 39, No. 2 (1996), pp. 464–82.
11. See, for example, J. B. Herman, "Are Situational Contingencies Limiting the Job Attitude–Job Performance Relationship?" *Organizational Behavior and Human Performance,* October 1973, pp. 208–24; M. M. Petty, G. W. McGee, and J. W. Cavender, "A Meta-Analysis of the Relationships between Individual Job Satisfaction and Individual Performance," *Academy of Management Review,* October 1984, pp. 712–21; C. N. Greene, "The Satisfaction–Performance Controversy," *Business Horizons,* February 1972, pp. 31–41; E. E. Lawler III, *Motivation and Organizations* (Monterey, CA: Brooks/Cole, 1973); A. H. Brayfield and W. H. Crockett, "Employee Attitudes and Employee Performance," *Psychological Bulletin,* September 1955, pp. 396–428; F. Herzberg, B. Mausner, R. O. Peterson, and D. F. Capwell, *Job Attitudes: Review of Research and Opinion* (Pittsburgh: Psychological Service of Pittsburgh, 1957); V. H. Vroom, *Work and Motivation* (New York: John Wiley & Sons, 1964); and G. P. Fournet, M. K. Distefano Jr., and M. W. Pryer, "Job Satisfaction: Issues and Problems," *Personnel Psychology,* Summer 1966, pp. 165–83.
12. Greene, "The Satisfaction–Performance Controversy"; Lawler, "Motivation and Organizations"; and Petty, McGee, and Cavender, "A Meta-Analysis of the Relationships between Individual Job Satisfaction and Individual Performance."
13. Rotter, "Generalized Expectancies for Internal versus External Control of Reinforcement"; Becker, Billings, and Gilbert, "Foci and Bases of Employee Commitment: Implications for Job Performance."
14. C. Ostroff, "The Relationship between Satisfaction, Attitudes, and Performance: An Organizational Level

Analysis," *Journal of Applied Psychology,* December 1992, pp. 963–74.
15. See, for example, W. Gallagher, "How We Become What We Are," *Atlantic Monthly,* September 1994, pp. 39–55.
16. See, for example, A. H. Buss, "Personality as Traits," *American Psychologist,* November 1989, pp. 1378–88. See also D. B. Turban and T. W. Dougherty, "Role of Protege Personality in Receipt of Mentoring and Career Success," *Academy of Management Journal* 37, No. 3 (1994), pp. 588–702.
17. S. P. Robbins, *Organizational Behavior: Concepts, Controversies, Applications,* 7th ed. (Upper Saddle River, NJ: Prentice Hall, 1996), p. 93.
18. I. B. Meyers, *Introduction to Type,* 6th ed. (Palo Alto, CA: Consulting Psychologists Press, Inc., 1998).
19. J. M. Digman, "Personality Structure: Emergence of the Five-Factor Model," in M. R. Rosenweig and L. W. Porter, eds., *Annual Review of Psychology,* vol. 41 (Palo Alto, CA.: Annual Reviews, 1990), pp. 417–40; O. P. John, "The Big Five Factor Taxonomy: Dimensions of Personality in the Natural Language and in Questionnaires," in L. A. Pervin, ed., *Handbook of Personality Theory and Research* (New York: Guilford Press, 1990), pp. 66–100; and M. K. Mount, M. R. Barrick, and J. P. Strauss, "Validity of Observer Ratings of the Big Five Personality Factors," *Journal of Applied Psychology,* April 1996, pp. 272–80.
20. See, for example, M. R. Barrick and M. K. Mount, "The Big Five Personality Dimensions and Job Performance: A Meta-Analysis," *Personnel Psychology* 44 (1991), pp. 1–26; and M. R. Barrick and M. K. Mount, "Autonomy as a Moderator of the Relationship between the Big Five Personality Dimensions and Job Performance," *Journal of Applied Psychology,* February 1993, pp. 111–18.
21. Barrick and Mount, "Autonomy as a Moderator of the Relationship between the Big Five Personality Dimensions and Job Performance."
22. This section is based on D. Goleman, *Emotional Intelligence* (New York: Bantam, 1995); J. D. Mayer and G. Geher, "Emotional Intelligence and Identification of Emotion," *Intelligence,* March–April 1996, pp. 89–113; J. Stuller, "EQ: Edging Toward Respectability," *Training,* June 1997, pp. 43–48; R. K. Cooper, "Applying Emotional Intelligence in the Workplace," *Training and Development,* December 1997, pp. 31–38; "HR Pulse: Emotional Intelligence," *HR Magazine,* January 1998, p. 19; M. Davies, L. Stankov, and R. D. Roberts, "Emotional Intelligence: In Search of an Elusive Construct," *Journal of Personality and Social Psychology,* October 1998, pp. 989–1015; and D. Goleman, *Working with Emotional Intelligence* (New York: Bantam, 1999).
23. J. Teresko, "The Magic of Common Sense," *Industry Week,* July 15, 1996, p. 21.
24. See, for instance, D. W. Organ and C. N. Greene, "Role Ambiguity, Locus of Control, and Work Satisfaction," *Journal of Applied Psychology,* February 1974, pp. 101–102; T. R. Mitchell, C. M. Smyser and S. E. Weed, "Locus of Control: Supervision and Work Satisfaction," *Academy of Management Journal,* September 1975, pp. 623–31; and J. Fierman, "What's Luck Got to Do with It?" *Fortune,* October 16, 1995, p. 149.
25. R. G. Vleeming, "Machiavellianism: A Preliminary Review," *Psychology Reports,* February 1979, pp. 295–310; see also J. Weber and G. McWilliams, "Cathy Abbott Is No Good Ol' Boy," *Business Week,* February 12, 1996, pp. 94–96; and R. D. Hof, K. Rebello, and P. Burrows, "Scott McNealy's Rising Sun," *Business Week,* January 22, 1996, pp. 68–73.
26. Based on J. Brockner, *Self-Esteem at Work* (Lexington, MA: Lexington Books, 1988), Chapters 1–4.
27. See K. Onstad, "No Jobs? No Problem!" *Canadian Business,* December 1995, p. 21; and J. Aley, "Wall Street's King Quant," *Fortune,* February 5, 1996, pp. 108–12.
28. T. Dalrymple, "Letting the Steam out of Self-Esteem," *Psychology Today,* September–October 1995, pp. 24–26.
29. M. Snyder, *Public Appearances/Private Realities: The Psychology of Self-Monitoring* (New York: W. H. Freeman, 1987).
30. Ibid.
31. See, for example, A. E. Sewer, "The Simplot Saga," *Fortune,* November 27, 1995, pp. 69–86.
32. R. N. Taylor and M. D. Dunnette, "Influence of Dogmatism, Risk-Taking Propensity, and Intelligence on Decision-Making Strategies for a Sample of Industrial Managers," *Journal of Applied Psychology,* August 1974, pp. 420–23.
33. I. L. Janis and L. Mann, *Decision Making: A Psychological Analysis of Conflict, Choice, and Commitment* (New York: Free Press, 1977).
34. N. Kogan and M. A. Wallach, "Group Risk Taking as a Function of Members' Anxiety and Defensiveness," *Journal of Personality,* March 1967, pp. 50–63.
35. J. L. Holland, *Making Vocational Choices: A Theory of Vocational Personalities and Work Environments,* 2nd ed. (Upper Saddle River, NJ: Prentice Hall, 1985).
36. See, for example, A. R. Spokane, "A Review of Research on Person-Environment Congruence in Holland's Theory of Careers," *Journal of Vocational Behavior,* June 1985, pp. 306–43; and D. Brown, "The Status of Holland's Theory of Career Choice," *Career Development Journal,* September 1987, pp. 13–23.
37. K. J. Jansen and A. Kristof-Brown, "Toward a Multi-Level Theory of Person-Environment Fit," *Academy of Management Proceedings from the Fifty-Eighth Annual Meeting of the Academy of Management,* San Diego, CA, August 7–12, 1998, pp. HR-FR1–FR-8.
38. See, for example, L. Brokaw, "Case in Point," *Inc.,* December 1995, pp. 88–92.
39. H. H. Kelley, "Attribution in Social Interaction," in E. Jones, et al., eds., *Behavior* (Morristown, NJ: General Learning Press, 1972).
40. See A. G. Miller and T. Lawson, "The Effect of an Informational Option on the Fundamental Attribution Error," *Personality and Social Psychology Bulletin,* June 1989, pp. 194–204.
41. J. M. Beyer, P. Chattopadhyay, E. George, W. H. Glick, and D. Pugliese, "The Selective Perception of Managers' Revisited," *Academy of Management Journal,* October 1997, pp. 716–37.
42. See, for example, L. Jussim, "Self-fulfilling Prophecies: A Theoretical and Integrative Review," *Psychological Review,* October 1986, pp. 429–45; and D. Eden, *Pygmalion in Management* (Lexington, MA: Lexington Books, 1990).
43. B. F. Skinner, *Contingencies of Reinforcement* (East Norwalk, CT: Appleton-Century-Crofts, 1971).

44. A. Bandura, *Social Learning Theory* (Upper Saddle River, NJ: Prentice Hall, 1977).
45. S. E. Asch, "Effects of Group Pressure upon the Modification and Distortion of Judgements," in H. Guetzkow, ed., *Groups, Leadership, and Men* (Pittsburgh: Carnegie Press, 1951), pp. 177–90.
46. Ibid.
47. See, for instance, E. J. Thomas and C. F. Fink, "Effects of Group Size," *Psychological Bulletin,* July 1963, pp. 371–84; and M. E. Shaw, *Group Dynamics: The Psychology of Small Group Behavior,* 3rd ed. (New York: McGraw-Hill, 1981).
48. See R. Albanese and D. D. Van Fleet, "Rational Behavior in Groups: The Free-Riding Tendency," *Academy of Management Review,* April 1985, pp. 244–55.
49. L. Berkowitz, "Group Standards, Cohesiveness, and Productivity," *Human Relations,* November 1954, pp. 509–19; and B. Mullen and C. Copper, "The Relation between Group Cohesiveness and Performance: An Integration," *Psychological Bulletin,* March 1994, pp. 210–17.
50. S. E. Seashore, *Group Cohesiveness in the Industrial Work Group* (Ann Arbor: University of Michigan, Survey Research Center, 1954).
51. The idea for this exercise came from J. Gandz and J. M. Howell, "Confronting Sex Role Stereotypes: The Janis/Jack Jerome Cases," *Organizational Behavior Teaching Review* 13, No. 4 (1988–1989), pp. 103–11.
52. C. Patton, "Working Woman 500, Anne Beiler, Chair and CEO, Auntie Anne's," *Working Woman,* June 1999, pp. 42–44.

Chapter 9

1. "Now That We're Not a Start-Up, How Do I Promote Teamwork?" *Inc.,* October 20, 1998, pp. 154–56.
2. C. Joinson, "Teams at Work," *HRMagazine,* May 1999, pp. 30–36.
3. See, for example, A. Edmondson, "Psychological Safety and Learning Behavior in Work Teams," *Administrative Science Quarterly,* June 1999, p. 350; D. W. Tjosvold, *Working Together to Get Things Done: Managing for Organizational Productivity* (Lexington, MA: Lexington Books, 1986); Tjosvold, *Organization: An Enduring Competitive Advantage* (New York: John Wiley & Sons, 1991); J. Lipnack and J. Stamps, *The TeamNet Factor* (Essex Junction, VT: Oliver Wright, 1993); and J. R. Katzenbach and D. K. Smith, *The Wisdom of Teams* (Boston: Harvard Business School Press, 1993); see also D. Richardson, "Teams Not Always the Best Way to Get Work Done," *HRNews,* August 1996, p. 11.
4. T. A. Stewart, "Telling Tales at BP Amoco," *Fortune,* June 7, 1999, pp. 220–24.
5. See, R. D. Banker, J. M. Field, R. G. Schroeder, and K. K. Sinha, "Impact of Work Teams on Manufacturing Performance: A Longitudinal Field Study," *Academy of Management Journal,* August 1996, pp. 867–90.
6. J. Mariotti, "A Company That Plays Together, Stays Together," *Industry Week,* March 19, 1999, p. 63; and M. A. Campion, and A. C. Higgs, "Design Work Teams to Increase Productivity and Satisfaction," *HRMagazine,* October 1995, pp. 101–107.
7. B. L. Kirkman and B. Rosen, "Beyond Self-Management: Antecedents and Consequences of Team Empowerment," *Academy of Management Journal,* February 1999, pp. 58–74; S. P. Robbins, *Organizational Behavior: Concepts, Controversies, Applications,* 8th ed (Upper Saddle River, NJ: Prentice Hall, 1998), p. 347. See also, G. M. Spreitzer, "Psychological Empowerment in the Workplace: Dimensions, Measurement, and Validation," *Academy of Management Journal* 38, No. 5 (1995), pp. 1442–65.
8. R. Taraschi, "Cutting the Ties That Bind," *Training and Development,* November 1998, pp. 12–14; B. W. Tuckman and M. A. C. Jensen, "Stages of Small-Group Development Revisited," *Group and Organizational Studies* 2, No. 3 (1977), pp. 419–27; and P. Buhler, "Group Membership," *Supervision,* May 1994, pp. 8–10.
9. T. Bragg, "Turn Around an Ineffective Team," *IIE Solutions,* May 1999, pp. 49–51; L. N. Jewell, and H. J. Reitz, *Group Effectiveness in Organizations* (Glenview, IL: Scott, Foresman, 1981); and M. Kaeter, "Repotting Mature Work Teams," *Training,* April 1994, pp. 54–56.
10. See, for instance, V. I. Sessa, "Using Perspective Taking to Manage Conflict and Affect in Teams," *Journal of Applied Behavioral Science,* March 1996, pp. 110–15.
11. Information for this section is based on Katzenbach and Smith, *The Wisdom of Teams,* pp. 21, 45, 85; and D. C. Kinlaw, *Developing Superior Work Teams* (Lexington, MA: Lexington Books, 1991), pp. 3–21.
12. M. B. Nelson, "Learning What 'Team' Really Means," *Newsweek,* July 19, 1999, p. 55.
13. C. Joinson, "Teams at Work," p. 32.
14. D. Richardson, "Teams Not Always the Best Way to Get Work Done," *HR News,* August 1996, p. 11; and "Where Teams Trip Up," *Inc.,* November 1995, p. 94.
15. H. Rothman, "The Power of Empowerment," *Nation's Business,* June 1993, pp. 49–51.
16. P. W. Mulvey, J. F. Veiga, and P. M. Elsass, "When Teammates Raise a White Flag," *Academy of Management Executives* 10, No. 1 (1996), pp. 40–50; J. H. Shonk, *Team-Based Organizations* (Homewood, IL: Business One Irwin, 1992); and M. A. Verespej, "When Workers Get New Roles," *Industry Week,* February 3, 1992, p. 11.
17. E. Hill Updike, D. Woodruff, and L. Armstrong, "Honda's Civic Lesson," *Business Week,* September 18, 1995, p. 71.
18. See, for example, C. J. Fausnaugh, "High-Performing Self-Managed Work Teams: A Comparison of Theory to Practice," *Management Learning,* June 1999, pp. 254–55; R. C. Ford and M. D. Fottler, "Empowerment: A Matter of Degree," *Academy of Management Executives* 9, No. 3 (1995), pp. 21–28; D. Barry, "Managing the Bossless Team," *Organizational Dynamics* 1 (Summer 1991), pp. 31–47; and J. R. Barker, "Tightening the Iron Cage: Concertive Control in Self-Managing Teams," *Administrative Science Quarterly,* September 1993, pp. 408–37.
19. For an interesting review of self-managed team behavior when evaluating one another, see C. P. Neck, M. L. Connerly, C. A. Zuniga, and S. Goel, "Family Therapy Meets Self-Managing Teams: Explaining Self-Managing Team Performance Through Team Member Perception," *Journal of Applied Behavioral Science,* June 1999, pp. 245–59; G. A. Neuman, S. H. Wagner, and N. D. Christiansen, "The

Relationship between Work-Team Personality Composition and the Job Performance of Teams," *Group & Organization Management,* March 1999, pp. 28–45; and V. U. Druskat and S. B. Wolff, "Effects and Timing of Developmental Peer Appraisals in Self-Managing Work Groups," *Journal of Applied Psychology,* February 1999, pp. 58–74.
20. See R. C. Liden, S. J. Wayne, and L. Bradway, "Connections Make the Difference," *HRMagazine,* February 1996, pp. 73–79; R. McGarvey, "More Power to Them," *Entrepreneur,* February 1995, pp. 73–75; J. Hillkirk, "Self-Directed Work Teams Give TI a Life," *USA Today,* December 20, 1993, p. B8; and M. A. Verespej, "Worker-Managers," *Industry Week,* May 16, 1994, p. 30.
21. See, for example, K. Labich, "Elite Teams Get the Job Done," *Fortune,* February 19, 1996, pp. 90–99; Sherman, "Secrets of HP's 'Muddled' Team"; and B. Dumaine, "The Trouble with Teams," *Fortune,* September 5, 1994, p. 92.
22. G. Taninecz, "Team Players," *Industry Week,* July 15, 1996, pp. 28–31; S. S. Brooks, "Managing Horizontal Revolution," *HRMagazine,* June 1995, pp. 52–58; and Lipnack and Stamps, *The TeamNet Factor,* pp. 14–17.
23. M. Loeb, "Empowerment That Pays Off," *Fortune,* March 20, 1995, p. 145.
24. D. R. Denison, S. L. Hart, and J. A. Kahn, "From Chimneys to Cross-Functional Teams: Developing and Validating a Diagnostic Model," *Academy of Management Journal,* August 1996, pp. 1005–23; and J. R. Katzenbach and J. A. Santamaria, "Firing up the Front Line," *Harvard Business Review,* May/June 1999, pp. 107–17.
25. T. B. Kinni, "Boundary-Busting Teamwork," *Industry Week,* March 21, 1994, pp. 72–78.
26. S. B. Eom, and C. K. Lee, "Virtual Teams: An Information Age Opportunity for Mobilizing Hidden Manpower," *SAM Advanced Management Journal,* Spring 1999, pp. 12–16; and A. M. Townsend, S. M. DeMarie, and A. R. Hendrickson, "Are You Ready for Virtual Teams?" *HRMagazine,* September 1996, pp. 123–26.
27. W. R. Pape, "Group Insurance," *Inc. Technology,* July 1997, pp. 29–31.
28. See M. A. Huselid and B. E. Becker, "The Impact of High Performance Work Systems, Implementation Effectiveness, and Alignment with Strategy on Shareholder Wealth," *Academy of Management Best paper Proceedings,* L. N. Dosier and J. B. Keys, eds., Boston, MA, August 8–13, 1997, pp. 144–47; M. R. Manning, and P. J. Schmidt, "Building Effective Work Teams: A Quick Exercise Based on a Scavenger Hunt," *Journal of Management Education,* August 1995, pp. 392–98; D. Vinokur-Kaplan, "Treatment Teams That Work (and Those That Don't): An Application of Hackman's Group Effectiveness Model to Interdisciplinary Teams in Psychiatric Hospitals," *Journal of Applied Behavior Science,* September 1995, pp. 303–27; B. Nelson, "Ways to Foster Team Spirit," *HRMagazine,* November 1995, pp. 47–50; E. Sundstrom, K. P. DeMeuse, and D. Futrell, "Work Teams," *American Psychologist,* February 1990, p. 120; C. E. Larson and F. M. J. LaFasto, *Teamwork* (Newbury Park, CA: Sage Publications, 1992); J. R. Hackman, ed., *Groups That Work (and Those That Don't)* (San Francisco: Jossey-Bass, 1990), and D. W. Tjosvold and M. M. Bass, *Leading the Team Organization* (Lexington, MA: Lexington Books, 1991).
29. M. A. Verespej, "Lessons from the Best," *Industry Week,* February 16, 1998, pp. 28–36.
30. "Job Morphing," *Wall Street Journal,* June 29, 1995, p. A1.
31. K. T. Dirks, "The Effects of Interpersonal Trust on Work Group Performance," *Journal of Applied Psychology,* June 1999, pp. 445–55.
32. Larson and LaFasto, *Teamwork,* p. 75.
33. See, for example, "Effects of Distribution of Feedback in Work Groups," *Academy of Management Journal* 37, No. 3 (1994), pp. 635–41.
34. Dumaine, "The Trouble with Teams," *Fortune.*
35. D. Harrington-Mackin, *The Team Building Tool Kit* (New York: AMACOM, 1994), p. 53.
36. See, for instance, B. L. Kirkman and D. L. Shapiro, "The Impact of Cultural Values on Employee Resistance to Teams: Toward a Model of Globalized Self-Managing Work Team Effectiveness," *Academy of Management Review,* July 1997, pp. 730–57.
37. T. D. Shellhardt, "To Be a Star among Equals, Be a Team Player," *Wall Street Journal,* April 20, 1994, p. B1.
38. Ibid.
39. Based on C. Margerison and D. McCann, *Team Management: Practical New Approaches* (London: Mercury Books, 1990).
40. See, for instance, T. A. Stewart, "The Great Conundrum—You vs. the Team," *Fortune,* November 25, 1996, p. 165.
41. Based on C. Margerison and D. McCann, *Team Management: Practical New Approaches.*
42. "Teaming for Success," *Training,* January 1994, p. 541.
43. See, for example, M. Cianni and D. Wnuck, "Individual Growth and Team Enhancement: Moving Toward a New Model of Career Development," *Academy of Management Executive,* February 2, 1997, pp. 105–15.
44. Information in this section is based on Kaeter, "Repotting Mature Work Teams." See also K. Dow Scott and A. Townsend, "Teams: Why Some Succeed and Others Fail," *HRMagazine,* August 1994, pp. 62–67.
45. D. C. Kinlaw, *Developing Superior Work Teams* (Lexington, MA: Lexington Books, 1991), p. 43.
46. B. Krone, "Total Quality Management: An American Odyssey," *Bureaucrat,* Fall 1990, p. 37.
47. M. A. Verespej, "Allegiance HealthCare Corporation," *Industry Week,* October 19, 1998, pp. 34–36; *Profiles in Quality: Blueprints for Action from 50 Leading Companies* (Boston: Allyn & Bacon, 1991), p. 37.
48. M. A. Verespej, "Allegiance HealthCare Corporation," p. 36.
49. See the review of the literature in S. E. Jackson, V. K. Stone, and E.B. Alvarez, "Socialization Amidst Diversity: The Impact of Demographics on Work Team Oldtimers and Newcomers," in L. L. Cummings and B. M. Staw, eds., *Research in Organizational Behavior,* Vol. 15 (Greenwich, CT: JAI Press, 1993), p. 64.
50. J. N. Choi and M. U. Kim, "The Organizational Application of Groupthink and Its Limitations in Organizations," *Journal of Applied Psychology,* April 1999, pp. 297–306.
51. J. W. Bishop and K. D. Scott, "How Commitment Affects Team Performance," *HRMagazine,* February 1997, pp. 107–11; and M. Mayo, J. C. Pastor, and J. R. Meindl, "The

Effects of Group Heterogeneity on the Self-Perceived Efficacy of Group Leaders," *Leadership Quarterly,* Summer 1996, pp. 265–84.

52. J. E. McGrath, *Groups: Interaction and Performance* (Upper Saddle River, NJ: Prentice Hall, 1984).
53. L. H. Pelled, K. M. Eisenhardt, and K. R. Xin, "Exploring the Black Box: An Analysis of Work Group Diversity, Conflict, and Performance," *Administrative Science Quarterly,* March 1999, pp. 1–28.
54. This idea is proposed in S. E. Jackson, V. K. Stone, and E. B. Alvarez, "Socialization Amidst Diversity," p. 68. See also A. B. Drexler and R. Forrester, "Interdependence: The Crux of Teamwork," *HRMagazine,* September 1998, pp. 52–61.
55. Case based on T. Feare, "Speeding HP Orders 'Out the Door in Four,'" *Modern Materials Management,* May 1999, pp. 40–43.

Chapter 10

1. Opening vignette based on K. Hein, "CEO's Speak," *Incentive,* May 1999, pp. 26–31; M. Larson, "Lantech's Kaizen Diary: Monday Through Friday," *Quality,* June 1998, p. 40; "Success of 'Kaizen' Approach Brings New Jobs to Lantech," *Business First: Weekly Business Newspaper of Greater Louisville,* February 8, 1998, p. 1; V. Alonzio, "Recognition? Who Needs It?" *Sales and Marketing Management,* February 1997, pp. 26–27; and P. Nulty, "Incentive Pay Can Be Crippling," *Fortune,* November 13, 1995, p. 235.
2. R. Katerberg and G. J. Blau, "An Examination of Level and Direction of Effort and Job Performance," *Academy of Management Journal,* June 1983, pp. 249–57.
3. A. Maslow, *Motivation and Personality* (New York: Harper & Row, 1954).
4. J. W. Marcum, "Maslow on Management," *National Productivity Review,* Summer 1999, p. 82; R. Zemke, "Maslow for a New Millennium," *Training,* December 1998, pp. 54–58; and M. Henricks, "Motivating Force," *Entrepreneur,* December 1995, pp. 70–72.
5. See, for example, E. E. Lawler III and J. L. Suttle, "A Causal Correlational Test of the Need Hierarchy Concept," *Organizational Behavior and Human Performance,* April 1972, pp. 265–87; and D. T. Hall and K. E. Nongaim, "An Examination of Maslow's Need Hierarchy in an Organizational Setting," *Organizational Behavior and Human Performance,* February 1968, pp. 12–35.
6. D. McGregor, *The Human Side of Enterprise* (New York: McGraw-Hill, 1960).
7. "The Way We Were," *Management Today,* June 1998, pp. 111–12.
8. F. Herzberg, B. Mausner, and B. Snyderman, *The Motivation to Work* (New York: John Wiley & Sons, 1959); and F. Herzberg, *The Managerial Choice: To Be Effective or To Be Human,* rev. ed. (Salt Lake City: Olympus, 1982).
9. See D. Fenn, "Redesigning Work," *Inc.,* June 1999, p. 82. For another viewpoint on satisfaction and the effect intelligence has on it, see Y. Ganzach, "Intelligence and Job Satisfaction," *Academy of Management Journal,* October 1998, pp. 526–39.
10. See also "Uninspiring Leadership," *Industry Week,* February 1, 1999, p. 11.
11. See, for instance, M. F. Gordon, N. M. Pryor, and B. V. Harris, "An Examination of Scaling Bias in Herzberg's Theory of Job Satisfaction," *Organizational Behavior and Human Performance,* February 1974, pp. 106–21; E. A. Locke and R. J. Whiting, "Sources of Satisfaction and Dissatisfaction among Solid Waste Management Employees," *Journal of Applied Psychology,* April 1974, pp. 145–56; and J. B. Miner, *Theories of Organizational Behavior* (Hinsdale, IL: Dryden Press, 1980), pp. 76–105.
12. D. C. McClelland, *The Achieving Society* (New York: Van Nostrand Reinhold, 1961); J. W. Atkinson and J. O. Raynor, *Motivation and Achievement* (Washington, DC: Winston, 1974); and D. C. McClelland, *Power: The Inner Experience* (New York: Free Press, 1969).
13. McClelland, *The Achieving Society.*
14. K. R. Thompson, W. A. Hochwarter, and N. J. Mathys, "Stretch Targets: What Makes Them Effective," *Academy of Management Executive,* August 1997, pp. 48–60.
15. J. S. Adams, "Inequity in Social Exchanges," in L. Berkowitz, ed., *Advances in Experimental Social Psychology,* vol. 2 (New York: Academic Press, 1965), pp. 267–300.
16. P. S. Goodman, "An Examination of Referents Used in the Evaluation of Pay," *Organizational Behavior and Human Performance,* October 1974, pp. 170–95; S. Ronen, "Equity Perception in Multiple Comparisons: A Field Study," *Human Relations,* April 1986, pp. 333–46; R. W. School, E. A. Cooper, and J. F. McKenna, "Referent Effects on Behavioral and Attitudinal Outcomes," *Personnel Psychology,* Spring 1987, pp. 113–27; and C. T. Kulik and M. L. Ambrose, "Personal and Situational Determinants of Referent Choice," *Academy of Management Review,* April 1992, pp. 212–37.
17. D. C. McClelland and D. G. Winter, *Motivating Economic Achievement* (New York: Free Press, 1969).
18. McClelland, *Power;* D. C. McClelland and D. H. Burnham, "Power Is the Great Motivator," *Harvard Business Review,* March–April 1976, pp. 100–10.
19. "McClelland: An Advocate of Power," *International Management,* July 1975, pp. 27–29.
20. D. Miron and D. C. McClelland, "The Impact of Achievement Motivation Training on Small Businesses," *California Management Review,* Summer 1979, pp. 13–28.
21. See P. P. Shah, "Who Are Employees' Social Referents? Using a Network Perspective to Determine Referent Others," *Academy of Management Journal,* June 1998, pp. 249–68.
22. P. S. Goodman and A. Friedman, "An Examination of Adams' Theory of Inequity," *Administrative Science Quarterly,* September 1971, pp. 271–88.
23. See, for example, M. R. Carrell, "A Longitudinal Field Assessment of Employee Perceptions of Equitable Treatment," *Organizational Behavior and Human Performance,* February 1978, pp. 108–18; R. G. Lord and J. A. Hohenfeld, "Longitudinal Field Assessment of Equity Effects on the Performance of Major League Baseball Players," *Journal of Applied Psychology,* February 1979, pp. 19–26; and J. E. Dittrich and M. R. Carrell, "Organizational Equity Perceptions, Employee Job Satisfaction, and Department Absence and Turnover Rates," *Organizational Behavior and Human Performance,* August 1979, pp. 97–132.
24. P. S. Goodman, "Social Comparison Process in Organizations," in B. M. Staw and G. R. Salancik, eds., *New*

Directions in Organizational Behavior (Chicago: St. Clair, 1977), pp. 97–132.

25. See J. R. Hackman and G. R. Oldham, "Motivation through the Design of Work: Test of a Theory," *Organizational Behavior and Human Performance,* August 1976, pp. 250–79; Y. Fried and G. R. Ferris, "The Validity of the Job Characteristics Model: A Review and Meta-Analysis," *Personnel Psychology,* Summer 1987, pp. 287–322; S. J. Zaccaro and E. F. Stone, "Incremental Validity of an Empirically Based Measure of Job Characteristics," *Journal of Applied Psychology,* May 1988, pp. 245–52; and R. W. Renn and R. J. Vandenberg, "The Critical Psychological States: An Under-represented Component in Job Characteristics Model Research," *Journal of Management,* February 1995, pp. 279–303.
26. J. R. Hackman, "Work Design," in J. R. Hackman and J. L. Suttle, eds., *Improving Life at Work* (Glenview, IL: Scott, Foresman, 1977), p. 129.
27. General support for the JCM is reported in Fried and Ferris, "The Validity of the Job Characteristics Model."
28. Ibid.; and "Small-Business Absenteeism Cost," *USA Today,* June 1, 1999, p. A1.
29. See "Job Characteristics Theory of Work Redesign," in J. B. Miner, *Theories of Organizational Behavior* (Hinsdale, IL: Dryden Press, 1980), pp. 231–66; Fried and Ferris, "The Validity of the Job Characteristics Model"; and Zaccaro and Stone, "Incremental Validity of an Empirically Based Measure of Job Characteristics."
30. See R. B. Dunham, "Measurement and Dimensionality of Job Characteristics," *Journal of Applied Psychology,* August 1976, pp. 404–409; J. L. Pierce and R. B. Dunham, "Task Design: A Literature Review," *Academy of Management Review,* January 1976, pp. 83–97; D. M. Rousseau, "Technological Differences in Job Characteristics, Employee Satisfaction, and Motivation: A Synthesis of Job Design Research and Sociotechnical Systems Theory," *Organizational Behavior and Human Performance,* October 1977, pp. 18–42.
31. All of the sources in note 51; and Y. Fried and G. R. Ferris, "The Dimensionality of Job Characteristics: Some Neglected Issues," *Journal of Applied Psychology,* August 1986, pp. 419–26.
32. R. B. Tiegs, L. E. Tetrick, and Y. Fried, "Growth Need Strength and Context Satisfactions as Moderators of the Relations of the Job Characteristics Model," *Journal of Management,* September 1992, pp. 575–93.
33. C. A. O'Reilly and D. F. Caldwell, "Informational Influence as a Determinant of Perceived Task Characteristics and Job Satisfaction," *Journal of Applied Psychology,* April 1979, pp. 157–65; R. V. Montagno, "The Effects of Comparison Others and Prior Experience on Response to Task Design," *Academy of Management Journal,* June 1985, pp. 491–98; and P. C. Bottger and I. K. H. Chew, "The Job Characteristics Model and Growth Satisfaction: Main Effects of Assimilation of Work Experience and Context Satisfaction," *Human Relations,* June 1986, pp. 575–94.
34. Fried and Ferris, "The Validity of the Job Characteristics Model"; and Hackman, "Work Design," pp. 132–33.
35. V. H. Vroom, *Work and Motivation* (New York: John Wiley & Sons, 1964).
36. See, for example, H. G. Henneman III and D. P. Schwab, "Evaluation of Research on Expectancy Theory Prediction of Employee Performance," *Psychological Bulletin,* July 1972, pp. 1–9; and L. Reinharth and M. Wahba, "Expectancy Theory as a Predictor of Work Motivation, Effort Expenditure, and Job Performance," *Academy of Management Journal,* September 1975, pp. 502–37.
37. See, for example, V. H. Vroom, "Organizational Choice: A Study of Pre- and Post-decision Processes," *Organizational Behavior and Human Performance,* April 1966, pp. 212–25; and L. W. Porter and E. E. Lawler III, *Managerial Attitudes and Performance* (Homewood, IL: Richard D. Irwin, 1968).
38. Among academicians these three variables are typically referred to as valence, instrumentality, and expectancy, respectively.
39. See T. A. Wright and R. Cropanzano, "Well-Being, Satisfaction and Job Performance: Another Look at the Happy/Productive Worker Thesis," *Academy of Management Best Paper Proceedings,* Boston, MA, L. N. Dosier and J. B. Keys, eds., August 8–13, 1997, pp. 364–69.
40. R. S. Fudge and J. S. Schlacter, "Motivating Employees to Act Ethically: An Expectancy Approach," *Journal of Business Ethics,* February 1999, pp. 295–304.
41. This four-step discussion was adapted from K. F. Taylor, "A Valence-Expectancy Approach to Work Motivation," *Personnel Practice Bulletin,* June 1974, pp. 142–48.
42. See also, N. H. Leonard, L. L. Beauvais, and R. W. School, "A Self-Concept–Based Model of Work Motivation," in D. P. Moore, ed., *Best Papers Proceedings: Academy of Management,* Vancouver, British Columbia, Canada, August 6–9, 1995, pp. 322–26.
43. See, for instance, M. Siegall, "The Simplistic Five: An Integrative Framework for Teaching Motivation," *Organizational Behavior Teaching Review* 12, No. 4 (1987–1988), pp. 141–43.
44. For an interesting application, see D. Lee-Ross, "Attitudes and Work Motivation of Subgroups of Seasonal Hotel Workers," *The Service Industries Journal,* June 1995, pp. 295–413.
45. See, for instance, J. L. Xie and G. Johns, "Job Scope and Stress: Can Job Scope Be Too High?" *Academy of Management Journal* 38, No. 5 (1995), pp. 1288–309.
46. J. Lynn, "Zap," *Entrepreneur,* December 1998, p. 36; "The Value of Flexibility," *Inc.,* April 1996, p. 114; and B. J. Wixom Jr., "Recognizing People in a World of Change," *HRMagazine,* June 1995, p. 65.
47. I. Harpaz, "The Importance of Work Goals: An International Perspective," *Journal of International Business Studies,* First Quarter 1990, pp. 75–93.
48. S. Shellenbarger, "Enter the 'New Hero': A Boss Who Knows You Have a Life," *Wall Street Journal,* May 8, 1996, p. B1.
49. G. Hofstede, "Motivation, Leadership, and Organizations: Do American Theories Apply Abroad?" *Organizational Dynamics,* Summer 1980, p. 55.
50. D. H. B. Walsh, F. Luthens, and S. M. Sommer, "Organizational Behavior Modification Goes to Russia: Replicating an Experimental Analysis across Cultures and Tasks," *Journal of Organizational Behavior Management,* Fall 1993, pp. 15–35; and J. R. Baum, J. D. Olian, M. Erez, and E. R. Schnell, "Nationality and Work Role Interactions: A Cultural Contrast of Israel and U.S. Entrepreneurs' versus Managers' Needs," *Journal of Business Venturing,* November 1993, pp. 499–512.

51. See, for instance, J. K. Giacobbe-Miller and D. J. Miller, "A Comparison of U.S. and Russian Pay Allocation Decisions and Distributive Justice Judgements," in Moore, ed., *Best Papers Proceedings: Academy of Management,* pp. 177–81.
52. A. Ignatius, "Now If Ms. Wong Insults a Customer, She Gets an Award," *Wall Street Journal,* January 24, 1989, p. A1.
53. R. K. Abbott, "Performance-Based Flex: A Tool for Managing Total Compensation Costs," *Compensation and Benefits Review,* March–April 1993, pp. 18–21; J. R. Schuster and P. K. Zingheim, "The New Variable Pay: Key Design Issues," *Compensation and Benefits Review,* March–April 1993, pp. 27–34; C. R. Williams and L. P. Livingstone, "Another Look at the Relationship between Performance and Voluntary Turnover," *Academy of Management Journal,* April 1994, pp. 269–98; and A. M. Dickinson and K. L. Gillette, "A Comparison of the Effects on Productivity: Piece Rate Pay versus Base Pay Plus Incentives," *Journal of Organizational Behavior Management,* Spring 1994, pp. 3–82.
54. See, for example, D. Fenn, "Compensation: Bonuses That Make Sense," *Inc.* March 1996, p. 95; J. H. Sheridan, "Yes to Team Incentives," *Industry Week,* March 4, 1996, p. 64; and H. N. Altmansberger and M. J. Wallace Jr., "Strategic Use of Goalsharing at Corning," *ACA Journal,* Winter 1995, pp. 64–71.
55. D. A. DeCenzo and S. P. Robbins, *Human Resource Management,* 6th ed. (New York: John Wiley & Sons, 1999), p. 116.
56. G. Grib and S. O'Donnell, "Pay Plans That Reward Employee Achievement," *HRMagazine,* July 1995, pp. 49–50.
57. F. Luthans and A. D. Stajkovic, "Reinforce for Performance: The Need to Go Beyond Pay and Even Rewards," *Academy of Management Executive,* May 1999, pp. 49–56.
58. "Consider Converting Merit Pay Raises to Other Rewards," *Financial Executive,* May/June 1999, p. 8.
59. "Compensation: Sales Managers as Team Players," *Inc.,* August 1994, p. 102.
60. D. Fenn, "Compensation: Goal-Driven Incentives," *Inc.,* August 1996, p. 91; and M. A. Verespej, "More Value for Compensation," *Industry Week,* June 17, 1996, p. 20.
61. S. Overman, "Saturn Teams Working and Profiting," *HRMagazine,* March 1995, p. 72.
62. D. J. Cira and E. R. Benjamin, "Competency-Based Pay: A Concept in Evolution," *Compensation and Benefits Review,* September/October 1998, p. 22.
63. M. E. Lattoni and A. Mercier, "Developing Competency-Based Organizations and Pay Systems," *Focus: A Review of Human Resource Management Issues in Canada* (Calgary, Canada: Towers Perrin, Summer 1994), p. 18.
64. Ibid.
65. S. W. Kelley, "Discretion and the Service Employee," *Journal of Retailing,* Spring 1993, pp. 104–26; S. S. Brooks, "Noncash Ways to Compensate Employees," *HRMagazine,* April 1994, pp. 38–43; and S. Greengard, "Leveraging a Low-Wage Work Force," *Personnel Journal,* January 1995, pp. 90–102.
66. "Raise Those Raises," *Psychology Today,* May/June 1999, p. 15. See also T. R. Mitchell and A. E. Mickel, "The Meaning of Money: An Individual-Difference Perspective," *Academy of Management Review,* June 1999, pp. 568–78.
67. "Pay Raises Are Not the Only Retention Tool," *HRMagazine,* April 1999, p. 28; "Reaching for the Top Shelf," *Canadian Business,* January 16, 1998, p. 67.
68. R. McGarvey, "Fire 'Em Up," *Entrepreneur,* March 1996, pp. 76–79.
69. C. Yang, A. T. Palmer, and A. Cuneo, "Low Wage Lessons," *Business Week,* November 11, 1996, pp. 108–116; and R. Henkoff, "Finding, Training, and Keeping the Best Service Workers," *Fortune,* October 5, 1994, pp. 110–22.
70. For an interesting perspective on this issue, see G. Dessler, "How to Earn Your Employees' Commitment," *Academy of Management Executive,* May 1999, pp. 58–66.
71. K. A. Dolan, "When Money Isn't Enough," *Forbes,* November 18, 1996, pp. 165, 168.
72. G. Fuchsberg, "Parallel Lines," *Wall Street Journal,* April 21, 1993, p. R4; and A. Penzias, "New Paths to Success," *Fortune,* June 12, 1995, pp. 90–94.
73. See, for instance, A. Saltzman, "Family Friendliness," *U.S. News & World Report,* February 22, 1993, pp. 59–66; M. A. Verespej, "People-First Policies," *Industry Week,* June 21, 1993, p. 20; and D. Stamps, "Taming Time with Flexible Work," *Training,* May 1995, pp. 60–66.
74. L. Daniel, "Feds and Families," *Government Executive,* April 1999, 41–46; and R. B. Durham, J. L. Pierce, and M. B. Castaneda, "Alternative Work Schedules: Two Field Experiments," *Personnel Psychology,* Summer 1987, pp. 215–42.
75. L. B. Ward, "If It's Friday, This Might Be Your Flex-Time Day Off," *New York Times,* March 31, 1996, p. F11.
76. M. F. J. Martens, F. J. N Nijhuis, M. P. J. Van Boxtel, and J. A. Knottnerus, "Flexible Work Schedules and Mental and Physical Health. A Study of a Working Population with NonTraditional Working Hours," *Journal of Organizational Behavior,* January 1999, pp. 35–46; and A. Shanley and W. Joel, "Assuring Alertness on the Job," *Chemical Engineering,* May 1999, p. 107.
77. A. R. Hochschild, "When Work Becomes Home and Home Becomes Work," *California Management Review,* Summer 1997, p. 85.
78. K. B. Hignite, "Hip Benefits," *Association Management,* February 1999, pp. 47–51; D. R. Dalton and D. J. Mesch, "The Impact of Flexible Scheduling on Employee Attendance and Turnover," *Administrative Science Quarterly,* June 1990, pp. 370–87; and K. S. Kush and L. K. Stroh, "Flextime: Myth or Reality?" *Business Horizons,* September–October 1994, p. 53.
79. Kush and Stroh, "Flextime."
80. Solomon, "Job Sharing," p. 90.
81. "Teaming up to Manage," *Working Woman,* September 1993, pp. 31–32.
82. S. Shellenbarger, "Two People, One Job: It Can Really Work," *Wall Street Journal,* December 7, 1994, p. B1.
83. D. C. D'Angelo, "Lifestyles," *Pennsylvania CPA Journal,* Spring 1999, pp. 16, 18; "Job-Sharing: Widely Offered, Little Used," *Training,* November 1994, p. 12.
84. Shellenbarger, "Two People, One Job."
85. See, for example, L. Grensing-Pophal, "Employing the Best People from Afar," *Workforce,* March 1997, pp. 30–38.
86. C. L. Dannhauser, "Who's in the Home Office?" *American Demographics,* June 1999, p. 51.

87. See, for instance, C. Keil, "Boundaryless Work Arrangements at Ceridan Employer Services," *Employment Relations Today,* Spring 1999, pp. 13–27; and T. Greene, "American Express: Don't Leave Home to Go to Work," *Network World,* March 8, 1999, p. 25.
88. Adapted from P. LaBarre, "Lighten Up!" *Industry Week,* February 5, 1996, p. 53.
89. V. Alonzo, "An Incentive to Embrace Family Values," *Sales and Sales Marketing Management,* July 1999, pp. 28–30.

Chapter 11

1. M. Ballon, "Extreme Managing," *Inc.,* July 1998, pp. 60–72; "Jack's Recipe," *Inc.,* July 1998, p. 63; and R. Ruggless, "D. L. Rogers Group," *Nation's Restaurant News,* January 1998, pp. 66–68.
2. S. Marino, "The Difference Between Managing and Leading," *Industry Week,* June 7, 1999, p. 10; N. Tichy and C. DeRose, "Roger Enrico's Master Class," *Fortune,* November 27, 1995, pp. 105–106.
3. J. Mariotti, "Leadership Matters," *Industry Week,* March 16, 1998, p. 70.
4. See S. A. Kirkpatrick and E. A. Locke, "Leadership: Do Traits Matter?" *Academy of Management Executive,* May 1991, pp. 48–60. See also M. D. Mumford, T. L. Gessner, M. S. Connelly, J. A. O'Connor, and T. C. Clifton, "Leadership and Destructive Acts: Individual and Situational Influences," *Leadership Quarterly 4,* No. 2 (1993), pp. 115–47.
5. S. Sherman, "How Tomorrow's Best Leaders Are Learning Their Stuff," *Fortune,* November 27, 1995, pp. 90–102.
6. Ibid.
7. R. J. Grossman, "Heirs Unapparent," *HRMagazine,* February 1999, pp. 36–44; and W. C. Byham, "Grooming Next Millennium Leaders," *HRMagazine,* February 1999, pp. 46–50.
8. K. Lewin and R. Lippitt, "An Experimental Approach to the Study of Autocracy and Democracy: A Preliminary Note," *Sociometry* 1 (1938), pp. 292–300; K. Lewin, "Field Theory and Experiment in Social Psychology: Concepts and Methods," *American Journal of Sociology* 44 (1939), pp. 868–96; K. Lewin, R. Lippitt, and R. K. White, "Patterns of Aggressive Behavior in Experimentally Created Social Climates," *Journal of Social Psychology* 10 (1939), pp. 271–301; and R. Lippitt, "An Experimental Study of the Effect of Democratic and Authoritarian Group Atmospheres," *University of Iowa Studies in Child Welfare* 16 (1940), pp. 43–95.
9. B. M. Bass, *Stodgill's Handbook of Leadership* (New York: Free Press, 1981), pp. 298–99.
10. R. Tannenbaum and W. H. Schmidt, "How to Choose a Leadership Pattern," *Harvard Business Review,* May–June 1973, pp. 162–80.
11. R. M. Stodgill and A. E. Coons, eds., *Leader Behavior: Its Description and Measurement,* Research Monograph No. 88 (Columbus: Ohio State University, Bureau of Business Research, 1951). For a more recent literature review of the Ohio State research, see S. Kerr, C. A. Schriesheim, C. J. Murphy, and R. M. Stodgill, "Toward a Contingency Theory of Leadership Based upon the Consideration and Initiating Structure Literature," *Organizational Behavior and Human Performance,* August 1974, pp. 62–82; and B. M. Fisher, "Consideration and Initiating Structure and Their Relationships with Leader Effectiveness: A Meta-Analysis," in F. Hoy, ed., *Proceedings of the 48th Annual Academy of Management Conference* (Anaheim, Calif.: 1988), pp. 201–205.
12. R. Kahn and D. Katz, "Leadership Practices in Relation to Productivity and Morale," in D. Cartwright and A. Zander, eds., *Group Dynamics: Research and Theory,* 2nd ed. (Elmsford, NY: Pow, Paterson, 1960).
13. R. R. Blake and J. S. Mouton, *The Managerial Grid III* (Houston: Gulf Publishing, 1984).
14. L. L. Larson, J. G. Hunt, and R. N. Osborn, "The Great Hi-Hi Leader Behavior Myth: A Lesson from Occam's Razor," *Academy of Management Journal,* December 1976, pp. 628–41; and P. C. Nystrom, "Managers and the Hi-Hi Leader Myth," *Academy of Management Journal,* June 1978, pp. 325–31.
15. See, for example, "The 3-D Theory of Leadership," in W. J. Reddin, *Managerial Effectiveness* (New York: McGraw-Hill, 1967).
16. F. E. Fiedler, *A Theory of Leadership Effectiveness* (New York: McGraw-Hill, 1967).
17. R. J. House, "A Path-Goal Theory of Leader Effectiveness," *Administrative Science Quarterly,* September 1971, pp. 321–38; R. J. House and T. R. Mitchell, "Path-Goal Theory of Leadership," *Journal of Contemporary Business,* Autumn 1974, p. 86; and R. J. House, "Retrospective Comment," in L. E. Boone and D. D. Bowen, eds., *The Great Writings in Management and Organizational Behavior,* 2nd ed. (New York: Random House, 1987), pp. 354–64.
18. L. H. Peters, D. D. Hartke, and T. J. Pholman, "Fiedler's Contingency Theory of Leadership: An Application of the Meta-Analysis Procedures of Schmidt and Hunter," *Psychological Bulletin,* March 1985, pp. 274–85.
19. See, for instance, R. W. Rice, "Psychometric Properties of the Esteem for the Least Preferred Co-Worker (LPC) Scale," *Academy of Management Review,* January 1978, pp. 106–18; C. A. Schriesheim, B. D. Bannister, and W. H. Money, "Psychometric Properties of the LPC Scale: An Extension of Rice's Review," *Academy of Management Review,* April 1979, pp. 287–90; E. H. Schein, *Organizational Psychology,* 3rd ed. (Upper Saddle River, NJ: Prentice Hall, 1980), pp. 116–17; and B. Kabanoff, "A Critique of Leader Match and Its Implications for Leadership Research," *Personnel Psychology,* Winter 1981, pp. 749–64.
20. J. Seltzer and J. W. Smither, "A Role Play Exercise to Introduce Students to Path-Goal Leadership," *Journal of Management Education,* August 1995, p. 381.
21. H. J. Klein and J. S. Kim, "A Field Study of the Influence of Situational Constraints, Leader-Member Exchange, and Goal Commitment on Performance," *Academy of Management Journal,* February 1998, pp. 86–95; J. Indrik, "Path-Goal Theory of Leadership: A Meta-Analysis," paper presented at the *National Academy of Management Conference,* Chicago, August 1986; R. T. Keller, "A Test of the Path-Goal Theory of Leadership with Need for Clarity as a Moderator in Research and Development Organizations," *Journal of Applied Psychology,* April 1989, pp. 208–12; J. C. Wofford and L. Z. Liska, "Path-Goal Theories of Leadership: A Meta-Analysis," *Journal of*

Management, Winter 1993, pp. 857–76; and S. Sagie and M. Koslowsky, "Organizational Attitudes and Behaviors as a Function of Participation in Strategic and Tactical Change Decisions: An Application of Path-Goal Theory," *Journal of Organizational Behavior,* January 1994, pp. 37–47.

22. V. H. Vroom and P. W. Yetton, *Leadership and Decision-Making* (Pittsburgh: University of Pittsburgh Press, 1973).
23. V. H. Vroom and A. G. Yago, *The New Leadership: Managing Participation in Organizations* (Upper Saddle River, NJ: Prentice Hall, 1988). See especially Chapter 8.
24. See, for example, R. H. G. Field, "A Test of the Vroom-Yetton Normative Model of Leadership," *Journal of Applied Psychology,* October 1982, pp. 523–32; C. R. Leana, "Power Relinquishment versus Power Sharing: Theoretical Clarification and Empirical Comparison of Delegation and Participation," *Journal of Applied Psychology,* May 1987, pp. 228–33; J. T. Ettling and A. G. Yago, "Participation under Conditions of Conflict: More on the Validity of the Vroom-Yetton Model," *Journal of Management Studies,* January 1988, pp. 73–83; and R. H. G. Field and R. J. House, "A Test of the Vroom-Yetton Model Using Manager and Subordinate Reports," *Journal of Applied Psychology,* June 1990, pp. 362–66.
25. For additional information about the exchanges that occur between the leader and the follower, see A. S. Phillips and A. G. Bedeian, "Leader-Follower Exchange Quality: The Role of Personal and Interpersonal Attributes," *Academy of Management Journal* 37, No. 4 (1994), pp. 990–1001; and T. A. Scandura and C. A. Schriesheim, "Leader-Member Exchange and Supervisor Career Mentoring as Complementary Constructs in Leadership Research," *Academy of Management Journal* 37, No. 6 (1994), pp. 1588–602.
26. P. Hersey and K. H. Blanchard, "So You Want to Know Your Leadership Style?" *Training and Development Journal,* February 1974, pp. 1–15; and Hersey and Blanchard, *Management of Organizational Behavior: Utilizing Human Resources,* 5th ed. (Upper Saddle River, NJ: Prentice Hall, 1988).
27. See, for example, C. F. Fernandez and R. P. Vecchio, "Situational Leadership Theory Revisited: A Test of an Across-Jobs Perspective," *Leadership Quarterly,* January 1997, p. 67.
28. Ibid., pp. 67–84; and C. L. Graeff, "Evolution of Situational Leadership Theory: A Critical Review," *Leadership Quarterly,* February 1997, pp. 153–70.
29. See R. H. Hambleton and R. Gumpert, "The Validity of Hersey and Blanchard's Theory of Leader Effectiveness," *Group and Organization Studies,* June 1982, pp. 225–42; C. L. Graeff, "The Situational Leadership Theory: A Critical Review," *Academy of Management Review,* April 1983, pp. 285–91; R. P. Vecchio, "Situational Leadership Theory: An Examination of a Prescriptive Theory," *Journal of Applied Psychology,* August 1987, p. 444–51; J. R. Goodson, G. W. McGee, and J. F. Cashman, "Situational Leadership Theory: A Test of Leadership Prescriptions," *Group and Organizational Studies,* December 1989, pp. 446–61; Blank, Weitzel, and Green, "A Test of the Situational Leadership Theory"; and P. R. Lucas, P. E. Messner, C. W. Ryan, and G. P. Sturm, "Preferred Leadership Style Differences: Perceptions of Defence Industry Labour and Management," *Leadership and Organization Development Journal,* December 1992, pp. 19–22.
30. J. A. Conger and R. N. Kanungo, "Behavioral Dimensions of Charismatic Leadership," in J. A. Conger, R. N. Kanungo, and Associates, *Charismatic Leadership* (San Francisco: Jossey-Bass, 1988), p. 79.
31. See B. Shamir, E. Zakay, E. Breinin, and M. Popper, "Correlates of Charismatic Leader Behavior in Military Units: Subordinates' Attitudes, Unit Characteristics, and Superiors' Appraisals of Leader performance," *Academy of Management Journal,* August 1998, pp. 387–409; and P. Sellers, "What Exactly Is Charisma?" *Fortune,* January 15, 1996, pp. 68–75.
32. R. J. House, "A 1976 Theory of Charismatic Leadership," in J. G. Hunt and L. L. Larson, eds., *Leadership: The Cutting Edge* (Carbondale, IL: Southern Illinois University Press, 1977), pp. 189–207.
33. W. Bennis, "The Four Competencies of Leadership," *Training and Development Journal,* August 1984, pp. 15–19; and M. Loeb, "Where Leaders Come From," *Fortune,* September 19, 1994, p. 241.
34. Conger and Kanungo, "Behavioral Dimensions of Charismatic Leadership," pp. 78–97.
35. D. A. Waldman and F. J. Yammarino, "CEO Charismatic Leadership: Levels-of-Management and Levels-of-Analysis Effects," *Academy of Management Review,* May 1998, pp. 266–285; R. J. House, J. Woycke, and E. M. Fodor, "Charismatic and Non-charismatic Leaders: Differences in Behavior and Effectiveness," in Conger, Kanungo, *Charismatic Leadership,* pp. 103–104; and B. R. Agle and J. A. Sonnenfeld, "Charismatic Chief Executive Officers: Are They More Effective? An Empirical Test of Charismatic Leadership Theory," in D. P. Moore, ed., *Academy of Management Best Papers Proceedings* 1994, August 14–17, 1994), pp. 2–6.
36. P. Burrows and P. Elstrom, "The Boss," *Business Week,* August 2, 1999, p. 78; Sellers, "What Exactly Is Charisma?" p. 75.
37. House, "A 1976 Theory of Charismatic Leadership."
38. Sellers, "What Exactly Is Charisma?" p. 68; R. Pillai, "Context and Charisma: The Role of Organic Structure, Collectivism, and Crisis in the Emergence of Charismatic Leadership," in D. P. Moore, ed., *Academy of Management Best Papers Proceedings,* August 6–9, 1995, p. 332; and D. Machan, "The Charisma Merchants," *Forbes,* January 23, 1989, pp. 100–101.
39. For an interesting perspective on CEO Failures and problems CEOs face, see R. Charan and G. Colvin, "Why CEOs Fail," *Fortune,* June 21, 1999, pp. 69–78; and P. Sellers, "CEOs in Denial," *Fortune,* June 21, 1999, pp. 80–82.
40. This definition is based on M. Sashkin, "The Visionary Leader," in J. A. Conger and R. N. Kanungo (eds.), *Charismatic Leadership,* pp. 124–25; B. Nanus, *Visionary Leadership* (New York: Free Press, 1992), p. 8; N. H. Snyder and M. Graves, "Leadership and Vision," *Business Horizons,* January–February 1994, p. 1; J. R. Lucas, "Anatomy of a Vision Statement," *Management Review,* February 1998, pp. 22–26; and S. Marino, "Where There Is No Visionary, Companies Falter," *Industry Week,* March 15, 1999, p. 20.
41. B. Nanus, *Visionary Leadership,* p. 8.

42. P. C. Nutt and R. W. Backoff, "Crafting Vision," *Journal of Management Inquiry,* December 1997, p. 309.
43. Ibid., pp. 312–14.
44. Based on M. Sashkin, "The Visionary Leader," pp. 128–30; and J. R. Baum, E. A. Locke, and S. A. Kirkpatrick, "A Longitudinal Study of the Relation of Vision and Vision Communication to Venture Growth in Entrepreneurial Firms," *Journal of Applied Psychology,* February 1998, pp. 43–54.
45. See, for instance, E. W. Book, "Leadership for the Millennium," *Working Woman,* March 1998, pp. 29–34; and "T. Stevens, "Follow the Leader," *Industry Week,* November 18, 1996, p. 16.
46. See J. M. Burns, *Leadership* (New York: Harper & Row, 1978); B. M. Bass, *Leadership and Performance beyond Expectations* (New York: Free Press, 1985); and B. M. Bass, "From Transactional to Transformational Leadership: Learning to Share the Vision," *Organizational Dynamics,* Winter 1990, pp. 19–31.
47. Sellers, "What Exactly Is Charisma?"; and M. A. Verespej, "Lead, Don't Manage," *Industry Week,* March 4, 1996, p. 55.
48. See, for instance, W. L. Gardner and B. J. Avolio, "The Charismatic Relationship: A Dramaturgical Perspective," *Academy of Management Review,* January 1998, pp. 32–58; F. J. Yammarino, A. J. Dubinsky, L. B. Comer, and M. A. Jolson, "Women and Transformational and Contingent Reward Leadership: A Multiple-Levels-of-Analysis Perspective," *Academy of Management Journal,* February 1997, pp. 205–22.
49. B. M. Bass, "Leadership: Good, Better, Best," *Organizational Dynamics,* Winter 1985, pp. 26–40; and J. Seltzer and B. M. Bass, "Transformational Leadership: Beyond Initiation and Consideration," *Journal of Management,* December 1990, pp. 693–703.
50. See B. J. Tepper, "Patterns of Downward Influence and Follower Conformity in Transactional and Transformational Leadership," in D. P. Moore, ed., *Academy of Management Best Papers Proceedings 1994,* August 14–17, 1994, pp. 267–71.
51. B. J. Avolio and B. M. Bass, "Transformational Leadership, Charisma and Beyond," working paper, School of Management, State University of New York, Binghamton, NY, 1985, p. 14; and S. Caminiti, "What Team Leaders Need to Know," *Fortune,* February 20, 1995, pp. 93–98.
52. Cited in B. M. Bass and B. J. Avolio, "Developing Transformational Leadership: 1992 and Beyond," *Journal of European Industrial Training,* January 1990, p. 23.
53. J. J. Hater and B. M. Bass, "Supervisors' Evaluation and Subordinates' Perceptions of Transformational and Transactional Leadership," *Journal of Applied Psychology,* November 1988, pp. 695–702.
54. Bass and Avolio, "Developing Transformational Leadership."
55. See, for instance, J. H. Zenger, E. Musselwhite, K. Hurson, and C. Perrin, *Leading Teams: Mastering the New Role* (Homewood, IL: Business One Irwin, 1994); and M. Frohman, "Nothing Kills Teams like Ill-Prepared Leaders," *Industry Week,* October 2, 1995, pp. 72–76.
56. S. Caminiti, "What Team Leaders Need to Know," *Fortune,* February 20, 1995, pp. 93–100.
57. Gary N. Powell, *Women and Men in Management,* 2nd ed. (Thousand Oaks, CA: Sage, 1993). See also, R. L. Kent and S. E. Moss, "Effects of Sex and Gender Role on Leader Emergence," *Academy of Management Journal* 37, No. 6 (1994), pp. 1335–46; and A. Fisher, "A Delicate Question: Why Are Women Bosses So Nasty to Me?" *Fortune,* April 14, 1997, p. 165.
58. S. P. Robbins, *Organizational Behavior: Concepts, Controversies, and Applications,* 8th ed. (Upper Saddle River, NJ: Prentice Hall, 1998), p. 431; J. Mariotti, "Women Reach for the Top," *Industry Week,* March 1, 1999, p. 66; K. Onstad, "You Say 'Tomato,'" *Canadian Business,* June 1996, p. 33; "Women Outscore Men in Management and Leadership Skills," *HRMagazine,* December 1996, p. 14; H. Collingwood, "Women as Managers: Not Just Different—Better," *Working Woman,* November 1995, p. 14; and D. Phillips, "The Gender Gap," *Entrepreneur,* May 1995, pp. 108–13.
59. H. Collingwood, "Women as Managers: Not Just Different—Better."
60. Ibid., p. 93.
61. Ibid., p. 100.
62. N. Steckler and N. Fondas, "Building Team Leader Effectiveness: A Diagnostic Tool," *Organizational Dynamics,* Winter 1995, p. 20. See also P. Kelly, "Lose the Boss," *Inc.,* December 1997, pp. 45–46; and J. Pfeffer and J. P. Veiga, "Putting People First for Organizational Success," *Academy of Management Executive,* May 1999, pp. 37–48.
63. R. S. Wellins, W. C. Byham, and G. R. Dixon, *Inside Teams* (San Francisco: Jossey-Bass, 1994), p. 318.
64. N. Steckler and N. Fondas, "Building Team Leader Effectiveness," p. 21.
65. I. Santillana, "Leadership in Latin America," *Latin Trade,* March 1998, p. 72.
66. For a review of the cross-cultural applicability of the leadership literature, see R. S. Bhagat, B. L. Kedia, S. E. Crawford, and M. R. Kaplan, "Cross-Cultural Issues in Organizational Psychology: Emergent Trends and Directions for Research in the 1990s," in C. L. Cooper and I. T. Robertson (eds.), *International Review of Industrial and Organizational Psychology,* vol. 5 (New York: John Wiley & Sons, 1990), pp. 79–89; and M. F. Peterson and J. G. Hunt, "International Perspectives on International Leadership," *Leadership Quarterly,* Fall 1997, pp. 203–31.
67. "Military-Style Management in China," *Asia Inc.,* March 1995, p. 70.
68. Cited in R. J. House and R. N. Aditya, "The Social Scientific Study of Leadership," p. 463.
69. R. J. House, "Leadership in the Twenty-First Century," in A. Howard (ed.), *The Changing Nature of Work* (San Francisco: Jossey-Bass, 1995), p. 442.
70. Ibid.
71. R. J. House and R. N. Aditya, "The Social Scientific Study of Leadership," p. 463.
72. R. J. House, "Leadership in the Twenty-First Century," p. 443.
73. S. Kerr and J. M. Jermier, "Substitutes for Leadership: Their Meaning and Measurement," *Organization Behavior and Human Performance,* December 1978, pp. 375–403; J. P. Howell and P. W. Dorfman, "Substitutes for Leadership: Test of a Construct," *Academy of Management Journal,*

December 1981, pp. 714–28; P. W. Howard and W. F. Joyce, "Substitutes for Leadership: A Statistical Refinement," paper presented at the 42nd Annual Academy of Management Conference, New York, August 1982; J. P. Howell, P. W. Dorfman, and S. Kerr, "Leadership and Substitutes for Leadership," *Journal of Applied Behavioral Science* 22, No. 1 (1986), pp. 29–46; and J. P. Howell, D. E. Bowen, P. W. Dorfman, S. Kerr, and P. M. Podsakoff, "Substitutes for Leadership: Effective Alternatives to Ineffective Leadership," *Organizational Dynamics,* Summer 1990, pp. 21–38.

74. Based on S. D. Boon and J. G. Holmes, "The Dynamics of Interpersonal Trust: Resolving Uncertainty in the Face of Risk," in R. A. Hinde and J. Groebel (eds.), *Cooperation and Prosocial Behavior* (Cambridge, UK: Cambridge University Press, 1991), p. 194; D. J. McAllister, "Affect- and Cognition-Based Trust as Foundations for Interpersonal Cooperation in Organizations," *Academy of Management Journal,* February 1995, p. 25; and D. M. Rousseau, S. B. Sitkin, R. S. Burt, and C. Camerer, "Not So Different After All: A Cross-Discipline View of Trust," *Academy of Management Review,* July 1998, pp. 393–404.
75. J. B. Rotter, "Interpersonal Trust, Trustworthiness, and Gullibility," *American Psychologist,* May 1980, pp. 1–7.
76. J. D. Lewis and A. Weigert, "Trust as a Social Reality," *Social Forces,* June 1985, p. 970.
77. J. K. Rempel, J. G. Holmes, and M. P. Zanna, "Trust in Close Relationships," *Journal of Personality and Social Psychology,* July 1985, p. 96.
78. M. Granovetter, "Economic Action and Social Structure: The Problem of Embeddedness," *American Journal of Sociology,* November 1985, p. 491.
79. R. C. Mayer, J. H. Davis, and F. D. Schoorman, "An Integrative Model of Organizational Trust," *Academy of Management Review,* July 1995, p. 712.
80. C. Johnson-George and W. Swap, "Measurement of Specific Interpersonal Trust: Construction and Validation of a Scale to Assess Trust in a Specific Other," *Journal of Personality and Social Psychology,* May 1982, p. 1306.
81. P. L. Schindler and C. C. Thomas, "The Structure of Interpersonal Trust in the Workplace," *Psychological Reports,* October 1993, pp. 563–73.
82. T. E. Becker, "Integrity in Organizations: Beyond Honesty and Conscientiousness," *Academy of Management Review,* January 1998, pp. 154–61. For a debate on Becker's article, see B. Barry and C. U. Stephens, "Objections to an Objectivist Approach to Integrity," *Academy of Management Review,* January 1998, pp. 162–69; and E. A. Locke and T. E. Becker, "Rebuttal to a Subjectivist Critique of an Objectivist Approach to Integrity in Organizations," *Academy of Management Review,* January 1998, pp. 170–75.
83. A. C. Wicks, S. L. Berman, and T. M. Jones, "The Structure of Optimal Trust: Moral and Strategic Implications," *Academy of Management Review,* January 1999, pp. 96–116; C. Braun, "Organizational Infidelity: How Violations of Trust Affect the Employee-Employer Relationship," *Academy of Management Executive,* November 1997, pp. 94–96; and J. K. Butler Jr. and R. S. Cantrell, "A Behavioral Decision Theory Approach to Modeling Dyadic Trust in Superiors and Subordinates," *Psychological Reports,* August 1984, pp. 19–28.
84. D. McGregor, *The Professional Manager* (New York: McGraw-Hill, 1967), p. 164.
85. B. Nanus, *The Leader's Edge: The Seven Keys to Leadership in a Turbulent World* (Chicago: Contemporary Books, 1989), p. 102.
86. D. E. Zand, *The Leadership Triad: Knowledge, Trust, and Power* (New York: Oxford Press, 1997), p. 89.
87. Based on L. T. Hosmer, "Trust: The Connecting Link between Organizational Theory and Philosophical Ethics," *Academy of Management Review,* April 1995, p. 393; and R. C. Mayer, J. H. Davis, and F. D. Schoorman, "An Integrative Model of Organizational Trust," *Academy of Management Review,* July 1995, p. 712.
88. M. Kouzes and B. Z. Posner, *Credibility: How Leaders Gain and Lose It, and Why People Demand It* (San Francisco: Jossey-Bass, 1993), p. 14.
89. J. Brockner, P. A. Siegel, J. P. Daly, T. Tyler, and C. Martin, "When Trust Matters: The Moderating Effect of Outcome Favorability," *Administrative Science Quarterly,* September 1997, p. 558. See also, W. H. Miller, "Leadership at a Crossroads," *Industry Week,* August 19, 1996, pp. 42–56.
90. Cited in C. Lee, "Trust Me," *Training,* January 1997, p. 32.
91. This section is based on D. Shapiro, B. H. Sheppard, and L. Cheraskin, "Business on a Handshake," *Negotiation Journal,* October 1992, pp. 365–77; and R. J. Lewicki and B. B. Bunker, "Developing and Maintaining Trust in Work Relationships," in R. M. Kramer and T. R. Tyler (eds.), *Trust in Organizations* (Thousand Oaks, CA: Sage, 1996), pp. 119–24.
92. Based on F. Bartolome, "Nobody Trust the Boss Completely—Now What?" *Harvard Business Review,* March–April 1989, p. 135–42; J. K. Butler, Jr., "Toward Understanding and Measuring Conditions of Trust: Evolution of a Condition of Trust Inventory," *Journal of Management,* September 1991, pp. 643–663; and J. Finegan, "Ready, Aim, Focus," *Inc.,* March 1997, p. 53.
93. N. Shirouzu, "Toyota Is Tightening Control of Key Suppliers in Bid to Block Encroachment by Foreign Firms," *Wall Street Journal,* August 3, 1999; p. A18; N. Shirouzu, "Toyota Plans An Expansion of Capacity Due to Demand," *Wall Street Journal,* June 29, 1999, p. A8; B. McClennan, "New Toyota Chief has U. S. Credentials," *Ward's Auto World,* June 1999, p. 42; E. Thornton, "Mystery at the Top," *Business Week,* April 26, 1999, p. 52; N. Shirouzu, "Top-Level Reshuffle Expected at Toyota," *Wall Street Journal,* April 8, 1999; E. Thornton, "This Isn't Your Simple Flat Tire," *Business Week,* February 1, 1999, p. 54; N. Shirouzu, "Toyota President Expected to Quit Post—Hiroshi Okuda Is to Become Auto Maker's Chairman; Firm to Revamp," *Wall Street Journal,* January 11, 1999; and A. Taylor, III, "Toyota's Boss Stands out in a Crowd," *Fortune,* November 25, 1996, pp. 116–22.

Chapter 12

1. Adapted from J. Bing, J. Zalesky, P. Gediman, and C. Abott, "To Russia with Fries," *Publishers Weekly,* April 12, 1999, p. 63; R. Legvold, "To Russia with Fries," *Foreign Affairs,* July/August, 1998, p. 133; and J. Cooney, "How a Big Mac Became the Symbol of Perestroika," *Ivey Business Quarterly,* Winter, 1997, pp. 77–78.

2. N. K. Austin, "The Skill Every Manager Must Master," *Working Woman,* May 1995, p. 29; and L. E. Penley, E. R. Alexander, I. E. Jernigan, and C. I. Henwood, "Communication Abilities of Managers: The Relationship to Performance," *Journal of Management,* March 1991, pp. 57–76.
3. D. K. Berlo, *The Process of Communication* (New York: Holt, Rinehart & Winston, 1960), pp. 30–32.
4. Ibid., p. 54.
5. Ibid., p. 103.
6. "Psst: Pass It on," *Entrepreneur,* April 1995, p. 64.
7. M. Henricks, "More Than Words," *Entrepreneur,* August 1995, pp. 54–57.
8. R. Stein, "Hands May Help Minds Grasp the Right Words," *The Washington Post,* November 30, 1998, p. A3.
9. A. Mehrabian, "Communication without Words," *Psychology Today,* September 1968, pp. 53–55.
10. "E-Legal," *Entrepreneur,* December 1998, p. 90.
11. J. DeLorean, quoted in S. P. Robbins, *The Administrative Process* (Upper Saddle River, NJ: Prentice Hall, 1976), p. 404.
12. M.J. Glauser, "Upward Information Flow in Organizations: Review and Conceptual Analysis," *Human Relations,* March 1984, pp. 613–43.
13. G. A. Miller, "The Magical Number Seven, Plus or Minus Two: Some Limits on Our Capacity for Processing Information," *The Psychological Review,* March 1956, pp. 81–97.
14. See, for instance, J. R. Gibb, "Defensive Communication," *Journal of Communication,* June 1961, pp. 141–48.
15. S. I. Hayakawa, *Language in Thought and Action* (New York: Harcourt Brace Jovanovich, 1949), p. 292.
16. Cited in J. J. Kilpatrick, "Uncommon Word Usage Can Enrich and Muddle Writing," *Seattle Times,* March 15, 1998, p. L4.
17. S. C. Bahls and J. E. Bahls, "Watch Your Language," *Entrepreneur,* December 1998, p. 78.
18. J. C. McCroskey, J. A. Daly, and G. Sorenson, "Personality Correlates of Communication Apprehension," *Human Communication Research,* Spring 1976, pp. 376–80.
19. B. H. Spitzberg and M. L. Hecht, "A Competent Model of Relational Competence," *Human Communication Research,* Summer 1984, pp. 575–99.
20. See, for example, L. Stafford and J. A. Daly, "Conversational Memory: The Effects of Instructional Set and Recall Mode on Memory for Natural Conversations," *Human Communication Research,* Spring 1984, pp. 379–402.
21. J. A. Daly and J. C. McCrosky, "Occupational Choice and Desirability as a Function of Communication Apprehension," paper presented at the annual meeting of the International Communication Association, Chicago, 1975.
22. J. A. Daly and M. D. Miller, "The Empirical Development of an Instrument of Writing Apprehension," *Research in the Teaching of English,* Winter 1975, pp. 242–49.
23. "Communication: Open Book Management 101," *Inc.,* August 1996, p. 92.
24. See, for instance, G. M. McEvoy, "Student Diary Keeping: Tool for Instructional Improvement," *Journal of Management Education,* May 1996, pp. 206–29.
25. T. D. Lewis and G. H. Graham, ASix Ways to Improve Your Communication Skills," *Internal Auditor,* May 1988, p. 25.
26. This section on gender differences in communications is based on D. Tannen, *You Just Don't Understand: Women and Men in Conversation* (New York: Ballantine Books, 1991); D. Tannen, *Talking from 9 to 5* (New York: Morrow, 1994); J. C. Tingley, *Genderflex: Men & Women Speak Other's Language at Work* (New York: American Management Association, 1994); C. Baher, "How to Avoid Communication Clashes," *HR Focus,* April 1994, p. 3; and "Communication: Bridging the Gender Gap," *HR Focus,* April 1994, p. 22.
27. See, for example, L. K. Larkey, "Toward a Theory of Communicative Interactions in Culturally Diverse Workgroups," *Academy of Management Review,* June 1996, pp. 463–91; R. V. Lindahl, "Automation Breaks the Language Barrier," *HRMagazine,* March 1996, pp. 79–82; D. Lindorff, "In Beijing, the Long March Is Just Starting," *Business Week,* February 12, 1996, p. 68; and L. Miller, "Two Aspects of Japanese and American Co-Worker Interaction: Giving Instructions and Creating Rapport," *Journal of Applied Behavioral Science,* June 1995, pp. 141–61.
28. Based on S. D. Saleh, "Relational Orientation and Organizational Functioning: A Cross-Cultural Perspective," *Canadian Journal of Administrative Sciences,* September 1987, pp. 276–93.
29. See, for example, J. D. Pettit Jr., B. C. Vaught, and R. L. Trewatha, "Interpersonal Skill Training: A Perspective for Success," *Business,* April–June 1990, pp. 8–14; and D. Milbank, "Managers Are Sent to 'Charm Schools' to Discover How to Polish up Their Acts," *Wall Street Journal,* December 14, 1990, p. B1.
30. C. Hymowitz, "Five Main Reasons Why Managers Fail," *Wall Street Journal,* May 2, 1988, p. B25.
31. D. Milbank, "Interpersonal Skills: Most Appreciated and Sought After in the 1990s," *Canadian Manager,* Spring 1993, p. 26.
32. L. Porter and L. E. McKibbin, *Future of Management Education and Development: Drift or Thrust into the 21st Century* (New York: McGraw-Hill, 1988).
33. S. P. Robbins and P. L. Hunsaker, *Training in Interpersonal Skills: TIPS for Managing People at Work,* 2nd ed. (Upper Saddle River, NJ: Prentice Hall, 1996); C. T. Lewis, J. E. Garcia, and S. M. Jobs, *Managerial Skills in Organizations* (Boston: Allyn & Bacon, 1990); D. A. Whetten and K. Cameron, *Developing Management Skills,* 3rd ed. (New York: HarperCollins, 1995); and A. C. Yrle, and W. P. Gale, "Using Interpersonal Skills to Manage More Effectively," *Supervisory Management,* April 1993, p. 4.
34. R. McGarvey, "Now Hear This," *Entrepreneur,* June 1996, pp. 87–89.
35. C. R. Rogers and R. E. Farson, *Active Listening* (Chicago: Industrial Relations Center of the University of Chicago, 1976).
36. S. P. Robbins, and P. L. Hunsaker, *Training in Interpersonal Skills,* 2nd ed., pp. 37–39.
37. C. Fisher, "Transmission of Positive and Negative Feedback to Subordinates," *Journal of Applied Psychology,* October 1979, pp. 433–540.
38. D. Llgen, C. D. Fisher, and M. S. Taylor, "Consequences of Individual Feedback on Behavior in Organizations," *Journal of Applied Psychology,* August 1979, pp. 349–71.

39. F. Bartolome, "Teaching about Whether to Give Negative Feedback," *The Organizational Behavior Teaching Review* 9, No. 2 (1986–1987), pp. 95–104.
40. K. Halperin, C. R. Snyder, R. J. Schenkel, and B. K. Houston, "Effect of Source Status and Message Favorability on Acceptance of Personality Feedback," *Journal of Applied Psychology,* February 1976, pp. 85–88.
41. C. R. Mill, "Feedback: The Art of Giving and Receiving Help," in L. Porter and C. R. Mill, eds., *The Reading Book for Human Relations Training* (Bethel, Maine: NTL Institute for Applied Behavioral Science, 1976), pp. 18–19.
42. Ibid.
43. Ibid.
44. Ibid.
45. K. S. Verderber and R. F. Verderber, *Inter-Act: Using Interpersonal Communication Skills,* 4th ed. (Belmont, CA: Wadsworth, 1986).
46. L. E. Bourne Jr. and C. V. Bunderson, "Effects of Delay of Information Feedback and Length of Post-Feedback Interval on Concept Identification," *Journal of Experimental Psychology,* January 1963, pp. 1–5.
47. Mill, "Feedback," pp. 18–19.
48. Verderber and Verderber, *Inter-Act.*
49. See, for example, W. A. Randolph, "Navigating the Journey to Empowerment," *Organizational Dynamics,* Spring 1995; pp. 19–32; R. Hanson, R. I. Porterfield, and K. Ames, "Employee Empowerment at Risk: Effects of Recent NLRB Rulings," *Academy of Management Executive,* April 1995, pp. 46–56; R. C. Ford and M. D. Fottler, "Empowerment: A Matter of Degree," *Academy of Management Executive,* August 1995, pp. 21–31; and J. S. McClenahen, "Empowerment's Downside," *Industry Week,* September 18, 1995, pp. 57–58.
50. B. K. Hackman and D. C. Dunphy, "Managerial Delegation," in G. C. Cooper and I. T. Robertson, eds., *International Review of Industrial and Organizational Psychology* (New York: John Wiley & Sons, 1990), pp. 35–37; and B. Marquand, "Effective Delegation," *Manage,* July 1993, pp. 10–12.
51. C. R. Leana, "Predictors and Consequences of Delegation," *Academy of Management Journal,* December 1986, pp. 754–74.
52. L. L. Steinmetz, *The Art and Skill of Delegation* (Boston: Addison-Wesley, 1976).
53. C. D. Pringle, "Seven Reasons Why Managers Don't Delegate," *Management Solutions,* November 1986, pp. 26–30.
54. Robbins and Hunsaker, *Training in Interpersonal Skills,* 2nd ed., pp. 93–95; R. T. Noel, "What You Say to Your Employees When You Delegate," *Supervisory Management,* December 1993, p. 13; and S. Caudron, "Delegate for Results," *Industry Week,* February 6, 1995, pp. 27–30.
55. K. W. Thomas and W. H. Schmidt, "A Survey of Managerial Interests with Respect to Conflict," *Academy of Management Journal,* June 1976, pp. 315–18.
56. Ibid.
57. This section is adapted from S. P. Robbins, *Managing Organizational Conflict: A Nontraditional Approach* (Upper Saddle River, NJ: Prentice Hall, 1977), pp. 11–14.
58. This section is drawn from K. W. Thomas, "Toward Multidimensional Values in Teaching: The Example of Conflict Behaviors," *Academy of Management Review,* July 1977, p. 487.
59. L. Greenhalgh, "Managing Conflict," *Sloan Management Review,* Summer 1986, pp. 45–51.
60. Robbins, *Managing Organizational Conflict,* pp. 31–55.
61. Kursh, "The Benefits of Poor Communication."
62. See, for instance, D. Tjosvold and D. W. Johnson, *Productive Conflict Management Perspectives for Organizations* (New York: Irvington Publishers, 1983).
63. S. P. Robbins, "Conflict Management and Conflict Resolution Are Not Synonymous Terms," *California Management Review,* Winter 1978, p. 71.
64. See E. Van de Vliert, A. Nauta, E. Giebels, and O. Janssen, "Constructive Conflict at Work," in L. N. Dosier and J. B. Keys, eds., *Academy of Management Best Paper Proceedings,* August 8–13, 1997, pp. 92–96.
65. Robbins, *Managing Organizational Conflict,* pp. 78–89; and S. Berglas, "Innovate: Harmony Is Death. Let Conflict Reign," *Inc.,* May 1997, pp. 56–58.
66. See also, J. M. Brett and T. Okumura, "Inter and Intra-Cultural Negotiation: U.S. and Japanese Negotiators," *Academy of Management Journal,* October 1998, pp. 495–510.
67. R. E. Walton and R. B. McKersie, *A Behavioral Theory of Labor Negotiations: An Analysis of a Social Interaction System* (New York: McGraw-Hill, 1965). See also, J. F. Brett, G. R. Northcraft, and R. L. Pinkley, "Stairways to Heaven: An Interlocking Self-Regulation Model of Negotiation," *Academy of Management Review,* July 1999, pp. 435–51.
68. N. Brodsky, "I've Got a Secret," *Inc.,* March 1998, p. 27.
69. K. W. Thomas, "Conflict and Negotiation Processes in Organizations," in M. D. Dunnette and L. M. Hough, eds. *Handbook of Industrial and Organizational Psychology,* vol. 3, 2nd ed. (Palo Alto, CA: Consulting Psychologists Press, 1992), pp. 651–717.
70. Based on R. Fisher and W. Ury, *Getting to Yes: Negotiating Agreement without Giving In* (Boston: Houghton Mifflin, 1981); J. A. Wall Jr. and M. W. Blum, "Negotiations," *Journal of Management,* June 1991, pp. 295–96; and M. H. Bazerman and M. A. Neale, *Negotiating Rationally* (New York: Free Press, 1992).
71. "How to Negotiate with Really Tough Guys," *Fortune,* May 27, 1996, pp. 173–74.
72. "Podium Fright," *Industry Week,* April 19, 1999, p. 11.
73. "Survey Shows Fundamental Managerial Skills Lacking," *Management Services,* January 1999, p. 3.
74. Ibid, and J. Lawn, "Better Presentation Skills Are Key to Career Growth," *Food Management,* May 1999, p. 10.
75. This material is based on Larry Laufer, *Presenting for Results Program,* copyright by the Applied Human Resource Systems, Inc., 1998; and K. Daley, "Presentation Skills: How To Be Focused, Forceful, Passionate, and Persuasive," *Information Executive,* September 1998.
76. "Classless Action," *Forbes,* November 6, 1995, p. 33.
77. E. Randall, "They Sell Suits with Soul," *Fast Company,* October 1998, p. 68; "HR Pulse: Emotional Intelligence," *HRMagazine,* January 1998, p. 19; and M. Henricks, "More Than Words," *Entrepreneur,* August 1995, pp. 54–57.

Chapter 13

1. Based on *Small Business 2000,* Show 109; and "SiloCaf Lookout Automation Software to Process More than 30 Percent of U.S. Coffee," *National Instruments,* March 18, 1998; pp. 1–2.
2. See J. H. Sheridan, "Nurturing World-Class Solutions," *Industry Week,* January 20, 1997, pp. 22–29; and K. A. Merchant, "The Control Function of Management," *Sloan Management Review,* Summer 1982, pp. 43–55.
3. E. Flamholtz, "Organizational Control Systems as a Managerial Tool," *California Management Review,* Winter 1979, p. 55.
4. W. G. Ouchi, "A Conceptual Framework for the Design of Organizational Control Mechanisms," *Management Science,* August 1979, pp. 833–38; and Ouchi, "Markets, Bureaucracies, and Clans," *Administrative Science Quarterly,* March 1980, pp. 129–41.
5. J. H. Sheridan, "Bonds of Trust," *Industry Week,* March 17, 1997, pp. 52–69; S. Tully, "Purchasing's New Muscle," *Fortune,* February 20, 1995, pp. 78–79.
6. W. Zellner, "Leave the Driving to Lentzsch," *Business Week,* March 18, 1996, pp. 66–67.
7. S. Kerr, "On the Folly of Rewarding A, while Hoping for B," *Academy of Management Journal,* December 1975, pp. 769–83.
8. D. Field, "Finance Chief Turning Profits and Heads at Boeing," *USA Today,* August 12, 1999, p. 5B; J. E. Garten, "Why the Global Economy Is Here to Stay," *Business Week,* March 23, 1998, p. 21; R. Stodgill, "Combat-Ready at McDonnell," *Business Week,* April 29, 1996, p. 39; and S. Greco, "Are We Making Money Yet?" *Inc.,* July 1996, pp. 53–61.
9. See, for instance, Zellner, "Leave the Driving to Lentzsch."
10. H. Koontz and R. W. Bradspies, "Managing through Feedforward Control," *Business Horizons,* June 1972, pp. 25–36.
11. G. Pitts, "From Potholes to Profits," *The Globe and Mail,* April 4, 1995, p. 18.
12. W. H. Newman, *Constructive Control: Design and Use of Control Systems* (Upper Saddle River, NJ: Prentice Hall, 1975), p. 33.
13. See, for example, Tully, "Purchasing's New Muscle," pp. 75–83.
14. See, for instance, S. Chandler, "How TWA Faced the Nightmare," *Business Week,* August 5, 1996, p. 30.
15. See, for instance, M. Kripalani, "A Traffic Jam of Auto Makers," *Business Week,* August 5, 1996, pp. 46–47.
16. Kripalani, "A Traffic Jam of Auto Makers," p. 46.
17. D. Freedman, "Bits to Ship," *Forbes ASAP,* December 5, 1994, pp. 28–31.
18. R. Frank, "As UPS Tries to Deliver More to Its Customers, Labor Problems Grow," *Wall Street Journal,* May 23, 1994, p. A1.
19. See, for instance, B. J. Jaworski and S. M. Young, "Dysfunctional Behavior and Management Control: An Empirical Study of Marketing Managers," *Accounting, Organizations and Society,* January 1992, pp. 17–35.
20. E. E. Lawler III and J. G. Rhode, *Information and Control in Organizations* (Santa Monica, CA: Goodyear, 1976), p. 108.
21. J. D. Thompson, *Organizations in Action* (New York: McGraw-Hill, 1967), p. 124.
22. J. Teresko, "Opening up the Plant Floor," *Industry Week,* May 20, 1996, p. 172; S. Lubove, "High-Tech Cops," *Forbes,* September 25, 1995, pp. 44–45; M. Meyer, "The Fear of Flaming," *Newsweek,* June 20, 1994, p. 54; and J. Ubois, "Plugged in Away from the Office," *Working Woman,* June 1994, pp. 60–61.
23. L. Smith, "What the Boss Knows about You," *Fortune,* August 1993, pp. 88–93; Z. Schiller and W. Konrad, "If You Light up on Sunday, Don't Come in on Monday," *Business Week,* August 26, 1991, pp. 68–72; and G. Bylinsky, "How Companies Spy on Employees," *Fortune,* November 4, 1991, pp. 131–40.
24. F. Jossi, "Eavesdropping in Cyberspace," *Business Ethics,* May–June 1994, pp. 22–25.
25. See, for example, R. Behar, "Drug Spies," *Fortune,* September 6, 1999, pp. 231–46.
26. R. Behar, "Who's Reading Your E-Mail?" *Fortune,* February 3, 1997, pp. 57–70.
27. "E-Mail Snooping Is OK in the Eyes of the Law," *Wall Street Journal,* March 19, 1996, p. A1.
28. Griffin, "Teaching Big Brother to be a Team Player," and "Privacy at Work? Don't Count on It," *Springfield News Leader,* May 26, 1997, p. 7A.
29. G. Bylinsky, "How Companies Spy on Employees," *Fortune,* November 4, 1991, pp. 131–40.
30. S. C. Bahls and J. E. Bahls, "Getting Personal," *Entrepreneur,* October 1997, pp. 76–78.
31. S. Greengard, "Privacy: Entitlement or Illusion?" *Personnel Journal,* May 1996, pp. 74–88.
32. See also, "Pot Smokers See Job Offers Go up in Smoke," *HRMagazine,* April 1999, p. 30.
33. This case is based on G. Lesser, "A Hard Rain's Gonna Fall," *Sky,* August 1996, p. 22.

Chapter 14

1. Opening vignette based on "French Rags Helps Clothes the Deal," *Apparel Industry Magazine,* May 1999, p. 14; material from *<http://www.frenchrags.com/articles/main.htm>* 1999, F. Musselman, "Stretching Beyond Her Gauge," *Apparel Industry Magazine,* April 1997, pp. 16–18; and H. Plotkin, "Riches to Rags," *Inc. Technology,* Summer 1995, pp. 62–67.
2. R. S. Russell and B. W. Taylor, III, *Operations Management* (Upper Saddle River, NJ: Prentice-Hall, 2000), p. 17.
3. J. H. Sheridan, "Productivity Payoff?" *Industry Week,* July 8, 1999, p. 22.
4. H. Schachter, "The Dispossessed," *Canadian Business,* May 1995, pp. 30–40.
5. J. E. Rigdon, "Give and Take," *Wall Street Journal,* November 14, 1994, p. A24.
6. J. Teresko, "Information Rich, Knowledge Poor," *Industry Week,* February 19, 1999, p. 19.
7. P. E. Ross, "Software as Career Threat," *Forbes,* May 22, 1995, pp. 240–46.
8. D. Hulme and P. Janssen, "Struggling to Acquire Expertise," *Asian Business,* July 1996, pp. 58–62.
9. See, for instance, N. F. Sullivan, *Technology Transfer: Making the Most of Your Intellectual Property* (London, England: Cambridge University Press, 1996); and A. A. Lado and G. S. Vozikis, "Transfer of Technology to Promote

Entrepreneurship in Developing Countries: An Integration and Proposed Framework," *Entrepreneurship Theory and Practice,* Winter 1996, pp. 55–72.

10. P. Gustavsson, P. Hansson, and L. Lundberg, "Technology, Resource Endowments and International Competitiveness," *European Economic Review,* August 1999, p. 1501.
11. This section based on D. Hulme and P. Janssen, "Struggling to Acquire Expertise." See also K. Ohlson, "Technology Transfer Aids Companies," *Industry Week,* July 5, 1999, pp. 33–38.
12. See, for example, R. A. Mamis, "Crash Course," *Inc.,* February 1995, pp. 54–63.
13. V. Raval, "Information Strategy in Service-Focused Organizations," *Information Strategy,* Fall 1999, p. 36.
14. J. T. Small and W. B. Lee, "In Search of an MIS," *MSU Business Topics,* Autumn 1975, pp. 47–55.
15. H. A. Simon, *Administrative Behavior,* 3rd ed. (New York: Free Press, 1976), p. 294; and J. Teresko, "Data Warehouses: Build Them for Decision-Making Power," *Industry Week,* March 18, 1996, pp. 43–46.
16. This section is based on J. W. Verity, "Getting Work to Go with the Flow," *Business Week,* June 21, 1993, pp. 156–61.
17. M. Hammer, "Reengineering Work: Don't Automate, Obliterate," *Harvard Business Review,* July–August 1990, p. 106.
18. J. H. Sheridan, "Workflow: Unsung Hero," *Industry Week,* July 5, 1999, p. 27; and J. H. Sheridan, "Lockheed Martin Corp.," *Industry Week,* October 19, 1998, p. 56.
19. R. B. Segal, "Why Workflow Works," *Mortgage Banking,* June 1999, p. 92.
20. B. Keyser, "Workflow Automation Frees up Company's Creativity," *InfoWorld,* October 12, 1998, p. 75.
21. R. Thompson, "Standing up To Software Piracy," *Computer Dealer News,* July 2, 1999, pp. 25; 31; and A. C. Trembly, "Cyber Crime Means Billions in Losses," *National Underwriter,* July 5, 1999, p. 37.
22. M. Mosquera, "The High Price of Software Piracy," *Computer Reseller News,* May 24, 1999, p. 76.
23. S. Boulton, "When Borrowing Is Steeling," *ENR,* March 15, 1999, p. 119.
24. M. Mosquera, "The High Price of Software Piracy."
25. A. Steel, "Software Piracy Creates Uneven Playing Field for Resellers," *Computer Dealer News,* July 2, 1999, p. 26.
26. W. A. Lo, and J. Choobinch, "Knowledge-Based Systems as Database Design Tools: A Comparative Study," *Journal of Database Management,* June–September 1999, p. 26; and G. R. Ungson, and J. D. Trudel, "The Emerging Knowledge-Based Economy," *IEEE Spectrum,* May 1999, p. 60.
27. F. L. Luconi, T. W. Malone, and M. S. S. Morton, "Expert Systems: The Next Challenge for Managers," *Sloan Management Review,* Summer 1996, pp. 3–14.
28. M. W. Davis, "Anatomy of Decision Support," *Datamation,* June 15, 1985, p. 201.
29. Cited in T. A. Stewart, "Brainpower," *Fortune,* June 3, 1991, p. 44.
30. G. Bylinsky, "Computers That Learn by Doing," *Fortune,* September 6, 1993, pp. 96–102; R. E. Calem, "To Catch a Thief," *Forbes ASAP,* June 5, 1995, pp. 44–45; and O. Port, "Computers That Think Are Almost Here," *Business Week,* July 17, 1995, pp. 68–73.
31. See, for example, K. Santa, S. Fatikow, and G. Felso, "Control of Microassembly-Robots by Using Fuzzy-Logic and Neural Networks," *Computers in Industry,* August 1999, pp. 219–27.
32. Bylinsky, "Computers That Learn by Doing."
33. J. Bartimo, "At These Shouting Matches, No One Says a Word," *Business Week,* June 11, 1990, p. 78; M. S. Poole, M. Holmes, and G. DeSanctis, "Conflict Management in a Computer-Supported Meeting Environment," *Management Science,* August 1991, pp. 926–53; A. R. Dennis and J. S. Valacich, "Computer Brainstorms: More Heads Are Better Than One," *Journal of Applied Psychology,* August 1993, pp. 531–37; R. B. Gallupe and W. H. Cooper, "Brainstorming Electronically," *Sloan Management Review,* Fall 1993, pp. 27–36; and R. B. Gallupe, W. H. Colper, M. L. Grise, and L. M. Bastianutti, "Blocking Electronic Brainstorms," *Journal of Applied Psychology,* February 1994, pp. 77–86.
34. W. R. Pape, "Beyond E-Mail," *Inc. Technology,* Summer 1995, p. 28.
35. M. E. Flatley and J. Hunter, "Electronic Mail, Bulletin Board Systems, Conferences: Connections for the Electronic Teaching/Learning Age," in N. J. Groneman, ed., *Technology in the Classroom* (Reston, VA: National Business Education Association, 1995), pp. 73–85.
36. A. L. Sprout, "Surprise! Software to Help You Manage," *Fortune,* April 17, 1995, pp. 197–202.
37. P. Engardio, "There's More Than One Way to Play Leapfrog," *Business Week/21st Century Capitalism,* November 18, 1994, pp. 162–65.
38. L. S. Gould, "GM's Metal Fabricating Division Stamps Its Approval of CAD/CAM," *Automotive Manufacturing and Production,* July 1999, pp. 46–48.
39. See, J. M. O'Brien, "Autodesk CAD-apults Into Low-End Market," *Computer Dealer News,* September 10, 1999, p. 11.
40. R. Mills, "CAD/CAM/CAE Drives Changes in Auto Industries," *Computer-Aided Engineering,* September 1999, pp. 20–26.
41. S. Lais, "Building Industry Braces for IT, Online Onslaught," *Computerworld,* August 23, 1999, p. 14.
42. G. Bylinsky, "The Digital Factory," *Fortune,* November 14, 1994, pp. 96–100.
43. P. Fuhrman, "New Way to Roll," *Forbes,* April 24, 1995, pp. 180–82.
44. J. Teresko, "New Eyes in Manufacturing," *Industry Week,* April 19, 1999, p. 49.
45. R. S. Russell and B. W. Taylor, III, *Operations Management,* p. 264.
46. W. Royal, "Stryker Corp." *Industry Week,* October 19, 1998, p. 72.
47. R. B. Tallian and M. A. Weinstein, "Flexible Automation Solutions for Today's Bakeries," *Robotics World,* May/June 1999, pp. 23–28.
48. "Flexible Industrial Robots," *Machine Design,* August 19, 1999, p. S16.
49. W. Pinkston, "Not Nearly as Cute as It Sounds, 'Urbie Is Anti-Terror Fighter—Georgia Tech Does Its Part to Make the World Safe by Rewiring Robot's Brain," *Wall Street Journal,* September 8, 1998, p. S1; and M. Geewax, "Robots to the Rescue," *The Sun,* August 8, 1999, p. 3C.

50. "Robot Orders Rocket to Record in First Quarter," *Robotics World,* July/August 1999, p. 12.
51. See, for instance, O. Port, "Moving Past the Assembly Line," *Business Week/Reinventing America Special Issue,* November 1992, pp. 177–80; D. M. Upton, "The Management of Manufacturing Flexibility," *California Management Review,* Winter 1994, pp. 72–89; Bylinsky, "The Digital Factory"; and N. Gross and P. Coy, "The Technology Paradox," *Business Week,* March 6, 1995, pp. 76–84.
52. See, for instance, T. Toth, F. Erdelyi, and F. Rayegani, "Intensity Type State Variables in the Integration of Planning and Controlling Manufacturing Processes," *Computers and Industrial Engineering,* October 1999, pp. 82–92.
53. S. S. Erengue, N. C. Simpson, and A. J. Vakharia, "Integrated Production/Distribution Planning in Supply Chains: An Invited Review," *European Journal of Operational Research,* June 1, 1999, p. 219.
54. S. Alexander, "Mass Customization," *Computerworld,* September 6, 1999, p. 54.
55. S. M. Silverman, "Retail Retold," *INC. Technology,* Summer 1995, pp. 23–24.
56. B. Ives and R. O. Mason, "Can Information Technology Revitalize Your Customer Service?" *Academy of Management Executive,* November 1990, pp. 52–69.
57. Ibid.
58. A. B. Gilbert, "Going Small Time," *Fortune,* September 27, 1999, pp. 262a–262f.
59. C. Cyr, "High Tech, High Impact: Creating Canada's Competitive Advantage through Technology Alliances," *Academy of Management Executive,* May 1999, pp. 17–28.
60. See, for instance, S. Dentzer, "Death of the Middleman?" *U.S. News & World Report,* May 22, 1995, p. 56.
61. See, for instance, J. W. Verity, "Planet Internet," *Business Week,* April 3, 1995, pp. 118–24; and B. Ziegler, "In Cyberspace the Web Delivers Junk Mail," *Wall Street Journal,* June 13, 1995, p. B1.
62. See, B. Schlender, "Larry Ellison: Oracle at Web Speed," *Fortune,* May 24, 1999, pp. 128–36.
63. "The Internet: Instant Access to Information," *Canadian Business,* May 1995, pp. 41–43.
64. R. D. Hof and L. Himelstein, "E-Bay vs. Amazon.com," *Business Week,* May 31, 1999, p. 129.
65. M. Sashkin and K. J. Kiser, *Putting Total Quality Management to Work* (San Francisco: Berrett-Koehler, 1993), p. 44.
66. T. Petzinger, Jr., "A Plant Manager Keeps Reinventing His Production Line," *Wall Street Journal,* September 19, 1997, p. B1.
67. M. Hammer and J. Champy, *Reengineering the Corporation: A Manifesto for Business Revolution* (New York: HarperBusiness, 1993). See also J. Champy, *Reengineering Management: The Mandate for New Leadership* (New York: HarperBusiness, 1995); and M. Hammer and S. A. Stanton, *The Reengineering Revolution* (New York: HarperBusiness, 1995).
68. R. Karlgaard, "ASAP Interview: Mike Hammer," *Forbes ASAP,* September 13, 1993, p. 70.
69. Ibid.
70. "The Age of Reengineering," *Across the Board,* June 1993, pp. 26–33.
71. "New Services Extend Supply Chain Management," *Automatic I. D. News,* August 1999, p. 14; and K. Hickey, "Pipeline to Pump," *Traffic World,* August 9, 1999, p. 38.
72. C. Stedman, "Baan Fills Supply-Chain Gap," *Computerworld,* August 9, 1999, p. 20; E. F. Moltzen, "IBM Assembles Bundles for Several ERP Server Solutions," *Computer Reseller News,* August 16, 1999, pp. 3; 8; and D. Kirkpatrick, "IBM from Big Blue Dinosaur to E-Business Animal," *Fortune,* April 26, 1999, p. 122.
73. This section drawn from R. S. Russell and B. W. Taylor, III, *Operations Management* (Upper Saddle River, NJ: Prentice Hall, 2000), pp. 373–74.
74. R. N. Frerichs, "Supply Chain Management," *Electronic Business,* August 1999, p. 8.
75. A. Mandel-Campbell, "Sweet Success," *Latin Trade,* February 1998, p. 26.
76. P. Ritchie, "McDonald's: A Winner through Logistics," *Journal of Physical Distribution and Logistics Management,* July 1990, pp. 21–24; and B. Lewis, "From Procedures to Hiring Practices, CIOs Can Learn a Lot from McDonald's," *InfoWorld,* August 9, 1999, p. 32.
77. See, for instance, E. H. Hall, Jr., "Just-in-Time Management: A Critical Assessment," *Academy of Management Executive,* November 1989, pp. 315–18.
78. P. A. Mason, "MRPII and Kanban Formulae," *Logistics Focus,* April 1999, p. 19; and G. Abdul-Nour, S. Lambert, and J. Drolet, "Adaptation of JIT Philosophy and Kanban Technique to a Small-Sized Manufacturing Firm: A Project Management Approach," *Computers and Industrial Engineering,* December 1998, pp. 419–22.
79. P. A. Mason and M. Parks, "The Implementation of Kanbans," *Logistics Focus,* May 1999, p. 20.
80. "Revamping the Supply Chain," *Manufacturing Engineering,* July 1998, p. 162.
81. E. E. Adams, Jr., and R. J. Ebert, *Production and Operations Management,* 5th ed. (Upper Saddle River, NJ: Prentice Hall, 1992), p. 33.
82. See, for instance, J. W. Weiss and R. K. Wysocki, *5-Phase Project Management* (Reading, Mass.: Addison-Wesley, 1992); J. K. Pinto, "The Power of Project Management," *Industry Week,* August 18, 1997, pp. 138–40; and T. D. Cartwright, "So You're Going to Manage a Project," *Training,* January 1998, pp. 62–67.
83. T. A. Stewart, "The Corporate Jungle Spawns a New Species: The Project Manager," *Fortune,* July 10, 1995, pp. 179–80.
84. Ibid.
85. D. Stamps, "Lights! Camera! Project Management!" *Training,* January 1997, p. 52.
86. T. A. Stewart, "The Corporate Jungle Spawns a New Species."
87. D. Stamps, "Lights! Camera! Project Management!" p. 52.
88. T. A. Stewart, "The Corporate Jungle Spawns a New Species."
89. D. Stamps, "Lights! Camera! Project Management!" p. 52.
90. See R. S. Russell and B. W. Taylor, III, *Operations Management,* p. 815.

91. E. Hazen, "Project Management Ensures On-Time Completion," *Transmission and Distribution,* April 1989, pp. 24–27.
92. L. Nakarmi, "Seoul Yanks the Chaebol's Leash," *Business Week,* October 30, 1995, p. 58.
93. This case based on materials collected from R. S. Russell and B. W. Taylor, III, *Operations Management* (Upper Saddle River, NJ: Prentice Hall, 2000), p. 257; E. P. Lima, "VW's Revolutionary Idea," *Industry Week,* March 17, 1997, pp. 62–67; J. H. Sheridan, "Bonds of Trust," *Industry Week,* March 17, 1997, pp. 52–62; R. Collins, K. Bechler, and S. Pires, "Outsourcing in the Automotive Industry: From JIT to Modular Consortia," *European Management Journal,* p. 11; and D. Woodruff, I. Katz, and K. Naughton, "VW's Factory of the Future," *Business Week,* October 7, 1996, pp. 52–56.

Photo Credits

Chapter 1
page 1 Cheryl Sheridan/Black Star
page 2 Cheryl Sheridan/Black Star
page 3 Jeff Vinnick/Archive Photos
page 5 Bill Cramer Photography
page 8 Stan Godlewski/Liaison Agency, Inc.
page 12 Robert Wright Photography
page 14 Ingersoll-Rand Company/All contents © copyright 1999, Ingersoll-Rand Company. All rights reserved.
page 17 Susan Harrison
page 19 Fritz Hoffman/Network Photographers

Chapter 2
page 45 Paul Souders/Liaison Agency, Inc.
page 46 Paul Souders/Liaison Agency, Inc.
page 50 Bernard Annebicque/Corbis Sygma Photo News
page 52 Reuters/Eriko Sugita/Archive Photos
page 55 © 1999 CDNow Online, Inc. All rights reserved.
page 62 Najlah Feanny/SABA Press Photos, Inc.
page 65 Martin Morrison
page 66 Coogan Photographic, © 2000, Dan Coogan.
page 67 Bebeto Matthews/AP/Wide World Photos

Chapter 3
page 79 Blake Little Photography
page 80 Blake Little Photography
page 83 Pam Francis/Liaison Agency, Inc.
page 90 The John Hopkins University
page 92 Frank LaBua/Pearson Education/PH College
page 96 Linda Farwell Photography
page 99 James Schnepf Photography, Inc. © James Schnepf.
page 101 Larry Evans/Black Star
page 103 Geoffrey Gilpin
page 104 S. Rubin/The Image Works

Chapter 4
page 113 Najlah Feanny/SABA Press Photos, Inc.
page 114 Najlah Feanny/SABA Press Photos, Inc.
page 116 Bill Bachmann/The Image Works
page 121 A. De Wilderberg/Liaison Agency, Inc.
page 122 William Neumann/William Neumann Photography
page 123 Vincent LaForet/Corbis Sygma
page 126 Jeanne Freibert/Corbis Sygma
page 129 PBJ Pictures/Liaison Agency, Inc.
page 132 Larry Ford Foto

Chapter 5
page 153 Jeff Sciortino Photography
page 154 Jeff Sciortino Photography
page 156 David Ulmer/Stock Boston
page 165 John Starkey/Black Star
page 169 Andy Freeberg Photography
page 172 Alisa Owens
page 173 Mark Katzman/Ferguson and Katzman Photography, Inc.
page 174 Amy's Ice Creams, Inc.

Chapter 6
page 183 HR Tech, LLC
page 184 HR Tech, LLC
page 188 William Thomas Cain/AP/Wide World Photos
page 193 Tomi/Photo Disc, Inc.
page 196 Jeff Zaruba/Marriott International, Inc. Courtesy Marriott International, Inc.
page 200 Robin Kalt
page 203 Saturn Corporation
page 205 Kevork Djansezian/AP/Wide World Photos
page 208 Todd Hougas/The New Britton Herald

Chapter 7
page 229 SuperStock, Inc.
page 230 SuperStock, Inc.
page 234 David Frazier/The Image Works
page 243 Bob Daemmrich/The Image Works
page 244 Angela Schwers
page 246 Jonathan Saunders

Chapter 8
page 255 John Abbott/John Abbott Photography
page 256 John Abbott/John Abbott Photography
page 258 Anders Grondstedt
page 261 Doug Mendez/SABA Press Photos, Inc.
page 265 Mark Peterson/SABA Press Photos, Inc.
page 270 Geoffroy de Boismenu/Outline/Corbis
page 274 B. Mahoney/The Image Works
page 278 Bayne Stanley/SABA Press Photos, Inc.

Chapter 9
page 287 Tape Resources, Inc.
page 288 Tape Resources, Inc.
page 293 Ben Coleman/Larime Photographic, Inc.
page 294 VeriFone, Inc.
page 296 Photo provided by James O. Fripp
page 298 Kevin Horan
page 301 Lockheed Martin Corporation
page 303 Allegiance Healthcare Corporation

Chapter 10
page 311 Lantech, Inc.
page 312 Lantech, Inc.
page 314 Wyatt McSpadden Photography
page 318 Forest McMullin Photography
page 323 Rahn & Associates
page 329 Brian Coats Photography
page 331 A. Ramey/PhotoEdit
page 332 Michelle Albert

Chapter 11
page 343 Photo courtesy of Jack Hartnett, D. L. Rogers Corp., Bedford, TX
page 344 Photo courtesy of Jack Hartnett, D. L. Rogers Corp., Bedford, TX

page 347 Munshi Ahmed Photography
page 351 James Sugar/Black Star
page 354 Steve Green/AP/Wide World Photos
page 358 Ann States/SABA Press Photos, Inc.
page 361 AP/Wide World Photos
page 365 Rene DeCarufel/Black Star
page 367 Photo provided by Betsy Reifsnider

Chapter 12 page 375 McDonald's Restaurants of Canada Limited
page 376 McDonald's Restaurants of Canada Limited
page 378 Robert Brenner/PhotoEdit
page 381 Keith Lampher/Liaison Agency, Inc.
page 385 Myrleen Ferguson/PhotoEdit
page 387 Robert J. Heckman
page 390 A. Ramey/PhotoEdit
page 398 Paul Avis/Liaison Agency, Inc.
page 400 Srdjan Ilic/AP/Wide World Photos
page 402 Stock Illustration Source, Inc.

Chapter 13 page 411 Bevil Knapp/Silocaf od New Orleans, Inc.
page 412 Bevil Knapp/Silocaf od New Orleans, Inc.
page 414 Bob Daemmrich/The Image Works
page 416 Phil Degginger/Tony Stone Images
page 421 Boeing Commercial Airplane Group. Used with permission of the Boeing Company.
page 424 Alan Pincus
page 425 Courtesy Reginaldo Manente/Volkswagen, Resende, Brazil
page 427 Kevin Jacobus/The Image Works

Chapter 14

page 437 Brian Leng Photography
page 438 Brian Leng Photography
page 440 Todd Bigelow Photography
page 443 Garry Connor/PhotoEdit
page 446 Don Seabrook/The Wenatchee World/AP/Wide World Photos
page 449 Tom Soblik/Black Star
page 455 John Abbott Photography
page 457 Eric O'Connell Photography
page 459 Chris Kartchner

Name/Organization Index

C

M

N

O

P

Glindex

a combined glossary/subject index

Change agent, 13, 232, 359
Change *An alteration of an organization's environment, structure, technology, or people,* 230
calm waters metaphor, 232–233
concluding remarks and/or chapter summary, 248–249
economy, the, 47–49, 231
external forces creating the need for, 231
innovation, stimulating, 245–248
internal forces creating the need for, 232
one manager's perspective, 244
organization development, 238–240
resistance to, 235–238
review and application questions, 249–250
stress, 240–245
white-water rapids metaphor, 233–234
workshop, management, 251–253
Channel *The medium by which a message travels,* 377–378
Charismatic leadership theory *The theory that followers make attributions of heroic or extraordinary leadership abilities when they observe certain behaviors,* 358–359
Chile, 53
China, 61, 329
Clan control *An approach to designing control systems in which employee behaviors are regulated by the shared values, norms, traditions, rituals, beliefs, and other aspects of the organization's culture,* 413, 414
Classical approach
general administrative theorists, 32
scientific management, 29–31
social events shaping management approaches, 39
subcategories, two, 28–29
Code of ethics *A formal document that states an organization's primary values and the ethical rules it expects managers and operatives to follow,* 60
Coercion and reducing resistance to change, 237, 238
Coercive power, 162
Cognitive component of an attitude *The beliefs, opinions, knowledge, and information held by a person,* 258
Cognitive dissonance *Any incompatibility between two or more attitudes or between behavior and attitudes,* 260
Cohesiveness, group, 280–281
Collaboration, 396
Collectivism, 297
College courses, 18–20
Colombia, 53
Combination strategy *The simultaneous pursuit by an organization of two or more of growth, stability, and retrenchment strategies,* 97
Commitment, 123, 258–259, 295
Communication apprehension *Communication anxiety,* 380, 382
Communication process
barriers to an effective, 380–385
concluding remarks and/or chapter summary, 404–405
conflict management, 397
electronic media, 380
gender issues, 385–386
grapevine, the, 379
importance of effective communication, 376
nonverbal cues, 379–380
resistance to change, reducing, 237
review and application questions, 405–406
seven parts of the, 377–378
technology, 445
workshop, management, 407–409
work teams, 295–296
written *vs.* verbal communications, 378–379
See also **Interpersonal skills**
Compensation administration *The process of determining a cost-effective pay structure that will attract and retain competent employees, provide an incentive for them to work hard, and ensure that pay levels will be perceived as fair,* 202–203, 330–331
See also **Motivation**
Competence, 14–15, 366
Competency-based compensation *A program that pays and rewards employees on the basis of skills, knowledge, or behaviors they possess,* 330–331
Competitive advantage, 99–100
Competitive intelligence *Accurate information about competitors that allows managers to anticipate competitors' actions rather than merely react to them,* 92–93
Competitive strategy *A strategy to position an organization in such a way that it will have a distinct advantage over its competition; three types are cost leadership, differentiation, and focus strategies,* 97
Compressed workweek, 333
Compromise, 396, 397
Computer-aided design (CAD) *Computational and graphics software allows the geometry of a product or component to be graphically displayed and manipulated on video monitors,* 448
Computer monitoring, 427–428
Conceptual skills *A manager's mental ability to coordinate all of the organization's interests and activities,* 13, 127–128
Concluder-producers, 299
Concurrent control *Control that takes place while an activity is in progress,* 420
Conflict *Perceived incompatible differences resulting in interference or opposition,* 393
managers, conflict, 363
players, who are the conflict, 397
sources of, 397–398
stimulating functional conflict, 398–399
styles, conflict-handling, 396–397
views of conflict, three, 394–395
which conflicts to handle, 397
Conforming and group decision-making, 130
Conscientiousness, 262
Consideration *The extent to which a leader has job relationships characterized by mutual trust, respect for employees' ideas, and regard for their feelings,* 348–349
Consistency, 259, 366
Constitution, U.S., 126
Consultation, process, 239
Contingency approach *The situational approach to management that replaces more simplistic systems and integrates much of management theory*
control systems, 422–424
decision making, 124–125
leadership, 350–357
organization design, 166–169
today's world, managing, 42–43
variables, four popular contingency, 42–43
Contingent workers *Part-time, temporary, and contract workers who are available for hire on an as-needed basis,* 67–69
Continuous improvement methods, 65–66, 302–303, 452–453, 456–457
Contract workers, 68
Control *The process of monitoring activities to ensure that they are being accomplished as planned and of correcting any significant deviations,* 7
approaches to designing control systems, three, 413
concluding remarks and/or chapter summary, 428–429
contingency factors of, 422–424
dysfunctional side of controls, 425–426
ethical issues, 426–428
managerial action, 419
measuring actual performance, 415–417
national differences, 424–425
one manager's perspective, 424
PERT program, 463

Economic order quantity model (EOQ) *A technique for balancing purchase, ordering, carrying, and stockout costs to derive the optimum quantity for a purchase order,* 149–151
Economics, college courses in, 19
Economy, the changing, 47–49, 231
Economy and effective control systems, 421
Education/communication and reducing resistance to change, 237
Effectiveness *Means doing the right thing; goal attainment,* 5–6, 421–422
Efficiency *Means doing the thing correctly; refers to the relationship between inputs and outputs. Seeks to minimize resource costs,* 5–6, 447–448, 454
Effort-performance linkage, 324
Electronic meeting *A type of nominal group technique in which participants are linked by computer,* 131–132
E-mail, 380, 427
Emotional stability, 263
Emotion intelligence (EI) *An assortment of noncognitive skills, capabilities, and competencies that influence a person's ability to cope with environmental demands and pressures,* 264
Emotions and effective communication, 380, 381–382, 385
Empathy, 264, 387–388
Employee assistance programs (EAPs) *Programs offered by organizations to help their employees overcome personal and health-related problems,* 208–209, 244–245
Employee benefits *Nonfinancial rewards designed to enrich employees' lives,* 203
Employee counseling *A process designed to help employees overcome performance-related problems,* 201–202
Employee oriented *The term used to describe a leader who emphasizes interpersonal relations, takes a personal interest in the needs of employees, and accepts individual differences,* 349
Employment planning *The process by which management ensures it has the right number and kinds of people in the right places at the right time, capable of helping the organization achieve its goals,* 187–189
  See also Human resource management (HRM)
Empowerment skills, 390–393
Encoding *The conversion of a message into some symbolic form,* 377
England, 52–53, 241, 329
Entrepreneurship *The process of initiating a business venture, organizing the necessary resources, and assuming the risks and rewards,* 9, 61–62, 103–105
Environment affecting structure, the organization's, 168–169
Environmental scanning *Screening large amounts of information to detect emerging trends and create a set of scenarios,* 91–93
Environmental sensitivity and charismatic leadership, 359
Epirit de corps, 33
Equity theory *Adam's theory that employees perceive what they get from a job situation (outcomes) in relation to what they put into it (inputs) and then compare their input-outcome ratio with input-outcome ratios of relevant others,* 33, 318–321
Escalation of commitment *An increased commitment to a previous decision despite negative information,* 123
Esteem needs, 314
Ethics *A set of rules or principles that define right and wrong conduct,* 59
  Bausch & Lomb, 125
  code of, 60
  competitive intelligence, 93
  contingent workforce, 69
  control systems, 426–428
  distorting information, 383
  incentive programs, 325
  leadership, gender differences in, 362
  orders, following, 158
  organization development, 240
  recruitment, 259
  salaries, executive, 16
  software, sharing, 445
  stress interviews, 194
  views of, three, 60
  work teams, 300
Ethnocentric view *A parochial view in which one sees one's own culture as better than any other,* 52
Europe, 68
Events *End points that represent the completion of major activities,* 462
Exceptions and effective control systems, 422
Expectancy theory *Vroom's theory that an individual tends to act in a certain way in the expectation that the act will be followed by a given outcome and according to the attractiveness of that outcome,* 324–327
Expert power, 162
Expert systems *Software programs to encode the relevant experience of an expert and allow a system to act like that expert in analyzing and solving ill-structured problems,* 445–446
Explorer-promoters, 298–299
Extinction, 275
Extroversion, 262

F

Facilitation/support and reducing resistance to change, 237
Fair Labor Standards, 40
Family-friendly benefits *A wide range of work and family programs to help employees; includes on-site day care, child and elder care, flexible work hours, job sharing, part-time employment, relocation programs, adoption benefits, parental leave, and other programs,* 62, 206–207
Feedback *The degree to which carrying out the work activities required by a job results in the individual's obtaining direct and clear information about the effectiveness of his or her performance,* 378
  communication barriers, overcoming, 383–384
  control systems, 420–421
  interpersonal skills, 388–390, 393
  job characteristics model, 321–323
  survey, 239
Feedforward control *Control that prevents anticipated problems,* 420
Fiedler contingency model *The theory that effective group performance depends on the proper match between the leader's style of interacting with employees and the degree to which the situation gives control and influence to the leader,* 351–353
Figurehead, 9
Filtering and effective communication, 380–381
Finland, 115
First-line managers *Supervisors responsible for directing the day-to-day activities of operative employees,* 4
Flexibility
  and effective control systems, 421
  manufacturing systems, 449–450
  motivation, 329, 333–335
  and rapid response systems, 67–69
Flexible manufacturing systems *Systems that integrate computer-aided design, engineering, and manufacturing to produce low-volume products at a cost comparable to what had once only been possible through mass production,* 449–450
Flextime, 334
Focus strategy *The strategy an organization follows when it wants to establish an advantage in a narrow market strategy,* 97
Forcing, 396
Forecast Pro, 447
Forensic Accountant Newsletter, 404
Forming *The first stage of work team development characterized by uncertainty about purpose, structure, and leadership,* 289
France, 30, 52, 66, 68
Franchising, 61

Functional conflict *Conflicts that support an organization's goals,* 394
Functional departmentalization *The grouping of activities by functions performed,* 163–164
Functional structure *An organization in which similar and related occupational specialties are grouped together,* 170
Functional teams *A work team composed of a manager and the employees in his or her unit and involved in efforts to improve work activities or to solve specific problems within the particular functional unit,* 291
Fundamental attribution error *The tendency to underestimate the influence of external factors and overestimate the influence of internal or personal factors when making judgments about the behavior of others,* 271

G

Gender differences in leadership, 362
Gender issues in the communication process, 385–386
General administrative theorists *Writers who developed general theories of what managers do and what constitutes good management practice,* 32
Geographic departmentalization *The grouping of activities by territory,* 164–165
Germany, 30, 66, 91, 105, 241
Global village *Refers to the concept of a boundaryless world; the production and marketing of goods and services worldwide*
managers, what effect does globalization have on, 51–54
multinational corporations, 49–50, 424
organizations, how does globalization effect, 50–51
Gnatt chart *A planning tool that shows in bar graph form when tasks are supposed to be done and compares that with the actual progress on each,* 459–460
Good work performance, 224
Grand strategies *The four primary types of strategies: growth, stability, retrenchment, and combination,* 95
Grapevine *An unofficial channel of communication,* 379
Graphic rating scales, 199
Group cohesiveness *The degree to which members of a group are attracted to each other and share goals,* 280–281
Groups *Two or more interacting and interdependent individuals who come together to achieve particular objectives*
cohesive, 280–281
decision-making, 128–132
norms, 278–279
ranking, group-order, 201
size of, 280
status, 279–280
why do people join, 276–277
See also **Work teams**
Groupthink *The withholding by group members of different views in order to appear to be in agreement,* 130
Groupware *Software programs developed to facilitate group interaction and decision making,* 447
Growth strategy *A strategy in which an organization attempts to increase the level of its operations; can take the form of increasing sales revenue, number of employees, or market share,* 95–96

H

Halo effect, 272
Hawthorne studies *A series of studies during the 1920s and 1930s that provided new insights into group norms and behaviors,* 35–36
Heuristics *Judgmental shortcuts,* 122–123
Hierarchy of needs theory *Maslow's theory that is a hierarchy of five human needs: physiological, safety, social, esteem, and self-actualization,* 314–315
Historical roots of contemporary management practices
building on history: studying management today, 40–43
classical approach, 28–32
human resources approach, 32–38
premodern area, 27–28
quantitative approach, 38–39
social events shaping management approaches, 39–40
How to Win Friends and Influence People (Carnegie), 36
Humanities/social science courses affecting management practices, 18–20
Human relations view of conflict *The view that conflict is natural and inevitable and has the potential to be a positive force,* 394
Human resource inventory report *A report listing the name, education, training, prior employer, languages spoken, and the likes of each employee in the organization,* 188
Human resource management (HRM), 184
compensation and benefits, 202–203
concluding remarks and/or chapter summary, 210–211
diversity, workplace, 203–204
employment planning, 187–189
family-friendly benefits, 206–207
issues facing today's managers, 203–209
key components, 185–186
legal environment of, 186–187
one manager's perspective, 200
orientation/training and development, 195–198
performance management, 198–202
recruitment and selection, 189–195
review and application questions, 211–212
sexual harassment, 204–206
unions and management, cooperation between, 207
violence, workplace, 208–209
workshop, management, 213–216
Human resources approach, 32
advocates of, early, 33–35
behavioral science theorists, 38
common thread linking advocates of, 37–38
Hawthorne studies, 35–36
history, management, 36–37
social events shaping management approaches, 39–40
Hungary, 61
Hygiene factors *Herzberg's term for factors, such as working conditions and salary, that, when adequate, may eliminate job dissatisfaction but do not necessarily increase job satisfaction,* 316–317

I

Iceberg metaphor, the organization as an, 257
Identification-based trust *Trust based on an emotional connection between the parties,* 368
Ill-structured problems *New problems in which information is ambiguous or incomplete,* 124
Image, presenting the right, 225
Immediate corrective action *Correcting a problem at once to get performance back on track,* 419
Impersonality, 34
Impression management *A technique that attempts to project the sort of image that will result in a favorable outcome,* 222
Improvement, continuous, 65–66, 302–303, 452–453, 456–457
Incentives, 312, 325
See also **Motivation**
Incubation and innovation, 246
India, 53, 83–84, 447
Individualism, 53
Individual ranking approach, 201
Individuals into team players, turning, 297–302

Industrial Revolution *The advent of machine power, mass production, and efficient transportation in the late eighteenth century in Great Britain,* 28, 48
Information *Analyzed and processed data,* 443
Information overload *The result of the situation of information exceeding processing capacity,* 380, 381
Information technology (IT), 55–56, 442–447
Initiating structure *The extent to which a leader defines and structures his or her role and the roles of employees to attain goals,* 348
Initiative, 33
Innovation *The process of taking a creative idea and turning it into a useful product, service, or method of operation,* 245–248, 298
Integrative bargaining *Negotiation in which there is at least one settlement that involves no loss to either party,* 401
Integrity, 365
Intelligence, competitive, 92–93
Interactionist view of conflict *The view that some conflict is necessary for an organization to perform effectively,* 394
Intergroup development *An activity that attempts to make several work groups become more cohesive,* 239
Internet, the, 56, 219, 452
Internships, 223
Interpersonal demands, 242
Interpersonal skills *A manager's ability to work with, understand, mentor, and motivate others, both individually and in groups,* 13
- active listening, 387–389
- concluding remarks and/or chapter summary, 404–405
- conflict, managing, 393–399
- empowerment skills, 390–393
- failure and poor, 386
- negotiation skills, 399–402
- one manager's perspective, 387
- presentations, effective, 402–404
- review and application questions, 405–406
- workshop, management, 407–409

Interviews, 193–195, 221–223
Intrapreneurs *Persons within an organization who demonstrate entrepreneurial characteristics,* 61–62
Inventory turnover ratios, 146
Ireland, 53
ISO 9000 series *Designed by the International Organization for Standardization, these standards reflect a process whereby independent auditors attest that a company's factory, laboratory, or office has met quality management standards,* 101–102

J

Japan
- communication process, 386
- decision making, 132–133
- downsizing, 67
- kanban, 456
- leaders, 364
- loyalty to the organization, 329
- stress, 241
- Taylor, F. W., 30
- total quality management, 64
- work teams, 298

Jargon *Technical language,* 382
Job analysis *An assessment of the kinds of skills, knowledge, and abilities needed to successfully perform each job in an organization,* 188
Job characteristics model (JCM) *Hackman and Oldham's job description model: The five core job dimensions are skill variety, task identity, task significance, autonomy, and feedback,* 321–323, 331
Job description *A written statement of what a jobholder does, how it is done, and why it is done,* 188
Job involvement, 258
Job-morphing, 295
Job satisfaction, 258
Job sharing *A type of part-time work that allows two or more workers to split a traditional 40-hour-a-week job,* 334
Job specification *A statement of the minimum acceptable qualifications that an incumbent must possess to perform a given job successfully,* 188
Just-in-time (JIT) inventory systems *Systems in which inventory items arrive when needed in the production process instead of being stored in stock,* 456

K

Kaizen *The Japanese term for an organization committed to continuous improvement,* 64, 66
Kanban *Japanese for card or signal; refers to a system of cards in shipping containers that uses the just-in-time concept (a card reorders a shipment when a container is opened),* 456
Karoshi *A Japanese term that refers to a sudden death caused by overworking,* 241
Knowledge-based trust *Trust based on behavioral predictability that comes from a history of interaction,* 367–368
Knowledge workers, 48
Korea, 364

L

Laissez-faire style of leadership *The term used to describe a leader who gives employees complete freedom to make decisions and to decide on work methods,* 347, 348
Language and effective communication, 380, 382, 384
Lateral thinking, 226
Layoffs, 66–67, 190, 191, 209
Leader-participation model *A leadership theory that provides a sequential set of rules for determining the form and amount of participation a leader should exercise in decision making according to different types of situations,* 355
Leaders *People who are able to influence others and who possess managerial authority,* 296, 345
Leading *Includes motivating employees, directing the activities of others, selecting the most effective communication channel, and resolving conflicts,* 7, 9
- behavioral theories, 345–350, 359
- charismatic leadership, 358–359
- concluding remarks and/or chapter summary, 369–370
- contingency theories of leadership, 350–357
- cultural dimensions of a country's environment, 363–364
- emerging approaches, 357–361
- Hartnett, Jack, 344
- managers *vs.* leaders, 344–345
- relationship between members and leaders, 352
- review and application questions, 370–371
- stress, 242
- teams, work, 361–363
- trait theories, 345
- transactional *vs.* transformational leaders, 360–361
- trust, 364–369
- visionary leadership, 359–360
- workshop, management, 372–374

Learning *Any relatively permanent change in behavior that occurs as a result of experience,* 273–276
Least-preferred co-worker questionnaire (LPC) *A questionnaire that measures whether a person is task or relationship oriented,* 351
Legislation
- Americans with Disabilities Act, 231
- human resource management, 187

Myers-Briggs type indicator (MBTI) *A method of identifying personality types,* 262, 263

N

National borders, management concepts and, 12
See also Cultural dimensions of a country's environment
National Labor Relations Board, 207
Need *An internal state that makes certain outcomes appear attractive,* 313–315, 317–318
Need-for-achievement concept, 329
Negative feedback, 388–390
Negative reinforcement, 275
Negotiation *A process in which two or more parties who have different preferences must make a joint decision and come to an agreement,* 9, 237–238, 399–402, 447
Netherlands, 53, 91
Networking, 227
Neural networks *Networks that use computer software to imitate the structure of brain cells and connections among them,* 445
New Deal, 40
New Zealand, 53, 329
Nominal group technique *A decision-making technique in which group members are physically present but operate independently,* 131–132
Nonprogrammed decisions *Decisions that must be custom-made to solve unique and nonrecurring problems,* 124, 126, 127
Nonverbal cues, 379–380
Norm *Acceptable standards shared by the members of a group,* 278–279
Norming *The third stage of work team development, in which close relationships develop and members begin to demonstrate cohesiveness,* 290
Not-for-profit *vs.* profit organizations, 10

O

Objectives, management by, 86–89, 414
Observation, measuring performance using personal, 416
Obsolescence, worker, 440–442
Openness to experience, 263
Open system *A system that dynamically interacts with its environment,* 41
Operant conditioning *A behavioral theory that argues that voluntary, or learned, behavior is a function of its consequences,* 273–274
Operating ratios, 146
Operations management, 439
Operations Research, 40
Operations research (OR), 38–40
Operations technology
- continuous improvement, 452–453, 456–457
- customer service, 450–451
- distribution, product, 451–452
- efficiency in product design, 447–448
- enhancing production processes, 448–450
- just-in-time inventory, 456
- process engineering, 453–454
- productivity and efficiency, 454
- supply chain management, 455–456

Operatives *People who work directly on a job or task and have no responsibility for overseeing the work of others,* 3–4
Opportunities, strategic *Positive external environmental factors,* 93–94, 365
Oral reports, 416
Order in Fayol's principles of management, 33
Orders, following, 158
Organic organization *An adhocracy; a structure that is low in specialization, formalization, and centralization,* 167
Organizational behavior (OB) *The study of the actions of people at work*
- concluding remarks and/or chapter summary, 281–282
- focus of, 257
- goals of, 257–261
- group behavior, 276–281
- learning, 273–276
- one manager's perspective, 258
- perception, 269–273
- personality, 261–268
- review and application questions, 283
- Wachner, Linda, 256
- workshop, management, 284–286

Organization *A systematic arrangement of people brought together to accomplish some specific purpose,* 3
Organization culture *A system of shared meaning within an organization that determines, in large degree, how employees act,* 174–176, 247–248, 392
Organization design *A process in which managers develop or change their organization's structure*
- authority and responsibility, 158–162
- boundaryless organization, 173–174
- bureaucracies, 170–172
- centralization and decentralization, 163–164
- chain of command, 156–157
- concluding remarks and/or chapter summary, 176–177
- contingency variables affecting structure, 166–169
- culture, organizational, 174–176
- departmentalization, 163–166
- Lipschultz, Levin, and Gray, 154
- one manager's perspective, 172
- review and application questions, 178
- simple structure, 169
- span of control, 157
- team-based structures, 172
- workshop, management, 179–181
- work specialization, 155–157

Organization development (OD) *An activity designed to facilitate planned, long-term organizationwide change that focuses on the attitudes and values of organizational members; essentially an effort to change an organization's culture,* 238–240
Organizing *Includes determining what tasks are to be done, who is to do them, how the tasks are to be grouped, who reports to whom, and where decisions are to be made,* 7
Outsourcing *An organization's use of outside firms for providing necessary products and services,* 67

P

Paired comparison approach, 201
Pakistan, 53
Parochialism *Refers to a narrow focus, in which one sees things solely through one's own eyes and within one's own perspective,* 52
Participation and reducing resistance to change, 237
Participative leader, 354
Part-time employees, 68, 224, 334
Path-goal theory *The theory that it is a leader's job to assist followers in attaining their goals and to provide the necessary direction and support,* 352–355
Pay-for-performance programs *Compensation plans, such as piece-rate plans, profit sharing, and the like that pay employees on the basis of some performance measure,* 330
Payoff matrices, 141–142
Perception, 246, 269–273
Performance management system *A process of establishing performance standards and evaluating performance in order to arrive at objective human resource decisions and to provide documentation to support personnel actions,* 198–202, 324, 415–417
Performance-simulation tests *Selection devices that are based on actual job behaviors, work sampling, and assessment centers,* 193
Performing *The fourth stage of work team development, in which the structure is fully functional and accepted by team members,* 290

Personal differences and conflicts, 397–398
Personal factors leading to stress, 242–243
Personality
categorizing traits, 261–262
cultural dimensions of a country's environment, 268
entrepreneurial, 104–105
locus of control, 264–265
Machiavellianism, 265
matching personalities and jobs, 266–268
predicting behaviors, 262–264
self-esteem, 265
self-monitoring, 265–266
value of a manager's understanding of personality differences, 268
PERT (program evaluation and review technique) *A flowchart-like diagram that depicts the sequence of activities needed to complete a project and the time or costs associated with each activity,* 460–463
Philippines, 53
Philosophy courses, 19
Physiological needs, 314
Plan-do-check-act (PDCA) cycle, 452–453
Planning *Includes defining goals, establishing strategy, and developing plans to coordinate activities,* 6–7, 80
career, 218
changes, 238–240
concluding remarks and/or chapter summary, 105–106
criticisms of formal, 82–83
employment, 187–189
entrepreneurship, 103–105
objectives, management by, 86–89
one manager's perspective, 103
organizational strategy, importance of an, 89–90
PERT program, 463
quality as a strategic weapon, 99–102
review and application questions, 107
strategic management process, 90–99
types of plans, 84–86
in uncertain environments, 81–84
workshop, management, 108–111
Policy *A general guide that establishes parameters for making decisions,* 125–126
Political science studies, 19
Political skills *A manager's ability to build a power base and establish the right connections,* 13
Portugal, 53
Position power, 352
Positive expectation, 365
Positive feedback, 388
Positive reinforcement, 275
Power *An individual's capacity to influence decisions,* 53, 160–162, 317–318, 352
Presentation skills, 402–404
Principles of management *Fayol's fundamental or universal principles of management practice,* 32, 33
Principles of Scientific Management, The (Taylor), 30
Privacy, control systems and an invasion of, 426
Problem *A discrepancy between an existing and a desired state of affairs,* 115–116, 124
Problem-solving teams *Work teams typically composed of five to twelve hourly employees from the same department who meet each week to discuss ways of improving quality, efficiency, and the work environment,* 291–292
Procedure *A series of interrelated sequential steps that can be used to respond to a well-structured problem,* 124–125
Process approach *The performance of planning, leading, and controlling activities is seen as circular and continuous,* 41
Process consultation *The use of consultants from outside an organization to help change agents within the organization assess process events such as workflow, informal intraunit relationships, and formal communications channels,* 239
Process departmentalization *The grouping of activities by work or customer flow,* 165, 166
Process engineering, work, 453–454
Process value analysis *Analysis of the organization as a series of processes in order to determine to what degree each adds value,* 454
Product departmentalization *The grouping of activities by product produced,* 164
Production oriented *The term used to describe a leader who emphasizes the technical or task aspects of a job, is concerned mainly with accomplishing tasks, and regards group members as a means to accomplishing goals,* 349
Productivity *Outputs (labor + capital + materials),* 439–440, 454
Professional employee organization (PEO), 184
Professional employees, 332–333
Profitability ratios, 146–147
Profit *vs.* not-for-profit organizations, 10
Program evaluation and review technique (PERT) *A flowchart-like diagram that depicts the sequence of activities needed to complete a project and the time or costs associated with each activity,* 460–463
Programmed decision *A repetitive decision that can be handled by a routine approach,* 124, 126
Project management *Task of getting the activities done on time, within budget, and according to specifications,* 457–463
Project *One-time only set of activities with a definite beginning and ending point in time,* 457
Psychology and Industrial Efficiency (Munsterberg), 34
Psychology courses, 20
Public speaking, 402–404
Punishment, 275

Q

Qualities of employees, 392
Quality circles *Work teams composed of eight to ten employees and supervisors who share an area of responsibility and who meet regularly to discuss quality programs, investigate the causes of the problem, recommend solutions, and take corrective actions but who have no authority,* 29
Quality control *Ensuring that what is produced meets some preestablished standard,* 457
benchmarking, 100–101
competitive advantage, 99–100
ISO 9000 series, 101–102
revolution, 63–64
six sigma, 102
total quality management, 63–64
Quality of life, 53, 329
Quantitative approach, 38–40
Queuing theory *A technique that balances the cost of having a waiting line against the cost of service to maintain that line,* 148–149

R

Range of variation *The acceptable parameters of variance between actual performance and the standard,* 417–419
Ratio analysis, 144–147
Rational *Describes choices that are consistent and value-maximizing within specified constraints,* 119
Readiness *The situational leadership model term for a follower's ability and willingness to perform,* 356–357
Realistic job preview (RJP) *Providing both positive and negative information about the job and the company during the job interview,* 195
Reasonable criteria and effective control systems, 422

Recruitment *The process of locating, identifying, and attracting capable applicants,* 189–190, 259
Referent *In equity theory, the other persons, the systems, or the personal experiences against which individuals compare themselves to assess equity,* 318–320
Referent power, 162
Reinforcement, 275
Reliability *The degree to which a selection device measures the same thing consistently,* 192
Remuneration, 33
Representative heuristics *The tendency for people to base judgments of probability on things with which they are familiar,* 122–123
Resistance to change, 235–238
Resource allocator, 9
Resources, analyzing/controlling organizational, 94, 225
Responsibility *An obligation to perform assigned activities,* 158, 388
résumé preparation, 219–224
Retention processes, 274
Retrenchment strategy *A strategy characteristic of a company that is reducing its size, usually in an environment of decline,* 97
Return-on-investment ratios, 146, 147
Reward power, 162
Reward systems, 300–301
See also **Motivation**
Rightsizing *Linking staffing levels to organizational goals,* 67
Rights view of ethics, 60
Ringisei *Japanese consensus-forming group decisions,* 132–133
Risk *The probability that a particular outcome will result from a given decision,* 119, 266
Robotics *Computer-controlled machines that manipulate materials and perform complex functions,* 446, 449
Role *A set of expected behavior patterns attributed to someone who occupies a given position in a social unit,* 8, 9, 242, 277, 288–289
Routineness of task technology, 43
Rule *An explicit statement that tells managers what they ought or ought not to do,* 125, 126
Russia, 30, 61

S

Safety needs, 314
Salaries, 16, 202–203, 330–331
See also **Motivation**
Scalar Chain, 33
Scanning, environmental, 91–92
Scheduling devices, 459–463
Scientific management *The use of the scientific method to define the one best way for a job to be done*
attention given to, 31
Gantt, Henry L., 31
Gilbreth, Frank and Lillian, 31
Taylor, Frederick W., 29–30
Security, 276
Selection process, employee, 190–195, 299–300
Selective perception and effective communication, 380, 381
Selectivity and judging others, 271, 272
Self-actualization needs, 314
Self-awareness, 264
Self-confidence and charismatic leadership, 359
Self-esteem *An individual's degree of like or dislike for him- or herself,* 265, 277
Self-fulfilling prophecy, 272
Self-interest concept, 329
Self-managed work teams *A formal group of employees that operates without a manager and is responsible for a complete work process or segment that delivers a product or service to an external or internal customer,* 292–293
Self-management, 264
Self-monitoring *A measure of an individual's ability to adjust his or her behavior to external, situational factors,* 265–266
Self-motivation, 264
Self-serving bias *The tendency for individuals to attribute their own successes to internal factors while putting the blame for failures on external factors,* 271
Sensitivity to differences, managerial, 63
Service organization *An organization that produces nonphysical outputs such as educational, medical, or transportation services,* 439
Sexual harassment *Sexually suggestive remarks, unwanted touching and sexual advances, requests for sexual favors, or other verbal and physical conduct of a sexual nature,* 204–206
Shaping behavior *Systematically reinforcing each successive step that moves an individual closer to a desired behavior,* 275, 299–301
Short-term plans *Plans that cover less than one year,* 84
Similarity, assumed, 271–272
Simple structure *An organization that is low in specialization and formalization but high in centralization,* 169
Singapore, 53, 442
Single-use plans *A plan that is used to meet the needs of a particular or unique situation,* 86
Situational approach, 42–43
Situational leadership *A model of leadership behavior that reflects how a leader should adjust his or her leadership style in accordance with the readiness of followers,* 355–357
Six sigma *A philosophy and measurement process that attempts to design in quality as a product is being made,* 102
Size of a group, 280
Size of the organization, 11–12, 43, 168, 392
Skills, management, 13–14, 226, 264, 321–323
Slack time *The time difference between the critical path and all other paths,* 463
Small business *Any independently owned and operated profit-seeking enterprise that has fewer than 500 employees,* 11–12
Social events shaping management approaches, 39–40
Social learning theory *The theory that people can learn through observation and direct experience,* 274–275
Social loafing *The tendency of an individual in a group to decrease his or her effort because responsibility and individual achievement cannot be measured,* 280
Social needs, 314
Social responsibility *A firm's obligation, beyond that required by the law and economics, to pursue long-term goals that are good for society,* 57–62
Social responsiveness *The ability of a firm to adapt to changing societal conditions,* 59
Social science/humanities courses affecting management practices, 18–20
Social Security, 203
Social skills, 264
Sociology studies, 20
Software, sharing, 445
South Africa, 53, 329
Span of control *The number of subordinates a manager can direct efficiently and effectively,* 157
Specific plans *Plans that have clearly defined objectives and leave no room for misinterpretation,* 85
Spokesperson, 9
Stability of tenure of personnel, 33
Stability strategy *A strategy that is characterized by an absence of significant change,* 96–97
Staff authority *Positions that have some authority but that are created to support,*

assist, and advise the holders of line authority, 159
Staffing. *See* Human resource management (HRM)
Stakeholders *Any group that is affected by organizational decisions and policies*, 41
Standing plan *A plan that is ongoing and provides guidance for repeatedly performed actions in an organization*, 86
Statistical reports, 416
Status *A prestige grading, position, or rank within a group*, 52, 276–277, 279–280
Stereotyping, 272
Storming, team *The second stage of work team development, characterized by intragroup conflict*, 290
Strategic alliances *A domestic and a foreign firm share the cost of developing new products or building production facilities in a foreign country*, 51
Strategic management process *A nine-step process that involves strategic planning, implementation, and evaluation*
  environment, analyze the, 91–93
  evaluate results, 99
  formulating strategies, 95–99
  implementation, 99
  mission statement, 90–91
  opportunities and threats, identify, 93–94
  resources, analyze the organization's, 94
  strengths and weaknesses, identify, 94
  SWOT analysis, 95
Strategic placement and effective control systems, 422
Strategic plans *Plans that are organizationwide, establish overall objectives, and position an organization in terms of its environment*, 84
Strengths, strategic *Internal resources that are available or things that an organization does well*, 94
Stress *A force or influences a person feels when he or she faces opportunities, constraints, or demands that he or she perceives to be both uncertain and important*, 194, 240–245
Structure, organizational
  conflict, sources of, 397
  divisional, 170
  environment affecting, 168–169
  functional, 170
  strategy affecting, 167–168
  stress, 242
  See also **Organization design**
Subordination of individual interests to the general interest, 33
Supply chain management *Management of the facilities, functions, and activities involved in producing and delivering a product or service, from suppliers to customers*, 455–456
Supportive leader, 354
Support/facilitation and reducing resistance to change, 237
Survey feedback *A method of assessing employees' attitudes about and perceptions of a change they are encountering by asking specific questions*, 239
Sweden, 173
Switzerland, 101
SWOT analysis *Analysis of an organization's strengths, weaknesses, opportunities, and threats in order to identify a strategic niche that the organization can exploit*, 95
Systems approach *Defines a system as a set of interrelated and interdependent parts arranged in a manner that produces a unified whole*, 41–42

T

Tactical plans *Plans that specify the details of how an organization's overall objectives are to be achieved*, 84
Task complexity, 392
Task demands, 241–242
Task identity, 321–323
Task significance, 321–323
Task structure, 352
Team-based structures *An organization that consists entirely of work groups, or teams*, 172
  See also **Work teams**
Team building *An activity that helps work groups set goals, develop positive interpersonal relationships, and clarify the role and responsibilities of each team member*, 239
Technical employees, 332–333
Technology *Any equipment, tools, or operating methods that are designed to make work more efficient; how an organization transforms its inputs into outputs*
  change, need for, 231
  concluding remarks and/or chapter summary, 464–465
  control systems, 425
  e-commerce, 56
  French, Brenda, 438
  information, 55–56, 442–447
  obsolescence, worker, 440–442
  one manager's perspective, 459
  and productivity, 439–440
  project management and control tools, 457–463
  review and application questions, 465
  structure, technology affecting, 168
  today's world, managing in, 54–57
  transfer, 442
  workshop, management, 466–468
  See also Operations technology
Technology transfer *Transfer of knowledge from one country to another for the development of new products or for improvements in a production process*, 442
Telecommuting *A system of working at home on a computer that is linked to the office*, 56–57, 334–335
Temporary employees, 68
Ten Commandments, 126
Theory of justice view of ethics, 60
Theory X *McGregor's term for the assumption that employees dislike work, are lazy, seek to avoid responsibility, and must be coerced to perform*, 315–316
Theory Y *McGregor's term for the assumption that employees are creative, seek responsibility, and can exercise self-direction*, 315–316
Therbligs *The Gilbreths' classification scheme for labeling 17 basic hand motions*, 31
Threats *Negative external environmental factors*, 93–94
Three-needs theory *McClelland's theory that the needs for achievement, power, and affiliation are major motives in work*, 317–319
360-degree appraisal, 199, 200
Thruster-organizers, 299
Timeliness and effective control systems, 421
Times-interest-earned ratios, 146
Titles, managerial, 4–5
Today's world, managing in
  common factors characterizing stars of the 2000s, 46
  concluding remarks and/or chapter summary, 70–72
  contingency approach, 42–43
  diversity affecting organizations, 62–63
  downsizing, 66–67
  economy, the changing, 47–49
  flexible and rapid response systems, 67–69
  global marketplace, 49–54
  human resource management, 203–209
  one manager's perspective, 65
  quality, 63–64
  quantum changes *vs.* continuous improvement, 65–66
  review and application questions, 72–73
  social responsibility, corporate, 57–62
  system approach, 41–42
  technology, 54–57
  workshop, management, 74–77

Top managers *Individuals who are responsible for making decisions about the direction of the organization and establishing policies that affect all organizational members,* 4–5
Total assets turnover ratios, 146
Total quality management (TQM) *A philosophy of management that is driven by customer needs and expectations and that is committed to continuous improvement,* 63–64
Traditional view of conflict *The view that all conflict is bad and must be avoided,* 394
Training, employee, 196–198
Trait theories of leadership *Theories that isolate characteristics that differentiate leaders from nonleaders,* 345
Transactional leaders *Leaders who guide or motivate their followers toward established goals by clarifying role and task requirements,* 360–361
Transformational leaders *Leaders who inspire followers to transcend their own self-interests for the good of the organization and are capable of having a profound and extraordinary effect on followers,* 360–361
Transformation process *The process through which an organization creates value by turning inputs (people, capital, equipment, materials) into outputs (goods or services),* 439
Transnational corporation (TNC) *A company that maintains significant operations in more than one country simultaneously and decentralizes decision making in each operation to the local country,* 50
Troubleshooters, 363
Trust, 295
Trust, in leaders *The belief in the integrity, character, and ability of a leader,* 364–369
Type A personality type *People who have a chronic sense of urgency and an excessive competitive drive,* 243
Type B personality type *People who are relaxed and easygoing and accept change easily,* 243

U

Uncertainty *A condition in which managers do not have full knowledge of the problem they face and cannot determine even a reasonable probability of alternative outcomes,* 43, 53, 119, 329
Understandability and effective control systems, 421
Unified commitment, 295
Uniformity, 452
Unions, 207
Unity of command, 33
Universal applicability of management activities
  decisions and dealing with change, 12–13
  level in the organization, 8, 10
  national borders, 12
  profit *vs.* not-for-profit, 10
  size of organization, 11–12
Upholder-maintainers, 299
Utilitarian view of ethics, 60

V

Validity *The proven relationship between a selection device and some relevant criterion,* 192
Variability, 452
Venezuela, 53, 329
Verbal intonation *An emphasis given to words or phrases that conveys meaning,* 379
Video conference, 132
Vietnam, 123
Violence, workplace, 208–209
Virtual team *An electronic meeting team; allows groups to meet without concern for space or time,* 294
Visible, staying, 225
Visionary leadership *The ability to create and articulate a realistic, credible, attractive vision of the future that grows out of, and improves upon, the present,* 359–360

W

Weaknesses *Resources that an organization lacks or activities that it does not do well,* 94
Wealth of Nations (Smith), 28, 155
Well-structured problems *Straightforward, familiar, easily defined problems,* 124
White-water rapids metaphor *A description of the organization as a small raft navigating a raging river,* 233–234
Withholding information, 383
Workflow automation *A method of improving the process of creating and transferring documents by automating the flow of information,* 443–444
Work group *A group that interacts primarily to share information and to make decisions that will help each member perform within his or her area of responsibility,* 290–291
Work process engineering *Radical or quantum change in an organization,* 65–66, 453–454
Workshop, management, 23–26
  change, 251–253
  communication process, 407–409
  control systems, 431–435
  decision-making process, 136–139
  human resources approach, 213–216
  leadership, 372–374
  motivation, 308–311
  organizational behavior, 284–286
  organization design, 179–181
  planning, 108–111
  technology, 466–468
  today's world, managing in, 74–77
  work teams, 307–310
Work specialization *A component of organization structure that involves having each discrete step of a job done by a different individual rather than having one individual do the whole job,* 155–157
Work teams *A group that engages in collective work that requires joint effort and generates a positive synergy*
  characteristics of high-performance, 294–297
  concluding remarks and/or chapter summary, 304–305
  continuous process improvement programs, 302–303
  cross-functional, 293–294
  diversity, workforce, 303–304
  functional, 291
  individuals into team players, turning, 297–302
  leadership, 361–363
  one manager's perspective, 296
  popularity of, 288–289
  problem-solving, 291–292
  review and application questions, 305–306
  self-managed, 292–293
  stages of team development, 289–290
  Tape Resources, Inc., 288
  types of, 291–294
  virtual, 294
  work groups *vs.*, 290–291
  workshop, management, 307–310
Written communications, 378–379, 416
Written tests, 192–193, 199

Z

Zero-sum conditions, 400

Class Notes

Class Notes

Class Notes

Class Notes

Class Notes

Class Notes

Class Notes

Class Notes